EYEWITNESS *TRAVEL GUIDES*

# FLORENCE & TUSCANY

*Main contributor:* CHRISTOPHER CATLING

DORLING KINDERSLEY
LONDON • NEW YORK • STUTTGART

A DORLING KINDERSLEY BOOK

PROJECT EDITOR Shirin Patel
ART EDITOR Pippa Hurst
EDITORS Maggie Crowley, Tom Fraser, Sasha Heseltine
US EDITORS Laaren Brown, Mary Ann Lynch
DESIGNERS Claire Edwards, Emma Hutton, Marisa Renzullo
MAP CO-ORDINATORS Simon Farbrother, David Pugh

MANAGING EDITOR Douglas Amrine
MANAGING ART EDITOR Gaye Allen
SENIOR EDITOR Helen Partington
SENIOR ART EDITOR Annette Jacobs
EDITORIAL DIRECTOR David Lamb
ART DIRECTOR Anne-Marie Bulat

PRODUCTION CONTROLLER Hilary Stephens
PICTURE RESEARCH Susan Mennell
DTP DESIGNER Siri Lowe

CONTRIBUTORS
Anthony Brierley, Kerry Fisher, Tim Jepson, Carolyn Pyrah

MAPS
Jan Clarke, James Mills-Hicks (Dorling Kindersley Cartography)

PHOTOGRAPHERS
Philip Enticknap, John Heseltine, Kim Sayer

ILLUSTRATORS
Stephen Conlin, Donati Giudici Associati srl,
Richard Draper, Robbie Polley

•

Film outputting bureau PLS (London)
Reproduced by Colourscan (Singapore)
Printed and bound by Graphicom (Italy)

First American Edition, 1994
2 4 6 8 10 9 7 5 3 1

Published in the United States by
Dorling Kindersley Publishing, Inc.,
95 Madison Avenue, New York, New York 10016


PUBLISHED IN GREAT BRITAIN BY DORLING KINDERSLEY LIMITED.
DISTRIBUTED BY HOUGHTON MIFFLIN COMPANY, BOSTON.

Library of Congress Cataloging-in-Publication Data
Catling, Chris.
Florence and Tuscany / Chris Catling.
p. cm. -- (Eyewitness travel guides)
Includes index.
ISBN 1-56458-502-6
1. Tuscany (Italy) -- Guidebooks. 2. Florence (Italy) -- Guidebooks.
I. Title. II. Series.
DG732.C37 1994 93-34986
914.5'504929--dc20 CIP

Every effort has been made to ensure that the information in this book is as up-to-date as possible at the time of going to press. However, details such as telephone numbers, opening hours, prices, gallery exhibits and travel information are liable to change. The publishers cannot accept responsibility for any consequences arising from the use of this book.

We would be delighted to receive any corrections and suggestions for incorporation in the next edition. Please write to:
Managing Editor, Eyewitness Travel Guides
Dorling Kindersley, 9 Henrietta Street, London WC2E 8PS.

THROUGHOUT THIS BOOK, FLOORS ARE REFERRED TO IN ACCORDANCE WITH EUROPEAN USAGE, I.E. THE "FIRST FLOOR" IS ONE FLOOR UP.

# CONTENTS

**Putto in Palazzo Vecchio**

## INTRODUCING FLORENCE AND TUSCANY

**Flag from Siena's Palio**

A Tuscan country scene in the Crete

Cheese seller in Siena

Panzanella salad

Fresco in Santa Maria Novella



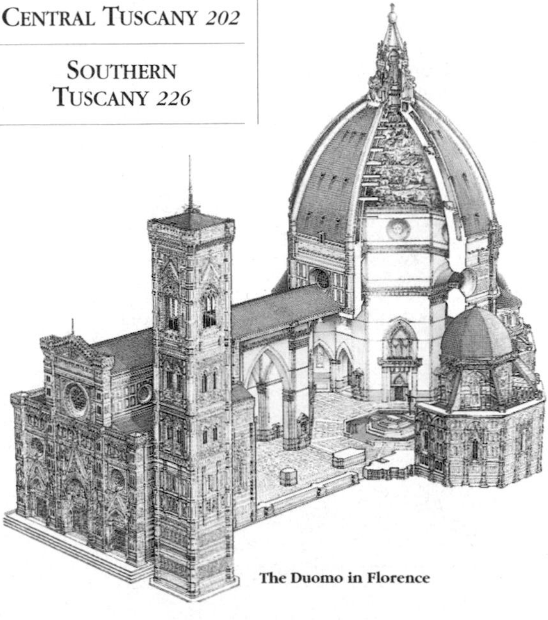

The Duomo in Florence

# How to Use this Guide

This guide helps you get the most from your stay in Florence and Tuscany. It provides both expert recommendations and detailed practical information. *Introducing Florence and Tuscany* maps the region and sets it in its historical and cultural context. *Florence Area by Area* and *Tuscany Area by Area* describe the important sights, with maps, pictures and detailed illustrations. Suggestions for food, drink, accommodation and shopping are in *Travelers' Needs*, and the *Survival Guide* has tips on everything from the Italian telephone system to getting to Tuscany and traveling around the region.

## Florence Area by Area

The historic center of the city has been divided into four sightseeing areas. Each has its own chapter, which opens with a list of the sights described. All the sights are numbered and plotted on an *Area Map*. The detailed information for each sight is presented in numerical order, making it easy to locate within the chapter.

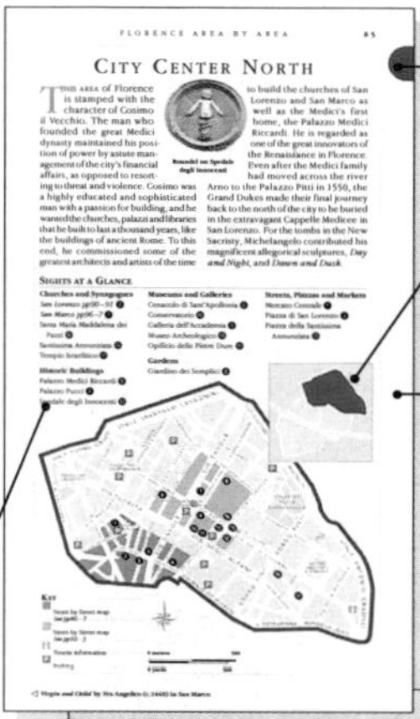

**All pages** relating to Florence have red thumb tabs.

**A locator map** shows where you are in relation to other areas of the city center.

**Sights at a Glance** lists the chapter's sights by category: Churches; Museums and Galleries; Historic Buildings; Streets and Piazzas.

**1 Area Map**
*For easy reference, the sights are numbered and located on a map. The sights are also shown on the* Florence Street Finder *on pages 136–41.*

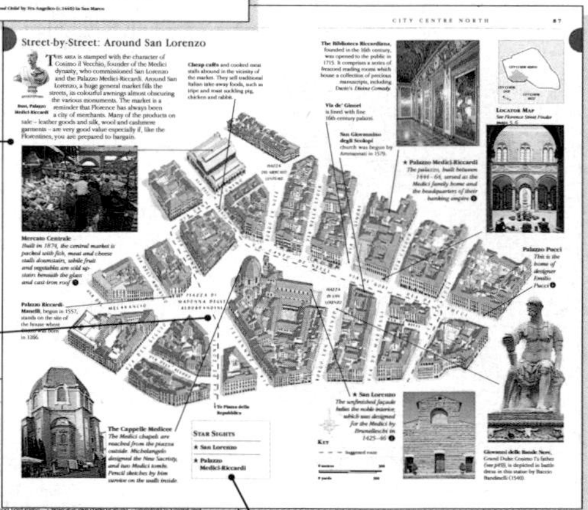

**2 Street-by-Street Map**
*This gives a bird's-eye view of the heart of each sightseeing area.*

**A suggested route** for a walk covers the more interesting streets in the area.

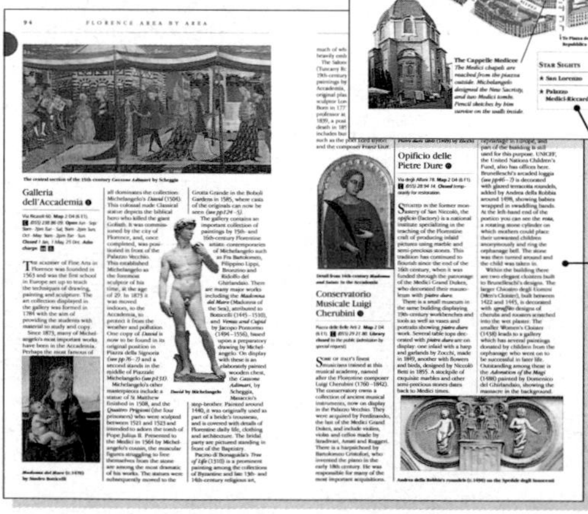

**Stars** indicate the sights that no visitor should miss.

**3 Detailed information on each sight**
*All the sights in Florence are described individually. Addresses, telephone numbers, opening hours and information on admission charges and wheelchair access are also provided.*

**1 Introduction**
*The landscape, history and character of each region is described here, showing how the area has developed over the centuries and what it offers to the visitor today.*

**TUSCANY AREA BY AREA**
In this book, Tuscany has been divided into five regions, each of which has a separate chapter. The most interesting sights to visit have been numbered on a *Pictorial Map.*

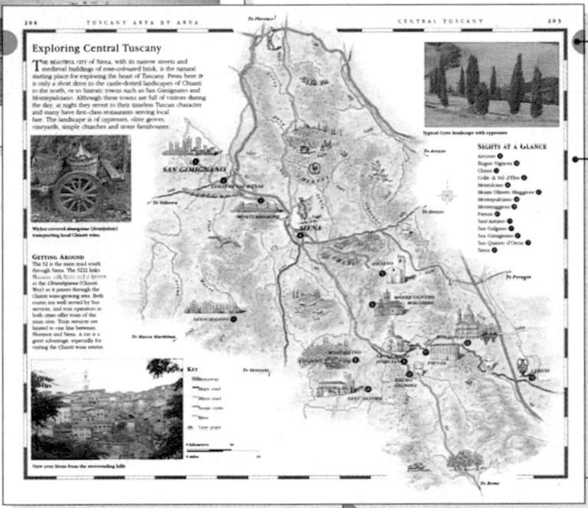


**Each area** of Tuscany can be quickly identified by its color coding.

**2 Pictorial Map**
*This shows the road network and gives an illustrated overview of the whole region. All the sights are numbered, and there are also useful tips on getting around the region by car, bus and train.*

**3 Detailed information on each sight**
*All the important towns and other places to visit are described individually. They are listed in order, following the numbering on the* Pictorial Map. *Within each town or city, there is detailed information on important buildings and other sights.*

**Stars** indicate the best features and works of art.

**For all the top sights,** a Visitor's Checklist provides the practical information you will need to plan your visit.

**4 The top sights**
*These are given two or more full pages. Historic buildings are dissected to reveal their interiors; museums and galleries have color-coded floorplans to help you locate the most interesting exhibits.*

# Introducing Florence and Tuscany

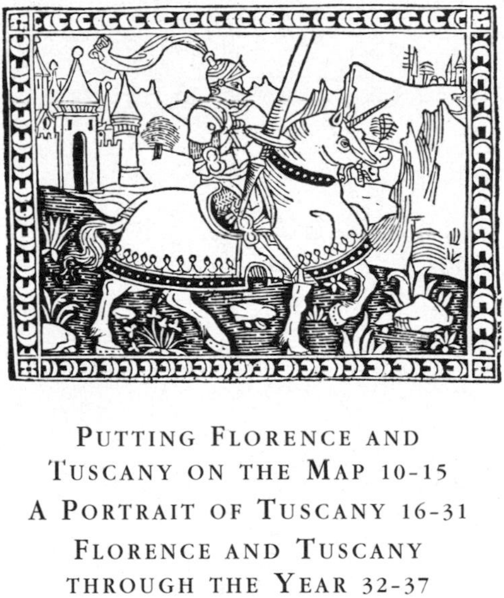

# Putting Florence and Tuscany on the Map

TUSCANY LIES IN CENTRAL ITALY, bordered by the regions of Emilia-Romagna, Marche, Umbria and Lazio. Along with Elba, several islands in the Ligurian Sea also form part of Tuscany. A region of rolling hills, mountains and rugged Mediterranean coastlines, Tuscany covers an area of 22,992 sq km (8,875 sq miles), and has a population of over 3.5 million. There are international airports at Pisa and Florence. Florence is about 2½ hours by train from Rome, and about 3 hours from Milan.

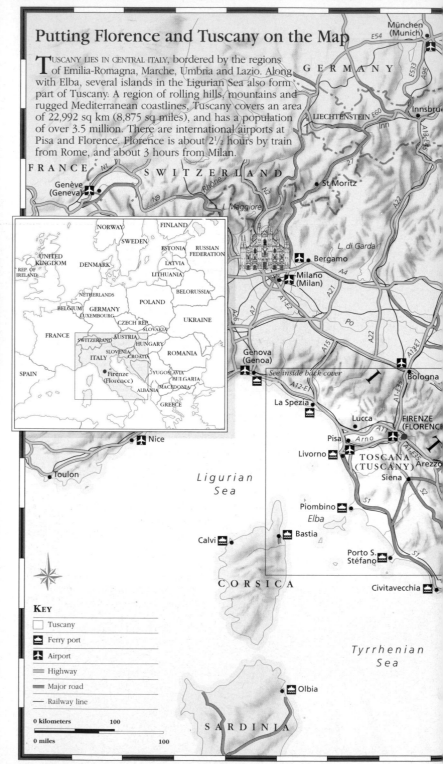

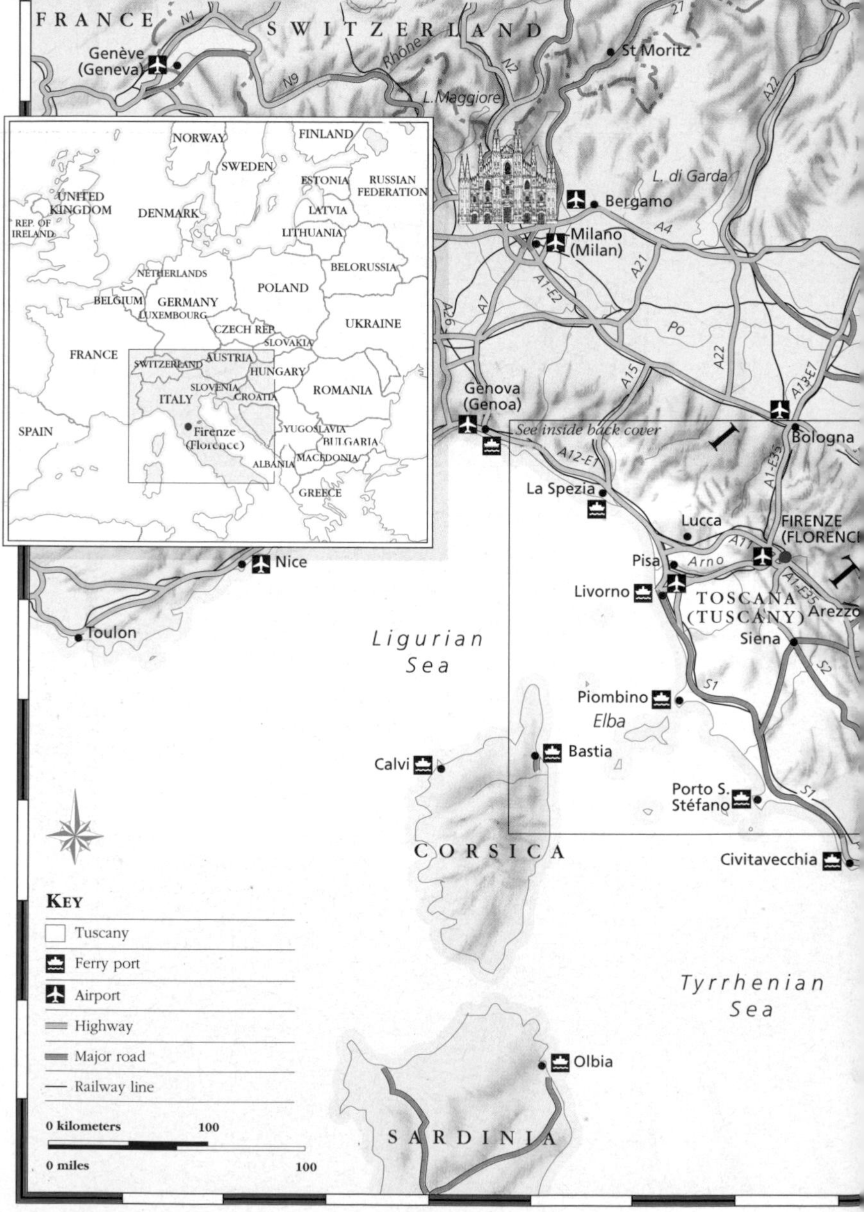

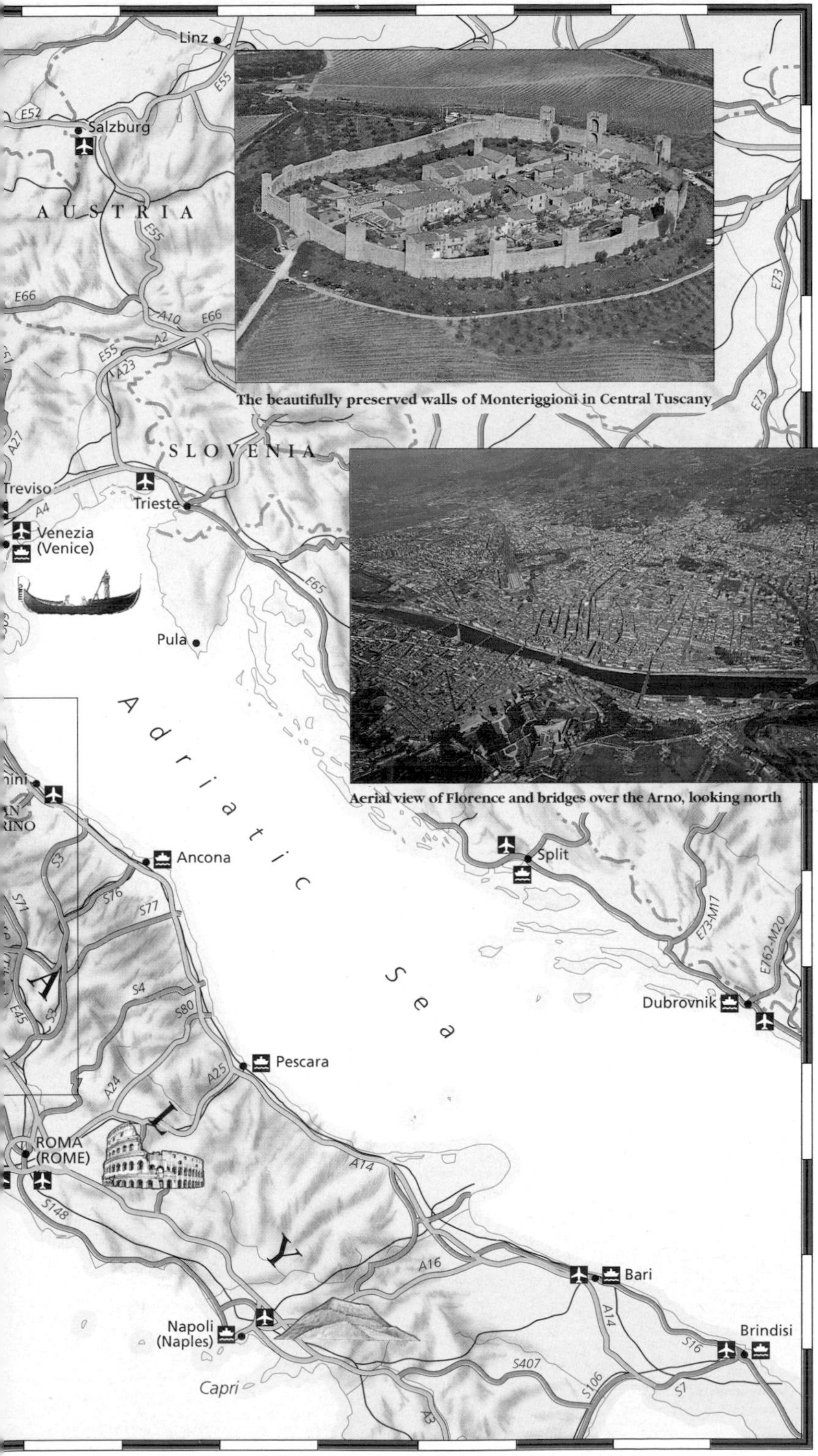


The beautifully preserved walls of Monteriggioni in Central Tuscany

Aerial view of Florence and bridges over the Arno, looking north

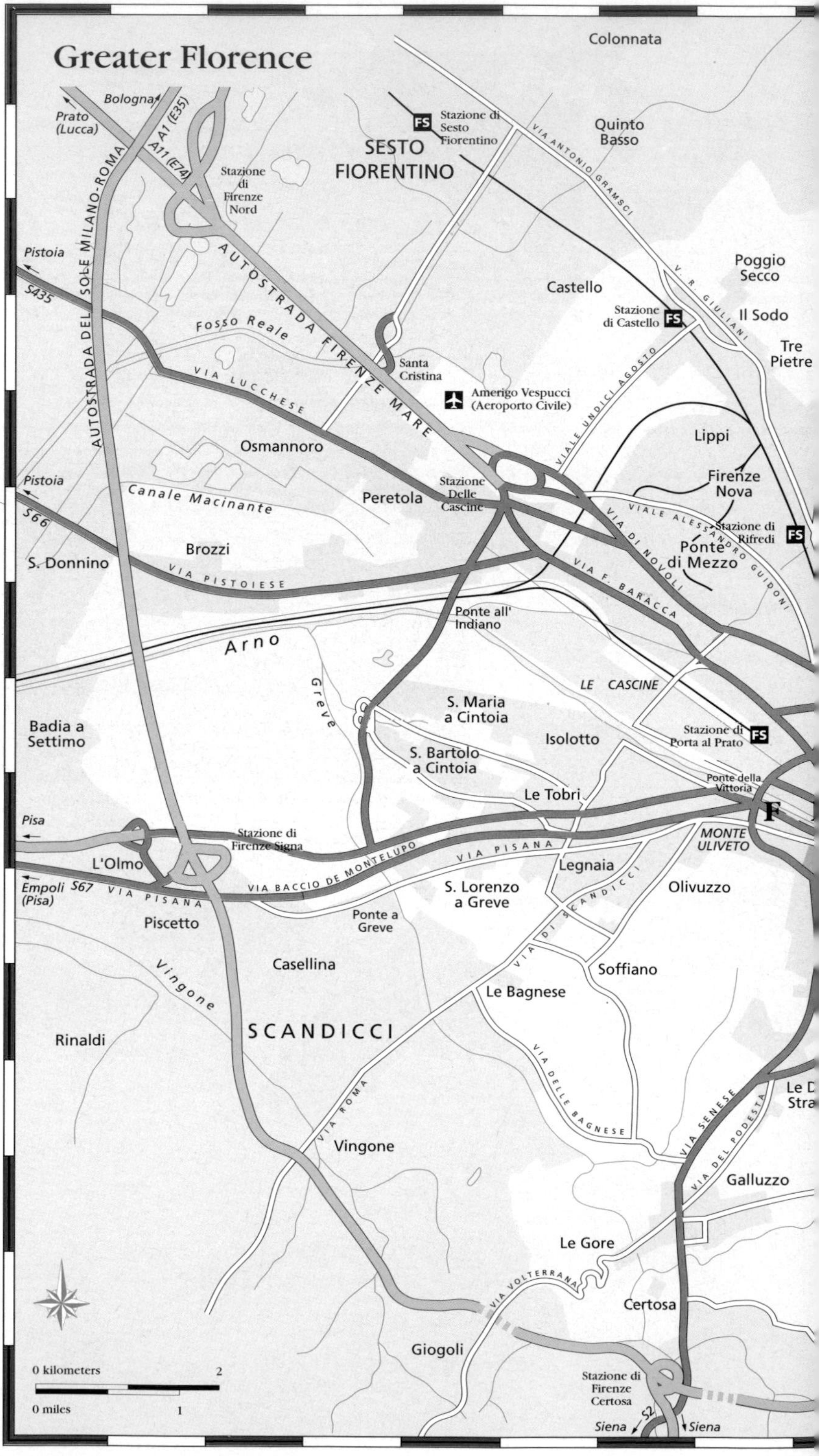
Greater Florence
Colonnata
Bologna
Prato (Lucca)
A1 (E35)
A11 (E74)
Stazione di Sesto Fiorentino
SESTO FIORENTINO
Quinto Basso
VIA ANTONIO GRAMSCI
Stazione di Firenze Nord
AUTOSTRADA DEL SOLE MILANO-ROMA
AUTOSTRADA FIRENZE MARE
Pistoia
S435
Poggio Secco
V. R. GIULIANI
Castello
Stazione di Castello
Il Sodo
Tre Pietre
Fosso Reale
Santa Cristina
VIA LUCCHESE
Amerigo Vespucci (Aeroporto Civile)
VIALE UNDICI AGOSTO
Lippi
Osmannoro
Pistoia
S66
Canale Macinante
Peretola
Stazione Delle Cascine
Firenze Nova
VIALE ALESSANDRO GUIDONI
VIA DI NOVOLI
Stazione di Rifredi
Ponte di Mezzo
Brozzi
S. Donnino
VIA PISTOIESE
VIA F. BARACCA
Ponte all' Indiano
Arno
Greve
LE CASCINE
S. Maria a Cintoia
Badia a Settimo
Isolotto
Stazione di Porta al Prato
S. Bartolo a Cintoia
Ponte della Vittoria
Le Tobri
Pisa
Stazione di Firenze Signa
MONTE ULIVETO
L'Olmo
VIA BACCIO DE MONTELUPO
VIA PISANA
Legnaia
Empoli (Pisa)
S67
S. Lorenzo a Greve
Olivuzzo
VIA DI SCANDICCI
Piscetto
Ponte a Greve
Casellina
Soffiano
Vingone
Le Bagnese
SCANDICCI
Rinaldi
VIA DELLE BAGNESE
VIA ROMA
VIA SENESE
VIA DEL PODESTA
Vingone
Galluzzo
Le Gore
VIA VOLTERRANA
Certosa
Giogoli
0 kilometers 2
0 miles 1
Stazione di Firenze Certosa
S2
Siena
Siena

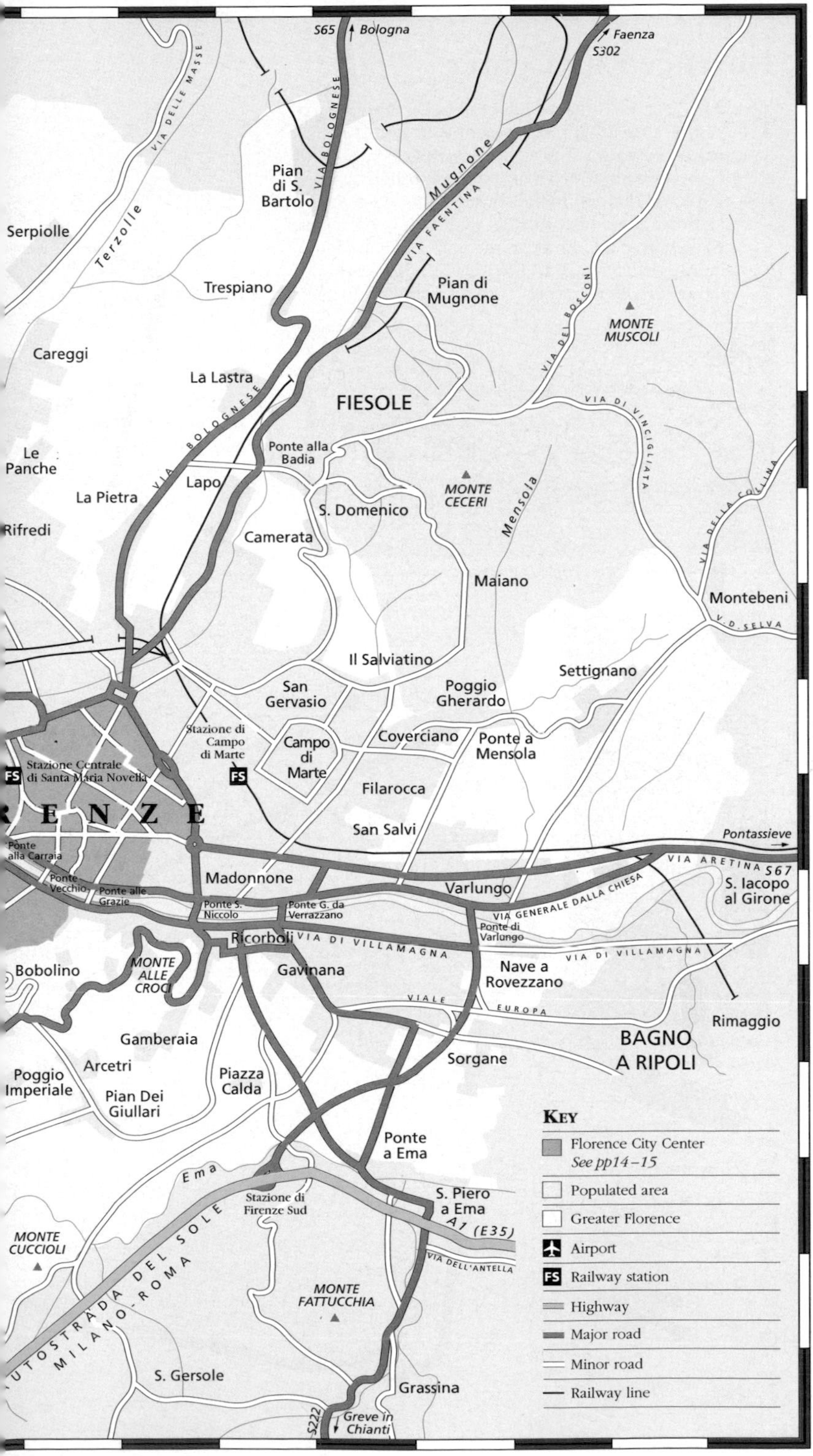
S65
Bologna
Faenza
S302
VIA DELLE MASSE
VIA BOLOGNESE
Pian di S. Bartolo
Mugnone
VIA FAENTINA
Serpiolle
Terzolle
Trespiano
Pian di Mugnone
MONTE MUSCOLI
VIA DEI BOSCONI
Careggi
La Lastra
FIESOLE
VIA DI VINCIGLIATA
Le Panche
Ponte alla Badia
Lapo
La Pietra
MONTE CECERI
Mensola
VIA DELLA COLLINA
S. Domenico
Rifredi
Camerata
Maiano
Montebeni
V. D. SELVA
Il Salviatino
Settignano
San Gervasio
Poggio Gherardo
Stazione di Campo di Marte
Campo di Marte
Coverciano
Ponte a Mensola
Stazione Centrale di Santa Maria Novella
Filarocca
RENZE
San Salvi
Pontassieve
Ponte alla Carraia
VIA ARETINA S67
Ponte Vecchio
Ponte alle Grazie
Madonnone
Varlungo
S. Iacopo al Girone
Ponte S. Niccolo
Ponte G. da Verrazzano
VIA GENERALE DALLA CHIESA
Ponte di Varlungo
Ricorboli
VIA DI VILLAMAGNA
Bobolino
MONTE ALLE CROCI
Gavinana
Nave a Rovezzano
VIALE EUROPA
Rimaggio
Gamberaia
BAGNO A RIPOLI
Arcetri
Sorgane
Poggio Imperiale
Piazza Calda
Pian Dei Giullari
Ponte a Ema
Ema
Stazione di Firenze Sud
S. Piero a Ema
A1 (E35)
MONTE CUCCIOLI
VIA DELL'ANTELLA
AUTOSTRADA DEL SOLE
MILANO-ROMA
MONTE FATTUCCHIA
S. Gersole
Grassina
S222
Greve in Chianti
KEY
Florence City Center
See pp14–15
Populated area
Greater Florence
Airport
Railway station
Highway
Major road
Minor road
Railway line

# Florence City Center

FLORENCE'S BEST SIGHTS are encompassed within such a compact area that the city seems to reveal its treasures at every step. The sights described in this book are grouped within four areas, each of which can be easily explored on foot. In the centre is the massive Duomo, providing a historical as well as a geographical focus to the city. Santa Croce to the east and San Marco to the north, with Santa Maria Novella to the west and the Palazzo Pitti in Oltrarno, mark the outlying areas.

**City Center West: Ponte Santa Trinita, with Ponte Vecchio behind**

**Oltrarno: taking a break in Piazza di Santo Spirito**

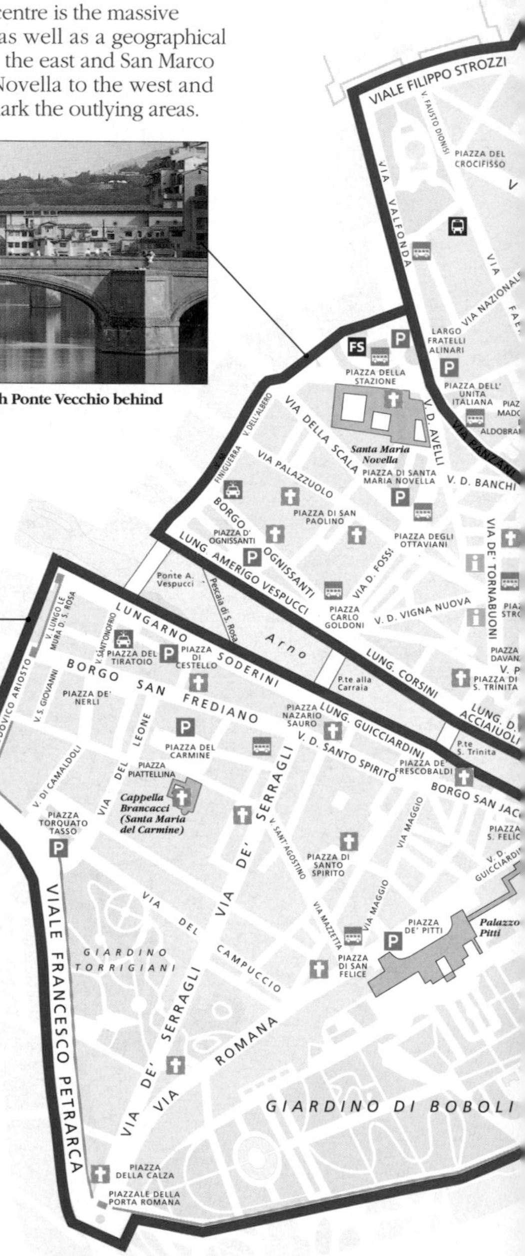


**KEY**

- Major sight
- Railway station
- Bus station
- Long-distance bus station
- Parking
- Tourist information
- Hospital with emergency room
- Police station
- Church
- Synagogue

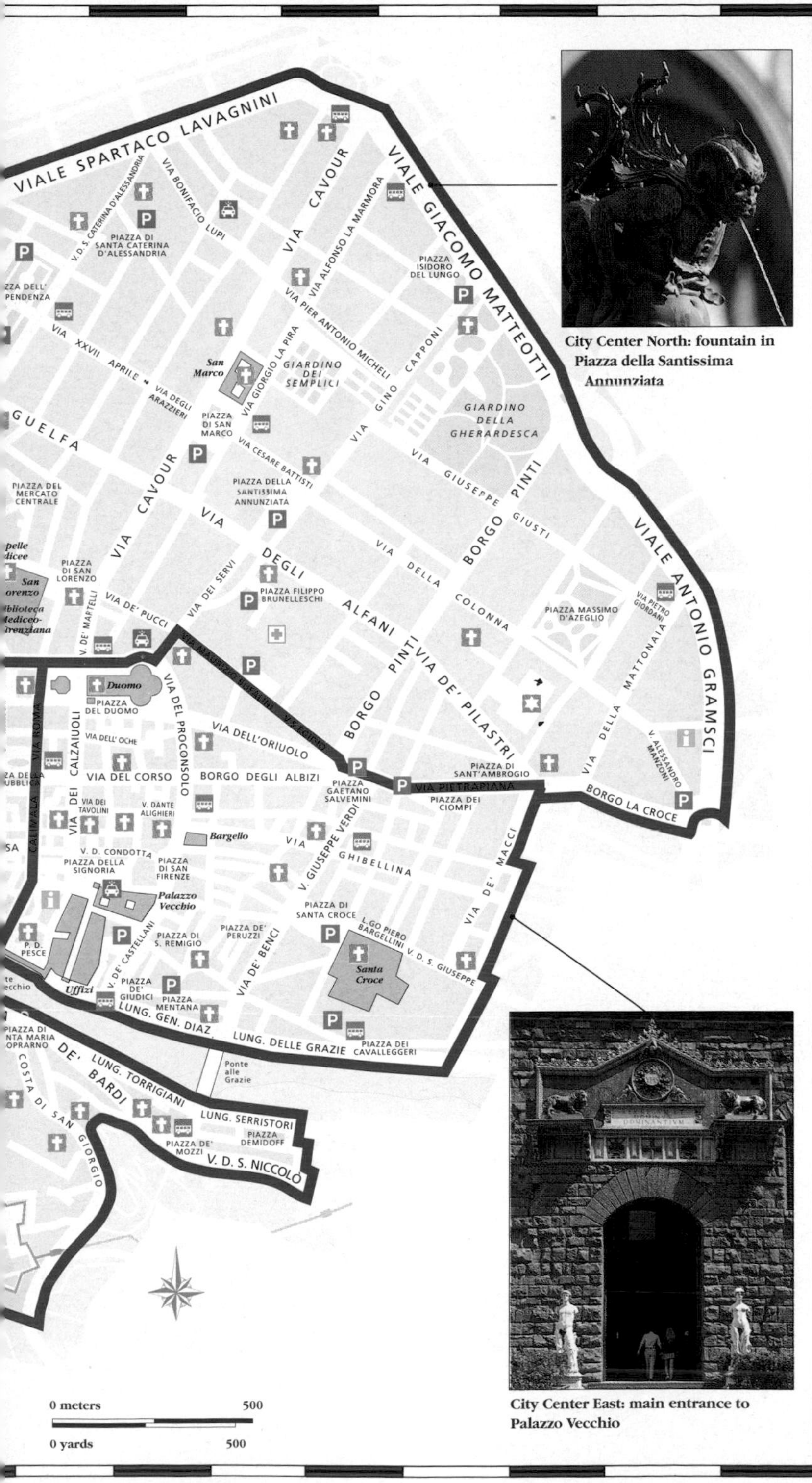


City Center North: fountain in Piazza della Santissima Annunziata

City Center East: main entrance to Palazzo Vecchio

# A Portrait of Tuscany

TUSCANY IS RENOWNED *throughout the world for its art, history and beautiful landscape. Here the past merges with the present to a remarkable degree, for its people pride themselves on their heritage. Independent and combative, for centuries they have preserved their surroundings and traditions, in which must lie much of Tuscany's eternal fascination for the outsider.*

The people of Tuscany are fiercely proud of their ancestry, which they trace back to the Etruscans. Geneticists have even discovered gene segments that are uniquely Tuscan: there are strong similarities between the faces carved on Etruscan cremation urns *(see pp40–41)* and those of the people on the streets of modern Tuscany.

A classic Tuscan face captured by Botticelli

This legacy also has a political significance. Tuscany still enjoys a kind of grass-roots democracy through referendums on such issues as whether to ban traffic from the center of Florence. Florentines will, however, take the law into their own hands, as they did when they fought the police in 1990 to prevent the closure of San Lorenzo market. Tuscans also scorn the government in Rome and its bureaucracy. Many people want the autonomy they enjoyed before Italy was united in 1870. This has been sharpened by the revelations of institutionalized corruption in Italy.

The Tuscan love of home has resulted in a strong *campanilismo*: parochialism defined by the sound of the local church bell (in the campanile or bell tower). Social anthropologists see in it a survival of medieval inter-city conflicts. It can be observed at many a Tuscan festival when, beneath the pageantry, there is a serious rivalry between a city's different quarters.

A timeless view and way of life: peaceful old age in Casole d'Elsa

◁ Brilliant, medieval-style pageantry before Siena's Palio *(see p218)*

A rare sight today – farming with oxen near Pienza

Even the working day of many Tuscans echoes that of their ancestors centuries ago. For people who work out in the fields, the day begins at sunrise, as early as 4:30am in summer. Farm and vineyard laborers will have completed a day's work by noon, when they retire indoors to eat and rest.

A cheese stand in Florence

Until the 1950s, most Tuscans were familiar with this pattern of life: the region still relied on a feudal system, *mezzadria*, whereby peasants working on the land without payment took a share of the crops as their reward. Today, agricultural produce remains an important ingredient in the Tuscan economy, but only 20 percent of Tuscans now work in agriculture. Many farming families left the land in favor of a stable income and a shorter working day as factory hands. Town dwellers have a much easier way of life, but the old rhythms prevail: the *siesta* period is still observed, so that almost everything closes for a few hours in the afternoon. Wise travelers soon learn that it pays to follow the same pattern, rising early to join the café throng before heading out to study ancient frescoes in peace. In the middle of Florence there are several lively early morning markets where you can buy fresh local produce *(see p267)*. Bargain hunters and food-loving Tuscans frequent them, but by 9am the vendors will have packed up and left.

Clerics in conversation, Colle di Val d'Elsa

Churches open at 8am, and, except on Sunday when mass is held, there will be few other people to disturb your thoughts if you stray into one. Today, very few Tuscans go regularly to church, and Sunday is spent visiting friends, watching sports or enjoying family lunch. After the burst of activity that marks the beginning of the day, Tuscan towns adopt a more sedate pace. New building is prohibited inside their walls, so that virtually everyone of school or working age travels out, by bus or car, to schools, offices or factories in the suburbs, leaving the old centers to visitors.

**The grape harvest in Chianti**

Some of the larger towns, particularly Pisa, Lucca, Florence and Siena, have resisted this tide, determined not to become museum cities dedicated entirely to tourism. They are thriving

**The hour for relaxing in Cortona**

service sectors, testimony to the same Tuscan flair for banking, insurance and accountancy that made the Medici family and the "Merchant of Prato" *(see p184)* some of the richest people in their time. It is, however, the lucky few who work in such beautiful towns. They practice as lawyers, architects, conservationists or designers and are often graduates of the renowned local universities: Pisa, Siena and Florence. For the great majority of Tuscans, however, the working day is spent in business areas, such as the one linking Prato to the Firenze Nuova (New Florence) suburbs west of the city. The Tuscan economy, however, still remains firmly rooted in craft traditions. The top designers from Milan use the textile factories of Prato and Florence for the execution of their designs. Gold working is not confined to the Ponte Vecchio workshops in Florence – Arezzo produces jewelry that is sold throughout Europe.

### THRIVING EXPORTS

Glass, marble and motorcycles are among Tuscany's most important industrial products, while its olive oil and wine are exported worldwide. This explains why Livorno, Tuscany's port, is the second busiest in Italy, while Pisa's Galileo Galilei airport is rapidly becoming a major air-freight distribution center.

Individual Tuscan artistry can best be admired in the heart of any Tuscan town during the evening promenade – the *passeggiata.* One moment the streets are empty, the next they are filled with elegant people strolling and chatting. The skill of *fare bella figura* ("looking good") is so prized that visitors will be judged by the same standard. It is an opportunity for you to join in the inherently Tuscan aspiration to create a civilized world.

**Italian chic, or *bella figura***

# A Tuscan Town Square

THE MAIN SQUARE OR PIAZZA of nearly every Tuscan town is the focus for much of the town's activities. It is here that the townsfolk gather around 6–7pm for the daily *passeggiata*, the traditional evening stroll, or to participate in local festivals and rallies. In most towns there are certain religious and civic buildings that are usually grouped around the piazza. Many of these buildings, you will notice, have standard features, such as the campanile, the *cortile* or the loggia, each of which fulfills a specific function. And often you will find that many of these buildings are still in use today, performing the same function for which they were originally built during the 13th–16th centuries.

**Town bell in the campanile**

**Wellhead**
*Water was a valuable resource that was protected by strict laws to prevent pollution.*

**Cortile**
*The arcaded courtyard, or* cortile, *of a palazzo served as an entrance hall shielded from the outside; it also provided a cool retreat.*

**Marble or hard sandstone paving**

**A palazzo** is any town house of stature. It is usually named after its owner.

**There are three floors** in most palazzi. Public reception rooms were on the middle floor, the *piano nobile.*

**The ground floor** was used for storage and workshops. Today many ground floors are rented to businesses, and the owners live above.

**Baptismal font**

**The Baptistry**, usually octagonal, was a separate building to the west of the church. After baptism, the infant was carried ceremoniously into the church for the first time.

**Stemmae**
*Stone-carved coats of arms, belonging to citizens who served as councilors and magistrates, are often seen on public buildings.*

**Festival in the Piazza**
*The prestigious buildings of the main piazza often form an appropriate backdrop to costumed tournaments involving jousting, archery and horsemanship, recalling the medieval arts of war.*

**Loggia**
*Many loggias, built to provide shelter from the sun or rain, now harbor colorful street markets.*

**The Palazzo del Comune** (town hall) often houses the Museo Civico (town museum) and the Pinacoteca (art gallery).

**The Duomo** (from Latin *Domus Dei* or House of God) is the cathedral, the focal point of the piazza. A smaller parish church is called a *pieve.*

**The campanile** rose high so that the town bells could be heard far and wide. The bells were rung to announce public meetings or mass, to sound the curfew or, when rung furiously *(a stormo),* to warn of impending danger.

**Side Chapel**
*Wealthy patrons paid for ornate tombs, paintings and frescoes in their own private chapels to commemorate their dead.*

# Understanding Architecture in Tuscany

**Romanesque capital**

The survival of so many fine Gothic and Renaissance buildings is part of Tuscany's immense appeal. Whole streets and squares, such as the Piazza dei Priori in Volterra *(see p163)* and the streets around the Mercato Nuovo in Florence, and even towns such as San Gimignano, have scarcely changed in appearance since the end of the 16th century. Simple clues, such as the shape of arches, windows and doorways, reveal the style of the building and when it was built.

**Gothic palazzi in Cortona**

## Romanesque (5th to mid-13th centuries)

The Tuscan Romanesque style developed from late Roman architecture. Early Tuscan churches, such as Sant'Antimo *(see pp42–3)*, have round arches, Roman style columns and arcades. Profuse surface decoration was introduced in the 12th century, resulting in the jewel-like church façades of Pisa and Lucca.

**A twisted knot**

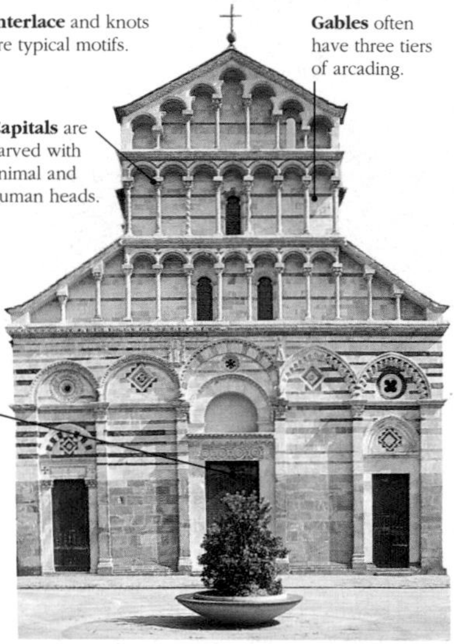

**Interlace** and knots are typical motifs.

**Gables** often have three tiers of arcading.

**Capitals** are carved with animal and human heads.

**The central portal** is flanked by smaller side doors.

***Pisa's San Paolo a Ripa d'Arno*** (see p157), *begun in 1210, has restrained geometric patterns on the lower façade and exuberant arcades above.*

**Marble patterning on stonework**

## Gothic (13th to mid-15th centuries)

Pointed arches are the key feature of Gothic architecture. The style was introduced to Tuscany by French Cistercian monks who built the abbey of San Galgano in 1218 *(see p220)*. Siena then made this style her own, using it for the city's Duomo, palazzi and civic buildings such as Palazzo Pubblico *(see pp214–19)*.

**Pinnacles**, like miniature spires, bristle from the roofline.

**Pointed gables**

**Gabled niches**, sheltering statues of saints or apostles, are a Gothic innovation.

**The crockets** are shaped like leaves and flowers.

***Santa Maria della Spina*** *(1230–1323), with its pointed gables and spiky pinnacles* (see p157), *is a typical example of Pisan Gothic architecture.*

**St. Luke, from Orsanmichele**

## Renaissance (15th and 16th Centuries)

Brunelleschi, the father of Renaissance architecture, was inspired by the purity and simplicity of Classical Roman buildings. This style is reflected in his first true Renaissance work, the loggia of the Spedale degli Innocenti in Florence (1419–24) *(see p95)*, with its elegant lines and simple arched bays. The style he created was adopted with enthusiasm by his fellow Florentines, who saw their city as the "new" Rome.

**Arch with teardrop keystone**

**Courtyard, Spedale degli Innocenti**

**Classical cornices** are molded in Roman style.

**String courses** define each story.

**Wedge-shaped** masonry around semi-circular window arches is characteristic of Renaissance buildings.

***Palazzo Strozzi*** (see p105) *is typical of many Tuscan Renaissance buildings. The rusticated stonework gives an impression of strength and stability.*

## Baroque (Late 16th and 17th Centuries)

The theatrical Baroque style, much favored by the popes in Rome, largely passed Tuscany by. Although a few churches in Florence were given new façades in the 17th century, the Florentine version of the Baroque style is very Classical in spirit and not as bold or as exuberant as elsewhere in Italy.

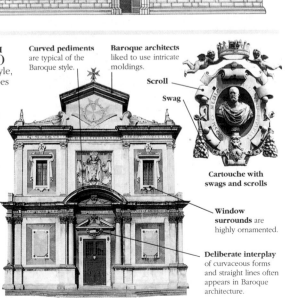

**Curved pediments** are typical of the Baroque style.

**Baroque architects** liked to use intricate moldings.

**Scroll**

**Swag**

**Cartouche with swags and scrolls**

**Window surrounds** are highly ornamented.

**Deliberate interplay** of curvaceous forms and straight lines often appears in Baroque architecture.

***Santo Stefano dei Cavalieri*** (see p153) *has columns and pilasters on its Baroque façade, which give the illusion of depth.*

# Understanding Art in Tuscany

TUSCANY WAS THE SCENE of one of the most influential and sustained artistic revolutions in history. Its masterpieces record the transition from the stylized charm of medieval art to the Classical beauty and richness of the High Renaissance.

## MEDIEVAL ART

Medieval art served as an aid to prayer and contemplation. The Virgin, patron saint of many Tuscan cities, including Siena, was often depicted as the Queen of Heaven, surrounded by adoring angels and saints.

**No detailed setting or background**

**Idealized figures**

**Gold,** symbolizing purity, was used lavishly.

**Lack of spatial depth**

**Unifying flow of drapery**

***Maestà*** *(1308–11)*
*The stylized figures in this detail from Duccio's huge altarpiece for Siena Cathedral are painted with great delicacy.*

**The figures** form a triangle, symbolizing the Holy Trinity. The viewer's eye is drawn upward to the figures of Christ and God the Father at the apex.

**The Virgin and St. John** are depicted as real people rather than idealized figures.

**Lorenzo Lenzi,** Masaccio's patron, kneels opposite his wife.

## RENAISSANCE ART

The artistic revolution known as the Renaissance, which spread throughout Europe from the 15th century onward, had its roots in Tuscany. Inspired by ancient Roman art, sculptors and painters brought about a "rebirth" of Classical ideals.

They were supported by wealthy and cultured patrons, themselves fascinated by the works of such Classical authors as Plato and Cicero. Nudes, landscapes, portraits, and scenes from mythology

***The Trinity*** *(c.1427)*
*Masaccio pioneered perspective in painting, using architectural illusion to create a three-dimensional effect* (see p110).

## TIMELINE OF GREAT TUSCAN ARTISTS

- **1260–1319** Duccio di Buoninsegna
- **1267–1337** Giotto di Bondone
- **1377–1455** Filippo Brunelleschi
- **1245–1315** Giovanni Pisano
- **1270–1348** Andrea Pisano
- **1374–1438** Jacopo della Quercia

1200 | 1250 | 1300 | 1350

- **1245–1302** Arnolfo di Cambio
- **1319–47** Ambrogio Lorenzetti
- **1378–1455** Lorenzo Ghiberti
- **1240–1302** Cimabue
- **1283–1344** Simone Martini
- **1386–1460** Donatello
- **1223–84** Nicola Pisano

☐ **Medieval Artists**

### MANNERIST ART

Mannerist artists used "hot" colors, elongated forms and deliberately contorted poses, often within complicated, large-scale compositions.

The twisted pose and vivid colors of Michelangelo's *Holy Family* *(see p81)* established the key features of the style. Few artists could match the monumental scale of his work, but Bronzino, Pontormo and Rosso Fiorentino brought new life to traditional biblical subjects by their skillful and dramatic composition.

**Statues of Roman gods** reflect a direct debt to Classical art.
**Writhing figures** create a sense of dramatic tension.
**Flesh and musculature** are painted in subtle gradations of light and shade.

***The Martyrdom of St. Lawrence*** *(1569)*
*With Mannerist bravura, Bronzino shows the human body in numerous poses* (see p90).

and everyday life became legitimate subjects for art.

Rejecting the stylized art of the medieval era, Renaissance artists studied anatomy in order to portray the human body more realistically, and strove to develop innovations to please their patrons. They learned how to apply the mathematics of linear perspective to their art to create the illusion of spatial depth. Painters set figures against recognizable landscapes or city backgrounds, and flattered their patrons by including them as onlookers or protagonists of the scene.

***La Maddalena* (1438), by Donatello**

The greatest Renaissance artists also added another dimension, that of psychological realism. It is evident in Donatello's sculpture *La Maddalena*, which vividly conveys the former prostitute's grief and penitence. Even when painting traditional subjects, they often tried to express the complexities of human character and emotion. The religious elements of the Virgin and Child theme gave way, for example, to an exploration of the mother-child relationship, as in the *Madonna and Child* (c.1455) by Fra Filippo Lippi *(see p82)*.

**Pallas**, symbolizing wisdom, tames the centaur, representing brute animal impulse.


***Pallas and the Centaur***
*Botticelli's allegory (1485) typifies the Renaissance interest in pagan myth.*

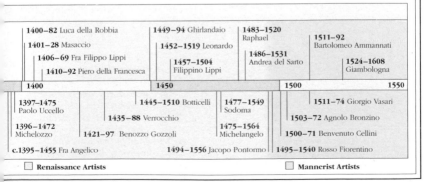

**1400–82** Luca della Robbia
**1401–28** Masaccio
**1406–69** Fra Filippo Lippi
**1410–92** Piero della Francesca
**1449–94** Ghirlandaio
**1452–1519** Leonardo
**1457–1504** Filippino Lippi
**1483–1520** Raphael
**1486–1531** Andrea del Sarto
**1511–92** Bartolomeo Ammannati
**1524–1608** Giambologna

**1400** — **1450** — **1500** — **1550**

**1397–1475** Paolo Uccello
**1396–1472** Michelozzo
**c.1395–1455** Fra Angelico
**1421–97** Benozzo Gozzoli
**1435–88** Verrocchio
**1445–1510** Botticelli
**1494–1556** Jacopo Pontormo
**1477–1549** Sodoma
**1475–1564** Michelangelo
**1511–74** Giorgio Vasari
**1503–72** Agnolo Bronzino
**1500–71** Benvenuto Cellini
**1495–1540** Rosso Fiorentino

☐ **Renaissance Artists** ☐ **Mannerist Artists**

# Renaissance Frescoes

FRESCOES DECORATE the walls of churches, public buildings and private palaces throughout Tuscany. Renaissance artists, in particular, favored the medium of fresco painting for decorating new buildings. The word *fresco,* meaning "fresh," refers to the technique of painting onto a thin layer of damp, freshly laid plaster. Pigments are drawn into the plaster by surface tension, and the color becomes fixed as the plaster dries. The pigments react with the lime in the plaster to produce strong, vivid colors. Because the colors do not lie on the surface, restorers are able to remove the superficial soot and grime that have accumulated over the years to reveal the original, embedded colors *(see pp54–5).*

**Chiaroscuro**
*This is a subtle method of contrasting light and dark for dramatic effect.*

**Jewellike Colors**
*Artists used rare, costly minerals to create bright, striking pigments. The blue of Mary's robe in Piero della Francesca's* Madonna del Parto *(c.1460)* (see p193) *is made from lapis lazuli.*

**Earth colors** such as reds and browns came from clay-based paints containing iron.

**White pigment** was used for important highlights because it reflects light.

**Use of Sinopia**
*The outlines of the fresco were drawn onto the plaster undercoat using a red pigment called* sinopia. *This layer was visible through the final plaster coat, guiding the artist as he painted in the details* (see p152).

**The Giornato**
*Once the final plaster coat was applied, artists had to work quickly before it dried. This meant painting a small area of plaster each day (the* giornato, *or daily portion). Joints between the sections were often concealed in borders, columns and frames.*

**Masons** left the bare wall surface uneven.

**The bare wall** was covered with coarse plaster, called *arriccio*, made of clay, hair, sand and lime.

**The artist** either sketched his design onto the *arriccio* using the pigment *sinopia*, and then painted directly onto the plaster, or he prepared a charcoal drawing on paper, which was copied onto the wall.

**The final fresco** was painted onto a top coat of fine, lime-based plaster, called *intonaco*.

**Workshop of Filippo Lippi**
*This fresco in the Duomo in Prato* (see p184) *shows the* Funeral of Santo Stefano. *The master artist concentrated on important features, such as faces and expressive gestures.*

**Apprentices**
*While learning their trade, apprentices painted drapery, backgrounds and architectural details in the style of their master.*

# What to Buy in Tuscany

As a center for high fashion and quality antiques, Florence is expensive but hard to beat. Bargains also abound, especially in leather goods and shoes. For food lovers there is a wide variety of wines, olive oils and preserves. Outside of Florence, small farm estates in Tuscany sell their produce, such as honey, liqueurs and wines, directly to the public, while many Tuscan towns have their own crafts and specialty foods. *(See also pp266–9.)*

**Desk organizer made of traditional hand-marbled paper**

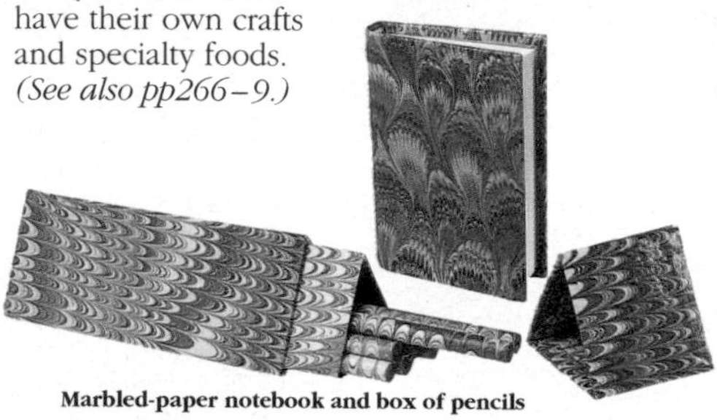

**Marbled-paper notebook and box of pencils**

**Colorful Stationery**
*Marbled paper is a Florentine specialty. You can buy it in sheets and notebooks, or shaped into carnival masks and even birds and flowers.*

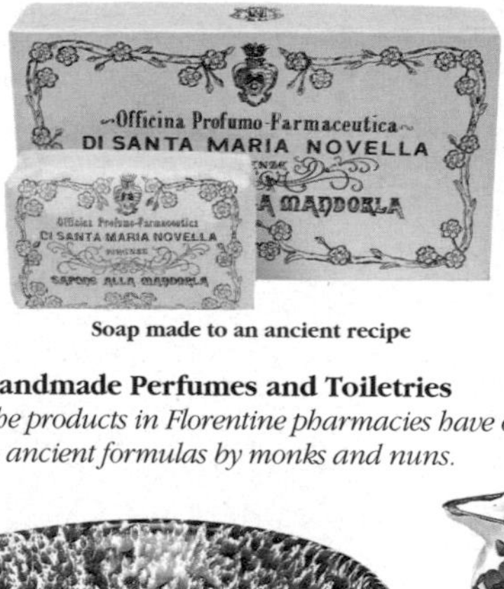


**Soap made to an ancient recipe**

**Floral air freshener**

**Greetings Cards**
*Beautifully illustrated cards are sold at bookshops and museums.*

**Handmade Perfumes and Toiletries**
*The products in Florentine pharmacies have often been made to ancient formulas by monks and nuns.*

**Hand-painted majolica**

**Alabaster figurine from Volterra**

**Terra-cotta and ceramic bowl**

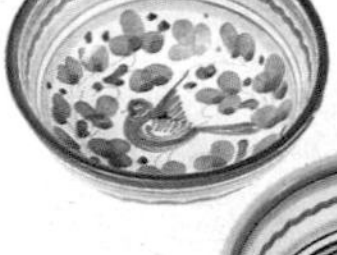

**Reproductions of Renaissance ceramics**

**Ceramics and Reproductions**
*Tuscan potters produce highly decorative pieces, from modern originals* (artistiche) *and Renaissance copies* (reproduzioni) *to attractive kitchenware. You can also buy copies of your favorite sculptures.*

Woven leatherwork handbag

Elegant briefcase

Small coin purse

## Quality Leather Goods

*Fine leather handbags, wallets and jackets are all remarkably good buys, but fake designer brands are also sold by street dealers and at market stalls.*

Belt with distinctive Gucci buckle

Handcrafted men's footwear

Beautifully made lady's shoes

Luxury charm bracelet

Designer silk scarf

## Fashion Accessories

*Florence has all the top names in fashion, including homegrown couturiers like Gucci.*

## Fashionable Footwear

*Even Hollywood movie stars come to Florence to buy shoes from boutiques such as Ferragamo's.*

Sunflower honey from Montalcino

Chocolate and biscuit cake

Red wine vinegar and fine olive oil

## Tuscan Delicacies

*Lovers of good food will want to visit an* alimentari *(grocer's) to choose from the fascinating range of stock available. Tuscan products to sample and take back home include bottled antipasti, fruity olive oils and a wide variety of candy and pastry.*

Artichoke hearts with peppers and olives

Sun-dried tomatoes in sunflower oil

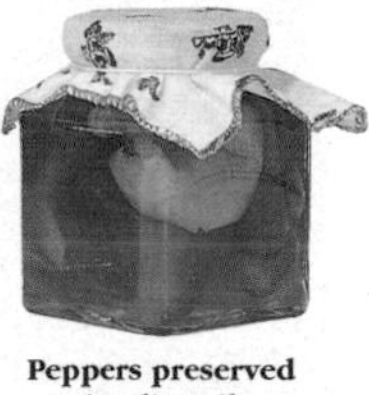

Peppers preserved in olive oil

# The Landscape of Tuscany

Tuscany is rich in wildlife, especially flowers and the insects that feed on them, including bees, crickets, cicadas and grasshoppers, whose song is heard during the summer months. For years Tuscan farmers were too poor to afford modern intensive agricultural methods, so the region was, until recently, still farmed by traditional methods. As a result, rural areas have remained relatively unspoiled, a safe haven for many species of animals and fauna – with the exception of the songbird, which has fallen victim to the Tuscan passion for hunting.

**Cypress Trees**
*The flame-shaped cypress is often planted as a windbreak in fields and along roadsides.*

**The Crete**
*The clay landscape south of Siena is one of bare hillocks and ravines, denuded of topsoil by heavy rain.*

**Terracing**
*The steep hillsides are farmed by cutting terraces and holding the soil in place with stone walls.*

**Building** on hilltops ensures a cooling wind in summer.

### Tuscan Farmland

A typical Tuscan farm will combine olive groves and vineyards with fields of corn and barley to feed the cattle and chickens.

**Garfagnana Landscape**
*Much of this region is an unspoiled national park where deer, boar, martens and eagles are protected.*

**Viticulture**
*Many families make their own wine, and every spare plot is planted with vines.*

**Olives**
*The olive tree, with its silver-backed leaves, is widely cultivated. Many farms sell home-produced olive oil.*

## TUSCAN WILDLIFE

The best time to see the Tuscan countryside is in May and June when all the flowers are in bloom. Fall rains bring a second burst of flowering later in the year, and then cyclamen carpet the woodland floors. Even winter has its flowers, such as hellebores and snowdrops.

### Animals, Birds and Insects

***Hummingbird** hawk moths hover in front of brightly colored flowers, feeding with their long tongues.*

***Swifts perform** aerial acrobatics at dusk, flying high above the city rooftops and towers.*

***The green lizard** feeds on grasshoppers and basks on walls in the sunlight.*

***Wild boars** are abundant but very shy as they are hunted for their tasty meat.*

### Roadside Flowers

***The blue chicory** plant flowers all summer and is used as animal fodder.*

***Pink, white and red** flowering mallows are a valuable food plant for bees.*

***The bloodred poppy** often grows alongside bright white oxeye daisies.*

***The almond-scented** bindweed attracts a multitude of different insects.*

# Florence and Tuscany Through the Year

Tuscany is most beautiful in May, when meadows and waysides are carpeted with the same bright flowers that Botticelli's Flora blithely scatters in *Primavera*, his celebration of spring *(see p82)*. Autumn is equally colorful, when the beech and chestnut woods turn a glorious blaze of seasonal red and gold.

The best months for escaping the heat and the crowds are May, September and October. Easter should be avoided, as also July and August, because of the long lines outside major museums. During August, when Tuscans head for the sea, you will find shops, bars and restarants closed. To see traditional festivities like the Palio in Siena or Arezzo's Joust of the Saracen, you will need to reserve accommodations a year ahead, but there are many other local festivals to enjoy. For information, inquire at main tourist offices *(see p273)*.

**A July harvest, medieval style**

## Spring

Tuscany begins to wake from winter as Easter approaches. The hillsides are vibrant with the soft green of new leaves and the scent of fresh growth. Even in the cities there is a sense of renewal as hanging baskets and window boxes are displayed outside from April onward, and wisteria and iris bloom in the public gardens.

Instead of winter's heavy game dishes, asparagus, a specialty of the Lucca area, begins to appear on restaurant menus, along with tender young beans, usually served in lemon juice and oil.

Except at Eastertime, the streets and main sights are rarely overcrowded, but the weather can be unpredictable and unseasonably wet.

**A window box in bloom: the first sign of spring in Cortona**

**"Explosion of the Carriage" festival**

### March

**Carnevale** *(Shrove Tuesday)*, Viareggio *(see p36)*.
**Scoppio del Carro**, or the Explosion of the Carriage *(Easter Sunday)*, Piazza del Duomo, Florence. An 18th-century gilded cart is pulled to the cathedral doors by white oxen, and a dove-shaped rocket swoops down a wire from above the high altar inside to ignite fireworks hidden in the cart. Ostensibly a celebration of the Resurrection, the ceremony has roots in pagan fertility rites. Many Tuscans still believe that a successful firework display means a good harvest.
**Festa degli Aquiloni**, or Kite Festival *(first Sunday after Easter)*, San Miniato *(see p159)*. Kite lovers perform aerial acrobatics on the Prato della Rocca, the grassy common above San Miniato.

### April

**Sagra Musicale Lucchese**, *(April–early July)* Lucca *(see pp174–5)*. This extensive festival of sacred music is held in the city's numerous Romanesque churches.
**Mostra Mercato Internazionale dell'Artigianato**, or Exhibition of Crafts *(last week)*, Fortezza da Basso, Florence. An important European exhibition of the work of artists and artisans.

### May

**Maggio Musicale**, Florence. This is the city's major arts festival, and it now lasts until early June, with concerts by the Orchestra Regionale Toscana, directed by Zubin Mehta, and other international performers. The festival has been extended to include dance (from classical ballet to experimental work) and other events.
**Festa del Grillo**, or the Cricket Festival *(first Sunday after Ascension Thursday)*, Le Cascine, Florence. The huge park to the west of Florence, where Shelley wrote *Ode to the West Wind*, is the setting for this festival. It is a celebration of the joys of spring, at which merchants sell crickets in tiny woven straw cages; these are then released to bring good luck.
**Balestro del Girifalco**, or Falcon Contest *(first Sunday after May 22)*, Massa Marittima *(see p37)*.

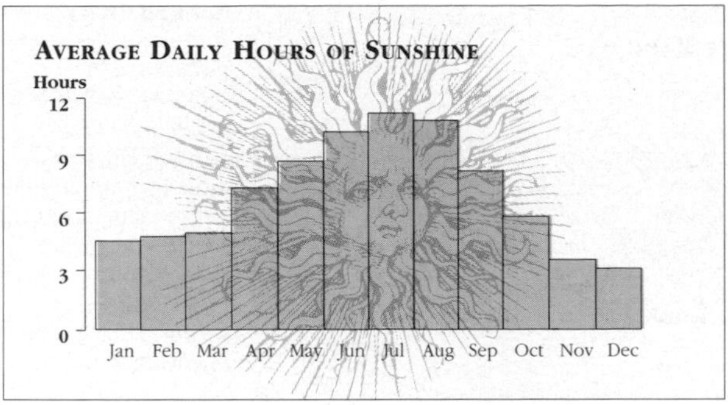


**Sunshine Chart**
*Tuscany has been praised for its light, which has a clear golden quality most noticeable when the intensely sunny days of high summer begin to shorten. Spring and fall days are still warm, with plenty of hours of sunshine to enjoy.*

## SUMMER

FROM JUNE onward, Tuscany's festive calendar becomes increasingly crowded with scores of small town festivals, many of them taking place around Midsummer Day, the feast of John the Baptist, on June 24. These provide an opportunity to sample local food and wine and join in the atmosphere, or to seek out some of the bigger festivals.

**A glorious crop of sunflowers in high summer**

### JUNE

**Calcio in Costume**, or Football (soccer) in Costume *(June 19, 24 and 28)*, Florence *(see p36)*.
**Estate Fiesolana**, or Fiesole Summer *(mid-June to end-August)* in Fiesole *(see p132)*. Festival of music, arts, drama, dance and film. Many events are staged in the amphitheater.
**Regata di San Ranieri** *(June 17)*, Pisa *(see p152)*. Boat races in costume and brilliant processions of colorfully decorated boats are held on the river Arno. After dark, its bankside buildings are illuminated by tens of thousands of flaming torches.
**Gioco del Ponte** or Game of the Bridge *(last Sunday in June)*, Pisa. A ritual battle played out on a bridge *(see p36)*.

**Celebrating a local saint's day on the streets of Siena**

### JULY

**Corsa del Palio** *(July 2 and August 16)*, Siena. This is Tuscany's most famous event *(see p218)*.
**Pistoia Blues** *(early July)*, Piazza del Duomo, Pistoia *(see pp182–3)*. Famous international festival of blues music, lasting for a week.
**Settimana Musicale Senese** *(last week)*, Siena *(see pp214–15)*. Throughout this "Musical Week," chamber music is performed by members of the renowned Accademia Musicale Chigiana in splendid settings, such as the Palazzo Chigi-Saraceni.

### AUGUST

**Festival Pucciniano** *(all month)*, Torre del Lago Puccini *(see p171)*. Performances of the composer's operas in an open-air theater by the lake where he lived.
**Rodeo** *(all month)*, Alberese. Cowboys of the Maremma *(see pp232–3)* demonstrate horse training and cattle herding.

**Italian ice cream, a feast for all ages**

**Cantiere Internazionale d'Arte** *(first half of August)*, Montepulciano *(see p223)*. Directed by the composer Hans Werner Henze, this is an important festival of new work by leading composers, dramatists and choreographers.
**Festa della Bistecca** *(August 15)*, Cortona *(see pp200–1)*. The Festival of the Beefsteak – a local specialty.
**Il Baccanale** *(penultimate Saturday)*, Montepulciano *(see p223)*. Feast of wine, food and song to celebrate the local Vino Nobile *(see p256)*.

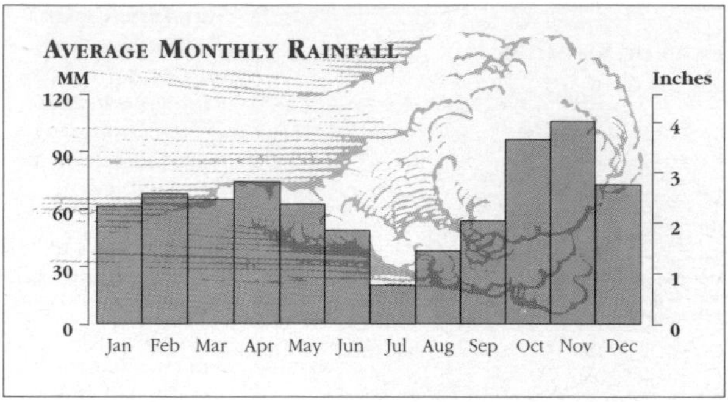


**Rainfall Chart**
*Autumn is the wettest time in Tuscany, with heavy downpours that can last for days, especially late in the season. Late summer storms often bring relief from the intense heat. Winter and spring usually have fairly low rainfall.*

## AUTUMN

AUTUMN IS THE SEASON of the *vendemmia*, the grape harvest, which is often used as an excuse for village festivities at which the local wines flow in quantity. The Tuscans are also passionate about fresh *funghi* (mushrooms), which will appear on restaurant menus and be sold in the markets. The first frosts will occur any time from the end of October, and at this point the great tracts of woodland all over Tuscany begin to turn brilliant shades of red and gold.

**Grape picking by hand in a Chianti vineyard**

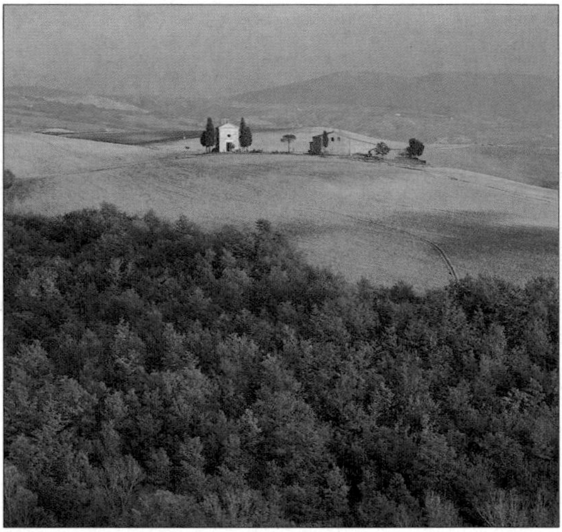

**Autumn in the Val d'Orcia, in southern Tuscany**

## SEPTEMBER

**Giostra del Saraceno** or the Joust of the Saracen *(first Sunday)*, Arezzo *(see p37)*.
**Festa della Rificolona** *(September 7)*, Piazza della Santissima Annunziata, Florence. Children from all over the city converge on the square, carrying candlelit paper lanterns to honor the eve of the birth of the Virgin.
**Palio della Balestra** or Crossbow Festival *(second Sunday)*, Sansepolcro *(see pp192–3)*. Costume parades and flag throwing accompany a crossbow competition between Sansepolcro and the Umbrian town of Gubbio.
**Luminara di Santa Croce** *(September 13)*, Lucca *(see pp174–5)*. The city's famous relic, the *Volto Santo*, a wooden statue of Christ, is paraded around by torchlight.
**Rassegna del Chianti Classico** *(second week)*, Greve in Chianti. The biggest Tuscan celebration of local wines.
**Mostra Mercato Internazionale dell'Antiquariato** *(Sep–Oct)*, Florence. A major biennial antiques fair.

## OCTOBER

**Amici della Musica** *(Oct–Apr)*, Florence. The "Friends of Music" concert season.
**Sagra del Tordo** or Festival of the Thrush *(last Sunday)*, Montalcino *(see p37)*.

**Participant in the Joust of the Saracen festival in Arezzo**

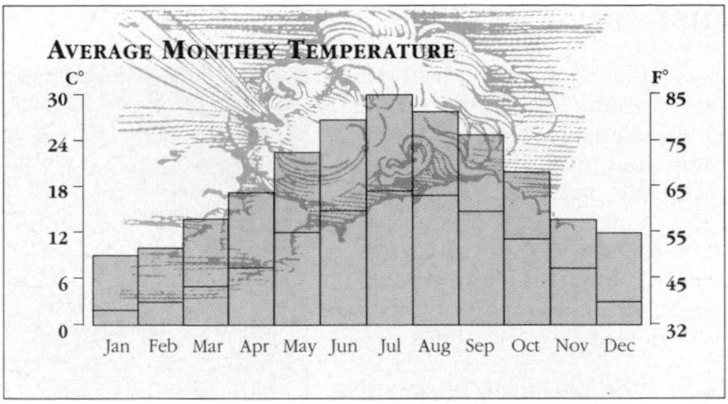


**Temperature Chart**
*July is the hottest, driest month, with June and August only marginally less so. These are the least comfortable months for sight-seeing. Choose late spring or early autumn for this, when you can also sit outside until late.*

## NOVEMBER

**Festival dei Popoli** *(Nov–Dec)*, Palazzo dei Congressi, Florence. Tuscany's most important film festival. Open to everyone, it shows films in their original language with Italian subtitles.

## WINTER

THIS CAN BE a good time to visit Florence and enjoy the city's museums and churches in tranquillity. It can be bitterly cold, but the skies are blue and the city is often bathed in golden sunlight, making this many photographers' favorite season. All over Tuscany, town squares are filled with the aroma of roasting chestnuts, and in December, the last of the olive crop is being harvested in the southernmost parts.

## DECEMBER

**Fiaccole di Natale**, or Festival of Christmas Torches *(Christmas Eve)*, Abbadia di San Salvatore, near Montalcino *(see p220)*. Carols and torchlight processions in memory of the shepherds from the first Christmas Eve.

## JANUARY

**Capodanno**. New Year's Day is celebrated with gusto all over Tuscany. There are fireworks displays, and volleys from hunters firing into the air and from exploding firecrackers: all are part of a ritual to frighten away the ghosts and spirits of the old year and welcome in the new.

**Roasting chestnuts, Montalcino**

**Pitti Immagine Uomo, Pitti Immagine Donna, Pitti Immagine Bimbo** *(throughout January)*, Fortezza da Basso, Florence. At these prestigious fashion shows, leading Italian designers and international couturiers present their spring and summer collections for men, women and children.

## FEBRUARY

**Carnevale** *(Shrove Tuesday)*, Viareggio *(see p171)*. The timing of carnival varies with Easter. This one is renowned throughout Italy for its amusing floats, often inspired by topical themes *(see p36)*.

There are many other opportunities to enjoy pre-Lent celebrations, such as the equally splendid carnival festivities that take place in San Gimignano and Arezzo.

### PUBLIC HOLIDAYS

**New Year's Day** (Jan 1)
**Epiphany** (Jan 6)
**Easter Monday**
**Liberation Day** (Apr 25)
**Labor Day** (May 1)
**Ferragosto** (Aug 15)
**All Saints' Day** (Nov 1)
**Immaculate Conception** (Dec 8)
**Christmas Day** (Dec 25)
**Santo Stefano** (Dec 26)

**Florence's Piazza di Santo Spirito in winter – serene and free of crowds**

# Festivals in Tuscany

Many Tuscan festivals celebrate battles and historical events that took place centuries ago; others have their origins in medieval tournaments. Yet they are not merely a pastiche of history, put on for the benefit of tourists. They are living festivals, mounted with an amazing degree of skill and commitment to authenticity and perfection. This can be seen in such details as the embroidery on the costumes worn by the participants and in the exhilarating displays of horsemanship, jousting and archery. Here is a selection of Tuscany's best.

Soccer in Costume at fever pitch

## Florence

Calcio in costume, or Soccer in Costume (June 19, 24 and 28), is usually held in Piazza di Santa Croce, but the venue varies. This ancient game, a combination of soccer and rugby, involves four teams of 27 men. Each team represents a medieval *rione* (district) of the city. Play is often violent and supporters are very partisan. The final is held on June 28, and the prize is a live cow.

Almost more spectacular than the match itself is the preceding procession, when Florentines march to the square dressed in Renaissance costume, with trumpets and drums. The game on June 24 coincides with midsummer and the feast of John the Baptist, the patron saint of Florence. These events are all celebrated by a fireworks display at 10pm, best seen from the north bank of the Arno, between Ponte Vecchio and Ponte alle Grazie.

## Western Tuscany

The last Sunday in June is the occasion for the Gioco del Ponte, or Game of the Bridge, in Pisa *(see pp152–3)*. This battle, in Renaissance costume, takes place between the Pisans who live north of the river Arno and those who live south. Arranged into teams, they attempt to push a seven-ton carriage over the historic Ponte di Mezzo (literally, the Middle Bridge), which divides the city. On the actual day, the river's banks are crowded with thousands of onlookers. This event probably has its roots in pre-Renaissance times, when there was no regular army and all citizens had to be trained and ready for war.

Some of the participants wear suits of antique armor that date from the 15th and 16th centuries, and their shields bear the colors of the city's different districts. This regalia is kept in the Museo Nazionale di San Matteo *(see p153)* when it is not in use.

Pisa's Game of the Bridge

## Northern Tuscany

Carnevale (Carnival) in Viareggio *(see p171)* on Shrove Tuesday is nationally renowned for its imaginative floats. These carry elaborate satirical models of politicians and other public figures. After courting controversy in recent years, however, this celebration is now more of a family event, but there is still an abundance of pointed visual jokes that can be appreciated by those in the know. The designers of the floats enjoy much flattery and prestige, and their creations remain on display all year. As elsewhere, the occasion is one of concentrated merrymaking, and it combines both ancient pagan rituals and Christian values.

One of the spectacular floats from the Viareggio Carnival

**Knights waiting to charge at the Joust of the Saracen in Arezzo**

## EASTERN TUSCANY

THE PIAZZA GRANDE in Arezzo *(see pp194–5)* is the scene of the Giostra del Saracino, or Joust of the Saracen. Held on the first Sunday in September, this tournament dates back to the Crusades in the Middle Ages, when all Christendom dedicated itself to driving the North African Arabs (the Moors) out of Europe.

There are lively and colorful processions to precede the event, in which eight costumed knights charge toward a wooden effigy of the Saracen. The aim is to try to hit the Saracen's shield with lances and then avoid a cat-o'-three-tails swinging back and unseating them. Each pair of knights represents one of Arezzo's four rival *contrade* (districts), and their supporters occupy a side each of Piazza Grande. They are quiet when their own *contrada* knights are jousting, but make as much noise as is possible to distract the opposition. The winner receives a gold lance.

**Archery at the Festival of the Thrush in Montalcino**

## CENTRAL TUSCANY

THE MOST IMPORTANT festival in this region is Siena's Palio *(see p218)*, but the Sagra del Tordo, or Festival of the Thrush, is also a great attraction. It takes place in Montalcino *(see pp220–21)* on the last Sunday in October. The 14th-century Fortezza (castle) is the setting for an archery contest which is fought in traditional costume by members of the town's four *contrade*. This is accompanied by considerable consumption of the local red Brunello wine and, much to the horror of many bird lovers, of charcoal-grilled thrush. The festival is essentially an excuse for gastronomic over-indulgence, and a celebration of its thriving local economy, which is based on olive oil and wine production. Brunello is widely regarded as one of the finest Italian wines.

Visitors are welcome to participate, and more conventional specialties, such as *porchetta* (roast suckling pig), are available for those who prefer not to eat songbirds. Archery competitions are also held in Montalcino during August to mark the beginning of the hunting season.

## SOUTHERN TUSCANY

BALESTRO DEL GIRIFALCO, or the Falcon Contest, takes place in Massa Marittima *(see p230)* on the first Sunday after the feast of San Bernardino (May 22) and again on the first Sunday in August. It is preceded by a long procession through the town of people in dazzling Renaissance costume, accompanied by flag waving and music. The contest itself is a test of ancient battle skills and the teams represent the town's three traditional historic divisions, which are known as *terzieri* or thirds. Marksmen come forward and try to shoot down a mechanical falcon, tethered on a wire, with their crossbows. Great precision is required to hit the target, and the whole contest is imbued with intense *terzieri* rivalry.

**Renaissance finery at the Falcon Contest in Massa Marittima**

# THE HISTORY OF FLORENCE AND TUSCANY

TUSCANY IS RICH in historical monuments. Etruscan walls encircle many of the region's hilltop towns, and the streets within are lined with medieval and Renaissance palazzi, town halls testifying to the ideals of democracy and self-government, and churches built on the ruins of ancient pagan temples. The countryside, too, is dotted with castles and fortified villages, symbols of the violence and intercommunal strife that tore Tuscany apart for so many years during the medieval period. Typical of these is the hilltop town of San Gimignano *(see pp208–11)*, with its defensive towers.

**The Marzocco lion, emblem of Florence**

Some of the most imposing castles, such as the Fortezza Medicea in Arezzo *(see p194)*, bear the name of the Medici family. Their coat of arms, found all over Tuscany, is a reminder of the role they played in the region's history. They presided over the simultaneous birth of Humanism and the Renaissance and, later, when they were Grand Dukes of Tuscany, patronized eminent scientists and engineers such as Galileo. Tuscany has also played a part in wider events: Napoleon was exiled to Elba, and Florence served briefly as capital of the newly united Italy (1865–71).

Much damage was done to Tuscany's art and monuments by World War II bombing and the floods of 1966. However, major restoration projects undertaken as a result have stimulated research into better scientific methods. In this way, Tuscany's artistic heritage continues to inspire contemporary life – something it has always done for the many creative people who live and work there and for its endless trail of admiring visitors.

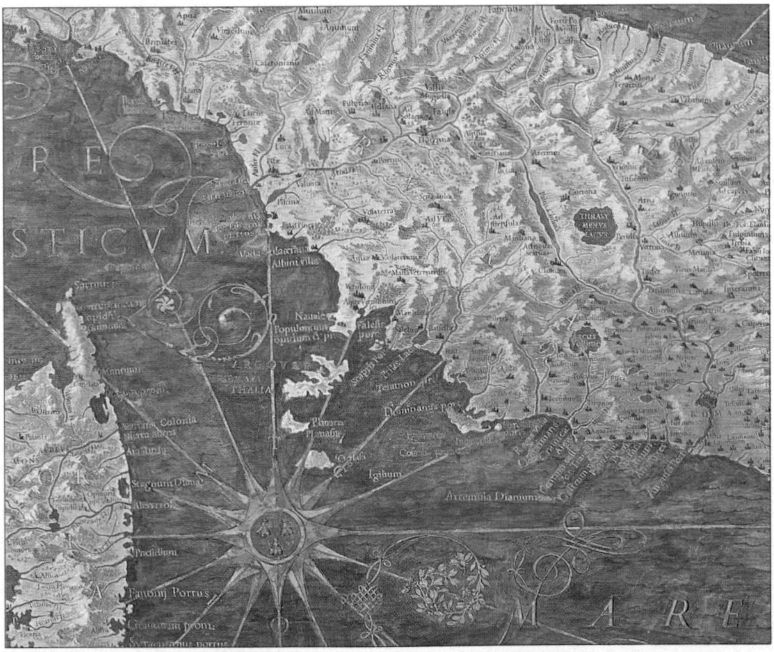


**16th-century map of Italy, showing Pisa and the river Arno leading to Florence**

◁ **San Gimignano, held by its patron saint, and little changed since Taddeo di Bartolo (1362–1422) painted it**

# Etruscan and Roman Tuscany

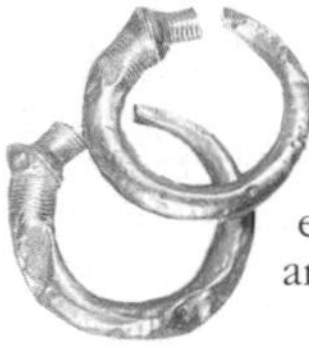

**Etruscan earrings worked in gold**

THE ETRUSCANS MIGRATED to Italy from Asia Minor around 900 BC, attracted to the area they called Etruria (now in Tuscany, Lazio and Umbria) by its mineral wealth. This they exploited to produce weapons, armor, tools and jewelry to trade with Greece. After a fierce war with Rome in 395 BC, the Etruscan civilization was eclipsed by Roman rule. Many aspects of Roman religion can be attributed to the Etruscans, including animal sacrifice and divination – reading the will of the gods in animal entrails or cloud patterns. Everyday Etruscan life and the preoccupation with the afterlife are reflected in detailed carved cremation urns and tombs like those at Volterra *(see pp162–3)*.

**Wax writing tablets** were used to keep household accounts.

**A covered wagon** carved on the urn shows the Etruscans were skilled at carpentry.

**The relief** depicts the last journey of the deceased into the underworld.

## Etruscan Cremation Urn

Much of what is known about the Etruscans comes from studying the contents of their tombs. This 1st-century BC terra-cotta cremation urn from Volterra is carved with scenes from Etruscan domestic life.

**Bronze Chimera** *(4th century BC)*
*The wounded chimera (part goat, lion and serpent) is a dramatic example of Etruscan bronze casting.*

**Athletic Games**
*Tomb paintings depicting chariot races, dancing and athletics suggest that the Etruscans had festivals similar to the Olympic Games of the ancient Greeks.*

## Timeline

**9th century BC** Earliest evidence of Etruscans on Elba

**508 BC** Lars Porsena, Etruscan ruler of Chiusi, leads an unsuccessful attack on Rome

**474 BC** Etruscans defeated in Asia Minor by their commercial rivals; trade with Greece suffers and Etruscan ports such as Populonia begin to decline

900 BC | 800 | 700 | 600 | 500 | 400 | 300

**7th century BC** Beginning of extensive maritime trade with Greece and the Near East

**6th century BC** Founding of the Dodecapolis, a confederation of the 12 most powerful Etruscan cities

*Coin from Populonia*

**395 BC** Rome captures Veii in Lazio, signaling the end of Etruscan independence

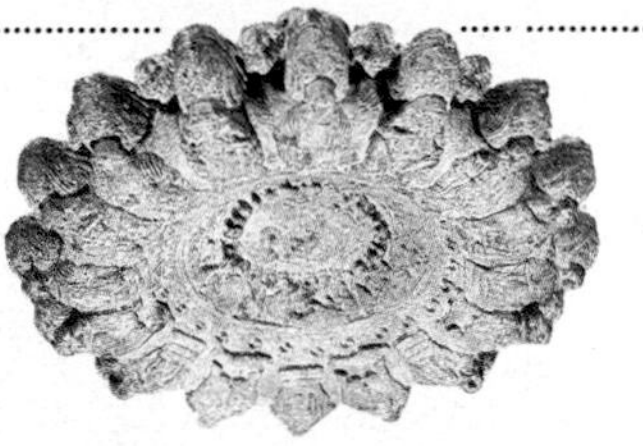

**Circular Chandelier**
*Sixteen oil lamps decorate the rim of this bronze chandelier, made around 300 BC.*

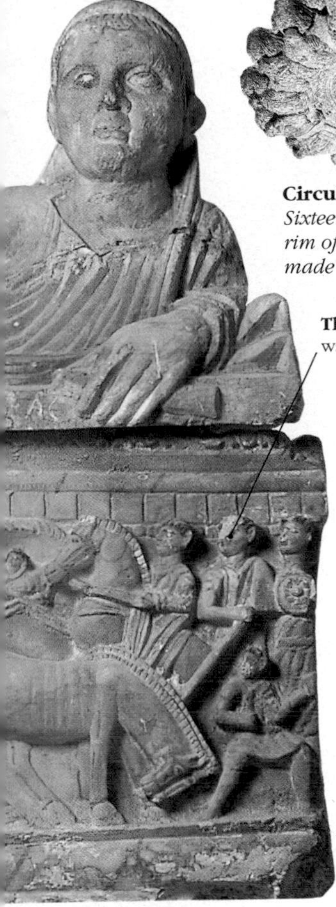

**The family** of the deceased watches the funeral cortège.

**Statue of Venus**
*Under Roman rule, the Etruscans adopted new deities like Venus, goddess of beauty.*

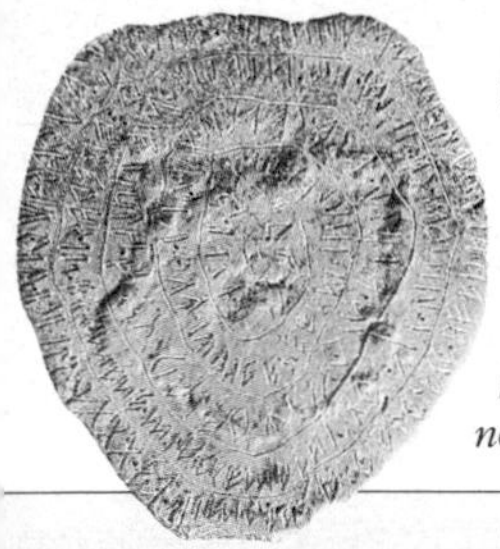

**Lead Tablet**
*Etruscan priests recorded details of their prayers and religious rites on lead tablets. However, their language has not yet been fully deciphered, and many of their beliefs and traditions are not completely understood.*

## Where to See Ancient Tuscany

The famous bronzes of the *Chimera* and the *Orator* are in Florence's Museo Archeologico *(p99)*. Good museum collections are in Fiesole *(pp132–3)*, Volterra *(p162)*, Chiusi *(p224)*, Cortona *(p200)* and Grosseto *(p234)*. There are tombs at Vetulonia *(p234)* and Sovana *(p234)*, and the ruins of an Etruscan town have been excavated near Roselle *(p234)*.

***Etruscan Rock-Cut Tomb***
*The tombs in Sovana date from the 3rd century BC* (p234).

***Roman Theater***
*The bath and theater complex excavated in Volterra was built after Rome conquered the city in the 4th century BC* (p163).

**205 BC** All Tuscany now under Roman control; the Etruscans forced to pay tribute in bronze, grain, weapons and iron

**90 BC** Etruscans granted Roman citizenship, marking the end of their existence as a distinct culture

**AD 250** Christianity brought to Florence by Eastern merchants; St. Minias martyred in the city

**AD 313** Constantine grants official status to Christianity

200 | 100 | AD 1 | 100 | 200 | 300 | 400

*Bronze of a Roman orator c. 300 BC*

**59 BC** Florentia (Florence) founded as a town for retired Roman army veterans

**20 BC** Military colony of Saena (Siena) founded

**AD 405** Flavius Stilicho defeats the Ostrogoths besieging Florence

# Early Medieval Tuscany

**Medieval carved stone lion**

THE CHURCH kept the flame of learning alive during the dark years when Tuscany was under attack from Teutonic tribes such as the Goths and Lombards. Charlemagne, responding to the pope's request for help, drove the Lombards out of Tuscany in the 8th century. He was crowned Holy Roman Emperor as his reward, but this was soon to spark off a long conflict between church and emperor about who should rule Italy.

**Mosaic Madonna**
*A 12th-century mosaic of the Virgin from Cortona* (see p200) *is typical of the Byzantine-influenced art of the early medieval period.*

**Early churche[s]** have simple wooden joists.

**The capitals** are carved with biblical scenes.

**Priests' quarters**

**Semicircular chapels** with limpet-shell roofs are a typical feature of the period.

**Knight on Horseback**
*This 11th-century carving from Sovana's cathedral symbolizes the conflict between pope and emperor over control of the church.*

**Chapel of Sant'Agata**
*Like most early churches in Tuscany, the 12th-century octagonal brick chapel in Pisa, with its pyramid-shaped roof, was built on the grave of a Christian saint martyred by the Romans* (see p152).

## TIMELINE

**552** Totila the Goth attacks Florence

**570** Lombards conquer northern Italy

*Carts used by Charlemagne's army in battle*

500 | 600 | 700 | 800

**774** Charlemagne, King of the Franks, begins a campaign to subjugate the Lombards

*7th-century Lombardic gold crown in Museo Archeologico, Florence* (see p99)

**800** Charlemagne crowned Holy Roman Emperor

**The bells in the campanile** were rung to call the village to church and prayer.

**The ambulatory** ran behind the altar and was used for processions.

**Countess Matilda**
*Matilda, the last of the Margraves, ruled Tuscany in the 11th-century and built many churches in the area.*

**Baptismal Font**
*Scenes taken from the lives of Moses and Christ adorn the 12th-century font at San Frediano, Lucca* (see pp174–5).

## SANT'ANTIMO *(see p224)*

Founded, according to legend, by Charlemagne in 781, the shape of the church demonstrates the influence of the Roman *basilica* (law court) on the design of early churches; the altar occupies the position of the magistrate's chair.

### WHERE TO SEE EARLY MEDIEVAL TUSCANY

Well-preserved early medieval churches are found throughout Tuscany: in San Piero a Grado *(see p157)*; Barga *(p170)*; Lucca *(pp174–5)*; San Quirico d'Orcia *(p221)*; Massa Marittima *(p230)*; Sovana *(p232)*; San Miniato al Monte in Florence *(p130)*; and in Fiesole *(p132)*.

***Castello di Romena***
*The 11th-century tower near Bibbiena was built by the Guidi family, who dominated the area.*

***Santi Apostoli in Florence***
*Founded in 786, the church includes columns from ancient Roman baths* (p109).

| 900 | 1000 | 1100 | 1200 |
|---|---|---|---|

**c.1025–30** Guido d'Arezzo invents a form of musical notation

**1062** Pisa captures Sicily and becomes the foremost Mediterranean port

**1063** Pisa Cathedral begun

**1115** Countess Matilda dies

**1125** Florence captures and destroys Fiesole

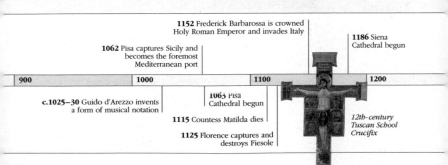

**1152** Frederick Barbarossa is crowned Holy Roman Emperor and invades Italy

**1186** Siena Cathedral begun

*12th-century Tuscan School Crucifix*

# Late Medieval Tuscany

During the 13th century Tuscany grew rich on textile manufacturing and trade. Commercial contact with the Arab world led the Pisan mathematician Fibonacci to introduce Arabic numerals to the West; a new understanding of geometry followed and Tuscan architects began to build ambitious new buildings. At the same time, Tuscan bankers developed the bookkeeping principles that still underlie modern accounting and banking practice. It was also an age of conflict. Cities and factions fought ruthlessly and incessantly to secure wealth and power.

**Defensive towers** protected the city.

**Contented citizens** had time for leisure.

**Condottieri** (mercenaries) were hired to settle conflicts.

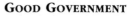

**Dante's Inferno**
*Dante* (in blue) *was caught in the Guelph-Ghibelline conflict and was exiled from Florence in 1302. He took revenge in his poetry, describing his enemies' torments in Hell.*

**Petrarch and Boccaccio**
*Petrarch and Boccaccio* (top and bottom left), *like Dante, wrote in the Tuscan dialect, not Latin. Petrarch's sonnets and Boccaccio's tales were very popular.*

## Good Government

Ambrogio Lorenzetti's early 14th-century allegorical fresco in Siena's Palazzo Pubblico *(see pp214–15)* shows thriving shops, fine buildings and dancing citizens, symbolizing the benefits of good government. Another fresco, *Bad Government,* shows rape, murder, robbery and ruin.

## Timeline

**1215** Start of conflict between Guelph supporters of the pope and Ghibelline supporters of the Holy Roman Emperor

**1252** First gold florin minted

**1260** Siena defeats Florence at Montaperti

**1278** Campo Santo begun in Pisa

1200 | 1220 | 1240 | 1260 | 1280

**1220** Frederick II of Germany is crowned Holy Roman Emperor and lays claim to Italy

**1224** St. Francis receives the "stigmata" (the wounds of Christ) at La Verna

*Florin stamped with the lily of Florence*

**1284** Pisan navy defeated by Genoa; the beginning of Pisa's decline as a port

**Wool Traders' Emblem**
*Luca della Robbia's roundel depicts the Lamb of God, symbol of the Calimala (wool importers), whose trade guild was the most powerful in Florence.*

**A building boom** resulted from increased prosperity.

**St. Francis (1181–1226)**
*From monasteries founded in Tuscany by St. Francis, the Franciscans brought about a major religious revival in reaction to the excesses of the church.*

**Bankers in Siena**
*Tuscan banks provided loans to popes, monarchs and merchants. Many bankers were ruined when Edward III of England defaulted on his debts in 1342.*

## Where to See Late Medieval Tuscany

San Gimignano's spectacular towers *(see pp208–11)* show what most Tuscan cities must have looked like during the Middle Ages. Siena has the best surviving late medieval town hall *(pp214–15)*, and Pisa's Leaning Tower, Duomo and Baptistry *(pp154–6)* reflect the willingness of architects of this period to experiment with new styles.

***Medieval building techniques***
*Rectangular putlog holes show where medieval builders placed their scaffolding timbers.*

***Lucignano***
*Some of Tuscany's best-preserved medieval architecture, including several defensive towers, can be seen in Lucignano* (p199).

**1294** Work begins on Florence's cathedral

**1299** Work begins on Palazzo Vecchio in Florence

**1300** Giovanni Pisano carves pulpit for Pisa's cathedral

**1302** Dante begins writing *The Divine Comedy*

**1345** Work begins on Florence's Ponte Vecchio

**1348–93** Black Death carries off half the Tuscan population

**1350** Pisa's Leaning Tower completed; Boccaccio begins writing *The Decameron*

*Sir John Hawkwood, English mercenary*

**1374** Death of Petrarch

**1377** Sir John Hawkwood appointed Captain General of Florence

**1300** | **1320** | **1340** | **1380**

# The Renaissance

**Della Robbia roundel from the Cappella de' Pazzi (1430)**

UNDER ASTUTE Medici leadership, Florence enjoyed a period of peace and prosperity. Rich bankers and merchants invested in fine palaces to replace their cramped tower houses and paid for the adornment of churches. The result was an outpouring of art and architecture, remarkable for its break with the Gothic past and its conscious attempt to give "rebirth" to Classical values. The rediscovery of works by ancient philosophers like Cicero and Plato profoundly influenced the intellectual preoccupations of the day. Their ideas inspired the Humanists, who emphasized the role of knowledge and reason in human affairs.

**Textile Market**
*The thriving Florentine textiles industry allowed the textile guilds and merchants like the dye importer Rucellai* (see p104) *to become patrons of the arts.*

**Terra-cotta roundels** of babies in swaddling bands, added by Andrea della Robbia in 1487, reflect the building's function as an orphanage.

**Classical arches** illustrate the Florentine passion for ancient Roman architecture.

## Spedale degli Innocenti

The archetypal Renaissance building, Brunelleschi's colonnade (1419–26) for the Spedale degli Innocenti *(see p95)* is a masterpiece of restrained Classical design. Europe's first orphanage, the Spedale is also a major social monument.

**Battle of San Romano** *(1456)*
*Florence hired* condottieri *(mercenaries) to fight its battles. Its citizens were therefore free to concentrate on making the city wealthy. Uccello's striking depiction of the Florentine victory over Siena in 1432 is an early attempt to master perspective.*

## Timeline

| 1400 | 1410 | 1420 | 1430 | 1440 |
|---|---|---|---|---|

**1402** Florence Baptistry doors competition *(see p66)*

**1406** Pisa falls to Florence

**1416** Donatello completes his *St. George (see p67)*

**1419** Work begins on the Spedale degli Innocenti

**1425–7** Masaccio paints *The Life of St. Peter* frescoes in Santa Maria del Carmine *(see pp126–7)*

*Cosimo il Vecchio*

**1434** Cosimo il Vecchio returns from exile

**1436** Brunelleschi completes dome for Florence cathedral *(see pp64–5)*. Work starts on San Marco *(see pp96–7)*

**Humanist Scholars**
*By studying a broad range of subjects, from art to politics, the Humanists fostered the idea of the Renaissance man, equally skilled in many activities.*

**Gray sandstone** and white plaster contrast radically with the rich surface ornamentation of late medieval architecture.

**Classical Corinthian capital**

**David** *(1475)*
*A favorite Florentine subject* (see p77), *Verrocchio's bronze emphasizes David's youth and vulnerability.*

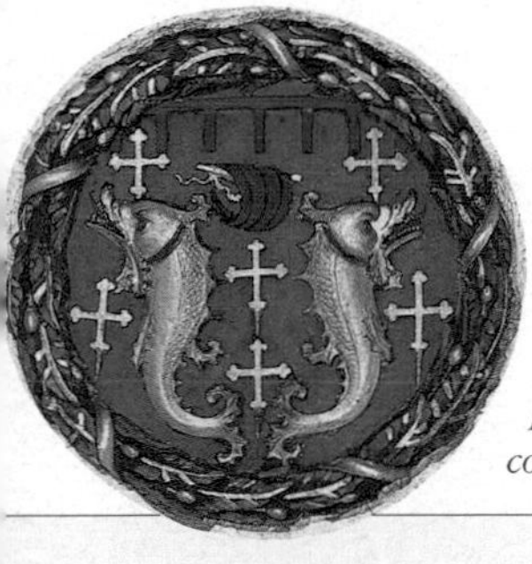

**Pazzi Family Emblem**
*The wealthy Pazzi were disgraced after trying to assassinate Lorenzo the Magnificent and seize control of Florence in 1478.*

### Where to See Renaissance Tuscany

Most of Florence was rebuilt during the Renaissance. Highlights include San Lorenzo *(see pp90–91)*, Masaccio's frescoes in the Brancacci Chapel *(pp126–7)*, many paintings in the Uffizi *(pp80–83)* and the sculptures at the Bargello *(pp68–9)*.

***Pienza Duomo*** *(1459)*
*Pope Pius II's plans for a model Renaissance city at Pienza* (p222) *were never fully realized.*

***San Marco Cloister*** *(1437)*
*Cosimo il Vecchio paid for Michelozzo's cloister* (pp96–7) *and used it as a retreat.*

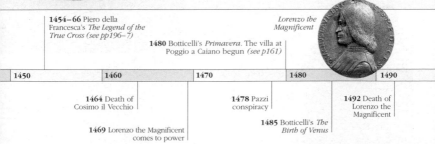

**1454–66** Piero della Francesca's *The Legend of the True Cross (see pp196–7)*

**1480** Botticelli's *Primavera*. The villa at Poggio a Caiano begun *(see p161)*

*Lorenzo the Magnificent*

| 1450 | 1460 | 1470 | 1480 | 1490 |
|---|---|---|---|---|

**1464** Death of Cosimo il Vecchio

**1469** Lorenzo the Magnificent comes to power

**1478** Pazzi conspiracy

**1485** Botticelli's *The Birth of Venus*

**1492** Death of Lorenzo the Magnificent

# The Medici of Florence

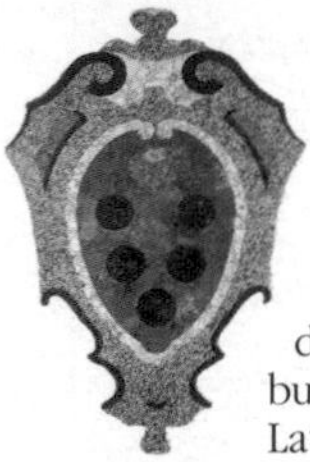

**Medici coat of arms, San Lorenzo**

THE MEDICI FAMILY held power in Florence almost continuously from 1434 until 1743. Their rule began discreetly enough with Cosimo il Vecchio, son of a self-made man, Giovanni di Bicci. For years, Cosimo and his descendants directed policy with popular support, but without ever being voted into office. Later generations gained titles and power but ruled by force. Two were elected pope and, after the Republic *(see pp50–51)*, the decadent Alessandro took the title Duke of Florence. From him control passed to Cosimo I, who was crowned Grand Duke of Tuscany.

**Giovanni di Bicci**
*An astute merchant banker, he founded the Medici fortune.*

**Lorenzo the Magnificent**
*A poet and statesman, Lorenzo was the model Renaissance man. One of his greatest achievements was to negotiate peace among the cities of northern Italy.*

Giovanni di Bicci (1360–1429)

① Cosimo il Vecchio (1389–1464)

② Piero the Gouty (1416–69)

③ Lorenzo the Magnificent (1449–92)

Giuliano (1453–78)

Giulio, Pope Clement V (1478–1534)

④ Piero (1472–1503)

⑤ Giovanni, Pope Leo X (1475–1521)

⑦ Giuliano, Duke of Nemours (1479–1516)

⑧ Alessandro, Duke of Florenc (1511–37: parentage uncertai

⑥ Lorenzo, Duke of Urbino (1492–1519)

Catherine, Duchess of Urbino *m* Henry II of France (1519–89)

**Catherine of France**
*Catherine married Henri II of France in 1533. She is shown with two of her sons, who both became French kings: Charles IX and Henri III. Yet another son became Francis II of France.*

**Pope Leo X**
*Elected pope when only 38, Leo's corrupt plans to fund the rebuilding of St. Peter's in Rome triggered a furious reaction that led to the birth of the Protestant movement.*

## Medici Patronage

As one of the most powerful families in Florence, the Medici were responsible for commissioning some of the greatest works of the Renaissance. Many artists flattered their patrons by placing them prominently in the foreground of their paintings. In Botticelli's *Adoration of the Magi* (1475), the gray-haired king who is pictured kneeling at the feet of the Virgin is Cosimo il Vecchio. The kneeling figure in the white robe is his grandson, Giuliano. The young man holding a sword, on the far left of the painting, is thought to be a rather idealized portrait of Lorenzo the Magnificent, Cosimo's other grandson.

***Adoration of the Magi* (1475) by Botticelli**

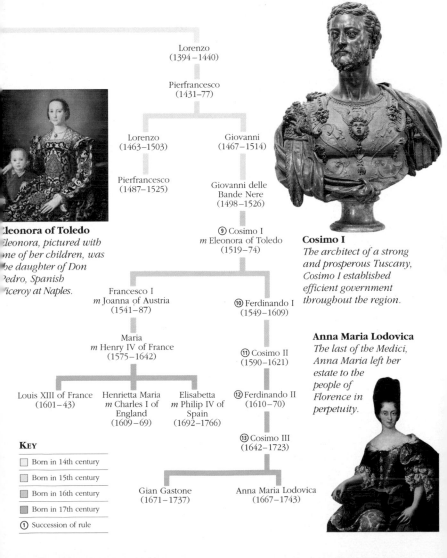

**leonora of Toledo**
*leonora, pictured with ne of her children, was he daughter of Don edro, Spanish iceroy at Naples.*

**Cosimo I**
*The architect of a strong and prosperous Tuscany, Cosimo I established efficient government throughout the region.*

Lorenzo (1394–1440)

Pierfrancesco (1431–77)

Lorenzo (1463–1503)

Pierfrancesco (1487–1525)

Giovanni (1467–1514)

Giovanni delle Bande Nere (1498–1526)

⑨ Cosimo I *m* Eleonora of Toledo (1519–74)

Francesco I *m* Joanna of Austria (1541–87)

Maria *m* Henry IV of France (1575–1642)

Louis XIII of France (1601–43)

Henrietta Maria *m* Charles I of England (1609–69)

Elisabetta *m* Philip IV of Spain (1692–1766)

⑩ Ferdinando I (1549–1609)

⑪ Cosimo II (1590–1621)

⑫ Ferdinando II (1610–70)

⑬ Cosimo III (1642–1723)

Gian Gastone (1671–1737)

Anna Maria Lodovica (1667–1743)

**Anna Maria Lodovica**
*The last of the Medici, Anna Maria left her estate to the people of Florence in perpetuity.*

**Key**

- Born in 14th century
- Born in 15th century
- Born in 16th century
- Born in 17th century
- ① Succession of rule

# The Florentine Republic

**Savonarola (1452–98)**

In 1494, when Piero de' Medici abandoned Florence to the invading troops of Charles VIII of France, the city was declared a Republic. Under the leadership of the religious fundamentalist Girolamo Savonarola the people were encouraged to believe that God was their only ruler. After his execution in 1498, the Republic survived 32 years of constant attack. Finally, in 1530, the Medici Pope, Clement VII, and the Holy Roman Emperor, Charles V of Spain, combined forces and returned the city to Medici rule.

**Palazzo Vecchio Frieze**

*The inscription, "Christ is King," on this Republican frieze implies that no mortal ruler has absolute power.*

**Charles VIII Enters Siena**

*When the French invaded Tuscan cities in 1494, Savonarola claimed it was God's punishment for the Tuscan obsession with profane books and art. He ordered such objects burned in "bonfires of vanity."*

**Judith and Holofernes**

*Donatello's statue of the virtuous Judith slaying the tyrant Holofernes was placed in front of the Palazzo Vecchio in 1494 to symbolize the end of Medici rule.*

### The Siege of Florence *(1529–30)*

Besieged by 40,000 papal and imperial troops, the citizens of Florence held out for ten months before starvation and disease led to their surrender. Vasari's fresco in the Palazzo Vecchio shows the full extent of the city's defenses and the scale of the enemy assault.

## Timeline

**1494** Charles VIII attacks Florence. Savonarola seizes power from Medici family

**1495**

**1498** Savonarola burned at the stake

*Chancellor Soderini*

**1502** Soderini elected first chancellor of the Republic

**1504** Michelangelo completes *David* *(see p77)*

**1505**

**1509** Pope Julius II begins driving the French from Italian soil

**1510**

**1512** Florence besieged by Cardinal Giovanni de' Medici

**1513** Giovanni de' Medici crowned Pope Leo X

**Execution of Savonarola**
*An inspirational orator who commanded great popular support, Savonarola's political enemies had him executed for heresy in 1498.*

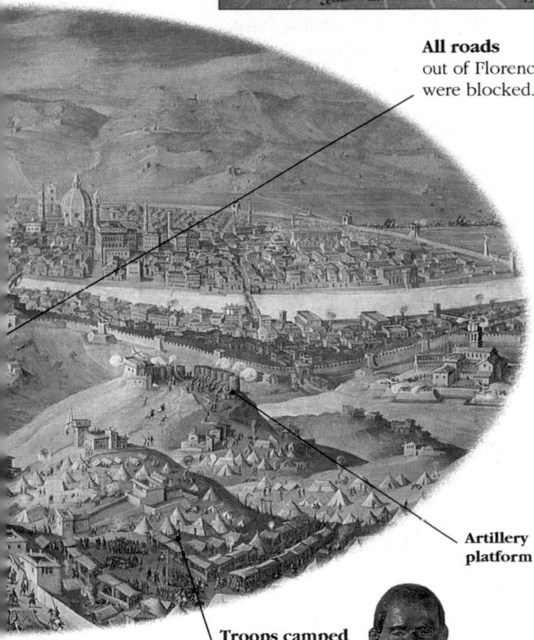
**All roads** out of Florence were blocked.
**Artillery platform**
**Troops camped** to the south.

**Niccolò Machiavelli**
*The author of* The Prince, *a treatise on the ruthless skills required to be a successful politician, was the last Republican chancellor.*

## WHERE TO SEE REPUBLICAN TUSCANY

A plaque in Piazza della Signoria *(see pp76–7)* marks the spot where Savonarola was executed; his cell can be seen in San Marco *(pp96–7)*. Michelangelo's *David (p94)* symbolizes the victory of the youthful Republic over tyranny. The Republican council met in the Salone dei Cinquecento *(p76)*.

***Tower of San Miniato***
*This was reinforced in 1530 as a gun platform* (pp130–31).

***Michelangelo's Sketches***
*During the siege of 1530, Michelangelo worked in the safety of the Cappelle Medicee* (pp90–91).

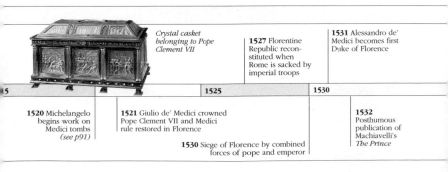

*Crystal casket belonging to Pope Clement VII*

**1527** Florentine Republic reconstituted when Rome is sacked by imperial troops

**1531** Alessandro de' Medici becomes first Duke of Florence

5 | 1525 | 1530

**1520** Michelangelo begins work on Medici tombs *(see p91)*

**1521** Giulio de' Medici crowned Pope Clement VII and Medici rule restored in Florence

**1530** Siege of Florence by combined forces of pope and emperor

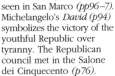

**1532** Posthumous publication of Machiavelli's *The Prince*

# The Grand Duchy

COSIMO I WAS CREATED GRAND DUKE of Tuscany in 1570, having forced Tuscany into a state of political unity for the first time. A period of prosperity followed, in spite of the corrupt and debauched nature of Cosimo's heirs. When the Medici line ended in 1737, the Grand Duchy was inherited by the Austrian Dukes of Lorraine. They were removed from power in 1860 during the Risorgimento, when the Italian people joined forces to overthrow their foreign rulers. From 1865–70, Florence was the nation's capital. With the final unification of Italy in 1870, however, the center of power returned to Rome.

**Leopoldo I and Family**
*Leopoldo I, later Emperor Leopold II of Austria, introduced many reforms, including abolition of the death penalty*

**The Church** rejected Galileo's discoveries.

**Galileo explains** his theory of gravity.

**Livorno Harbor**
*Livorno became a free port in 1608: ships from every nation were granted equal docking rights, and the resulting influx of Jewish and Moorish refugees contributed to the city's prosperity.*

**The Old Market**
*Florence's Old Market was knocked down in 1865, when the city was briefly the Italian capital. In its place is the triumphal arch of the Piazza della Repubblica* (see p112).

## THE AGE OF SCIENCE

Galileo was one of several brilliant scientists who benefited from Medici patronage during the 17th century, making Tuscany a center of scientific innovation. His experiments and astronomical observations laid the foundations for modern empirical science, but led to his persecution for contradicting the teachings of the Roman Catholic Church.

## TIMELINE

**1537** Cosimo I elected Duke of Florence

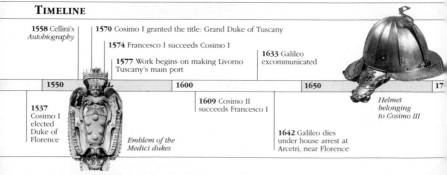

**1558** Cellini's *Autobiography*

**1570** Cosimo I granted the title: Grand Duke of Tuscany

**1574** Francesco I succeeds Cosimo I

**1577** Work begins on making Livorno Tuscany's main port

**1609** Cosimo II succeeds Francesco I

**1633** Galileo excommunicated

**1642** Galileo dies under house arrest at Arcetri, near Florence

1550 | 1600 | 1650 | 17

*Emblem of the Medici dukes*

*Helmet belonging to Cosimo III*

**The Grand Tour**
*It became fashionable for wealthy 18th-century European aristocrats to visit Tuscany. This detail from Zoffani's* Tribuna *(1770) shows a tour of the Uffizi.*

**Galileo conducted** his experiments using specially designed equipment *(see p74).*

**Cosimo II** gave refuge to Galileo after the Church accused him of heresy.

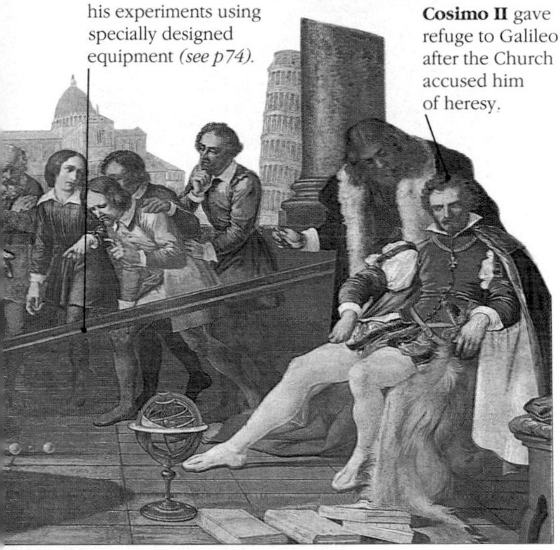

**National Rule**
*Florence ran up huge debts while serving as the Italian capital. This cartoon shows a protest against the seat of power (the Palazzo Vecchio) being transferred to Rome.*

## Where to See Grand Duchy Tuscany

The Uffizi art collection *(see pp80–83)* was assembled by the Medici at this time, along with the collections in the Palazzo Pitti *(pp120–23)*, the building from which the Grand Dukes ruled Tuscany for over 300 years. The story of Galileo and his contemporaries is told in the Museo di Storia della Scienza in Florence *(p74)*. The frescoes of the Sala del Risorgimento, in the Palazzo Pubblico, Siena *(p214)*, depict the events that preceded the final unification of Italy.

***Palazzzo del Cavalieri***
*Francavilla's statue of Cosimo I (1596) marks the entrance to Vasari's ornate Palazzo* (p152).

***Napoleon's Bathroom***
*Napoleon never used this bathroom (1790–99), built for him at the Palazzo Pitti* (pp120–23).

**1765** Grand Duke Leopoldo I introduces many social reforms

**1796** Napoleon's first Italian campaign

**1799** France defeats Austria: Tuscany ruled by Louis de Bourbon, then by Napoleon's sister, Elisa Baciocchi

**1815** Napoleon defeated at Waterloo

**1822** Shelley drowns near Livorno

**1840** Ruskin visits Florence

1750 | 1800 | 1850

**1814** Napoleon exiled to Elba

**1743** Death of Anna Maria Lodovica, last of the Medici

**1737** End of Medici dynasty; rule passes to Austrian House of Lorraine

*John Ruskin (1819–1900), who revived critical interest in the Renaissance*

**1865** Florence chosen as capital of new Italian state

**1871** Italian capital returns to Rome

# The Modern Era

**Traffic Control**
*In 1988 Florence banned cars from the city center.*

THE 20TH CENTURY has seen many threats to Florence's fragile artistic heritage. The city's historic bridges, except for the Ponte Vecchio, were destroyed during World War II, and worse was to come in 1966 from devastating floods. Traffic and pollution have also taken their toll, leading to tough environmental controls aimed at preserving the historic city center. Fortunately, the city has energetically risen to these challenges. It continues to thrive both on its proud heritage and as a living, working city with a robust commercial and industrial base.

**La Bohème** *(1896)*
*This popular opera by Puccini, Tuscany's greatest composer, often features in the region's music festivals* (see p33).

**Firenze Nuova**
*Florentine commerce and industry are moving to the suburb of "New Florence," leaving the city center free for cultural and creative enterprises.*

## ART RESTORATION

Great pride is taken in Tuscany's artistic heritage, and modern scientific methods are used to analyze frescoes before restoration, such as *The Procession of the Magi* *(see p89)*. These methods include computer-aided mapping of the pigments and plotting any structural damage.

## TIMELINE

*Domenico Tiburzi, folk hero and notorious Maremman bandit*

**1896** First performance of Puccini's *La Bohème*

**1896** Domenico Tiburzi is caught and shot after 24 years on the run

**1915** Italy enters World War I on the side of the Allies (France, Britain and Russia)

**1922** Mussolini heads Italy's first Fascist government

1890 | 1900 | 1910 | 1920

*Benito Mussolini*

**The 1966 Floods**
*On November 4, floodwater from the Arno rose to 6 m (19.5 ft) above street level. Many art treasures were ruined; some are still in restoration.*

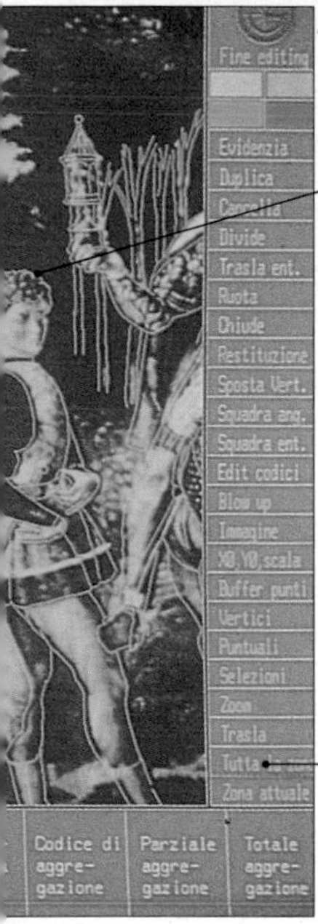


**A scanned image** lets restorers trace existing outlines and reconstruct damaged areas.

**Commands for operating the computer program**

**Fashion**
*Many Florentine designers have become household names. These include Pucci, who invented the "Palazzo Pajamas," Gucci, Ferragamo* (see p266) *and, more recently, rising stars like Daelli and Coveri.*

**Tourism**
*Florence and Tuscany have long been popular destinations for tourists* (see p53). *Florence now receives some 5 million visitors each year.*

## WHERE TO SEE MODERN FLORENCE

The shops of Via de' Tornabuoni and Via della Vigna Nuova *(see p105)* sell the best in Florentine fashion. Exhibitions of photographs at the Museo Alinari *(p104)* illustrate the city as it has developed during the 20th century. Cimabue's ruined *Crucifixion (p72)* in Santa Croce is displayed as a reminder of the 1966 floods.

***Train station*** *(1935)*
*The Functionalist station is the city center's only notable modern building* (see p113).

***San Giovanni Battista*** *(1964)*
*Giovanni Michelucci's modern church stands near Amerigo Vespucci airport.*

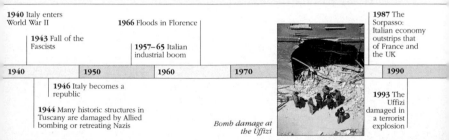

**1940** Italy enters World War II

**1943** Fall of the Fascists

**1944** Many historic structures in Tuscany are damaged by Allied bombing or retreating Nazis

**1946** Italy becomes a republic

**1957–65** Italian industrial boom

**1966** Floods in Florence

**1987** The Sorpasso: Italian economy outstrips that of France and the UK

**1993** The Uffizi damaged in a terrorist explosion

| 1940 | 1950 | 1960 | 1970 | 1990 |
|---|---|---|---|---|

*Bomb damage at the Uffizi*

# FLORENCE AREA BY AREA

# Florence at a Glance

HISTORIC FLORENCE is fairly compact, and the sights described on the following pages are easily reached on foot or by bus. The sights are grouped within the four areas shown on the map below, each of which has its own section within this book. Most visitors head first for City Center East, with the magnificent Duomo, the heart of the city. City Center North is associated with the Medici, while City Center West has smart shops. Across the Ponte Vecchio is Oltrarno, with the treasures of the Palazzo Pitti.

**PAGES 100–113**
*Street Finder maps*
*1, 3, 5, 6*

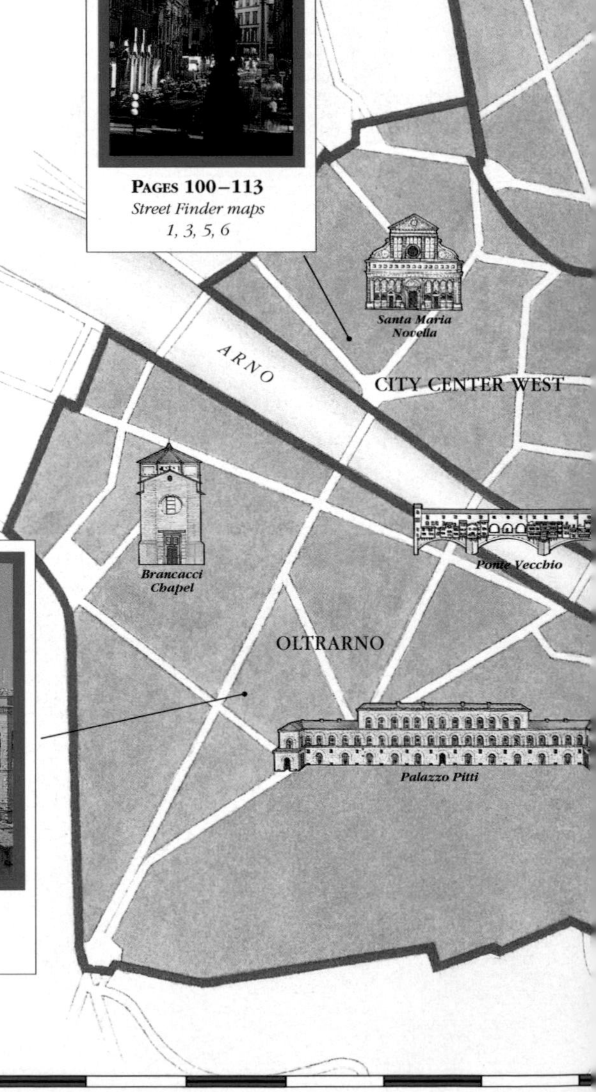

**PAGES 114–127**
*Street Finder maps*
*3, 4, 5*

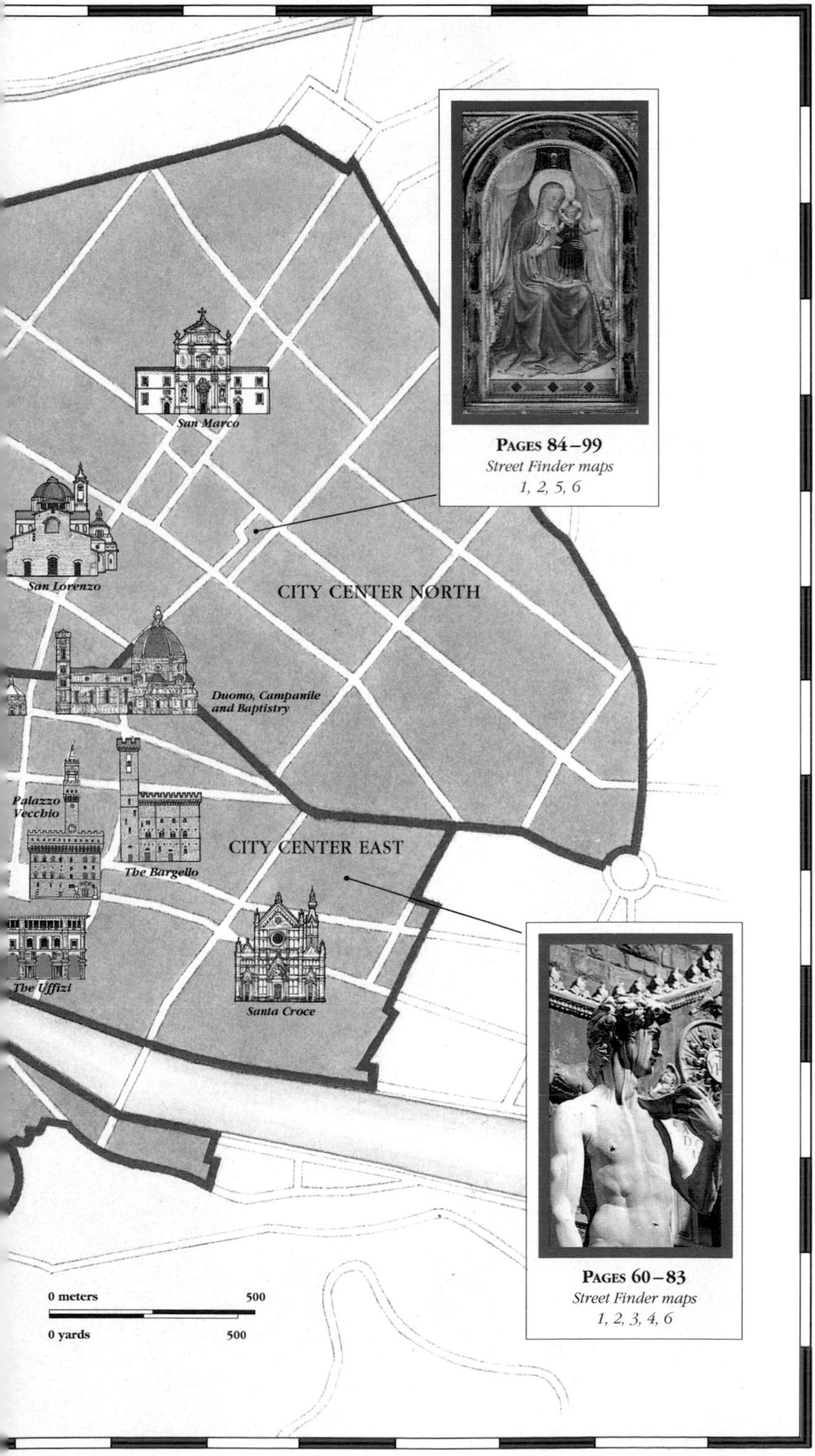
San Marco
San Lorenzo
CITY CENTER NORTH
Duomo, Campanile and Baptistry
Palazzo Vecchio
The Bargello
CITY CENTER EAST
The Uffizi
Santa Croce
PAGES 84–99
Street Finder maps
1, 2, 5, 6
PAGES 60–83
Street Finder maps
1, 2, 3, 4, 6
0 meters 500
0 yards 500

# City Center East

The dominant building in this part of Florence is the magnificent Duomo, the first place most people will visit when they arrive in the city. Traffic is now banned in the Piazza del Duomo, which makes it easier to appreciate the immensity of this great building. It is, in fact, so large that a comprehensive view is impossible from such close quarters. As you wander the streets to the south you will continually catch glimpses of its multicolored marble cladding.

**Duomo clock, decorated in 1443 by Paolo Uccello**

The area's other major church, Santa Croce, containing the tombs and monuments of many great Florentines, sits at the center of the traditional artisans' quarter. These streets have few prestigious palaces, but there is a lively and attractive sense of community. It is here that you will find distinctive neighborhood shops and restoration workshops where specialists continue to repair the many books and works of art damaged in the 1966 floods *(see pp54–5).*

## Sights at a Glance

**Museums and Galleries**
*The Bargello pp68–9* ❻
Casa di Dante ❹
Museo di Firenze com'era ❽
Museo Horne ⓬
Museo dell'Opera del Duomo ❷
Museo di Storia della Scienza ⓭
Palazzo Nonfinito ❼
*Palazzo Vecchio pp78–9* ⓱
*The Uffizi pp80–83* ⓲

**Churches**
Badia Fiorentina ❺
Casa Buonarroti ❿
*Duomo, Campanile and Baptistry pp64–5* ❶
Orsanmichele ❸
*Santa Croce pp72–3* ⓫
Santo Stefano al Ponte ⓮

**Historic Streets and Piazzas**
*Piazza della Signoria pp76–7* ⓰

**Shops**
Erboristeria ⓯

**Ice Cream Parlors**
Bar Vivoli Gelateria ❾

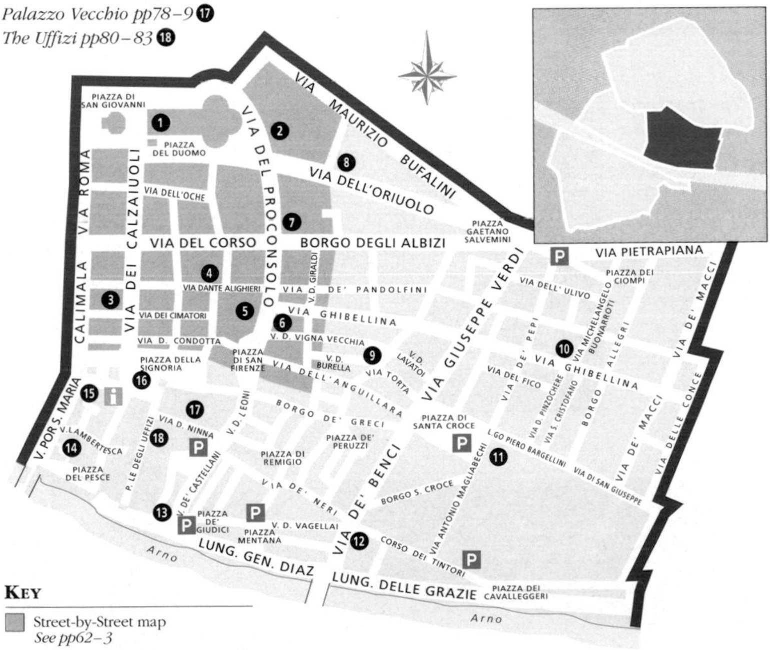


**Key**

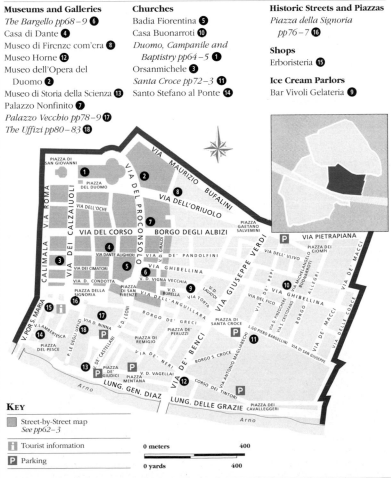

Street-by-Street map *See pp62–3*

Tourist information

Parking

0 meters 400

0 yards 400

◁ Michelangelo's *David* in Piazza della Signoria

# Street-by-Street: Around the Duomo

**Statue on Orsanmichele façade**

MUCH OF FLORENCE WAS REBUILT during the Renaissance, but the eastern part of the city retains a distinctly medieval feel. With its confusing maze of tiny alleyways and hidden lanes, it would still be recognizable to Dante. His house, the Casa di Dante, still stands near the Badia Fiorentina, where he first glimpsed his beloved, Beatrice Portinari *(see p70)*. He would also recognize the Bargello, across the road from the Badia, and, of course, the Baptistry. Onc of thc oldest streets is the Borgo degli Albizi. Now lined with Renaissance palaces, it follows the line of the ancient Roman road to Rome.

**The dome**, completed in 1436, was designed by Brunelleschi to dwarf even the great buildings of ancient Greece and Rome.

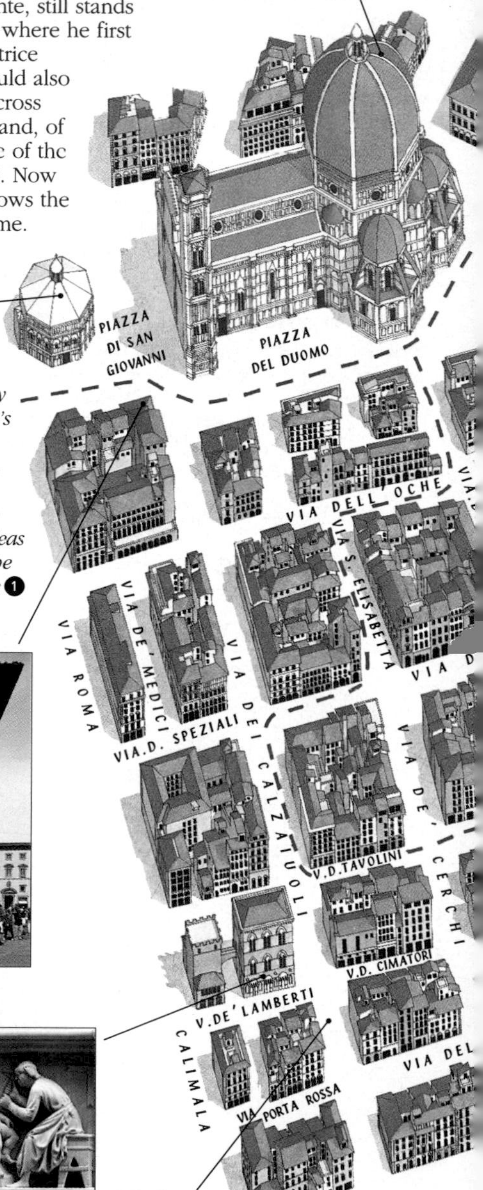


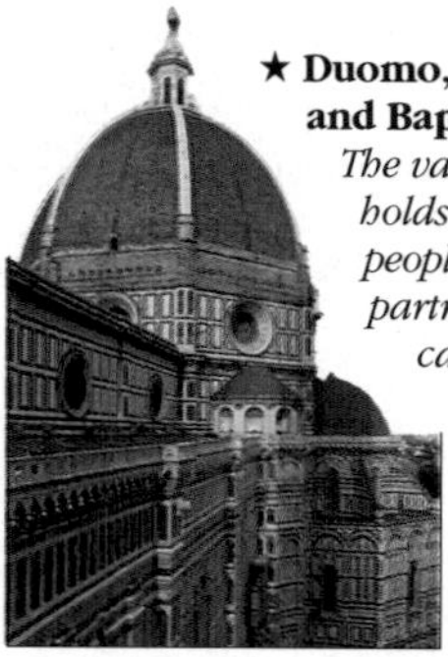

**★ Duomo, Campanile and Baptistry**
*The vast Duomo holds up to 20,000 people. It is elegantly partnered by Giotto's campanile and the Baptistry, whose doors demonstrate the artistic ideas that led to the Renaissance* ❶

**The Loggia del Bigallo** was built for the Misericordia by Alberto Arnoldi in 1358. During the 15th century, abandoned children were displayed here for three days. If, after this time, their parents had not claimed them, they were sent to foster homes.

**★ Orsanmichele**
*The carvings on the walls of this Gothic church depict the activities and patron saints of the city's trade guilds, such as the Masons and Carpenters* ❸

**Via dei Calzaiuoli**, lined with smart shops, is the focus of the *passeggiata*, the traditional evening stroll.

**★ Museo dell'Opera del Duomo**
*Works removed from the Duomo, Campanile and Baptistry, like this panel by Verrocchio, are displayed here* ❷

**Locator Map**
*See Florence Street Finder map 6*

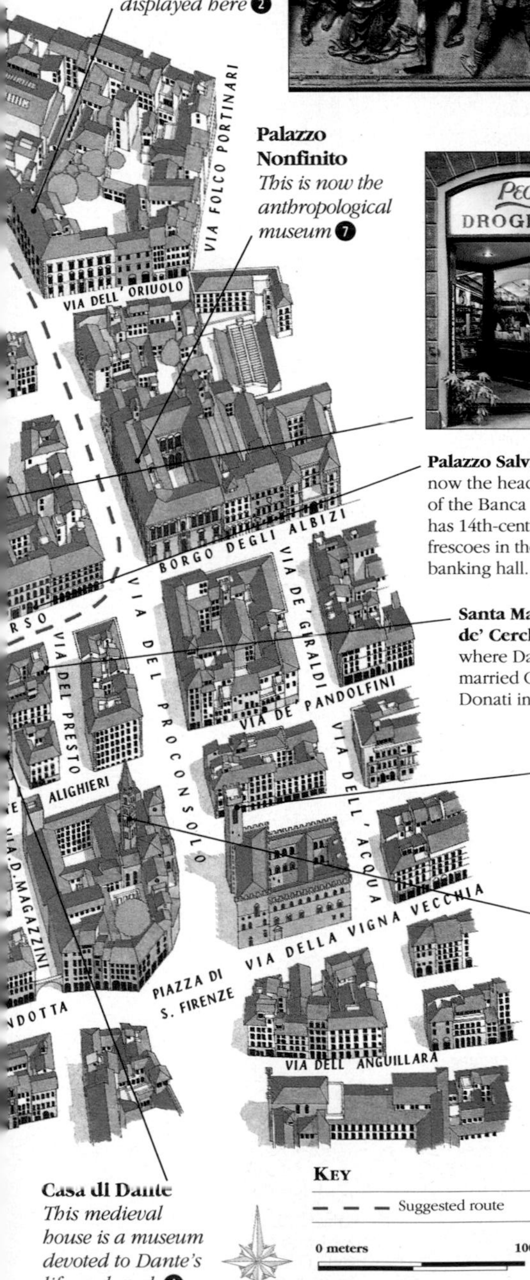


**Palazzo Nonfinito**
*This is now the anthropological museum* ❼

**Pegna**, a mini-supermarket tucked away in the Via della Studio, sells a range of gourmet treats including chocolate, honey, wine, balsamic vinegar and olive oil *(see p267).*

**Palazzo Salviati**, now the head office of the Banca Toscana, has 14th-century frescoes in the main banking hall.

**Santa Margherita dc' Cerchi** is where Dante married Gemma Donati in 1285.

**★ The Bargello**
*The city's old prison is home to a rich collection of applied arts and sculpture, like this figure by Cellini (1500–71)* ❻

**Badia Fiorentina**
*The Badia's bell regulated daily life in medieval Florence* ❺

**Casa di Dante**
*This medieval house is a museum devoted to Dante's life and work* ❹

**Key**

— — — Suggested route

0 meters 100

0 yards 100

**Star Sights**

- ★ **Duomo, Campanile and Baptistry**
- ★ **The Bargello**
- ★ **Museo dell'Opera del Duomo**
- ★ **Orsanmichele**

# Duomo, Campanile and Baptistry ❶

SET IN THE HEART of Florence, Santa Maria del Fiore – the Duomo, or cathedral, of Florence – dominates the city with its enormous dome. Its sheer size was typical of Florentine determination to lead in all things, and to this day, no other building stands taller in the city. The Baptistry with its celebrated doors *(see p66)* is one of Florence's oldest buildings, dating perhaps to the 4th century. In his capacity as city architect, Giotto designed the Campanile in 1334; it was completed in 1359, 22 years after his death.

**The Campanile**
*At 85 m (276 ft), the Campanile is 6 m (20 ft) shorter than the dome. It is clad in white, green and pink Tuscan marble.*

**★ Baptistry Ceiling**
*Colorful 13th-century mosaics illustrating the Last Judgment are set above the large octagonal font where many famous Florentines, including Dante, were baptized.*

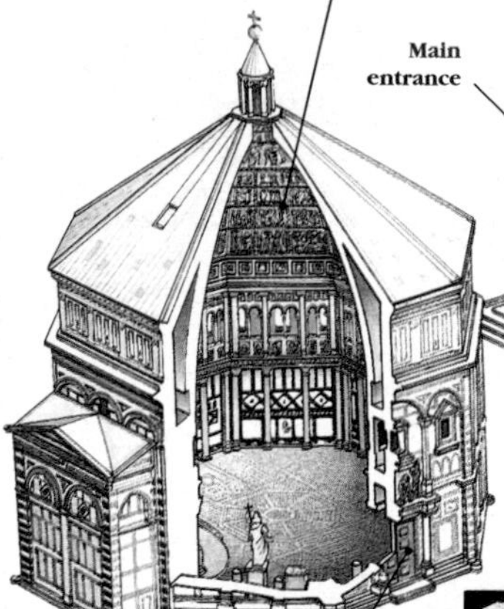

**The Neo-Gothic marble façade** echoes the style of Giotto's Campanile, but was only added in 1871–87.

**The terra-cotta panels** with bas-reliefs are by Andrea Pisano.

**Steps to Santa Reparata**
*The crypt contains the remains of the 4th-century church of Santa Reparata, demolished in 1296 to make way for the cathedral.*

**STAR FEATURES**

- ★ **Brunelleschi's Dome**
- ★ **Baptistry Ceiling**

**The top of the dome** offers spectacular views over the city.

**★ Brunelleschi's Dome**
*Brunelleschi's revolutionary achievement was to build the largest dome of its time without scaffolding. As you climb the 463 steps to the top, you can see how an inner shell provides a platform for the timbers that support the outer shell.*

**Bricks of varying size** were set in a self-supporting herringbone pattern – a technique Brunelleschi copied from the Pantheon in Rome.

***Last Judgment* frescoes by Vasari**

**The octagonal marble sanctuary** around the High Altar was decorated by Baccio Bandinelli.

**Marble Pavement**
*As you climb up to the dome, you can see that the 16th-century marble pavement is laid out as a maze.*

### Visitors' Checklist

Piazza del Duomo. **Map** 2 D5 (6 D2). *1, 6, 7, 11, 12, 14.* **Duomo** *(055) 29 45 14.* **Open** *9:30am–6pm daily.* *8am, 8:30am, 9:30am, 10am Mon–Sat; 10:30am, noon Sun & religious hols.* **Crypt *open*** *10am–5pm Mon–Sat.* ***Closed*** *religious hols.* ***Adm charge.*** **Campanile** *(055) 230 28 85.* ***Open*** *Apr–Sep: 8:30am–7:30pm; Oct: 9am–6pm; Nov–Mar: 9am–5pm (last adm: 40 mins before closing).* ***Closed*** *Jan 1, Easter Sun, Sep 8, Dec 25.* ***Adm charge.*** **Baptistry *open*** *1–6pm Mon–Sat, 9am–1pm Sun and religious hols.* ***Closed*** *Easter Sun.* *11am, 11:30am Mon–Sat.*

**Chapels at the East End**
*The three apses house five chapels each and are crowned by a miniature copy of the dome. The 15th-century stained glass is by Lorenzo Ghiberti.*

### Timeline

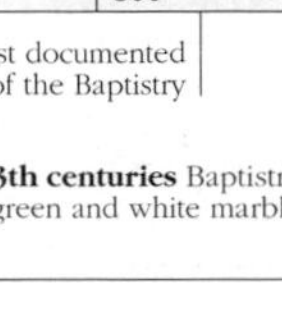

*Panel from South Doors*

**4th–5th centuries** The Baptistry and Santa Reparata church built

**897** First documented record of the Baptistry

**11th–13th centuries** Baptistry re-clad in green and white marble

**1209** Zodiac pavement laid in Baptistry

**1271** *The Last Judgment* completed on Baptistry ceiling

**1296** Arnolfo di Cambio begins the new cathedral on the site of Santa Reparata

**1338** Andrea Pisano's South Doors added

**1359** Giotto's Campanile completed

**1403–24** Ghiberti's North Doors added

**1425–52** Ghiberti's East Doors, the "Gate of Paradise," added

**1436** Dome completed

**1887** Long-delayed completion of the cathedral façade

400 | 600 | 800 | 1000 | 1200 | 1400 | 1600 | 1800

# The East Doors of the Baptistry

Lorenzo Ghiberti

Ghiberti's winning panel

LORENZO GHIBERTI'S celebrated doors were commissioned in 1401 to mark Florence's deliverance from the plague. Ghiberti was chosen after a competition involving seven leading artists, including Donatello and Brunelleschi. Ghiberti's and Brunelleschi's trial panels *(see p69)* are so different from Florentine Gothic art of the time that they are often regarded as the first products of the Renaissance.

**The "Gate of Paradise"**
*Having spent 21 years on the North Doors, Ghiberti worked on the East Doors from 1424 to 1452. Michelangelo enthusiastically dubbed them the "Gate of Paradise." The original panels are in the Museo dell'Opera del Duomo; those on the Baptistry are copies.*

**The jagged rocks**, symbolizing Abraham's pain, are carefully arranged to emphasize the sacrificial act.

**Abraham and the Sacrifice of Isaac**

**Architecture** is used to create the illusion of spatial depth. Ghiberti was a master of perspective.

**Joseph Sold into Slavery and Recognized by his Brothers**

### Key to the East Doors

| | |
|---|---|
| 1 | 2 |
| 3 | 4 |
| 5 | 6 |
| 7 | 8 |
| 9 | 10 |

**1** Adam and Eve are Expelled from Eden
**2** Cain Murders his Brother, Abel
**3** The Drunkenness of Noah and his Sacrifice
**4** Abraham and the Sacrifice of Isaac
**5** Esau and Jacob
**6** Joseph Sold into Slavery
**7** Moses Receives the Ten Commandments
**8** The Fall of Jericho
**9** The Battle with the Philistines
**10** Solomon and the Queen of Sheba

## Duomo, Campanile and Baptistry ❶

*See pp64–5.*

## Museo dell'Opera del Duomo ❷

Piazza del Duomo 9. **Map** 2 D5 (6 E2). *(055) 230 28 85.* ***Open*** *Apr–Oct: 9am–7:30pm Mon–Sat; Nov–Mar: 9am–6pm Mon–Sat.* ***Closed*** *Dec 25, Jan 1, Easter Sun.* ***Adm charge****.*

THE CATHEDRAL Works Museum houses items removed for protection from the exteriors of the Duomo, Campanile and Baptistry, notably the Ghiberti panels from the Baptistry doors.

Michelangelo carved his *David (see p77)* in the courtyard in 1501–4. Dotted with Roman sarcophagi, it now contains a Baroque figure group centered on St. John the Baptist ascending to heaven.

**Pulley used to build Brunelleschi's dome**

By its side is a small bust of Brunelleschi, architect of the cathedral dome. The museum's first room is devoted to Brunelleschi. It contains tools used by 15th-century masons and models for the construction of the cathedral dome.

The main ground-floor room has a facsimile of Arnolfo di Cambio's original façade for the cathedral, along with statues carved for its niches. Some are by Arnolfo himself, including the Gothic *Madonna of the Glass Eyes.*

Nearby are Bernardo Ciuffagni's *St. Matthew*, Nanni di Banco's *St. Luke* and, most striking of all, Donatello's *St. John*. The three were carved between 1408 and 1415 for a competition, declared void when Ciuffagni was accused of cheating by copying Donatello's *St. John*. The prize, the commission to carve *St. Mark*, was given by default to Niccolò Lamberti. Michelangelo also copied Donatello's saint when carving his famous *Moses* (1503–13). His *Pietà* is featured on the staircase. The hooded figure of Nicodemus is widely believed to be a self-portrait. That Mary Magdalene is the inferior work of a pupil is strikingly obvious.

**Carving from della Robbia's choir loft in the Museo dell'Opera del Duomo**

The first room on the upper floor is dominated by two choir lofts, dating to the 1430s, by Donatello and Luca della Robbia. Carved in crisp white marble and decorated with colored glass and mosaic, both depict children dancing and playing musical instruments. But while della Robbia's figures seem innocent, Donatello's look like frenzied participants in some primitive ritual.

Among a number of works by Donatello are his statue of *La Maddalena* (1455) *(see p25)* and several Old Testament figures, including the prophet Abakuk (1423–5), affectionately known by Florentines as *lo zuccone* (bone-head).

Ghiberti's Baptistry door panels are exhibited in the next room. Only four of them are on show; the others are being cleaned and regilded.

**St. George on the façade of Orsanmichele**

## Orsanmichele ❸

Via Calzaiuoli. **Map** 3 C1 (6 D3). *(055) 28 47 15.* ***Open*** *9am–noon, 4–6pm daily.*

THE NAME is a corruption of *Orto di San Michele*, a monastic garden long since vanished. Orsanmichele was built in 1337 as a grain market, but scarcely was it finished than it was converted into a church. The open arcades became windows, and though these have since been bricked in, the original Gothic tracery can still be seen.

The exterior walls have 14 niches, each containing a statue of the patron saint of one of Florence's major *Arti* (guilds).

The interior has two parallel naves. To the right stands an extraordinary 1350s altar by Andrea Orcagna. It is covered in cherubs, encrusted with colored marble and glass, and bristling with carved reliefs.

Close by is Bernardo Daddi's *Virgin and Child* (1348), its frame beautifully carved with angels.

# The Bargello 6

Built in 1255 as the city's town hall, the Bargello is the oldest seat of government surviving in Florence. In the 16th century it was the residence of the chief of police and a prison: executions took place here until 1786. After extensive renovation, it became one of Italy's first national museums in 1865. The Bargello houses a superb collection of Florentine Renaissance sculpture, with rooms dedicated to the work of Michelangelo, Donatello, Giambologna and Cellini, as well as a collection of Mannerist bronzes.

**Mercury by Giambologna**
*Giambologna's famous 1564 bronze shows an athletic youth poised for flight.*

## Gallery Guide

*The gallery is on three floors. To the right of the entrance hall, the Michelangelo Room is presided over by his* Bacchus *(1497). The courtyard staircase leads up to the Upper Loggia, filled with statues of birds by Giambologna. To the right is the Donatello Room, which also contains the panels for the Baptistry doors competition of 1401. The Magdalen Chapel and Islamic Room are also on the first floor. The Verrocchio Room, the Arms and Armor Collection and the Room of the Small Bronzes are on the second floor.*

**The courtyard** was once the place of execution.

**★ Bacchus by Michelangelo**
*The Roman god of wine with a small satyr was Michelangelo's first major work (1497). The modeling is Classical, but the unsteady, drunken posture mocks the poise of ancient works.*

**Key**

- Ground floor
- First floor
- Second floor
- Temporary exhibitions
- Non-exhibition space

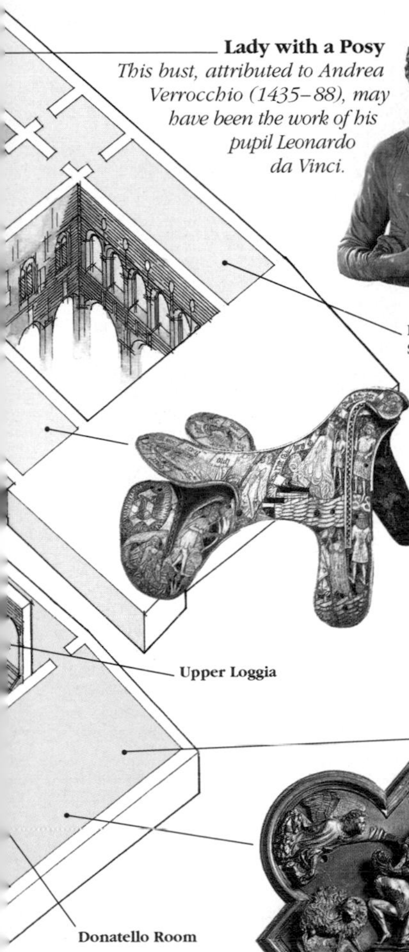

**Lady with a Posy**
*This bust, attributed to Andrea Verrocchio (1435–88), may have been the work of his pupil Leonardo da Vinci.*

**VISITORS' CHECKLIST**

Via del Proconsolo 4. **Map** 4 D1 (6 E3). *(055) 238 86 06.* 19. ***Open*** *9am–2pm Tue–Sun.* ***Closed*** *Dec 25, Jan 1, Apr 25, May 1 (some rooms may be closed during winter).* ***Adm charge.*** *ground floor only.*

**Ivory Saddle**
*Made for the Medici, this saddle inlaid with ivory was used during jousts in 15th-century Florence.*

**★ David by Donatello**
*Cast during the 1430s, Donatello's famous bronze was the first nude statue by a Western artist since Classical times* (see pp46–7).

**★ Baptistry Doors Competition Panel**
*Brunelleschi's bronze panel depicting Abraham about to slay Isaac was made in 1401 for the Baptistry doors competition* (see p66).

**The Bargello** has a daunting and heavily fortified façade.

**STAR EXHIBITS**

- **★ Baptistry Doors Competition Panel**
- **★ David by Donatello**
- **★ Bacchus by Michelangelo**

**BARGELLO PRISON**

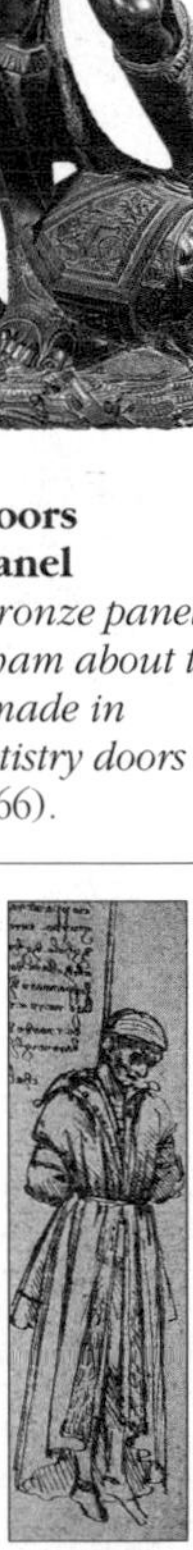

Among the notorious figures executed here was Bernardo Baroncelli. He went to the gallows in 1478 for his part in the failed attempt to assassinate Lorenzo the Magnificent in the Pazzi conspiracy *(see p47)*. Baroncelli's body, hanging from a window in the Bargello as a warning to other anti-Medici conspirators, was sketched by Leonardo da Vinci.

## Casa di Dante ❹

Via Santa Margherita 1. **Map** 4 D1 (6 E3). *(055) 21 94 16.* ***Open*** *9am–1pm Wed–Mon.*

IT IS UNCERTAIN whether the poet Dante (1265–1321) was actually born here, but at least the house looks the part. In 1911, the remains of a 13th-century tower house were cleverly restored to give the building its rambling appearance.

**Bust of Dante on the façade of Casa di Dante**

Inside, there is a small museum dedicated to Dante's life and work, but it contains nothing of any real historical significance. The downstairs rooms are used for exhibitions of modern art and sculpture.

Just a short stroll north of the house is the parish church of Santa Margherita de' Cerchi, built during the 11th century. It is here that Dante is said to have first caught sight of Beatrice Portinari, whom he idealized in his poetry. The church, which is often used for Baroque chamber music and organ recitals, contains a fine altarpiece by Neri di Bicci (1418–91).

## Badia Fiorentina ❺

Via del Proconsolo. **Map** 4 D1 (6 E3). *(055) 28 73 89.* ***Open*** *5–7pm Thu–Tue.*

THE ABBEY, one of Florence's oldest churches, was founded in 978 by Willa, the widow of Count Uberto of Tuscany. Their son, Count Ugo, was buried inside the church in 1001. His splendid tomb was carved by Mino da Fiesole and dates from 1469–81. Mino also carved the altarpiece and, in the right transept, the tomb of Bernardo Giugni, the Florentine statesman, with its fine effigy of Justice.

Filippino Lippi's *The Virgin Appearing to St. Bernard* (1485) also enlivens an otherwise drab interior. Its remarkable detail, particularly in the landscape, makes it one of the most significant works of the 15th century.

The peaceful Chiostro degli Aranci is hard to find. Look for a door to the right of the altar. Sadly, the orange trees that the monks once cultivated are no longer here.

The two-tier cloister, built by Rossellino in 1435–40, has a well-preserved fresco cycle showing scenes from the life of St. Benedict. Dating to the 15th century, it was restored as recently as 1973. An early fresco by Bronzino (1503–72) can also be seen in the north walkway. Excellent views of the hexagonal campanile, mentioned in Dante's *Paradiso*, can be had from the cloister.

In the 14th century, a series of readings and lectures devoted to Dante's work were given at the Badia by the poet Boccaccio. In keeping with the spirit of these meetings, the abbey is today often used for talks and concerts.

## The Bargello ❻

*See pp68–9.*

## Palazzo Nonfinito ❼

Via del Proconsolo 12. **Map** 2 D5 (6 E2). *(055) 239 64 49.* ***Open*** *9am–1pm Thu–Sat & every 3rd Sun of month.* ***Closed*** *Jan 1, Apr 25, Easter Sun, May 1, Jun 24, Aug 13–17, Dec 8, Dec 25–26.*

THE PALAZZO NONFINITO (Unfinished Palace) was begun by Buontalenti in 1593 and was still incomplete when it became Italy's first museum of anthropology and ethnology in 1869. The most striking architectural feature is an imposing inner courtyard usually attributed to Cigoli (1559–1613).

The museum's opening hours are severely restricted. However, it's worth setting aside some time to see the collection of art from Italy's former African colonies, and material brought back by Captain Cook, the 18th-century British explorer, from the last of his Pacific voyages.

***The Virgin Appearing to St. Bernard* (1485) by Filippino Lippi**

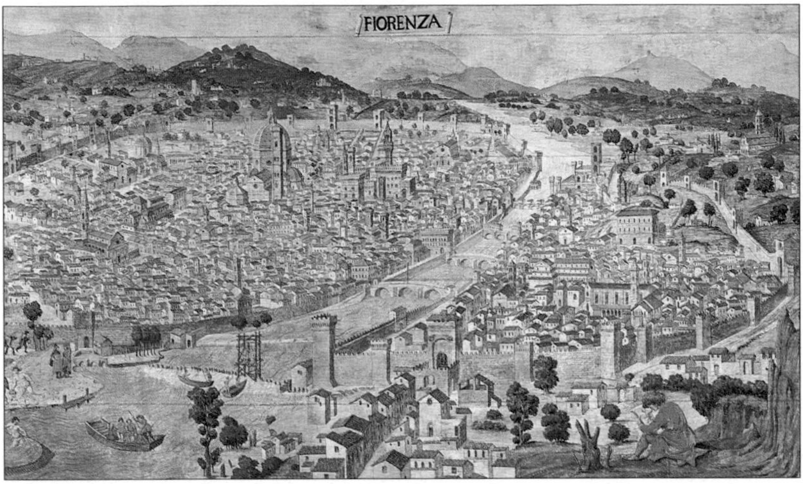


**19th-century copy of the *Pianta della Catena*, showing Florence's cityscape**

## Museo di Firenze com'era 8

Via dell'Oriuolo 4. **Map** 2 D5 (6 F2). *(055) 239 84 83.* ***Open*** *9am–2pm Mon–Wed, Fri & Sat, 8am–1pm Sun.* ***Closed*** *Jan 1, Easter Sun, May 1, Aug 15, Dec 25.* ***Adm charge***.

THE MUSEUM traces the development of the city through drawings, plans and paintings. One of the most fascinating exhibits is the *Pianta della Catena*, a 19th-century copy of a woodcut made around 1470, showing Florence at the height of the Renaissance. Its name refers to the chainlike border that surrounds the whole image. Try spotting the buildings that still stand, for instance the Palazzo Pitti, and picturing those that had yet to be built, such as the Uffizi.

The Palazzo Pitti is depicted again in the delightful sequence of lunettes made by the Flemish artist Giusto Utens in 1599. They show all the Medici villas and gardens, with fascinating vignettes of rural life *(see p121 and 161)*.

One room is devoted to a plan devised by Giuseppe Poggi, once the city architect, for remodeling central Florence during its brief stint as the Italian capital in 1865–71. If the plan had been implemented, vast areas of the center would have been destroyed. Demolition was halted following an international outcry, but not before buildings had been cleared for the new Piazza della Repubblica *(see p112)* and the 14th-century walls had been torn down.

## Bar Vivoli Gelateria 9

Via Isola delle Stinche 7. **Map** 4 D1 (6 F3). *(055) 29 23 34.* ***Open*** *8am–1am Tue–Sun.*

**Bar Vivoli Gelateria**

THIS TINY ice cream parlor attracts large crowds and long lines for its rich iced concoctions. Vivoli claims to make the "best ice cream in the world," and the walls of the bar are covered in press clippings from ice cream connoisseurs that strongly support this view.

The bar stands at the heart of the colorful Santa Croce district, with its narrow alleys and tiny squares. Here, you will find small shops that serve the local community, rather than cater to tourists, and scores of little workshops where craftsmen make picture frames or mend furniture. Via Torta is typical of the area.

## Casa Buonarroti 10

Via Ghibellina 70. **Map** 4 E1. *(055) 24 17 52.* ***Open*** *9:30am–1:30pm Wed–Mon.* ***Closed*** *Jan 1, Easter Sun, May 1, Aug 15, Dec 25.* ***Adm charge***.

MICHELANGELO (whose surname was Buonarroti) lived briefly in this group of three houses that he bought as an investment in 1508. Subsequent generations of his descendants added what they could to a significant collection of his works.

Among these is his earliest known work, the *Madonna della Scala*, a marble *tavoletta*, or rectangular relief, carved in 1490–92. There is also a relief from 1492, showing *The Battle of the Centaurs*, and the design, never used, for the façade of San Lorenzo, shown in a wooden model.

# Santa Croce ⓫

THE MAGNIFICENT GOTHIC CHURCH of Santa Croce (1294) contains the tombs of many famous Florentines, including Michelangelo and Galileo. The spacious, airy interior is enhanced by the radiant frescoes of Giotto and his gifted pupil, Taddeo Gaddi, painted early in the 14th century. Incorporated into the cloister beside the church is Brunelleschi's Classical Cappella de' Pazzi (Pazzi Chapel), a masterpiece of Renaissance architecture. The rest of the monastic buildings scattered around the cloister form a museum of religious painting and sculpture.

**The façade** was reclad with colored marble in 1863; paid for by an English benefactor, Francis Sloane.

**Galileo's Tomb**
*Condemned by the church in 1616, Galileo was denied a Christian burial until 1737, when this tomb by Giulio Foggini was erected.*

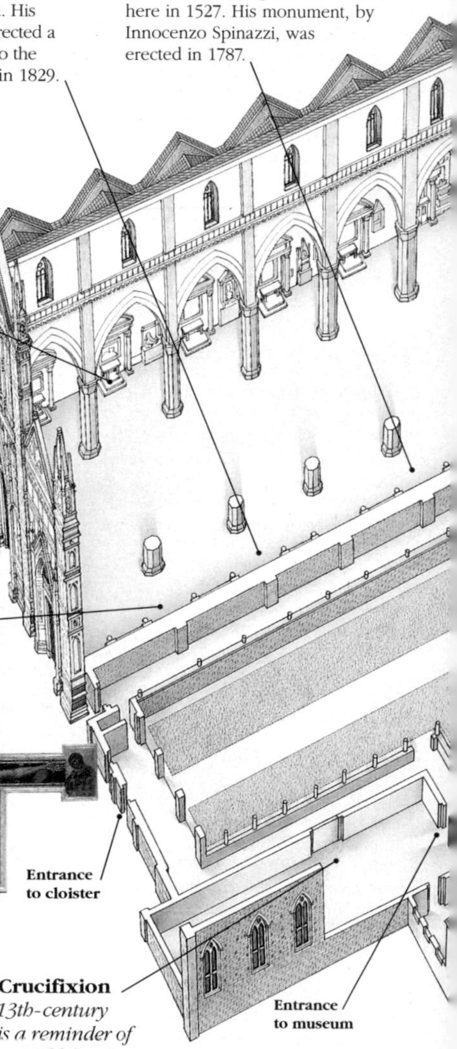


**Dante** died in exile in 1321 and is buried in Ravenna. His admirers erected a memorial to the great poet in 1829.

**Machiavelli** *(see p51)* was buried here in 1527. His monument, by Innocenzo Spinazzi, was erected in 1787.

**Michelangelo's Tomb**
*Michelangelo never completed the* Pietà *he planned for his own tomb* (see p67). *This monument was designed in 1570 by Vasari. The figures are Painting, Architecture and Sculpture.*

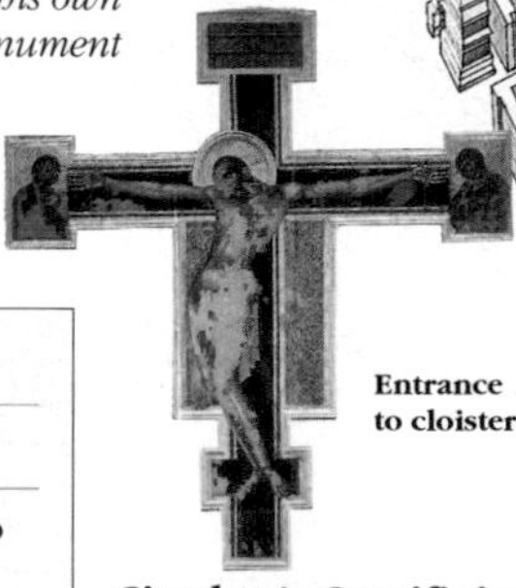

**Cimabue's Crucifixion**
*This ruined 13th-century masterpiece is a reminder of the destructive 1966 floods.*

**STAR FEATURES**

- ★ **Cappella de' Pazzi**
- ★ **Tomb of Leonardo Bruni**
- ★ **Fresco by Gaddi in Baroncelli Chapel**

**Donatello's Crucifix** (1425) in the first Bardi Chapel provoked Brunelleschi to say that Christ looked like a peasant. Challenged to do better, Brunelleschi carved his own version, which now hangs in Santa Maria Novella.

**In the second Bardi Chapel** Giotto's frescoes (1317) depict scenes from the Life of St. Francis.

**The Neo-Gothic campanile** was added in 1842.

## Visitors' Checklist

Piazza di Santa Croce. **Map** 4 E1 (6 F4). *(055) 24 46 19.* *12, 14, 19, 23, 31, 32.* **Basilica** ***open*** *8–12:30am, 3–6:30pm Mon–Sun (Jul–Sep: 8am–6:30pm).* *9am, 6pm Mon–Sat & 8am, 9:30am, 11am, noon, 6pm Sun and religious hols.* **Museum, Cloister, Cappella de' Pazzi** ***open*** *10–12:30am, 2:30–6:30pm (Nov–Mar: 3–5pm) Thu–Tue (last adm: 15 mins before closing).* ***Closed*** *Jan 1, Dec 25.* ***Adm charge.***

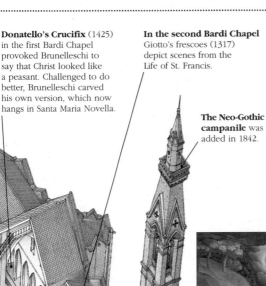

**★ Fresco by Gaddi in Baroncelli Chapel**
*This image of an angel appearing to sleeping shepherds (1338) was the first true night scene depicted in fresco.*

**★ Tomb of Leonardo Bruni**
*Rossellino's effigy (1447) of the great Humanist, depicted in serene old age, is a triumph of realistic portraiture.*

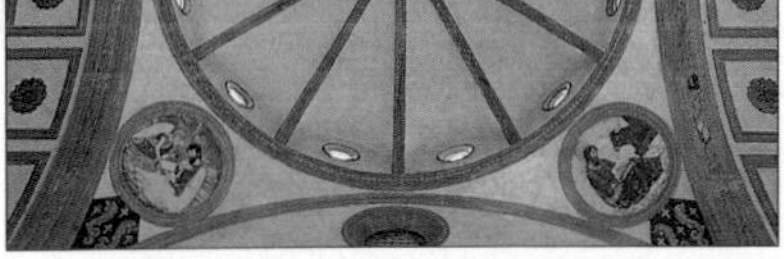

**★ Cappella de' Pazzi**
*Brunelleschi designed this domed chapel in 1430. Delicate gray stonework frames white plaster inset with Luca della Robbia's terra-cotta roundels of the apostles.*

Museo Horne

## Santa Croce ⓫

*See pp72–3.*

## Museo Horne ⓬

Via de' Benci 6. **Map** 4 D1 (6 F4). *(055) 24 46 61.* ***Open*** *9am–1pm Mon–Sat.* ***Closed*** *Jan 1, May 1, Aug 15, Nov 1, Dec 25–26.* ***Adm charge.***

THE MUSEUM'S small collection of paintings, sculpture and decorative arts was left to the city by Herbert Percy Horne (1844–1916), the English art historian. It is housed in a splendid example of a Renaissance *palazzino* (small town house), built in 1489 for the wealthy Alberti family.

The arrangement of rooms, with a working and storage area at ground level and grander apartments above, is typical of many Renaissance houses. The Alberti family, who grew wealthy from the city's thriving cloth trade, had wool-dyeing vats in the basement and drying racks in the courtyard.

Most of the museum's major artifacts, including a number of important 17th- and 18th-century drawings, are now housed in the Uffizi. However, the collection still boasts at least one major exhibit: Giotto's 13th-century *St. Stephen* polyptych (an altarpiece with more than three panels). There is also a *Madonna and Child* attributed to Simone Martini (1283–1344) and *Madonna* by Bernardo Daddi (c.1312–48).

The kitchen, which was built on the top floor to stop fumes from passing through the entire house, contains Horne's collection of Renaissance pots and cooking utensils.

## Museo di Storia della Scienza ⓭

Piazza de' Guidici 1. **Map** 4 D1 (6 E4). *(055) 29 34 93.* ***Open*** *9:30am–1pm Mon–Sat, 2–5pm Mon, Wed, Fri.* ***Closed*** *Jan 1, Apr 25, May 1, Jun 24, Dec 8, Dec 25–26.* ***Adm charge.***

THIS SMALL MUSEUM is something of a shrine to the Pisa-born scientist, Galileo Galilei (1564–1642). Exhibits include his telescopes and the lens he used to discover the largest moons of Jupiter.

The museum also features large-scale reconstructions of his experiments into motion, weight, velocity and acceleration. These are sometimes demonstrated by the attendants.

In memory of Galileo, Florence founded the world's first scientific institution, the Accademia del Cimento (Academy for Experimentation), in 1657. A number of the academy's inventions, including early thermometers, barometers and hygrometers, are on exhibit here. Equally fascinating are the enormous globes and spheres made in Florence during the 16th and 17th centuries to illustrate the motion of the planets and stars.

Be sure to see Lopo Homem's map of the world, dating to 1554, and the nautical instruments invented by Sir Robert Dudley, the Elizabethan marine engineer. He was employed by the Medici dukes to build the harbor at Livorno from 1607–21 *(see p158)*.

Galileo Galilei (1564–1642), court mathematician to the Medici

## Santo Stefano al Ponte ⓮

Piazza Santo Stefano al Ponte. **Map** 3 C1 (6 D4). ***Closed*** *temporarily.*

ST. STEPHEN "by the bridge," dating to 969, is so called because of its proximity to the Ponte Vecchio. The Romanesque façade, dating

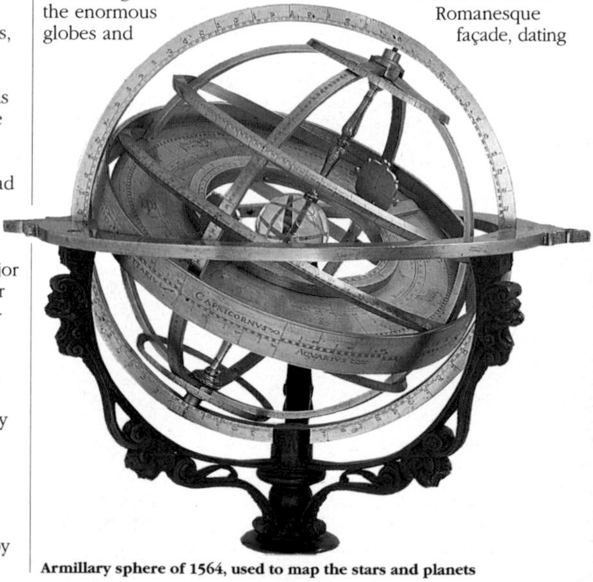



Armillary sphere of 1564, used to map the stars and planets

### Mapping the World

The same preoccupation with space that made Florentine artists such masters of perspective also made them excellent navigators and mapmakers. Florentine cartographers based their maps on the observations and navigational records of early explorers. That is how America came to be named after the Florentine Amerigo Vespucci rather than Christopher Columbus. When Columbus returned from his transatlantic voyage, King Ferdinand of Spain hired Vespucci, an expert navigator, to check whether Columbus really had discovered a new route to the Indies. Vespucci was the first to realize that Columbus had come upon a new continent and he described his own voyage in a series of letters to Piero de' Medici. As soon as the letters were made public, Florentine cartographers rushed out revised maps of the world based on Vespucci's account. Out of loyalty to a fellow Florentine, they named the New World Amerigo, which was later corrupted to America.

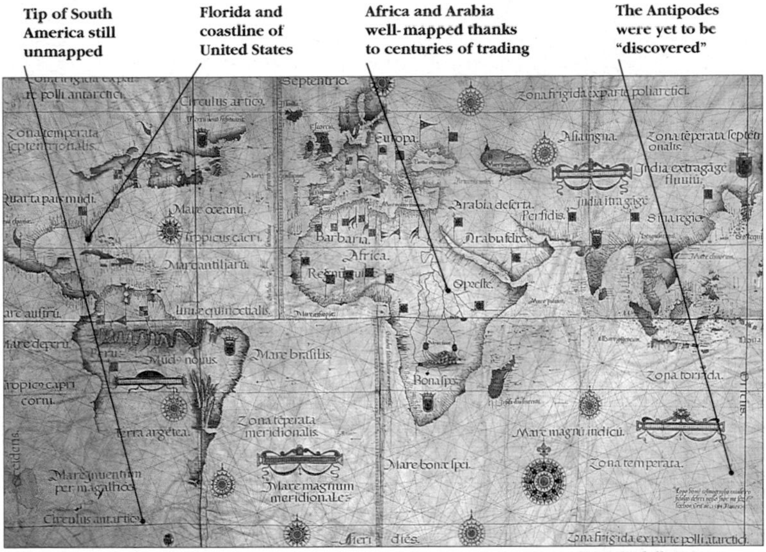


**16th-century map by the Portuguese cartographer Lopo Homem, in the Museo di Storia della Scienza**

to around 1233, is its most important architectural feature. Florentines, however, know the church better as a place for top-quality orchestral concerts, organized by the Amici della Musica. Details are posted at the entrance.

## Erboristeria ⓯

Spezieria–Erboristeria Palazzo Vecchio. Via Vaccherecccia 9r. **Map** 3 C1 (6 D3). ☎ *(055) 239 60 55.* ***Open*** *Mar–Oct: 9am–2pm, 3–7:30pm daily (Nov–Feb: Tue–Sat).*

This ancient herbalist's shop, known as the Palazzo Vecchio, is hidden among the pavement cafés that line the Via Vaccherecccia, off Piazza della Signoria. It has a lovely frescoed interior. Several such shops in Florence sell herbal soaps, potpourri, cosmetics and fragrances made to ancient recipes by monks and nuns in various parts of Tuscany. Another *erboristeria* is just around the corner at Calimala 4r: the Erboristeria della Antica Farmacia del Cinghiale (Herbalist at the Old Boar Pharmacy), which takes its name from the famous bronze boar in the Mercato Nuovo opposite *(see p112).*

## Piazza della Signoria ⓰

*See pp76–7.*

## Palazzo Vecchio ⓱

*See pp78–9.*

## The Uffizi ⓲

*See pp80–83.*

**Arno façade of the Uffizi with the Vasari Corridor *(pp106–7)* above**

# Piazza della Signoria ⑯

THE PIAZZA IS A UNIQUE outdoor sculpture gallery and, with the Palazzo Vecchio *(see pp78–9)*, has been at the heart of Florentine politics since the 14th century. Citizens gathered here when called to a *parlamento* (a public meeting) by the Palazzo's great bell. The statues, some original, some copies, commemorate events in the city's history. Many are linked to the rise and fall of the Florentine Republic *(pp50–51)*, during which the religious leader Savonarola was burned at the stake here.

**Salone dei Cinquecento**
*This vast council chamber, built in 1495, is decorated with Vasari's frescoes on the history of Florence.*

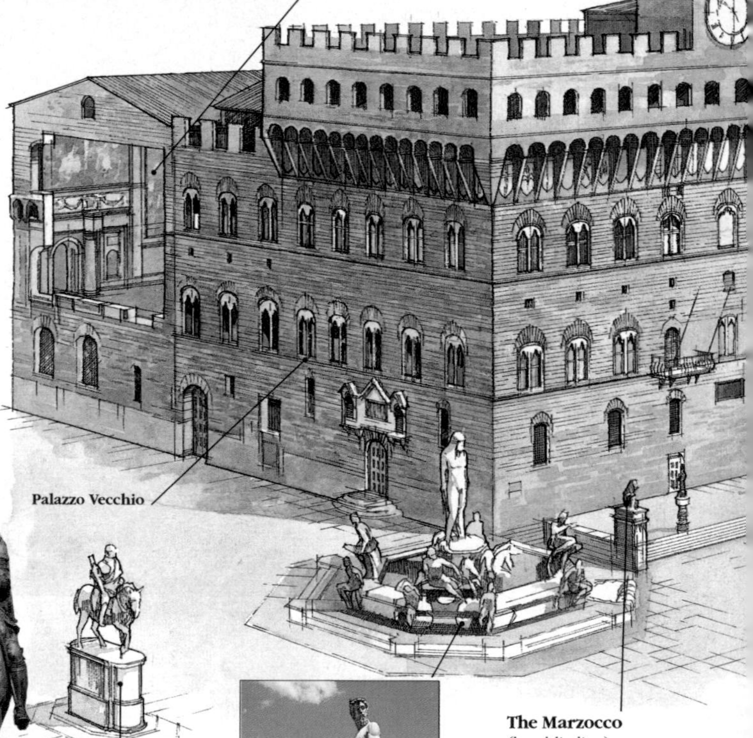

**The Marzocco** (heraldic lion) was carved in the 15th century by Donatello.

**Grand Duke Cosimo I**
*Giambologna's equestrian statue (1595) celebrates the man who subjugated all Tuscany under his military rule* (see pp52–3).

**★ Neptune Fountain**
*Ammannati's Mannerist fountain (1575) of the Roman sea god surrounded by water nymphs commemorates Tuscan naval victories.*

**VISITORS' CHECKLIST**

**Map** 4 D1 (6 D3). 🚌 *19.*
*Pedestrian area.*

**Pageantry**
*For centuries the piazza has been the city's venue for public rallies and festivities, as shown in this 18th-century engraving.*

**★ Perseus**
*Cellini's bronze statue (1554) of Perseus beheading Medusa, the snake-headed monster, was intended to warn Cosimo I's enemies of their probable fate.*

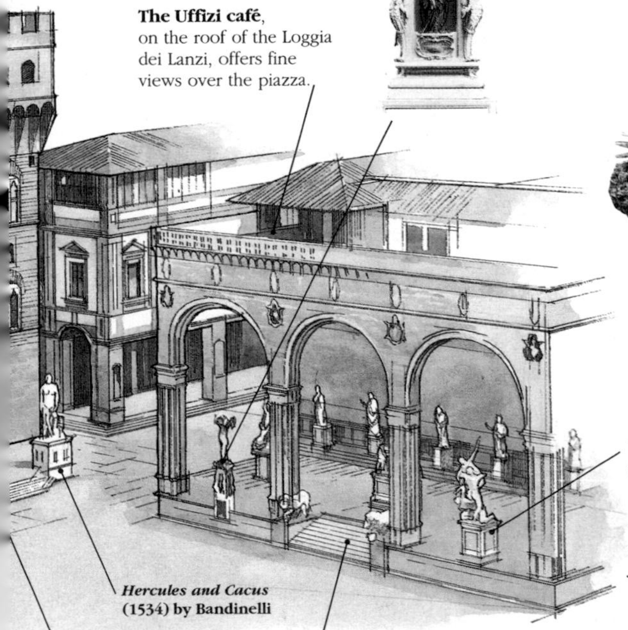

**The Uffizi café**, on the roof of the Loggia dei Lanzi, offers fine views over the piazza.

**★ The Rape of the Sabine Women** *(1583)*
*The writhing figures in Giambologna's famous statue were carved from a single block of flawed marble.*

***Hercules and Cacus*** **(1534) by Bandinelli**

**The Loggia dei Lanzi** (1382), by Orcagna, is named after Cosimo I's bodyguards, the Lancers. The back wall is lined with ancient Roman statues of priestesses.

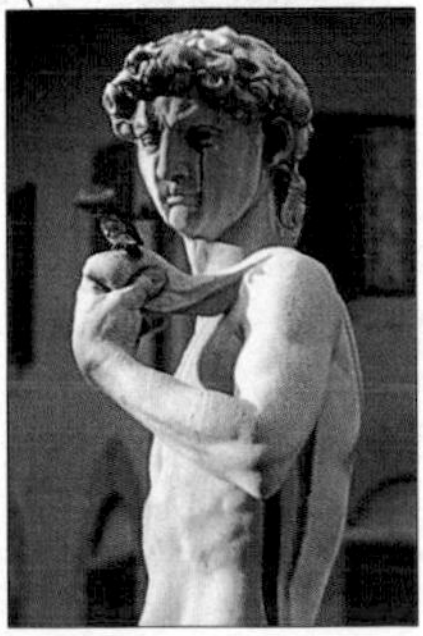

**★ David** *(1501)*
*Michelangelo's celebrated statue* (see p94) *refers to David's victory over the giant Goliath, and symbolizes Republican triumph over tyranny.*

**STAR FEATURES**

- **★ David by Michelangelo**
- **★ Neptune Fountain by Ammannati**
- **★ The Rape of the Sabine Women by Giambologna**
- **★ Perseus by Cellini**

# Palazzo Vecchio 17

THE PALAZZO VECCHIO ("Old Palace") still fulfills its original role as Florence's town hall. It was completed in 1322 when a huge bell, used to call citizens to meetings or warn of fire, flood or enemy attack, was hauled to the top of the imposing bell tower. The palazzo has retained its medieval appearance, but much of the interior was remodeled for Duke Cosimo I when he moved into the palace in 1540. Leonardo da Vinci and Michelangelo were asked to redecorate the interior, but it was Vasari who finally undertook the work. His many frescoes (1563–5) glorify Cosimo and his creation of the Grand Duchy of Tuscany.

**★ Sala dei Gigli (Room of the Lilies)**
*Gold fleurs-de-lis, emblems of Florence, cover the walls between Ghirlandaio's frescoes (1485) of Roman statesmen.*

**PALACE GUIDE**
*The palazzo is entered via a courtyard. A monumental staircase leads to the first-floor council chamber, Salone dei Cinquecento, with its frescoed walls and marble statues. Above this is a suite of decorated rooms once used by the rulers of Florence. A one-way system guides visitors through the palazzo's corridors.*

**Heraldic Frieze**
*Shields on the façade symbolize episodes in Florentine history. The crossed keys represent Medici papal rule.*

**★ Cortile and Putto Fountain**
*Vasari's courtyard, with its copy of Verrocchio's Putto Fountain, dates to 1565.*

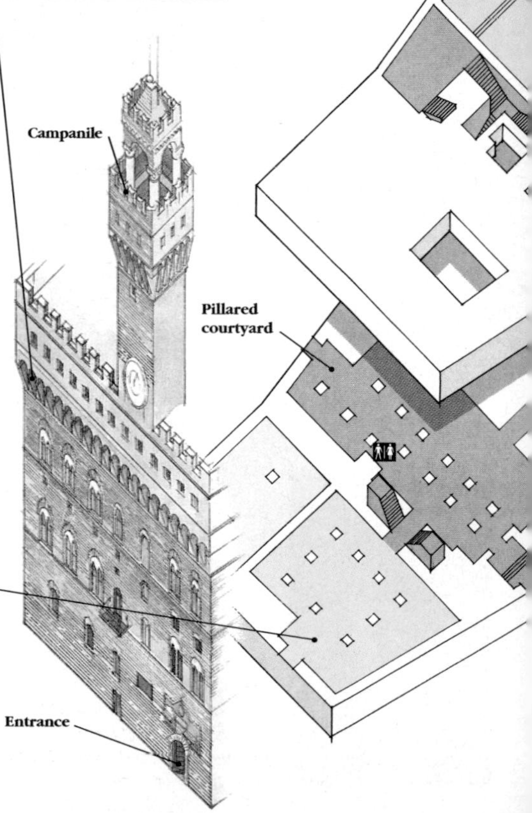


**KEY TO FLOORPLAN**

- Ground floor
- First floor
- Second floor
- Temporary exhibitions
- Nonexhibition space

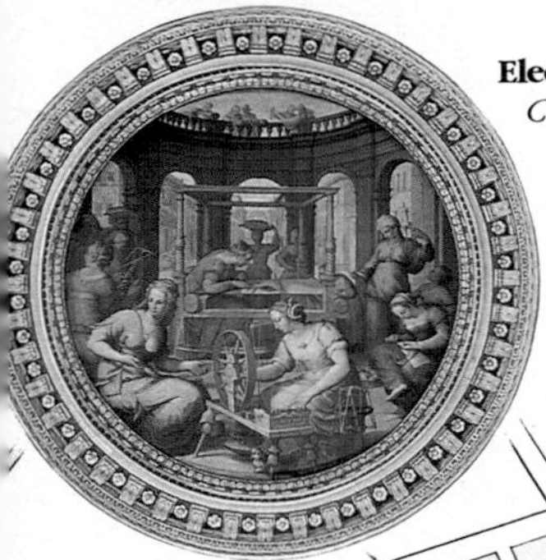

**Eleonora di Toledo's Rooms**
*Cosimo I's wife had a suite of rooms decorated with scenes of virtuous women. Penelope, wife of the Greek hero Odysseus, is shown waiting faithfully for her husband to return.*

**VISITORS' CHECKLIST**

Piazza della Signoria.
**Map** 4 D1 (6 D3). *(055) 276 84 65.* *19, 23, 31, 32.*
***Open*** *9am–7pm Mon–Wed, Fri, Sat 8am–1pm Sun (last adm: 1 hour before closing).*
***Closed*** *Dec 25, Jan 1, Easter Sun, May 1, Aug 15.* ***Adm charge***.

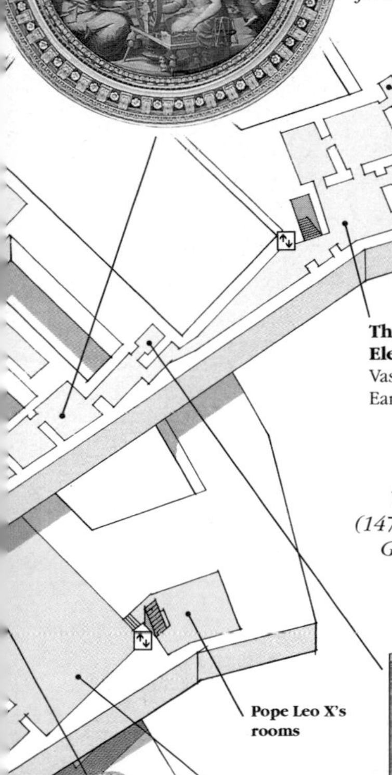

**The Quartiere degli Elementi** contains Vasari's allegories of Earth, Fire, Air and Water.

**Putto with Dolphin**
*Verrocchio's bronze fountain head (1470) is displayed in the Terrazzo di Giunone. The small room next door has fine views of San Miniato al Monte.*

**Pope Leo X's rooms**

**The Salone dei Cinquecento** was a meeting place for the leaders of the Florentine Republic *(see pp50–51).*

**Cappella di Eleonora**
*Egyptian soldiers pursuing Moses drown in the Red Sea, in the biblical frescoes (1540–45) by Bronzino in Eleonora di Toledo's chapel.*

**★ Victory by Michelangelo**
*Michelangelo's nephew presented this statue (1533–4), intended for the tomb of Pope Julius II, to Cosimo I in 1565, following the Duke's military triumph over Siena.*

**STAR FEATURES**

**★ Cortile and Putto Fountain**

**★ Victory by Michelangelo**

**★ Sala dei Gigli**

# The Uffizi 18

The Uffizi was built in 1560–80 as a suite of offices *(uffici)* for Duke Cosimo I's new Tuscan administration *(see p48)*. The architect, Vasari, used iron reinforcement to create an almost continuous wall of glass on the upper story. From 1581 Cosimo's heirs, beginning with Francesco I, used this well-lit space to display the Medici family art treasures, creating what is now the oldest gallery in the world.

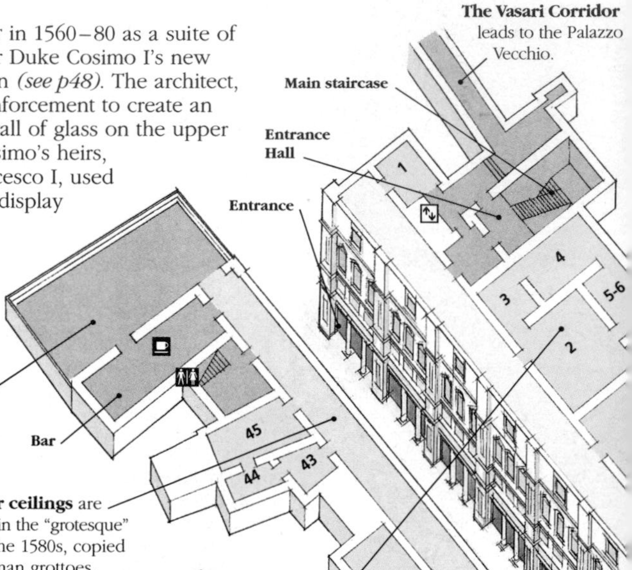
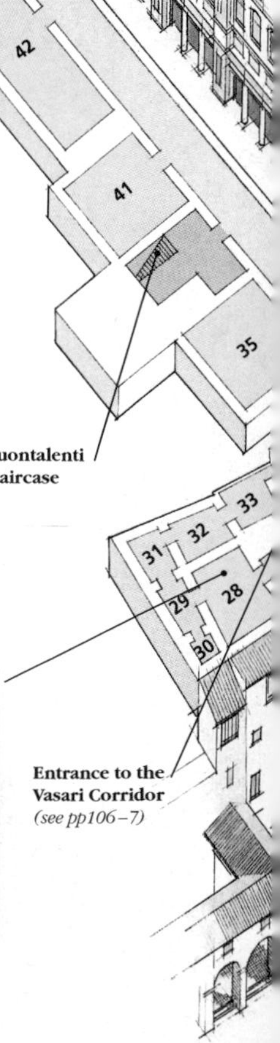


**The Vasari Corridor** leads to the Palazzo Vecchio.

**Main staircase**

**Entrance Hall**

**Entrance**

**The café terrace** merits a visit for its unusual views of the Piazza della Signoria *(see pp76–7)*.

**Bar**

**Corridor ceilings** are frescoed in the "grotesque" style of the 1580s, copied from Roman grottoes.

**Buontalenti staircase**

**Entrance to the Vasari Corridor** *(see pp106–7)*

## Gallery Guide

*The Uffizi art collection is housed on the top floor of the building. Ancient Greek and Roman sculptures are displayed in the broad corridor running around the inner side of the horseshoe-shaped building. The paintings are hung in a series of rooms off the main corridor, in chronological order, to reveal the development of Florentine art from Gothic to High Renaissance and beyond. Most of the best-known paintings are grouped in rooms 7–18.*

**The Ognissanti Madonna**
*Giotto's grasp of spatial depth in this altarpiece (1310) was a milestone in the mastery of perspective.*

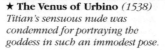

★ **The Venus of Urbino** *(1538)*
*Titian's sensuous nude was condemned for portraying the goddess in such an immodest pose.*

## Star Paintings

- ★ **The Duke and Duchess of Urbino by Piero della Francesca**
- ★ **The Birth of Venus by Botticelli**
- ★ **The Holy Family by Michelangelo**
- ★ **The Venus of Urbino by Titian**

**★ The Duke and Duchess of Urbino** *(1460)*
*Piero della Francesca's panels are among the first true Renaissance portraits. He even recorded the Duke's hooked nose – broken by a sword blow.*

### Visitors' Checklist

Loggiato degli Uffizi 6.
**Map** 4 D1 (6 D4).
*(055) 238 86 51.* *3, 13, 14, 15, 18, 19, 23, 31, 32.*
***Open*** *9am–7pm Tue–Sat, 9am–2pm Sun (last adm: 30 mins before closing).*
***Closed*** *Jan 1, May 1, Dec 25.*
***Adm charge***.
**Rooms 26–33 & 41–5** ***closed*** *temporarily for restoration.*
**The Vasari Corridor** ***closed*** *temporarily for restoration.*

**★ The Birth of Venus** *(1485)*
*Botticelli's captivating image shows the Roman goddess of love, born in a storm in the Aegean sea. She is blown ashore by the winds and greeted by nymphs, ready to wrap her in a cloak.*

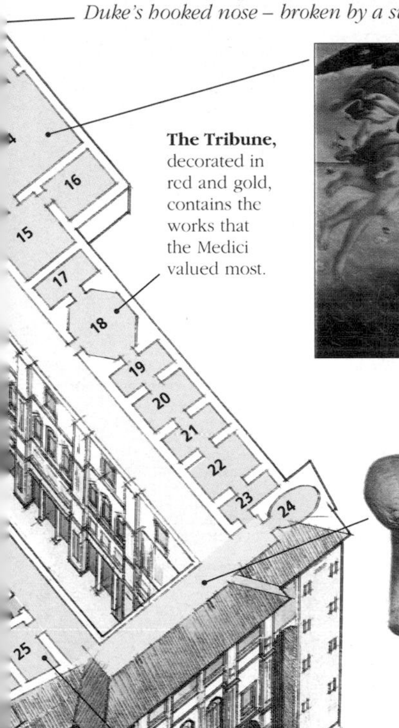


**The Tribune,** decorated in red and gold, contains the works that the Medici valued most.

**Vasari's Classical Arno façade**

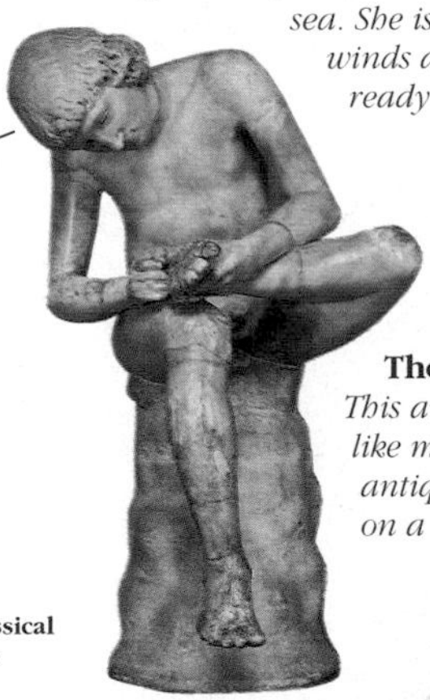

**Boy Removing a Thorn from his Foot**
*This ancient Roman statue is, like many of the collection's antique sculptures, based on a Greek original.*

**★ The Holy Family** *(1508)*
*Michelangelo's painting, the first to break with the convention of showing Christ on the Virgin's lap, inspired Mannerist artists through its expressive handling of color and posture* (see p25).

**Key**

- East Corridor
- West Corridor
- Arno Corridor
- Gallery Rooms 1–45
- Non-exhibition space

# Exploring the Uffizi's Collection

The Uffizi offers an unrivaled opportunity to see some of the greatest works of the Renaissance. The collection was born from the immense wealth of the Medici family *(see pp48–9)*, who commissioned work from many great Florentine masters. Francesco I housed the family collection at the Uffizi in 1581. His descendants added to it until 1737, when Anna Maria Lodovica, last of the Medici, bequeathed it to the people of Florence.

## Gothic Art

Following the collection of antiquities in room 1, the gallery's next six rooms are devoted to Tuscan Gothic art from the 12th to 14th centuries.

Giotto (1266–1337) introduced a degree of naturalism that was new in Tuscan art. The angels and saints in his *Ognissanti Madonna* (1310), in room 2, express a range of human emotions, from awe and reverence to puzzlement. The throne in this painting, and the temple in Lorenzetti's *Presentation in the Temple* (1342) in room 3, show a concern for three-dimensional depth quite at odds with the flatness of much Gothic art.

Giotto's naturalism extends throughout the works in room 4, devoted to the 14th-century Florentine School. One of the most obvious examples is the *Pietà* (1360–65), attributed to Giottino. Look at the difference between the characters' expressions, their medieval, rather than Biblical, style of dress and the blood, still fresh on the cross.

## Early Renaissance

A better understanding of geometry and perspective allowed Renaissance artists to create an illusion of space and depth in their works. Paolo Uccello (1397–1475) was obsessed with perspective; witness his nightmarish *The Battle of San Romano* (1456) *(see p46)* in room 7.

Also in this room are two panels by Piero della Francesca (1410–92), depicting the Duke and Duchess of Urbino on one side and representations of their virtues on the other. Painted between 1465 and 1470, these are two of the first Renaissance portraits.

If these works seem coldly experimental, Fra Filippo Lippi's *Madonna and Child with Angels* (1455–66), in room 8, is a masterpiece of warmth and humanity. Like so many Renaissance artists, Lippi uses a religious subject to celebrate earthly delights, such as feminine beauty and the Tuscan landscape.

***Madonna and Child with Angels* (1455–66) by Fra Filippo Lippi**

## Botticelli

The Botticelli paintings in rooms 10–14 are the highlight of the Uffizi's collection. The brilliant colors and crisp draftsmanship of, for instance, *The Birth of Venus* (about 1485) *(see p81)*, are a reminder that Renaissance artists often experimented with

***Primavera* (1480) by Botticelli**

new pigments to achieve striking color effects. The subject of this painting, the Roman goddess Venus, is also significant. By painting Venus instead of the Christian Virgin, Botticelli expressed the fascination with Classical mythology common to many Renaissance artists.

The same is true of his other famous work, *Primavera* (about 1480). It breaks with the tradition of Christian religious painting by illustrating a pagan rite of spring. Other works to see here include the *Adoration of the Magi* (about 1475), a thinly disguised Medici family portrait *(see p49)*.

### Leonardo da Vinci

**Detail from *The Annunciation* (1472–5) by Leonardo da Vinci**

Room 15 contains works attributed to the young Leonardo. Still under the influence of his teachers, he was already developing his own masterly style, as in *The Annunciation* (1472–5) and the unfinished *Adoration of the Magi* (1481).

### The Tribune

The octagonal tribune, with its mother-of-pearl ceiling, was designed in 1584 by Buontalenti so that Francesco I could display all his favorite works from the Medici collection in one room.

Notable paintings include Bronzino's portrait (1545) of Eleonora di Toledo with her son, Giovanni *(see p49)*, and the same artist's portrait of Bia, Cosimo I's illegitimate daughter. It was painted just before her

**Portrait of *Bia* (1542) by Bronzino**

early death in 1542. *The Medici Venus*, probably dating to the 1st century BC, is a Roman copy of the Greek original by Praxiteles. A small room off the Tribune contains a copy of the Hellenistic sculpture, *The Hermaphrodite*.

### Non-Florentine Art

The works in rooms 19 to 23 show how rapidly the artistic ideas and techniques of the Renaissance spread beyond Florence. Umbrian artists like Perugino (1446–1523) and Northern European painters such as Dürer (1471–1528) are well represented.

### The Arno Corridor

The corridor overlooking the Arno, which links the east and west wings of the Uffizi, offers fine views of the hills to the south of Florence.

The ancient Roman statues displayed here were mainly collected by the Medici during the 15th century. Their anatomical precision and faithful portraiture were much admired and copied by Renaissance artists, who saw themselves as giving rebirth to Classical perfection in art.

The Roman statues were equally popular during the 17th and 18th centuries with visitors on their way to Rome on the Grand Tour *(see p53)*. The Renaissance works, which attract visitors today, were largely ignored until John Ruskin, the art historian, wrote about them in the 1840s.

### High Renaissance and Mannerism

Michelangelo's *The Holy Family* (1506–8), in room 25, is striking for its vibrant colors and the unusually twisted pose of the Virgin *(see p81)*. This painting proved to be enormously influential with the next generation of Tuscan artists, notably Bronzino (1503–72), Pontormo (1494–1556) and Parmigianino (1503–40). The latter's *Madonna of the Long Neck* (about 1534) in room 29, with its contorted anatomy and bright, unnatural colors, is a remarkable example of what came to be known as the Mannerist style.

Two other masterpieces of the High Renaissance are located nearby. Raphael's tender *Madonna of the Goldfinch* (1506), in room 26, still shows signs of earthquake damage dating to 1547. Titian's *The Venus of Urbino* (1538), said to be one of the most beautiful nudes ever painted, is in room 28.

***Madonna of the Goldfinch* (1506) by Raphael**

### Later Paintings

Rooms 41–45 of the Uffizi hold paintings acquired by the Medici in the 17th and 18th centuries. These include works by Rubens (1577–1640) and Van Dyck (1599–1641) in room 41 (sometimes closed); Caravaggio (1573–1610) in room 43; and Rembrandt (1606–69) in room 44.

# City Center North

**Roundel on Spedale degli Innocenti**

This area of Florence is stamped with the character of Cosimo il Vecchio. The man who founded the great Medici dynasty maintained his position of power by astute management of the city's financial affairs, as opposed to resorting to threat and violence. Cosimo was a highly educated and sophisticated man with a passion for building, and he wanted the churches, palazzi and libraries that he built to last a thousand years, like the buildings of ancient Rome. To this end, he commissioned some of the greatest architects and artists of the time to build the churches of San Lorenzo and San Marco as well as the Medici's first home, the Palazzo Medici Riccardi. He is regarded as one of the great innovators of the Renaissance in Florence. Even after the Medici family had moved across the river Arno to the Palazzo Pitti in 1550, the Grand Dukes made their final journey back to the north of the city to be buried in the extravagant Cappelle Medicee in San Lorenzo. For the tombs in the New Sacristy, Michelangelo contributed his magnificent allegorical sculptures, *Day and Night* and *Dawn and Dusk*.

## Sights at a Glance

**Churches and Synagogues**
*San Lorenzo pp90–91* 2
*San Marco pp96–7* 7
Santa Maria Maddalena dei Pazzi 16
Santissima Annunziata 14
Tempio Israelitico 17

**Historic Buildings**
Palazzo Medici Riccardi 5
Palazzo Pucci 4
Spedale degli Innocenti 12

**Museums and Galleries**
Cenacolo di Sant'Apollonia 6
Conservatorio 10
Galleria dell'Accademia 9
Museo Archeologico 15
Opificio delle Pietre Dure 11

**Gardens**
Giardino dei Semplici 8

**Streets, Piazzas and Markets**
Mercato Centrale 1
Piazza di San Lorenzo 3
Piazza della Santissima Annunziata 13

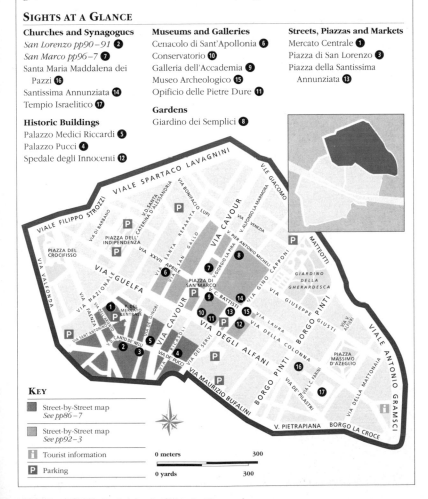

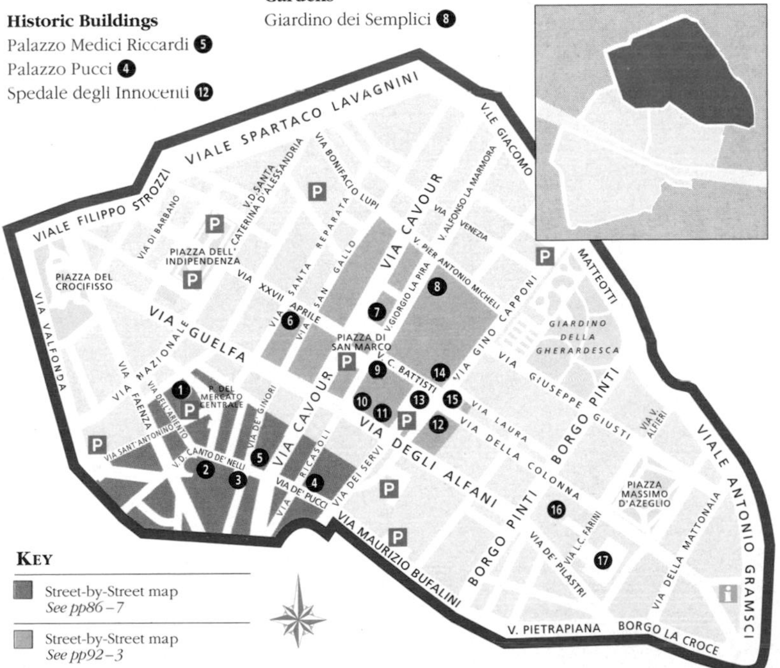


**Key**

Street-by-Street map *See pp86–7*

Street-by-Street map *See pp92–3*

Tourist information

Parking

0 meters 300

0 yards 300

◁ ***Virgin and Child*** **by Fra Angelico (c.1440) in San Marco**

# Street-by-Street: Around San Lorenzo

**Bust, Palazzo Medici Riccardi**

THIS AREA is stamped with the character of Cosimo il Vecchio, founder of the Medici dynasty, who commissioned San Lorenzo and the Palazzo Medici Riccardi. Around San Lorenzo, a huge general market fills the streets, its colorful awnings almost obscuring the various monuments. The market is a reminder that Florence has always been a city of merchants. Many of the products for sale – leather goods and silk, wool and cashmere garments – are very good buys, especially if, like the Florentines, you are prepared to bargain.

**Inexpensive cafés** and cooked meat stands abound in the vicinity of the market. They sell traditional Italian take-out foods, such as tripe and roast pork, chicken and rabbit.

**Mercato Centrale**
*Built in 1874, the central market is packed with fish, meat and cheese vendors downstairs, while fruit and vegetables are sold upstairs beneath the glass and cast-iron roof* ❶

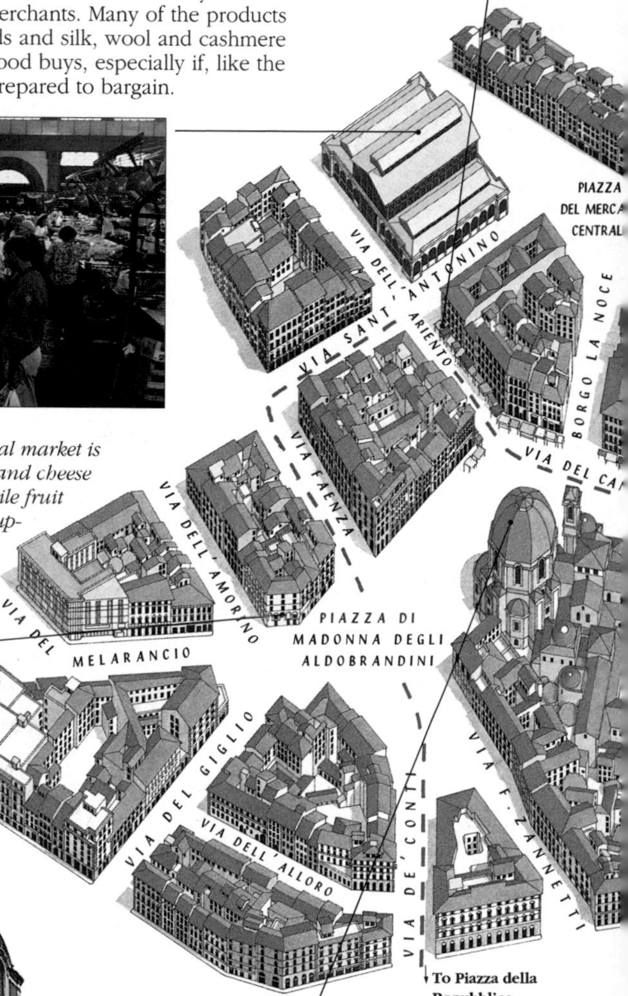


**Palazzo Riccardi-Manelli**, begun in 1557, stands on the site of the house where Giotto was born in 1266.

**The Cappelle Medicee** are situated in San Lorenzo, but are reached from a separate entrance in Piazza di Madonna degli Aldobrandini. Michelangelo designed the New Sacristy and two Medici tombs. Some of his pencil sketches survive on the walls inside.

**STAR SIGHTS**

★ **San Lorenzo**

★ **Palazzo Medici Riccardi**

**The Biblioteca Riccardiana**, founded in the 16th century, was opened to the public in 1715. It comprises a series of frescoed reading rooms that house a collection of precious manuscripts, including Dante's *Divine Comedy*.

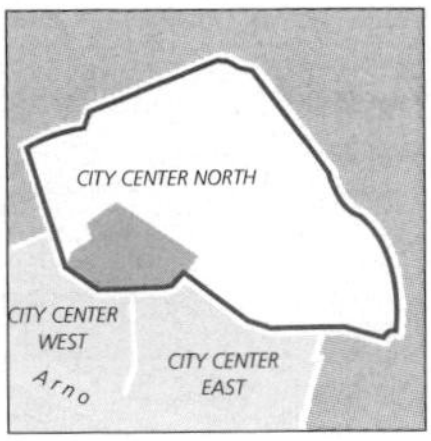


**LOCATOR MAP**
*See Florence Street Finder maps 5, 6*

**Via de' Ginori** is lined with fine 16th-century palazzi.

**San Giovannino degli Scolopi** church was begun by Ammannati in 1579.

**★ Palazzo Medici Riccardi**
*The palazzo, built between 1444 and 1464, served as the Medici family home and the headquarters of their banking empire* ❺

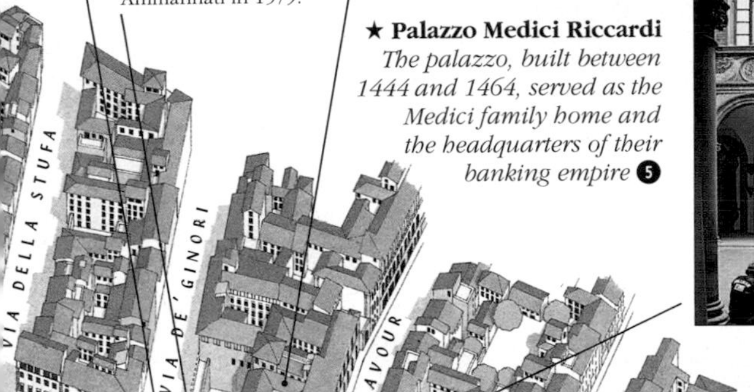


**Palazzo Pucci**
*This is the home of designer Emilio Pucci* ❹

**★ San Lorenzo**
*The unfinished façade belies the noble interior, which was designed for the Medici by Brunelleschi in 1425–46* ❷

**Giovanni delle Bande Nere**, Grand Duke Cosimo I's father *(see p49)*, is depicted in battle dress in this statue by Baccio Bandinelli (1540).

**KEY**

— — — Suggested route

0 meters 100

0 yards 100

Mercato Centrale

## Mercato Centrale ❶

Via dell'Ariento 10–14. **Map** 1 C4 (5 C1). ***Open*** *7am–2pm daily & 4–8pm Sat (exc mid-Jun–mid-Sep).* **Underground parking garage *open*** *7am–8:30pm Mon–Sat.*

RIGHT IN THE HEART of the San Lorenzo street market is Florence's busiest food market, the bustling Mercato Centrale. It is housed in a vast two-story building made of cast iron and glass, which was built in 1874 by Giuseppe Mengoni. During restoration in 1980, a mezzanine floor was constructed and a parking garage was added in the basement. On the ground floor are hundreds of stalls selling meat, poultry, fish, cheese and typical Tuscan takeout foods, such as *porchetta* (roast suckling pig), *lampredotto* (pig's intestines) and *trippa* (tripe). Fruit, vegetables and flowers are sold on the top floor.

## San Lorenzo ❷

*See pp90–91.*

## Piazza di San Lorenzo ❸

**Map** 1 C5 (6 D1). *summer: 7am–8pm; winter: 8am–8pm Tue–Sat.*

AT THE WESTERN END of the piazza, near the entrance to San Lorenzo church, there is a statue of Giovanni delle Bande Nere, mercenary and father of Cosimo I, first Medici Grand Duke *(see p49)*. It was carved by Baccio Bandinelli in 1540, and is almost hidden from view among the market stalls stretching all the way up the side of San Lorenzo church and into the streets leading off the piazza. The stalls closest to the church cater mostly to tourists, selling leather goods, T-shirts and souvenirs. In the streets around the market, everything from lentils to bargain-priced clothes is sold. The neighboring shops have become an integral part of the market, selling cheeses, hams, home-baked bread, pastries, fabrics and table linen.

San Lorenzo street market

Statue of Giovanni delle Bande Nere in Piazza di San Lorenzo

## Palazzo Pucci ❹

Via de' Pucci 6. **Map** 2 D5 (6 E1). *(055) 28 30 61.* **Showroom *open*** *by appt.*

THE PALAZZO PUCCI is the ancestral home of clothes designer Emilio Pucci, Marchese di Barsento. The Pucci family, traditionally friends and allies of the Medici, feature prominently in Florence's history, and this large palace was built in the 16th century to plans by Bartolomeo Ammannati.

Emilio Pucci's boutique is at Via della Vigna Nuova 97–99r. Haute couture clients are fitted in the palatial rooms which are above the showroom. Pucci is most famous for smart but casual clothes, and designed the stylish blue uniforms worn by Florentine traffic police, the *vigili urbani (see p276).*

## Palazzo Medici Riccardi ❺

Via Cavour 1. **Map** 2 D5 (6 D1). *(055) 276 03 40.* **Cappella dei Magi** ***open*** *9am–1pm, 3–6pm Thu–Tue (9am–1pm Sun & public hols).* ***Adm charge.*** **Sala Luca Giordano** ***open*** *9am–6pm Thu–Tue (9am–noon Sun).*

HOME OF THE MEDICI for 100 years from 1444, the palazzo was later acquired by the Riccardi family and now houses government offices. It was built to an austere design by Michelozzo for Cosimo il Vecchio, who rejected Brunelleschi's original plans for the palazzo as being too flamboyant – Cosimo did not want to be seen flaunting his wealth to his rivals. The windows on either side of the entrance were added in 1517 and designed by Michelangelo.

Through the main door, the courtyard walls are covered in ancient Roman masonry fragments. The roundels above the arcade show scenes copied from antique intaglios, carved gem-stones collected by the Medici, now on display in the Museo degli Argenti *(see p123)*. Donatello's statue of David (now in the Bargello, *see pp68–9)*, was originally here, but today the place of honor is given to Bandinelli's marble statue of *Orpheus*.

Only two rooms in the palazzo are open to the public. In the Cappella dei Magi is a colorful fresco of *The Procession of the Magi* painted by Benozzo Gozzoli in 1459–60, which depicts several members of the Medici dynasty *(see pp48–9)*. Gozzoli's self-portrait can be picked out by his name written around the rim of his cap. The Sala di Luca Giordano is named after the Neapolitan artist who painted its walls with *The Apotheosis of the Medici* in High Baroque style in 1683.

**Statuary in the garden of the Palazzo Medici Riccardi**

***The Last Supper* (1445–50) by Andrea del Castagno in Sant'Apollonia**

## Cenacolo di Sant'Apollonia ❻

Via XXVII Aprile 1. **Map** 2 D4. *(055) 238 85.* ***Open*** *9am–2pm Tue–Sun.*

THE CLOISTER and refectory of what was originally a convent for the Camaldolite order of nuns are now used by the students of Florence University. The main wall of the refectory is decorated with a fresco of *The Last Supper* painted in 1445–50, one of the few surviving works by Andrea del Castagno, pupil of Masaccio and among the first Renaissance artists to begin to experiment with perspective.

Here Judas sits isolated in the foreground of the picture, disrupting its balance and breaking up the long white strip of tablecloth. He is shown in profile with the face of a satyr: a mythological creature, half-man, half-goat, often used in Renaissance paintings to represent evil.

## San Marco ❼

*See pp96–7.*

## Giardino dei Semplici ❽

Via Micheli 3. **Map** 2 E4. *(055) 275 74 02.* ***Open*** *9am–noon Mon, Wed, Fri & Sat (also Sun late Apr–early May).* ***Closed*** *Dec 24–26, Dec 31, Jan 1, Jan 6, Apr 25, Easter Mon, May 1, Aug 13–17, Nov 1.*

**Giardino dei Semplici**

THE WORD "SEMPLICI" refers to the raw ingredients, "simples," used by medieval apothecaries in preparing medicine – thus the Giardino dei Semplici was where medicinal herbs were grown and studied. It was set up in 1545 by Niccolò Tribolo for Cosimo I in the area between Via Micheli, Via Giorgio la Pira and Via Gino Capponi. The garden retains its original layout, but now the collection includes tropical plants as well as flora native to Tuscany.

Around the garden are small theme museums: a geology collection includes fossils; the mineralogy section shows the geological structure of Elba, whose ores attracted bronze traders in the 10th century BC. The botanical museum has specimens of rare plants.

# San Lorenzo ❷

San Lorenzo was the parish church of the Medici family, who lavished their wealth on its adornment. Brunelleschi rebuilt the church in Renaissance Classical style in 1419, although the façade was never completed. In 1520 Michelangelo began work on the Medici tombs in the New Sacristy and designed the Biblioteca Mediceo-Laurenziana (Laurentian Library) in 1524 to house the manuscripts collected by the Medici. The family mausoleum, the Cappella dei Principi (Chapel of the Princes), was added in 1604.

**★ Cappella dei Principi**
*The marble decoration of the Medici mausoleum, begun in 1604 by Matteo Nigetti, was not completed until 1962.*

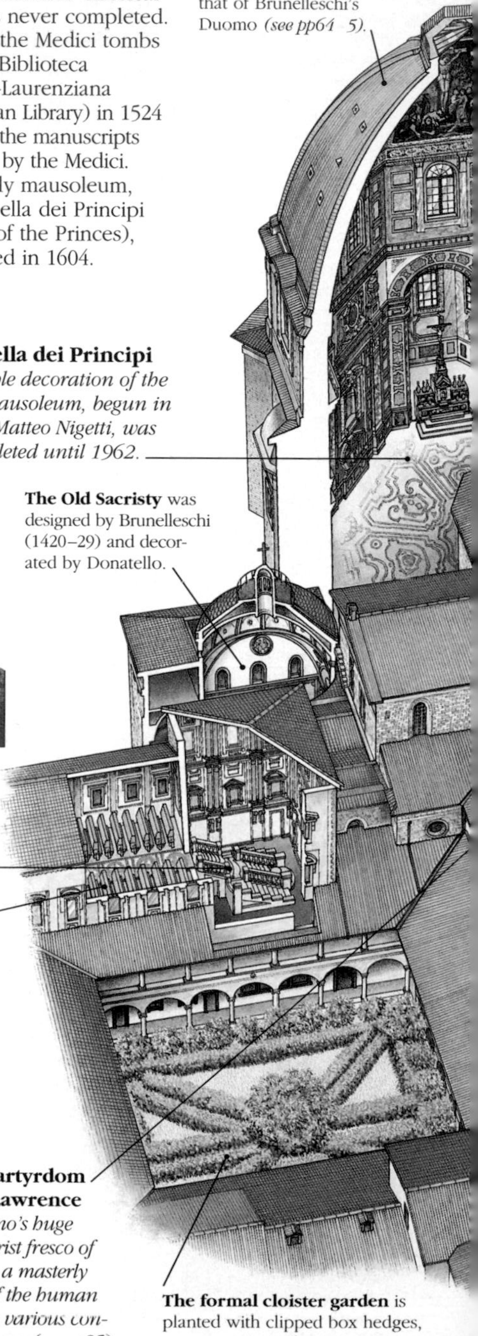

**The huge dome** by Buontalenti echoes that of Brunelleschi's Duomo *(see pp64–5)*.

**The Old Sacristy** was designed by Brunelleschi (1420–29) and decorated by Donatello.

**★ Michelangelo's Staircase**
*The elaborate* pietra serena *sandstone staircase to the Biblioteca is one of Michelangelo's most innovative designs. It was built by Ammannati in 1559.*

**Michelangelo** designed the desks and ceiling of the Biblioteca, which is entered from Manetti's graceful, tiered cloister, built in 1462.

**The Martyrdom of St. Lawrence**
*Bronzino's huge Mannerist fresco of 1569 is a masterly study of the human form in various contorted poses* (see p25).

**The formal cloister garden** is planted with clipped box hedges, pomegranate and orange trees.

**★ Medici Tombs**
*Michelangelo's monumental funerary figures, symbolizing Night, Day, Dawn and Dusk, are among his greatest works.*

**Six Grand Dukes** are buried in the Cappella dei Principi.

**The belltower** was built in 1740.

**A simple stone** slab marks the unostentatious grave of Cosimo il Vecchio (1389–1464), founder of the Medici dynasty.

**Michelangelo** submitted several designs for the façade of San Lorenzo, but it remains unfinished.

**Entrance to church**

### Visitors' Checklist

Piazza di San Lorenzo (Basilica and Biblioteca), Piazza di Madonna degli Aldobrandini (Cappelle Medicee). **Map** 1 C5 (6 D1).
*many routes.*
**Basilica** *(055) 21 66 34.*
***Open*** *7:30am–noon, 3:30–6:30pm.* *8am, 9:30am, 6pm Mon–Sun; also 11am Sun and religious hols.*
**Biblioteca** *(055) 21 44 43.*
***Open*** *9am–1pm Mon–Sat.*
**Cappelle Medicee** *(055) 238 85.* ***Open*** *9am–2pm Tue–Sun (last adm: 30 mins before closing).*
***Closed*** *Jan 1, May 1, Dec 25.*
***Adm charge.***

**Donatello's Pulpits**
*Donatello was 74 when he began work on the bronze pulpits in the nave in 1460; they depict Christ's Passion and Resurrection.*

**St. Joseph and Christ in the Workshop**
*Pietro Annigoni (1910–88) is one of the few modern artists to exhibit in Florence.*

### Star Features

- ★ Cappella dei Principi
- ★ Michelangelo's Staircase
- ★ Medici Tombs by Michelangelo

# Street-by-Street: Around San Marco

THE BUILDINGS IN THIS PART of Florence once stood on the fringes of the city, serving as stables and barracks. The Medici menagerie, including lions, elephants and giraffes, was housed here. Today it is the student quarter, and Piazza di San Marco is usually filled with young people waiting for lectures at the university or at the Accademia di Belle Arti. This is the world's oldest art school, set up in 1563, with Michelangelo as a founder *(see p94).*

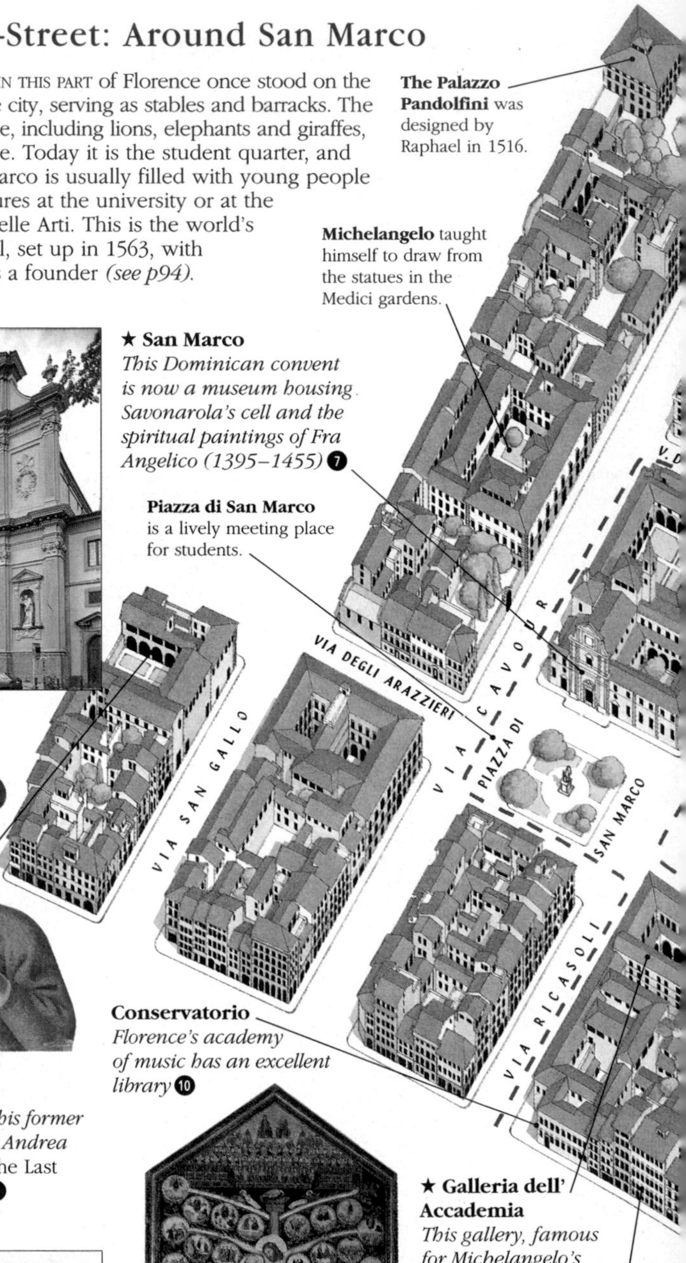


**The Palazzo Pandolfini** was designed by Raphael in 1516.

**Michelangelo** taught himself to draw from the statues in the Medici gardens.

**★ San Marco**
*This Dominican convent is now a museum housing Savonarola's cell and the spiritual paintings of Fra Angelico (1395–1455)* ❼

**Piazza di San Marco** is a lively meeting place for students.

**Cenacolo di Sant'Apollonia**
*The refectory of this former convent features Andrea del Castagno's* The Last Supper *(1450)* ❻

**Conservatorio**
*Florence's academy of music has an excellent library* ❿

**★ Galleria dell' Accademia**
*This gallery, famous for Michelangelo's* David, *also contains Bonaguida's* Tree of the Cross *(1330)* ❾

**Opificio delle Pietre Dure**
*Precious mosaics are restored here* ⓫

**STAR SIGHTS**

- ★ **Galleria dell' Accademia**
- ★ **San Marco**
- ★ **Spedale degli Innocenti**

**Santissima Annunziata**
*The Medici funded the rebuilding of this church, begun in 1444 by Michelozzo. The atrium was frescoed by Andrea del Sarto* ⓮

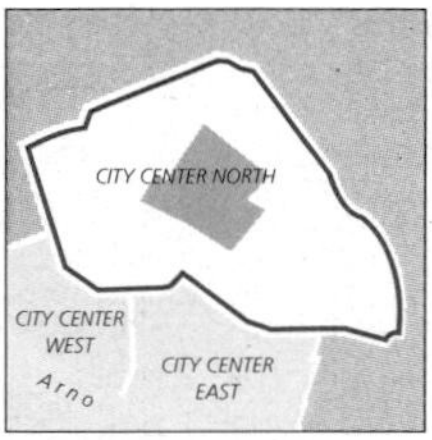


**LOCATOR MAP**
*See Florence Street Finder map 2*

**Giardino dei Semplici**
*Research into plant remedies has been undertaken here since 1545* ❽

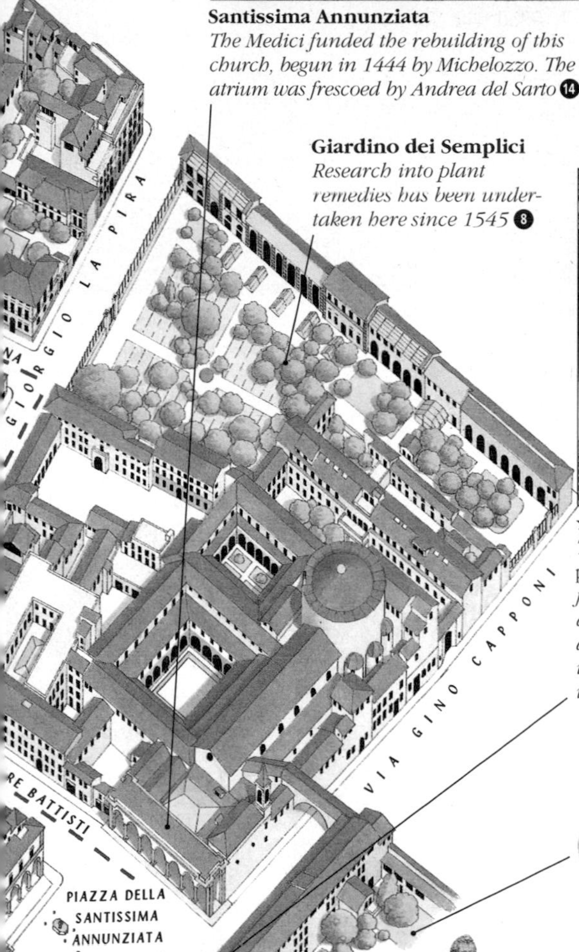

**★ Spedale degli Innocenti**
*The city orphanage* (see pp46–7) *was Brunelleschi's first completed Classical design. Andrea della Robbia added cameos of swaddled infants in the 1480s, as an inspiration to charity* ⓬

**Museo Archeologico**
*Etruscan vases and bronzes form part of this major collection* ⓯

**Grand Duke Ferdinando I** was Giambologna's last statue and was cast by Tacca in 1608, using the bronze from cannons captured as battle trophies by the Tuscan navy.

**KEY**

— — — Suggested route

0 meters 50

0 yards 50

**The central section of the 15th-century *Cassone Adimari* by Scheggia**

# Galleria dell'Accademia ❾

Via Ricasoli 60. **Map** 2 D4 (6 E1). *(055) 238 86 09.* ***Open*** *Apr–Sep: 9am–7pm Tue–Sat, 9am–2pm Sun; Oct–Mar: 9am–2pm Tue–Sun.* ***Closed*** *Jan 1, May 1, Dec 25.* ***Adm charge.***

THE ACADEMY of Fine Arts in Florence was founded in 1563 and was the first school in Europe set up to teach the techniques of drawing, painting and sculpture. The art collection displayed in the gallery was formed in 1784 with the aim of providing the students with material to study and copy.

Since 1873, many of Michelangelo's most important works have been in the Accademia. Perhaps the most famous of all dominates the collection: Michelangelo's *David* (1504). This colossal nude Classical statue depicts the biblical hero who killed the giant Goliath. It was commissioned by the city of Florence, and, once completed, was positioned in front of the Palazzo Vecchio. This established Michelangelo as the foremost sculptor of his time, at the age of 29. In 1873 it was moved indoors, to the Accademia, to protect it from the weather and pollution. One copy of *David* is now to be found in its original position in Piazza della Signoria *(see pp76–7)* and a second stands in the middle of Piazzale Michelangelo *(see p131)*.

***Madonna del Mare* (c.1470) by Sandro Botticelli**

Michelangelo's other masterpieces include a statue of St. Matthew finished in 1508, and the *Quattro Prigioni* (the four prisoners) who were sculpted between 1521 and 1523 and intended to adorn the tomb of Pope Julius II. Presented to the Medici in 1564 by Michelangelo's cousin, the muscular figures struggling to free themselves from the stone are among the most dramatic of his works. The statues were subsequently moved to the Grotta Grande in the Boboli Gardens in 1585, where casts of the originals can now be seen *(see pp124–5)*.

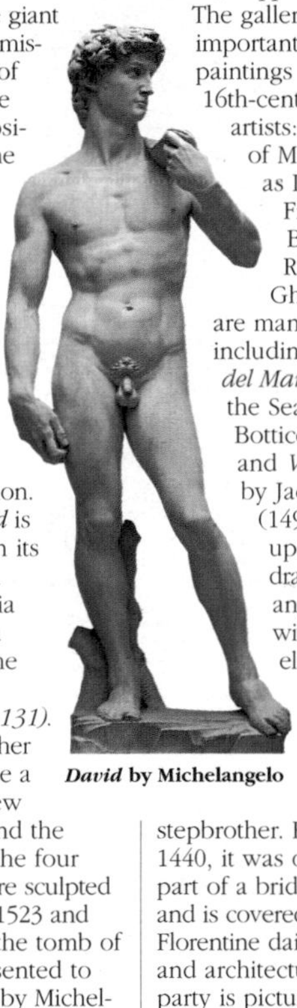

***David* by Michelangelo**

The gallery contains an important collection of paintings by 15th- and 16th-century Florentine artists: contemporaries of Michelangelo such as Fra Bartolomeo, Filippino Lippi, Bronzino and Ridolfo del Ghirlandaio. There are many major works, including the *Madonna del Mare* (Madonna of the Sea), attributed to Botticelli (1445–1510), and *Venus and Cupid* by Jacopo Pontormo (1494–1556), based upon a preparatory drawing by Michelangelo. On display with these is an elaborately painted wooden chest, the *Cassone Adimari*, by Scheggia, Masaccio's stepbrother. Painted around 1440, it was originally used as part of a bride's trousseau, and is covered with details of Florentine daily life, clothing and architecture. The bridal party is pictured standing in front of the Baptistry.

Pacino di Bonaguida's *Tree of Life* (1310) is a prominent painting among the collections of Byzantine and late 13th- and 14th-century religious art, much of which is stylized and heavily embossed with gold.

The Salone della Toscana (Tuscany Room) is full of 19th-century sculpture and paintings by members of the Accademia, and a series of original plaster models by the sculptor Lorenzo Bartolini. Born in 1777, he became professor at the Accademia in 1839, a post he held until his death in 1850. His work includes busts of major figures such as the poet Lord Byron and the composer Franz Liszt.

**Detail from 14th-century *Madonna and Saints* in the Accademia**

## Conservatorio Musicale Luigi Cherubini ⑩

Piazza delle Belle Arti 2. **Map** 2 D4 (6 E1). *(055) 29 21 80.* **Library** ***closed*** *to the public (admission by special request).*

Some of Italy's finest musicians trained at this musical academy, named after the Florentine composer Luigi Cherubini (1760–1842). The conservatory owns a collection of ancient musical instruments, now on display in the Palazzo Vecchio. They were acquired by Ferdinando, the last of the Medici Grand Dukes, and include violins, violas and cellos made by Stradivari, Amati and Ruggeri. There is a harpsichord by Bartolomeo Cristofori, who invented the piano in the early 18th century. He was responsible for many of the most important acquisitions. The conservatory has one of the best music libraries in Italy, holding many original manuscripts by composers like Monteverdi and Rossini.

***Pietre dure* table (1849) by Zocchi**

## Opificio delle Pietre Dure ⑪

Via degli Alfani 78. **Map** 2 D4 (6 F1). *(055) 28 94 14.* ***Closed*** *temporarily for restoration.*

Situated in the former monastery of San Niccolò, the *opificio* (factory) is a national institute specializing in the teaching of the Florentine craft of producing inlaid pictures using marble and semi-precious stones. This tradition has continued to flourish since the end of the 16th century, when it was funded through the patronage of the Medici Grand Dukes, who decorated their mausoleum with *pietre dure*.

There is a small museum in the same building displaying 19th-century workbenches and tools as well as vases and portraits showing *pietre dure* work. Several tabletops decorated with *pietre dure* are on display: one inlaid with a harp and garlands by Zocchi, made in 1849, another with flowers and birds, designed by Niccolò Betti in 1855. A stockpile of exquisite marbles and other semi-precious stones dates back to Medici times.

## Spedale degli Innocenti ⑫

Piazza della Santissima Annunziata 12. **Map** 2 D4. *(055) 247 79 52.* ***Open*** *8:30am–2pm Mon, Tue, Thu–Sat, 8am–1pm Sun.* ***Closed*** *public hols.* ***Adm charge.***

The "hospital" is named after Herod's biblical Massacre of the Innocents following the birth of Jesus. It opened in 1444 as the first orphanage in Europe, and part of the building is still used for this purpose. UNICEF, the United Nations Children's Fund, also has offices here. Brunelleschi's arcaded loggia *(see pp46–7)* features glazed terra-cotta roundels, added by Andrea della Robbia around 1498, showing babies wrapped in swaddling bands. At the left-hand end of the portico you can see the *rota*, a rotating stone cylinder on which mothers could place their unwanted children anonymously and ring the orphanage bell. The stone was then turned around and the child was taken in.

Within the building there are two elegant cloisters built to Brunelleschi's designs. The larger Chiostro degli Uomini (Men's Cloister), built between 1422 and 1445, is decorated with *sgraffito* designs of cherubs and roosters scratched into the wet plaster. The smaller Women's Cloister (1438) leads to a gallery that has several paintings donated by children from the orphanage who went on to be successful in later life. Outstanding among these is the *Adoration of the Magi* (1488) painted by Domenico del Ghirlandaio, showing the massacre in the background.

**Andrea della Robbia's roundels (c.1490) on the Spedale degli Innocenti**

# San Marco 7

**Dominican friar in gray habit**

The convent of San Marco was founded in the 13th century and enlarged in 1437 when Dominican monks from nearby Fiesole moved there at the invitation of Cosimo il Vecchio. He paid a considerable sum to have the convent rebuilt by his favorite architect, Michelozzo, whose simple cloisters and cells are the setting for a remarkable series of devotional frescoes (c.1438–45) by Fra Angelico.

**The Mocking of Christ**
*Fra Angelico's beautiful allegorical fresco (c.1442) shows Jesus blindfolded and being struck by a Roman guard.*

**Cells 38 and 39** were reserved for Cosimo il Vecchio when he retreated to the convent to find spiritual sustenance and peace.

**Cells 12 to 14** contain relics of the religious fanatic Savonarola, made prior of San Marco in 1491 *(see pp50–51).*

**An ancient cedar** stands in Michelozzo's Sant'Antonino cloister.

**Entrance to San Marco**

**Entrance to Museo di San Marco**

**Sant'Antonino cloister**

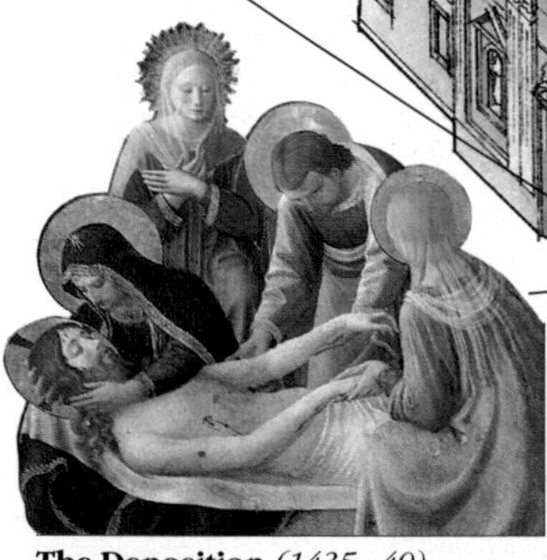

**The Deposition** *(1435–40)*
*This poignant scene of the dead Christ, and other works by Fra Angelico and his School, are displayed in the former Pilgrims' Hospice.*

**Key to Floorplan**

- Ground floor
- First floor
- Non-exhibition space

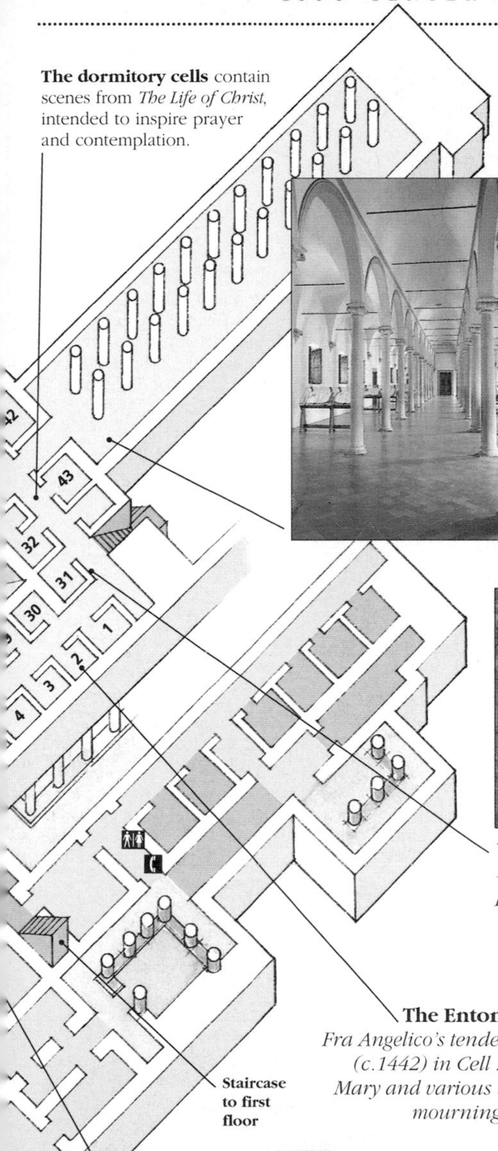


**The dormitory cells** contain scenes from *The Life of Christ*, intended to inspire prayer and contemplation.

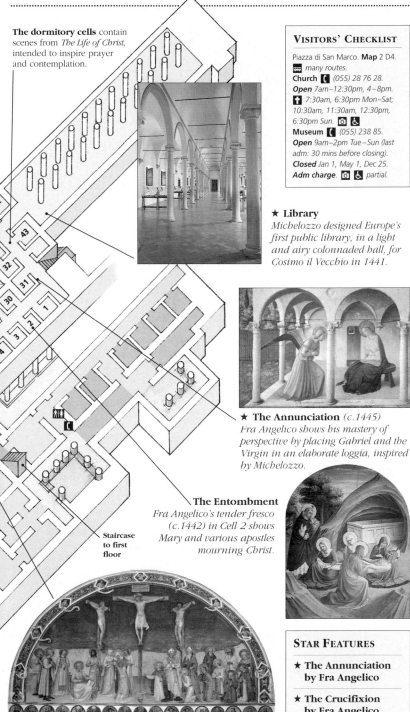

### Visitors' Checklist

Piazza di San Marco. **Map** 2 D4.
*many routes.*
**Church** *(055) 28 76 28.*
***Open*** *7am–12:30pm, 4–8pm.*
*7:30am, 6:30pm Mon–Sat; 10:30am, 11:30am, 12:30pm, 6:30pm Sun.*
**Museum** *(055) 238 85.*
***Open*** *9am–2pm Tue–Sun (last adm: 30 mins before closing).*
***Closed*** *Jan 1, May 1, Dec 25.*
***Adm charge****.* *partial.*

**★ Library**
*Michelozzo designed Europe's first public library, in a light and airy colonnaded hall, for Cosimo il Vecchio in 1441.*

**★ The Annunciation** *(c.1445)*
*Fra Angelico shows his mastery of perspective by placing Gabriel and the Virgin in an elaborate loggia, inspired by Michelozzo.*

**The Entombment**
*Fra Angelico's tender fresco (c.1442) in Cell 2 shows Mary and various apostles mourning Christ.*

**Staircase to first floor**

**★ The Crucifixion** *(1441–42)*
*Fra Angelico was moved to tears as he painted this image of the Crucifixion of Christ in the Chapter House.*

### Star Features

- **★ The Annunciation by Fra Angelico**
- **★ The Crucifixion by Fra Angelico**
- **★ Library by Michelozzo**

**Mannerist fountain by Pietro Tacca in Piazza della Santissima Annunziata**

## Piazza della Santissima Annunziata ⓭

**Map** 2 D4.

THE DELICATE nine-bay arcade on the eastern side of this elegant square was designed by Brunelleschi in 1419 and forms the façade to the Spedale degli Innocenti *(see p46)*. Brunelleschi's round arches gave rise to the Classical style widely copied by many other Renaissance architects. In the center of the square is an equestrian statue of Duke Ferdinando I, started by Giambologna toward the end of his long career. It was finished in 1608 by his assistant, Pietro Tacca, who also designed the two highly stylized Mannerist bronze fountains in the square.

A fair is held annually in the piazza on the feast of the Annunciation, March 25, when homemade sweet cookies called *brigidini* are sold from the stands.

## Santissima Annunziata ⓮

Piazza della Santissima Annunziata. **Map** 2 E4. *(055) 239 80 34.* ***Open*** *7am–12:30pm, 4–6:30pm Mon–Sat & 4–5:30pm Sun.*

THE CHURCH of the Holy Annunciation was founded by the Servite order in 1250 and later rebuilt by Michelozzo between 1444 and 1481. There is a series of early 16th-century frescoes in the atrium by Mannerist artists Rosso Fiorentino, Andrea del Sarto and Jacopo Pontormo, but many of these frescoes have suffered from dampness and are fading. The most celebrated are *The Journey of the Magi* (1511) and *The Birth of the Virgin* (1514) by del Sarto.

The interior is dark and heavily decorated, with a frescoed ceiling completed by Pietro Giambelli in 1669.

The church also boasts one of the most revered shrines in Florence, a painting of the Virgin Mary begun in 1252 by a monk. Devout Florentines believe the picture was finished by an angel, and many newlywed couples traditionally come here after their wedding ceremony to present a bouquet of flowers to the Virgin and pray for a long and fruitful marriage. Nine chapels radiate from the sanctuary. The central one was reconstructed by Giambologna to use as his tomb and it contains several bronze reliefs and a crucifix sculpted by him.

Through the door in the north transept of the church is the Chiostro dei Morti (Cloister of the Dead), so called because it was originally used as a burial ground and is packed with memorial stones. The fresco above the entrance porch is by Andrea del Sarto. Painted in 1525, it shows the Holy Family resting on their flight to Egypt and is usually known as *The Madonna del Sacco*, since Joseph is depicted leaning on a sack.

The Cappella di San Luca off the cloister has belonged to the Accademia delle Arte del Disegno since 1565, and a service dedicated to artists is held every year on St. Luke's day, October 18. Benvenuto Cellini is one of the artists buried in the vault.

***The Birth of the Virgin* (1514) by Andrea del Sarto**

The François Vase, covered in figures from Greek mythology

## Museo Archeologico ⓯

Via della Colonna 38. **Map** 2 E4. *(055) 235 75.* ***Open*** *8:30am–2pm Tue–Sat, 8:30am–1pm Sun.* ***Closed*** *some public hols.* ***Adm charge.***

The archaeological Museum is in a palazzo built by Giulio Parigi for the Princess Maria Maddalena de' Medici in 1620. It now exhibits outstanding collections of Etruscan, Greek, Roman and ancient Egyptian artifacts.

A section on the second floor is dedicated to Greek vases, with a room devoted to the François Vase, found in an Etruscan tomb at Fonte Rotella near Chiusi *(see p224)*. Painted and signed in 570 BC, it is decorated with six rows of black and red figures depicting scenes from Greek mythology. The Etruscan collection was very badly damaged by the 1966 flood and only a fraction is now on display, although restoration work is being continued.

In addition to the splendid series of bronze Etruscan statues, on the first floor of the museum there are two famous bronzes. The *Chimera (see p40)*, sculpted in the 4th century BC, is a mythical lion with a goat's head imposed on its body and a serpent for a tail, shown here cowering in terror. It was plowed up in a field near Arezzo in 1553 and presented to Cosimo I de' Medici by Giorgio Vasari, the artist, author and critic. The *Arringatore* (Orator) was found c.1566 near Lake Trasimeno in central Italy and is inscribed with the name of a powerful Etruscan aristocrat, Aulus Metullus. The sculpture dates from the 1st century BC, and the figure, shown dressed in a Roman toga, appears to be addressing his audience.

Part of the Egyptian collection was acquired during a joint French and Tuscan expedition in 1829. It is rich in wooden, cloth and bone artifacts, preserved in the dry atmosphere of the desert tombs in which they were found. They include a near-complete chariot of bone and wood dating to c.15th century BC, which was found in a tomb near Thebes, along with textiles, ropes, furniture, hats, purses and baskets.

Bronze Etruscan warrior

## Santa Maria Maddalena dei Pazzi ⓰

Borgo Pinti 58. **Map** 2 F5. *(055) 247 84 20.* **Church and chapter house *open*** *9am–noon, 5–7pm daily.*

This former convent has been restored following the floods of 1966. Originally run by the Cistercian order, it was taken over by Carmelites in 1628, and Augustinian monks have lived here since 1926. The chapter house, which is entered from the crypt, contains the famous *Crucifixion and Saints* fresco painted in 1493–6 by Perugino (his real name was Pietro Vannucci), who was one of the founders of the Umbrian School of artists. This beautiful and well-preserved fresco is regarded as a masterpiece, bearing all Perugino's trademarks, most notably the background, which is a detailed landscape of wooded hills and winding streams painted in soft blues and greens. The main chapel, decorated with colored marble by Ciro Ferri (1675), is one of the best examples of the High Baroque style in a Florentine church. In 1492 Giuliano da Sangallo designed the church's unusual portico, with its square-topped, Ionic-style arcades.

## Tempio Israelitico ⓱

Via Farini 4. **Map** 2 F5. *(055) 24 52 52.* **Synagogue and Museum *open*** *10am–1pm, 2–5pm Sun–Thu, 10am–1pm Fri (Oct– Mar: 11am–1pm, 2–5pm Mon–Thu, 10am–1pm Fri, Sun).* ***Closed*** *Jewish hols.*

Interior of the Tempio Israelitico

The green copper-covered dome of Florence's main synagogue stands out on the horizon as you look down on the city from the surrounding hills. As elsewhere in Europe, Jews in Florence were alternately welcomed and persecuted over the years. In the early 17th century they flocked to Livorno and then to Florence when it was freed from its strong political ties with Spain by Grand Duke Ferdinando I (1549–1609).

In the Inquisition, Grand Duke Cosimo III (1642–1723) passed laws forbidding Christians to work for Jewish families and businesses. In the 1860s the Jewish ghetto was cleared to make way for the Piazza della Repubblica *(see p112)*. The synagogue was built by Marco Treves in 1874–82 in Spanish-Moorish style. It has a museum of ritual objects dating to the 17th century.

# CITY CENTER WEST

Detail from Strozzi Chapel in Santa Maria Novella

AT ONE END of this part of Florence is the main railway station – a rare example of modern architecture in the city center. At the other end, a magnet for visitors and Florentines alike, is the Ponte Vecchio, the city's oldest bridge. It is lined with jewelers' shops, here since 1593, and presents a scene little changed since.

Between these two focal points there is something to interest everyone, from the frescoes of Santa Maria Novella and Santa Trìnita to the Palazzo Davanzati, which provides an insight into the surprisingly luxurious living conditions enjoyed by the wealthier medieval Florentines. Nearby is Piazza della Repubblica, laid out as part of the grandiose plans to remodel Florence when it was briefly the nation's capital. Although many locals consider it an eyesore, the cafés here have always been very popular. This is also the part of Florence to shop, from the cheap merchandise of the Mercato Nuovo to the elegant creations of the top couturiers in Via della Vigna Nuova and Via de' Tornabuoni. In the smaller streets off these, the local artisans still continue Florence's proud tradition of fine craftsmanship, from stonecutting to restoration work.

## SIGHTS AT A GLANCE

**Museums and Galleries**
Museo Marino Marini (San Pancrazio) 1
Palazzo Davanzati 10
Palazzo Rucellai (Museo Alinari) 2

**Churches**
Ognissanti 16
Santi Apostoli 8
*Santa Maria Novella pp110–11* 17
Santa Trìnita 7

**Historic Buildings**
Palazzo Antinori 14
Palazzo di Parte Guelfa 11
Palazzo Strozzi 5
Stazione Centrale di Santa Maria Novella 18

**Historic Streets and Piazzas**
Piazza della Repubblica 13
Piazza di Santa Trìnita 6
Via dei Fossi 15
Via de' Tornabuoni 4
Via della Vigna Nuova 3

**Bridges**
*Ponte Vecchio pp106–7* 9

**Markets**
Mercato Nuovo 12

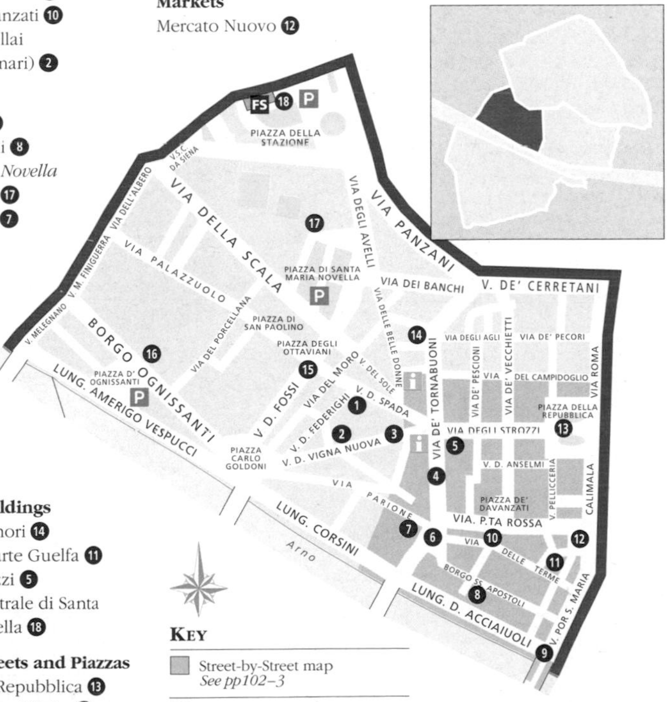


**KEY**

Street-by-Street map *See pp102–3*

Tourist information

Parking

Railway station

0 meters 400

0 yards 400

◁ **View from Ponte Santa Trìnita toward Piazza di Santa Trìnita**

# Street-by-Street: Around Piazza della Repubblica

Underlying the street plan of modern Florence is the far older pattern of the ancient Roman city founded on the banks of the Arno. Nowhere is this more evident than in the rectilinear grid of narrow streets in the western half of the city center. Here the streets lead north from the river Arno to the Piazza della Repubblica, once the site of the forum, the main square of the ancient Roman city. It later became the city's main food market *(see p52)* until the city authorities decided to tidy it up in the 1860s, building the triumphal arch that now stands in today's café-filled square.

**Palazzo Strozzi**
*This monumental palazzo dominates the square* ❺

**Piazza di Santa Trìnita**
*The square is marked by an ancient Roman column* ❻

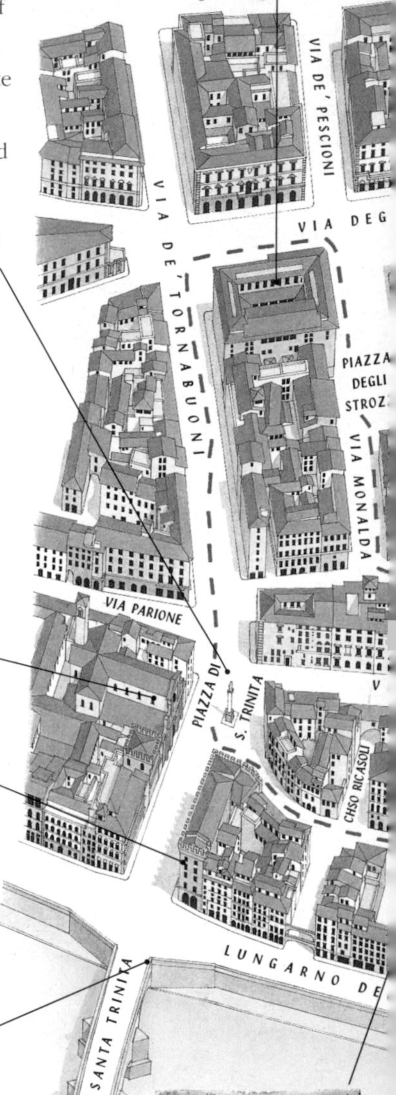

**★ Santa Trìnita**
*Ghirlandaio's frescoes,* The Life of St. Francis *(1483), depict scenes that took place in this area. Here, a child is restored to life after falling from the Palazzo Spini-Ferroni* ❼

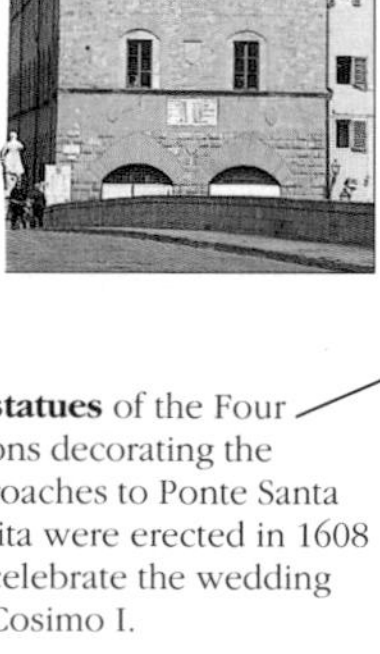

**Palazzo Spini-Ferroni,** a medieval palazzo featured in Ghirlandaio's frescoes in Santa Trìnita, now houses the fashion boutique of Salvatore Ferragamo *(see p108).*

**The statues** of the Four Seasons decorating the approaches to Ponte Santa Trìnita were erected in 1608 to celebrate the wedding of Cosimo I.

**Key**

— — — Suggested route

0 meters 200

0 yards 200

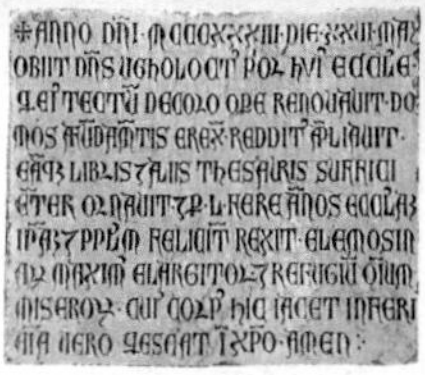

**Santi Apostoli**
*A plaque claims Charlemagne as founder* ❽

Piazza della Repubblica
*The Roman-style triumphal arch celebrates Florence's stint as Italy's capital (1865–71)* ⓭

**Locator Map**
*See Florence Street Finder maps 5, 6*

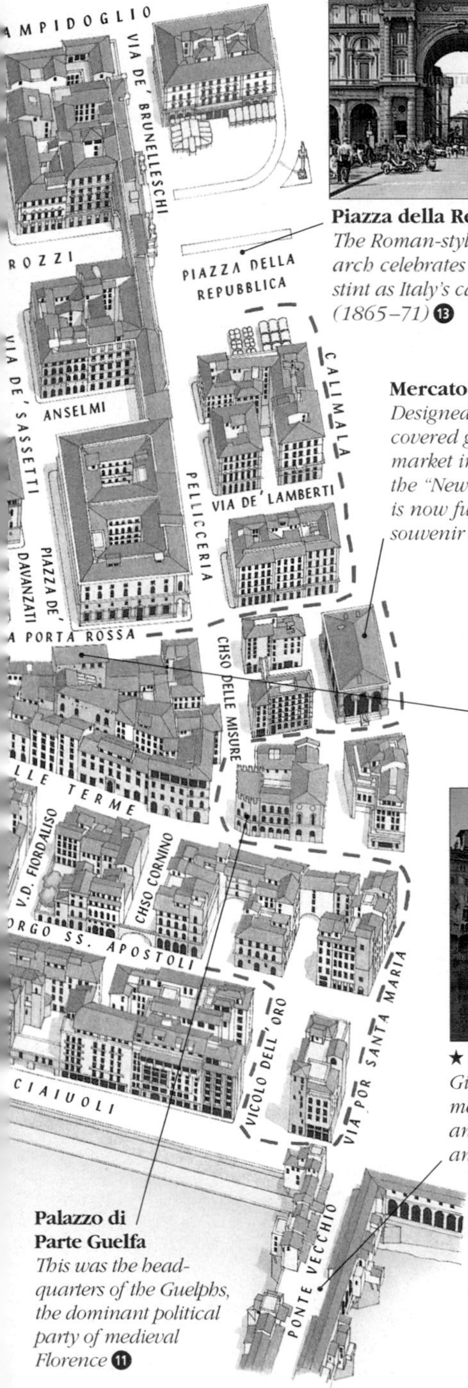


**Mercato Nuovo**
*Designed as a covered general market in 1547, the "New Market" is now full of souvenir stands* ⓬

**★ Palazzo Davanzati**
*Frescoes with exotic birds decorate the Sala dei Papagalli, which was once the dining room of this 14th-century palazzo* ❿

**★ Ponte Vecchio**
*Giotto's pupil Taddeo Gaddi designed this medieval bridge in 1345. It is the oldest – and most popular – of Florence's bridges and retains many of its original features* ❾

**Palazzo di Parte Guelfa**
*This was the headquarters of the Guelphs, the dominant political party of medieval Florence* ⓫

**Star Sights**

- ★ Palazzo Davanzati
- ★ Ponte Vecchio
- ★ Santa Trìnita

## Museo Marino Marini (San Pancrazio) ❶

Piazza San Pancrazio. **Map** 1 B5 (5 B2). (055) 21 94 32. ***Open*** *10am–1pm, 3–6pm (Jun–Aug: 4–7pm) Wed–Mon.* ***Closed*** *Dec 25, May 1, 2 weeks in Aug.* ***Adm charge.***

THE FORMER CHURCH of San Pancrazio has been turned into a museum devoted to the work of Italy's best-known abstract artist, Marino Marini (1901–80). Marini was born in Pistoia, where more of his work can be seen in the Palazzo del Comune and in the newly-opened Centro Marino Marini *(see p182).* Marini studied art in Florence before moving on to teaching in Monza and at the prestigious Brera Academy in Milan. He is noted for rugged and elemental bronzes, many of them on the theme of horse and rider, which express a range of moods and experiences, from somber weariness to joyous eroticism.

San Pancrazio itself is one of the oldest churches in Florence. It was founded in the 9th century, though its most attractive features are from the Renaissance period, including a graceful Classical façade and porch (1461–7) by Leon Battista Alberti.

San Pancrazio was the parish church of the wealthy merchant Giovanni Rucellai. Inside, in the Cappella di San Sepolcro, built by Alberti in 1467, is Rucellai's tomb, which is modeled on the Holy Sepulcher in Jerusalem (the tomb of Christ).

**Bronze statue, *Cavaliere* (1949), by Marini in the Museo Marino Marini**

**19th-century view of Lungarno degli Acciaiuoli, from Museo Alinari**

## Palazzo Rucellai (Museo Alinari) ❷

Via della Vigna Nuova 16r. **Map** 1 C5 (5 B2). *(055) 21 33 70.* ***Open*** *10am–7:30pm Thu–Tue, 10–11:30pm Fri & Sat.* ***Closed*** *some public hols.* ***Adm charge.***

BUILT IN 1446–57, this is one of the most ornate Renaissance palaces in the city. It was commissioned by Giovanni Rucellai, whose enormous wealth derived from the family business, the import of a rare and costly red dye made from lichen found only on the island of Majorca. The dye was called *oricello*, from which the name Rucellai is derived.

Giovanni commissioned several buildings from the architect Leon Battista Alberti, who went on to write the influential treatise on architecture called *De Re Aedificatoria* (Concerning Architecture) in 1452. He designed this palace almost as a textbook illustration of the major Classical orders. In ascending order of complexity, the pilaster strips on the ground floor are Doric, those above are Ionic and those on the top floor are Corinthian.

Two symbols are carved into the entablature: the Rucellai's billowing sails of Fortune and the ring symbol of the Medici family. The ring is a reminder that Bernardo Rucellai formed an alliance with the Medici in the 1460s by marrying Lorenzo de' Medici's sister, Lucrezia. The Loggia del Rucellai, opposite the palace, was built to commemorate the marriage.

The palazzo now houses the Museo Alinari. The Alinari brothers began taking pictures of Florence in the 1840s, not long after the invention of photography. The firm they set up in 1852 specialized in supplying top-quality prints, postcards and art books to foreigners on the Grand Tour who flocked to the city during the 19th century. The museum mounts changing exhibitions of pictures drawn from its photographic archives, providing a fascinating insight into the social history of Florence over the last 150 years.

## Via della Vigna Nuova ❸

**Map** 3 B1 (5 B3).

Reflecting its associations with wealthy Renaissance Florentines, such as the Rucellai, Via della Vigna Nuova, like nearby Via de' Tornabuoni, has a number of fashionable clothing stores. These include Enrico Coveri (No. 27–29r), Naj Oleari (No. 35r) and Giorgio Armani (No. 51r). Another shop not to miss is Emilio Paoli (No. 26r), which specializes in woven straw goods of the type once sold in the Mercato Nuovo *(see p112)*, including hats, toys, sculptures and furniture.

**Armani shop, Via della Vigna Nuova**

## Via de' Tornabuoni ❹

**Map** 1 C5 (5 C2).

Via de' Tornabuoni is the most elegant shopping street in Florence. Leading jewelers and couturiers have boutiques here, including Salvatore Ferragamo (No. 14r), Bijoux Casciou (No. 32r), Ugolini (No. 20–22r), and Gucci (No. 73r). Valentino is in nearby Via della Vigna Nuova (47r). Farther up is the excellent Seeber bookshop (No. 68r), founded in 1865 for the expatriate community and still selling publications in many languages. La Giocosa (No. 83r) is a fashionable café where the famous Negroni cocktail (Campari, vermouth and gin) was invented.

### The Biggest Palazzo in Florence

The Strozzi family were exiled from Florence in 1434 for their opposition to the Medici, but in 1466 the banker Filippo Strozzi, having built up a fortune in Naples, returned to the city, determined to outdo his great rivals. He became a man obsessed. For years he bought up and demolished other palaces around his home. At last, he acquired enough land to achieve his ambition: to build the biggest palace ever seen in Florence. Having spent so much money to get this far, nothing was left to chance. Astrologers were brought in to choose the most favorable day on which to lay the foundation stone, and the walls of the monumental palace began to rise in 1489. Two years later Filippo Strozzi was dead, and, though his heirs struggled on with the building, the cost of pursuing Filippo's grandiose vision finally left them penniless and bankrupt.

**Filippo Strozzi (1428–91)**

## Palazzo Strozzi ❺

Piazza degli Strozzi. **Map** 3 C1 (5 C3). **Piccolo Museo di Palazzo Strozzi** ***closed*** *for restoration.*

The Strozzi palace is awesome because of its sheer size: 15 buildings were demolished to make way for it, and although it is only three stories high, each floor is as tall as a normal palazzo. The palace was commissioned by the wealthy banker Filippo Strozzi, but he died in 1491, only two years after the foundation stone was laid.

The building was not completed until 1536, and three major architects had a hand in its design – Giuliano da Sangallo, Benedetto da Maiano and Simone del Pollaiuolo (also known as Cronaca). The exterior, built of huge rusticated masonry blocks, remains unspoiled. Be sure to see the original Renaissance torch-holders, lamps and rings for tethering horses, which adorn the corners and façades.

To the left of the courtyard entrance, the Piccolo Museo di Palazzo Strozzi explains the building's history through models and drawings. The elegance of the courtyard itself has been destroyed by a huge iron fire escape, constructed when the building was converted to a major exhibition site. The Biennale dell'Antiquariato, one of Italy's biggest antiques fairs, is held here every alternate year in September–October *(see p34)*.

The palace also houses various scholarly institutes and an excellent library, the Gabinetto Vieusseux, named after the 19th-century Swiss scholar Gian Pietro Vieusseux. He founded a scientific and literary association in 1818, which was attended by, among others, the French author Stendhal.

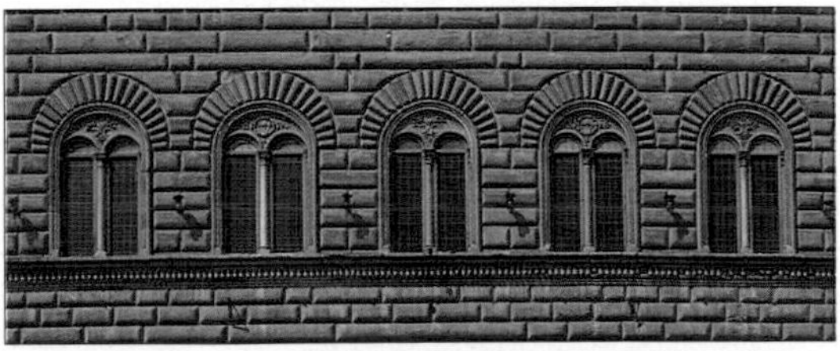

**Exterior of Palazzo Strozzi, with masonry block rustication**

# Ponte Vecchio ❾

The ponte vecchio, or Old Bridge – indeed, the oldest bridge in Florence – was built in 1345. It was the only bridge in the city to escape being blown up during World War II. There have always been workshops on the bridge, but the butchers, tanners and blacksmiths who were here originally (and who used the river as a convenient garbage dump) were evicted by Duke Ferdinando I in 1593 because of the noise and stench they created. The workshops were rebuilt and rented to the more decorous goldsmiths, and the shops lining and overhanging the bridge continue to specialize in new and antique jewelry to this day.

**Private Corridor**
*The aerial corridor built by Vasari along the eastern side of the bridge is hung with the self-portraits of many great artists, including Rembrandt, Rubens and Hogarth.*

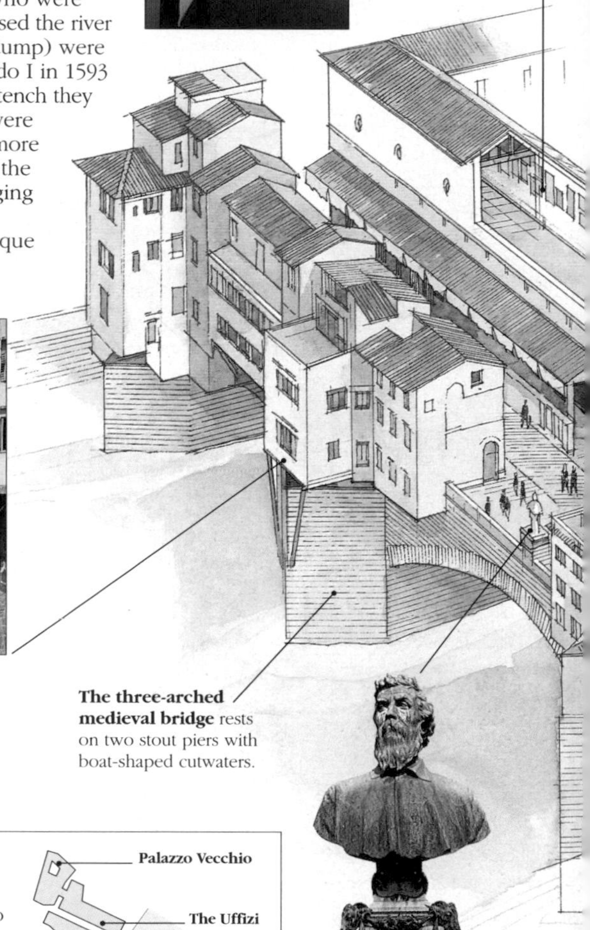

**Medieval Workshops**
*Some of the oldest workshops have rear extensions overhanging the river, supported by timber brackets called* sporti.

**The three-arched medieval bridge** rests on two stout piers with boat-shaped cutwaters.

**Bust of Cellini**
*A bust of Benvenuto Cellini (1500–71), the most famous of all Florentine goldsmiths, was placed in the middle of the bridge in 1900.*

## Vasari's Corridor

The Corridoio Vasariano was built in 1565 by Giorgio Vasari, court architect to the Medici dukes. The elevated corridor links the Palazzo Vecchio to the Palazzo Pitti, via the Uffizi. This private walkway allowed members of the Medici family to move about between their various residences, admiring the paintings on the corridor's walls, without having to step into the street below and mix with the crowds.

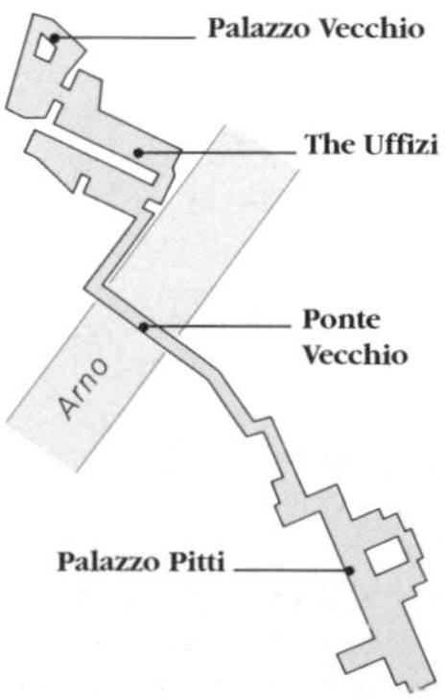

**★ Bridge at Sunset**
*The Ponte Vecchio is especially attractive when viewed in the setting sun from Ponte Santa Trinita, or from one of the river embankments.*

**Visitors' Checklist**

**Map** 3 C1 (5 C4). *Several to the bridge. Pedestrian area.*

**Mannelli Tower**
*This medieval tower was built to defend the bridge. The Mannelli family stubbornly refused to demolish it to make way for the Vasari Corridor.*

**★ Jewelers' Shops**
*The shops sell everything from affordable modern earrings to precious antique rings.*

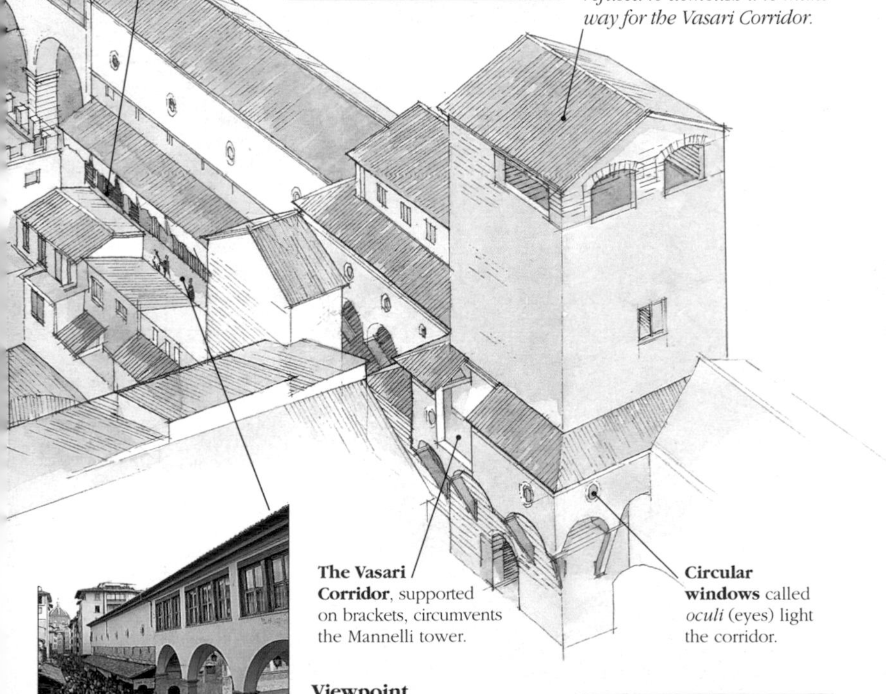

**The Vasari Corridor**, supported on brackets, circumvents the Mannelli tower.

**Circular windows** called *oculi* (eyes) light the corridor.

**Viewpoint**
*There are few better places for enjoying the river views; street performers, portrait painters and street traders gather on the bridge, adding to the color and bustle.*

**Star Features**

**★ Jewelers' Shops**

**★ Bridge at Sunset**

Piazza di Santa Trìnita

## Piazza di Santa Trìnita ❻

**Map** 3C1 (5C3).

NOBLE PALAZZI line this busy square. To the south is the Palazzo Spini-Ferroni, originally built in 1290 but much rebuilt in the 19th century; today the ground floor houses the famous boutique of Salvatore Ferragamo *(see p266)*, specializing in shoes and leather goods. To the north, on the corner with Via delle Terme, is the Palazzo Bartolini-Salimbeni. Built during 1520–29, it is one of the city's best examples of High Renaissance architecture. In between the two palazzi is a column of oriental granite originally from the Baths of Caracalla in Rome and given to Cosimo I by Pope Pius IV in 1560. The figure of Justice on top was made in 1581.

Just south of the square is the Ponte Santa Trìnita, considered the most beautiful bridge in Florence. It affords fine views of the surrounding hills and especially of the Ponte Vecchio *(see pp106–7)*. It was originally built in wood in 1252, and then rebuilt by Ammannati in 1567 as a monument to Cosimo I's defeat of Siena. Michelangelo is credited with the elegant design, based on an intriguing elliptical curve echoing those on the famous Medici tombs *(see p91)*. The statues of the Four Seasons at each end were added in 1608 for Cosimo II's marriage to Maria of Austria. The bridge was restored after it was blown up by the Germans in 1944, and the statues were dredged up from the riverbed.

Look west from here to the golden yellow Palazzo Corsini (1648–56), with statues on the roof balustrade. It is one of the best examples of Baroque architecture in Florence.

Ponte Santa Trìnita

## Santa Trìnita ❼

Piazza di Santa Trìnita. **Map** 3 C1 (5 C3). *(055) 21 69 12.*
***Open*** *7:15am–noon, 4–7pm (Sun: 4–5:30pm) daily.*

The nave of Santa Trìnita

THE ORIGINAL CHURCH, built in the second half of the 11th century by the Vallombrosan monastic order, was very plain – a reflection of the austerity of the order, which was founded in Florence in 1092 to restore the simplicity of monastic rule. Gradually, the building became more ornate, with a Baroque façade added in 1593. Inside, the east wall shows traces of its Romanesque predecessor.

Ghirlandaio's frescoes in the Sassetti Chapel (right of the High Altar) show what the church looked like in 1483–6. In one scene, St. Francis of Assisi performs a miracle in the Piazza di Santa Trìnita, with the church and the Palazzo Spini-Ferroni in the background. The donors of the chapel, Francesco Sassetti and his wife Nera Corsi, are portrayed on either side of the altar. In another scene, St. Francis is receiving the Rule of the Franciscan Order from Pope

Honorius III in the Piazza della Signoria. Sassetti, who was general manager of the Medici bank, is shown with his son, Teodoro, and with Lorenzo de' Medici to his right, along with Antonio Pucci. Lorenzo's sons are climbing up steps with their tutors, led by the Humanist scholar Agnolo Poliziano, or Politian. The altar painting, *The Adoration of the Shepherds* (1485), is also by Ghirlandaio; he is the first, dark-haired shepherd. The black sarcophagi of Sassetti and his wife are by Giuliano da Sangallo.

## Santi Apostoli ❽

Piazza del Limbo. **Map** 3 C1 (5 C4). ☎ *(055) 29 06 42.* ***Open*** *3–7pm daily, 9am–12:30pm Sun.*

THE LITTLE CHURCH of the Holy Apostles is, along with the Baptistry, among the oldest surviving churches in Florence. Florentines like to think that the church was founded in AD 800 by the first Holy Roman Emperor, Charlemagne, but it more likely dates to 1059–1100. The church has a simple Romanesque façade and the basilican plan typical of early Christian churches, but with 16th-century side aisles.

Santi Apostoli fronts Piazza del Limbo, so called because there was a cemetery here for infants who died before being baptized. Hence, according to Roman Catholic belief, their souls dwelt in limbo – halfway between heaven and hell.

**Della Robbia glazed terra-cotta tabernacle in Santi Apostoli**

## Ponte Vecchio ❾

*See pp106–7.*

**Fresco in a bedroom in the Palazzo Davanzati**

## Palazzo Davanzati ❿

Via Porta Rossa 13. **Map** 3 C1 (5 C3). ☎ *(055) 238 86 10.* ***Open*** *9am–2pm Tue–Sun.* ***Closed*** *Mon & some public hols.* ***Adm charge.***

ALSO KNOWN as the Museo dell'Antica Casa Fiorentina, the Palazzo Davanzati is preserved as a typical house of wealthy Florentines of the 14th century. The entrance courtyard was designed to trap unwanted visitors; "pelting holes" in the vaulted ceiling were used for dropping missiles. In the peaceful inner courtyard, a staircase links all the floors. In one corner is a well and a pulley system so buckets of water could be raised to each floor – this private water supply was quite a luxury since most households had to carry all their water from a public fountain.

**Emblem of the Guelphs**

The main living room on the first floor looks plain, but the hooks high up beneath the ceiling show that the walls would have been hung with tapestries. This and adjacent rooms are now used to display a fine collection of antique lace. The dining room has gorgeous frescoes imitating wall hangings and is decorated with parrot motifs – hence its name: Sala dei Pappagalli. Many rooms have bathrooms attached, and are decorated with frescoes of scenes from a French romance. The kitchen was built on the top floor, so smoke and smells did not spread throughout the house.

## Palazzo di Parte Guelfa ⓫

Piazza di Parte Guelfa. **Map** 3 C1 (6 D3). ***Closed*** *to the public.*

THIS DISTINCTIVE building served as the headquarters of the Guelph party and the residence of its captains from around 1266, after the Guelphs began to emerge as the stronger of the two medieval factions struggling for control over Florence. In the complex politics of the period, the Guelphs supported the Pope and the Ghibellines took the side of the Holy Roman Emperor in the dispute over who should rule northern Italy *(see p44).*

The lower part of the building dates to the 13th century, but the upper part was added by Brunelleschi in 1431. There are *stemmae* (coats-of-arms) under the crenellations. The elegant open staircase, added in 1589, is by Vasari.

# Santa Maria Novella ⓱

The gothic church of Santa Maria Novella contains some of the most important works of art in Florence. The church was built by the Dominicans from 1279 to 1357. Beside the church is a cemetery walled in with *avelli* (grave niches), which continue along the façade and the wall beyond. The cloisters form a museum. Here, the frescoes in the Spanish Chapel show the Dominicans as whippets – *domini canes* or hounds of God – rounding up the "stray sheep."

**Green Cloister**
*The name comes from the green tinge to Uccello's* Noah and the Flood *frescoes, unfortunately damaged by the 1966 floods.*

**★ Spanish Chapel**
*The chapel used by the Spanish courtiers of Eleonora of Toledo, the wife of Cosimo I* (see p49)*, has dramatic frescoes on the theme of salvation and damnation.*

**★ The Trinity**
*Masaccio's pioneering work is a masterpiece of perspective and portraiture* (see p24).

**The billowing sail** emblem of the Rucellai *(see p104)* appears on the façade because they paid for its completion in 1470.

**Alberti added the volutes** in 1458–70 to hide the roofs over the side chapels.

**Strozzi Chapel**
*The 14th-century frescoes by Nardo di Cione and his brother, Andrea Orcagna, were inspired by Dante's epic poem,* The Divine Comedy. *Dante himself is portrayed in the* Paradise *fresco on the left, along with members of the Strozzi family.*

### VISITORS' CHECKLIST

Piazza di Santa Maria Novella. **Map** 1 B5 (5 B1). *(055) 21 01 13 (church), (055) 28 21 87 (museum). major routes.* **Church** ***open*** *7–11:30am, 3:30–6pm Mon–Sat, 8am–noon, 3:30–5pm Sun and religious hols.* *7:30am, 8:30am, 6pm Mon–Sat; 8:30am, 10:30am, noon, 6pm Sun & religious hols.* **Museum** ***open*** *9am–2pm Mon–Thu & Sat, 8am–1pm Sun (last adm: 1 hour before closing).* ***Closed*** *Dec 25, Jan 1, Easter Sun, May 1, Aug 15.* ***Adm charge.***

**The arcade arches** are emphasized by gray and white banding.

**★ Tornabuoni Chapel**
*Ghirlandaio's famous fresco cycle,* The Life of John the Baptist *(1485), portrays Florentine aristocrats and contemporary costumes and furnishings. Opposite is his other masterpiece,* The Life of the Virgin.

**★ Filippo Strozzi Chapel**
*Filippino Lippi's dramatic frescoes show St. John raising Drusiana from the dead and St. Philip slaying a dragon. Boccaccio set the beginning of* The Decameron *in this chapel.*

**The walls** of the old cemetery are decorated with the emblems and badges of wealthy Florentines.

**Interior**
*The nave piers are spaced closer at the east end to create the illusion of an exceptionally long church.*

### STAR FEATURES

- ★ **The Trinity by Masaccio**
- ★ **Filippo Strozzi Chapel**
- ★ **Tornabuoni Chapel**
- ★ **Spanish Chapel**

## Mercato Nuovo ⓬

**Map** 3 C1 (6 D3). ***Open*** *Apr–Oct: 9am–7pm daily; Nov–Mar: 9am–7pm Tue–Sat.*

The Mercato Nuovo (New Market) is sometimes called the "Straw Market" because goods woven out of straw, such as hats and baskets, were sold here from the end of the 19th century until the 1960s. In fact, it was originally built in 1547–51 as a central market for silk and other luxury goods. Today's stallholders sell leather goods and souvenirs, and on summer evenings street performers entertain visitors.

To the south of the market is a little fountain called Il Porcellino. This is a 17th-century copy in bronze of the Roman marble statue of a wild boar that can be seen in the Uffizi. Its snout gleams like gold, thanks to the superstition that any visitor who rubs it will return to Florence some day. Coins dropped in the water basin below are collected and distributed to the city's charities.

**Bronze boar in Mercato Nuovo**

## Piazza della Repubblica ⓭

**Map** 1 C5 (6 D3).

Until 1890, when the present square was laid out, this had been the site of the Mercato Vecchio (Old Market) and before that of the ancient Roman forum. A single column from the old market still stands on the square, topped by an 18th-century statue of Abundance. Dominating the western side of the square is a triumphal arch built in 1895 to celebrate the fact that Florence was then the capital of Italy. The demolition of the Old Market was intended as the first step in a wholesale remodeling of Florence, but leading members of the English community led an international campaign opposing this grand plan, which would have led to the destruction of almost every historic building in the city center. Fortunately, the campaign was successful and the demolition halted.

**One of the many pavement cafés in Piazza della Repubblica**

The square, popular with both tourists and locals, is lined with pavement cafés, such as the very smart Gilli (No. 39r) or the Giubbe Rosse (No. 13–14r), so called because of the red jackets of the waiters. In the early part of this century, the Giubbe Rosse was the haunt of writers and artists, including those of Italy's avant-garde Futurist movement. UPIM, one of Florence's department stores *(see p269)*, is on the eastern side of the square.

## Palazzo Antinori ⓮

Piazza Antinori 3. **Map** 1 C5 (5 C2). ***Not open*** *to the public.*
**Cantinetta Antinori** ***open*** *12:30–2:30pm, 7–10:30pm Mon–Fri.*

The Palazzo Antinori, originally the Palazzo Boni e Martelli, was built in 1461–6 and with its elegant courtyard is considered one of the finest small Renaissance *palazzi* of Florence. It was acquired by the Antinori family in 1506 and has remained with them since.

The family owns large and productive estates all over Tuscany and in the neighboring region of Umbria, producing a range of well-regarded wines, olive oils and liqueurs. You can sample these in the frescoed wine bar to the right of the courtyard, the Cantinetta Antinori.

The wine bar also specializes in typical Tuscan cuisine, with dishes such as *crostini alla toscana,* together with traditional cheeses and a range of other produce from the Antinori estates.

## Via dei Fossi ⓯

**Map** 1 B5 (5 B3).

**Shop in Via dei Fossi selling reproduction statuary**

Via dei Fossi and the nearby streets contain some of the most absorbing shops in Florence, many of them specializing in antiques and works of art and statuary, and in classic Florentine products. Bottega Artigiana del Libro (Lungarno Corsini 40r) stocks handmade marbled papers, albums, notebooks and carnival masks. Fallani Best (Borgo Ognissanti 15r) has Art Nouveau and Art Deco furnishings and sculpture, and Antonio Frilli (Via dei Fossi 26r) specializes in marble sculpture – original Art Nouveau works and copies of famous Renaissance pieces. Neri (Via dei Fossi 57r) also sells top-quality antiques and G. Lisio (Via dei Fossi 41r), makes handwoven tapestries and rich Renaissance-style fabrics. Attached to the convent of the same name, the frescoed Farmacia di Santa Maria Novella (Via della Scala 16r) dates to the 16th century and sells toiletries and liqueurs made by Dominican monks. *(See also pp266–7.)*

**The cloister of Ognissanti with 17th-century frescoes**

## Ognissanti ⓰

Borgo Ognissanti 42. **Map** 1 B5 (5 A2). *(055) 239 87 00.* ***Open*** *7:50am–noon, 4–6:30pm.*

The church of All Saints, or Ognissanti, was the parish church of the merchant family of the Vespucci, one of whose members, the 15th-century navigator Amerigo, gave his name to the New World. Amerigo is depicted in Ghirlandaio's fresco of the *Madonna della Misericordia* (1472) in the second chapel on the right – he is the boy between the Virgin and the old man in the red cloak.

Amerigo Vespucci was the first to realize that the land discovered by Columbus was a completely new continent, not the eastern shore of the Indies. He made two voyages following Columbus's route, and because the letters he sent back enabled cartographers to draw the first maps *(see p75)* of the new land, it was given his name.

Ognissanti is also the burial place of Sandro Botticelli. His fresco of *St. Augustine* (1480) can be seen on the south wall. It is complemented by Ghirlandaio's *St. Jerome* (1480) on the opposite wall.

Alongside the church is a delightful cloister and refectory, containing Ghirlandaio's fresco *The Last Supper* (1480), with its charming background of birds and trees.

## Santa Maria Novella ⓱

*See pp110–11.*

## Stazione di Santa Maria Novella ⓲

**Map** 1 B4 (5 B1). *(055) 28 87 85.* ***Closed*** *1:30–4:15am.* **Train information** ***open*** *7am–9pm daily.* **Shops** ***open*** *6am–9pm Wed–Mon, 6am–7:30pm Tue.* ***open*** *9am–9pm daily.* **Bank** ***open*** *8:20am–1:20pm Mon–Fri.* **Drugstore** ***open*** *24 hours.*

The central railway station is considered one of the finest examples of modern architecture in Italy *(see p55)*. It was designed in 1935 by a group of young Tuscan artists, including Giovanni Michelucci and Piero Berardi, who subscribed to the "Functionalist" view that the form of a building should reflect the purpose for which it was built.

**Ghirlandaio's *Madonna della Misericordia* (1472) in Ognissanti, with the boy Amerigo Vespucci**

# OLTRARNO

OLTRARNO MEANS "over the Arno," and living on the south bank of the river was once considered a sign of inferiority. Here lived people who did not have sufficient wealth to build their own palazzo within the city center. That stigma did not change until the household of the Medici Grand Dukes moved to Oltrarno in 1550.

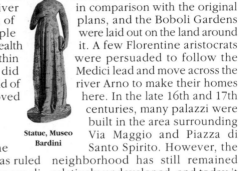

Statue, Museo Bardini

### MEDICI POWER BASE

The Palazzo Pitti became the base from which Tuscany was ruled for the next 300 years. Eleonora di Toledo, the Spanish wife of Cosimo I, purchased the Palazzo Pitti in 1549. Suffering from a wasting disease, perhaps malaria or tuberculosis, Eleonora persuaded Cosimo that her health might well improve if they lived in the relatively rural setting of Oltrarno. Over the years the Palazzo Pitti increased almost threefold in size in comparison with the original plans, and the Boboli Gardens were laid out on the land around it. A few Florentine aristocrats were persuaded to follow the Medici lead and move across the river Arno to make their homes here. In the late 16th and 17th centuries, many palazzi were built in the area surrounding Via Maggio and Piazza di Santo Spirito. However, the neighborhood has still remained relatively undeveloped, and today it is primarily a quiet area full of artisan workshops and antique shops, contrasting with the elegant palazzi and the unfinished austere façade of Santo Spirito. It is a fascinating area to wander around and discover the true character of Florence.

## SIGHTS AT A GLANCE

**Churches**

*Brancacci Chapel pp126–7* 10
Santa Felìcita 5
San Frediano in Cestello 11
Santo Spirito 1

**Museums and Galleries**

Cenacolo di Santo Spirito 2
Museo Bardini 8
Museo "La Specola" 9
*Palazzo Pitti pp120–21* 6

**Gardens**

*Boboli Gardens pp124–5* 7

**Streets and Piazzas**

Piazza di Santo Spirito 3
Via Maggio 4

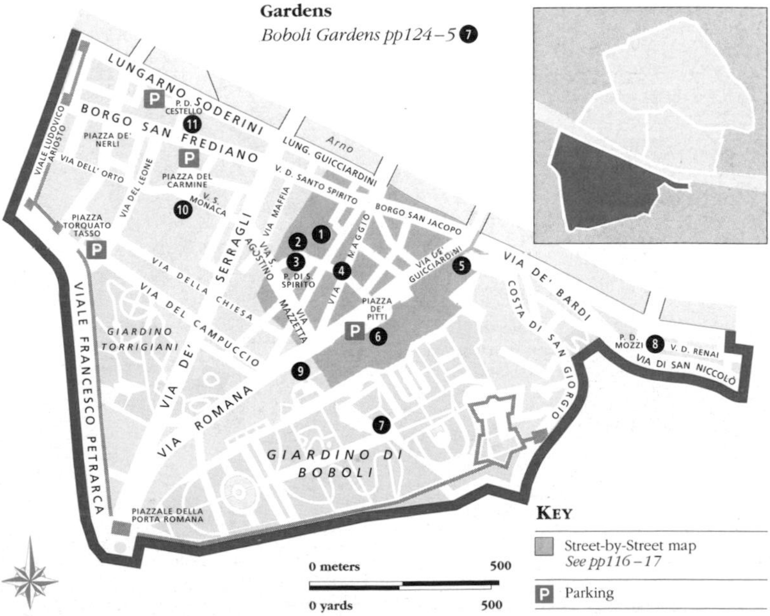


0 meters 500

0 yards 500

**KEY**

Street-by-Street map
*See pp116–17*

P Parking

Rooftops of the Oltrarno and the spire and dome of Santo Spirito

# Street-by-Street: Oltrarno

**Medici coat of arms**

For the most part, the Oltrarno area consists of relatively small houses and shops selling antiques, bric-a-brac and food. The Via Maggio breaks this pattern, with its numerous imposing 16th-century palazzi close to the Medici's Palazzo Pitti. As it is one of the main routes into the city, the road is busy and there is constant traffic noise. Step into the side streets, however, and you quickly escape the noise and bustle to discover traditional Florence; the restaurants are authentic and reasonably priced, and the area is full of workshops restoring antique furniture.

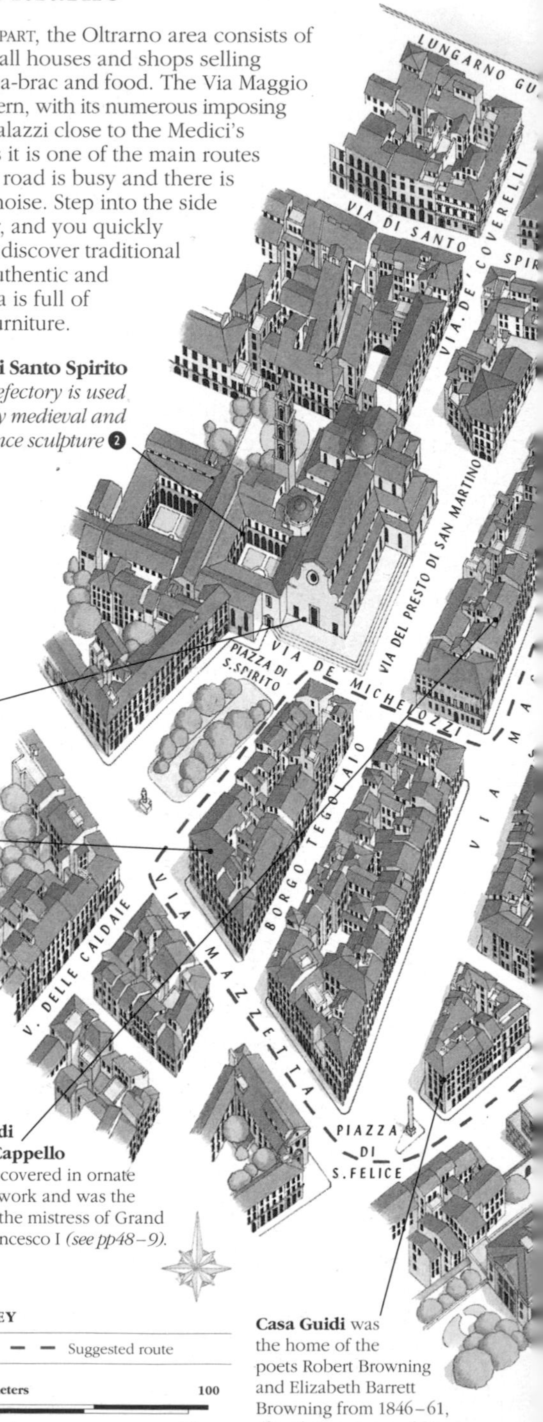


**Cenacolo di Santo Spirito**
*The old refectory is used to display medieval and Renaissance sculpture* ❷

**Santo Spirito**
*Simplicity is the keynote of Brunelleschi's last church. It was completed after his death in 1446* ❶

**Palazzo Guadagni** (1500) was the first in the city to be built with a rooftop loggia, setting a trend among the aristocracy.

**Palazzo di Bianca Cappello** (1579) is covered in ornate *sgraffito* work and was the home of the mistress of Grand Duke Francesco I *(see pp48–9)*.

**Casa Guidi** was the home of the poets Robert Browning and Elizabeth Barrett Browning from 1846–61, after their secret wedding.

**Star Sights**

- ★ **Palazzo Pitti**
- ★ **Boboli Gardens**

**Key**

— — — Suggested route

0 meters 100

0 yards 100

**The fountain** and gargoyle in Piazza de' Frescobaldi were designed by Buontalenti in the 16th century.

**LOCATOR MAP**
*See Florence Street Finder map 5*

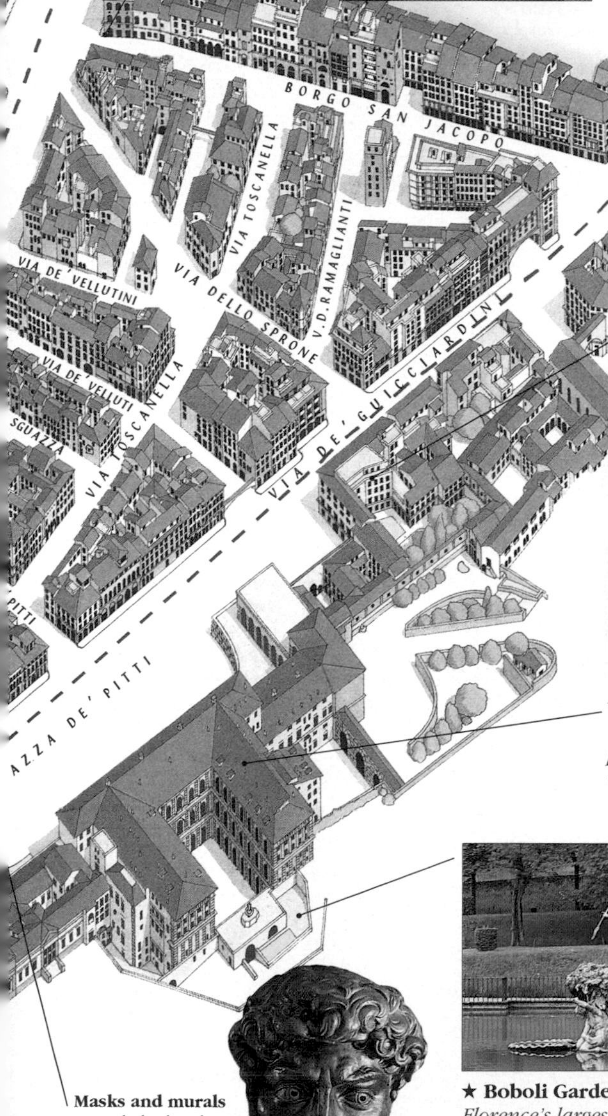

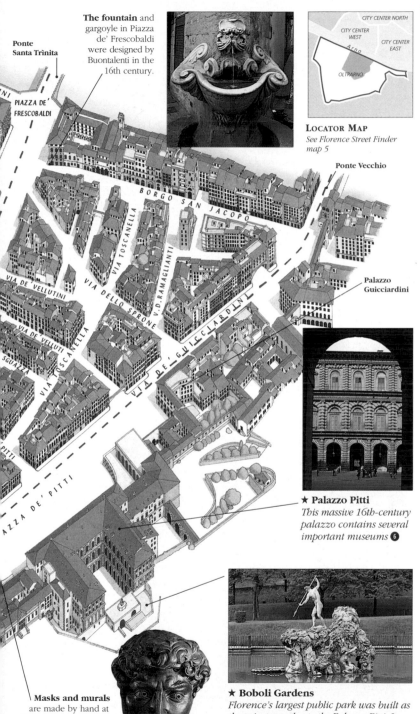

**Ponte Santa Trìnita**

**Ponte Vecchio**

**Palazzo Guicciardini**

**★ Palazzo Pitti**
*This massive 16th-century palazzo contains several important museums* ❻

**★ Boboli Gardens**
*Florence's largest public park was built as the private garden to the Palazzo Pitti. It contains Classical sculptures such as Stoldo Lorenzi's* Neptune *(1588) spearing fish* ❼

**Masks and murals** are made by hand at Frieze of Papier-Mâché, one of the unusual shops in Piazza de' Pitti.

## Santo Spirito ❶

Piazza di Santo Spirito. **Map** 3 B2 (5 A4). *(055) 21 00 30.* ***Open*** *8:30am–noon, 4–5:30pm Thu–Tue.*

THE AUGUSTINIAN foundation of this church dates from 1250. The present building has an unfinished 18th-century façade, dominating the northern end of Piazza di Santo Spirito. The church was designed by Brunelleschi in 1435, but not completed until the late 15th century, well after his death.

Inside, the harmony of the proportions has been somewhat spoiled by the elaborate Baroque baldacchino and the High Altar, which was finished in 1607 by Giovanni Caccini. The church has 38 side altars, decorated with 15th- and 16th-century Renaissance paintings and sculpture, among them works by Cosimo Rosselli, Domenico Ghirlandaio and Filippino Lippi. The latter painted a magnificent *Madonna and Child* (1466) for the Nerli Chapel in the south transept.

In the north aisle, a door beneath the organ leads to a vestibule with an ornate coffered ceiling. It was designed by Simone del Pollaiuolo, more commonly known as Cronaca, in 1491. The sacristy adjoining the vestibule was designed by Giuliano da Sangallo in 1489.

## Cenacolo di Santo Spirito ❷

Piazza di Santo Spirito 29. **Map** 3 B1 (5 B4). *(055) 28 70 43.* ***Open*** *10am–1pm Tue–Sun.* ***Closed*** *public hols.* ***Adm charge****.*

ALL THAT SURVIVES of the monastery that stood next to Santo Spirito is the refectory *(cenacolo)*, now run as a small museum. Inside is a dramatic fresco, *The Crucifixion* (1360–65), which is attributed to the followers of Andrea Orcagna and his brother Nardo di Cione. In a city that has a wealth of Renaissance painting, this is a rare and beautiful example of High Gothic religious work.

The Fondazione Salvatore Romano, a collection of 11th-century Romanesque sculpture, is displayed in the monastic buildings alongside.

Colonnaded aisle in Santo Spirito

The façade of Palazzo Guadagni

## Piazza di Santo Spirito ❸

**Map** 3 B2 (5 A4). *2nd Sun of month.*

THIS PART OF FLORENCE is best appreciated by wandering around the square and its market, looking at the many furniture restorers' workshops and medieval palazzi. The biggest house in the square is the Palazzo Guadagni at No. 10, on the corner with Via Mazzetta. It was built around 1505, probably to the designs of Cronaca. The windows have distinctive stone surrounds with teardrop-shaped keystones. The top floor forms an open loggia, the first of its kind to be built in the city. The loggia set a fashion among 16th-century Florentine aristocrats, who incorporated the design into their own palazzi.

## Via Maggio ❹

**Map** 3 B2 (5 B5).

OPENED IN THE mid-13th century, this road became a fashionable residential area after the Medici Grand Dukes moved to the Palazzo Pitti in 1550 *(see pp120–21)*. It is lined with 15th- and 16th-century palazzi, such as the Palazzo Ricasoli at No. 7, and antique shops. Via Maggio runs into Piazza di San Felice, where a plaque marks the Casa Guidi. The English poets Elizabeth and Robert Browning rented an apartment there after eloping in 1847. Inspired by Tuscan art and landscape, this is where they wrote much of their best poetry.

**The Virgin from *The Annunciation* (1528) by Pontormo**

## Santa Felìcita ❺

Piazza di Santa Felicita. **Map** 3 C2 (5 C5). *(055) 21 30 18.* ***Open*** *8am–noon, 3:30–6:30pm.*

THERE HAS BEEN a church on this site since the 4th century AD. A new one was built in the 11th century and remodeled in 1736–9 by Ferdinando Ruggieri, retaining some original Gothic features as well as the porch added by Vasari in 1564.

The Capponi family chapel to the right of the entrance contains two masterpieces by the Mannerist artist Jacopo da Pontormo: *The Annunciation* and *The Deposition*. Painted between 1525 and 1528, the frescoes make use of vivid colors such as light green, salmon pink, apricot and gold. The roundels around the base of the ceiling vault depict the Four Evangelists, also painted by Pontormo, with help from his pupil Agnolo Bronzino.

## Palazzo Pitti ❻

*See pp120–23.*

## Boboli Gardens ❼

*See pp124–5.*

## Museo Bardini ❽

Piazza de' Mozzi 1. **Map** 4 D2 (6 E5). *(055) 234 24 27.* ***Open*** *9am–2pm Mon, Tue & Thu–Sat, 8am–1pm Sun.* ***Closed*** *Jan 1, Easter Sun, May 1, Aug 15, Dec 25.* ***Adm charge.***

STEFANO BARDINI WAS a 19th-century antiquarian and avid collector of architectural materials – mostly salvaged from the churches and palazzi demolished when the Piazza della Repubblica was built in the 1860s *(see p112)*. In 1883 he built his palazzo in Piazza de' Mozzi almost entirely from recycled medieval and Renaissance masonry, including carved doorways, chimney pieces and staircases as well as painted and coffered ceilings. The rooms overflow with an unusual mixture of sculpture, statues, paintings, armor, musical instruments, ceramics and antique furnishings. In 1922 this collection of antiquities was bequeathed to the people of Florence.

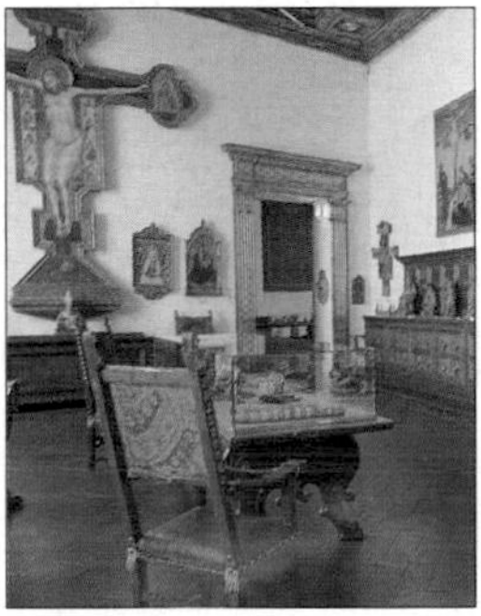

**Museo Bardini, Piazza de' Mozzi**

## Museo "La Specola" ❾

Via Romana 17. **Map** 3 B2 (5 B5). *(055) 22 24 51.* ***Open*** *9am–noon Thu–Tue (9am–1pm Sun).* ***Closed*** *May 1, Aug 13–17, Dec 25.* ***Adm charge.***

THIS UNUSUAL museum is in the Palazzo Rottigiani, built in 1775 and now used by the natural science faculty of Florence University. The name "la Specola" refers to the observatory built on the roof of the building by Grand Duke Pietro Leopoldo in the late 18th century. It now contains the museum, which has a zoological section exhibiting vast numbers of preserved animals, insects and fish, and an anatomical section with some extremely realistic 18th-century wax models showing various grotesque aspects of human physiology and disease.

## Brancacci Chapel ❿

*See pp126–7.*

## San Frediano in Cestello ⓫

Piazza di Cestello. **Map** 3 B1 (5 A3). *(055) 21 58 16.* ***Open*** *9am–noon, 4:30–5:30pm Mon–Sat, 4:30–6pm Sun.*

THE SAN FREDIANO area, with its small, low houses, has long been associated with the wool and leather industries. The parish church of San Frediano in Cestello stands beside the Arno looking across the river. It has a bare stone exterior with a large dome that is a local landmark. It was rebuilt on the site of an older church in 1680–89 by Antonio Maria Ferri: the fresco and stuccowork inside are typical of the late 17th and early 18th centuries. Nearby is a well-preserved stretch of the 14th-century city walls. The Porta San Frediano, built in 1324, has a tower overlooking the road to Pisa. Its wooden doors have retained all their original 14th-century locks and detailed ironwork.

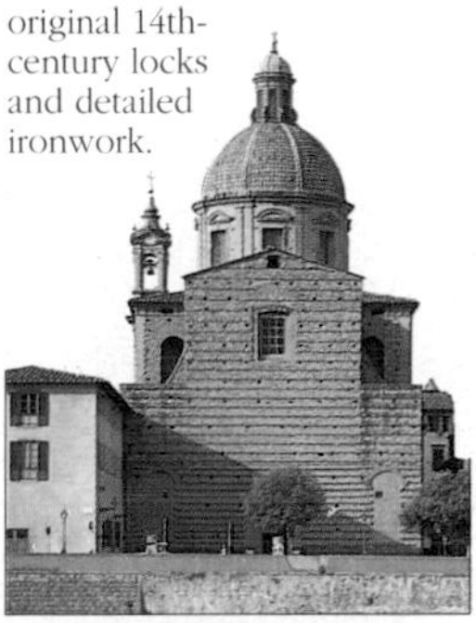

**The dome and plain façade of San Frediano in Cestello**

# Palazzo Pitti 6

THE PALAZZO PITTI was originally built for the banker Luca Pitti. The huge scale of the building, begun in 1457, illustrated Pitti's determination to outrival the Medici family. Ironically, they later purchased the palazzo when building costs bankrupted Pitti's heirs. In 1550 it became the main residence of the Medici, and subsequently all the rulers of the city lived here. Today the richly decorated rooms exhibit treasures from the Medici collections *(see pp122–3).*

**Inner Courtyard**
*Ammannati designed the courtyard in 1560–70. The Artichoke Fountain by Francesco Susini (1641) was topped by a bronze artichoke, since lost.*

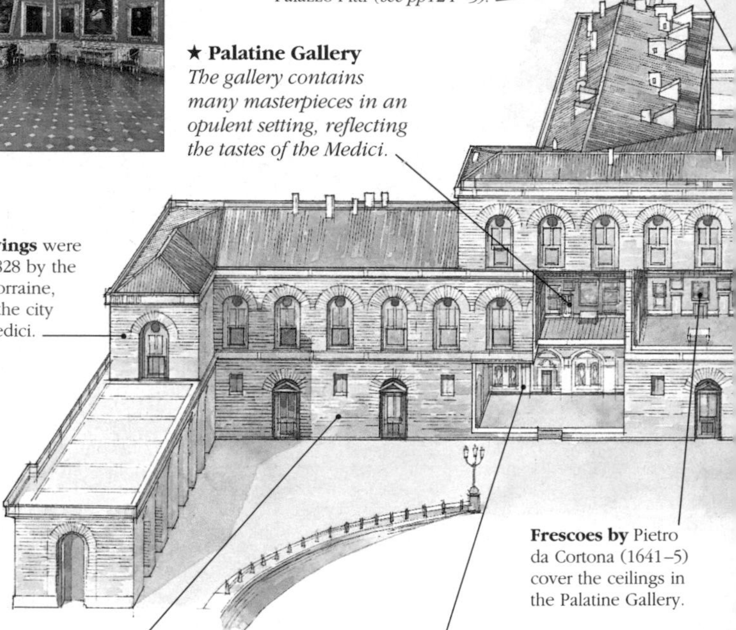

**The Boboli Gardens** were laid out where stone had been quarried to build the Palazzo Pitti *(see pp124–5).*

**★ Palatine Gallery**
*The gallery contains many masterpieces in an opulent setting, reflecting the tastes of the Medici.*

**The side wings** were added in 1828 by the Dukes of Lorraine, who ruled the city after the Medici.

**Frescoes by** Pietro da Cortona (1641–5) cover the ceilings in the Palatine Gallery.

**Brunelleschi** designed the façade of the palazzo, but it was later extended to 200 m (650 ft), three times its original length.

**★ Museo degli Argenti**
*Along with silverware, the museum displays gold, stone and glassware. This view of Piazza della Signoria* (see pp76–7) *is made of precious stones.*

**STAR SIGHTS**

**★ Palatine Gallery**

**★ Museo degli Argenti**

**Galleria d'Arte Moderna**
*The gallery, on the second floor of the palazzo, spans the years from 1784 to 1924.* The Tuscan Maremma *(c.1850), by Giovanni Fattori, is a highlight of the collection.*

**Galleria del Costume**
*The clothes reflect changing fashion at the court of the Grand Dukes during the 18th and 19th centuries.*

## Visitors' Checklist

Piazza Pitti. **Map** 3 C2 (5 B5).
*3, 15, 31, 32.*
**Palatine Gallery** *(055) 21 03 23.* ***Open*** *9am–2pm Tue–Sun (last adm: 30 mins before closing).*
**Appartamenti Monumentali** *as above.* ***Open*** *Apr–Dec: 9am–2pm Tue–Sun (last adm: 1 hr before closing).*
**Galleria del Costume** (entrance in the Boboli Gardens, *see p125*).
**Museo degli Argenti** *(055) 21 25 57.* ***Open*** *9am–2pm Tue–Sun (last adm: 30 mins before closing).*
**Galleria d'Arte Moderna** *(055) 28 70 96.* ***Open*** *9am–2pm Tue–Sun (last adm: 30 mins before closing).*
***All museums closed*** *public hols.*
***Adm charge*** *for each museum.*
**Palatine Gallery** *ticket admits to* **Appartamenti Monumentali**.
**Museo degli Argenti** *ticket admits to* **Galleria del Costume**.

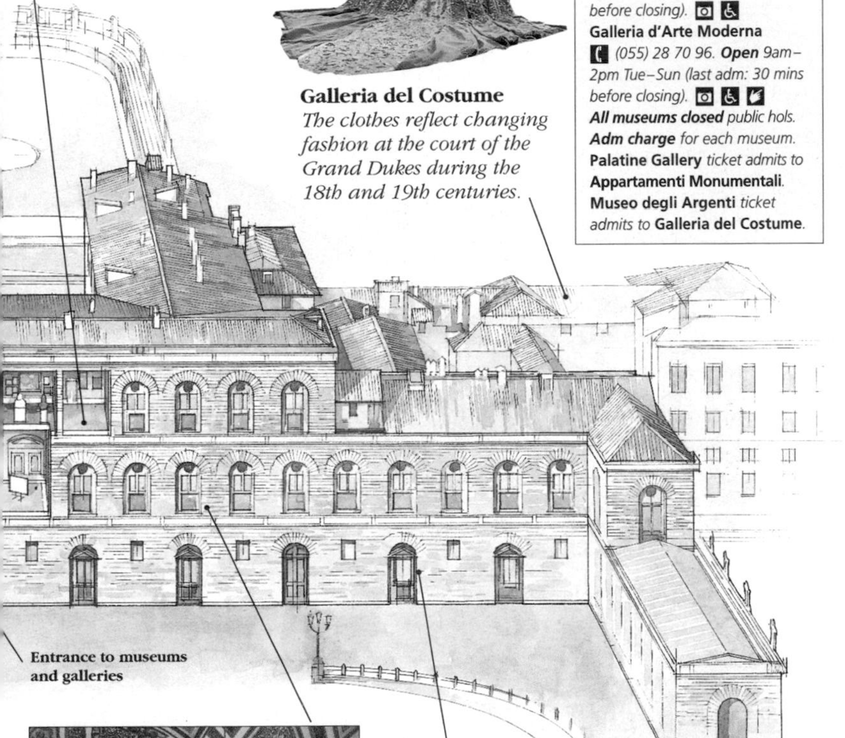

**Entrance to museums and galleries**

**Massive Windows**
*The windows of the Palazzo Pitti were built to be larger than the main door of the Palazzo Medici Riccardi.*

**Appartamenti Monumentali**
*The south wing was used for ceremonial occasions and receiving ambassadors.*

# Exploring the Palazzo Pitti

THE PALATINE GALLERY was added to the Palazzo Pitti by the Medici family in the 17th century. The frescoed walls were hung with masterpieces from their private collection and the gallery was opened to the public in 1833. Other attractions in the Palazzo include the richly refurbished state apartments, the Medici collection of jewelry and treasures, the gallery of modern art and an exhibition of 18th- and 19th-century costumes.

## THE PALATINE GALLERY

THE GALLERY CONTAINS a superb collection of works dating from the Renaissance and Baroque. They are hung as the 17th- and 18th-century Medici Grand Dukes wished, placed purely for their effect, regardless of subject or chronology. The decoration of the rooms in the gallery reflects the tastes and preoccupations of the time. Rooms 1 to 5 are painted with Baroque ceiling frescoes begun by Pietro da Cortona between 1641–7, and finished by his pupil Ciro Ferri in 1665. They allegorize the education of a prince by the gods. In Room 1, the prince is torn from the love of Venus by Minerva (knowledge) and in the following rooms he is taught science by Apollo, war by Mars and leadership by Jupiter. Finally Saturn welcomes him to Mount Olympus, home of the gods in Roman mythology.

The other rooms in the gallery were private apartments and range from the opulence of the formal drawing rooms to the severity of Napoleon's bathroom (Room 27) *(see p53)*, in a suite of rooms designed by Giuseppe Cacialli for the emperor in 1813 following his conquest of northern Italy.

***Mary Magdalene*** **by Titian (c.1535)**

Although some of the Medici collection has been transferred to the Uffizi over the years, the Palatine Gallery is still packed with masterpieces by artists such as Botticelli, Perugino, Titian, Andrea del Sarto, Pontormo, Tintoretto, Veronese, Caravaggio, Rubens and Van Dyck, among others. There are approximately 1,000 paintings here, providing a vast survey of 16th- and 17th-century European painting.

The Sala di Venere (Venus) is dominated by the statue of *Venus Italica* by Antonio Canova, commissioned by Napoleon in 1810 as a replacement for *The Medici Venus* in the Uffizi Gallery, which was to be taken to Paris. Napoleon was not normally so generous, as his agents were renowned for stealing a large number of fine works of art from Italy during the Napoleonic Wars.

Several of Titian's works in the following rooms were commissioned by the Duke of Urbino. *La Bella* (1536) is a portrait of a lovely but unknown woman, whom he also used as a model in other paintings. His portrait, *Mary Magdalene*, in the Sala di Apollo, was painted between 1530–35 in an overtly sensual manner, bathed in soft light.

Some of Raphael's best High Renaissance work is in the Palatine, including *Portrait of a Woman* (c.1516) and

### THE PALATINE GALLERY

*The gallery is on the first floor of the Palazzo Pitti.*

***Madonna of the Chair*** **by Raphael (c.1516)**

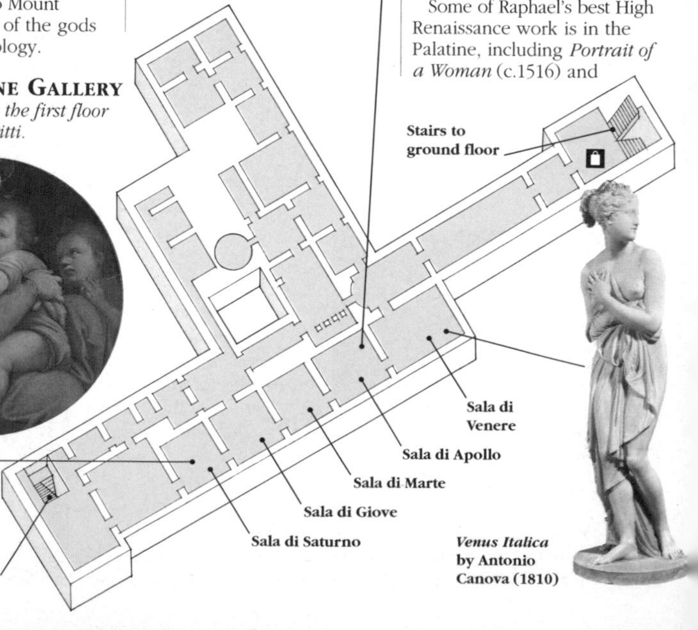


***Venus Italica*** **by Antonio Canova (1810)**

*Madonna of the Chair* (c.1510) in the *tondo* (roundel) form popularized during the Renaissance.

*The Consequences of War* by Peter Paul Rubens (1638) is an allegorical painting of the Thirty Years War (1618–48), showing Venus preventing Mars from unleashing his fury on the cowering, beleaguered figure of Europe, completely robed in black mourning.

### Appartamenti Monumentali

**The Throne Room**

The state apartments on the first floor of the south wing of the palazzo were built in the 17th century. They are decorated with frescoes by various Florentine artists and a series of portraits of the Medici by the Flemish painter Justus Sustermans, who worked at the court between 1619–81. In the late 18th and early 19th centuries, the apartments were completely revamped in Neo-Classical style by the Dukes of Lorraine when they succeeded the Medici dynasty as the rulers of Florence *(see pp52–3)*.

The apartments are lavishly appointed with ornate gold and white stuccowork ceilings and rich decoration, as on the walls of the Parrot Room, which are covered with an opulent crimson fabric detailed with a bird design. The apartments have now been extensively restored in accordance with the original plans and designs.

### Museo degli Argenti

This museum is on the ground and mezzanine floors, below the Palatine Gallery, in the rooms used by the Medici as their summer apartments. It displays the massive private wealth of the Medici dynasty: the collection encompasses rare and beautiful examples of ancient Roman glassware, ivory, carpets, crystal and amber and fine works by Florentine and German goldsmiths. The feature of the collection is 16 *pietre dure* vases displayed in the Sala Buia. These belonged to Lorenzo the Magnificent and are from the ancient Roman and Byzantine periods.

**14th-century gold and jasper vase**

The family's lavish tastes are reflected in the museum's polished ebony furniture inlaid with semi-precious marbles and stones. Portraits of the Medici hang throughout the rooms, including a series of the Grand Duchesses, and Cosimo I and his family carved in an onyx cameo.

### Galleria d'Arte Moderna

Here the paintings span the period from 1784 to 1924; many of them were collected by the Dukes of Lorraine to decorate the Palazzo Pitti. The present museum has combined this collection with pictures donated by the state and various private collectors. The museum contains Neo-Classical, Romantic and religious works, but probably the most important collection is of the group of late 19th-century artists known as the *Macchiaioli* (spot-makers), similar to French Impressionists. The *Macchiaioli* used bright splashes of color to represent the sun-dappled Tuscan landscape. This collection was given to the city of Florence in 1897 by the art critic Diego Martelli, and includes paintings by Giovanni Fattori *(see p121)* and Giovanni Boldini. Two works by Camille Pissarro hang in the same room.

### Galleria del Costume

Opened in 1983, the gallery is on the ground floor of the Palazzo Meridiana. This was designed in 1776 by Gaspare Maria Paoletti for the Royal Family; they lived here until the abolition of the monarchy. The exhibits reflect the changing tastes in the courtly fashion of the late 18th century up to the 1920s. Some of the rooms have been restored to correspond to a 1911 inventory, with original furniture and wall hangings.

***The Italian Camp after the Battle of Magenta* (c.1855) by Giovanni Fattori**

# Boboli Gardens 7

The Boboli Gardens were laid out for the Medici after they bought the Palazzo Pitti in 1549. An excellent example of stylized Renaissance gardening, they were opened to the public in 1766. The more formal parts of the garden, nearest the palazzo, consist of box hedges clipped into symmetrical geometric patterns. These lead to wilder groves of holly and cypress trees, planted to create a contrast between artifice and nature. Statues of varying styles and periods are dotted around, and the vistas were planned to give views over Florence.

**★ Amphitheater**
*Stone for the Palazzo Pitti was quarried here and the hollow was turned into a stage for the very first opera performances.*

**Kaffeehaus**
*The Rococo-style pavilion, built in 1776 by Zanobi del Rosso, now houses a coffeehouse. It is open during the summer.*

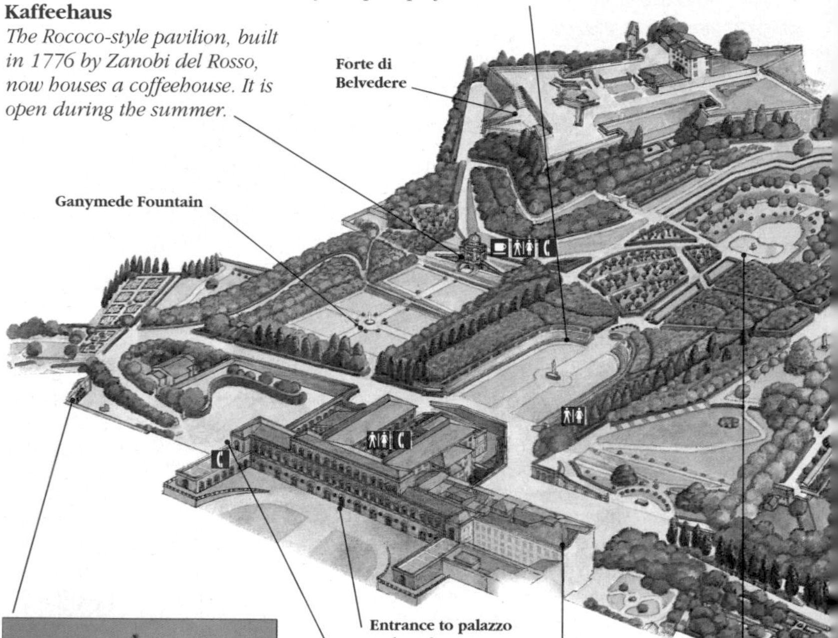

**Forte di Belvedere**

**Ganymede Fountain**

**Entrance to palazzo and gardens**

**Galleria del Costume**

**The Neptune Fountain** was built between 1565–8 by Stoldo Lorenzi.

**★ La Grotta Grande**
*The casts of Michelangelo's* Quattro Prigioni (see p94) *are built into the walls of this Mannerist folly (1583–8), which also houses Vincenzo de' Rossi's* Paris with Helen of Troy *(1560) and* Venus Bathing *(1565) by Giambologna.*

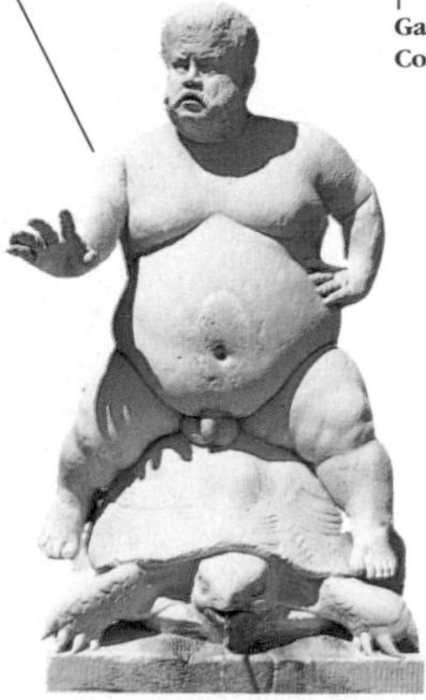

**Bacchus Fountain** *(1560)*
*A copy of the original by Valerio Cioli, the statue shows Pietro Barbino, Cosimo I's court dwarf, as Bacchus, the Roman god of wine, astride a turtle.*

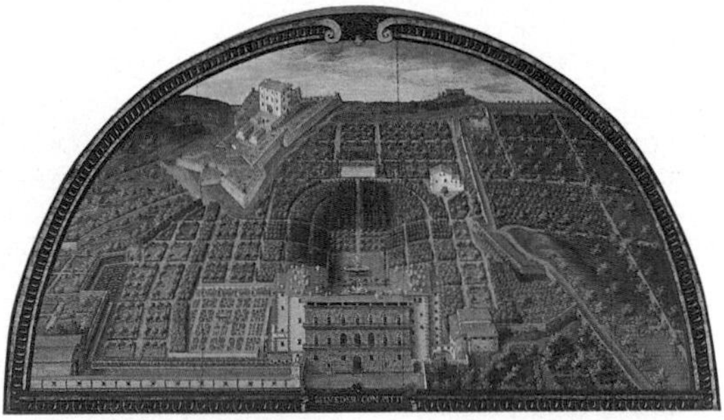

**Lunette of Boboli Gardens**
*The Flemish artist Giusto Utens painted this picture of the Palazzo Pitti and Boboli Gardens in 1599.*

### Visitors' Checklist

Piazza de' Pitti. **Map** 3 B2 (5 B5). **Boboli Gardens** *(055) 21 34 40.* *many routes.* **Open** *9am–1 hour before sunset (Jun–Sep: 9am–8pm) (last adm: 30 mins before closing).* **Closed** *1st & 4th Mon of month.* **Adm charge.**
**Galleria del Costume** *(055) 21 25 57.* **Open** *9am–2pm Tue–Sun (last adm: 30 mins before closing).* **Closed** *public hols.* **Adm charge.**

**Viottolone**
*The avenue of cypress trees, planted in 1637, is lined with Classical statues.*

**★ L'Isolotto (Little Island)**
*Statues of dancing peasants surround the moated garden, with a copy of Giambologna's* Oceanus Fountain *(1576) as the centerpiece. The original is now in the Bargello* (see pp68–9).

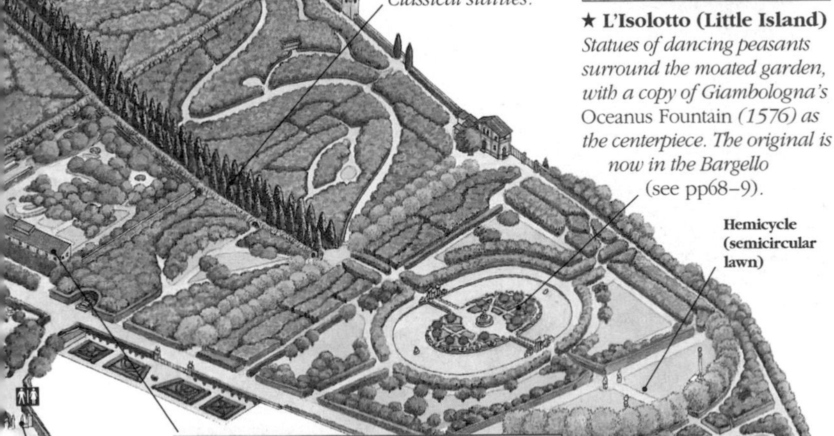

**The Porcelain Museum** in the Rose Garden is temporarily closed.

**Hemicycle (semicircular lawn)**

**Entrance**

**Orangery**
*Zanobi del Rosso's Orangery (1785) was built to protect rare, tender plants from frost.*

### Star Features

- **★ Amphitheater**
- **★ La Grotta Grande**
- **★ L'Isolotto (Little Island)**

# Brancacci Chapel ⑩

THE CHURCH of Santa Maria del Carmine is famous for *The Life of St. Peter* frescoes in the Brancacci Chapel, commissioned by the Florentine merchant Felice Brancacci around 1424. Masolino began the work in 1425, but many of the scenes are by his pupil, Masaccio, who died before completing the cycle. Filippino Lippi finished the work 50 years later, in 1480. Masaccio's use of perspective in *The Tribute Money* and the tragic realism of his figures in *The Expulsion of Adam and Eve* placed him at the vanguard of Renaissance painting. Many great artists, including Leonardo and Michelangelo, later visited the chapel to study his pioneering work.

**St. Peter Heals the Sick**
*Masaccio's realistic portrayal of cripples and beggars was revolutionary in his time.*

**In every scene**, St. Peter is distinguished from the crowds as the figure in the orange cloak.

**The grouping** of stylized figures in Masaccio's frescoes reflects his interest in the sculpture of his contemporary Donatello *(see p69)*.

**Masaccio's simple style** allows us to focus on the figures central to the frescoes without distracting detail.

**Expulsion of Adam and Eve**
*Masaccio's ability to express emotion is well illustrated by his harrowing portrait of Adam and Eve being driven out of the Garden of Eden, their faces wracked by misery, shame and the burden of self-knowledge.*

### Key to the Frescoes: Artists and Subjects

☐ Masolino

☐ Masaccio

☐ Lippi

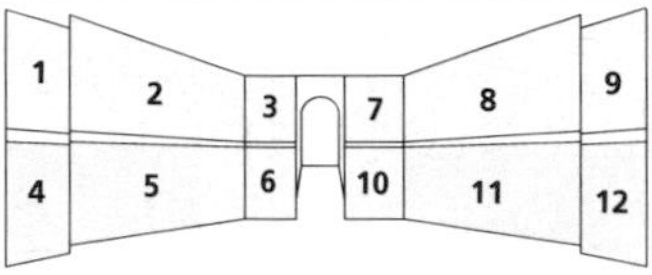

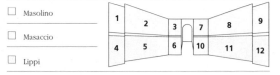

1 Expulsion of Adam and Eve
2 The Tribute Money
3 St. Peter Preaching
4 St. Peter Visited by St. Paul
5 Raising the Emperor's Son; St. Peter Enthroned
6 St. Peter Healing the Sick
7 St. Peter Baptizing the Converts
8 St. Peter Healing the Cripple; Raising Tabitha
9 Temptation of Adam and Eve
10 St. Peter and St. John Giving Alms
11 Crucifixion; Before the Proconsul
12 The Release of St. Peter

### Visitors' Checklist

Piazza del Carmine. **Map** 3 A1 (5 A4). *(055) 238 21 95.* *15.* **Open** *10am–4:30pm Mon, Wed–Sat, 1–4:30pm Sun.* **Closed** *Easter Sun, Dec 25.* **Adm charge**.

**Masolino's *Temptation of Adam and Eve*** is gentle and decorous, in contrast with the emotional force of Masaccio's painting on the opposite wall.

**Woman in a Turban**
*The freshness of Masaccio's original colors is seen in this rediscovered roundel, hidden behind the altar for 500 years.*

**St. Peter** is depicted against a background of Florentine buildings.

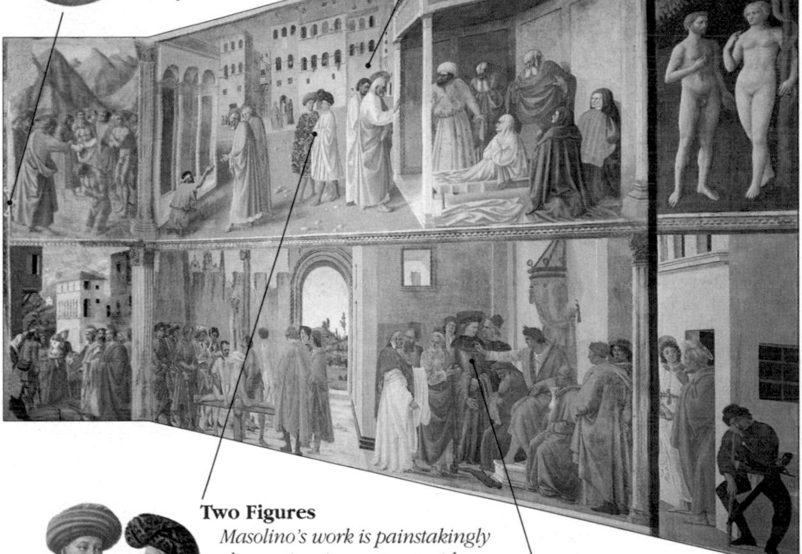

**Two Figures**
*Masolino's work is painstakingly decorative, in contrast with Masaccio's simpler style.*

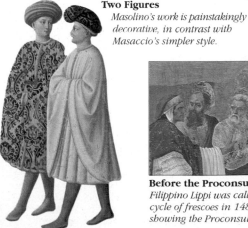

**Before the Proconsul**
*Filippino Lippi was called in to complete the unfinished cycle of frescoes in 1480. He added this emotional scene showing the Proconsul sentencing St. Peter to death.*

# Two Guided Walks

In Florence the countryside is never very far away, and you can be walking down the quiet, rural lanes within just a few minutes of leaving the Ponte Vecchio *(see pp106–7)*, in the bustling heart of the city. The first walk is popular with the Florentines, who like to stroll on a Sunday beneath the city walls, taking in the panoramic views that can be enjoyed from San Miniato al Monte and the Piazzale Michelangelo. Depending on the time of day, the pleasure is enhanced by the sound of church bells ringing out across the city. Fiesole, the setting for the second walk, is 8 km (5 miles) north of Florence. It was once a powerful Etruscan city, but was later eclipsed by the rise of Florence, so that it is now merely a village. There are archaeological remains to provide a hint of its previous glory and, on a clear day, wonderful views across the red, tiled rooftops of Florence and of the cypress-dotted hills of the Mugello.

**Bust, Museo Faesulanum**

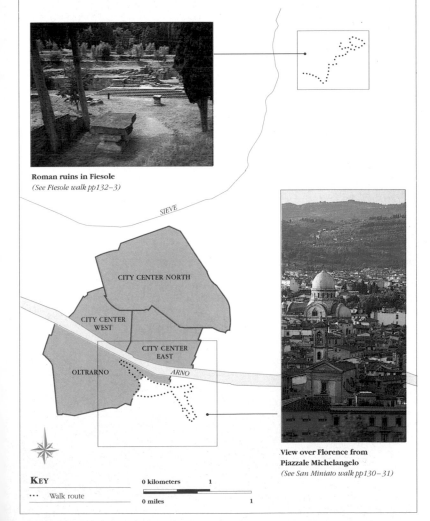

**Roman ruins in Fiesole**
*(See Fiesole walk pp132–3)*

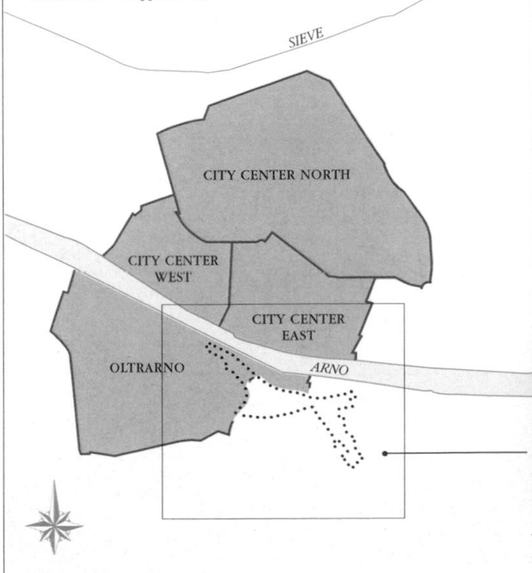

**View over Florence from Piazzale Michelangelo**
*(See San Miniato walk pp130–31)*

**Key**

··· Walk route

0 kilometers 1

0 miles 1

◁ **Looking up the steps to the church of San Miniato al Monte**

# A Two-Hour Walk to San Miniato al Monte

THIS WALK TAKES YOU from the center of Florence to the exquisitely decorated church of San Miniato al Monte high on a hill in the south of the city. The route follows quiet lanes along the city walls, and then takes in the bustling Piazzale Michelangelo, packed with souvenir stalls, before returning to the town center.

**The façade of San Miniato al Monte ⑧**

**No. 19 Costa di San Giorgio ③**

From the Ponte Vecchio ① walk south down Via de' Guicciardini and take the second left turn into the square fronting Santa Felìcita ②. On the left of the church, take the steep road to the right, Costa di San Giorgio. No. 19 ③ was once the home of Galileo. The Porta San Giorgio (St. George's Gate) ④ is at the end of the lane.

Built in 1260, this is the oldest city gate to survive in Florence. The weathered fresco within the arch is *The Virgin with St. George and St. Leonard* by Bicci di Lorenzo (1460). On the outer face of the arch is a carving of St. George fighting the dragon, a copy of the original 1284 work, which has been removed and is currently being restored.

The Forte di Belvedere ⑤ is to the right through the gate, and was designed by Bernardo Buontalenti in 1590. Originally the fortress was built to guard the city against attack from its political rivals, but it soon became a private refuge for the Medici Grand Dukes. From here there are extensive views over the Boboli Gardens ⑥ below, and across to the olive groves and cypress trees in the countryside south of the city. Head downhill along Via di Belvedere, which runs along a stretch of city walls (to the left) dating from 1258. Porta San Miniato ⑦, a small arch in the wall, is situated at the bottom of the hill.

### San Miniato al Monte

Turn right into Via del Monte alle Croci and walk uphill for 500 m (550 yds) to the Viale Galileo Galilei. Bear right and cross the road to the vast stone steps leading to the terrace in front of San Miniato al Monte ⑧. Catch your breath and admire the view of the Forte di Belvedere.

San Miniato al Monte is one of the most unspoiled of all the Romanesque churches in Tuscany. It was built in 1018 over the shrine of the early Christian martyr, San Miniato (St. Minias). He was a rich Armenian merchant beheaded for his beliefs by Emperor Decius in the 3rd century. The façade was begun around 1090 and has geometric patterning in green-gray and white marble, typical of the Romanesque style. The statue on the gable shows an eagle carrying a

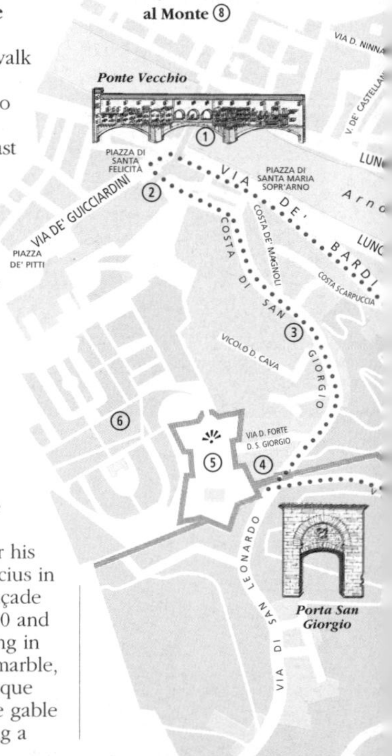

**View across to San Miniato al Monte from Forte di Belvedere ⑤**

bale of cloth, the symbol of the powerful Arte di Calimala (guild of wool importers) who financed the church in the Middle Ages. The restored 13th-century mosaic below the gable shows Christ, the Virgin and St. Minias. Inside the church there is a Byzantine-style mosaic in the apse, again of St. Minias with Christ and the Virgin. Below this is the crypt, built using columns salvaged from ancient Roman buildings. The floor of the nave is covered with seven marble mosaic panels of lions, doves and the signs of the Zodiac (1207); similar intarsia work panels can be seen on the raised marble choir and pulpit. In the north wall is the funeral chapel of the 25-year-old Cardinal of Portugal, Iacopo di Lusitania, who died in Florence in 1439. Antonio Rossellino carved the figure of the cardinal guarded by angels on the elaborate marble tomb (1466). The terra-cotta roundels on the ceiling, showing the Holy Spirit and Virtues, were painted by Luca della Robbia (1461).

**13th-century mosaic on San Miniato façade**

Outside, the massive bell tower was begun in 1523 by Baccio d'Agnolo, but was never finished. Cannons were installed here to shoot at the Medici troops during the Siege of Florence *(see pp50–51)*. The cemetery (9) surrounding the church opened in 1854 and this contains tombs the size of miniature houses, built so large to show off family wealth.

**San Salvatore al Monte (10)**

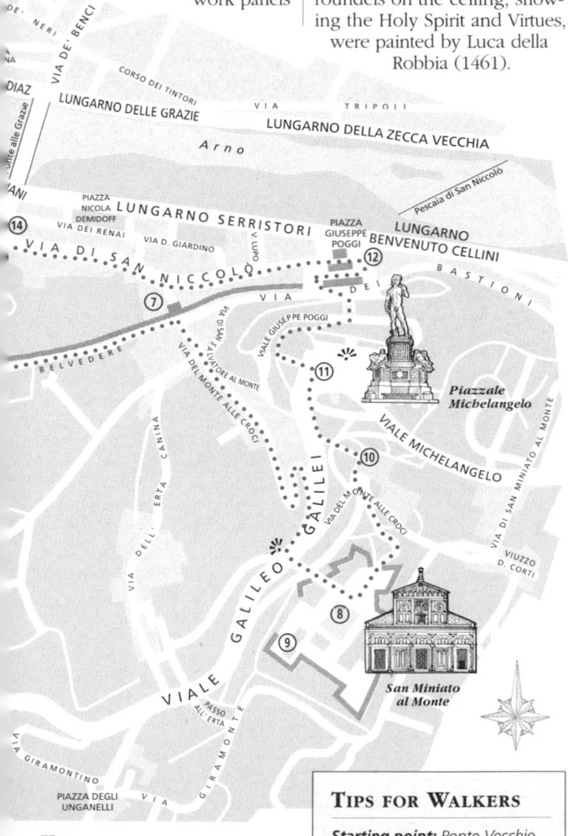


**Key**

• • • Walk route

View point

**0 meters** **500**

**0 yards** **500**

### Tips for Walkers

***Starting point:*** *Ponte Vecchio.*
***Length:*** *3 km (2 miles).*
***San Miniato al Monte:*** *Open 8am–noon & 2–7pm summer; 8am–noon & 2:30–6pm winter.*
***Stopping-off points:*** *There are several cafés along the route.*

Leave San Miniato by an arch in the buildings to the west and follow the path to the church of San Salvatore al Monte (10). Here steps lead down to the Viale Galileo Galilei; take a right turn to reach Piazzale Michelangelo (11). The piazzale, laid out in the 1860s by Giuseppe Poggi, is dotted with copies of Michelangelo's famous statues. It has far-reaching views over the rooftops of central Florence.

Either take the No. 13 bus back to the city center, or the stone steps on the west side of the piazza down to Porta San Niccolò (12), a 14th-century gateway in the city wall. Go left along Via di San Niccolò and Via de' Bardi, lined with medieval buildings. This includes the 13th-century Palazzo de' Mozzi (13) on Via de' Bardi; the Museo Bardini (14) *(see p119)* is opposite. From here, return along the Arno to Ponte Vecchio (1).

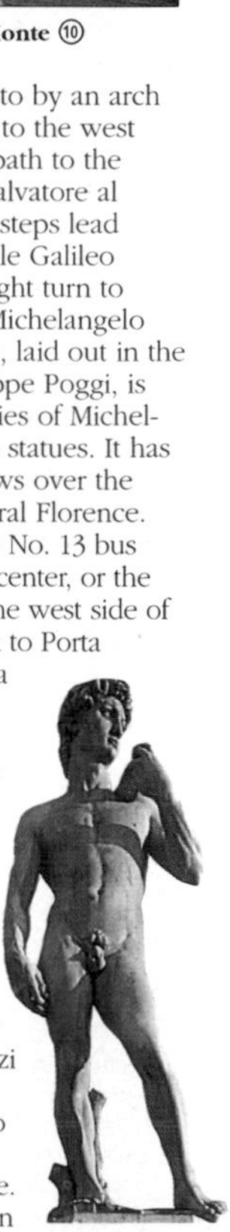

***David*** **in Piazzale Michelangelo (11)**

# A Two-Hour Walk through Fiesole

THE VILLAGE OF FIESOLE stands in the foothills of the Mugello region, 8 km (5 miles) north of Florence, and has substantial Roman and Etruscan remains. The area has been a popular summer retreat since the 15th century, thanks to its fresh breezes and hilltop position.

The bell tower of the Duomo ②

**Piazza Mino da Fiesole**

The No. 7 bus arrives in Fiesole's main square ① after a 30-minute journey from Florence through countryside dotted with villas. Settled in the 7th century BC, Fiesole was a powerful force in central Italy by the 5th century BC. It began to decline after the Romans founded Florence in the 1st century BC, but kept its independence until 1125, when Florentine troops razed most of the city. The Duomo of San Romolo ② in the piazza was begun in 1028 and has a massive bell tower. The bare Romanesque interior has columns which are topped with reused Roman capitals.

### Tips for Walkers

***Starting point:*** *Piazza Mino da Fiesole.*
***Length:*** *1.5 km (1 mile).*
*Allow at least 2 hours for the walk to include time to visit the various museums. Note that Via di San Francesco is steep.*
***Badia Fiesolana:*** *Open Sunday morning for services.*
***Getting there:*** *No. 7 bus from Santa Maria Novella bus station, Piazza del Duomo or Piazza di San Marco in Florence.*
***Stopping-off points:*** *There are several cafés around Piazza Mino da Fiesole.*

From here, walk up the square to the front of the 14th-century Palazzo Comunale ③. Here there is a bronze statue of King Vittorio Emanuele II and Garibaldi, called *Incontro di Teano* (Meeting at Teano) ④. Returning to the church, take the first right turning, down Via Dupre, to the Roman theater ⑤ and into the archeological park.

**The bronze statue *Incontro di Teano* ④**

After its defeat by Florence in 1125, Fiesole went into a decline, and many Etruscan and Roman remains went undisturbed until excavation in the 1870s. The Teatro, built in the 1st century BC, is used for the annual Estate Fiesolana festival *(see pp36–7)*. Its tiers of stone seats can hold 3,000 spectators. Next to the theater is the Museo Faesulanum ⑥, built in 1912–14. Inside are finds from the Bronze Age onward: coins, jewelry and ceramics, bronzes and marble sculpture. The building is a copy of the 1st-century Roman temple whose remains are in the northern part of the complex. It is built on Etruscan foundations, and part of the Roman frieze dating from the 1st century BC is still intact. There are some partly restored Roman baths close by ⑦, and, at

**Roman theater complex ⑤**

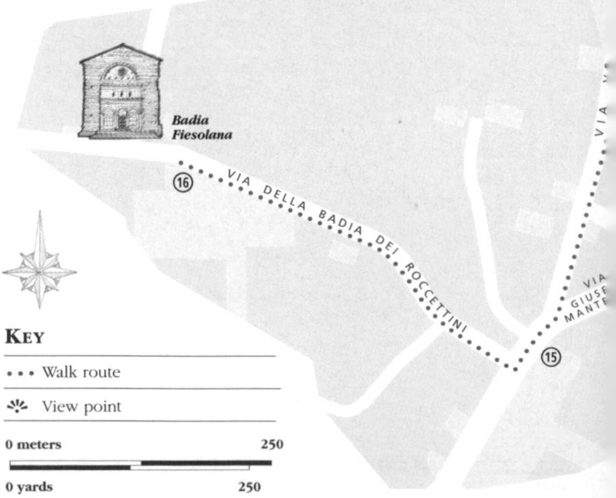

the northern edge of the park, 4th-century BC Etruscan walls ⑧. From the theater turn into Via Dupre to Museo Bandini ⑨ to the right, with a collection of medieval religious paintings built up by local aristocrat Angelo Bandini in the 19th century.

Back in Piazza Mino da Fiesole, turn right down Via di San Francesco to the left of the Palazzo Vescovile ⑩. There are views over Florence and back to Fiesole ⑪ on the road up to Sant'Alessandro church ⑫, which has a Neo-Classical façade combined with a 9th-century Romanesque interior. Original Roman columns used in the nave are made out of *cipollino* (onion ring) marble. From here continue up to San Francesco ⑬, a Franciscan friary founded in 1399 and restored in 1907. It has a pretty cloister and a museum of artifacts collected by the monks.

Fiesole from Via di San Francesco

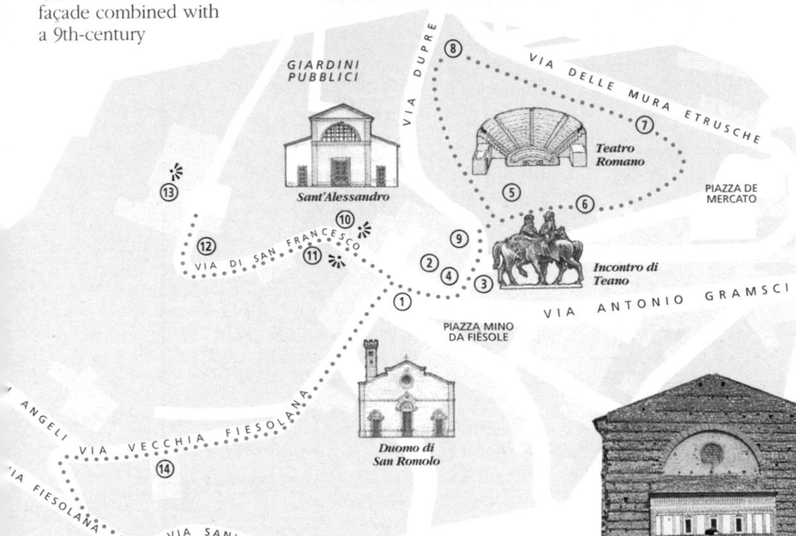

Façade of Badia Fiesolana ⑯

The 15th-century church of San Francesco ⑬

## From Fiesole to San Domenico

Retrace your steps or walk through the park back to the town center. Continue down Via Vecchia Fiesolana. On the left is the Villa Medici ⑭, built in 1461 by Michelozzo for Cosimo de' Medici. Walk down Via Bandini and Via Vecchia Fiesolana to San Domenico. In this little hamlet is the 15th-century church of San Domenico ⑮, with two good works by Fra Angelico, Domenican prior of the monastery here until 1437. The *Madonna with Angels* and *The Crucifixion* are in the chapter house and were both painted around 1430.

Opposite, Via della Badia dei Roccettini leads to the Badia Fiesolana ⑯, a pretty church with a Romanesque façade of inlaid marble. The interior is decorated with local gray sandstone, *pietra serena*. The No. 7 bus back to Florence can be caught from the village square in San Domenico.

# Florence Street Finder

Map references given for sights, restaurants, hotels and shops in Florence refer to the maps in the *Florence Street Finder* *(see* How the Map References Work *opposite).*

Where two map references are provided, the second (in brackets) relates to the large-scale maps, 5 and 6.

A complete index of street names is on pages 142–3. The key map below shows the area of Florence covered by each of the six maps in the *Florence Street Finder.* The maps encompass the four city-center areas (color-coded pink), which include all the sights. *(See also* Florence City Center, *pp14–15.)*

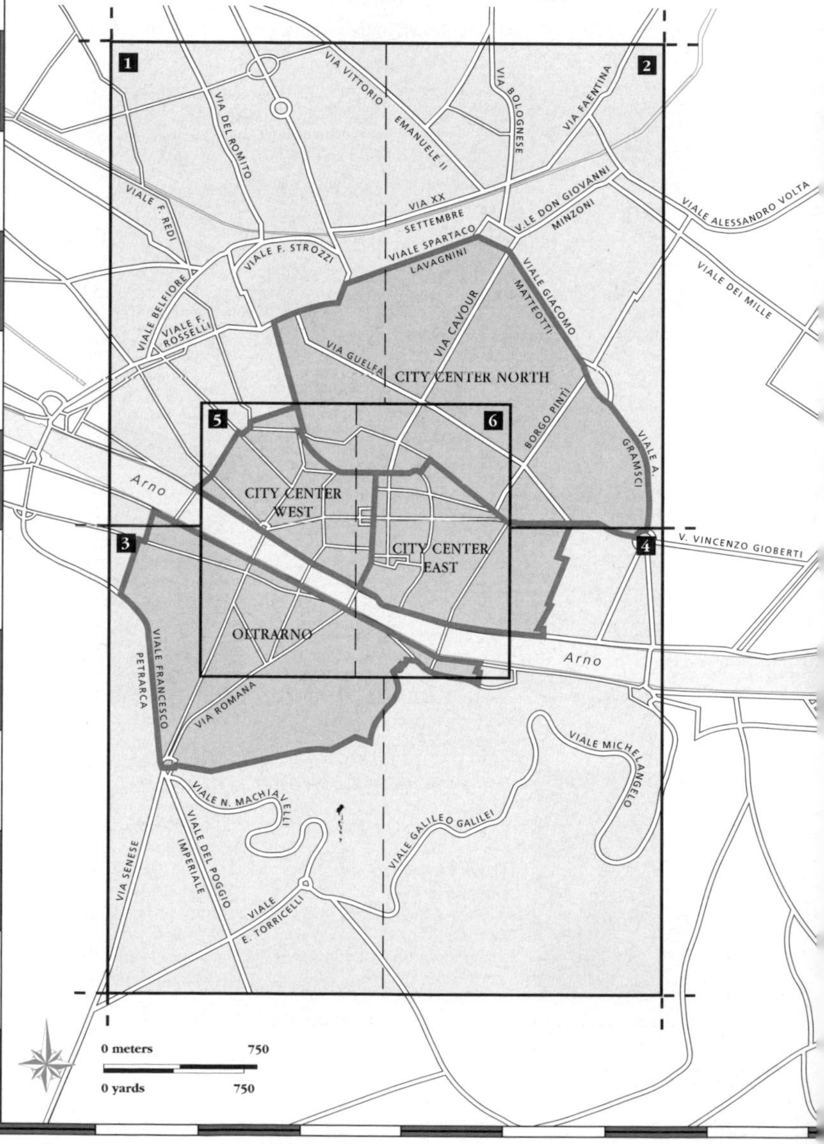

## How the Map References Work

**The first figure** tells you which Street Finder map to turn to.

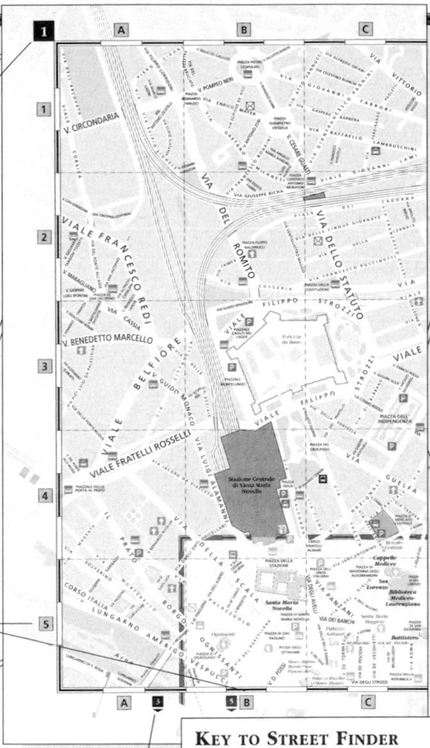


### Ognissanti 16

Borgo Ognissanti 42. **Map** 1 B5 (5 A2) (055) 239 87 00.
***Open*** *7:50am–noon, 4–6:30pm.*

**The letter and number** are a grid reference. You will find the letters at the top and bottom of the map and the numbers at the sides.

**The map** continues on map 3 of the Street Finder.

**The second reference** refers to the large-scale maps of Florence (5 & 6). It is read in exactly the same way as the first.

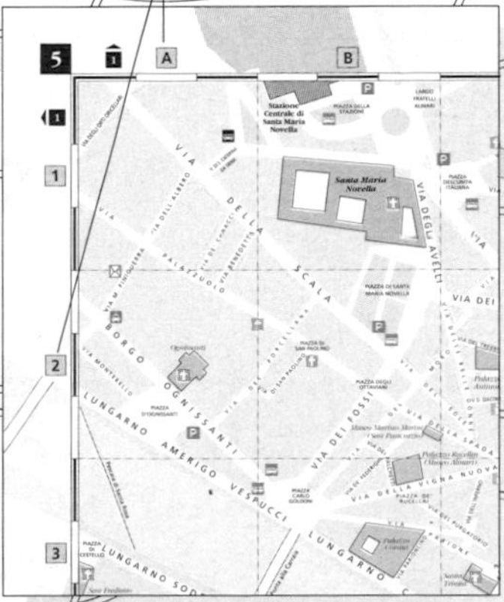

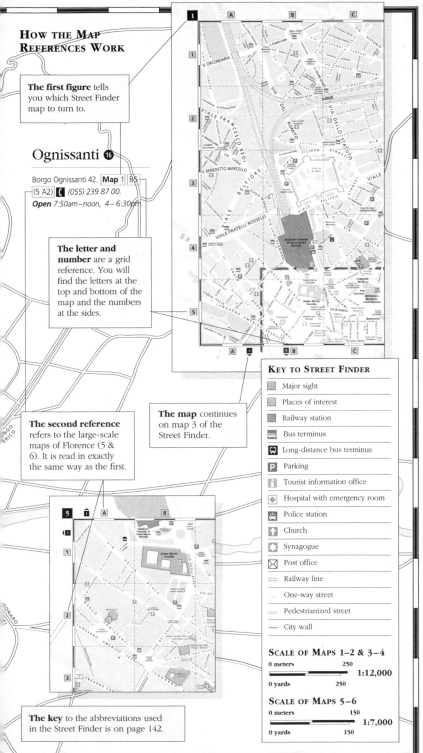

**The key** to the abbreviations used in the Street Finder is on page 142.

### Key to Street Finder

- Major sight
- Places of interest
- Railway station
- Bus terminus
- Long-distance bus terminus
- Parking
- Tourist information office
- Hospital with emergency room
- Police station
- Church
- Synagogue
- Post office
- Railway line
- One-way street
- Pedestrianized street
- City wall

### Scale of Maps 1–2 & 3–4

0 meters 250
**1:12,000**
0 yards 250

### Scale of Maps 5–6

0 meters 150
**1:7,000**
0 yards 150

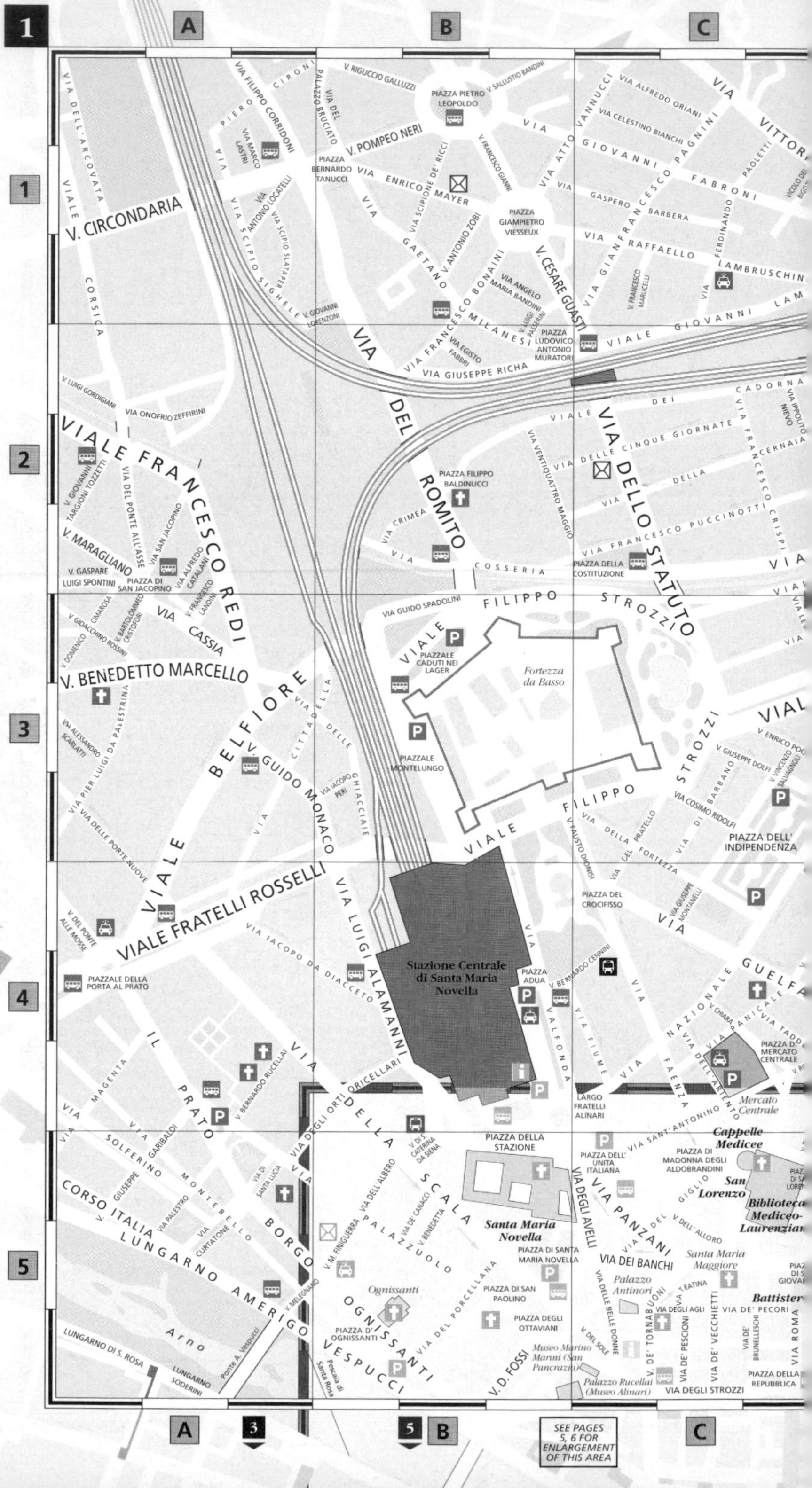
1
A
B
C
1
2
3
4
5
V. CIRCONDARIA
VIALE CORSICA
VIA DELL'ARCOVATA
VIA PIERO CIRONI
VIA FILIPPO CORRIDONI
VIA MARCO LASTRI
VIA ANTONIO LOCATELLI
VIA SCIPIO SLATAPER
VIA SCIPIO SIGHELE
V. GIOVANNI LORENZONI
V. RIGUCCIO GALLUZZI
VIA DEL PALAZZO BRUCIATO
PIAZZA PIETRO LEOPOLDO
V. SALLUSTIO BANDINI
V. POMPEO NERI
PIAZZA BERNARDO TANUCCI
VIA ENRICO MAYER
VIA SCIPIONE DE' RICCI
V. FRANCESCO GIANNI
VIA GAETANO MILANESI
V. ANTONIO ZOBI
PIAZZA GIAMPIETRO VIESSEUX
VIA ANGELO MARIA BANDINI
VIA FRANCESCO BONAINI
VIA EGISTO FABBRI
V. LUIGI PASSERINI
V. CESARE GUASTI
PIAZZA LUDOVICO ANTONIO MURATORI
VIA GIUSEPPE RICHA
VIA ATTO VANNUCCI
VIA ALFREDO ORIANI
VIA CELESTINO BIANCHI
VIA GIOVANNI FABRONI
VIA FRANCESCO PAGNINI
VIA GASPERO BARBERA
VIA RAFFAELLO LAMBRUSCHINI
VIA GIANFRANCESCO
V. FRANCESCO MARUCELLI
VIA FERDINANDO PAOLETTI
VIA VITTORIO
VIALE GIOVANNI LAM
VIA DEL ROMITO
VIA DELLO STATUTO
VIALE DEI CADORNA
VIA IPPOLITO NIEVO
VIA DELLE CINQUE GIORNATE
VIA DELLA CERNAIA
VIA FRANCESCO CRISPI
VIA FRANCESCO PUCCINOTTI
VIA VENTIQUATTRO MAGGIO
PIAZZA FILIPPO BALDINUCCI
VIA CRIMEA
VIA COSSERIA
PIAZZA DELLA COSTITUZIONE
V. LUIGI GORDIGIANI
VIA ONOFRIO ZEFFIRINI
VIALE FRANCESCO REDI
V. GIOVANNI TARGIONI TOZZETTI
VIA DEL PONTE ALL'ASSE
VIA SAN JACOPINO
V. MARAGLIANO
V. GASPARE LUIGI SPONTINI
PIAZZA DI SAN JACOPINO
VIA ALFREDO CATALANI
V. FRANCESCO LANDINI
VIA CIMAROSA
V. BARTOLOMMEO CRISTOFORI
V. GIOACCHINO ROSSINI
V. DOMENICO
VIA CASSIA
V. BENEDETTO MARCELLO
VIALE BELFIORE
VIA PIER LUIGI DA PALESTRINA
VIA ALESSANDRO SCARLATTI
V. GUIDO MONACO
VIA DELLA CITTADELLA
VIA DELLE GHIACCIAIE
VIA JACOPO PERI
VIA DELLE PORTE NUOVE
VIA GUIDO SPADOLINI
VIALE FILIPPO STROZZI
PIAZZALE CADUTI NEI LAGER
Fortezza da Basso
PIAZZALE MONTELUNGO
V. ENRICO POGGI
VIA GIUSEPPE DOLFI
V. VINCENZO SALVAGNOLI
VIA COSIMO RIDOLFI
VIA DI BARBANO
VIA DEL PRATELLO
VIA DELLA FORTEZZA
V. FAUSTO DIONISI
PIAZZA DELL' INDIPENDENZA
PIAZZA DEL CROCIFISSO
VIA GIUSEPPE MONTANELLI
VIALE FRATELLI ROSSELLI
VIA LUIGI ALAMANNI
V. DEL PONTE ALLE MOSSE
VIA JACOPO DA DIACCETO
PIAZZALE DELLA PORTA AL PRATO
Stazione Centrale di Santa Maria Novella
PIAZZA ADUA
V. BERNARDO CENNINI
VIA VALFONDA
VIA FIUME
VIA NAZIONALE
VIA GUELFA
V. CHIARA
VIA PANICALE
VIA TADDEA
PIAZZA DEL MERCATO CENTRALE
VIA FAENZA
VIA DELL'ARIENTO
Mercato Centrale
IL PRATO
VIA MAGENTA
V. BERNARDO RUCELLAI
VIA DEGLI ORTI ORICELLARI
VIA DELLA SCALA
LARGO FRATELLI ALINARI
VIA SANT'ANTONINO
VIA SOLFERINO
VIA GIUSEPPE GARIBALDI
VIA MONTEBELLO
VIA DI SANTA LUCIA
VIA PALESTRO
V. CURTATONE
CORSO ITALIA
BORGO OGNISSANTI
LUNGARNO AMERIGO VESPUCCI
Arno
LUNGARNO DI S. ROSA
LUNGARNO SODERINI
Ponte A. Vespucci
Pescaia di Santa Rosa
V. MELEGNANO
V. DI S. CATERINA DA SIENA
VIA DELL'ALBERO
V. DE' CANACCI
V. BENEDETTA
VIA PALAZZUOLO
V. M. FINIGUERRA
Ognissanti
PIAZZA D' OGNISSANTI
VIA DEL PORCELLANA
PIAZZA DELLA STAZIONE
Santa Maria Novella
PIAZZA DI SANTA MARIA NOVELLA
PIAZZA DI SAN PAOLINO
PIAZZA DEGLI OTTAVIANI
PIAZZA DELL' UNITA ITALIANA
VIA DEGLI AVELLI
VIA PANZANI
VIA DEI BANCHI
VIA DEL GIGLIO
V. DELL'ALLORO
Palazzo Antinori
VIA DELLE BELLE DONNE
V. DEL SOLE
V. D. FOSSI
Museo Marino Marini (San Pancrazio)
Palazzo Rucellai (Museo Alinari)
V. DE' TORNABUONI
VIA DEGLI AGLI
V. TEATINA
VIA DE' PESCIONI
VIA DE' VECCHIETTI
VIA DEGLI STROZZI
VIA DE' PECORI
VIA DE' BRUNELLESCHI
VIA ROMA
PIAZZA DELLA REPUBBLICA
Santa Maria Maggiore
PIAZZA DI MADONNA DEGLI ALDOBRANDINI
Cappelle Medicee
San Lorenzo
Biblioteca Medicea-Laurenziana
Battistero
3
5
SEE PAGES 5, 6 FOR ENLARGEMENT OF THIS AREA

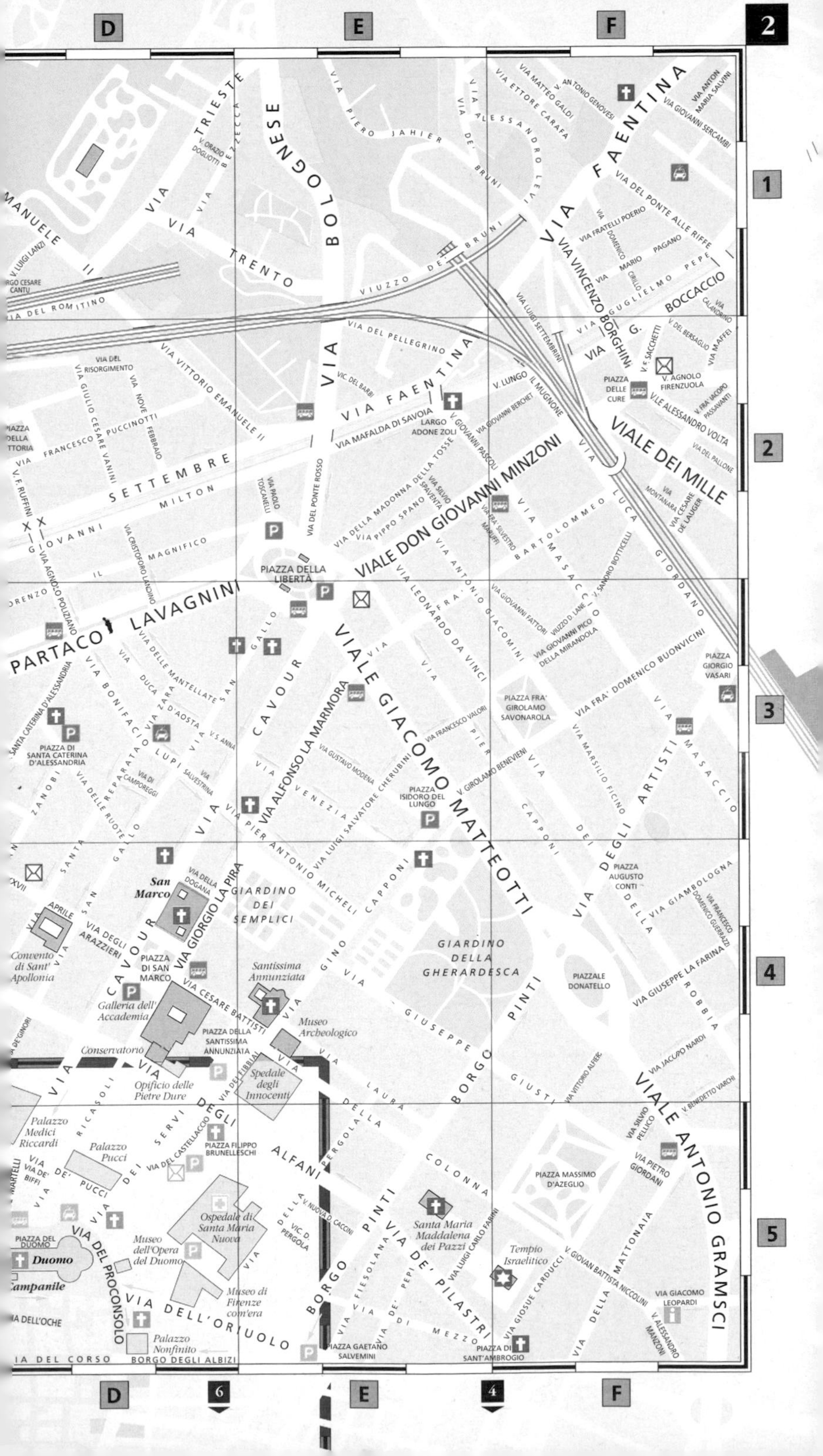
2
D
E
F
1
2
3
4
5
6
4
VIA TRIESTE
VIA BOLOGNESE
VIA PIERO JAHIER
VIA ALESSANDRO DE' BRUNI
VIA ETTORE CARAFA
VIA MATTEO GALDI
V. ANTONIO GENOVESI
VIA FAENTINA
VIA ANTON MARIA SALVINI
VIA GIOVANNI SERCAMBI
VIA ALESSANDRO LEVI
VIA DEL PONTE ALLE RIFFE
VIA FRATELLI POERIO
VIA DOMENICO CIRILLO
VIA MARIO PAGANO
VIA GUGLIELMO PEPE
VIA G. BOCCACCIO
VIA VINCENZO BORGHINI
VIA LUIGI SETTEMBRINI
VIA TRENTO
VIUZZO DE' BRUNI
VIA DEL ROMITINO
VIA DEL PELLEGRINO
VIA DEL RISORGIMENTO
VIA VITTORIO EMANUELE II
VIA GIULIO CESARE VANINI
VIA NOVE FEBBRAIO
VIA FRANCESCO PUCCINOTTI
VIA XX SETTEMBRE
VIA MILTON
VIA GIOVANNI
VIA CRISTOFORO LANDINO
IL MAGNIFICO
VIA AGNOLO POLIZIANO
VIA PAOLO TOSCANELLI
VIA DEL PONTE ROSSO
VIA MAFALDA DI SAVOIA
LARGO ADONE ZOLI
V. GIOVANNI PASCOLI
VIA GIOVANNI BERCHET
V. LUNGO IL MUGNONE
PIAZZA DELLE CURE
V. AGNOLO FIRENZUOLA
V.LE ALESSANDRO VOLTA
VIA DEL PALLONE
VIALE DEI MILLE
VIA MONTANARA
VIA CESARE DE LAUGER
VIALE DON GIOVANNI MINZONI
VIA DELLA MADONNA DELLA TOSSE
VIA SILVIO SPAVENTA
VIA PIPPO SPANO
VIA FRA' SILVESTRO MARUFFI
VIA BARTOLOMMEO
VIA LUCA GIORDANO
VIA MASACCIO
V. SANDRO BOTTICELLI
PIAZZA DELLA LIBERTÀ
VIALE SPARTACO LAVAGNINI
VIA LEONARDO DA VINCI
VIA ANTONIO GIACOMINI
VIA GIOVANNI FATTORI
VIA GIOVANNI PICO DELLA MIRANDOLA
VIA FRA' DOMENICO BUONVICINI
PIAZZA GIORGIO VASARI
VIALE GIACOMO MATTEOTTI
VIA ALFONSO LA MARMORA
VIA CAVOUR
VIA SAN GALLO
VIA DELLE MANTELLATE
VIA DUCA D'AOSTA
VIA BONIFACIO LUPI
V.S. ANNA
VIA SALVESTRINA
VIA DI CAMPOREGGI
PIAZZA DI SANTA CATERINA D'ALESSANDRIA
VIA SANTA REPARATA
VIA DELLE RUOTE
PIAZZA FRA' GIROLAMO SAVONAROLA
VIA FRANCESCO VALORI
VIA GUSTAVO MODENA
VIA LUIGI SALVATORE CHERUBINI
VIA VENEZIA
PIAZZA ISIDORO DEL LUNGO
V. GIROLAMO BENIVIENI
VIA PIER CAPPONI
VIA MARSILIO FICINO
VIA DEGLI ARTISTI
VIA PIER ANTONIO MICHELI
PIAZZA AUGUSTO CONTI
VIA DELLA ROBBIA
VIA GIAMBOLOGNA
VIA FRANCESCO DOMENICO GUERRAZZI
San Marco
VIA DELLA DOGANA
VIA GIORGIO LA PIRA
GIARDINO DEI SEMPLICI
GIARDINO DELLA GHERARDESCA
PIAZZALE DONATELLO
VIA GIUSEPPE LA FARINA
Convento di Sant' Apollonia
VIA DEGLI ARAZZIERI
PIAZZA DI SAN MARCO
Santissima Annunziata
Galleria dell' Accademia
VIA CESARE BATTISTI
PIAZZA DELLA SANTISSIMA ANNUNZIATA
Museo Archeologico
VIA GINO CAPPONI
VIA GIUSEPPE GIUSTI
BORGO PINTI
VIA JACOPO NARDI
V. BENEDETTO VARCHI
VIA VITTORIO ALFIERI
Conservatorio
Opificio delle Pietre Dure
VIA DEI FIBBIAI
Spedale degli Innocenti
VIA DELLA COLONNA
VIA LAURA
VIA RICASOLI
VIA DEGLI ALFANI
VIA DEI SERVI
VIA DEL CASTELLACCIO
PIAZZA FILIPPO BRUNELLESCHI
VIA DELLA PERGOLA
VIALE ANTONIO GRAMSCI
VIA SILVIO PELLICO
VIA PIETRO GIORDANI
PIAZZA MASSIMO D'AZEGLIO
Palazzo Medici Riccardi
Palazzo Pucci
VIA DE' PUCCI
VIA DE' BIFFI
Ospedale di Santa Maria Nuova
V. NUOVA D. CACCINI
VIC. D. PERGOLA
Santa Maria Maddalena dei Pazzi
VIA LUIGI CARLO FARINI
Tempio Israelitico
PIAZZA DEL DUOMO
Duomo
Campanile
VIA DEL PROCONSOLO
Museo dell'Opera del Duomo
Museo di Firenze com'era
VIA DELL'ORIUOLO
VIA DE' PEPI
VIA DE' PILASTRI
VIA FIESOLANA
VIA DE' MEZZO
VIA GIOSUE CARDUCCI
V. GIOVAN BATTISTA NICCOLINI
VIA DELLA MATTONAIA
VIA GIACOMO LEOPARDI
V. ALESSANDRO MANZONI
Palazzo Nonfinito
VIA DEL CORSO
BORGO DEGLI ALBIZI
PIAZZA GAETANO SALVEMINI
PIAZZA DI SANT'AMBROGIO
VIA DELL'OCHE

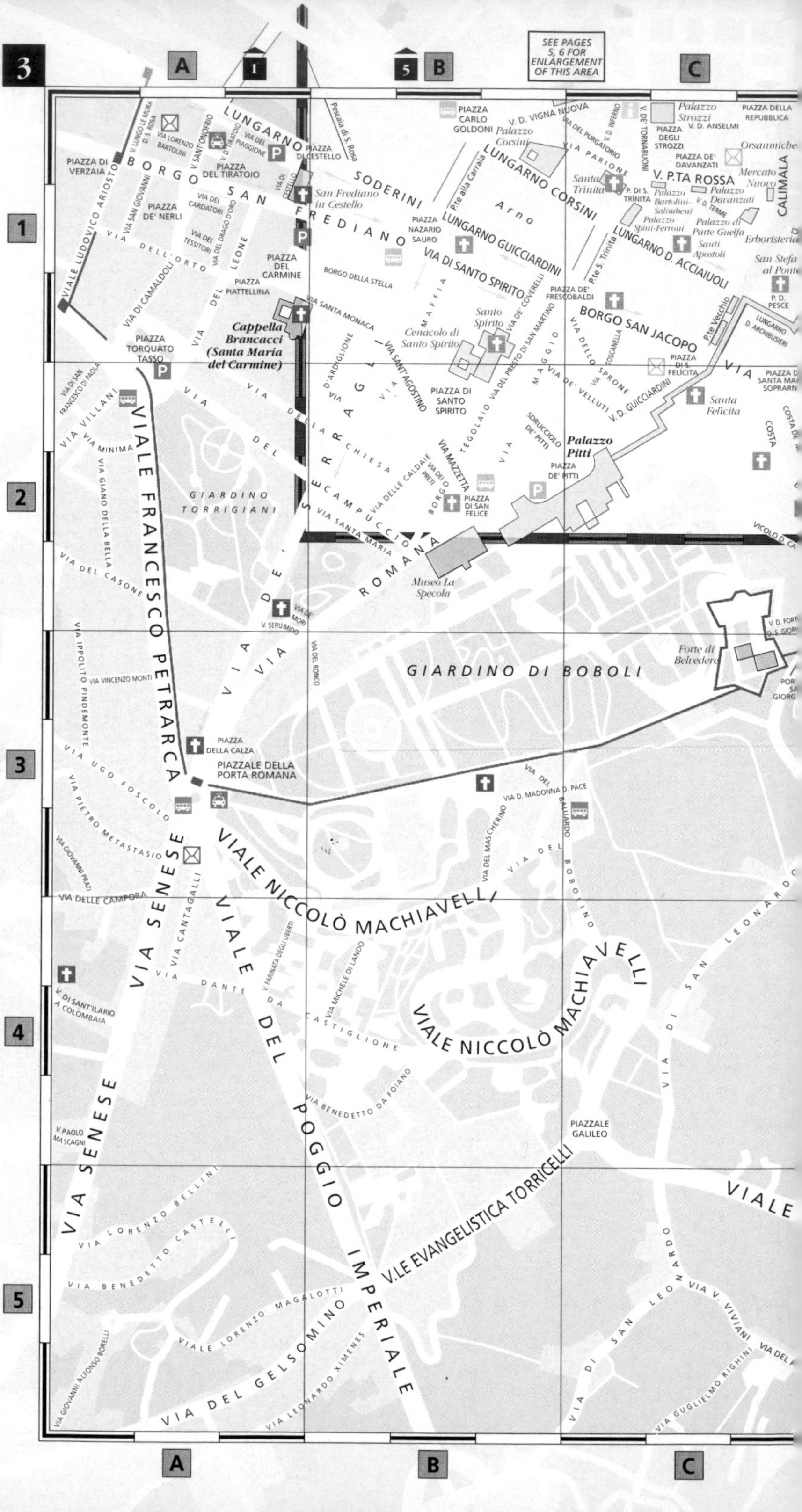

3
A
1
5
B
C
SEE PAGES 5, 6 FOR ENLARGEMENT OF THIS AREA
1
2
3
4
5
LUNGARNO SODERINI
BORGO SAN FREDIANO
VIALE LUDOVICO ARIOSTO
PIAZZA DI VERZAIA
PIAZZA DEL TIRATOIO
PIAZZA DE' NERLI
PIAZZA DI CESTELLO
San Frediano in Cestello
PIAZZA DEL CARMINE
PIAZZA PIATTELLINA
PIAZZA TORQUATO TASSO
Cappella Brancacci (Santa Maria del Carmine)
VIA DELL'ORTO
VIA DEL LEONE
VIA DI CAMALDOLI
BORGO DELLA STELLA
VIA SANTA MONACA
PIAZZA CARLO GOLDONI
Palazzo Corsini
LUNGARNO CORSINI
LUNGARNO GUICCIARDINI
Arno
PIAZZA NAZARIO SAURO
VIA DI SANTO SPIRITO
Cenacolo di Santo Spirito
Santo Spirito
PIAZZA DI SANTO SPIRITO
VIA MAGGIO
PIAZZA DE' FRESCOBALDI
BORGO SAN JACOPO
LUNGARNO D. ACCIAIUOLI
Santa Trinita
Palazzo Strozzi
PIAZZA DEGLI STROZZI
PIAZZA DE' DAVANZATI
V. P.TA ROSSA
Palazzo Davanzati
Palazzo di Parte Guelfa
Palazzo Spini-Feroni
Santi Apostoli
Orsanmichele
Mercato Nuovo
CALIMALA
PIAZZA DELLA REPUBBLICA
Erboristeria
San Stefano al Ponte
P.te Vecchio
PIAZZA DI S. FELICITA
Santa Felicita
VIA DE' GUICCIARDINI
Palazzo Pitti
PIAZZA DE' PITTI
PIAZZA DI SAN FELICE
VIA MAZZETTA
VIA ROMANA
Museo La Specola
VIA DEL CAMPUCCIO
VIA DE' SERRAGLI
VIA DELLA CHIESA
VIA SANTA MARIA
GIARDINO TORRIGIANI
VIA VILLANI
VIA DEL CASONE
VIALE FRANCESCO PETRARCA
VIA IPPOLITO PINDEMONTE
VIA VINCENZO MONTI
GIARDINO DI BOBOLI
Forte di Belvedere
VIA DEL RONCO
PIAZZA DELLA CALZA
PIAZZALE DELLA PORTA ROMANA
VIA UGO FOSCOLO
VIA PIETRO METASTASIO
VIA DELLE CAMPORA
VIA SENESE
VIA CANTAGALLI
VIALE NICCOLÒ MACHIAVELLI
VIA D. MADONNA D. PACE
VIA DEL BALUARDO
VIA DEL MASCHERINO
VIA DEL BOBOLINO
VIA DANTE DA CASTIGLIONE
VIA MICHELE DI LANDO
VIALE DEL POGGIO IMPERIALE
VIA BENEDETTO DA FOIANO
PIAZZALE GALILEO
VIA DI SAN LEONARDO
V.LE EVANGELISTICA TORRICELLI
VIALE
VIA LORENZO BELLINI
VIA BENEDETTO CASTELLI
VIALE LORENZO MAGALOTTI
VIA DEL GELSOMINO
VIA LEONARDO XIMENES
VIA GIOVANNI ALFONSO BORELLI
VIA V. VIVIANI
VIA GUGLIELMO RIGHINI
V. DI SANT'ILARIO A COLOMBAIA
V. PAOLO MASCAGNI
A
B
C

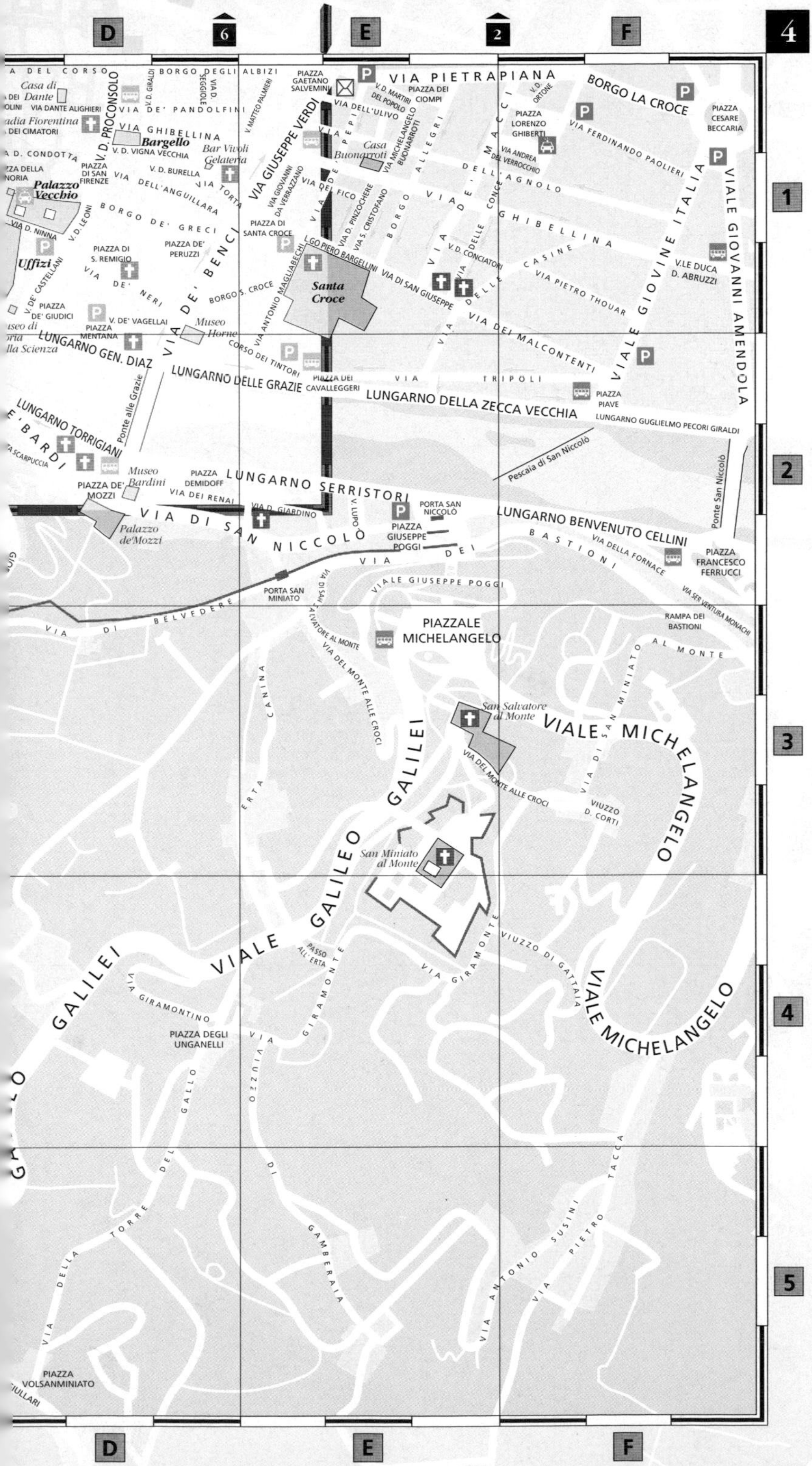

D
6
E
2
F
4
1
2
3
4
5
VIA PIETRAPIANA
BORGO LA CROCE
PIAZZA CESARE BECCARIA
BORGO DEGLI ALBIZI
PIAZZA GAETANO SALVEMINI
PIAZZA DEI CIOMPI
VIA DELL'ULIVO
V. D. MARTIRI DEL POPOLO
VIA MICHELANGELO BUONARROTI
PIAZZA LORENZO GHIBERTI
VIA FERDINANDO PAOLIERI
VIA ANDREA DEL VERROCCHIO
V. D. ORTONE
Casa di Dante
VIA DANTE ALIGHIERI
Badia Fiorentina
V. DEI CIMATORI
VIA DE' PANDOLFINI
V. D. PROCONSOLO
VIA GHIBELLINA
Bargello
V. D. VIGNA VECCHIA
V. MATTEO PALMIERI
VIA GIUSEPPE VERDI
Bar Vivoli Gelateria
VIA DE' PEPI
Casa Buonarroti
VIA ALLEGRI
VIA DE' MACCI
VIA DELL'AGNOLO
VIA D. CONDOTTA
PIAZZA DI SAN FIRENZE
V. D. BURELLA
VIA DELL'ANGUILLARA
VIA TORTA
VIA GIOVANNI DA VERRAZZANO
VIA DEL FICO
Palazzo Vecchio
BORGO DE' GRECI
PIAZZA DI SANTA CROCE
V. D. LEONI
V. D. NINNA
PIAZZA DE' PERUZZI
VIA DE' BENCI
VIA D. PINZOCHERE
VIA S. CRISTOFANO
BORGO
VIA DELLE CONCE
GHIBELLINA
VIALE GIOVINE ITALIA
VIALE GIOVANNI AMENDOLA
V.LE DUCA D. ABRUZZI
Uffizi
PIAZZA DI S. REMIGIO
L.GO PIERO BARGELLINI
VIA DI SAN GIUSEPPE
V. D. CONCIATORI
VIA DELLE CASINE
VIA PIETRO THOUAR
VIA DE' NERI
BORGO S. CROCE
Santa Croce
VIA ANTONIO MAGLIABECHI
V. DE' CASTELLANI
PIAZZA DE' GIUDICI
V. DE' VAGELLAI
Museo Horne
VIA DEI MALCONTENTI
Museo di Storia della Scienza
PIAZZA MENTANA
LUNGARNO GEN. DIAZ
CORSO DEI TINTORI
LUNGARNO DELLE GRAZIE
PIAZZA DEI CAVALLEGGERI
VIA TRIPOLI
LUNGARNO DELLA ZECCA VECCHIA
PIAZZA PIAVE
LUNGARNO GUGLIELMO PECORI GIRALDI
Ponte alle Grazie
LUNGARNO TORRIGIANI
V. DE' BARDI
V. DI SCARPUCCIA
Museo Bardini
PIAZZA DEMIDOFF
LUNGARNO SERRISTORI
Pescaia di San Niccolò
Ponte San Niccolò
PIAZZA DE' MOZZI
VIA DEI RENAI
V. D. GIARDINO
V. LUPO
PORTA SAN NICCOLÒ
LUNGARNO BENVENUTO CELLINI
Palazzo de'Mozzi
VIA DI SAN NICCOLÒ
PIAZZA GIUSEPPE POGGI
VIA DEI BASTIONI
VIA DELLA FORNACE
PIAZZA FRANCESCO FERRUCCI
VIALE GIUSEPPE POGGI
VIA SER VENTURA MONACHI
PORTA SAN MINIATO
VIA DI BELVEDERE
VIA DI SALVATORE AL MONTE
PIAZZALE MICHELANGELO
RAMPA DEI BASTIONI
VIA DEL MONTE ALLE CROCI
VIA DI SAN MINIATO AL MONTE
ERTA CANINA
San Salvatore al Monte
VIALE MICHELANGELO
VIALE GALILEO GALILEI
VIA DEL MONTE ALLE CROCI
VIUZZO D. CORTI
San Miniato al Monte
PASSO ALL' ERTA
VIUZZO DI GATTAIA
VIA GIRAMONTE
VIA GIRAMONTINO
PIAZZA DEGLI UNGANELLI
VIUZZO
VIA DEL GALLO
VIA DELLA TORRE DEL GALLO
VIA DI GAMBERAIA
VIA ANTONIO SUSINI
VIA PIETRO TACCA
PIAZZA VOLSANMINIATO
GIULLARI

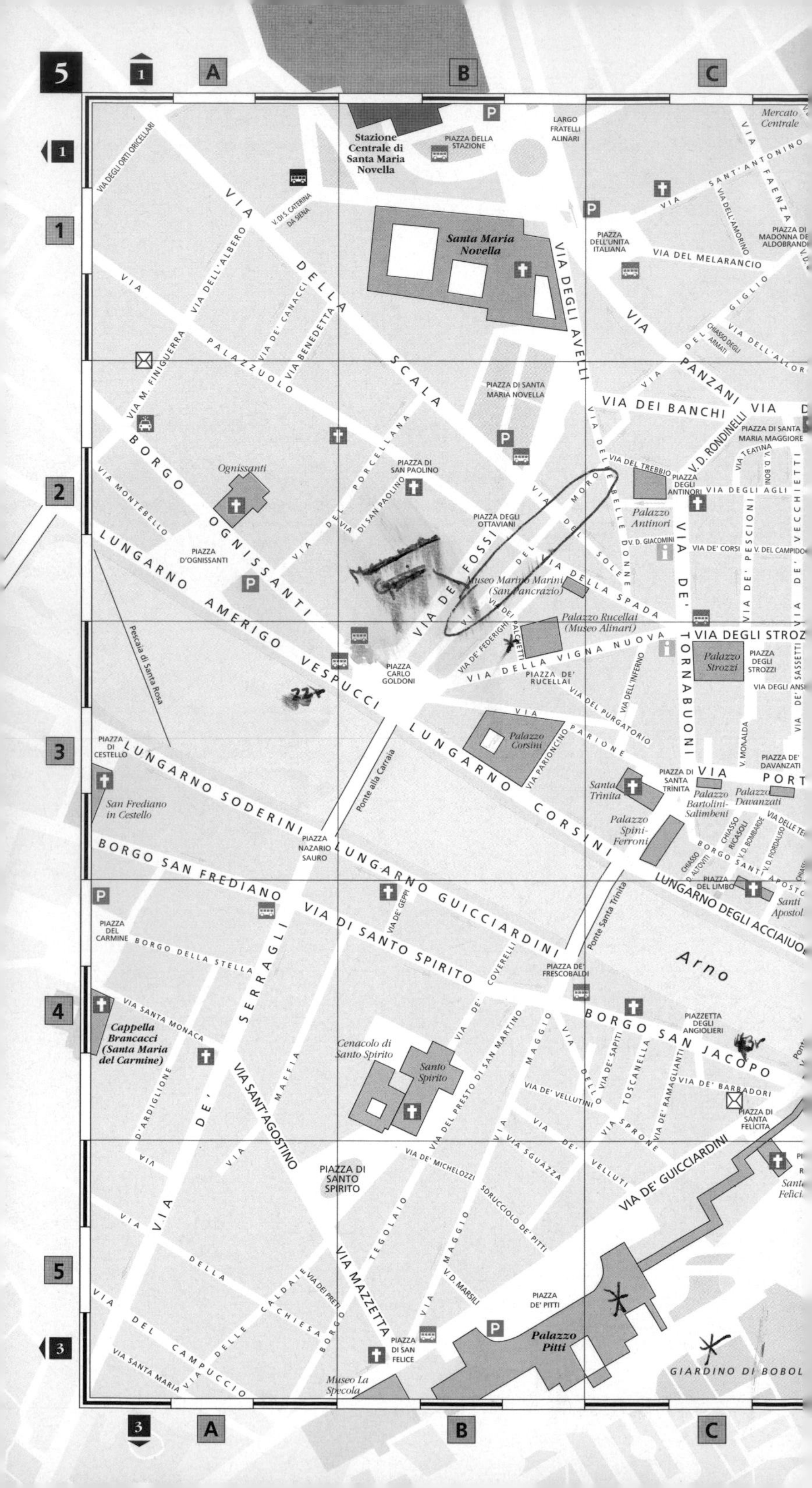
5
A
B
C
1
2
3
4
5
Stazione Centrale di Santa Maria Novella
PIAZZA DELLA STAZIONE
LARGO FRATELLI ALINARI
Mercato Centrale
VIA SANT'ANTONINO
VIA FAENZA
VIA DELL'AMORINO
PIAZZA DI MADONNA DEGLI ALDOBRANDINI
VIA DEGLI ORTI ORICELLARI
V. DI S. CATERINA DA SIENA
VIA DELLA SCALA
Santa Maria Novella
VIA DEGLI AVELLI
PIAZZA DELL'UNITÀ ITALIANA
VIA DEL MELARANCIO
VIA DELL'ALBERO
VIA DE' CANACCI
VIA BENEDETTA
VIA PALAZZUOLO
VIA PANZANI
VIA DEL GIGLIO
CHIASSO DEGLI ARMATI
VIA DELL'ALLORO
VIA M. FINIGUERRA
PIAZZA DI SANTA MARIA NOVELLA
VIA DEI BANCHI
VIA DELLE BELLE DONNE
V. D. RONDINELLI
PIAZZA DI SANTA MARIA MAGGIORE
VIA TEATINA
V. D. BONI
BORGO OGNISSANTI
Ognissanti
VIA DEL PORCELLANA
PIAZZA DI SAN PAOLINO
VIA DI SAN PAOLINO
VIA DEL MORO
VIA DEL TREBBIO
PIAZZA DEGLI ANTINORI
VIA DEGLI AGLI
VIA MONTEBELLO
PIAZZA DEGLI OTTAVIANI
Palazzo Antinori
VIA DEL SOLE
V. D. GIACOMINI
VIA DE' CORSI
V. DEL CAMPIDOGLIO
VIA DE' PESCIONI
VIA DE' VECCHIETTI
LUNGARNO AMERIGO VESPUCCI
PIAZZA D'OGNISSANTI
VIA DE' FOSSI
Museo Marino Marini (San Pancrazio)
VIA DELLA SPADA
VIA DE' TORNABUONI
VIA DE' FEDERIGHI
VIA DEI PALCHETTI
Palazzo Rucellai (Museo Alinari)
VIA DEGLI STROZZI
Palazzo Strozzi
PIAZZA DEGLI STROZZI
VIA DEGLI ANSELMI
VIA DE' SASSETTI
Pescaia di Santa Rosa
VIA DELLA VIGNA NUOVA
PIAZZA CARLO GOLDONI
PIAZZA DE' RUCELLAI
VIA DELL'INFERNO
VIA DEL PURGATORIO
VIA PARIONE
Palazzo Corsini
VIA PARIONCINO
V. MONALDA
PIAZZA DE' DAVANZATI
PIAZZA DI CESTELLO
LUNGARNO SODERINI
San Frediano in Cestello
Ponte alla Carraia
LUNGARNO CORSINI
PIAZZA DI SANTA TRINITA
VIA PORTA ROSSA
Santa Trinita
Palazzo Bartolini-Salimbeni
Palazzo Davanzati
Palazzo Spini-Ferroni
CHIASSO RICASOLI
V. D. BOMBARDE
V. D. FIORDALISO
VIA DELLE TERME
CHIASSO D. ALTOVITI
BORGO SANTI APOSTOLI
PIAZZA DEL LIMBO
Santi Apostoli
BORGO SAN FREDIANO
PIAZZA NAZARIO SAURO
LUNGARNO GUICCIARDINI
LUNGARNO DEGLI ACCIAIUOLI
VIA DE' GEPPI
Ponte Santa Trinita
VIA DI SANTO SPIRITO
PIAZZA DEL CARMINE
BORGO DELLA STELLA
VIA DEI SERRAGLI
Arno
VIA DE' COVERELLI
PIAZZA DE' FRESCOBALDI
BORGO SAN JACOPO
Ponte Vecchio
PIAZZETTA DEGLI ANGIOLIERI
Cappella Brancacci (Santa Maria del Carmine)
VIA SANTA MONACA
VIA MAFFIA
VIA SANT'AGOSTINO
VIA D'ARDIGLIONE
Cenacolo di Santo Spirito
Santo Spirito
VIA DEL PRESTO DI SAN MARTINO
VIA MAGGIO
VIA DELLO SPRONE
VIA DE' SAPITI
VIA TOSCANELLA
VIA DE' RAMAGLIANTI
VIA DE' BARBADORI
VIA DE' VELLUTINI
VIA DE' VELLUTI
PIAZZA DI SANTA FELICITA
VIA DE' GUICCIARDINI
PIAZZA DI SANTO SPIRITO
VIA DE' MICHELOZZI
VIA SGUAZZA
SDRUCCIOLO DE' PITTI
Santa Felicita
VIA DELLA CHIESA
VIA DELLE CALDAIE
VIA DEI PRETI
BORGO TEGOLAIO
VIA MAZZETTA
V. D. MARSILI
PIAZZA DE' PITTI
VIA DEL CAMPUCCIO
VIA DELLE CAMPORA
VIA SANTA MARIA
PIAZZA DI SAN FELICE
Palazzo Pitti
Museo La Specola
GIARDINO DI BOBOLI

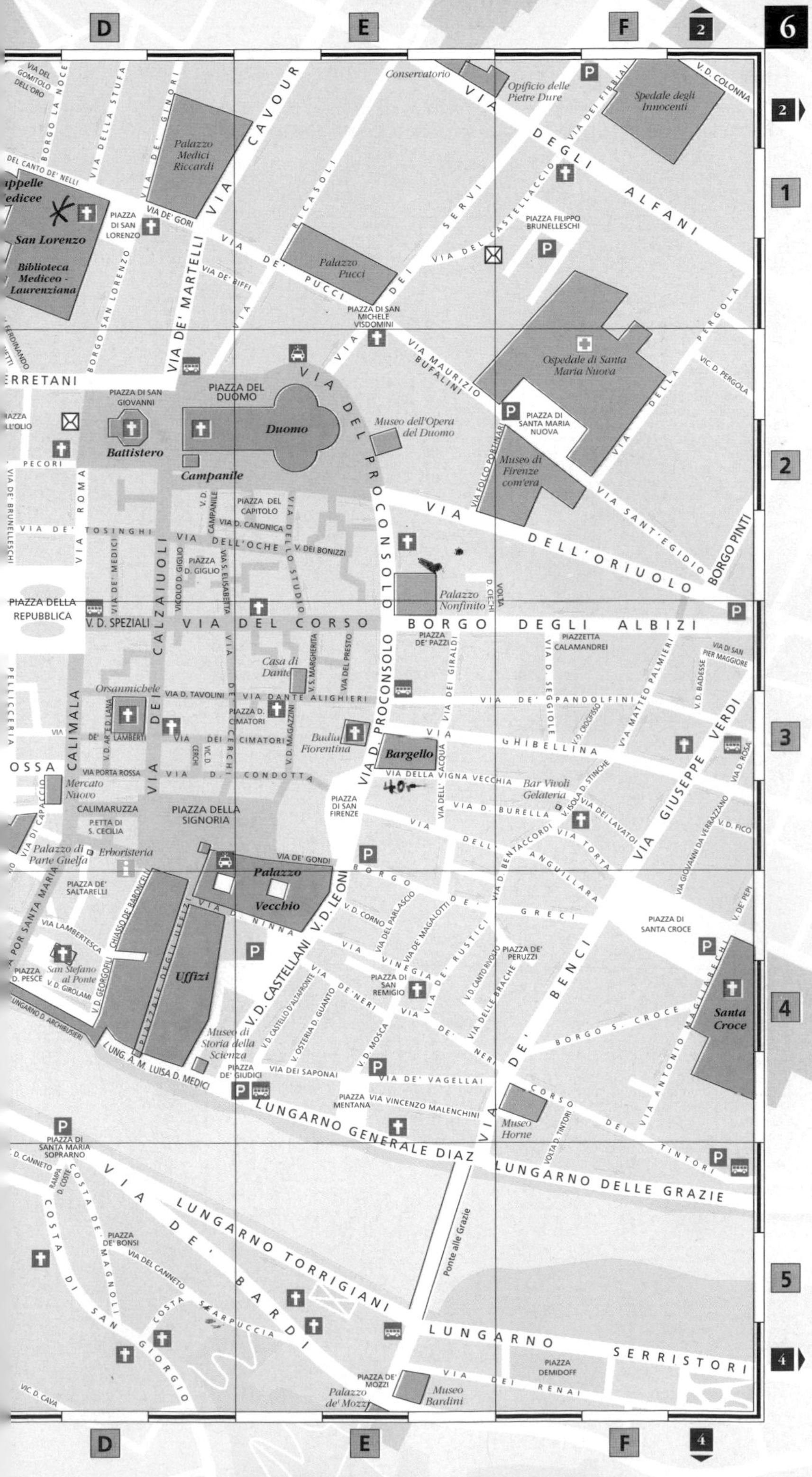
6
D
E
F
2
1
2
3
4
5
4
Conservatorio
Opificio delle Pietre Dure
Spedale degli Innocenti
V. D. COLONNA
VIA DEI FIBBIAI
VIA DEGLI ALFANI
VIA DEL GOMITOLO DELL'ORO
BORGO LA NOCE
VIA DELLA STUFA
VIA DE' GINORI
Palazzo Medici Riccardi
VIA CAVOUR
VIA RICASOLI
VIA DEI SERVI
VIA DEL CASTELLACCIO
PIAZZA FILIPPO BRUNELLESCHI
DEL CANTO DE' NELLI
Cappelle Medicee
San Lorenzo
Biblioteca Mediceo - Laurenziana
PIAZZA DI SAN LORENZO
VIA DE' GORI
VIA DE' MARTELLI
VIA DE' PUCCI
VIA DE' BIFFI
Palazzo Pucci
BORGO SAN LORENZO
PIAZZA DI SAN MICHELE VISDOMINI
VIA MAURIZIO BUFALINI
Ospedale di Santa Maria Nuova
VIA DELLA PERGOLA
VIC. D. PERGOLA
CERRETANI
PIAZZA DI SAN GIOVANNI
PIAZZA DEL DUOMO
VIA DEL PROCONSOLO
Duomo
Battistero
Campanile
Museo dell'Opera del Duomo
PIAZZA DI SANTA MARIA NUOVA
VIA FOLCO PORTINARI
Museo di Firenze com'era
VIA DELLA
VIA SANT'EGIDIO
BORGO PINTI
PIAZZA DELL'OLIO
PECORI
VIA DE' BRUNELLESCHI
VIA ROMA
VIA DE' TOSINGHI
V. D. CAMPANILE
PIAZZA DEL CAPITOLO
VIA D. CANONICA
VIA DELLO STUDIO
VIA DELL'OCHE
V. DEI BONIZZI
VIA DELL'ORIUOLO
VIA DE' CALZAIUOLI
VIA DE' MEDICI
VICOLO D. GIGLIO
PIAZZA D. GIGLIO
VIA S. ELISABETTA
Palazzo Nonfinito
VOLTA D. CIECHI
PIAZZA DELLA REPUBBLICA
V. D. SPEZIALI
VIA DEL CORSO
BORGO DEGLI ALBIZI
PELLICCERIA
PIAZZA DE' PAZZI
PIAZZETTA CALAMANDREI
VIA DI SAN PIER MAGGIORE
Casa di Dante
V. S. MARGHERITA
VIA DEL PRESTO
VIA DEI GIRALDI
VIA D. SEGGIOLE
VIA MATTEO PALMIERI
V. D. BADESSE
Orsanmichele
VIA D. TAVOLINI
VIA DANTE ALIGHIERI
VIA DE' PANDOLFINI
CALIMALA
VIA D. ARTE D. LANA
VIA DEI CERCHI
PIAZZA D. CIMATORI
VIA D. MAGAZZINI
V. D. CROCIFISSO
VIA GIUSEPPE VERDI
DE' LAMBERTI
VIA DEI CIMATORI
Badia Fiorentina
VIA D. PROCONSOLO
VIA GHIBELLINA
VIA D. ROSA
VIA DELL'ACQUA
Bargello
ROSSA
VIA PORTA ROSSA
VIA D. CONDOTTA
VIA DELLA VIGNA VECCHIA
Bar Vivoli Gelateria
V. ISOLA D. STINCHE
Mercato Nuovo
CALIMARUZZA
PIAZZA DELLA SIGNORIA
PIAZZA DI SAN FIRENZE
VIA D. BURELLA
VIA DEI LAVATOI
VIA GIOVANNI DA VERRAZZANO
V. D. FICO
P.ETTA DI S. CECILIA
VIA DI CAPACCIO
VIA DELL'ANGUILLARA
VIA TORTA
VIA DE' BENTACCORDI
Palazzo di Parte Guelfa
Erboristeria
VIA DE' GONDI
BORGO DEI GRECI
Palazzo Vecchio
PIAZZA DE' SALTARELLI
CHIASSO DE' BARONCELLI
VIA DELLA NINNA
V. D. LEONI
V. D. CORNO
VIA DEL PARLASCIO
VIA DE' MAGALOTTI
PIAZZA DI SANTA CROCE
VIA DE' PEPI
POR SANTA MARIA
VIA LAMBERTESCA
VIA VINEGIA
VIA DE' RUSTICI
VIA DEL CANTO RIVOLTO
PIAZZA DE' PERUZZI
VIA DE' BENCI
PIAZZA D. PESCE
San Stefano al Ponte
V. D. GIROLAMI
V. D. GEORGOFILI
PIAZZALE DEGLI UFFIZI
Uffizi
V. D. CASTELLANI
VIA D. CASTELLO D'ALTAFRONTE
VIA DE' NERI
PIAZZA DI SAN REMIGIO
VIA DELLE BRACHE
Santa Croce
BORGO S. CROCE
LUNGARNO D. ARCHIBUSIERI
Museo di Storia della Scienza
V. OSTERIA D. GUANTO
V. D. MOSCA
VIA ANTONIO MAGLIABECHI
L'UNG. A. M. LUISA D. MEDICI
PIAZZA DE' GIUDICI
VIA DEI SAPONAI
VIA DE' VAGELLAI
CORSO DEI TINTORI
PIAZZA MENTANA
VIA VINCENZO MALENCHINI
LUNGARNO GENERALE DIAZ
Museo Horne
VOLTA D. TINTORI
PIAZZA DI SANTA MARIA SOPRARNO
V. D. CANNETO
RAMPA D. COSTE
COSTA DE' MAGNOLI
VIA DE' BARDI
LUNGARNO TORRIGIANI
Ponte alle Grazie
LUNGARNO DELLE GRAZIE
PIAZZA DE' BONSI
VIA DEL CANNETO
COSTA DI SAN GIORGIO
COSTA SCARPUCCIA
LUNGARNO SERRISTORI
PIAZZA DEMIDOFF
PIAZZA DE' MOZZI
Palazzo de' Mozzi
Museo Bardini
VIA DEI RENAI
VIC. D. CAVA

# Street Finder Index

**Key to Abbreviations Used in the Street Finder**

| | | | | | | | |
|---|---|---|---|---|---|---|---|
| **d.** | di, del, dell', dello, della, dei, de', delle, degli | **Lung.** | Lungarno | **P.te** | Ponte | **V.** | Via |
| | | **P.** | Piazza | **S.** | San, Sant', Santa, Santo | **Vic.** | Vicolo |
| | | **P.ta** | Porta | **SS.** | Santi, Santissima | **V.le** | Viale |

Map references in parentheses refer to the larger scale map.

# Tuscany Area by Area

# Tuscany at a Glance

TUSCANY IS RICH IN CULTURE and landscape. Out of Florence, most visitors' first port of call is Pisa, in Western Tuscany, with its Leaning Tower. Northern Tuscany has mountains and beaches, and Eastern Tuscany the lush forests of the Mugello. Siena and San Gimignano in Central Tuscany draw their own visitors, while Southern Tuscany, with its sparse vegetation and unspoiled beaches, is more off the beaten track.

Sights in Tuscany are grouped within their own sections in this book, corresponding with the color-coded map below.

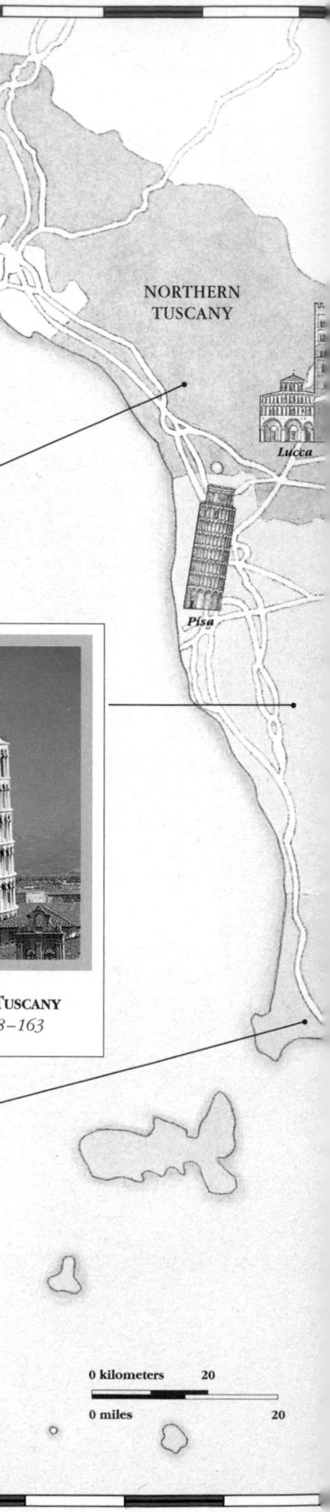

**NORTHERN TUSCANY**
*Pages 164–185*

**WESTERN TUSCANY**
*Pages 148–163*

**SOUTHERN TUSCANY**
*Pages 226–237*

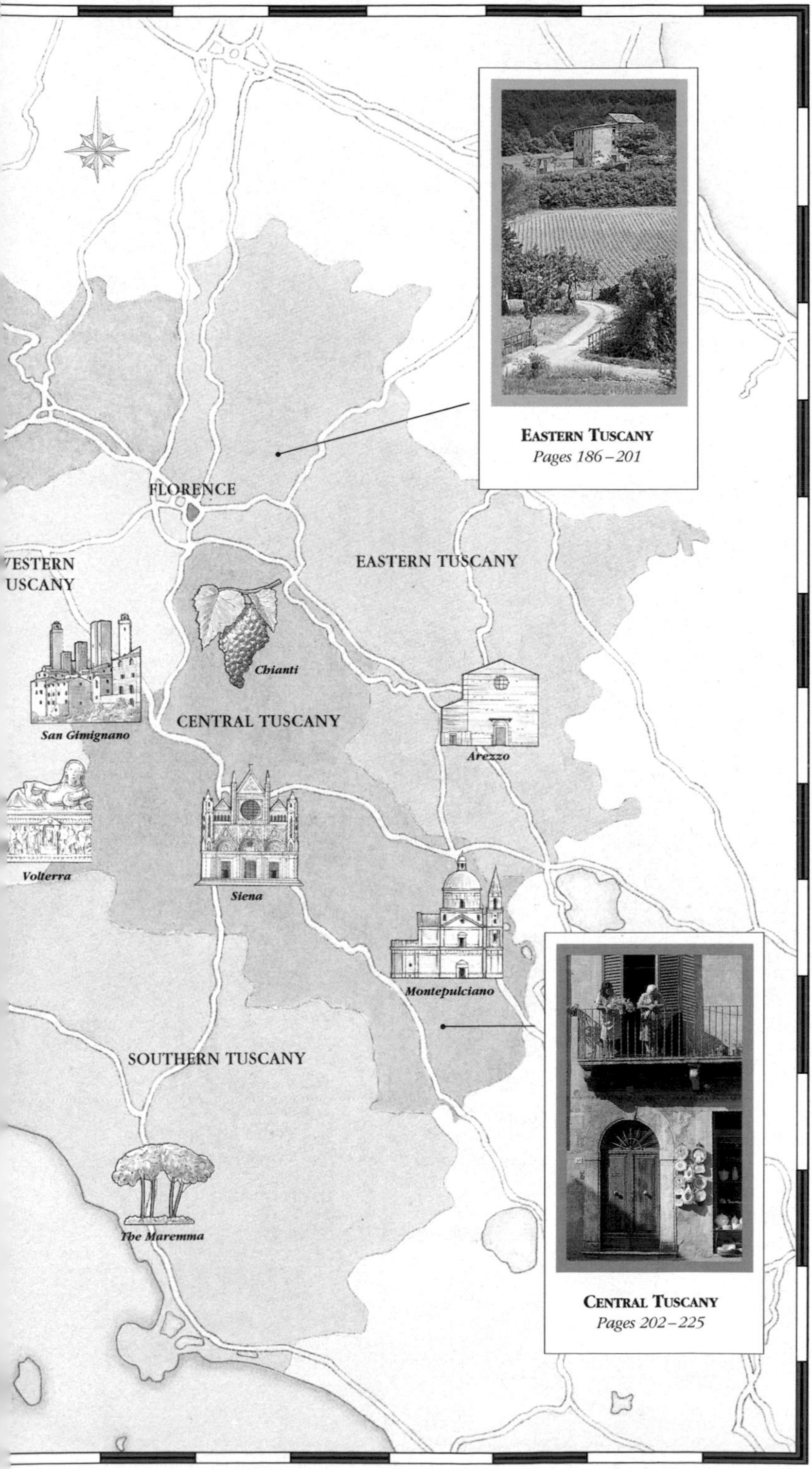
EASTERN TUSCANY
Pages 186–201
FLORENCE
EASTERN TUSCANY
WESTERN
TUSCANY
Chianti
San Gimignano
CENTRAL TUSCANY
Arezzo
Volterra
Siena
Montepulciano
SOUTHERN TUSCANY
The Maremma
CENTRAL TUSCANY
Pages 202–225

# WESTERN TUSCANY

TUSCANY'S HARDWORKING ECONOMIC ENGINE, *this area is characterized by its factories and ports, particularly Livorno. There are also some extraordinary sights, most famously the Leaning Tower of Pisa. To the south, the windswept ancient Etruscan town of Volterra, standing high on a barren plateau, has some of the finest museums and medieval architecture in Italy.*

From the 11th to the 13th centuries, when at the height of its powers, Pisa dominated the Western Mediterranean. Its strong navy opened up extensive trading links with North Africa, and brought to Italy the benefits of Arabic scientific and artistic achievement.

These new ideas had a profound effect on 12th- and 13th-century architects working in western Tuscany. Many of the era's splendid buildings, for instance Pisa's Duomo, Baptistry and Campanile, are decorated with complex geometric patterns made from beautiful inlaid marble, alternating with bizarre arabesques.

During the 16th century the Arno estuary began to silt up, ending Pisan supremacy. In 1571, work began to establish Livorno as the region's main port. This proved so successful that it remains Italy's second-busiest port. Pisa, meanwhile, has become the gateway to Tuscany following the extensive development of Galileo Galilei airport. The Arno valley is mainly an industrial area, with huge factories producing glass, furniture, motorcycles, leather and textiles. Even so, there are some rewarding sights lurking within the urban sprawl, like the Romanesque church of San Piero a Grado or the entertaining museum in Vinci, which contains models of many of Leonardo da Vinci's brilliant inventions.

South of the Arno valley, the landscape is pleasant but unremarkable, consisting of rolling hills and expanses of agricultural land. But the imposing ancient town of Volterra, with its unmatched collection of Etruscan artifacts, demands a visit.

**Landscape of rolling hills near Volterra**

◁ **The Leaning Tower, rising above the terra-cotta roofs of Pisa**

# Exploring Western Tuscany

PISA, WITH ITS WORLD-FAMOUS LEANING TOWER, and Volterra, with a wealth of ancient Etruscan remains, are the highlights of the region. There is, however, much more to see, especially in the gentle hilly countryside that rises on either side of the Arno valley. It was here that Renaissance architects pioneered new styles of villa building; their work can be admired at Poggio a Caiano and Artimino. San Miniato is gloriously sited on a hilltop commanding extensive views; the museum in Vinci, on the other side of the valley, celebrates the inventive genius of Leonardo da Vinci.

## Sights at a Glance

- Artimino ⓫
- Capraia ❼
- Certosa di Pisa ❺
- Empoli ❾
- Livorno ❻
- Marina di Pisa ❸
- Pisa ❶
- Poggio a Caiano ⓬
- San Miniato ❽
- San Piero a Grado ❹
- Tenuta di San Rossore ❷
- Vinci ❿
- Volterra ⓭

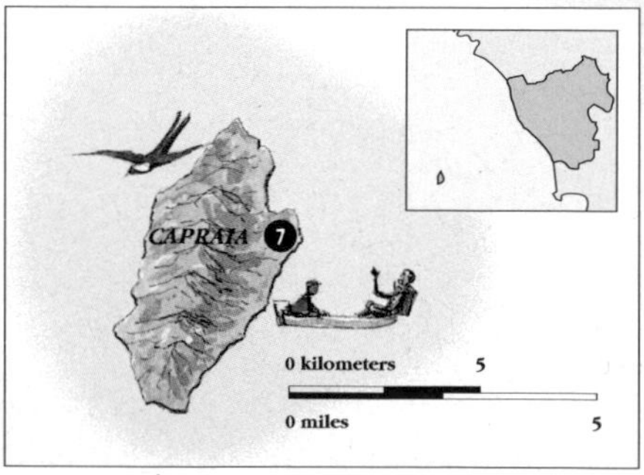

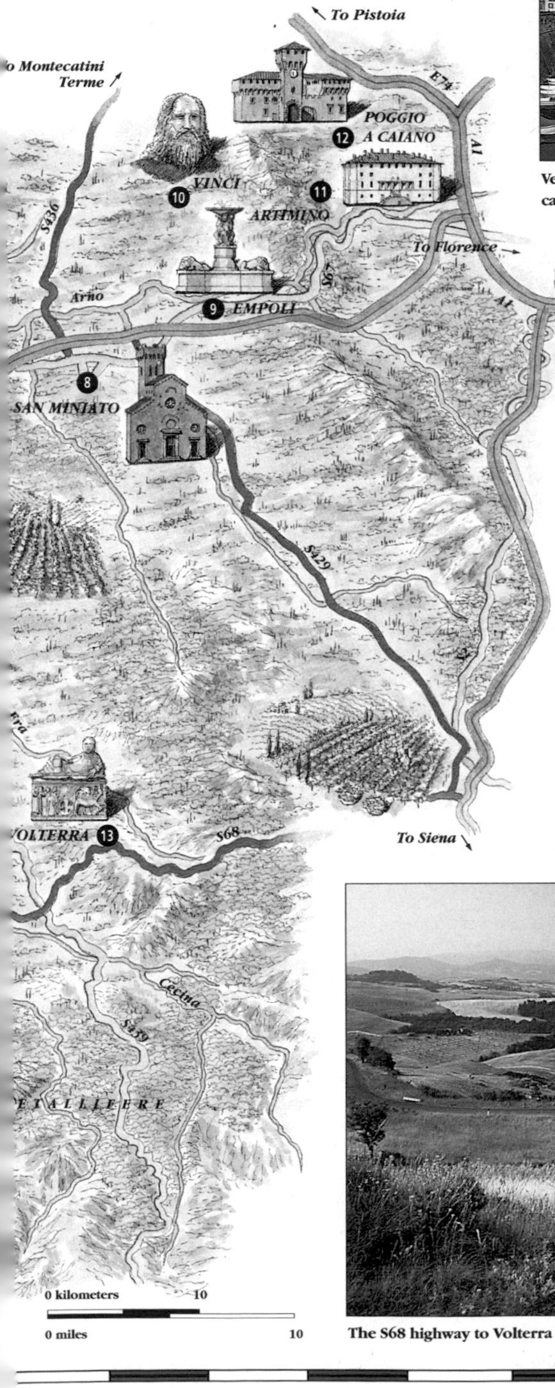

**Venezia Nuova in Livorno, with its canals and waterways**

## Getting Around

Western Tuscany has a number of busy roads. A new express route links Pisa with Florence, but travelers may find the old S67 a more convenient way of reaching the sights lining the Arno valley toward Florence. The S1 coastal road skirts Livorno on its way to Rome.

The region is well served by buses and trains. A regular rail service runs between Florence and Pisa, stopping at the major Arno valley towns.

It can be difficult to reach Volterra, as there is no train service, but several buses depart each day from Florence, Pisa and Livorno.

### Key

- Highway
- Major road
- Minor road
- River

**The S68 highway to Volterra**

# Pisa ❶

**Inlaid marble, Duomo façade**

FROM THE 11TH TO THE 13TH CENTURIES, Pisa's navy was responsible for the city's dominance in the Western Mediterranean. Trading links with Spain and North Africa led to a scientific and cultural revolution *(see p44)* reflected in the splendid buildings of the era: the Duomo, Baptistry and Campanile. Pisa's decline was assured when the Arno began to silt up. Salt marsh, partly a nature reserve, now divides the city from the sea.

**Campo dei Miracoli**

### Campo dei Miracoli

*See pp154–5.*

### Museo delle Sinopie

Piazza del Duomo. (050) 56 05 47. ***Open** daily. **Adm charge.***

This fascinating museum displays sketches from the fresco cycle that once covered the walls of the Camposanto cemetery *(see pp154–5).*

The frescoes, by a number of artists, disintegrated when the cemetery was bombed in 1944, although the underlying sketches survived. They were removed from the walls for conservation before being rehoused in the museum. There are also displays showing how fresco artists went about their work.

### Museo dell'Opera del Duomo

Piazza Arcivescovado 6. *(050) 56 18 20. **Open** daily. **Adm charge.***

Housed in the cathedral's 13th-century former Chapter House, the museum was opened in 1986. All the exhibits were formerly in the Duomo and Baptistry, but they are now excellently presented in new modern displays. Exhibits such as the intricately inlaid marble arabesque panels and fine Corinthian capitals reveal the twin influences of Rome and Islam on Pisan architects in the 12th and 13th centuries. Be sure to see the imposing 10th-century hippogriff (half horse, half gryphon); this statue, cast in bronze by Islamic craftsmen, was looted by Pisan adventurers during the wars against the Saracens.

The museum also contains 13th-century statues and sculptures by Nicola and Giovanni Pisano, including Giovanni's ivory *Virgin and Child* (1300) carved for the Duomo's High Altar. There are paintings from the 15th to 18th centuries, a fine Roman and Etruscan archaeological collection, and ecclesiastical treasures and vestments dating from the 12th century.

The museum cloister offers a wonderful view of the Leaning Tower *(see p156).*

**10th-century bronze hippogriff**

### Piazza dei Cavalieri

The Piazza dei Cavalieri stands at the heart of Pisa's student quarter. The huge building on the north side of the square, covered in exuberant black and white *sgraffito* decoration (designs scratched into wet plaster), is the Palazzo dei Cavalieri and houses one of Pisa University's most prestigious colleges: the Scuola Normale Superiore.

The site was originally occupied by Pisa's medieval town hall, but Cosimo I ordered its destruction when the city fell under Florentine rule. The council chamber, however, was spared and is now a lecture hall. The present flamboyant building was designed by Vasari in 1562, as the headquarters of the Cavalieri di San Stefano, an order of knights created by Cosimo in 1561. An equestrian statue of Cosimo by Pietro Francavilla (1596) stands outside. Santo Stefano dei

***Virgin and Child*** **polyptych (1321) by Simone Martini**

**VISITORS' CHECKLIST**

**Road map** B2. 98,929. Galileo Galilei. FS Pisa Centrale, Viale Gramsci. Piazza del Duomo. (050) 56 04 64. Piazza della Stazione. (050) 422 91. Wed, Sat. ***Shops closed*** *Mon morning.* *Gioco del Ponte* (see p36).

Cavalieri (1565–9), the knights' church, stands next to the Palazzo dei Cavalieri. Also designed by Vasari, it has a splendid gilded and coffered ceiling. The walls are hung with figureheads and battle standards. There is also a splendid organ (look for notices of recitals).

On the other side of the Palazzo dei Cavalieri is the Palazzo dell'Orologio, incorporating the medieval town jail. The building, now a library, was the scene of a most shameful historical episode. In 1288 Count Ugolino, mayor of Pisa, was accused of treachery and walled up with his sons and grandsons. The entire male side of the Ugolino family was wiped out.

### Museo Nazionale di San Matteo

Lungarno Mediceo. *(050) 54 18 65.* ***Open*** *Tue–Sun.* ***Adm charge.***

The medieval convent of San Matteo, with its elegant Gothic façade, is located alongside the Arno. For many years, the museum inside has been partially closed. A large number of the exhibits are poorly labeled and the various rooms leading off the peaceful cloister are unnumbered. Nevertheless, the museum presents a unique opportunity to examine the vast range of Pisan and Florentine art from the 12th to the 17th centuries.

Most of the earliest works portray the Virgin and Child. These include Simone Martini's fine polyptych (1321) and a 14th-century statue, the *Madonna del Latte*, attributed to Nino Pisano, another member of the talented family of sculptors. The half-length statue, in gilded marble, shows Christ feeding at his mother's breast. A number of early Renaissance pieces deserve to be sought out, particularly Masaccio's *St. Paul* (1426), Gentile da Fabriano's radiant 15th-century *Madonna and Child*, and Donatello's reliquary bust of *San Rossore* (1424–7).

**Grand Duke Cosimo I**

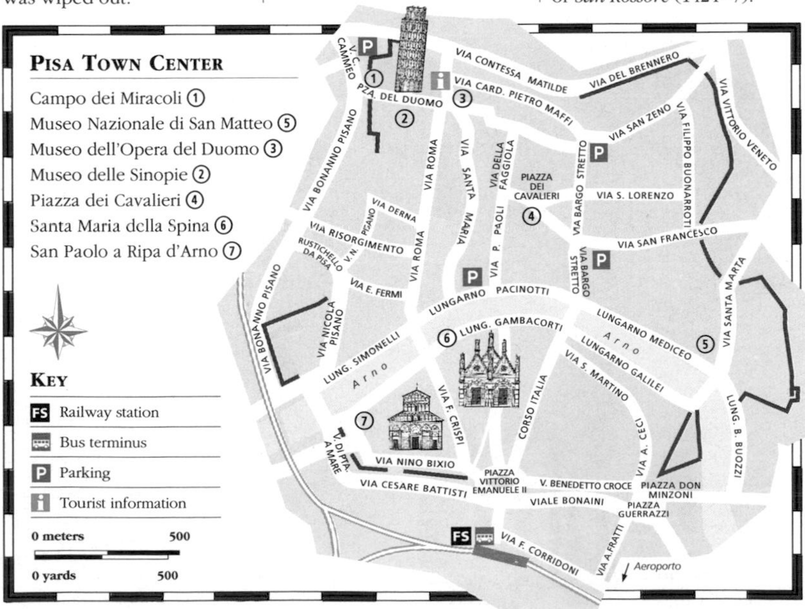

# Campo dei Miracoli

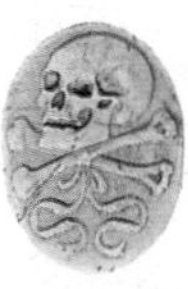

**Cemetery memorial**

PISA'S WORLD-FAMOUS Leaning Tower is just one of the splendid religious buildings that rise from the emerald green lawns of the "Field of Miracles." Lying to the northwest of the city center, it is partnered by the Duomo, begun in 1063, the Baptistry of 1152–1284 and the Campo Santo cemetery begun in 1278. These buildings combine definite Moorish elements, such as inlaid marble in geometric patterns (arabesques), with delicate Romanesque colonnading and spiky Gothic niches and pinnacles.

**Campo Santo**
*The cemetery contains earth from the Holy Land and carved Roman sarcophagi.*

**The Triumph of Death**
*These late 14th-century frescoes depict various allegorical scenes, such as this of a knight and lady overwhelmed by the stench of an open grave.*

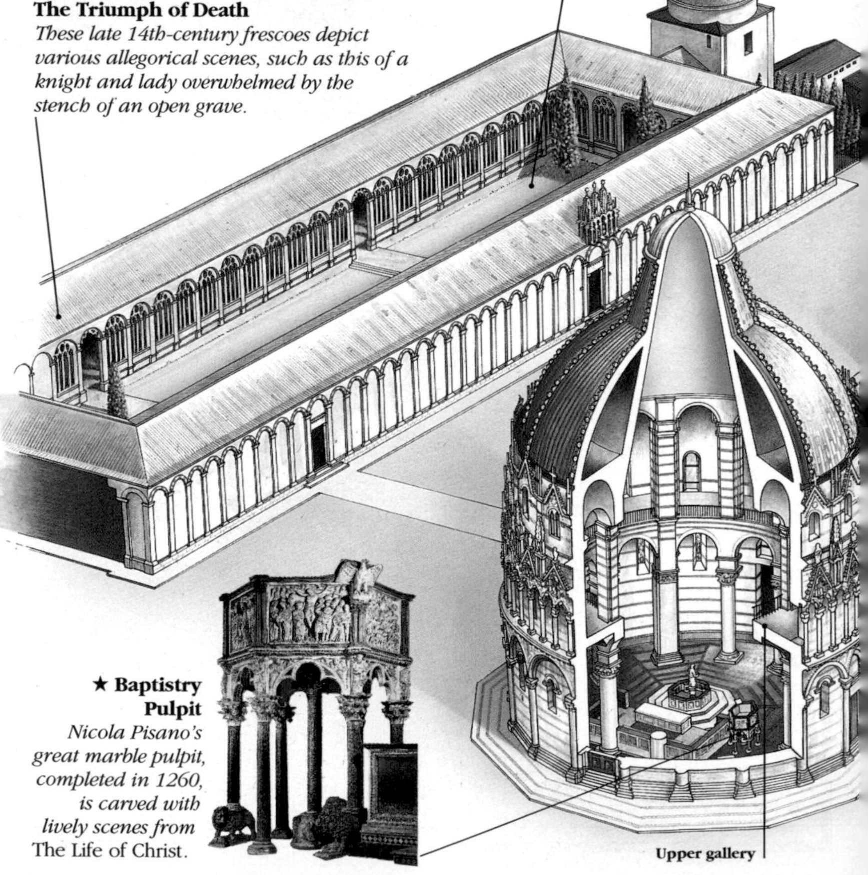


**★ Baptistry Pulpit**
*Nicola Pisano's great marble pulpit, completed in 1260, is carved with lively scenes from* The Life of Christ.

**★ Portale di San Ranieri**
*Bonanno Pisano's bronze panels for the south transept doors depict* The Life of Christ. *Palm trees and Moorish buildings show Arabic influence.*

**VISITORS' CHECKLIST**

Piazza dei Miracoli. *(050) 56 09 21.* *1.* **Duomo open** *7:45am–12:45pm, 3–6:45pm (Nov–Feb: 3–4:45pm).* *8am, 9am, 9:30am Mon–Fri, 8am, 9am, 10am, 11am, noon Sat & Sun.* **Baptistry and Campo Santo open** *8am–7:40pm (Nov–Feb: 9am–4:40pm).* **Leaning Tower** ***not open*** *to the public.*

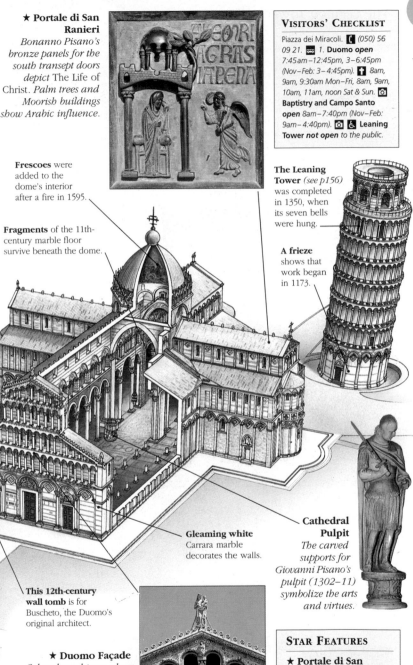

**Frescoes** were added to the dome's interior after a fire in 1595.

**Fragments** of the 11th-century marble floor survive beneath the dome.

**The Leaning Tower** *(see p156)* was completed in 1350, when its seven bells were hung.

**A frieze** shows that work began in 1173.

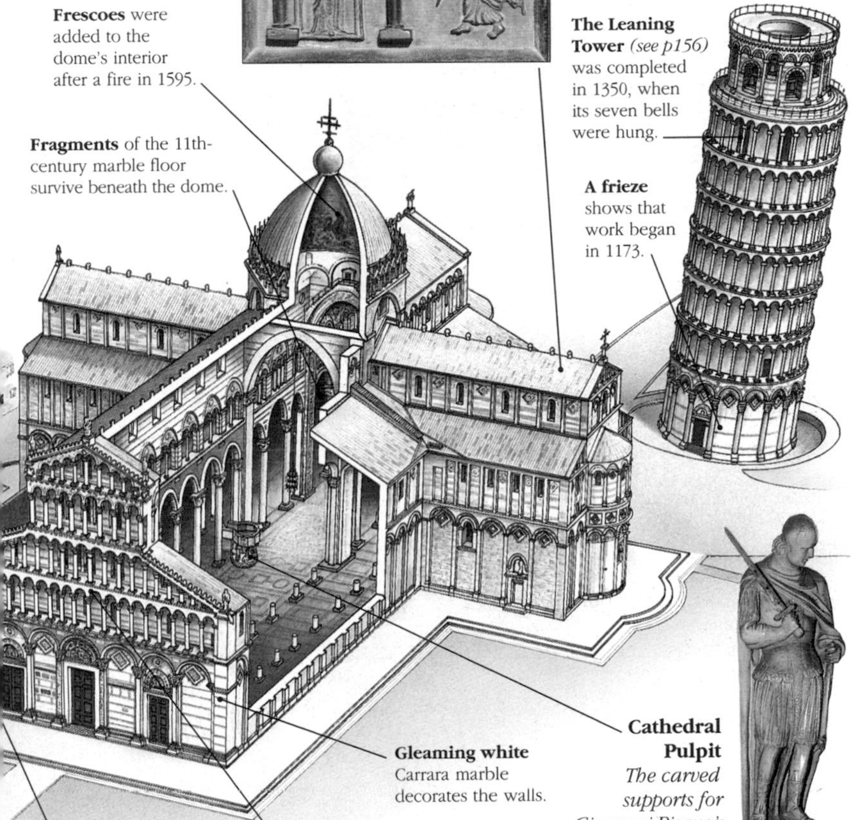

**Cathedral Pulpit**
*The carved supports for Giovanni Pisano's pulpit (1302–11) symbolize the arts and virtues.*

**Gleaming white** Carrara marble decorates the walls.

**This 12th-century wall tomb** is for Buscheto, the Duomo's original architect.

**★ Duomo Façade**
*Colored sandstone, glass and majolica plates decorate the flamboyant 12th-century façade. Its patterned surface includes knots, flowers and animals in inlaid marble.*

**STAR FEATURES**

- **★ Portale di San Ranieri**
- **★ Baptistry Pulpit by Nicola Pisano**
- **★ Duomo Façade**

# The Leaning Tower of Pisa

All the buildings of the Campo dei Miracoli lean because of their shallow foundations and sandy silt subsoil, but none tilts so famously as the Torre Pendente – the Leaning Tower. Begun in 1173, the tower began to tip sideways before the third story was completed. Even so, construction continued until its completion in 1350. Recently the tilt has increased, so the tower is closed to the public until ways to prevent further leaning – and total collapse – are found.

**Belfry**
*The bell chamber at the top of the tower is smaller in diameter than the other seven stories. Its addition in 1350 brought the total height to 54.5 m (179 ft).*

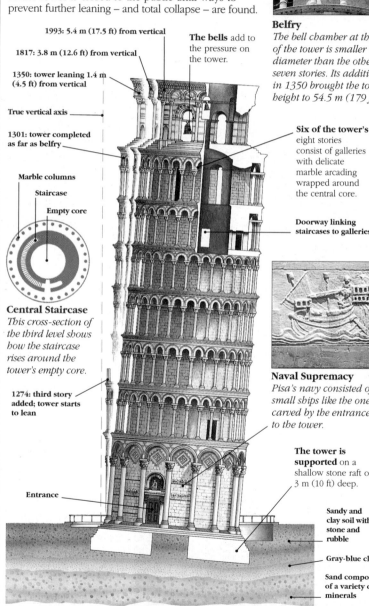

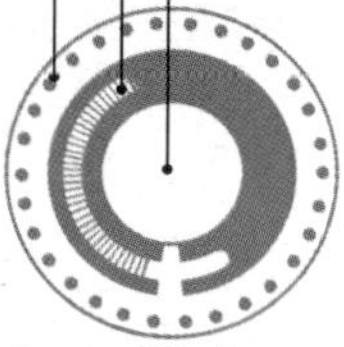


**Central Staircase**
*This cross-section of the third level shows how the staircase rises around the tower's empty core.*

**Naval Supremacy**
*Pisa's navy consisted of small ships like the one carved by the entrance to the tower.*

**Santa Maria della Spina by the river Arno in Pisa**

### Santa Maria della Spina

Lungarno Gambacorti. (050) 53 24 74. **Open** *by appt.*

The roofline of this tiny church bristles with spiky Gothic pinnacles, miniature spires and niches sheltering statues of apostles and saints. All of this is highly appropriate for a church that was built to house an unusual precious relic: a thorn taken from the Crown of Thorns forced onto Christ's head during the cruel mock coronation that preceded His crucifixion.

### San Paolo a Ripa d'Arno

Piazza San Paolo a Ripa d'Arno. (050) 415 15. **Open** *by appt.*

Worth visiting almost solely for its impressive 12th-century façade, this church was built in the same Pisan Romanesque style as the Duomo *(see pp154–5)*.

The Romanesque chapel *(see p42)* at the east end is dedicated to St. Agatha. Built entirely from bricks, with a cone-shaped roof, Islamic influence is said to account for its highly distinctive octagonal shape.

## Tenuta di San Rossore ❷

**Road map** B2. *Pisa.* *(050) 52 55 00.* **Open** *Sun and public hols.*

NORTH OF THE ARNO, the Tenuta di San Rossore is part of a vast nature reserve, the Parco Naturale di San Rossore, stretching to the north of Tuscany. Wild boar and deer are rumored to roam among the pine forests and salt marsh. Gombo, to the west, is where the English poet Shelley's drowned body was found in 1822. His friends built his funeral pyre there.

## Marina di Pisa ❸

**Road map** B2. *3,000.* *Sun in summer, Tue in winter.*

**Moorings at Marina di Pisa, at the mouth of the river Arno**

MUCH OF THE salt marsh to the west of Pisa has now been drained and reclaimed, and a large US Air Force base (Camp Darby) now occupies the area south of the Arno. There are extensive sandy beaches on the Arno estuary, and here lies Marina di Pisa, a seaside resort with some pretty Art Nouveau houses, backed by pine woods.

On the drive there you may catch sight of grazing camels – these are the descendants of a large herd established under Duke Ferdinand II in the mid-17th century. The village of Tirrenia, with its sandy beaches, lies 5 km (3 miles) south of Marina di Pisa.

## San Piero a Grado ❹

**Road map** B2. ***Open*** *daily.*

SAN PIERO is a handsome 11th-century church built on the spot where St. Peter is supposed to have first set foot on Italian soil in AD 42. According to the Book of Acts in the New Testament, he arrived at a set of landing steps by the Arno. Archaeologists have discovered the foundations of Roman port buildings underneath the present church, which stands at the point where the Arno once flowed into the sea. Silt deposits mean that the church now stands some 6 km (3.5 miles) from the shore.

An unusual feature of the church is the lack of any façade. Instead, it has semicircular apses at both the east and west ends. The exterior is decorated with blind arcading and with Moorish-style ceramic plates set into the masonry around the eaves – a decoration that it shares with the Duomo in San Miniato *(see p159)*.

The present church was built during the reign of Pope John XVIII (1004–9) and the varied capitals of the nave come from ancient Roman buildings. High up on the nave walls there are frescoes by Deodato Orlandi, painted around 1300, on *The Life of St. Peter*. These are interspersed with portraits of all the popes from St. Peter to John XVII.

**Interior of San Piero a Grado, with frescoes by Deodati Orlandi**

**The 18th-century Certosa di Pisa**

## Certosa di Pisa ⑤

**Road map** C2. *from Pisa.* *(050) 93 84 30.* ***Open** by appt.* ***Adm charge**.*

FOUNDED in 1366, this Carthusian monastery was rebuilt in flamboyant late Baroque style during the 18th century. The splendid church is richly decorated with frescoes, stuccowork and colorful marble.

Part of the monastery buildings are devoted to the University of Pisa's **Museo di Storia Naturale**. Exhibits include anatomical wax models dating to the 16th century.

Nearby you can see the **Pieve di Calci**, a fine 11th-century Romanesque church. The unfinished campanile stands alongside.

### Museo di Storia Naturale

Certosa di Pisa. *(050) 93 70 92.* ***Open** 1st week in Dec, one week in Apr.* *partial.*

### Pieve di Calci

Piazza della Propositura, Calci. ***Open** daily.*

## Livorno ⑥

**Road map** B3. *168,370.* FS *Piazza Cavour 6. (0586) 89 81 11.* *Fri.*

THE FACT THAT LIVORNO is now a bustling city, Italy's second busiest container port, is thanks to Cosimo I. In 1571 he chose Livorno, then a tiny fishing village, as the site for Tuscany's new port after Pisa's harbor silted up. From 1607–21 the English marine engineer Sir Robert Dudley built the great sea wall that protects the harbor.

In 1608 Livorno was declared a free port, open to all traders, regardless of religion or race. Jews, Protestants, Arabs, Turks and others who came here, fleeing wars or religious persecution, contributed greatly to the city's success.

### Piazza Grande

When the architect Buontalenti planned the new city of Livorno in 1576, he envisaged the huge Piazza Grande at the heart of a network of wide avenues.

The square's original appearance has, however, been lost. This is partly due to controversial postwar rebuilding, which cut the square into two halves: the present Piazza Grande, to the south, and the Largo Municipio, to the north.

### Duomo

Piazza Grande. ***Open** daily.*

A prominent victim of Livorno's wartime bombing was the late 16th-century cathedral by Pieroni and Cantagallina. It was rebuilt in 1959, retaining the original entrance portico, with its Doric arcades.

The original building was designed by Inigo Jones, who served his apprenticeship under the architect Buontalenti. Jones later used an almost identical design for the arcades of his Covent Garden piazza in London.

### Piazza Micheli

The piazza, with its views of the 16th-century Fortezza Vecchia, contains Livorno's best-known monument: the *Monumento dei Quattro Mori*.

Bandini's bronze figure of Duke Ferdinand I dates from 1595; but Pietro Tacca's four Moorish slaves, also cast in bronze, were not added until 1626. Naked and manacled, the dejected slaves are a stark reminder that Livorno once had a thriving slave market.

**Venezia Nuova canals**

### Venezia Nuova

Originally laid out in the middle of the 17th century, this area, which includes the 18th-century octagonal church of Santa Caterina, is spread among a handful of canals, reminiscent of Venetian waterways. Although it only covers a few blocks, Venezia Nuova is one of the city's most scenic areas.

***Monumento dei Quattro Mori*** **by Bandini and Tacca in Piazza Micheli**

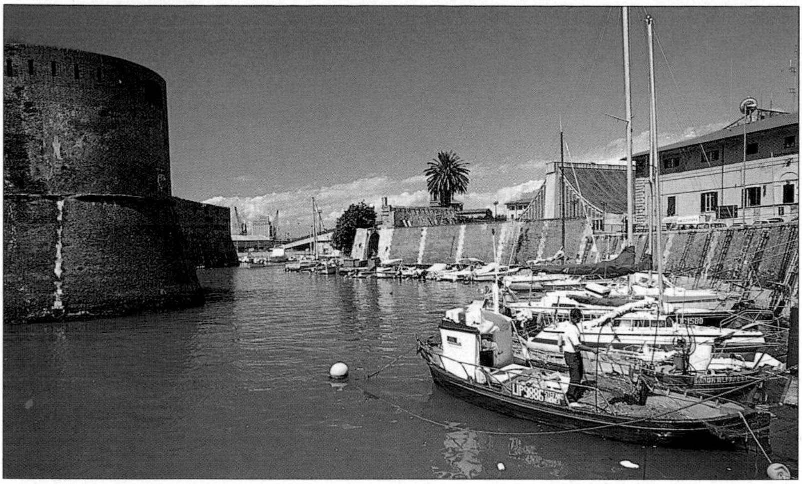

Fortezza Vecchia, Livorno harbor

The Fortezza Nuova, surrounded by a moat, dates from 1590. Its interior has been converted to a public park.

**Piazza XX Settembre**

Lying south of the Fortezza Nuova, the piazza is renowned for its bustling "American Market." The market's name derives from the large assortment of American army surplus goods that could be bought here after World War II.

A US army base, Camp Darby, still operates to the north of Livorno.

**English Cemetery**

Via Giuseppe Verdi 63. (0586) 89 73 24. **Open** by appt.

The 19th-century memorials to British and American emigrés, long untended, are considerably overgrown. Among them is the grave of Tobias Smollett (1721–71), the misanthropic Scottish novelist. He claimed to live in Italy for health reasons, but constantly complained about the place.

**Museo Civico**

Viale della Libertà 30. (0586) 80 80 01. **Open** *Tue–Sun.* **Adm charge**.

Housed in the 19th-century Villa Fabricotti, the Museo Civico contains several paintings by Giovanni Fattori (1825–1908) *(see p123)*. He was a leading artist of the *Macchiaioli* School, similar to the French Impressionists.

## Capraia 7

*from Livorno.* *300.*
*Agenzia Viaggi Parco. (0586) 90 50 71.*

THIS TINY mountainous island appeals mainly to bird watchers and divers who go to explore the rocky coastline.

Nearby Gorgona, a penal colony, can also be visited by booking in advance. Contact tourist information in Livorno.

## San Miniato 8

**Road map** C2. *3,852.*
*Piazza del Popolo 3. (0571) 427 45.* *Tue.*

SAN MINIATO SUFFERS from its proximity to the vast industrial development of the Arno valley. Straddling the crest of one of the region's highest hills, it manages, however, to remain somewhat aloof. There are a number of fine historic buildings, including the 13th-century Rocca (castle) built for Frederick II (1194–1250), the German Holy Roman Emperor.

The town played a major part in Frederick's Italian military campaigns. He dreamed of rebuilding the ancient Roman empire that lay divided between papal and Imperial authority. To this end, he conquered large areas of Italy. His battles fueled fierce local struggles between the imperial Ghibellines and the papal Guelphs *(see p44)*.

Local people still refer to the town as San Miniato *al Tedesco* (of the German).

Façade of Duomo in San Miniato

**Duomo**

Piazza del Duomo. **Open** *daily.*

Only the red-brick façade survives from the original 12th-century building. The majolica plates set within it show evidence of trade with Spain or North Africa. They seem to represent the North Star and the constellations of Ursus Major and Minor: key reference points for early navigators.

The campanile, the Torre di Matilda, is named in honor of the great Countess Matilda *(see p43)*, who was born in Livorno in 1046.

### Piazza della Repubblica

The Piazza della Repubblica (also known as the Piazza del Seminario) occupies a long, narrow space dominated by the decorated façade of the 17th-century seminary. The frescoes and *sgraffito* (scenes scratched out of plaster) on the façade show allegories of the Virtues painted below quotations from key religious texts, for instance, the writings of Pope Gregory (540–604).

To the right of the seminary are several well-restored 15th-century shops. Buildings like these can be seen in many medieval frescoes, such as Lorenzetti's 14th-century *Good Government* *(see p44)*.

**Façade of the seminary in Piazza della Repubblica**

### Museo Diocesano d'Arte Sacra

Piazza Duomo. (0571) 41 82 71. ***Open** Mar–Oct: Tue–Sun; Nov–Feb: Sat & Sun.* ***Adm charge**.*

Located next to the Duomo, the Museo Diocesano d'Arte Sacra contains a number of important 15th-century works. These include a *Crucifixion* by Filippo Lippi, a terra-cotta bust of Christ attributed to Verrocchio, and Andrea del Castagno's *Virgin of the Holy Girdle.*

### Rocca

A staircase behind the Museo Diocesano leads toward Frederick II's ruined 13th-century Rocca (castle). While the remains are run-down, the site offers extraordinary views along the entire Arno valley, from Fiesole to Pisa.

**Piazza Farinata degli Uberti in Empoli**

## Empoli 9

**Road map** C2. *43,500.* FS *Piazza Farinata degli Uberti 3. (0571) 70 78 54. Thu.*

An industrial town, specializing in textiles and glass manufacturing, Empoli is worth visiting for the excellent Museo della Collegiata.

### Piazza Farinata degli Uberti

Empoli's arcaded main square is surrounded by a number of 12th-century buildings, notably the church of Sant'Andrea, with its black and white marble façade. The large fountain dating from 1827, with water nymphs and lions, is by Luigi Pampaloni.

### Museo della Collegiata di Sant'Andrea

Piazza della Propositura. *(0571) 762 84.* ***Open** Tue–Sun.* ***Adm charge**.*

The museum contains an unusually rich collection of Renaissance paintings and sculpture. Of particular interest are Masolino's *Pietà* fresco (1425) and a marble font by Rossellino, dating from 1447.

***Pietà* by Masolino in Museo della Collegiata**

### Santo Stefano

Via dei Neri. ***Open** Sat & Sun (at Mass) or by appt.*

Visitors to Santo Stefano can see fresco fragments by Masolino, dating from 1424, and two 15th-century Annunciation statues by Rossellino. Bicci di Lorenzo's painting, *St. Nicholas of Tolentino* (1445), in the second chapel on the north side, shows Empoli as it was in the mid-15th century.

## Vinci 10

**Road map** C2. *2,000. Piazza del Castello. (0571) 560 55. Wed.*

This hilltop town was the birthplace of Leonardo da Vinci (1452–1519). To celebrate his genius, the 13th-century castle in the center of the town was restored in 1952 to create the **Museo Leonardiano**. Among the displays are wooden models of Leonardo's machines and inventions, based on drawings from his notebooks, shown alongside. These range from his conception of a car, to an armored tank and even a machine gun. A pair of skis, designed for walking on water, show that he could occasionally miss the mark. The museum is best avoided on Sundays, when it can be extremely crowded.

Close to the museum is Santo Stefano church and the font in which Leonardo was baptized. His actual birthplace, the **Casa di Leonardo**, is 2 km (1.25 miles) from the town center at Anchiano. This simple farmhouse is worth visiting if you feel like a pleasant, undemanding walk through some beautiful poppy fields; but don't expect to find a major collection on display. The main exhibits are a few reproduction drawings and explanatory panels.

**Museo Leonardiano**
Castello dei Conti Guidi. *(0571) 560 55.* ***Open*** *daily.* ***Adm charge.***

**Casa di Leonardo**
Anchiano. *(0571) 560 55.*
***Open*** *Thu–Tue.*

**Model bicycle based on drawings by Leonardo, Museo Leonardiano**

## Artimino ⓫

**Road map** C2. *Tue.*

ARTIMINO IS A FINE example of a *borgo*, a small fortified hamlet. Despite its proximity to the big industrial conglomerations of Florence and Prato, the stupendous views from this hilltop site are of wooded green hills, with not a factory in sight.

The hamlet itself is only remarkable for the unspoiled Romanesque church of San Leonardo. Outside the walls, however, higher up the hill, lies the **Villa di Artimino**, designed by Buontalenti in 1594 for Grand Duke Ferdinando I. It is often referred to as the "Villa of a Hundred Chimneys," because of the numerous and highly ornate chimney pots crowding the roofline. The building is today used as a conference center, but the Museo Archeologico Etrusco in the basement, which exhibits Etruscan and Roman artifacts from nearby excavations, is open to the public.

Lovers of the work of Pontormo (1494–1557) should set aside time to visit the church of **San Michele** in Carmignano, only 5 km (3 miles) north of Artimino. It contains his great masterpiece, *The Visitation* (1530).

**Villa di Artimino**
*(055) 879 20 40 (villa), 871 81 24 (museum).* **Villa *open*** *by appt.*
**Museo Archeologico Etrusco *open*** *Thu–Tue.* ***Adm charge.***

**San Michele**
Piazza SS. Francesco e Michele 1, Carmignano. ***Open*** *daily.*

## Poggio a Caiano ⓬

**Road map** C2. *(055) 87 70 12.* ***Open*** *daily.* ***Adm charge.***

THE VILLA di Poggio a Caiano, built by Giuliano da Sangallo for Lorenzo de' Medici *(see p48)* in 1480, was the first Italian villa to be designed in the Renaissance style. Its original severity is now softened by the graceful, curved staircase (added in 1802–7) leading up to the villa terrace, with its views of the gardens and parkland beyond.

**Villa di Artimino**

The villa's principal room is the barrel-vaulted *salone*, with its 16th-century frescoes by Andrea del Sarto and Franciabigio. They were commissioned by the future Leo X, the Medici pope, to portray his family as great statesmen in the manner of such ancient Roman figures as Julius Caesar and Cicero.

The *salone* also contains Pontormo's colorful *Conette* fresco (1521). Surrounding the circular window of the end wall, it portrays the Roman garden deities, Vertumnus and Pomona – a perfect evocation of a Tuscan summer afternoon.

Among the other rooms is the bedchamber of Bianca Cappello, mistress and later wife of Grand Duke Francesco I. The couple died here within a few hours of each other, presumably poisoned. They may, however, simply have succumbed to a lethal viral infection.

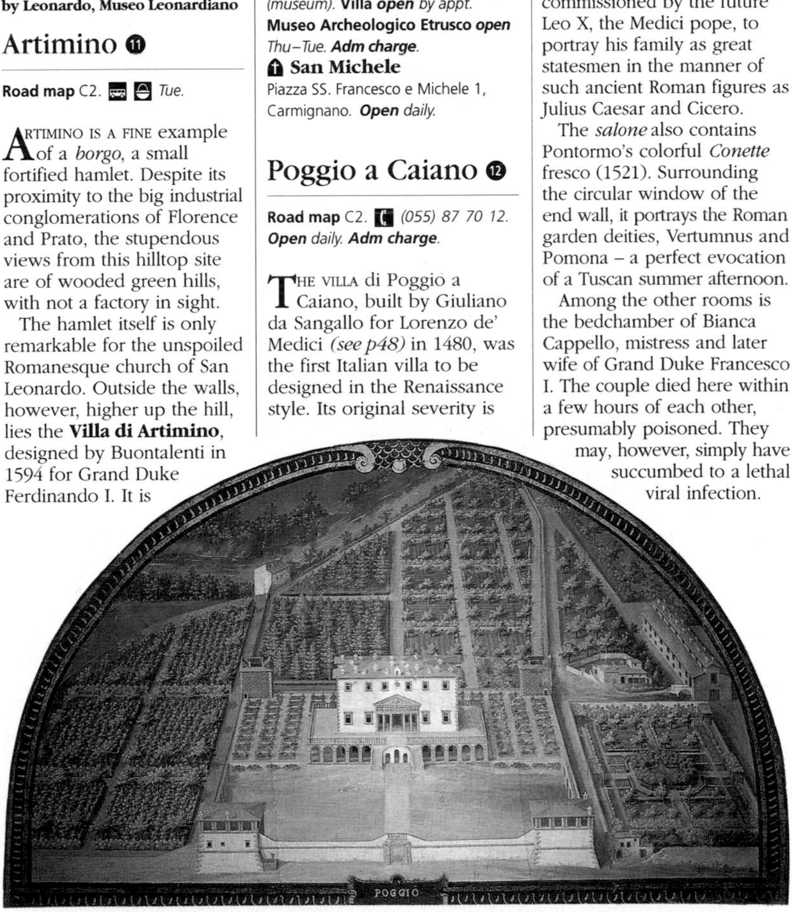


***Villa di Poggio a Caiano*** **from the set of lunettes by Giusto Utens** ***(see p71)***

# Volterra ⓭

**Stucco figure in the Duomo**

SITUATED, LIKE MANY ETRUSCAN CITIES, on a high plateau, Volterra offers uninterrupted views over the surrounding hills. In many places the ancient Etruscan walls still stand. Volterra's famous Museo Guarnacci contains one of the best collections of Etruscan artifacts in Italy. Many of the exhibits were gathered from the numerous local tombs. After its museums and medieval buildings, the city is famous for its craftsmen who carve beautiful white statues from locally mined alabaster.

### Museo Etrusco Guarnacci

Via Don Minzoni 15. (0588) 863 47.
**Open** *daily.* **Adm charge.** *partial.*

***Ombra della Sera***

The pride of the Guarnacci Museum is its collection of 600 Etruscan funerary urns. Adorned with detailed carving, they offer a unique insight into Etruscan customs and beliefs *(see pp40–41).*

The museum's two principal exhibits are located on the first floor. Room 20 contains the terra-cotta "Married Couple" urn. The elderly couple on the lid are portrayed extremely realistically, with strikingly haggard and careworn faces.

Room 22 contains an even more unusual exhibit, the elongated bronze figure known as the *Ombra della Sera* (Shadow of the Evening). This intriguing name was bestowed by the poet Gabriele d'Annunzio, who said the bronze reminded him of the shadow thrown by a human figure in the dying light of the evening sun. It is probably a votive figure dating to the 3rd century BC, but it is difficult to date it with any certainty; unusually, it was cast with no clothes or jewelry to indicate rank, status or date. It is only by chance that this remarkable figure has managed to survive. It was plowed up by a farmer in 1879 and used as a fireplace poker until someone recognized it as a masterpiece of Etruscan art.

**Detail from *The Deposition* (1521) by Rosso Fiorentino**

### Pinacoteca e Museo Civico

Via dei Sarti 1. (0588) 875 80.
**Open** *daily.* **Adm charge.**

Volterra's excellent art gallery is situated in the 15th-century Palazzo Minucci-Solaini.

The best works are by Florentine artists. Ghirlandaio's *Christ in Majesty* (1492) shows Christ hovering above an idealized Tuscan landscape. The San Giusto monastery, for which it was intended, was abandoned after a landslide like the one shown in the middle distance and beyond. Luca Signorelli's *Madonna and Child with Saints* (1491) states his debt to Roman art through the reliefs on the base of the Virgin's throne. His *Annunciation,* painted in the same year, is a beautifully balanced composition.

The museum's main exhibit is Rosso Fiorentino's *The Deposition* (1521) – a major Mannerist painting *(see p25).* Attention is focused on the grief-stricken figures in the foreground and the pallid, empty shell of Christ's body, its dead weight symbolizing that His spirit is elsewhere.

### Duomo

Piazza San Giovanni. **Open** *daily.*

Work on Volterra's cathedral began in the 1200s and continued intermittently over the next two centuries.

To the right of the high altar stands a Romanesque wood carving of *The Deposition* (1228). The altar itself is flanked by graceful marble angels carved by Mino da Fiesole in 1471; they face the same artist's elegant tabernacle, carved with figures of Faith, Hope and Charity.

The nave, remodeled in 1581, has an unusual coffered ceiling with stucco figures of bishops and saints painted in rich blue and gold. The pulpit, in the middle of the nave, dates to 1584, but was created using sculptural reliefs from the late 12th and early 13th centuries. The *Last Supper* panel, facing into the nave and thought to be the work of the Pisan artist Guglielmo

**View from Volterra over the surrounding landscape**

**Detail from one of the panels decorating the Duomo pulpit**

Pisano, has a number of humorous details, including a monster snapping at the heels of Judas. Nearby, in the north aisle, Fra Bartolomeo's *The Annunciation* (1497) hangs above one of the side chapel altars.

More sculptures are housed in the oratory off the north aisle, near the main entrance. The best is a tableau of the Epiphany, preserved behind glass. The remarkably humane painted terra-cotta figures of the Virgin and Child in the foreground are believed to be by Zaccaria da Volterra (1473–1544), a local sculptor.

### Museo d'Arte Sacra

Via Roma 13. *(0588) 862 90.*
***Open** daily. **Adm charge.***

This museum, housed in the Palazzo Arcivescovile, contains a variety of sculpture and architectural fragments removed from the Duomo and a number of local churches. The most important exhibit is a 15th-century della Robbia terra-cotta of St. Linus, Volterra's patron saint.

The collection also has a range of church bells from the 11th to 15th centuries, some church silver and several illuminated manuscripts.

### Teatro Romano

Viale Ferrucci. *(0588) 860 50.*
***Open** mid-Mar–Nov daily.*
***Adm charge.***

Situated just outside the city walls, the ancient Roman theater, dating to the first century BC, is one of the best preserved in Italy. Enough of the original structure, for instance the 5-meter-high (16.5 ft) Corinthian columns, has survived to enable an almost complete reconstruction.

## VISITORS' CHECKLIST

**Road map** C3. *12,871.*
*Via Giusto Turazza 2. (0588) 861 50. Sat. Astiludio (1st Sun in Sep).*

### Piazza dei Priori

This fine square, with excellent views of the Roman theater, is dominated by the Palazzo dei Priori, dating to 1208. A sober building, it is said to have been the model for the Palazzo Vecchio in Florence *(see pp78–9).*

The 13th-century Porcellino tower, on the other side of the square, is named after the small pig, now almost worn away, carved at its base.

**Plaque outside the Palazzo dei Priori**

### Arco Etrusco

One of Volterra's more unusual sights, the Etruscan arch is in fact part Roman. Only the columns and the severely weathered basalt heads, representing Etruscan gods, date to the 6th century BC original. The features of each head are now barely visible.

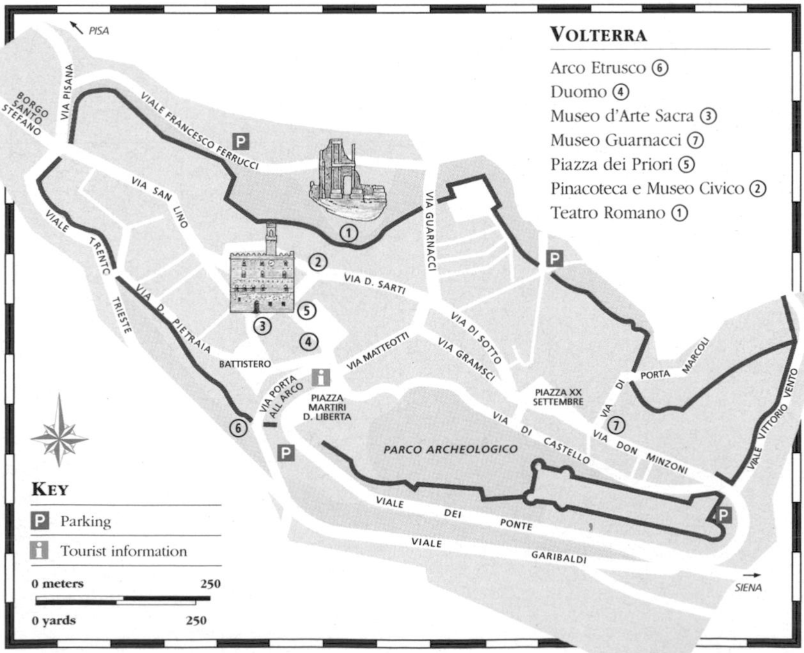

# NORTHERN TUSCANY

OF ALL THE REGIONS OF TUSCANY, *this one offers something for everyone. The historic towns are rich in art, architecture and music festivals, while many sporting activities can be enjoyed along the coast or in the mountains. The landscape, too, is marked by a vast range of features, from marble quarries to market gardens, and from mountain ranges and nature reserves to beaches.*

The heavily populated Lucchese plain between Florence and Lucca is dominated by industry: the textile factories of Prato produce three out of every four woolen garments exported from Italy. But in spite of their large suburbs, cities such as Prato, Pistoia and, above all, Lucca have rewarding churches, museums and galleries within their historic city centers.

The land between the cities is fertile and is therefore intensively cultivated. Asparagus and cut flowers are two of the most important crops, and the wholesale flower market at Pescia is one of the biggest in Italy. East of Lucca toward Pescia are garden centers and nurseries where huge quantities of young trees and shrubs are grown in long, neat rows.

North of the Lucchese plain the scenery is very different again. A series of foothills is covered in olive groves that produce some of the finest oil in Italy. Then, the land rises up to the wild and mountainous areas of the Garfagnana, the Alpi Apuane (Apuan Alps) and the Lunigiana, with its fortified towns and castles built by the Dukes of Malaspina. Here you will find some of Tuscany's highest peaks, rising to 2,000 m (6,550 ft) or more. Vast areas of the mountains are designated as nature parks and the wild scenery attracts ramblers, trekkers and riders as well as hang-gliding enthusiasts.

Finally, the coastal area, known as the Versilia, includes some of Italy's most elegant and popular beach resorts. It stretches from the famous marble-quarrying town of Carrara in the north down to the area's main town, Viareggio, and to Torre del Lago Puccini, the lakeside home of Giacomo Puccini, where he wrote nearly all his operas.

**Lucca's Piazza del Mercato, echoing the shape of the original Roman amphitheater**

◁ **The village of Vagli di Sotto on Lago di Vagli in the Parco Naturale delle Alpi Apuane**

# Exploring Northern Tuscany

THE BEAUTIFUL TOWN of Lucca is a favorite base for exploring. Northward, industrial suburbs give way to the olive groves, chestnut woods and bare mountains of the Alpi Apuane and the Garfagnana region, a popular area for outdoor sports, from trekking and canoeing to skiing. Castles dot the rugged Lunigiana, while beaches line the Versilia. Due east are large towns with historic centers: Pistoia and Prato.

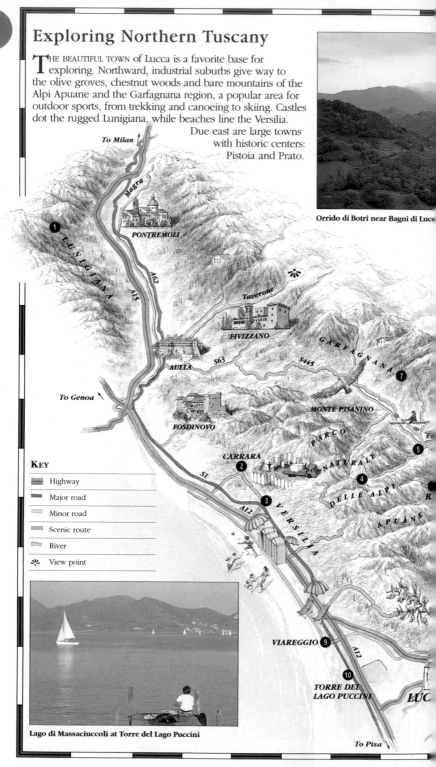

**Orrido di Botri near Bagni di Lucc**

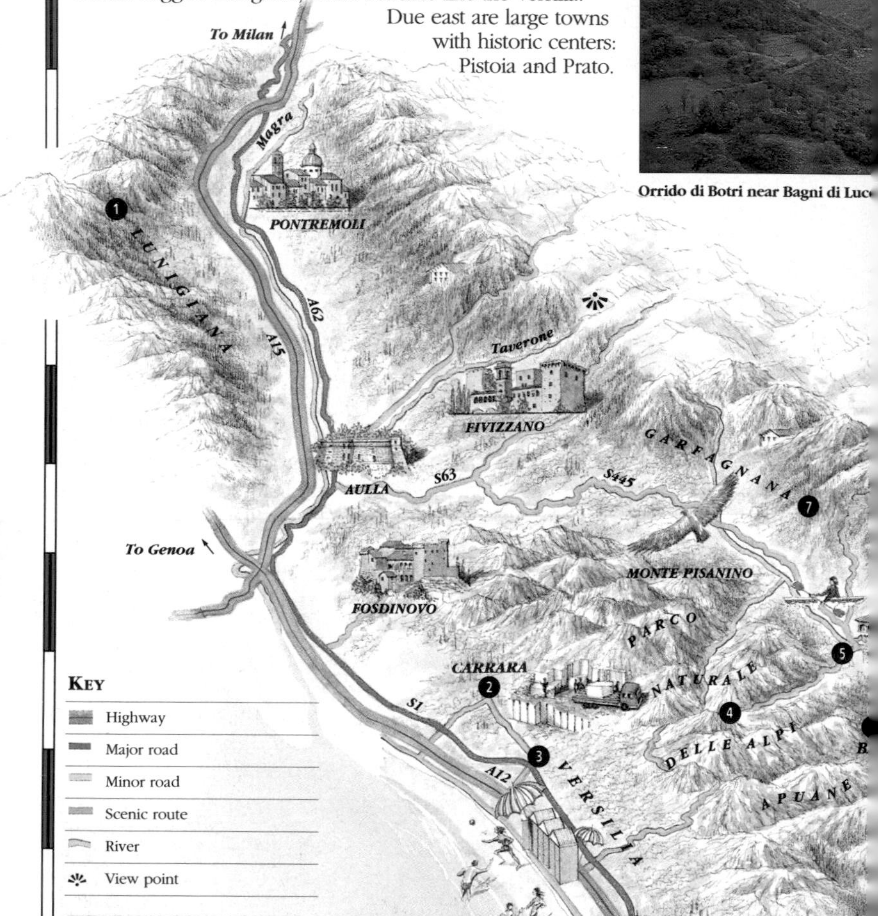


**KEY**

- Highway
- Major road
- Minor road
- Scenic route
- River
- View point

**Lago di Massaciuccoli at Torre del Lago Puccini**

## Getting Around

Lucca, Montecatini Terme, Prato and Pistoia are all on the A11 autostrada and are easy to reach by car from Pisa, Florence and other major cities outside Tuscany, such as Bologna. There are several trains a day between Pisa and Florence via Lucca, Montecatini Terme, Prato and Pistoia, and along the coast between Pisa and Carrara. From Lucca you can also travel by train up the Serchio valley to Castelnuovo di Garfagnana. But, since this is a mountainous region, much of it is accessible only by car.

## Sights at a Glance

Bagni di Lucca 8
Barga 6
Carrara 2
Castelnuovo di Garfagnana 5
Collodi 12
The Garfagnana 7
Lucca 11
The Lunigiana 1
Montecatini Terme 14
Parco Naturale delle Alpi Apuane 4
Pescia 13
Pistoia 15
Prato 16
Torre del Lago Puccini 10
The Versilia 3
Viareggio 9

The hamlet of Montefegatesi in the Alpi Apuane

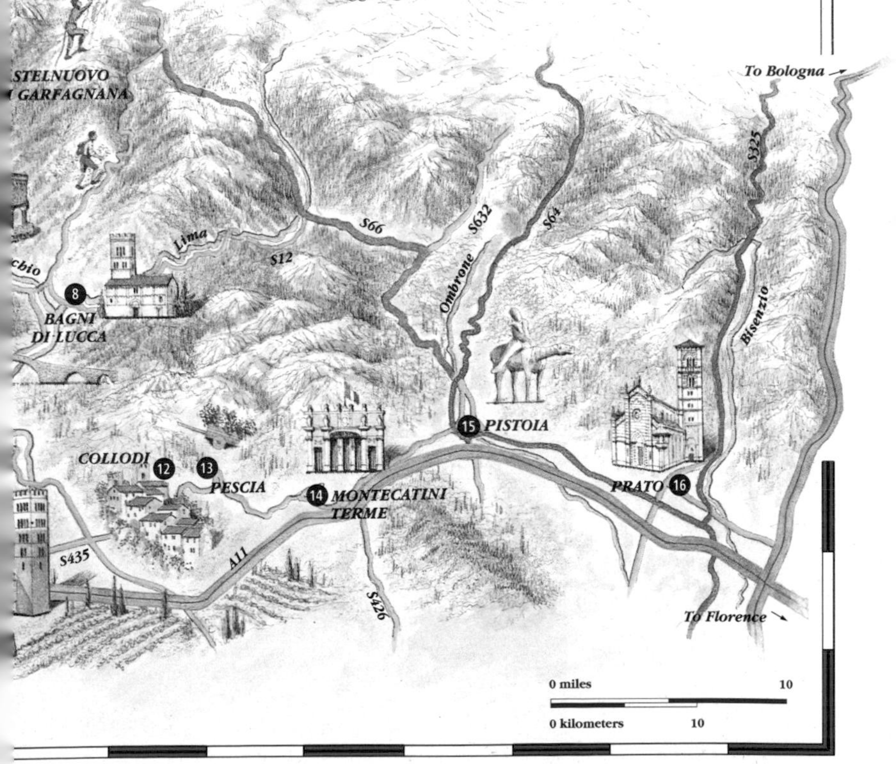

**Sun, sand and sea – essential components of a holiday at a beach resort of the Versilia**

## The Lunigiana ❶

**Road map** A1. FS 🚌 *Aulla.*
ℹ *Aulla. (0187) 40 01 11.*

THE LUNIGIANA (Land of the Moon) region takes its name from the port of Luni – so called because of the moonlike luminescence of the marble shipped from here in Roman times. From the 16th century onward, the Dukes of Malaspina built castles here and fortified villages against bandits. Malaspina castles can be seen at Massa, Fosdinovo, Aulla, Fivizzano and Verrucola.

At Pontremoli, the 14th-century Castello del Piagnaro houses the **Museo delle Statue-Stele Lunigianesi**, which shows prehistoric carved stone figures from the region.

**Museo delle Statue-Stele Lunigianesi**
Castello del Piagnaro, Pontremoli.
☎ *(0187) 83 14 39.* ***Open*** *Tue–Sun.* ***Adm charge***.

## Carrara ❷

**Road map** B1. 👥 *11,600.* FS 🚌
ℹ *Piazza Gino Menconi 6b. (0585) 63 22 18.* 🛒 *Mon.*

CARRARA IS WORLD-FAMOUS for its white marble. The 300 or so quarries near the town date to Roman times, making this the oldest industrial site in continuous use in the world. In Carrara itself there are numerous showrooms and workshops, where the marble is sawed into sheets or sculpted into statues and ornaments. Many of these workshops welcome visitors. You can also discover more about the techniques of crafting marble at the **Museo Civico del Marmo**.

Carrara's **Duomo** uses the local marble to good effect in its Pisan-Romanesque façade with its lovely rose window. In the same square is the house where Michelangelo used to stay on his visits to buy marble for his sculptures. The façade is marked by a plaque and by carvings of the sculptor's tools.

Tour buses from Carrara make regular visits to the quarries at Colonnata and at Fantiscritti, where a small museum displays various marble-quarrying techniques. You can also drive there, following the numerous signs that say "Cave di Marmo."

**Museo Civico del Marmo**
Viale XX Settembre. ☎ *(0585) 84 57 46.* ***Open*** *Mon–Sat.*

**Duomo**
Piazza del Duomo. ***Open*** *daily.*

## The Versilia ❸

**Road map** B2. FS 🚌 *Viareggio.*
ℹ *Viareggio. (0584) 96 22 33.*

THE VERSILIA, sometimes called the Tuscan Riviera because of the many beach resorts that line this 30-km (18-mile) strip, stretches from Marina di Carrara in the north down to Marina di Torre del

**A quarry in the marble-bearing hills around Carrara**

Lago Puccini. In the 1820s, towns such as Massa, Pietra Santa and Camaiore developed marinas and resorts along the part of the coast they controlled. These inland towns are linked by roads to the coastal areas. Here villas and hotels with fine walled gardens line the streets, with the mountains of the Alpi Apuane as a backdrop.

The beaches are divided into numerous recreational establishments run by hotels or private operators, who charge for use of the beach and its facilities. Forte dei Marmi is perhaps the most beautiful of these resorts, the favorite of wealthy Florentines and Milanese.

**Poster for the Versilia**

**The Turrite Secca valley in the Parco Naturale delle Alpi Apuane**

## Parco Naturale delle Alpi Apuane ❹

**Road map** B1. FS 🚌 *Castelnuovo di Garfagnana.* ℹ *Castelnuovo di Garfagnana. (0583) 64 43 54.*

THE PARCO NATURALE delle Alpi Apuane, northwest of Castelnuovo di Garfagnana, was designated a nature reserve in 1985. Monte Pisanino, the highest peak in this region at 1,945 m (6,320 ft), stands above Lago di Vagli, which is an artificial lake covering the drowned village of Fabbrica. Nearby are Vagli di Sotto *(see p164)* and Vagli di Sopra, ancient villages with rugged stone houses.

To the south, in the valley of the Turrite Secca, a spectacular mountain road leads to Seravezza, passing through a white-walled tunnel, the Galleria del Cipollaio. Northwest, at Arni, are the Marmitte dei Giganti (Giants' Cooking Pots), great hollows left by the glacial meltwaters of the Ice Age.

Southeast at Calomini is a 12th-century rock-cut hermitage, home to a Capuchin monk. Farther on is the Grotta del Vento (Cave of the Wind), at Fornovolasco. To the east, past Barga, at Coreglia Antelminelli, is the **Museo della Figurina di Gesso**, devoted to the history of locally manufactured plaster figurines, once sold by traders all over Europe.

**The 13th-century Rocca at Castelnuovo di Garfagnana**

### Museo della Figurina di Gesso

Via del Mangano 17, Coreglia Antelminelli. ☎ *(0583) 780 82.* ***Open*** *Jun–Sep: daily; Oct–May: Mon–Sat.* ***Adm charge.***

## Castelnuovo di Garfagnana ❺

**Road map** B1. *6,300.* FS 🚌 ℹ *Loggiato Porta 10. (0583) 64 43 54.* *Thu.*

VISITORS to the Garfagnana use the town as a base from which to explore. Information is available at the **Cooperativa Garfagnana Vacanze**, which offers guided excursions. The 13th-century Rocca (castle) is now the town hall. Ludovico Ariosto, author of the epic poem *Orlando Furioso* (1516), lived here between 1522 and 1525.

### Cooperativa Garfagnana Vacanze

Piazza delle Erbe 1. ☎ *(0583) 651 69.* ***Open Mon–Sat.***

## Barga ❻

**Road map** C1. *5,000.* FS
*Piazza Angelio 4. (0583) 72 34 99.*
*Sat.*

Barga is the most attractive of the towns that line the Serchio valley leading northward from Lucca, and it makes an excellent base for touring the Garfagnana region. The little walled town with its steep streets paved with stone is the setting for a highly regarded opera festival held in July in the 18th-century Teatro dell'Accademia dei Differenti.

**View over Barga rooftops**

### Duomo

Propositura. ***Open** daily.*

Barga's Duomo stands on a grassy terrace at the highest point in the town. There are glorious views from here of the gleaming white marble and limestone peaks of the Alpi Apuane.

The 11th-century Duomo is dedicated to San Cristofano (St. Christopher). The exterior is decorated with interesting Romanesque carvings of interlaced knots, wild beasts and knights in armor. Over the north portal, a frieze thought to be a scene from a folk tale depicts a banquet.

Inside, there is a huge wooden statue of St. Christopher, dating to the 12th century, and a gilded tabernacle guarded by two charming terra-cotta angels by Luca della Robbia.

Most impressive of all is the massive marble pulpit, standing fully 5 m (16.5 ft) tall, supported by pillars which in turn rest on the back of man-eating lions. The pulpit is the work of Guido Bigarelli of Como and dates from the early 13th century. The lively sculptures on the upper part depict the Evangelists, the Three Magi, the Annunciation, the Nativity and the Baptism of Christ.

## The Garfagnana ❼

**Road map** C1. FS *Castelnuovo di Garfagnana.* *Castelnuovo di Garfagnana. (0583) 64 43 54.*

This mountainous region can be explored from Barga, Seravezza, or Castelnuovo di Garfagnana *(see p169)*. Here too is the Parco Naturale delle Alpi Apuane *(see p169)*. From Castelnuovo a scenic drive takes you to the Alpe Tre Potenze. You can return via San Pellegrino in Alpe with its **Museo Etnografico**, and also visit the nature park, **Parco dell'Orecchiella** and the **Orto Botanico Pánia di Corfino** with its collection of local Alpines.

**Romanesque sculpture in Pieve di Brancoli**

### Museo Etnografico

Via del Voltone 15, San Pellegrino in Alpe. *(0583) 64 90 72. **Open** Jul–Aug: daily. **Adm charge**.*

### Parco dell'Orecchiella

**Centro Visitatori**, Orecchiella. *(0583) 61 90 98. **Open** Jul–mid-Sep: daily; Nov–Jun: by appt.*

### Orto Botanico Pánia di Corfino

Parco dell'Orecchiella. *(0583) 61 90 98. **Open** mid-Jun–mid-Sep: daily.*

## Bagni di Lucca ❽

**Road map** C2. *7,402.*
*Via Umberto I, 139. (0583) 879 46.* *Wed, Sat.*

Visitors come to Bagni di Lucca because of its lime sulfate springs. In the 19th century it was one of Europe's most fashionable spa towns *(see p181)*: the Casino, built in 1837, was the first to be licensed in Europe. Also from that time are the Neo-Gothic **English Church** of 1839, the elegant **Palazzo del Circolo dei Forestieri** restaurant and the **Cimitero Anglicano** (Protestant Cemetery). Bagni di Lucca makes a good base for exploring the surrounding hills, cloaked in chestnut woods. You can walk to Montefegatesi, a hamlet surrounded by the peaks of the Alpi Apuane, and then continue to Orrido di Botri, a dramatic gorge. To the south of Bagni is San Giorgio or **Pieve di Brancoli**, one of many Romanesque churches in the area founded during the reign of Countess Matilda (1046–1115) *(see p43)*.

The Ponte della Maddalena is a humpbacked bridge across the River Serchio just north of the village of Borgo a Mozzano. It is popularly called Ponte del Diavolo (Devil's Bridge) because, according to local legend, the Devil offered to build the bridge in return

**Ponte della Maddalena or "Devil's Bridge" near Bagni di Lucca**

**A seaside café in the popular beach resort of Viareggio**

for possession of the first soul to cross it; the shrewd villagers agreed and, when it was finished, sent a dog across.

**English Church**
Via Crawford. (0583) 862 00.
***Open** by appt.*

**Palazzo del Circolo dei Forestieri**
Piazza Varraud 10. *(0583) 860 38. **Open** Tue–Sun.*

**Cimitero Anglicano**
Via Letizia. *(0583) 862 00.*
***Open** by appt.*

**Pieve di Brancoli**
*Vinchiana. **Open** daily.*

## Viareggio ❾

**Road map** B2. *55,000.*
*Viale Carducci 10. (0584) 96 22 33. Thu.*

VIAREGGIO IS FAMOUS for its elegant "Liberty" style (Art Nouveau) villas and hotels. They were built in the 1920s after the original boardwalk and timber chalets of the resort went up in flames in 1917. One example is the Gran Caffè Margherita, designed by the prolific Galileo Chini *(see p190)*. The harbor has an interesting mix of boatyards, luxury yachts and fishing boats, and there are fine views of the Versilia coastline from here. Viareggio's carnival is famous throughout Italy *(see p36)*.

## Torre del Lago Puccini ❿

**Road map** B2. *10,000.*
*Via Marconi 225. (0584) 35 98 93. Fri.*

THE COMPOSER Giacomo Puccini (1858–1924) *(see p175)* lived here, beside Lago di Massaciuccoli, to indulge his passion for shooting waterfowl. Puccini and his wife are buried in the house, now the **Museo Villa Puccini**, in the mausoleum between the piano room, where he composed all but the last of his operas, and the gun room, where he kept his rifle ("my second favorite instrument"). The operas are performed in the open-air lakeside theater in summer *(see p33)*. The reed-fringed lake is now a nature reserve for rare and migrating birds.

**Museo Villa Puccini**
Viale Puccini 264. *(0584) 34 14 45.*
***Open** Jul–Aug: daily; Sep–Jun: Tue–Sun. **Adm charge**.*

**Near Puccini's lakeside home at Torre del Lago Puccini**

# Street-by-Street: Lucca ⓫

Lucca became a colony of ancient Rome in 180 BC, and the town's Roman legacy is still evident in the regular grid pattern of its streets. The remarkable elliptical shape of the Piazza del Mercato *(see p165)* is a survival of the amphitheater. The name of the church of San Michele in Foro indicates that it stands beside the Roman forum, laid out as the city's main square in ancient times and still serving that function to this day. San Michele is just one of Lucca's many churches built in the 12th and 13th centuries in the elaborate Pisan-Romanesque style.

**Most of** the Renaissance palazzi of Piazza San Michele are now offices.

**Casa di Puccini**
*This plaque marks the birthplace of Giacomo Puccini (1858–1924), composer of some of the world's most popular operas.*

**★ San Michele in Foro**
*The Madonna on the southwest corner of the church is a copy of the original inside, carved by Matteo Civitali (1436–1501).*

**The Palazzo Ducale**, once home to Lucca's rulers, has a Mannerist colonnade by Ammannati (1578).

**San Giovanni (1187)**

**Piazza Napoleone**
*The square is named after Napoleon, whose sister, Elisa Baciocchi, was ruler of Lucca (1805–15). The statue is of her successor, Marie Louise de Bourbon.*

**Star Sights**

- ★ **San Martino**
- ★ **San Michele in Foro**

**Via Fillungo**
*Several storefronts in Lucca's main shopping street are decorated with Art Nouveau details.*

## VISITORS' CHECKLIST

**Road map** C2. 100,000. FS *Piazza Ricasoli.* *Piazzale Verdi.* *Piazzale Verdi 2. (0583) 41 96 89.* *Wed, Sat. Antiques market: 3rd weekend of month.* *Palio della Balestra (Jul 12); Estate Musicale (Jul–Sep); Luminara di Santa Croce (Sep 13).*

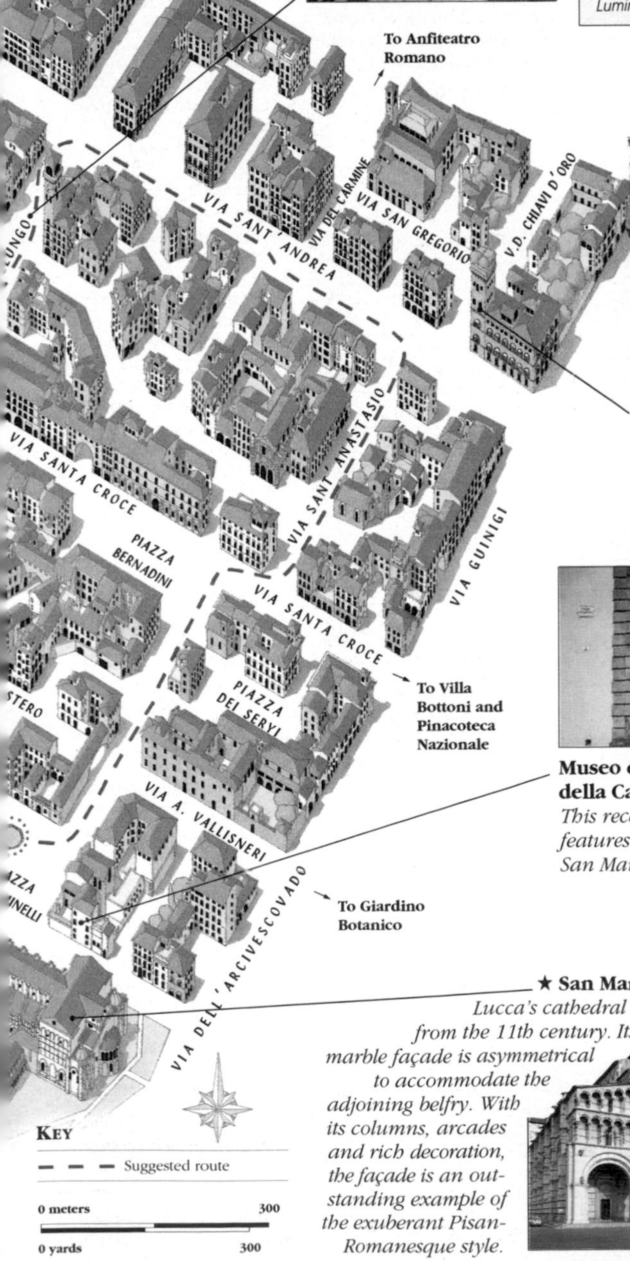

**Torre dei Guinigi**
*This medieval tower with oak trees growing at the top is a familiar landmark of Lucca.*

**Museo dell'Opera della Cattedrale**
*This recently opened museum features the treasures of San Martino.*

**★ San Martino**
*Lucca's cathedral dates from the 11th century. Its marble façade is asymmetrical to accommodate the adjoining belfry. With its columns, arcades and rich decoration, the façade is an outstanding example of the exuberant Pisan-Romanesque style.*

# Exploring Lucca

**Mosaic in San Frediano**

LUCCA IS ENCLOSED by massive red brick walls, which help to give the city its special character by shutting out traffic and the modern world. Built in 1504–1645, the walls are among the best-preserved Renaissance defenses in Europe. Within these walls, Lucca is a peaceful city of narrow lanes, preserving intact its original ancient Roman street plan. Unlike several of Tuscany's hilltop cities, Lucca is flat: many locals use bicycles, which lends the city added charm.

**Lucca viewed from the top of the Guinigi Tower**

### San Martino
*See pp176–7.*

### Anfiteatro Romano
Piazza del Mercato.

Almost no original stone of the ancient Roman amphitheater survives: its remains were gradually stolen for use elsewhere, leaving the atmospheric arena-shaped Piazza del Mercato of today *(see p165).* The piazza is enclosed by medieval houses that were built up against the walls of the amphitheater, its shape perfectly preserved, and form a striking reminder that Lucca was founded by the Romans around 180 BC. Low archways at north, south, east and west mark the gates through which beasts and gladiators would once have entered the arena.

### Palazzo dei Guinigi
Via Sant'Andrea. *(0583) 485 24.* ***Tower open** daily.* ***Adm charge**.*

The house is one of several in Lucca that once belonged to the powerful Guinigi family, rulers of the city in the 15th century. The Guinigi kept Florence at bay, so that Lucca, remarkably, was never conquered by the Medici, remaining proudly independent till the end of the 18th century.

The red brick palazzo, built in the late 14th century, has late-Gothic pointed windows. The striking 41-m (133-ft) defensive tower alongside, the Torre del Guinigi, has a small roof garden, hence the ilex (holm oak) trees sprouting incongruously at the top.

### Giardino Botanico
Via dell'Orto Botanico 14. *(0583) 44 21 60.* ***Open** Mon–Sat.* ***Adm charge**.*

Lucca's delightful botanical garden, tucked into an angle of the city walls, was laid out in 1820. It displays a wide range of Tuscan plants, from alpines to coastal species.

### Museo della Cattedrale
Via Arcivescovado. *(0583) 49 05 30.* ***Open** Tue–Sun.* ***Adm charge**.*

The museum, housed in the 14th-century former Archbishop's Palace, displays the treasures of the Duomo, San Martino. These include the 11th-century carved stone head of a king from the original cathedral façade. There is also a very rare 12th-century Limoges enamel casket, possibly for a relic of St. Thomas Becket. The Croce di Pisani made by Vincenzo di Michele in 1411 is a masterpiece of the goldsmith's art. It shows Christ hanging from the Tree of Redemption, surrounded by angels, the Virgin, St. John and the other Evangelists.

### Museo Nazionale Guinigi
Via della Quarquonia. *(0583) 460 33.* ***Open** Tue–Sun.* ***Adm charge**.*

This massive Renaissance villa was built for Paolo Guinigi, who ruled Lucca from 1400 to 1430. The ground floor contains sculpture from Lucca and the surrounding area, including fine Romanesque reliefs from Lucca's churches. The picture gallery on the floor above displays paintings, furnishings, and choir stalls from Lucca's cathedral, inlaid with marquetry views of the city in 1529.

**Romanesque lion at Museo Nazionale Guinigi**

**The beautiful galleried staircase at Palazzo Pfanner**

### Palazzo Pfanner

***Closed** for restoration.*

The Palazzo Pfanner is an imposing house built in 1667. It has one of Tuscany's most delightful formal gardens to the rear. (The garden can also be viewed while walking along the Ramparts.) Laid out in the 18th century, the garden's central avenue is lined with Baroque statues of the gods and goddesses of ancient Roman mythology, alternating with lemon trees in huge terra-cotta pots.

The house itself contains a rich collection of court costume of the 18th and 19th centuries. Many garments on display are made of silk, whose production and export made Lucca families wealthy.

### Piazza Napoleone and Piazza del Giglio

These two squares are almost one. The first was laid out in 1806 when Lucca was under the imposed rule of Elisa Baciocchi, Napoleon's sister. The statue in the square is of her successor, Marie Louise de Bourbon. She faces the massive Palazzo Ducale, with its elegant colonnade built by Ammannati in 1578. Behind her is the Piazza del Giglio, with the Teatro del Giglio (1817) on the south side of the square. The theater saw the first performance in Italy of Rossini's last opera *William Tell* (1831). Today it is famous for its productions of operas by Puccini, who was born in Lucca.

### Casa di Puccini

Corte San Lorenzo 9 (Via di Poggio). *(0583) 58 40 28.* ***Open** Tue–Sun.* ***Adm charge**.*

**The composer Giacomo Puccini**

The house in which Giacomo Puccini (1858–1924) was born is now a shrine to the great opera composer. The fine 15th-century house has portraits of Puccini, costume designs for his operas and the piano he used when composing his last opera, *Turandot*. Left unfinished at his death, it was completed by Franco Alfano and given its first performance two years later at La Scala, Milan.

### Pinacoteca Nazionale

Via Galli Tassi 43. *(0583) 555 70.* ***Open** Tue–Sun.* ***Adm charge**.*

Lucca's picture gallery is in the impressive 17th-century Palazzo Manzi, with paintings and furnishings of the same period, typical of the time when Mannerism was being superseded by Baroque and Rococo art. There are also works by Bronzino, Pontormo, Sodoma, Andrea del Sarto, Tintoretto and Salvatore Rosa, including Medici portraits.

### Ramparts

*Complete circuit: 4.2 km (2.5 miles).*
*(0583) 462 57 for guided tours.*

A promenade runs along the top of the city walls, built in 1504–1645. Marie Louise de Bourbon made the Ramparts into a public park in the early 19th century, with a double avenue of trees. It makes a delightful walk with fine views, including glimpses into private gardens. There are occasional guided tours of the chambers and passages inside one of the bastions.

**The Porta San Donato along the tree-lined Ramparts walk**

## San Martino

**Threshing, the Labor of September**

Lucca's extraordinary cathedral, with its façade abutting incongruously onto the campanile, is dedicated to St. Martin. He is the Roman soldier depicted on the façade, dividing his cloak with a sword to share with a needy beggar. This and other scenes from the life of the saint form part of the complex decorations covering the 13th-century façade. There are also reliefs depicting *The Labors of the Months* and intricate panels of inlaid pink, green and white marble showing hunting scenes, peacocks and flowers.

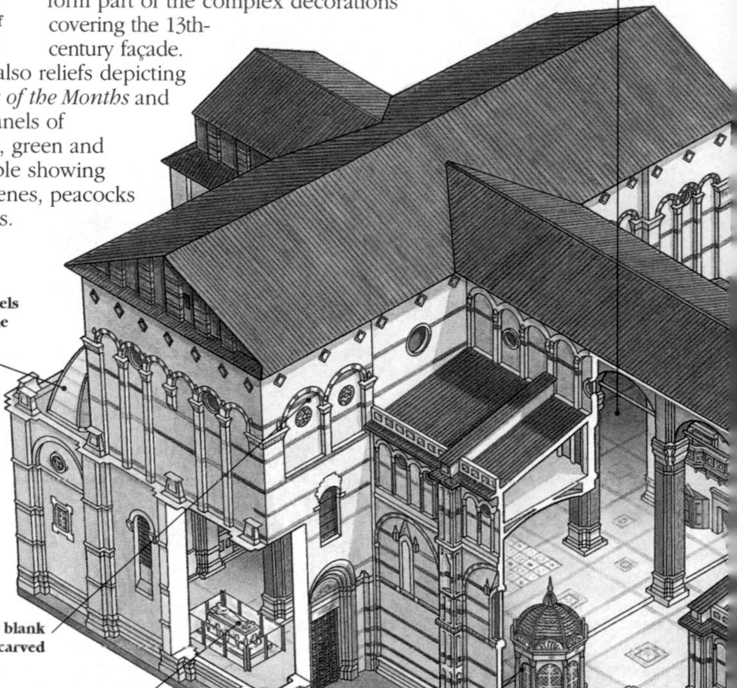

**The altar painting** in the Sacristy, *The Madonna and Saints* (1449–94), is by Ghirlandaio.

**Domed chapels encircling the apse**

**Romanesque blank arcades and carved capitals**

**Matteo Civitali's marble Tempietto (1184)**

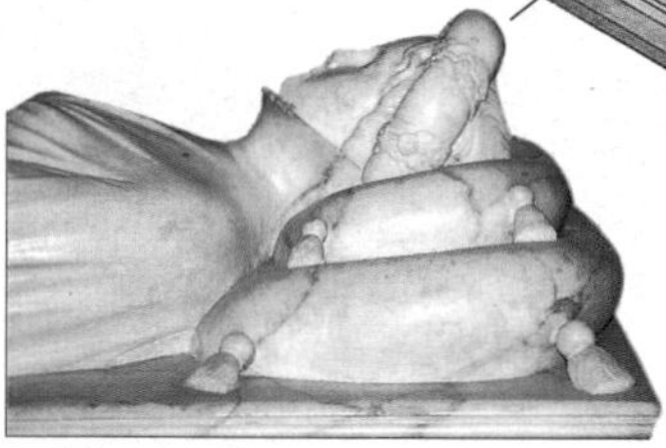

**★ Tomb of Ilaria del Carretto**
*This beautiful portrait in marble by Jacopo della Quercia (1405–6) is of the youthful bride of Paolo Guinigi.*

**★ Volto Santo**
*This highly revered 13th-century wooden effigy was believed by medieval pilgrims to be carved by Christ's follower, Nicodemus, at the time of the Crucifixion.*

**Star Features**

- ★ **Façade**
- ★ **Volto Santo**
- ★ **Tomb of Ilaria del Carretto**

**★ Façade**
*The gabled façade has three tiers of ornate colonnading (1204). Every one of the carved columns is different, and there are lively hunting scenes above them.*

**The campanile** was built in 1060 as a defensive tower. The upper two tiers were added in 1261 when the tower was joined to the cathedral.

**VISITORS' CHECKLIST**

Piazza San Martino. ☎ *(0583) 95 70 68.* **Open** *Jun–Sep: 7am–12:30pm, 3–7pm; Oct–May: 6am–noon, 3–6pm.* ✝ *7:30am, 9am, 6pm Mon–Sat, 8am, 10:30am, noon Sun & religious hols.* 📷

**St. Martin**
*This sculpture of the saint dividing his cloak to share it is a copy. The 13th-century original is now just inside the cathedral entrance.*

**Circular** clerestory windows, in the nave and above the aisle roof, light the unusually tall nave of the cross-shaped church.

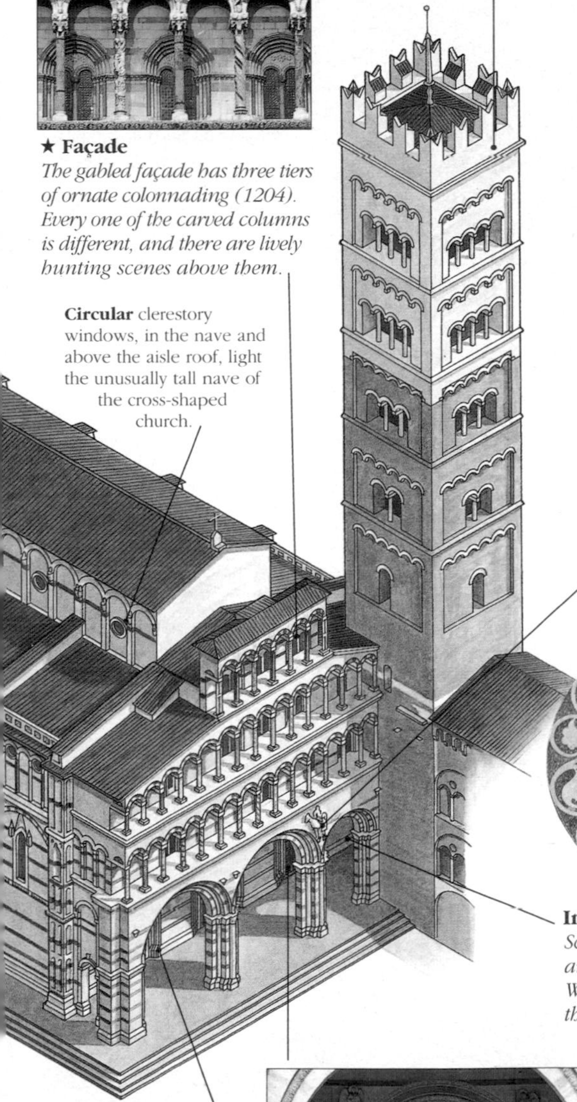

**Inlaid Marble**
*Scenes from daily life, myths and poems cover the façade. Watch for the maze pattern on the right pier of the porch.*

**Nicola Pisano** (1200–78) carved *The Journey of the Magi* and *The Deposition* around the left doorway.

**Doorway Sculptures**
*This 13th-century relief depicts the beheading of St. Regulus.* The Labors of the Months *around the central door show the tasks appropriate to each season.*

**Apostles from the mosaic on the façade of San Frediano in Lucca**

### San Frediano

Piazza San Frediano. ***Open*** *daily.*

The striking façade of Lucca's San Frediano church features a colorful 13th-century mosaic, *The Ascension,* by the School of Berlinghieri. Inside, to the right, is a splendid Romanesque font, which could easily be mistaken for a fountain, because it is so big and impressive. The sides are carved with scenes from *The Life of Christ* and the story of Moses. One dramatic scene shows Moses and his followers dressed in 12th-century armor, looking like Crusaders, as they pass through the divided Red Sea with an entourage of camels.

Amico Aspertini's frescoes (1508–9) in the second chapel in the north aisle tell the story of Lucca's precious relic, the Volto Santo *(see p176),* and give a good idea what the city looked like in the early 16th century.

Also in the church is a colored wooden statue of the Virgin, carved by Matteo Civitali, and an altarpiece carved from a single block of marble by Jacopo della Quercia in the Cappella Trenta. It is carved in the shape of a polyptych with five Gothic-spired niches.

### San Michele in Foro

Piazza San Michele. ***Open*** *daily.*

As its name suggests, the church stands on the site of the ancient Roman forum. It has a wonderfully rich Pisan Romanesque façade that competes in splendor with that of San Martino *(see pp176–7).* John Ruskin, the English artist and art historian whose work did so much to revive interest in Italian art during the 19th century *(see p53),* spent many hours sketching the rich mixture of twisted marble columns and Cosmati work (inlaid marble). The façade is almost barbaric in its exuberance, and the inlaid marble scenes depict wild beasts and huntsmen on horseback rather than Christian subjects. Only the huge winged figure of St. Michael, standing on the pediment and flanked by two angels, marks this as a church. The splendor of the façade, built over a long period from the 11th to the 14th centuries, is matched by the arcading of the bell tower.

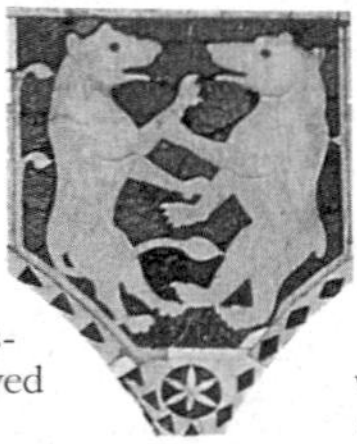

**Detail from façade of San Michele in Foro**

The interior has little of interest except for Filippino Lippi's recently restored *Saints Helena, Jerome, Sebastian and Roch,* among the most beautiful of his paintings.

The square outside is circled by 15th- and 16th-century palazzi, which are now mostly occupied by banks, while the portico of the Palazzo Pretorio to the south shelters a 19th-century statue of Lucca's greatest artist and architect, Matteo Civitali (1436–1501).

### Via Fillungo

Lucca's principal shopping street winds its way through the heart of the city toward the Anfiteatro Romano *(see p174).* It is a good place to stroll in the cool of the early evening. The upper end, toward San Frediano church, has several shops with Art Nouveau ironwork, while San Cristoforo, the 13th-century church halfway down the street, holds exhibitions of work by local artists.

### Villa Bottini

Via Elisa. *(0583) 49 14 49.*

**Garden *open*** *Mon–Sat.*

The pretty walled garden of this late 16th-century building is open to the public. It is also used occasionally in summer for outdoor concerts.

**Villa Bottini and garden**

# A Day Out around Lucca

This driving tour takes you by a scenic route to the best of the villas around Lucca.

After leaving Lucca, the first stop is the Romanesque church of San Giorgio at Pieve di Brancoli; then comes the ancient humpbacked Ponte della Maddalena, also known as Devil's Bridge. In the spa town of Bagni di Lucca, the pretty suspension bridge across the Lima dates from 1840.

On reaching Collodi, explore the village on foot, as the streets are too steep and narrow for cars. The Villa Garzoni, with its splendid gardens, lies below the town, and Pinocchio Park is on the other side of the road. Continue to the Villa Torrigiani, which is set in a fine park and contains porcelain and furnishings from the 13th to 18th centuries. The tour ends at the 17th-century Villa Mansi, with its Baroque façade and a garden enlivened by statues of Diana and other pagan deities.

**Bagni di Lucca ③**
Drive along the S12 for 5 km (3 miles) to the spa town. Then continue along the same road through the town.

**Villa Garzoni ④**
Turn left at the T-junction on the S12 for Abetone, then right for Collodi and the Villa Garzoni, with its terraced gardens.

**Ponte della Maddalena ②**
Continue for 8 km (5 miles) on the S12 to the bridge.

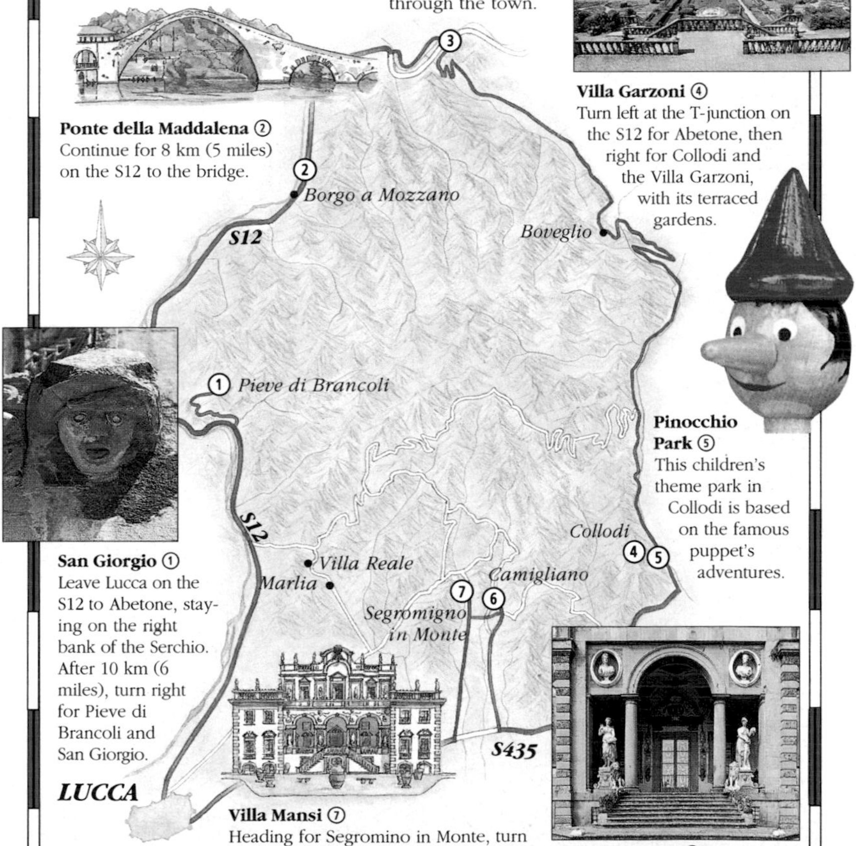


**Pinocchio Park ⑤**
This children's theme park in Collodi is based on the famous puppet's adventures.

**San Giorgio ①**
Leave Lucca on the S12 to Abetone, staying on the right bank of the Serchio. After 10 km (6 miles), turn right for Pieve di Brancoli and San Giorgio.

**Villa Mansi ⑦**
Heading for Segromino in Monte, turn right at the first junction into Via Piaggiori; then follow signs to Villa Mansi.

**Villa Torrigiani ⑥**
South of Collodi, turn right on the S435 for Lucca. After Borgonuovo, turn right for Camigliano Santa Gemma and left after 1.5 km (1 mile) for the villa.

**Key**

Tour route

Other roads

0 kilometers 5

0 miles 2

**Terme Tettuccio, Montecatini's oldest and most famous spa, rebuilt in 1925–8**

## Collodi ⓬

**Map** C2. 3,000.

THERE ARE two main sights in this little town: the **Villa Garzoni** with its theatrical terraced gardens tumbling down the hillside and, for children, the **Pinocchio Park** *(see p179)*.

The author of *The Adventures of Pinocchio* (1881), Carlo Lorenzini, was born in Florence but his uncle was custodian of the Villa Garzoni and Lorenzini frequently stayed there as a child. Fond memories led him to use Collodi as his pen name and in 1956 the town decided to repay the compliment by setting up the theme park.

The park consists of gardens featuring mosaics and sculptural tableaux based on the adventures of the puppet, plus a maze, playground, exhibition center and children's restaurant.

**Villa Garzoni**
*(0572) 42 85 79.* **Villa *open*** *Jun–Sep daily; Oct–May: Sat, Sun & public hols.* ***Adm charge*****. Garden *open*** *daily.* ***Adm charge****.*

**Pinocchio Park**
*(0572) 42 93 42.* ***Open*** *daily.* ***Adm charge****.*

## Pescia ⓭

**Map** C2. *18,123.* *Piazza Mazzini. (0572) 49 22 44.* *Sat.*

PESCIA'S wholesale flower market is one of Italy's biggest. The town itself is rather scruffy, but there are some interesting sights to visit.

In the church of **San Francesco** are frescoes on *The Life of St. Francis* (1235) by Bonaventura Berlinghieri (1235–74). The artist knew St. Francis *(see p45)*, who had died nine years earlier, and it is claimed that the frescoes are an accurate portrait of the saint. The **Duomo,** remodeled in Baroque style by Antonio Ferri in 1693, has a massive campanile that was originally built as a tower within the city walls. It was given its onion-dome "cap" in 1771.

There is a small collection of religious paintings and illuminated manuscripts in the **Museo Civico**, and the **Museo Archeologico della Valdinievole** displays material excavated from nearby Valdinievole, the pretty "Vale of Mist."

**San Francesco**
Piazza San Francesco. ***Open*** *daily.*

**Duomo**
Piazza del Duomo. ***Open*** *daily.*

**Museo Civico**
Palazzo Galeotti, Piazza Santo Stefano 1. *(0572) 49 00 57.* ***Open*** *Wed–Sat.*

**Museo Archeologico della Valdinievole**
Piazza Leonardo da Vinci 1. *(0572) 47 75 33.* ***Open*** *Mon–Sat.*

**The Pescia river, running through a fertile, cultivated landscape**

## Montecatini Terme ⓮

**Map** C2. *22,500* *Viale Verdi 66. (0572) 77 22 44.* *Thu.*

OF ALL TUSCANY'S many spa towns, Montecatini Terme is the most interesting to visit. It has beautiful formal gardens and the varied architecture of its several spa establishments is particularly distinguished.

Terme Leopoldine (1926), built in the style of a Classical temple, is named after Grand Duke Leopoldo I, who first

**Theater building in Montecatini Alto's main square**

encouraged the development of Montecatini Terme in the 18th century.

The most splendid is the Neo-Classical Terme Tettuccio (1925–8) with its circular, marble-lined pools, fountains and Art Nouveau tiles depicting languorous nymphs.

Terme Torretta, named after its mock medieval tower, is noted for its afternoon concerts, while Terme Tamerici has well-tended gardens.

Visitors can obtain day tickets to the spas to drink the waters and relax in the reading, writing and music rooms. More information is available from the Direzione delle Terme at Viale Verdi 41.

A popular excursion from Montecatini Terme is to take the funicular railway up to the ancient fortified village of Montecatini Alto. In the quiet main piazza, there are antique shops and well-regarded restaurants with outdoor tables. From the Rocca (castle) you can take in sweeping views over the mountainous countryside, known locally as "Little Switzerland."

Nearby at Ponte Buggianese, in **San Michele** church, you can see modern frescoes by the Florentine artist Pietro Annigoni (1910–88) on the theme of Christ's Passion.

At Monsummano Terme, another of Tuscany's well known spa towns, the **Grotta Giusti** spa prescribes the inhalation of vapors from hot sulfurous springs found in the nearby caves.

Above Monsummano Terme is the fortified hilltop village of Monsummano Alto with its once strategically placed but now ruined castle. Today, few people live in the sleepy village, with its pretty 12th-century church and crumbling houses, but there are some fine views from here.

**San Michele**
Ponte Buggianese. ***Open*** *daily.*

**Grotta Giusti**
Monsummano Terme. *(0572) 510 08.* ***Open*** *Apr–Nov.*
***Adm charge.***

**The Terme Tamerici, built in Neo-Gothic style in the early 20th century**

## TAKING THE WATERS IN TUSCANY

The therapeutic value of bathing was first recognized by the ancient Romans. They were also the first to exploit the hot springs of volcanic origin that they found all over Tuscany. Here they built bath complexes where the army veterans who settled in towns such as Florence and Siena could relax. Some of these spas, such as Saturnia *(see p234)*, are still called by their original Roman names.

Other spas came into prominence during the Middle Ages and Renaissance: St. Catherine of Siena (1347–80) *(see p215)*, who suffered from scrofula, a form of tuberculosis, and Lorenzo de' Medici (1449–92), who was arthritic, both bathed in the sulfurous hot springs at Bagno Vignoni *(see p222)* to relieve their ailments. Tuscan spas really came into their own in the early 19th century when Bagni di Lucca was one of the most fashionable spa centers in Europe, frequented by emperors, kings and aristocrats *(see p170)*. However, spa culture in the 19th century had more to do with social life: flirtation and gambling took precedence over health cures.

**1920s spa poster**

Today treatments such as inhaling sulfur-laden steam, drinking the mineral-rich waters, hydromassage, bathing and application of mud packs are prescribed for disorders ranging from liver complaints to skin conditions and asthma. Many visitors still continue the tradition of coming to fashionable spas such as Montecatini Terme or Monsummano Terme, not just for the benefits of therapeutic treatment but also for relaxation and in search of companionship.

# Pistoia ⓯

**The Cappella del Tau symbol**

THE CITIZENS OF PISTOIA acquired a reputation for viciousness and intrigue in the 13th century, and the taint has never quite disappeared. The cause was a feud between two of the city's rival factions, the Bianchi and Neri (Blacks and Whites), that spread to involve other cities. Assassination in Pistoia's narrow alleyways was commonplace. The favored weapon was a tiny but deadly dagger called the *pistole*, made by the city's ironworkers, who also specialized in surgical instruments. The city still thrives on metalworking: everything from buses to mattress springs is made here. Its historic center has several fine buildings.

**Baptistry opposite the Cattedrale**

### Cattedrale di San Zeno

Piazza del Duomo. ***Open** daily.*
*side entrance.*

Piazza del Duomo, the city's main square, is dominated by the Cattedrale di San Zeno and its bulky campanile, which was originally built in the 12th century as a defensive watch-tower in the city walls.

The interior is rich in funerary monuments. The finest of these, in the south aisle, is the tomb of Cino da Pistoia. He was a friend of Dante and a fellow poet, and is depicted in a relief (1337) lecturing to a class of young boys.

Nearby is the chapel of St. James and its extraordinary silver altar decorated with over 600 statues and reliefs. The earliest of these date from 1287, but the altar was not completed until 1456. During that time, nearly every silversmith of note in Tuscany contributed to the extraordinarily rich design. Among them was Brunelleschi, who began his career working in metal before switching to architecture. Also in Piazza del Duomo, facing the Cattedrale, is the octagonal Baptistry, which was completed in 1359.

### Museo della Cattedrale

Palazzo dei Vescovi, Piazza del Duomo. *(0573) 36 92 72.* ***Open** Tue, Thu & Fri.* ***Adm charge**.*
*partial.*

Just next to the Cattedrale, housed in the well-restored Palazzo dei Vescovi (Bishop's Palace), is the Museo della Cattedrale. In the basement, you can see the excavated remains of Roman buildings, and upstairs there are some fine reliquaries, crucifixes and chalices made by local goldsmiths during the 13th–15th centuries.

### Museo Civico

Palazzo del Comune, Piazza del Duomo. *(0573) 37 11.* ***Open** Tue–Sun.* ***Adm charge**.*

On the opposite side of the square is the Palazzo del Comune (Town Hall), which has the Museo Civico upstairs. Exhibits here range from medieval altar paintings to the work of 20th-century Pistoian artists, architects and sculptors.

### Centro Marino Marini

Palazzo del Tau, Corso Silvano Fedi 72. *(0573) 302 85.* ***Open** Tue–Sun.*

The work of Marino Marini (1901–80), Pistoia's best-known 20th-century artist, is now housed in a museum dedicated to him in the Palazzo del Tau.

On display here are drawings and casts, which trace the development of his style. Marini specialized in sculpting primitive forms in bronze or clay. Favorite subjects for his work were a horse and rider *(see p104)*, and also Pomona, the ancient Roman goddess of fertility.

***Pomona* by Marino Marini**

### Cappella del Tau

Corso Silvano Fedi 70. ***Open** Tue–Sat.*

Opposite the Museo Civico is the Cappella del Tau, so called because the monks who built it wore on their cloaks the letter T (*tau* in Greek), symbolizing a crutch.

Inside the chapel there are frescoes on *The Creation* and the life of St. Anthony Abbot, who founded the order, which is dedicated to tending the sick and crippled.

***The Fall*, in the Cappella del Tau**

### San Giovanni Fuorcivitas

Via Cavour. ***Open** daily.*

Just north of the Cappella del Tau is the 12th-century church of San Giovanni Fuorcivitas ("St. John outside the city," since the church once stood beyond the city walls). Its north flank is strikingly clad in banded marble, and there is a Romanesque relief of *The Last Supper* over the portal. Inside is Giovanni Pisano's holy water basin, carved in marble with figures of the Virtues, and an equally masterly pulpit by Guglielmo

**Detail of frieze (1514–25) by Giovanni della Robbia, Ospedale del Ceppo**

da Pisa, carved in 1270 with New Testament scenes. Both works are among the finest of this period, when artists were reviving the art of carving.

### Sant'Andrea

Via Sant'Andrea 21. ***Open*** *daily.*

The church of Sant'Andrea is reached by walking through Piazza della Sala, the site of Pistoia's lively open-air market. There is a good Romanesque relief of *The Journey of the Magi* over the portal, and inside is Giovanni Pisano's pulpit (completed in 1301). This is considered by some to be his masterpiece, even more accomplished than the pulpit he made in 1302 for Pisa cathedral *(see p155).* It is decorated with reliefs depicting scenes from *The Life of Christ.*

### San Bartolomeo in Pantano

Piazza San Bartolomeo 6. ***Open*** *daily.*

The beautiful Romanesque church of San Bartolomeo in Pantano, dating from 760, houses another celebrated pulpit, carved in 1250 by Guido da Como.

### Ospedale del Ceppo

Piazza Giovanni XXIII.

This hospital and orphanage, founded in 1277, was named after the *ceppo*, or hollowed-out tree trunk, that was used in medieval times to collect donations for its work. The striking façade of the main building features colored terra-cotta panels (1514–25) by Giovanni della Robbia illustrating the Seven Works of Corporeal Mercy. The portico is by Michelozzo.

**VISITORS' CHECKLIST**

**Road map** C2. *93,000.*
FS *Piazza Dante Alighieri.*
*Piazza San Francesco.*
*Palazzo dei Vescovi, Piazza del Duomo. (0573) 216 22.* *Wed & Sat.* ***Early closing*** *Sat afternoon (summer), Mon morning (winter).*
*Giostro dell'Orso (25 Jul).*

### Zoo

Via Pieve a Celle 160a. *(0573) 93 92 19.* ***Open*** *daily.* ***Adm charge.***

There is a small but well-maintained zoo just 4 km (2.5 miles) to the northwest of Pistoia at La Verginina.

**Façade of San Bartolomeo**

**PISTOIA CITY CENTER**

Cappella del Tau ⑧
Cattedrale and Baptistry ⑥
Centro Marino Marini ⑨
Museo della Cattedrale ⑤
Museo Civico ④
Ospedale del Ceppo ②
Sant'Andrea ①
San Bartolomeo in Pantano ③
San Giovanni Fuorcivitas ⑦

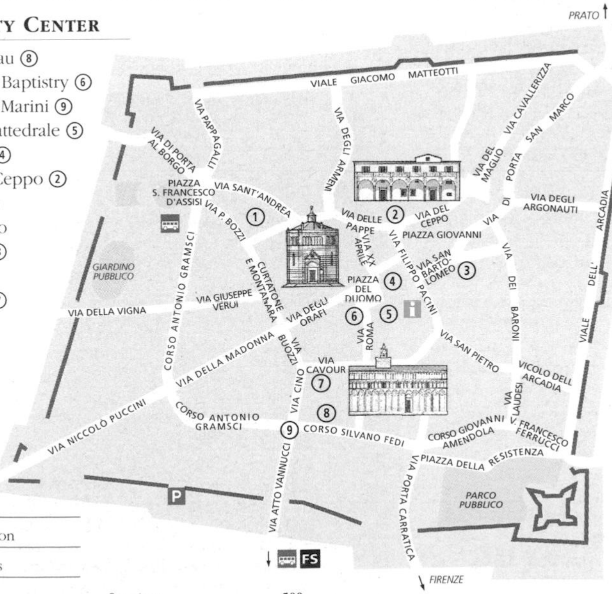


**KEY**

FS Railway station
Bus terminus
P Parking
Tourist information

# Prato ⑯

PRATO HAS BEEN ONE OF ITALY'S most important textile-manufacturing cities since the 13th century. One of its most famous citizens was the immensely wealthy Francesco di Marco Datini (1330–1410), who has been immortalized by Iris Origo in *The Merchant of Prato* (1957). Datini left all his money to charity, and the city contains several reminders of him, particularly in his own Palazzo Datini. Prato also attracts pilgrims from all over Italy, who come to see the Virgin's Girdle, a prized relic kept in the Duomo and shown five times a year.

***Madonna del Ceppo* by Fra Filippo Lippi in the Museo Civico**

**Duomo façade and pulpit**

### Duomo

Piazza del Duomo. ***Open** daily.*

The Duomo stands on the main square, with the Pulpit of the Holy Girdle to the right of its façade, its frieze of dancing cherubs designed by Donatello (1438). Inside, the first chapel on the left holds the Virgin's Girdle, which is displayed to the public from the pulpit on Easter Sunday, May 1, August 15, September 8 and Christmas Day. Frescoes in the chapel by Agnolo Gaddi (1392–5) relate how the girdle reached Prato. When a local merchant married a Palestinian woman in 1141, she brought it with her. She had inherited it from the Apostle Thomas, who was given it by the Virgin before her Assumption. Also in the Duomo is Fra Filippo Lippi's masterpiece, *The Life of John the Baptist* (1452–66); Salome is a portrait of Lippi's mistress, Lucrezia Buti.

### Museo dell'Opera del Duomo

Piazza del Duomo 49. *(0574) 293 39.* ***Open** Wed–Mon.* ***Adm charge**.*

Besides Donatello's original panels for the Holy Girdle pulpit (sadly corroded by pollution), the museum houses the splendid reliquary (1446) made for the girdle by Maso di Bartolomeo, and *St. Lucy* by Filippino Lippi, the son of Fra Filippo Lippi and Lucrezia Buti.

### Piazza del Comune

The maze of streets around the Duomo contains several important buildings. The city's main street, Via Mazzoni, leads west to the little Piazza del Comune with its pretty Bacchus fountain. The original, made in 1659 by Ferdinando Tacca, is in the nearby Palazzo Comunale.

### Museo Civico

Palazzo Pretorio, Piazza del Comune. *(0574) 45 23 02.* ***Open** Wed–Mon.* ***Adm charge**.*

Opposite the Palazzo Comunale is the austere medieval Palazzo Pretorio, housing the Museo Civico. On display are the altar painting *The Story of the Holy Girdle* by Bernardo Daddi (1312–48) and Fra Filippo Lippi's *Madonna del Ceppo*, featuring a portrait of Francesco Datini, a major patron of the Ceppo charity *(see p183)*.

### Palazzo Datini

Via Ser Lapo Mazzei 43. *(0574) 213 91.* ***Open** Mon–Sat.*

This house where Francesco Datini lived is now a museum. Its archive contains 140,000 business letters and Datini's account books, on which Iris Origo based her biography.

***The Story of the Holy Girdle* by Bernardo Daddi in the Museo Civico**

### Santa Maria delle Carceri

Piazza delle Carceri. **Open** *daily.*

Prato's most important church stands on the site of a prison *(carceri)* on whose wall an image of the Virgin miraculously appeared in 1484. The serene domed church (1485–1506), with its harmoniously proportioned interior, is a fine work by the Renaissance architect Giuliano da Sangallo. Inside, the blue and white glazed terra-cotta roundels of the Evangelists (1490) are by Andrea della Robbia.

### Castello dell'Imperatore

Piazza delle Carceri. *(0574) 382 07.* **Open** *Wed–Mon.*

This imposing castle opposite Santa Maria delle Carceri was built by the German Holy Roman Emperor, Frederick II, in 1237 during his campaign to conquer Italy.

### Museo del Tessuto

Viale della Repubblica 9. *(0574) 57 03 52.* **Open** *by appt.*

The history of Prato's textile industry, the basis of its wealth, is charted in a textile museum located on the city's southern outskirts. The displays include historic looms and examples of different types of cloth, including lush Renaissance embroidery, velvets, lace and damask.

**Castello dell'Imperatore (1237), built by Frederick II**

### Visitors' Checklist

**Road map** D2. *167,580.* *Prato Centrale and Porta al Serraglio.* *Piazza Ciardi and Piazza San Francesco.* *Via Cairoli 48. (0574) 241 12.* *Mon.* **Early closing** *Mon morning (winter); Sat afternoon (summer).*

### Centro per l'Arte Contemporanea Luigi Pecci

Viale della Repubblica 277. *(0574) 57 06 20.* **Open** *Wed–Mon.* **Adm charge.**

To the west of the city, near the Prato Est Autostrada exit, this important cultural center is an interesting modern building in its own right (1988). It is used for changing displays of contemporary art, concerts and films.

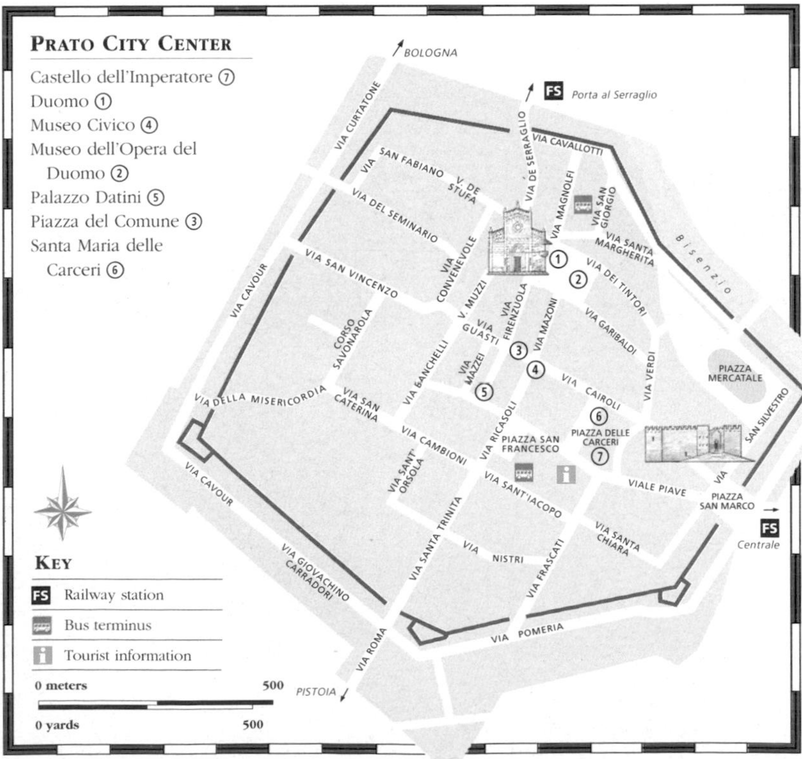

# EASTERN TUSCANY

FROM THE FORESTS *of the Mugello and the Casentino to the heights of La Verna, this is an area of outstanding natural beauty. Hermits and mystics have long favored its more remote reaches, where ancient monastic orders continue to flourish. Only this part of Tuscany could have produced an enigmatic artist like Piero della Francesca, whose celebrated frescoes decorate San Francesco in Arezzo.*

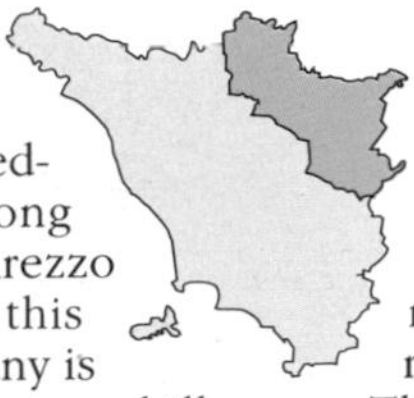

Eastern Tuscany's main transport route, the A1 Autostrada, channels speeding traffic southward along the Arno valley toward Arezzo and Rome. Away from this busy artery, Eastern Tuscany is a little-visited region of steep hills cloaked in beech, oak and chestnut trees. It is particularly attractive in autumn, when the huge forests of the Mugello and the Casentino take on fiery shades of red and gold. This is also the season when mushrooms and truffles abound. Driving through the region at this time of year, you'll see them for sale at roadside stands.

The tiny mountain pastures to the east of the region are grazed both by sheep, whose milk is made into cheese, and by beautiful white cattle, which were once highly prized by the Romans as sacrificial beasts.

This is also a land of saints, hermits and monasteries. The mountaintop sanctuary of La Verna is reputed to be the place where St. Francis received the stigmata – marks resembling Christ's wounds.

The 11th-century hermitage at Camaldoli was intended as the site for a Benedictine order that wished to live in complete isolation, but proved so popular for religious excursions that a visitors' center soon had to be built nearby. The monastery at Vallombrosa has such glorious woodlands that John Milton was moved to describe them in his epic poem *Paradise Lost* (1667).

For art lovers, eastern Tuscany is the region of Piero della Francesca. His frescoes in Arezzo, largely ignored until the late 19th century, form one of the world's greatest fresco cycles.

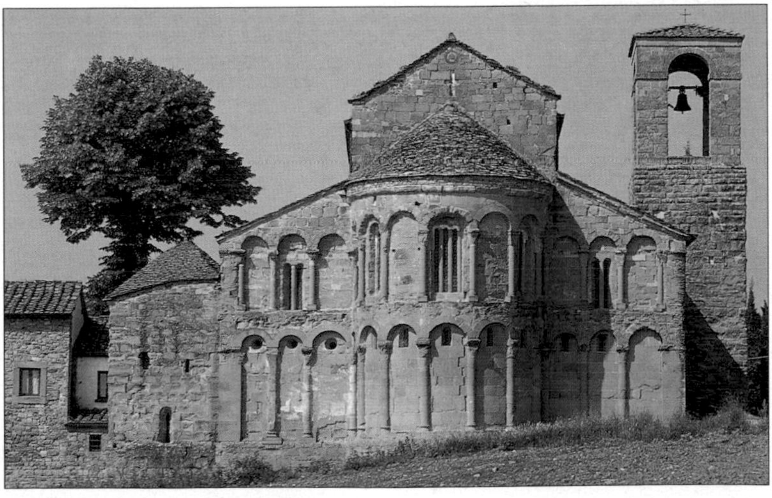

**Pieve di Santi Ippolito e Donato in Bibbiena**

◁ **Fertile countryside surrounding Monterchi**

# Exploring Eastern Tuscany

THE ANCIENT CITY OF AREZZO and the hilltop town of Cortona, with its steep streets, narrow, ladderlike alleys and ancient houses, will amply satisfy visitors in search of culture, art and architecture. The region will also appeal to those who love nature. The woodlands, meadows and streams are ideal for exploring on foot. There are plenty of well-marked paths and picnic areas to encourage you, especially within the beautiful ancient forests surrounding the monasteries at Vallombrosa and Camaldoli.

**KEY**

- Highway
- Major road
- Minor road
- River
- View point

0 kilometers 10

0 miles 10

**Cortona, with its steep streets and medieval towers**

## GETTING AROUND

The region's main highways, the A1 Autostrada and the S71, linking Bibbiena, Poppi and the Casentino, offer swift access to most of the region. The remaining roads are delightfully rural, particularly the S70, with its fine views near Vallombrosa, but be prepared for steep gradients and hairpin bends. Some roads in the Casentino are very narrow. There are passing places, but a speed limit of 40 km/h (25 mph) means you should leave plenty of time for your journey.

Bus and rail transportation is very limited. An intercity train service links Florence to Arezzo, from where there are irregular bus services to other major towns in the region.

## Sights at a Glance

- Anghiari 12
- Arezzo 14
- Bibbiena 7
- Borgo San Lorenzo 2
- Camaldoli 5
- Caprese Michelangelo 10
- The Casentino 9
- Cortona 17
- La Verna 8
- Lucignano 16
- Monte San Savino 15
- Monterchi 13
- The Mugello 1
- Poppi 6
- Sansepolcro 11
- Stia 4
- Vallombrosa 3

Ancient forest in the Casentino: a rich ecological enclave

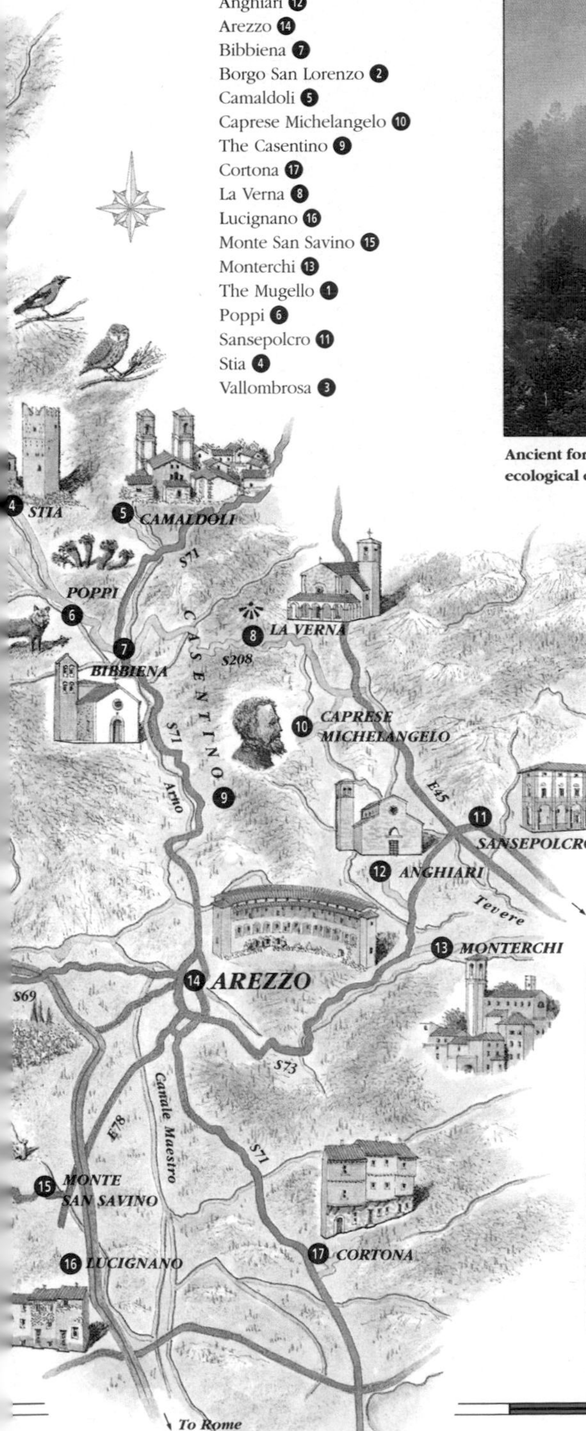

Medieval street in Monte San Savino

## The Mugello ❶

**Road map** D2. [FS] [bus] *Borgo San Lorenzo.* [i] *Piazza Dante 29, Borgo San Lorenzo. (055) 845 87 93.*

THE MUGELLO is the area to the north and east of Florence, and is ideal to see by car. The scenic S65 passes the **Parco Demidoff** at Pratolino, to the south of the region. Here you can see a giant statue of the mountain god, Appennino, carved by Giambologna in 1580. Just to the north, the **Convento di Montesenario** offers fine views over the entire region. Farther east lies the wine town of Rufina, with its **Museo della Vita e del Vino della Val di Sieve**.

**Parco Demidoff**
Via Fiorentina 6, Pratolino. *(055) 40 94 27.* ***Open*** *May–Sep: Fri–Sun.* ***Adm charge.***

**Convento di Montesenario**
Via Montesenario 1, Bivigliano. *(055) 40 64 41.* **Church *open*** *daily.* **Convent *open*** *by request.*

**Museo della Vita e del Vino della Val di Sieve**
Villa di Poggio Reale, Rufina. *(055) 889 79 32.* ***Closed*** *for restoration.*

## Borgo San Lorenzo ❷

**Road map** D2. *15,285.* [FS] [bus] *Via Palmiro Togliatti 45. (055) 84 55 51.* *Tue.*

SUBSTANTIALLY REBUILT after an earthquake in 1919, this is the largest town of the Mugello. The parish church, the **Pieve di San Lorenzo**, has an odd Romanesque campanile, circular in its lower stages and hexagonal above. In the apse, the wall paintings (1906) are by the Art Nouveau artist Galileo Chini. He also worked on the Tabernacle of St. Francis (1926), a shrine outside the church, and the Santuario del Santissimo Crocifisso, a church on the edge of town.

**Tabernacle of St. Francis in Borgo San Lorenzo**

**Woodland landscape at Vallombrosa**

To the west are **Castello del Trebbio**, with 15th-century gardens, and the castellated **Villa di Cafaggiolo**, with its bulging clock tower. Among the first Medici villas, both were built by Michelozzo di Bartolommeo (1396–1472) for Cosimo il Vecchio.

**Pieve di San Lorenzo**
Via Cocchi 4. ***Open*** *daily.*

**Castello del Trebbio**
San Piero a Sieve. *(055) 845 87 93 (Mon, Wed, Fri mornings).* ***Open*** *by appt.* ***Adm charge.*** *partial.*

**Villa di Cafaggiolo**
Cafaggiolo, Barberino di Mugello. ***Open*** *by appt.* *(055) 845 87 93 (Mon, Wed, Fri mornings).* ***Adm charge.*** *partial.*

## Vallombrosa ❸

**Road map** D2. *from Florence.* *(055) 86 20 29.* **Church *open*** *daily.* **Abbey *open*** *by appt.*

LIKE THE MONASTERIES of the Casentino *(see p192)*, the abbey buildings at Vallombrosa are surrounded by woodland. The routes to this sight are all very scenic.

The Vallombrosan order was founded by Saint Giovanni Gualberto Visdomini in 1038. He aimed to persuade like-minded aristocrats to join him in relinquishing their wealth and adopting a life of great austerity. Contrary to these worthy ideals, the order grew wealthy and powerful during the 16th and 17th centuries. It was then that today's fortress-like abbey was built. Today, the order comprises some 20 monks.

In 1638 the English poet John Milton (1608–74) visited the abbey. The beautiful scenery of this area inspired a passage in his epic poem, *Paradise Lost.*

Façade of Santa Maria Assunta in Stia

## Stia ❹

**Road map** D2. 3,017.
Piazza Tanucci 65. (0575) 50 41 06.
Tue.

STIA IS A BUSTLING, attractive village on the Arno. In the main piazza is the Romanesque church of **Santa Maria Assunta**, with a rather plain façade. Inside is a 16th-century terra-cotta *Madonna and Child* by Andrea della Robbia.

There are two medieval Guidi family castles close by: **Castello di Palagio**, with an attractive garden, and the **Castello di Porciano**, which houses an agricultural museum.

**Santa Maria Assunta**
Piazza Tanucci. **Open** *daily.*

**Castello di Palagio**
Via Vittorio Veneto. *(0575) 58 22 74.* **Open** *Jul–Sep: Fri–Sun.* **Adm charge**.

**Castello di Porciano**
Porciano. *(0575) 58 26 35.* **Open** *mid-May–mid-Oct: Sun.*

## Camaldoli ❺

**Road map** E2. *from Bibbiena.* *(0575) 55 60 12.* **Monastery and hermitage** ***open*** *daily.* **Museo Ornitologico Forestale** ***open*** *Jun–Sep: daily; Oct–May: by appt.* **Adm charge**.

THE MONASTERY was founded in 1046 and today houses 40 Carthusian monks. Visitors to Camaldoli will want to see not only the monastery but the original *eremo* (hermitage), 2.5 km (1.5 miles) away. A narrow, winding road leads up from the monastic complex to the hermitage through thick forest. This ancient woodland, which is some of the most ecologically rich in Europe, was declared a National Park in 1991.

The hermitage dates back to 1012 when San Romualdo (St. Rumbold) came here with a small group of followers, to cut themselves off completely from the outside world.

Today's monks lead a more gregarious life, running a small café in the monastery below. As you descend to the monastery complex you will also pass numerous picnic spots and some of the many local footpaths.

The monks still tend the magnificent beech and chestnut woodland that surrounds the ancient monastery, as their predecessors have for nearly 1,000 years. A pharmacy, dating to 1543, now sells soaps, toiletries and liqueurs made by the monks.

There is a small ornithological museum across the road from the monastery, opposite the parking lot, which illustrates the area's rich bird life.

## Poppi ❻

**Road map** E2. *6,700.*
*Via Nazionale, Badia Prataglia (mid-Jun – mid-Sep). (0575) 55 90 54.*
*Tue.*

THE OLDER PART of Poppi is located high above the town's bus and train termini. Its splendid castle, the imposing **Castello di Poppi**, can be seen from as far away as Bibbiena *(see p192)*. Just south of the town is the **Zoo Fauna Europa**, which specializes in the conservation of endangered European species like the Apennine wolf and the lynx.

Visible from Poppi, a short drive to the northwest up the Arno valley, is the 11th-century **Castello di Romena** where Dante stayed as a guest of the local rulers in the early 14th century. Romena's *pieve*, dating to 1152, is a typical example of a Romanesque village church.

**Castello di Poppi**
*(0575) 52 02 94.* **Open** *Apr–Sep: daily; Oct–Mar: Sat & Sun, or by appt.* **Adm charge**.

**Zoo Fauna Europa**
Poppi. *(0575) 52 90 79.* **Open** *daily.* **Adm charge**.

**Castello di Romena**
Pratovecchio. *(0575) 586 33.* **Open** *daily.*

Castello di Poppi, which towers over Poppi and overlooks the entire Casentino

Casentino landscape

## Bibbiena 7

**Road map** E2. *11,000.* *Via Berni 29. (0575) 59 30 98.* *Thu.*

One of the oldest towns in the region, Bibbiena was in medieval times the subject of intense territorial feuding between Arezzo and Florence. It is now the commercial center of the Casentino region, surrounded by a haphazard expanse of factories and industrial buildings.

The town's main attraction is the **Pieve di Santi Ippolito e Donato**. Dating back to the 12th century, this church contains some fine Siena School paintings and an altarpiece by Bicci di Lorenzo (1373–1452).

Bibbiena's main square, the Piazza Tarlati, offers excellent views of Poppi *(see p191).*

**Pieve di Santi Ippolito e Donato**

Piazza Tarlati. ***Open** daily.*

## La Verna 8

**Road map** E2. *from Bibbiena.* *(0575) 59 93 56.* ***Open** daily.* *partial.*

The rocky outcrop on which La Verna monastery stands, called La Senna, was split, according to legend, by an earthquake when Christ died on the cross. The site was given to St. Francis by the local ruler, Count Orlando Cattani, in 1213, and it was here, in 1224, that the saint was miraculously marked with the stigmata – the wounds of Christ.

Today, the monastery is both a popular tourist sight and a charismatic religious center. Its modern buildings are not particularly attractive, but they contain numerous sculptures by the della Robbia workshops. There are several signposted paths through the surrounding woodland, leading to some excellent viewpoints.

## The Casentino 9

**Road map** E2. FS *from Bibbiena.* *Bibbiena.*

The vast Casentino region, an area of tiny villages dotted among hills covered with ancient woodland, lies to the north of Arezzo. The river Arno has its source here, on the slopes of Monte Falterona. Countless streams run down the region's valleys to join it, creating stunning waterfalls.

A favorite destination for walkers, the area is renowned for its abundant autumn mushroom crop *(see p198).*

The monastery at La Verna, founded by St. Francis in 1213

## Caprese Michelangelo 10

**Road map** E2. *1760.* *from Arezzo.* *Via Capoluogo. (0575) 79 39 12.*

Michelangelo Buonarroti was born in Caprese on March 6, 1475, while his father served briefly as the town's *podestà* – a job combining the functions of mayor, magistrate and chief of police. His birthplace, the rustic Casa del Podestà, is now the **Museo Michelangelo**, containing photographs and copies of the artist's work. The town walls are dotted with modern sculptures and have fine views over the local alpine landscape. Michelangelo attributed his keen mind to the mountain air he breathed here as an infant.

Michelangelo Buonarroti (1475–1564)

**Museo Michelangelo**

Casa del Podestà, Via Capoluogo 1. *(0575) 79 39 12.* ***Open** daily.*

## Sansepolcro 11

**Road map** E3. *15,700.* *Via della Fonte 5. (0575) 74 05 36.* *Tue, Sat.*

Sansepolcro is a busy industrial town, famous as the birthplace of the artist Piero della Francesca (1410–92). Most visitors come to see the collection of his work at the **Museo Civico**.

Housed in the 14th-century Palazzo Comunale, the museum's most famous exhibit is Piero's fresco, *The Resurrection* (1463), in which a curiously impassive Christ strides out of his tomb. The sleeping soldiers at his feet, in their Renaissance armor, seem trapped in time, while the Son of God takes possession of a primitive, eternal landscape. Several other works by Piero are displayed in the same room, notably the *Madonna della Misericordia* (1462).

Sansepolcro is home to a number of other major works. Chief among these are Luca Signorelli's 15th-century *Crucifixion* (also in the Museo Civico) and Rosso Fiorentino's Mannerist *Deposition* in **San Lorenzo** church.

**Museo Civico**
Via Aggiunti 65. (0575) 73 22 18.
**Open** daily. **Adm charge**.

**San Lorenzo**
Via Santa Croce. **Open** by appt.
(0575) 74 05 36.

Anghiari, a typical medieval walled town

## Anghiari ⓬

**Road map** E3. 5,874.
Via Matteotti 103. (0575) 74 92 79. Wed.

The battle of Anghiari, between Florence and Milan in 1440, was to have been the subject of a fresco by Leonardo in Florence's Palazzo Vecchio. It was, however, never painted – one of the greatest "lost" works of the Renaissance. Today, this historic little town sits peacefully amid fields of tobacco, a traditional crop of the upper valley of the river Tevere (Tiber), which rises nearby on the slopes of Monte Fumaiolo.

**Museo dell'Alta Valle del Tevere**
Piazza Mameli 16. (0575) 78 80 01. **Open** daily.
Several major works, such as Jacopo della Quercia's fine wooden *Madonna* (1420), can be seen here. There are also displays of locally made furniture and toys.

**Santa Maria delle Grazie**
Propositura. **Open** daily.
The town's main church, dating to the 18th century, contains a high altar and tabernacle from the della Robbia workshops. There is also a 15th-century *Madonna and Child* painted by Matteo di Giovanni.

**Museo della Misericordia**
Via Francesco Nenci 13. (0575) 78 95 77. **Open** by appt.
The Misericordia, a charitable organization, was founded in the 13th century to look after ailing pilgrims on their way to Rome. Today it operates Tuscany's efficient ambulance service *(see p277)*. This small museum records its work.

***The Resurrection*** **(1463) by Piero della Francesca in Sansepolcro**

## Monterchi ⓭

**Road map** E3. 1,910.
Arezzo. Sun.

The cemetery chapel at Monterchi was the site chosen in 1460 by Piero della Francesca for his *Madonna del Parto* (Pregnant Madonna) *(see p26)*, possibly because his mother may be buried here. The recently restored fresco is now in the **Museo Madonna del Parto**.

A work of haunting ambiguity, it simultaneously captures the Virgin's pride in the impending birth, the weariness of pregnancy and the sorrow borne of knowing that her child will be no ordinary man.

**Museo Madonna del Parto**
Via Reglia 1. (0575) 707 13.
**Open** Tue–Sun. **Adm charge**.

# Arezzo ⓮

ONE OF THE WEALTHIEST CITIES in Tuscany, Arezzo produces gold jewelry for shops all over Europe. It is famous for Piero della Francesca's frescoes in San Francesco. War damage has led to much rebuilding – broad avenues have replaced many of the medieval alleys. The Chimera fountain near the station remains, however, a firm reminder of the city's past. It is a copy of an Etruscan bronze *(see p40)* cast here in 380 BC.

**Chimera fountain**

### San Francesco

*See pp196–7.*

### Pieve di Santa Maria

Corso Italia 7. ***Open** daily.*

Arezzo's main shopping street, Corso Italia, leads uphill to the Pieve di Santa Maria, with one of Tuscany's most ornate Romanesque façades. The complex filigree of interlaced arches has, however, weathered badly.

The splendid campanile, the "tower of a hundred holes," dates from 1330. Its name derives from the many arches running through it.

### Piazza Grande

The square is famous for its regular antiques market *(see p268).* On the west side, the façade of the Palazzo della Fraternità dei Laici is decorated with a relief of the Virgin (1434) by Bernardo Rossellino. The lower half of the building dates from 1377. The belfry and clock tower date from 1552.

The north side of the square is occupied by a handsome arcade designed by Vasari in 1573.

### Fortezza Medicea e Parco il Prato

*(0575) 37 76 66.* ***Open** daily.*

Antonio da Sangallo the Younger's imposing fortress was built for Cosimo I during the 16th century. It was partly demolished in the 18th century, leaving only the ramparts intact. With its excellent views across the Arno valley, it remains an excellent spot for a picnic.

The same can be said of the city's large public park, the Parco il Prato, with its extensive lawns. It contains a huge statue (1928) of the great poet Petrarch. The house where he was born stands at the entrance to the park.

### Duomo

Piazza del Duomo. ***Open** daily.*

Begun in 1278, the Duomo remained incomplete until 1510; its façade dates to 1914. A huge building, its Gothic interior is lit through windows containing beautiful 16th-century stained glass by Guillaume de Marcillat, a French artist who settled in Arezzo.

High on the wall to the left of the 15th-century High Altar can be seen the tomb of Guido Tarlati, bishop and ruler of Arezzo from 1312 until his death in 1327. Carved reliefs depict scenes from his unconventional life. Next to the tomb is a small fresco of Mary Magdalene by Piero della Francesca (1410–92).

**Duomo façade, completed as recently as 1914**

The Lady Chapel, fronted by an intricate wrought-iron screen (1796), contains a terracotta *Assumption* by Andrea della Robbia (1435–1525).

### Museo del Duomo

Piazzetta behind the Duomo 13.

*(0575) 239 91.* ***Open** Thu–Sat.* ***Adm charge**.*

Among the artifacts removed from the cathedral are three wooden crucifixes, dating from the 12th and 13th centuries. The oldest of these was painted by Margaritone di Arezzo in 1264.

Also of interest are Bernardo Rossellino's terracotta bas-relief of *The Annunciation* (1434), a number of frescoes by Vasari (1512–74) and an *Annunciation* by Spinello Aretino (1373–1410). Vasari and Aretino were born locally.

**Apse of Pieve di Santa Maria and Palazzo della Fraternità dei Laici in Piazza Grande**

### Casa del Vasari

Via XX Settembre 55. (0575) 30 03 01. ***Open** daily.*

Vasari (1512–74) built this house for himself in 1540 and decorated the ceilings and walls with portraits of fellow artists, friends and mentors. He also painted himself looking out of one of the windows. Vasari was a prolific painter and architect, and is most famous for his book, *Lives of the Most Excellent Painters, Sculptors and Architects* (1530). A contemporary account of many great Renaissance artists, it has, in spite of revealing an often cavalier attitude to the truth, led to Vasari being described as the first art historian.

**Detail of fresco from Casa del Vasari**

### Museo Statale d'Arte Medioevale e Moderna

Via di San Lorentino 8. *(0575) 30 03 01.* ***Open** daily. **Adm charge**.*

The museum is housed in the graceful 15th-century Palazzo Bruni. Its courtyard contains architectural fragments and sculptures dating from the 10th to the 17th centuries.

The varied collection includes one of the best displays of majolica pottery in Italy. There are also a number of terracottas by Andrea della Robbia and his followers; frescoes by Vasari and Signorelli; and paintings by 19th- and 20th-century artists, including members of the Italian *Macchiaioli* School *(see p123)*.

### Anfiteatro Romano e Museo Archeologico

Via Margaritone 10. *(0575) 208 82.* ***Open** daily. **Adm charge** for Museo Archeologico.*

A ruined Roman amphitheater stands near the Museo Archeologico, to the south of Arezzo.

Famous for its extensive collection of Roman Aretine ware, the museum has a display showing how this high quality red-glazed pottery was produced during the 1st century BC and exported throughout the Roman Empire.

**1st-century BC Aretine ware**

> **VISITORS' CHECKLIST**
>
> **Road map** E3. 92,000. FS *Piazza della Repubblica.* *Piazza della Repubblica 22. (0575) 37 76 78.* *Sat.* *Giostra del Saracino (last Sun in Aug and 1st Sun in Sep). **Early closing** Sat (Mon am in winter).*

### Santa Maria delle Grazie

Via di Santa Maria. ***Open** daily.*

Completed in 1449 and set in its own walled garden, this jewel of a church, fronted by Benedetto da Maiano's pretty loggia (1482), stands on the south-eastern outskirts of the town. The High Altar, by Andrea della Robbia (1435–1525), encloses Parri di Spinello's fresco of the Virgin (1430). A damaged fresco by Lorentino d'Arezzo (1430–1505) is on the right of the altar.

## AREZZO

Anfiteatro Romano e Museo Archeologico ⑨
Casa del Vasari ①
Duomo ④
Fortezza Medicea e Parco il Prato ⑧
Museo del Duomo ③
Museo Statale d'Arte Medioevale e Moderna ⑦
Piazza Grande ⑦
Pieve di Santa Maria ⑥
San Francesco ⑤

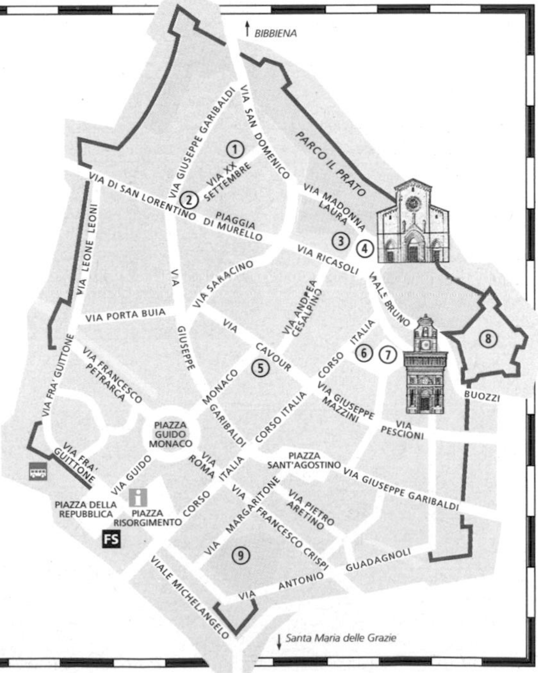


**KEY**

FS Railway station
Bus terminus
Tourist information

0 meters 500
0 yards 500

# San Francesco

THE 13TH-CENTURY CHURCH of San Francesco contains Piero della Francesca's frescoes, *The Legend of the True Cross* (1452–66), his masterpiece and one of Italy's greatest fresco cycles. The frescoes show how the Cross, made from the tree that bore the forbidden fruit Eve tempted Adam to eat, was found near Jerusalem by the Empress Helena. Her son, the Emperor Constantine, adopted it as his battle emblem. In reality, Constantine granted the Christian faith official recognition through the Edict of Milan, signed in 313. He is said to have bequeathed the Empire to the Church in 337, although this was still hotly disputed when Piero painted the frescoes.

**Exaggerated Hats**
*Piero often depicted historical figures in Renaissance garb.*

**Painted Crucifix**
*The 13th-century Crucifix forms the focal point of the fresco cycle. The figure at the foot of the Cross represents St. Francis, to whom the church is dedicated.*

**The Cross** returns to Jerusalem.

**Judas reveals** where the Cross is hidden.

**The Empress Helena** watches the Cross being dug up. The town shown in the background, symbolizing Jerusalem, is an accurate representation of 15th-century Arezzo.

**The Annunciation**, with its stately figures and aura of serenity, is typical of Piero's enigmatic style.

**The Defeat of Chosroes**
*The battle scene shows the chaos of Renaissance warfare. Piero was influenced by ancient Roman carving, especially the battle scenes that often decorated sarcophagi.*

**The Death of Adam**
*This vivid portrayal of Adam and Eve in old age illustrates Piero's masterly treatment of anatomy. He was one of the first Renaissance artists to paint nude figures.*

### Visitors' Checklist

Piazza San Francesco, Arezzo.
(0575) 206 30. **Open** 8:30am–noon, 1:30–6:30pm daily.
10am, 11am, 6pm daily.

**The prophets** appear to play no part in the narrative cycle; their presence may be for purely decorative reasons.

**The buildings** in the fresco reflect the newly fashionable Renaissance style in architecture *(see p23).*

**The wood** of the Cross is buried in a pit.

**Constantine dreams** of the Cross on the eve of battle.

**Constantine adopts** the Cross as his battle emblem.

**The Queen of Sheba** recognizes the wood of the Cross.

**Solomon's Handshake**
*The Queen's handshake with Solomon, King of Israel, symbolizes 15th-century hopes for a union between the Orthodox and Western churches.*

## Mushrooms in Tuscany

**Champignon**
*(Marasmius oreades)*

THE PEOPLE OF TUSCANY consider mushrooms a great delicacy. Collecting fungi can be dangerous, unless you are an expert, but you can sample the best varieties in the region's restaurants. The smaller edible varieties are sometimes chopped and combined with mashed garlic to make a pasta sauce. As appetizers, many menus include *funghi trifolati* (sautéed mushrooms with garlic and parsley), or the region's most popular mushrooms, porcini, served *in gratella* (grilled). The prized truffle is often simply grated over homemade pasta; it has a pronounced flavor and should be used sparingly.

**Gathering chanterelles *(right)* and saddle fungus *(left)***

**Cauliflower fungus**
*(Sparassis crispa)*

**Field blewit**
*(Lepista personata)*

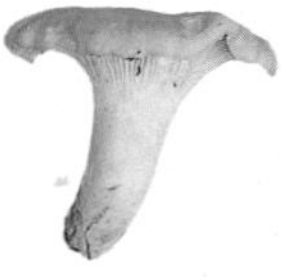

**Chanterelle**
*(Cantharellus cibarius)*

**Parasol**
*(Lepiota procera)*

**Cepe**
*(Boletus edulis)*

**Oyster**
*(Pleurotus ostreatus)*

**Morel**
*(Morchella esculanta)*

**Champignon**
*(Marasmius oreades)*

### THE BEST TUSCAN MUSHROOMS

Prized species have a rich flavor and a firm texture. They are sold from mid-September to late November at shops and markets in the Casentino (see p192) and the Maremma (pp232–3).

**Porcini**
*This popular mushroom, also known in the US as cepe, is one of the few wild species available all year, either fresh or dried.*

## Monte San Savino ⓯

**Road map** E3. 7,794. FS
Piazza Gamurrini 25. (0575) 84 30 98. Wed.

THE TOWN stands on the western edge of the Valdichiana, once a marshy and malaria-ridden plain that was drained by Cosimo I in the 16th century. It is now rich farmland, used to rear cattle whose meat is made into *Bistecca alla Fiorentina*, the famous beefsteaks served in Florentine restaurants *(p255)*.

Agriculture has made the town prosperous, and its streets are lined with handsome buildings and churches. Some of these are by the High Renaissance sculptor and architect Andrea Contucci, known as Sansovino (1460–1529), who was born in the town; a number are by Antonio da Sangallo the Elder (1455–1537), his contemporary.

The town's main street, Corso Sangallo, starts at the Porta Fiorentina town gate, built in 1550 to Giorgo Vasari's design. The street leads past the 14th-century Cassero, or Citadel, whose exterior walls are now almost entirely hidden by 17th-century houses. There are good views from the interior, which contains the tourist office and the small **Museo di Ceramica** with its extensive collection of local work. Farther up the street is the handsome Classical Loggia dei Mercanti (1518–20), designed by Sansovino, and the Palazzo Comunale, originally built as the Palazzo di Monte by Sangallo for Cardinal Antonio di Monte in 1515. Sansovino's house can be seen in the Piazza di Monte. He laid out the square, built the fine double loggia with Ionic columns that fronts **Sant'Agostino** church and went on to design the cloister standing alongside it. Inside the church is a series of 15th-century frescoes illustrating scenes from *The Life of Christ*, and Vasari's *Assumption* altarpiece (1539). Sansovino's worn tomb slab lies beneath the pulpit.

Lucignano, with its circular street plan

Locally made vase, Museo di Ceramica

Corso Sangallo in Monte San Savino

**Museo di Ceramica**
Piazza Gamurrini. (0575) 84 30 98. ***Open*** *Jun–Oct: daily; Nov–May: Sat & Sun.* ***Adm charge***.

**Sant'Agostino**
Piazza di Monte. ***Open*** *daily.*

## Lucignano ⓰

**Road map** E3. 3,349.
Piazza del Tribunale 1. (0575) 83 61 28. Thu.

AN ATTRACTIVE medieval town, Lucignano contains many well-preserved 14th-century houses. The street plan is extremely unusual, consisting of a series of four concentric rings encircling the hill upon which the town sits, sheltered by its ancient walls. There are four small piazzas at the center.

The **Collegiata** is fronted by some attractive steps whose circular shape reflects the town's street plan. Completed by Orazio Porta in 1594, the church contains fine gilded wooden angels that were added in 1706.

The 14th-century Palazzo Comunale houses the **Museo Comunale**. Its highlight is a massive gold reliquary, 2.5 m (8 ft) high, to which numerous artists contributed over the period 1350–1471. Because of its shape, it is known as the *Tree of Lucignano*.

Also of note are two 14th-century paintings by Luca Signorelli: a lunette showing St. Francis of Assisi miraculously receiving the wounds of Christ to his hands and feet, and a *Madonna and Child*. There are several fine 13th- to 15th-century Siena School paintings and a small painting of the Madonna by Lippo Vanni (1341–75).

The vaulted ceiling of the main chamber, the Sala del Tribunale, has frescoes of famous biblical figures and characters from Classical mythology painted from 1438–65 by various Siena School artists.

**Collegiata**
Costa San Michele. ***Open*** *daily.*

**Museo Comunale**
Piazza del Tribunale 22. (0575) 83 61 28. ***Open*** *Tue–Sun.* ***Adm charge***.

# Cortona 17

Cortona is one of the oldest cities in Tuscany. It was founded by the Etruscans *(see p40)*, whose work can still be seen in the foundations of the town's massive stone walls. The city was a major seat of power during the medieval period, able to hold its own against larger towns like Siena and Arezzo; its decline followed defeat by Naples in 1409, after which it was sold to Florence and lost its autonomy. The main street, Via Nazionale, is remarkably flat in comparison with the rest of Cortona. The numerous ladderlike alleys leading off it, for instance, the Vicolo del Precipizio (Precipice Alley), are far more typical.

**Palazzo Comunale**

### Palazzo Comunale

***Not open** to the public.*

Dating to the 13th-century, the building was enlarged at the beginning of the 16th century, to incorporate the distinctive tower. Its ancient steps are the ideal place to linger in the early evening.

### Museo dell'Accademia Etrusca

Palazzo Casali, Piazza Signorelli 9. *(0575) 63 04 15.* ***Open** Tue–Sun.* ***Adm charge**.*

This is one of the region's most rewarding museums. It contains a number of major Etruscan artifacts, including a unique bronze chandelier *(see p41)* dating to the 4th century BC. There are also various Egyptian objects, notably a wooden model funerary boat dating to the second millennium BC.

The beautiful fresco of Polymnia, muse of song, on the west wall of the main hall, was once believed to be 1st- or 2nd-century Roman. It is now known to be a brilliant 18th-century fake.

### Duomo

Piazza del Duomo. ***Open** daily.*

The present Duomo was designed by Giuliano da Sangallo in the 16th century. Remains of an earlier Romanesque building were incorporated into the west façade. The entrance is through an attractive doorway (1550) by Cristofanello.

### Museo Diocesano

Piazza del Duomo 1. *(0575) 628 30.* ***Open** Tue–Sun.* ***Adm charge**.*

Housed in the 16th-century church of Gesù, the museum contains several masterpieces. Chief among these are Fra Angelico's *Annunciation* (1428–30), a *Crucifixion* by Pietro Lorenzetti (c.1280–1348) and a *Deposition* by Luca Signorelli (1441–1523). There is also a Roman sarcophagus, featuring Lapiths and centaurs, which was much admired by Donatello and Brunelleschi.

**Medieval houses in Via Janelli**

### Via Janelli

The medieval houses in this short street are some of the oldest to survive in Italy. A striking feature is their overhanging upper stories, built out on massive timbers.

### San Francesco

Via Maffei. ***Open** daily.*

The church was built in 1245 by Brother Elias, a native of Cortona, who succeeded St. Francis as leader of the Franciscan order. He and Luca Signorelli (1441–1523), also born locally, are buried here.

The church contains an *Annunciation*, the last work by Pietro da Cortona (1596–1669) and a 10th-century ivory reliquary, brought back from Constantinople by Brother Elias. It is displayed in Bernardino Radi's 17th-century marble tabernacle.

***The Annunciation*** **(1428–30) by Fra Angelico in the Museo Diocesano**

### Piazza Garibaldi

Located on the eastern edge of town, this square is a favorite haunt of American students, who come to Cortona each summer. It offers superb views, notably of the handsome Renaissance church of Santa Maria delle Grazie al Calcinaio.

### Via Crucis and Santa Margherita

The Via Crucis, a long uphill lane with gardens on either side, leading to the 19th-century church of Santa Margherita, was laid out as a war memorial in 1947. It is decorated with Futurist mosaics depicting episodes in Christ's Passion by Gino Severini (1883–1966).

The church, rebuilt from 1856–97 in the Romanesque-Gothic style, has excellent views over the surrounding countryside. Inside, to the right of the altar, lie a number of Turkish battle standards and lanterns captured during 18th-century naval battles. A single rose window remains from the original church.

**Santa Maria delle Grazie**

### Santa Maria delle Grazie

*Calcinaio.* ***Open*** *daily.*

A pleasant 15-minute stroll from the center of town, this remarkable Renaissance church (1485) is one of the few surviving works by Francesco di Giorgio Martini (1439–1502). The building is opened on request – ask at the caretaker's house, beyond a garden to the right of the main entrance.

The attractive high altar (1519), built by Bernardino Covatti, contains a 15th-century image of the Madonna del Calcinaio. The stained glass is by Guillaume de Marcillat *(see p194)*.

### Visitors' Checklist

**Road map** E3. *22,620.*
FS *Camucia, 5 km (3 miles) SE Cortona.* *Piazza Garibaldi.* *Via Nazionale. (0575) 63 03 52.* *Sat.* *Sagra della Bistecca (Aug 15).* ***Shops closed*** *Mon am.*

### Tanella di Pitagora

*On the road to Sodo.* ***Open*** *daily.*

One of several restored Etruscan tombs on the plain below the town, "Pythagoras's tomb" draws its name from a confusion between Cortona and Crotone, Pythagoras's birthplace. It is referred to as a "melon" tomb because of the grassy mound that has been built up around it.

**Tanella di Pitagora, a typical Etruscan "melon" tomb**

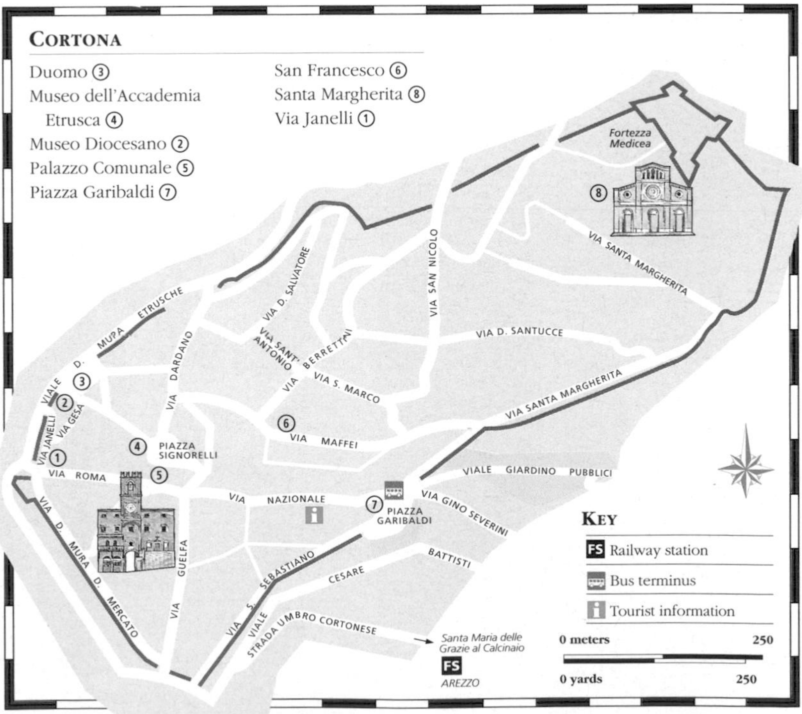

37

# Central Tuscany

*With Siena at its heart, this is an agricultural area of great scenic beauty, noted for its historic walled towns such as San Gimignano and Pienza. To the north of Siena is the Chianti Classico region, where some of Italy's best wines are produced; to the south is the Crete, with landscapes characterized by round clay hills, eroded of topsoil by heavy rain over the centuries.*

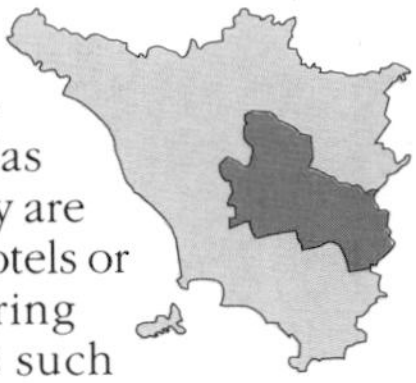

The vine-clad hills to the north of Siena are dotted with farmhouses, villas and baronial castles. Many are now turned into luxury hotels or rental apartments, offering various leisure facilities such as tennis courts, swimming pools and riding stables: this is now one of the most popular areas for family vacations in the Tuscan countryside.

To the south of Siena, in the Crete, shepherds tend sheep whose milk is used to produce the pecorino cheese popular throughout Tuscany. Cypress trees, planted to provide windbreaks along roads and around isolated farms, are an important sculptural feature in this empty and primeval landscape.

Linking the two regions is the S2 highway, an ancient road along which pilgrims made their way in the Middle Ages, followed by travelers on the Grand Tour *(see p53)* in the 18th and 19th centuries. Romanesque churches line the roads, and the valleys and passes are defended by castles and garrison towns, most of which have hardly changed over the years.

### Constant Conflict

The history of the region is of a long feud between the two city states of Florence and Siena. Siena's finest hour was its victory in the Battle of Montaperti in 1260, but when Siena finally succumbed to the Black Death, and subsequently to a crushing defeat by Florence in the siege of 1554–5, the city went into decline.

As several other Central Tuscan cities experienced the same fate, this lovely region became a forgotten backwater, frozen in time. But after centuries of neglect, the graceful late-medieval buildings in many of the towns are now being well restored, making this the most architecturally rewarding part of Tuscany to explore.

**The beautifully preserved fortified town of Monteriggioni**

**◁ A house in San Quirico d'Orcia, bathed in the morning light**

# Exploring Central Tuscany

THE BEAUTIFUL CITY of Siena, with its narrow streets and medieval buildings of rose-colored brick, is the natural starting place for exploring the heart of Tuscany. From here it is only a short drive to the castle-dotted landscapes of Chianti to the north, or to historic towns such as San Gimignano and Montepulciano. Although these towns are full of visitors during the day, at night they revert to their timeless Tuscan character and many have first-class restaurants serving local fare. The landscape is of cypresses, olive groves, vineyards, simple churches and stone farmhouses.

**Wicker-covered *damigiane* (demijohns) transporting local Chianti wine**

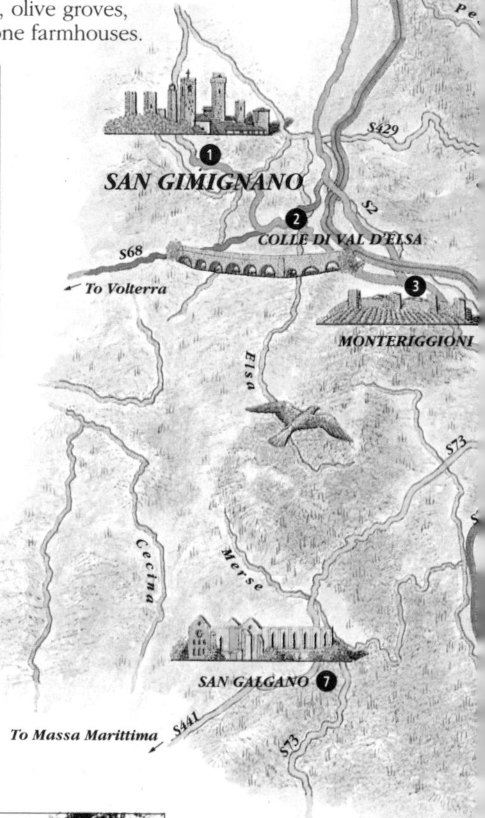


## GETTING AROUND

The S2 is the main road south through Siena. The S222 links Florence with Siena and is known as the *Chiantigiana* (Chianti Way) as it passes through the Chianti wine-growing area. Both routes are well served by bus services, and tour operators in both cities offer tours of the main sites. Train services are limited to one line between Florence and Siena. A car is a great advantage, especially for visiting the Chianti wine estates.

**View over Siena from the surrounding hills**

KEY

To Grosseto

- Highway
- Major road
- Minor road
- Scenic route
- River
- View point

0 kilometers 10

0 miles 10

Typical Crete landscape with cypresses

## Sights at a Glance

Asciano 5
Bagno Vignoni 10
Chiusi 13
Colle di Val d'Elsa 2
Montalcino 8
Monte Oliveto Maggiore 6
Montepulciano 12
Monteriggioni 3
Pienza 11
Sant'Antimo 14
San Galgano 7
San Gimignano 1
San Quirico d'Orcia 9
Siena 4

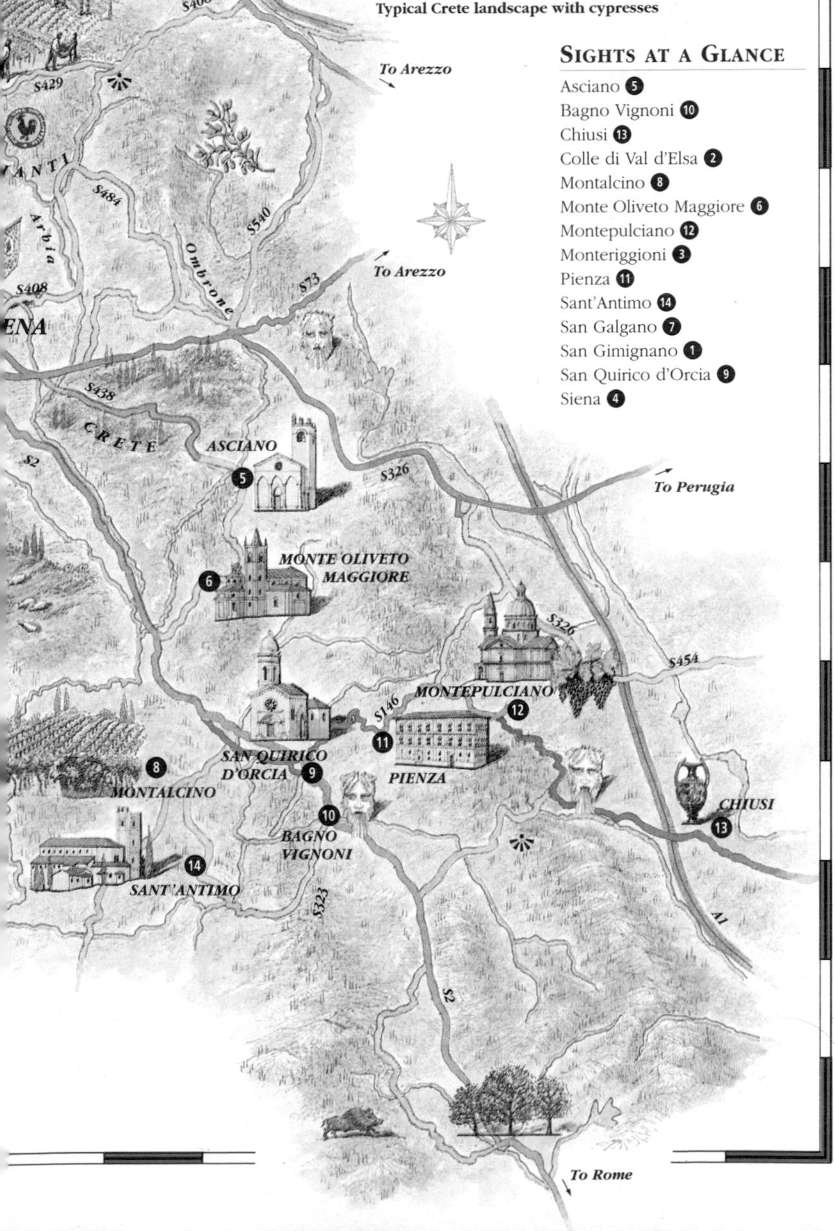

**Palazzo Campana, the gateway to Colle Alta**

## San Gimignano ❶

*See pp 208–11.*

## Colle di Val d'Elsa ❷

**Road map** C3. *17,200.* FS
*Via Campana 18. (0577) 92 27 91.*
*Fri.*

COLLE DI VAL D'ELSA has two separate parts – a lower and an upper town. Colle Alta, the upper town, is of great medieval architectural interest. Arnolfo di Cambio, who built the Palazzo Vecchio in Florence *(see pp 78–9)*, was born here in 1232. In the modern lower town, shops sell locally made crystal.

### Palazzo Campana

***Not open** to the public.*
This Mannerist palazzo was built on a viaduct in 1539 by Baccio d'Agnolo, forming a gateway to Colle Alta.

### Duomo

Piazza del Duomo. ***Open** daily.*
*(0577) 92 31 25.*
The Duomo has a marble Renaissance pulpit carved with bas-reliefs of the Madonna (1465), attributed to Giuliano da Maiano. The façade was rebuilt in 1603.

### Museo Archeologico

Palazzo Pretorio, Piazza del Duomo.
*(0577) 92 29 54. **Open** Tue–Sun.*
***Adm charge**.*
The museum, in the upper rooms of the palazzo, has a collection of cremation urns from local Etruscan tombs. The building was once a jail: political slogans written on the walls by Communists survive from the 1920s.

### Museo d'Arte Sacra

Via del Castello 27. *(0577) 92 31 25. **Closed** temporarily.*
Housed in the former bishop's palace, the museum features 14th-century frescoes of hunting scenes by Bartolo di Fredi, Sienese paintings and a collection of Etruscan pottery.

***Sgraffito* cherub, Museo Civico**

### Museo Civico

Via del Castello 31. *(0577) 92 38 88. **Open** Apr–Sep Tue–Sun; Oct–Mar Sat, Sun & public hols only.*
***Adm charge**.*
The museum is in the Palazzo dei Priori, whose façade is decorated with *sgraffito* work scratched in the plaster, incorporating cherubs and Medici coats of arms. There is a small collection of Siena School paintings, Etruscan pottery and scale models of the old town of Colle Alta. The chapel next to the main room has a portico decorated with frescoes by Simone Ferri in 1581.

### Santa Maria in Canonica

Via del Castello. ***Open** daily.*
The Romanesque church has a simple bell tower, and the stone façade is decorated with brickwork. The interior was altered in the 17th century, and now contains a tabernacle by Pier Francesco Fiorentino, showing scenes from the lives of the Madonna and Child.

### Porta Nova

Via Gracco del Secco. ***Open** daily.*
The Porta Nova is a large Renaissance fortress, designed by Giuliano da Sangallo in the 15th century to guard against attack from the Volterra road. There are two heavily fortified cylindrical towers on the outside of the building.

## Monteriggioni ❸

**Road map** D3. *720.*

MONTERIGGIONI is a gem of a medieval hilltop town. It was built in 1203 and ten years later became a garrison town. It is totally encircled by high walls with 14 heavily fortified towers, built to guard the northern borders of Siena's territory against invasion by Florentine armies.

Dante was sufficiently impressed to use the town as a simile for the abyss at the

**Craft shop in the main piazza of Monteriggioni**

heart of his *Inferno*, which compares Monteriggioni's "ring-shaped citadel . . . crowned with towers" to giants standing in a moat.

The walls, which are still perfectly preserved, are best viewed from the direction of the Colle di Val d'Elsa road. Within the walls, the sleepy village consists of a large piazza, a pretty Romanesque church, a few houses, some craft shops and restaurants, as well as shops selling many of the excellent local Castello di Monteriggioni wines.

*Temptation of St. Benedict* **(1508) by Sodoma in Monte Oliveto Maggiore**

## Siena ❹

*See pp212–19.*

## Asciano ❺

**Road map** D3. *6,250.* FS
*Corso Matteotti. (0577) 71 95 10.*
*Sat.*

THE ROAD from Siena to Asciano passes through the strange Crete landscape of clay hills, almost bare of vegetation and looking like massive anthills. Asciano itself is medieval and retains much of its fortified wall, built in 1351. The main street, Corso Matteotti, is lined with smart shops and Classical palazzi. At the top of the street, in Piazza della Basilica, there is a large fountain built in 1472. Facing it is the late 13th-century Romanesque **Basilica di Sant'Agata**.

**The Romanesque Basilica di Sant'Agata in Asciano**

Alongside the church is the **Museo d'Arte Sacra**, which houses a collection of late Siena School masterpieces, including Ambrogio Lorenzetti's unusual *St. Michael the Archangel* and Duccio's *Madonna and Child.*

The **Museo Archeologico** is in the old San Bernardino church and displays local Etruscan finds from the **Necropoli di Poggio Pinci**, 5 km (3 miles) east of the village. The artifacts come from tombs built between the 7th and 4th centuries BC. On Via Mameli, the **Museo Amos Cassioli** has a display of portraits by Cassioli, who lived here from 1832–91, and other modern works by local artists.

**Basilica di Sant'Agata**
Piazza della Basilica. ***Open*** *daily.*

**Museo d'Arte Sacra**
Piazza della Basilica. *(0577) 71 82 07.* ***Open*** *by appt.*

**Museo Archeologico**
Corso Matteotti 46. ***Open*** *Tue–Sun.* ***Adm charge.***

**Necropoli di Poggio Pinci**
Poggio Pinci. *(0577) 71 81 12.* ***Open*** *by appt.*

**Museo Amos Cassioli**
Via Mameli. *(0577) 71 87 45.* ***Open*** *Tue–Sun.* ***Adm charge.***

## Monte Oliveto Maggiore ❻

**Road map** D3. *(0577) 70 70 17.* ***Open*** *daily.*

THE APPROACH to the abbey of Monte Oliveto Maggiore is through thick cypresses, with stunning views of eroded cliffs and sheer drops to the valley floor. It was founded in 1313 by the Olivetan order, which was dedicated to restoring the simplicity of Benedictine monastic rule. The 15th-century rose-pink abbey church is a Baroque building with outstanding choir stalls of inlaid wood.

Alongside is the Great Cloister (1427–74), whose walls are covered by a cycle of frescoes on the life of St. Benedict, begun by Luca Signorelli, a pupil of Piero della Francesca, in 1495. He completed nine panels; the remaining 27 were finished by Sodoma in 1508. The cycle, which begins on the east wall with Benedict's early life, is considered a masterpiece of fresco painting for its combination of architectural and naturalistic detail.

# Street-by-Street: San Gimignano ❶

THE DISTINCTIVE SKYLINE of San Gimignano must have been a welcome sight to the faithful in medieval times, for the town lay on the main pilgrim route from northern Europe to Rome. This gave rise to its great prosperity at that time, when its population was twice what it is today. The plague of 1348, and later the diversion of the pilgrim route, led to its economic decline. However, since World War II it has been recovering rapidly, thanks to tourism and local wine production. For a small town, San Gimignano is rich in works of art, and good shops and restaurants.

**Sant'Agostino**
*Here Bartolo di Fredi painted* Christ, Man of Sorrows.

La Buca, Via San Giovanni, selling local wine and wild boar ham

**★ Collegiata**
*This 11th-century church is covered in delightful frescoes, including* The Creation *(1367) by Bartolo di Fredi.*

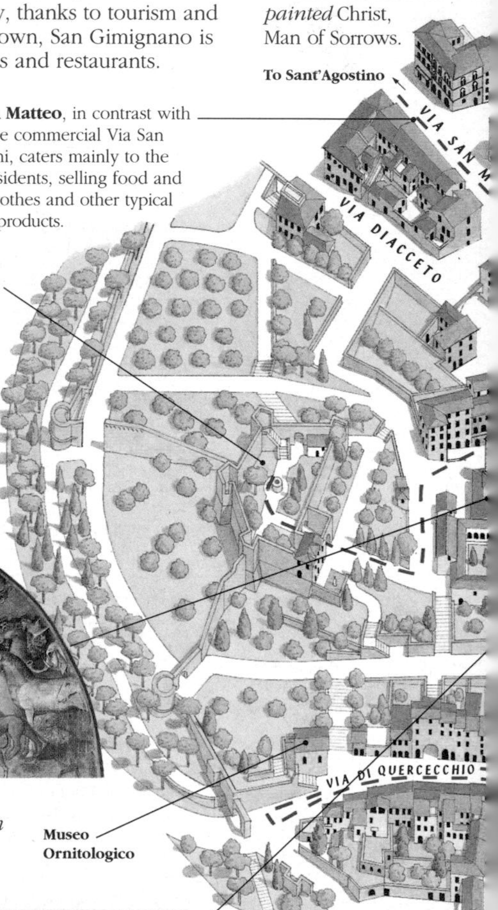


**Via San Matteo**, in contrast with the more commercial Via San Giovanni, caters mainly to the local residents, selling food and wine, clothes and other typical Tuscan products.

**Rocca (1353)**

**Museo Ornitologico**

**Museo d'Arte Sacra e Museo Etrusco**
*The museum contains precious Etruscan and religious works of art.*

**STAR SIGHTS**

- ★ Collegiata
- ★ Piazza del Duomo
- ★ Palazzo del Popolo

**KEY**

— — — Suggested route

0 meters 250

0 yards 250

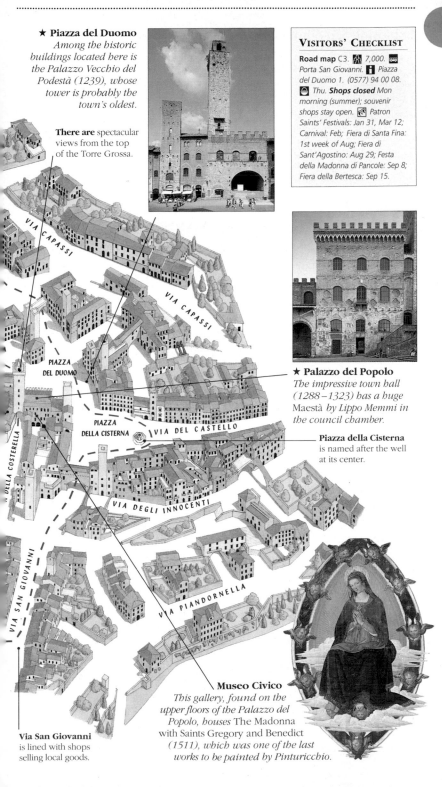

**★ Piazza del Duomo**
*Among the historic buildings located here is the Palazzo Vecchio del Podestà (1239), whose tower is probably the town's oldest.*

## VISITORS' CHECKLIST

**Road map** C3. 7,000. Porta San Giovanni. Piazza del Duomo 1. (0577) 94 00 08. Thu. ***Shops closed*** *Mon morning (summer); souvenir shops stay open. Patron Saints' Festivals: Jan 31, Mar 12; Carnival: Feb; Fiera di Santa Fina: 1st week of Aug; Fiera di Sant'Agostino: Aug 29; Festa della Madonna di Pancole: Sep 8; Fiera della Bertesca: Sep 15.*

**There are** spectacular views from the top of the Torre Grossa.

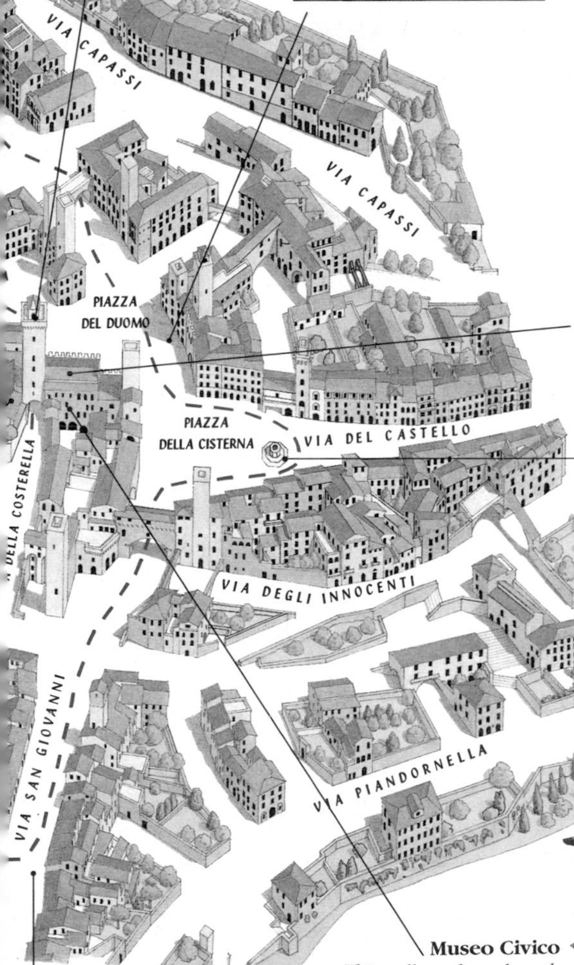

**★ Palazzo del Popolo**
*The impressive town hall (1288–1323) has a huge* Maestà *by Lippo Memmi in the council chamber.*

**Piazza della Cisterna** is named after the well at its center.

**Museo Civico**
*This gallery, found on the upper floors of the Palazzo del Popolo, houses* The Madonna with Saints Gregory and Benedict *(1511), which was one of the last works to be painted by Pinturicchio.*

**Via San Giovanni** is lined with shops selling local goods.

# Exploring San Gimignano

**Fresco in Sant'Agostino**

The "city of beautiful towers" is one of the best-preserved medieval towns in Tuscany. Its stunning skyline bristles with tall towers dating from the 13th century: 14 of the original 76 have survived. These windowless towers were built to serve both as private fortresses and symbols of their owners' wealth. In the Piazza della Cisterna, ringed by a jumble of unspoiled 13th- and 14th-century palazzi, is a wellhead built in 1237. Shops, galleries and jewelers line the two main streets, Via San Matteo and Via San Giovanni, which still retain their medieval feel.

**San Gimignano's skyline, almost unchanged since the Middle Ages**

### Palazzo Vecchio del Podestà

Piazza del Duomo. (0577) 94 03 16. ***Open*** *daily.*

The Palazzo Vecchio del Podestà (the old mayor's palace) is in a group of public buildings clustered around the central Piazza del Duomo. It has a vaulted loggia and the 51-m (166-ft) Torre della Rognosa, one of the oldest towers in San Gimignano. A law was passed in 1255 forbidding any private citizen to build a higher tower, but the rule was often broken by rival families.

### Museo Civico

Palazzo del Popolo, Piazza del Duomo. *(0577) 94 03 40.* **Museum & tower *open*** *daily (Nov–Mar: Tue–Sun).* ***Adm charge.***

The Museo is on the south side of the Piazza del Duomo, in the Palazzo del Popolo (town hall). Its tower, finished in 1311, is the tallest in the city, at 54 m (175 ft). This is open to the public, and the views from the top are quite stunning. Worn frescoes in the courtyard feature the coats of arms of city mayors and magistrates, as well as a 14th-century *Virgin and Child* by Taddeo di Bartolo. The first public room is the Sala di Dante, where an inscription records the poet's plea to the city council in 1300 to support the Guelph (pro-pope) alliance led by Florence. The walls are covered with hunting scenes and a huge *Virgin Enthroned* by Lippo Memmi (1317).

The floor above has a small art collection, which includes Pinturicchio's *Madonna with Saints Gregory and Benedict* (1511), painted against a landscape of blues and greens. The painting of *San Gimignano and His Miracles* by Taddeo di Bartolo shows the saint holding the town – recognizably the same city we see today. The *Wedding Scene* frescoes by Memmo di Filippucci (early 14th century) show a couple sharing a bath and going to bed – an unusual record of life in a wealthy household in 14th-century Tuscany.

**12th-century well and medieval palazzi in the triangular Piazza della Cisterna**

### Museo d'Arte Sacra e Museo Etrusco

Piazza Pecori. *(0577) 94 03 16.* ***Open*** *Apr–Oct: daily; Nov–Mar: Tue–Sun.* ***Adm charge.***

The museum is entered from the Piazza Pecori, where street performers entertain visitors in summer. A chapel on the ground floor contains elaborate tomb slabs. The first floor houses paintings, sculpture and liturgical objects from the Collegiata and a small collection of local Etruscan treasures. A marble bust (1493) by Benedetto da Maiano commemorates the life of scholar Onofrio di Pietro.

### Collegiata

Piazza del Duomo. ***Open*** *daily.*

The plain façade of this 12th-century Romanesque church belies its exotic interior; it is one of the most frescoed churches in Italy. The arches bordering the central aisle are painted in striking blue and white stripes, and the deep blue paint of the vaulted roof is speckled with gold stars. The aisle walls are extensively covered with dramatic fresco cycles of scenes from the Bible. In the north aisle the frescoes are on three levels and comprise 26 episodes

**The ceiling of the Collegiata, painted with gold stars**

from the Old Testament, including *The Creation of Adam and Eve, Noah and His Ark, Moses Crossing the Red Sea* and *The Afflictions of Job*, finished by Bartolo di Fredi in 1367. On the opposite walls are scenes from the life of Christ, dated 1333–41, now attributed to Lippo Memmi, a pupil of Simone Martini. At the back of the church, on the nave walls, are scenes from *The Last Judgment*, painted by Taddeo di Bartolo (1393–6). They depict the souls of the damned being tortured in hell by devils relishing their task.

The tiny Santa Fina chapel, off the south aisle, is covered with a cycle of frescoes by Ghirlandaio (1475) telling the life story of St. Fina; legend has it that she spent most of her short life in prayer. The towers of San Gimignano appear in the background of the funeral scene.

Under an arch to the left of the Collegiata is a courtyard containing the loggia to the Baptistry, frescoed with an *Annunciation* painted in 1482 by Ghirlandaio.

### Rocca

Piazza Propositura. ***Open*** *daily.*

The Rocca, or fortress, was built in 1353. It now has only one surviving tower following its dismantling by Cosimo I de' Medici in the 16th century. It encloses a public garden filled with fig and olive trees, and commands superb views over the vineyards where wine has been produced for hundreds of years.

### Sant'Agostino

Piazza Sant'Agostino. ***Open*** *daily.*

This church was consecrated in 1298 and has a simple façade, contrasting markedly with the heavily decorated Rococo interior (c.1740) by Vanvitelli, architect to the kings of Naples. Above the main altar is the *Coronation of the Virgin* by Piero del Pollaiuolo, dated 1483, and the choir is entirely covered in a cycle of frescoes of *The Life of St. Augustine* (1465), executed by the Florentine artist Benozzo Gozzoli and a group of his assistants.

In the Cappella di San Bartolo, to the right of the main entrance, is an elaborate marble altar completed by Benedetto da Maiano in 1495. The bas-relief carvings show the miracles performed by St. Bartholomew, all topped by flying angels and a roundel of the Madonna and Child.

**Detail from *The Life of St. Augustine***

### Museo Ornitologico

Via Quercecchio. *(0577) 94 13 88.* ***Open*** *daily (Nov–Mar: Tue–Sun).* ***Adm charge.***

The museum is in an elaborate 18th-century Baroque church. This is in total contrast to the sturdy cases of mounted birds that form the collection, put together by a local dignitary.

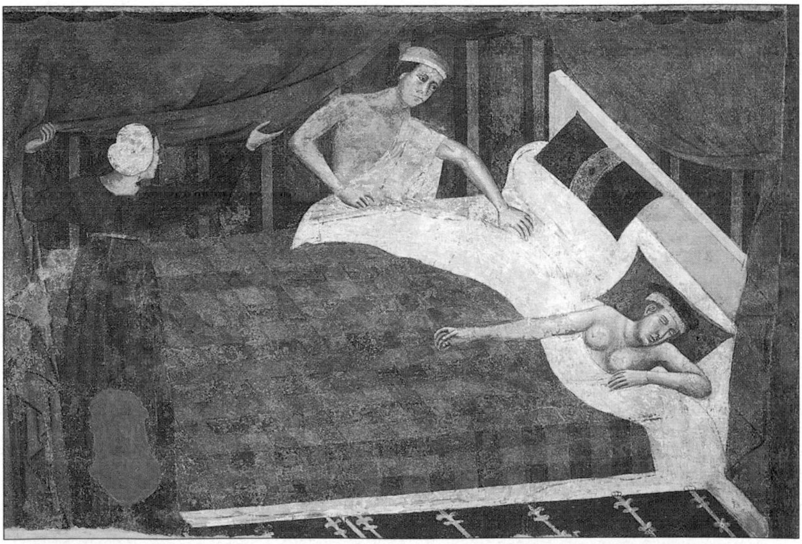

**Fresco from the early 14th-century *Wedding Scene* cycle by Memmo di Filippucci in the Museo Civico**

# Street-by-Street: Siena ❹

**Unicorn *contrada* symbol**

THE PRINCIPAL SIGHTS of Siena are found in the network of narrow streets and alleys around the fan-shaped Piazza del Campo. Scarcely any street is level, as Siena, like Rome, is built on seven hills. This adds to the pleasure of exploring: one minute the city spreads before you and the next you are in a warren of medieval houses. Packed into Siena are the 17 *contrade* (parishes) whose animal symbols are everywhere on carvings, plaques and car stickers.

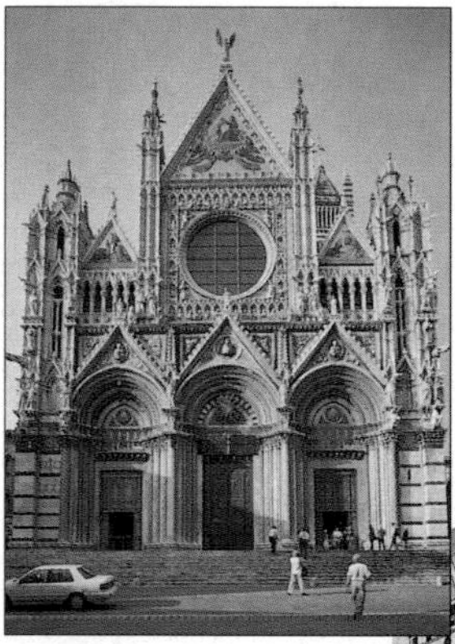

**★ Duomo**
*Statues of prophets carved by Giovanni Pisano in the 1290s fill the Gothic niches of the marble façade* (see pp216–17).

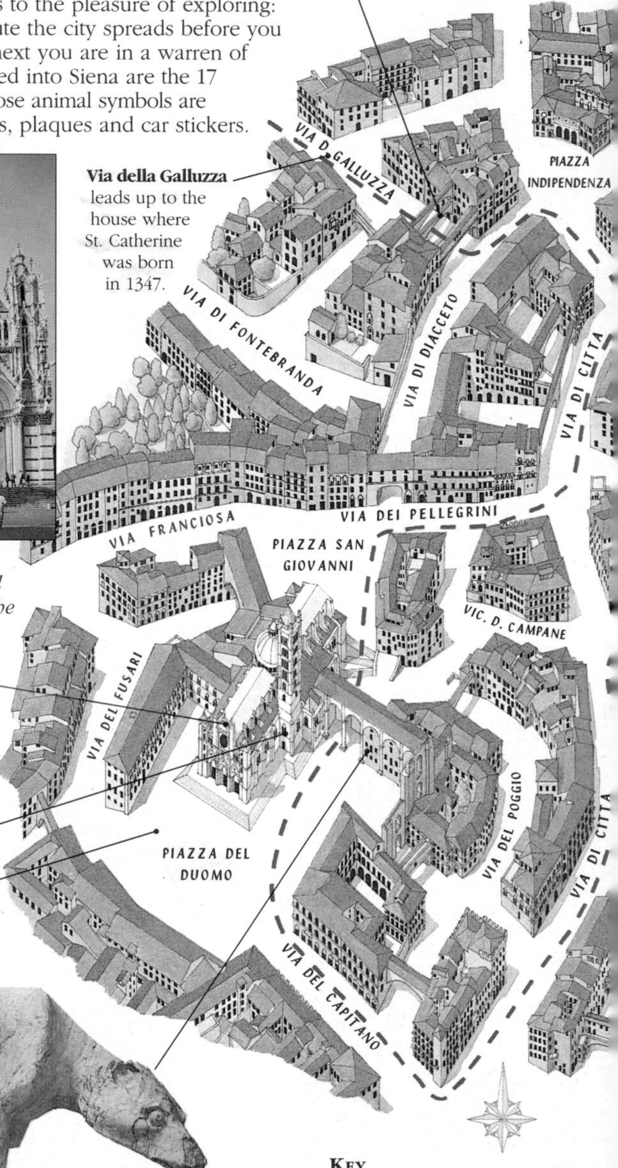


**Aerial bridges** and corridors linking buildings on opposite sides of the street are characteristic of Siena.

**Via della Galluzza** leads up to the house where St. Catherine was born in 1347.

**Each tier** of the Duomo's bell tower has one window fewer than the floor above.

**Cafés and shops** fill the streets near the Duomo square.

**Museo dell'Opera del Duomo**
*Statues of a wolf suckling Remus abound; legend tells that his son Senius founded the city of Siena.*

**KEY**

— — — Suggested route

0 meters 300

0 yards 300

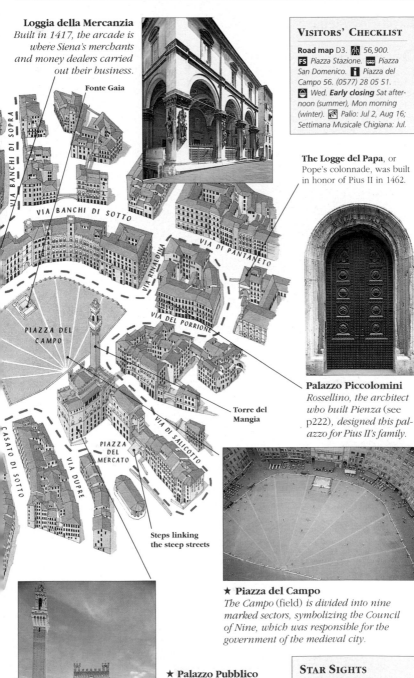

**Loggia della Mercanzia**
*Built in 1417, the arcade is where Siena's merchants and money dealers carried out their business.*

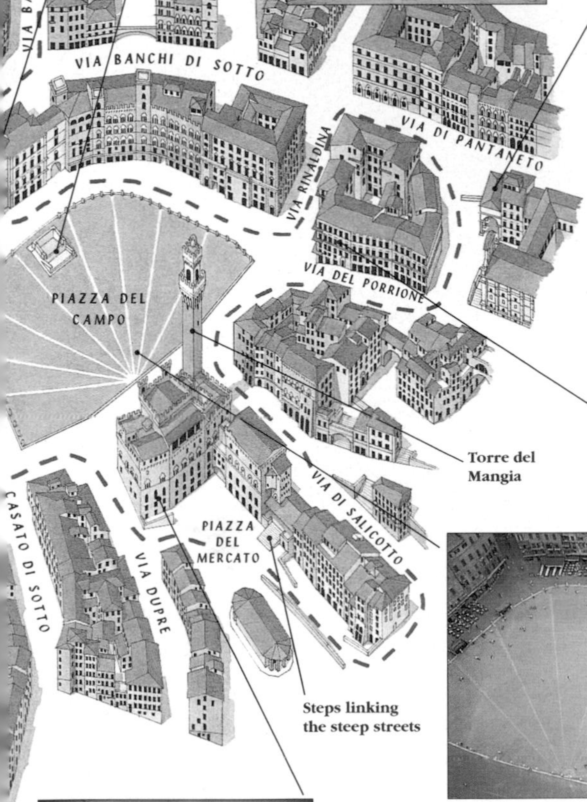


## Visitors' Checklist

**Road map** D3. *56,900.* *Piazza Stazione.* *Piazza San Domenico.* *Piazza del Campo 56. (0577) 28 05 51.* *Wed.* ***Early closing*** *Sat afternoon (summer), Mon morning (winter).* *Palio: Jul 2, Aug 16; Settimana Musicale Chigiana: Jul.*

**The Logge del Papa**, or Pope's colonnade, was built in honor of Pius II in 1462.

**Palazzo Piccolomini**
*Rossellino, the architect who built Pienza* (see p222), *designed this palazzo for Pius II's family.*

**★ Piazza del Campo**
*The Campo* (field) *is divided into nine marked sectors, symbolizing the Council of Nine, which was responsible for the government of the medieval city.*

**★ Palazzo Pubblico**
*The graceful Gothic town hall was completed in 1342. At 102 m (330 ft), the bell tower is the second highest medieval tower ever built in Italy.*

## Star Sights

- **★ Duomo**
- **★ Piazza del Campo**
- **★ Palazzo Pubblico**

# Exploring Siena

SIENA IS A CITY OF STEEP medieval alleys surrounding the Piazza del Campo. The buildings around the square symbolize the golden age of the city between 1260 and 1348, when wealthy citizens contributed to a major program of civic building. Siena's decline began in 1348 when the Black Death hit the city, killing a third of the population; 200 years later many more died in an 18-month siege ending in defeat by the Florentines. The victors repressed all further building and development, and so Siena has remained frozen in time, full of medieval buildings that have recently been renovated.

**Aerial view of Siena's Piazza del Campo and surrounding palazzi**

### Piazza del Campo

The shell-shaped 12th-century Piazza del Campo is bordered by elegant palazzi. It has an elaborate fountain as its focal point, the Fonte Gaia, a rectangular marble basin decorated by statues. The fountain now seen in the square is a 19th-century copy of the original, which was carved by Jacopo della Quercia in 1409–19. This was removed to preserve it from the ravages of the weather.

The reliefs on the fountain depict Adam and Eve, the Madonna and Child, and the Virtues. Water is fed into it by a 25-km-long (15 mile) aqueduct, which has brought fresh water into the city from the hills since the 14th century.

### Torre del Mangia

Piazza del Campo. ***Open*** *daily.* ***Adm charge***.

The bell tower to the left of the Palazzo Pubblico is the second highest in Italy, at 102 m (330 ft). Built by the brothers Muccio and Francesco di Rinaldo between 1338–48, it is named after the first bell ringer, who was nicknamed *Mangiaguadagni* (literally "eat the profits") because of his great idleness. (It was the bell ringer's responsibility to toll the nightly curfew and warn the citizens of impending danger.) There are 505 steps to the top of the tower, which has views across Tuscany.

**Fonte Gaia in Piazza del Campo**

### Palazzo Pubblico

Piazza del Campo 1. *(0577) 29 22 63.* **Museo Civico** ***open*** *daily.* ***Adm charge***.

The Palazzo Pubblico still serves as the town hall, but the medieval state rooms are open to the public. The main council chamber is called the Sala del Mappamondo, named after a map of the world painted by Ambrogio Lorenzetti in the early 14th century. One wall is covered by the *Maestà* (Virgin in Majesty) by Simone Martini, a prominent artist of the Siena School. Painted in 1315, it depicts the Virgin Mary as the Queen of Heaven, attended by the apostles, saints and angels. Opposite is Martini's unusual fresco of mercenary Guidoriccio da Fogliano (1330), mounted and in full battle dress.

The walls of the chapel alongside are covered with frescoes of the *Life of the Virgin* (1407) by Taddeo di Bartolo, and the choir stalls (1428) are decorated by wooden panels inlaid with biblical scenes.

The Sala della Pace contains the famous *Allegory of Good and Bad Government*, a pair of allegorical frescoes by Ambrogio Lorenzetti, finished in 1338. They form one of the most important series of secular paintings from the Middle Ages. In *The Good*

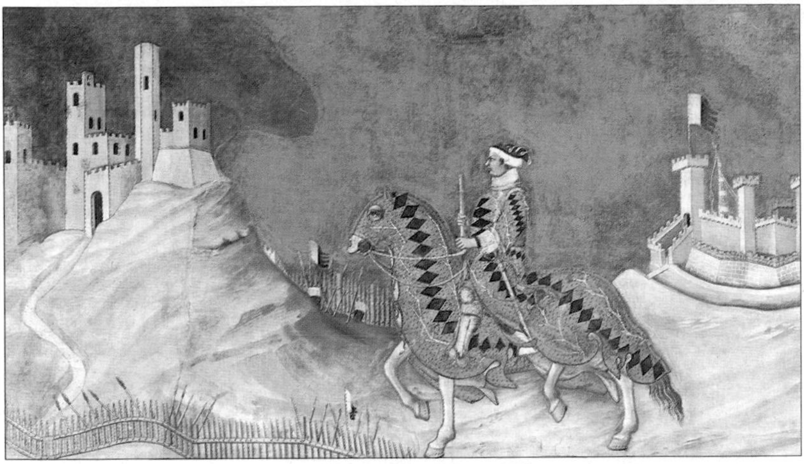

***Guidoriccio da Fogliano*** **by Simone Martini (1330) in the Palazzo Pubblico**

*Government (see pp44–5)* civic life flourishes, while *The Bad Government* reveals trash-strewn streets and ruins.

The Sala del Risorgimento is covered with late 19th-century frescoes illustrating the events leading up to the unification of Italy under King Vittorio Emanuele II *(see pp52–3).*

### Palazzo Piccolomini

Via Rinaldina. (0577) 412 71. **Open** *Mon–Sat.* **Adm charge**.

Siena's most imposing private palazzo was built for the very wealthy Piccolomini family in the 1460s by Rossellino. It now contains the Sienese state archives, account books and taxation documents dating back to the 13th century. Other unusual records include a will attributed to Boccaccio and examples of medieval bookbinding. Some of these books are decorated with pictures painted by Siena School artists.

**Pisano's *Simone* (c.1300) in the Museo dell'Opera del Duomo**

### Pinacoteca Nazionale

Via San Pietro 29. (0577) 28 11 61. **Open** *daily.* **Adm charge**.

Housed in the 14th-century Palazzo Buonsignori, this gallery contains works by the Siena School. Lorenzetti's *Two Views*, painted in the 14th century, are early examples of landscape painting and Pietro da Domenico's *Adoration of the Shepherds* (1510) shows how the art of the Siena School remained stylized long after Renaissance naturalism had influenced the rest of Europe *(see p46)*. There is a striking *Deposition* (1502) by Sodoma.

### Duomo

*See pp216–17.*

### Museo dell'Opera del Duomo

Piazza del Duomo 8. (0577) 28 30 48. **Open** *daily.* **Adm charge**.

The museum is built into the unfinished side aisle of the Duomo *(see pp216–17)*. Part of it is devoted to the sculpture removed from the exterior of the Duomo, including Gothic statues by Giovanni Pisano (1250–1314), which had been badly eroded over many years of exposure to the weather.

Duccio's huge double-sided *Maestà*, considered one of the best Siena School works, has a first-floor room to itself. Painted in the years between 1308–11 and placed on the high altar in the Duomo, it depicts the Madonna and Child on one side and scenes from *The Life of Christ* on the other. The two halves of the *Maestà* were separated in 1771 to allow both faces to be exhibited. On the top floor, stairs lead off the Sala dei Parati to a loggia with views of the town and surrounding countryside.

**Cloister of Casa di Santa Caterina**

### Casa di Santa Caterina

Costa di Sant'Antonio. (0577) 441 77. **Open** *daily.*

Siena's patron saint, Catherine Benincasa (1347–80), was the daughter of a tradesman. She took the veil at the age of eight, and experienced many visions of God, from whom she also received the stigmata. Her eloquence persuaded Gregory XI to return the seat of the papacy to Rome in 1376, after 67 years of exile in Avignon. She died in Rome and was canonized in 1461. Today, Catherine's house is surrounded by chapels and cloisters. It is decorated with paintings of incidents from her life by a range of artists, including Francesco Vanni and Pietro Sorri, who were among her contemporaries.

# Siena Duomo

SIENA'S DUOMO (1136–1382) is one of the most spectacular in Italy, and one of the few to have been built south of the Alps in full Gothic style. Many ordinary citizens helped to cart the black and white stone used in its construction from quarries on the outskirts of the city. In 1339, the Sienese decided to build a new nave to the south with the aim of making it the biggest church in Christendom. This plan came to nothing when plague hit the city soon afterward, killing off much of the population. The uncompleted nave now contains a museum of Gothic sculpture.

**★ Pulpit Panels**
*Carved by Nicola Pisano in 1265–8, the panels on the octagonal pulpit depict scenes from* The Life of Christ.

**★ Inlaid Marble Floor**
The Massacre of the Innocents *is one of a series of scenes in inlaid marble covering the floor. Other themes include medieval astrology and alchemy.*

**Nave**
*Black and white marble pillars support the vault.*

**Chapel of St. John the Baptist**

**STAR FEATURES**

**★ Inlaid Marble Floor**

**★ Piccolomini Library**

**★ Pulpit Panels by Pisano**

**★ Piccolomini Library**
*Pinturicchio's frescoes (1509) portray the life of Pope Pius II* (see p222). *Here he presides at the betrothal of Frederick III to Eleonora of Portugal.*

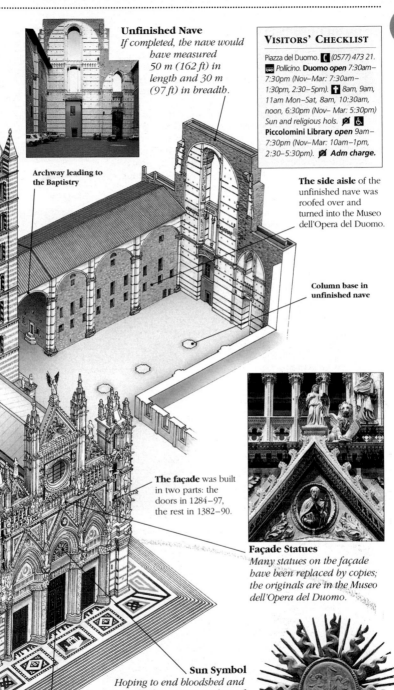

**Unfinished Nave**
*If completed, the nave would have measured 50 m (162 ft) in length and 30 m (97 ft) in breadth.*

### Visitors' Checklist

Piazza del Duomo. (0577) 473 21. *Pollicino.* **Duomo open** 7:30am–7:30pm (Nov–Mar: 7:30am–1:30pm, 2:30–5pm). 8am, 9am, 11am Mon–Sat, 8am, 10:30am, noon, 6:30pm (Nov– Mar: 5:30pm) Sun and religious hols. **Piccolomini Library open** 9am–7:30pm (Nov–Mar: 10am–1pm, 2:30–5:30pm). ***Adm charge.***

**Archway leading to the Baptistry**

**The side aisle** of the unfinished nave was roofed over and turned into the Museo dell'Opera del Duomo.

**Column base in unfinished nave**

**The façade** was built in two parts: the doors in 1284–97, the rest in 1382–90.

**Entrance to Duomo**

**Façade Statues**
*Many statues on the façade have been replaced by copies; the originals are in the Museo dell'Opera del Duomo.*

**Sun Symbol**
*Hoping to end bloodshed and rivalry, St. Bernardino of Siena (1380–1444) wanted the feuding Sienese to give up all loyalty to their* contrada *emblems and unite under this symbol of the risen Christ.*

## The Sienese Palio

**One of the *contrada* symbols**

THE PALIO IS TUSCANY'S most celebrated festival and takes place on July 2 and August 16 each year in the Campo *(see p214)*. It is a bareback horse race and was first recorded in 1283, but may have had its origins in Roman military training. The jockeys represent the 17 *contrade* or districts; the horses are chosen by the drawing of straws and are then blessed at the local *contrada* churches. The races are preceded by heavy betting and pageantry, but only last about 90 seconds each. The winner is awarded a *palio* (banner).

**Ringside View**
*Huge sums are paid for a view of the races.*

**Flag-Throwing**
*The Sienese display their flag-throwing skills in the procession and pageantry before the race.*

**Medieval Knight**
*The traditional outfits worn in the processions are all handmade.*

**Galloping toward the finish**

**Racing Crowds**
*Thousands of people cram into the piazza to watch the race, and rivalry is intense between competitors.*

**Traditional drummer taking part in prerace pageant**

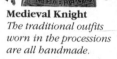

**View across the Campo during a race**

The façade of San Domenico

## San Domenico

Piazza San Domenico. ***Open*** *daily.*

This barnlike Gothic church was begun in 1226 and its bell tower was added in 1340. Inside is an exquisite chapel dedicated to St. Catherine *(see p215)*. It was built in 1460 to store her preserved head, which is now kept in a gilded marble tabernacle on the altar. This is surrounded by frescoes, painted by Sodoma in 1526, showing Catherine in a state of religious fervor. The marble pavement is attributed to Giovanni di Stefano.

Catherine experienced many of her visions and received her stigmata in the Cappella delle Volte at the west end of the church. Here there is an authenticated portrait of her by contemporary Andrea Vanni, dated around 1380.

## Fortezza Medicea

Viale Maccari. **Fortezza *open*** *daily.* **Enoteca *open*** *3pm–midnight.* **Theater *open*** *Jun–Sep: daily.* ***Adm charge.***

This huge red-brick fortress was built for Cosimo I by Baldassarre Lanci in 1560, following Siena's defeat by the Florentines in the 1554–5 war. More than 8,000 Sienese died either from battle wounds or from starvation and disease during the 18-month siege, reducing the town's population to a mere 6,000. The town was repressed by its Florentine masters, its banking and wool industries suppressed and all building work ended.

The fortress now houses an open-air theater, and from the entrance bastions there are glorious views of the countryside. The Enoteca Italica is in one of the bastions on the Lizza; the garden fronts the fort. It is a wine shop, offering tourists the chance both to taste and to buy from a comprehensive list of quality wines from all over Italy.

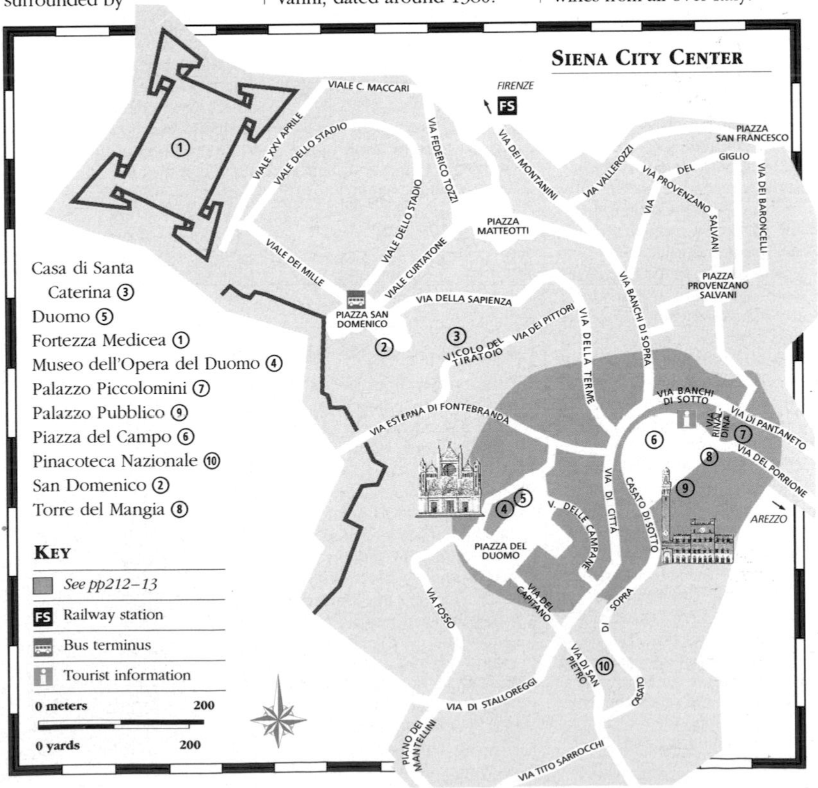

**The ruined abbey at San Galgano, surrounded by dense woodland**

## San Galgano ❼

**Road map** D4. 🚌 *from Siena.* 📞 *(0577) 75 10 44.* **Abbey and oratory** ***open*** *daily.*

THE RUINED Cistercian abbey is in dense woodland in a superb setting. It is very remote but well worth the effort of getting there for the beauty of the surroundings and the majesty of the ruined, roofless building. Begun in 1218, the abbey is Gothic in style; unusual in Tuscany, this reflects the French origins of the Cistercian monks who designed and built it.

The monks avoided contact with civilization and divided their lives between prayer and labor, clearing the hills of vegetation to graze their sheep. Despite the Cistercian emphasis on poverty, the monks became wealthy from the sale of wool; by the middle of the 14th century, the abbey was corruptly administered and gradually fell into decline.

In the late 14th century, the English mercenary Sir John Hawkwood sacked the abbey and by 1397 the abbot was the sole occupant. Residents increased for a time, but the abbey was eventually dissolved in 1652. Empty for many years, the cloister and other monastic buildings alongside the church are now being restored for the Olivetan order of nuns.

On a hill above the abbey is the beehive-shaped chapel of Montesiepi, built around 1185, on the site of St. Galgano's hermitage, a few years after his death in 1181.

St. Galgano's sword stands embedded in a stone just inside the door of the circular oratory. The 14th-century stone walls of the side chapel are covered with frescoes showing scenes from Galgano's life by Ambrogio Lorenzetti (1344); some are now in poor condition.

The shop alongside the chapel sells locally made herbs, wines, olive oils and toiletries along with books on the history of the region.

## Montalcino ❽

**Road map** D4. 5,100. 🚌 ℹ *Costa del Municipio 8. (0577) 84 93 31.* *Fri.*

MONTALCINO'S foremost activity is wine producing, evident from the great number of shops where you can both sample and buy the excellent local Brunello wines.

The town is of timeless character and the streets are narrow, winding and steep. The highest point is the 14th-century **Fortezza** and its impressive ramparts, built by Cosimo I in 1571. There is an Enoteca (wine

### THE LEGEND OF ST. GALGANO

Galgano was born in 1148, the son of noble parents, and grew into a brave but dissolute young knight. He saw his life as futile and turned to God, renouncing the material world. When he tried to break his sword against a rock as a symbol of his rejection of war, it was swallowed by the stone. This he interpreted as a sign of God's approval. He built a hut on the site of today's chapel at Montesiepi, and died a hermit in 1181. In 1185 Pope Urban III declared him a saint and an example to all Christian knights.

Montalcino's 14th-century Fortezza

shop) on the grounds of the Fortezza, where Brunello wines are for sale.

Inside the fortress there is an ancient Sienese battle standard, a reminder that the town gave refuge to a band of rebels after Florence conquered Siena in 1555. In remembrance of this, flag-bearers from the village of Montalcino lead the parade before the Palio in Siena every year *(see p218)*.

As you walk down into the town from the Fortezza, the monastery of Sant'Agostino and its 14th-century church are on the right. Just beyond, the **Palazzo Vescovile** (bishop's palace) houses a mixture of archaeological finds from local excavations. There is a collection of Siena School painting, sculpture from the 12th–14th centuries, including terra-cottas by Andrea della Robbia, and several paintings by Sodoma (1477–1549). On the Piazza del Popolo, the **Palazzo Comunale** sometimes hosts wine exhibitions.

The Duomo, San Salvatore, was designed in 1818–32 by Agostino Fantastici, and replaced the original Romanesque church building.

**Fortezza**
Piazzale della Fortezza. *(0577) 84 92 11.* **Enoteca** ***open*** *mid-Jul–mid-Sep: daily; mid-Sep–mid-Jul: Tue–Sun.* ***Adm charge*** for ramparts.

**Palazzo Vescovile**
Via Spagni 4. *(0577) 84 81 35.*
**Museo Civico, Museo Diocesano, Museo Archeologico** ***open*** *Tue–Sun.* ***Adm charge.***

**Palazzo Comunale**
Costa del Municipio 1. *(0577) 84 82 46.* ***Open*** *Tue–Fri.*

Flower-covered house in the pretty town of Montalcino

## San Quirico d'Orcia 9

**Road map** E4. *2,390.*
*Via Dante Alighieri 33. (0577) 89 72 11. 2nd and 4th Tue of month.*

Collegiata in San Quirico

STANDING JUST INSIDE the city walls, San Quirico d'Orcia's pride is the **Collegiata**, featuring three ornately carved Romanesque portals built onto an 8th-century structure. Begun in 1080, the capitals and lintels of the portals are carved with details of dragons, mermaids and other beasts. The church commemorates the 3rd-century martyr St. Quiricus, who was killed at the age of five by the Romans for declaring himself a Christian. He is depicted in the elaborate altar piece by Sano di Pietro, along with the Virgin and Child and other saints.

Next to the church is the 17th-century **Palazzo Chigi**, whose frescoed interior has recently been restored. The **Horti Leonini** nearby is a 16th-century garden of box hedges nestling within the town walls. It was intended as a refuge for pilgrims and travelers, and is now used as a public sculpture garden during the summer months.

**Collegiata**
Via Dante Alighieri. *(0577) 89 75 06.* ***Open*** *daily.*

**Palazzo Chigi**
Via Dante Alighieri. ***Open*** *early 1996 following restoration.*

**Horti Leonini**
Piazza Libertà. *(0577) 89 75 06.* ***Open*** *daily.*

**The Terme di Bagno Vignoni**

## Bagno Vignoni ⑩

**Road map** D4. *32.* *from Siena.*

This is a tiny medieval spa village that consists of a handful of houses built around a huge piazza containing an arcaded, stone-lined pool. Constructed by the Medici, it is full of hot sulfurous water that bubbles up to the surface from the volcanic rocks deep underground. The healing quality of the water has been known since Roman times and, according to legend, famous people who have sought a cure in Bagno Vignoni include St. Catherine of Siena *(see p215)* and Lorenzo the Magnificent, to relieve his arthritis. The pool is no longer open for swimming but is still well worth a visit to admire the architecture. There are sulfur pools on the grounds of the Posta Marcucci hotel, which are open for swimming.

## Pienza ⑪

**Road map** E4. *1,300.* *Piazza Pio II. (0578) 74 85 02.* *Fri.*

The center of Pienza was completely redesigned in Renaissance times by Pope Pius II *(see p47)*. Born here in 1405, when it was called Corsignano, Aeneas Sylvius Piccolomini became known as a leading Humanist scholar and philosopher. He was elected pope in 1458 and in the following year decided to commission a new center in Corsignano and rename it Pienza in his own honor. He planned to transform his birthplace into a model Renaissance town, but the grand scheme never progressed beyond the handful of buildings around the Piazza Pio II. The architect Bernardo Rossellino was commissioned to build a Duomo, papal palace and town hall, which were completed in three years. Subsequently Rossellino was caught embezzling papal funds, but Pius II forgave him because he was so delighted with his new buildings.

Away from the grandeur of the main square, Pienza is a quiet agricultural town with shops selling local produce like *pecorino*, cheese made from sheep's milk *(see p255)*.

### Duomo

Piazza Pio II. ***Open*** *daily.*

The Duomo was built by the architect Rossellino in 1459, and is now suffering from serious subsidence at its eastern end. There are cracks in the walls and floor of the nave, but this does not detract at all from the splendid Classical proportions of this Renaissance church. It is flooded with light from the vast stained-glass windows requested by Pius II; he wanted a *domus vitrea* (literally "a house of glass"), which would symbolize the spirit of intellectual enlightenment of the Humanist age.

**Coat of arms of Pope Pius II**

### Palazzo Piccolomini

Piazza Pio II. *(0578) 74 85 03.* ***Open*** *Tue–Sun.* ***Adm charge.***

The palazzo is next door to the Duomo and was home to Pius II's descendants until 1968. Rossellino's design for the building was influenced by Leon Battista Alberti's Palazzo Rucellai in Florence *(see p104)*. The apartments open to the public include Pius II's bedroom and library, which are full of his personal possessions. At the rear of the palazzo there is an ornate arcaded courtyard and a triple-tiered loggia looking out on the garden. From here there are spectacular views across to the wooded slopes of the volcano, Monte Amiata.

**Courtyard in Palazzo Piccolomini**

### Pieve di Corsignano

Via delle Fonti. *(0578) 74 82 03.* ***Open*** *by appt.*

Pope Pius II was baptized in this 11th-century Romanesque parish church on the outskirts of Pienza. It has an unusual round tower and a doorway decorated with flower motifs.

**Pienza's piazza and Duomo, designed by Rossellino (1459)**

The church of Madonna di San Biagio on the outskirts of Montepulciano

## Montepulciano ⓬

**Road map** E4. *14,000.*
*Via Ricci 9. (0578) 75 86 87.*
*Thu.*

MONTEPULCIANO is built along a narrow limestone ridge and, at 605 m (1,950 ft) above sea level, is one of the highest of Tuscany's hilltop towns. The town is encircled by walls and fortifications designed by Antonio da Sangallo the Elder in 1511 for Cosimo I. Inside the walls the streets are crammed with Renaissance-style palazzi and churches, but the town is chiefly known for its good local Vino Nobile wines *(see p256)*. A long, winding street called the Corso climbs up into the main square, which crowns the summit of the hill.

On the Corso is the Art Deco Caffè Poliziano, which has an art gallery in the basement. In July the café hosts a jazz festival and the town fills with musicians who perform at the Cantiere Internazionale d'Arte *(see p33)*, an arts festival directed by the German composer Hans Werner Henze.

In August there are two festivals: the Bruscello takes place on the 14th, 15th and 16th, when hordes of actors reenact scenes from the town's turbulent history. For the Bravio delle Botti, on the last Sunday in August, there is a parade through the streets followed by a barrel race and a banquet to end the day.

### Madonna di San Biagio

Via di San Biagio 14. ***Open*** *daily.*

This beautiful pilgrimage church is on the outskirts of Montepulciano, perched on a platform below the city walls. Built of honey- and cream-colored travertine, it is Sangallo's masterpiece, a Renaissance gem begun in 1518. The project occupied him until his death in 1534.

### Palazzo Bucelli

Via di Gracciano del Corso 73. ***Closed.***

The lower façade of the palazzo (1648) is studded with ancient Etruscan reliefs and funerary urns collected by its 18th-century antiquarian owner, Pietro Bucelli.

### Sant'Agostino

Piazza Michelozzo. ***Open*** *daily.*

Michelozzo built the church in 1427, with an elaborate carved portal featuring the Virgin and Child flanked by St. John and St. Augustine.

### Palazzo Comunale

Piazza Grande 1. *(0578) 75 70 34.*
**Tower *open*** *Mon–Sat.*

In the 15th century, Michelozzo added a tower and façade to the original Gothic town hall. The building is now a smaller version of the Palazzo Vecchio *(see pp78–9)*. On a clear day, the views that can be seen from the tower are superb.

### Palazzo Tarugi

Piazza Grande. ***Closed.***

The imposing 16th-century palazzo is next to the town hall and is currently undergoing restoration to the façade.

### Duomo

Piazza Grande. ***Open*** *daily.*

The Duomo was designed between 1592 and 1630 by Ippolito Scalza. The façade is unfinished and plain, but the interior is Classical in proportions. It is the setting for an earlier masterpiece from the Siena School, the *Assumption of the Virgin* triptych painted by Taddeo di Bartolo in 1401. Placed over the High Altar, it is rich in bright, jewel-like colors and heavily embossed with gold leaf.

Taddeo di Bartolo's triptych (1401)

### Santa Maria dei Servi

Via del Poliziano. ***Open*** *by appt.*

The Corso continues from the Piazza up to the Gothic church of Santa Maria dei Servi. The wine bar alongside sells Vino Nobile from medieval storage cellars cut out of the limestone cliffs below the town.

**Etruscan frieze in the Museo Nazionale Etrusco in Chiusi**

## Chiusi ⓭

**Road map** E4. 10,000. FS
*Via Porsenna 73. (0578) 22 76 67.*
*Tue.*

CHIUSI WAS ONE of the most powerful cities in the Etruscan league, reaching the height of its influence in the 7th and 6th centuries BC *(see pp40–41)*. There is a large number of Etruscan tombs in the surrounding countryside.

### Museo Nazionale Etrusco

Via Porsenna 2. *(0578) 201 77.* ***Open** daily. **Adm charge**.*

The museum was founded in 1871 and is now packed with cremation urns, vases decorated with black figures, and Bucchero ware, burnished to resemble bronze. Most of these were excavated from tombs in the area. Arrangements can be made at the museum to visit local tombs.

### Duomo

Piazza del Duomo. ***Open** daily.*

The Romanesque cathedral is opposite the museum and built from recycled Roman pillars and capitals. The decorations on the nave walls appear to be mosaics, but in fact were painted by Arturo Viligiardi in 1887. There is an authentic Roman mosaic underneath the high altar.

### Museo della Cattedrale

Piazza del Duomo. *(0578) 22 64 90.* ***Open** daily. **Adm charge**.* *partial.*

The museum, found in the cloister of the cathedral, has a display of Roman, Lombardic and medieval sculpture. In this museum, visits can be arranged to the underground galleries beneath the city, dug by the Etruscans and used as catacombs by early Christians in the 3rd–5th centuries.

## Sant'Antimo ⓮

**Road map** D4. ***Custodian** (0577) 83 56 59. **Open** daily.*

THIS BEAUTIFUL abbey church *(see pp42–3)* has inspired many poets and painters; it enchants everyone who goes there. The ancient church, built of creamy travertine, is set against a background of tree-clad hills in the Starcia valley. The very earliest surviving church on the site dates back to the 9th century, but local people prefer to think the church was founded by the Holy Roman Emperor, Charlemagne, in 781. The main part of the church was built in 1118 in the French Romanesque style, and the exterior is decorated with interlaced blank arcades carved with the symbols of the four Evangelists.

The soft, honey-colored alabaster interior has an odd luminous quality that is seen to change according to time of day and season. The capitals in the nave are carved with geometric designs, leaf motifs and biblical scenes. Recorded plainsong echoes around the walls, adding to the eerie atmosphere.

The Augustinian monks who tend the church sing Gregorian chants at mass every Sunday and there are organ concerts in the church during July and August.

**The beautiful abbey church of Sant'Antimo**

# A Day Out in Chianti

THIS TOUR TAKES IN the main villages of the Chianti Classico wine region. Castles and wine estates line the route, and vineyards offer tastings and sell direct to the public. Look for signs along the way saying "vendita diretta."

The first stop after leaving Siena is the Castello di Brolio, which has been owned by the Ricasoli family since 1167. From Brolio, drive to Gaiole, diverting to see the 13th-century castle at Meleto. Gaiole is a very quiet agricultural town with a stream running down the main street; wine can be sampled here at the local cooperative. In Badia a Coltibuono there is a restaurant *(see p262)* and a Romanesque church, and Radda in Chianti offers lovely views over the Parco Naturale della Viriglia. At Castellina in Chianti, there is a 15th-century underground passage, built for defense purposes, and the Enoteca Vini Gallo Nero (Via della Rocca 13) is a showcase for the region's wines *(see pp256–7)*.

**Badia a Coltibuono ④**
At the crossroads in Gaiole, follow the signs to Montevarchi and bear to the left off the main road before heading right toward the village of Badia.

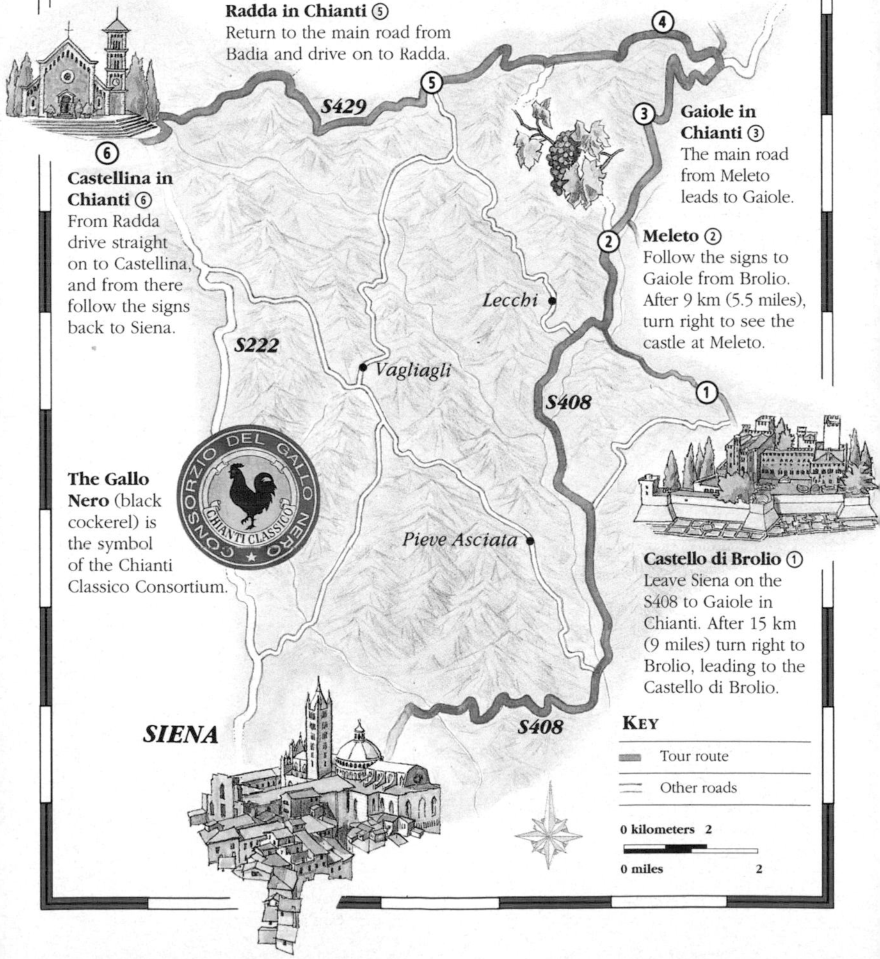


**Radda in Chianti ⑤**
Return to the main road from Badia and drive on to Radda.

**Gaiole in Chianti ③**
The main road from Meleto leads to Gaiole.

**Castellina in Chianti ⑥**
From Radda drive straight on to Castellina, and from there follow the signs back to Siena.

**Meleto ②**
Follow the signs to Gaiole from Brolio. After 9 km (5.5 miles), turn right to see the castle at Meleto.

**The Gallo Nero** (black cockerel) is the symbol of the Chianti Classico Consortium.

**Castello di Brolio ①**
Leave Siena on the S408 to Gaiole in Chianti. After 15 km (9 miles) turn right to Brolio, leading to the Castello di Brolio.

**KEY**

Tour route

Other roads

**0 kilometers 2**

**0 miles 2**

# SOUTHERN TUSCANY

THE SOUTHERNMOST PART *of Tuscany has a different feel from any other Tuscan region. Thanks to the hotter, drier and sunnier climate, the hills are cloaked in aromatic Mediterranean scrub, known as* macchia. *Palm trees grow in the towns and along the edge of the sandy beaches, and great strands of prickly pear cactus are traditionally used to mark field boundaries in the countryside.*

The coastline, lined with fishing villages and beaches, is very popular in the summer, with numerous vacation villages and caravan sites. Resorts such as Monte Argentario have a much more exclusive image, and are favored by the wealthy, yacht-owning Italians from Rome and Milan. Inland, the region's wild and unspoiled hills are popular with sportsmen, who come to hunt for wild boar and deer.

The transformation of the marshy coastal strip, known as the Maremma, into a vacation playground is a recent development. The ancient Etruscans, followed by the Romans *(see p40)*, drained its swamps to create richly fertile farming land. After the collapse of the Roman Empire, the drainage channels became choked, turning the Maremma into an inhospitable wilderness of marshland and stagnant pools plagued by malaria-carrying mosquitoes. Redraining of the land began again in the late 18th century and, with the help of insecticides, the malaria mosquito was finally eliminated in the 1950s.

### LITTLE DEVELOPMENT

The region slumbered from Roman times and for long periods was virtually uninhabited except for farmers and fishermen. Consequently there are few cities or major architectural and artistic monuments. On the other hand, archaeological remains have survived because there were few people here to salvage the stone for new buildings. Because intensive farming is limited, the region is still rich in wildlife, from butterflies and orchids to tortoises and porcupines.

**Detail of Romanesque *tympanum* on the Duomo at Massa Marittima**

◁ **The Strada Panoramica at Monte Argentario**

# Exploring Southern Tuscany

Statue above gateway, Orbetello

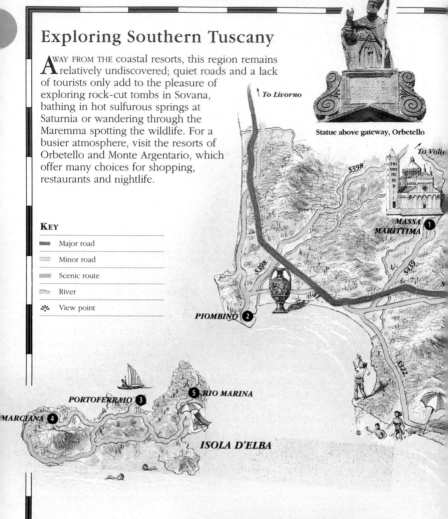

AWAY FROM THE coastal resorts, this region remains relatively undiscovered; quiet roads and a lack of tourists only add to the pleasure of exploring rock-cut tombs in Sovana, bathing in hot sulfurous springs at Saturnia or wandering through the Maremma spotting the wildlife. For a busier atmosphere, visit the resorts of Orbetello and Monte Argentario, which offer many choices for shopping, restaurants and nightlife.

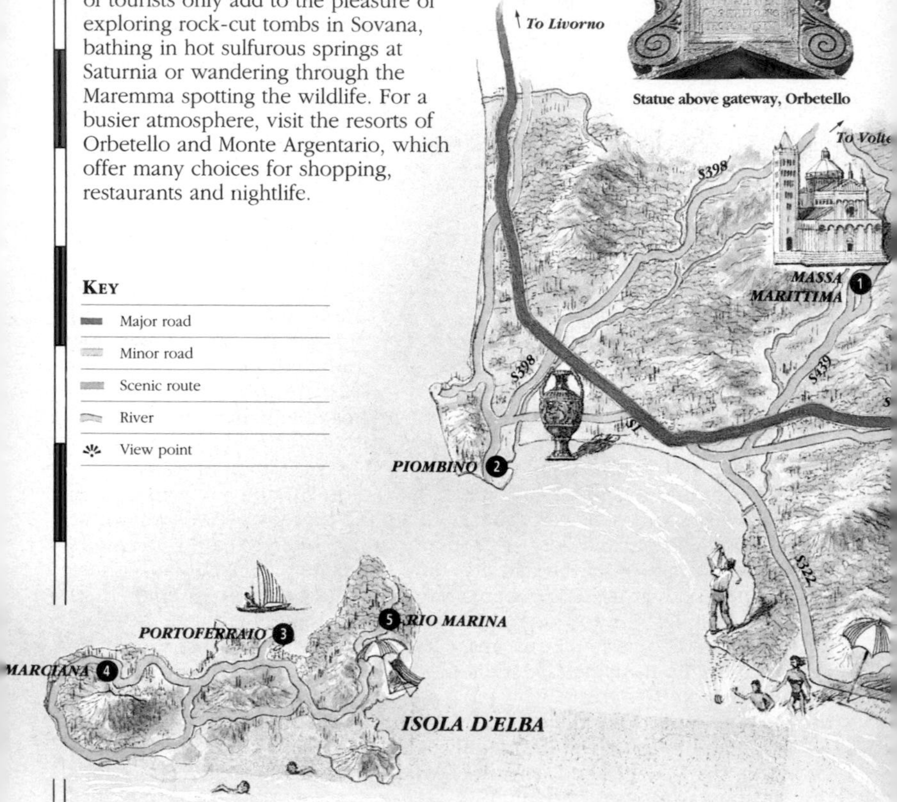


**KEY**

- Major road
- Minor road
- Scenic route
- River
- View point

**GETTING AROUND**

The S1 coastal route cannot handle the traffic in summer and is best avoided. A busy railway line runs alongside; most trains stop at Grosseto and Orbetello, and buses from Grosseto serve most towns in the area. Vehicle and passenger ferries depart from Piombino to Elba every 30 minutes during the day in summer. Bus services from Portoferraio cover all parts of the island.

View across the rooftops of Massa Marittima to the hills beyond

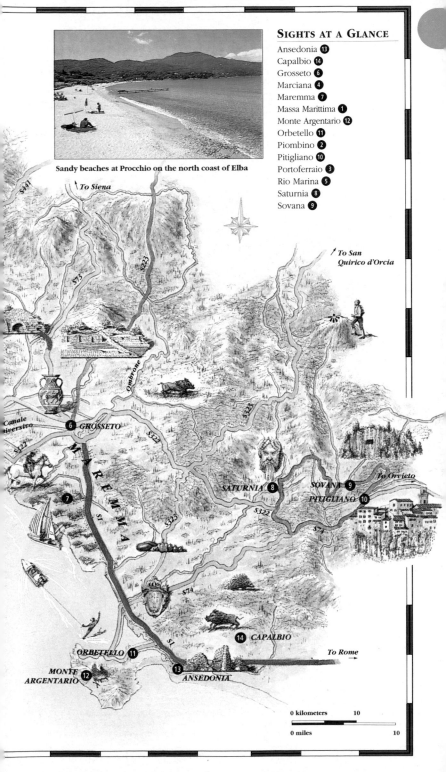

Sandy beaches at Procchio on the north coast of Elba

## Sights at a Glance



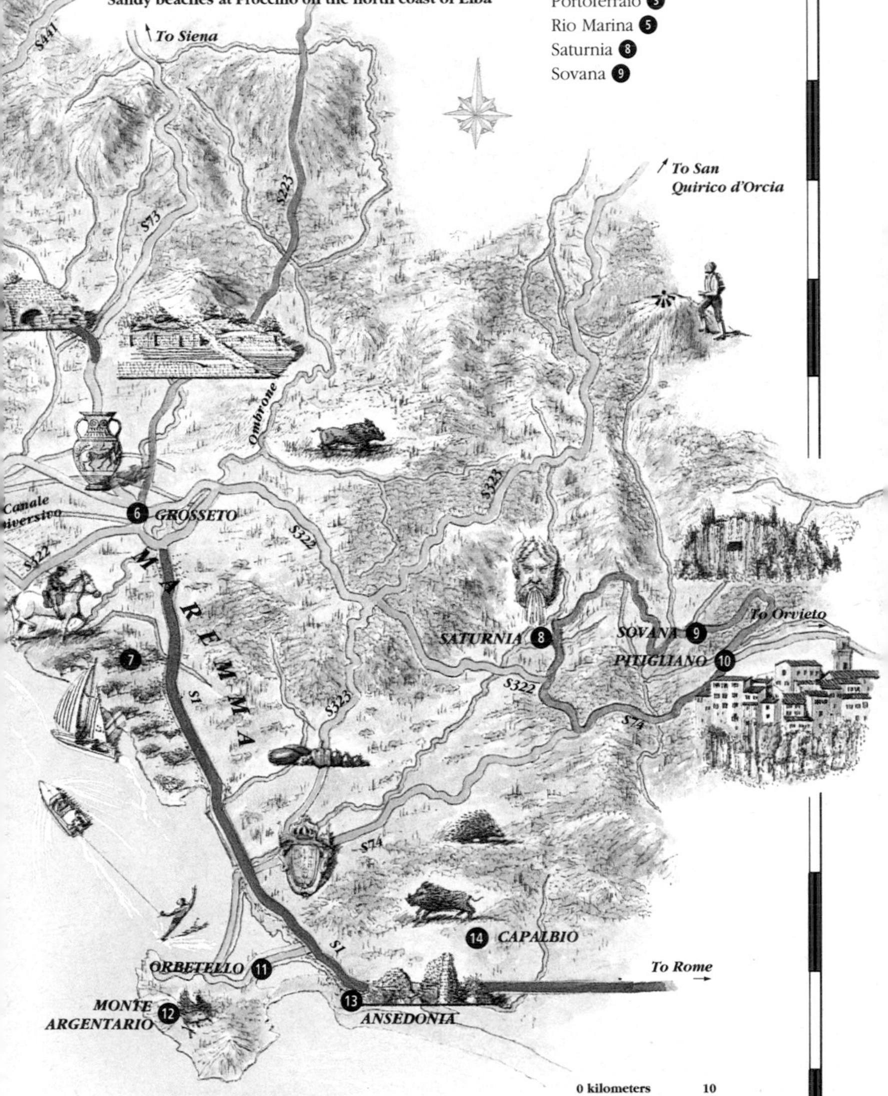

## Massa Marittima ❶

**Road map** C4. *9,469.* *Palazzo del Podestà, Piazza Garibaldi. (0566) 90 22 89.* *Wed.*

SET IN THE Colline Metallifere (metal-bearing hills), from which lead, copper and silver ores were mined, Massa Marittima is far from being a grimy industrial town. Its history is closely associated with mining, and there are some excellent examples of Romanesque architecture.

### Duomo

The Romanesque cathedral is dedicated to St. Cerbone, a 6th-century saint whose story is told in stone above the door.

### Museo Archeologico

Palazzo del Podestà, Piazza Garibaldi. *(0566) 90 22 89.* ***Open*** *Tue–Sun (Jul & Aug: daily).* ***Adm charge****.*

This 13th-century building has an archeological museum with material from Paleolithic to Roman times.

### Museo della Miniera

Via Corridoni. *(0566) 90 22 89.* ***Open*** *Tue–Sun (Jul & Aug: daily).* ***Adm charge****.*

This museum of mining is partially located within a worked-out mine shaft and has exhibits explaining the techniques of mining and the minerals found locally.

**The skyline of Massa Marittima**

## Piombino ❷

**Road map** C4. *36,550.* FS *Piazzale Premuda, Porto. (0565) 22 44 32.* *Wed.*

PIOMBINO is a busy town dominated by iron- and steelworks. It is at the end of the Massoncello peninsula and was originally an island.

## A Day Out on Elba

ELBA'S MOST FAMOUS RESIDENT was Napoleon, who spent nine months here after the fall of Paris in 1814. Today the island is mainly populated by tourists, who come by ferry from Piombino, 10 km (6 miles) away on the mainland. The main town is Portoferraio, with an old port and a modern seafront with smart hotels. The landscape of the island is varied: on the west coast there are sandy beaches, suitable for all water sports; inland, olive groves and vineyards line hillsides, and vegetation covers the mountains. The east coast is more rugged, with high cliffs and stony beaches.

**Marciana Marina** ③
Return to the main road and follow the coast past Procchio, with its long sandy bays. From here it is 7.5 km (4.5 miles) to the marina.

**Marciana Alta** ④
From the marina, take the main road into the hills to the old medieval town. After 8 km (5 miles) turn left onto a minor road. It leads to the cable car up to the top of Monte Capanne.

**Marina di Campo** ⑤ Stay on the coast road, around the west end of the island, until Marina di Campo.

**KEY**

Tour route

Other roads

0 kilometers 2

0 miles 2

It is the main port for ferries to Elba, which run every half hour in summer and also at frequent intervals in winter. Nearby are the ruins of Etruscan Populonia and the **Museo Etrusco Gasparri**, which contains bronze and terra-cotta works found in the surrounding necropoli.

**Museo Etrusco Gasparri**
Populonia. *(0565) 294 36.* ***Open** daily.* ***Adm charge**.*

## Portoferraio ❸

**Road map** B4. *11,500.* *Calata Italia 26. (0565) 91 46 71.* *Fri.*

THE FERRY from Piombino brings visitors to Elba here from the mainland. The town has a pretty harbor but the principal sights are Napoleon's two houses.

In the center of Portoferraio is the **Palazzina Napoleonica** (also known as the Villetta dei Mulini), a modest house built around two windmills. **Villa San Martino**, his country residence, had a Classical façade imposed on it by Russian emigré, Prince Demidoff, in 1851.

Egyptian-style frescoes in the house, painted in 1814, are a reminder of Napoleon's Nile campaigns of 1798–9.

**Palazzina Napoleonica**
Forte Stella. *(0565) 91 58 46.* ***Open** Tue–Sun (Jul & Aug: daily).* ***Adm charge**.*

**Villa San Martino**
San Martino. *(0565) 91 46 88.* ***Open** Tue–Sun (Jul & Aug: daily).* ***Adm charge**.*

## Marciana ❹

**Road map** B4. *2,200.* *Municipio, Marciana Alta. (0565) 90 10 15.*

ON ELBA'S northwest coast is Marciana Marina, and farther inland the well-preserved medieval town of Marciana Alta. The **Museo Civico Archeologico** houses exhibits from Etruscan ships wrecked off Elba. From here, take the cable car up Monte Capanne, Elba's highest peak at 1,018 m (3,300 ft).

**Shady beaches and inlets at Marciana Marina on Elba**

**Museo Civico Archeologico**
Via del Pretorio, Marciana Alta. *(0565) 90 12 15.* ***Open** daily.* ***Adm charge**.*

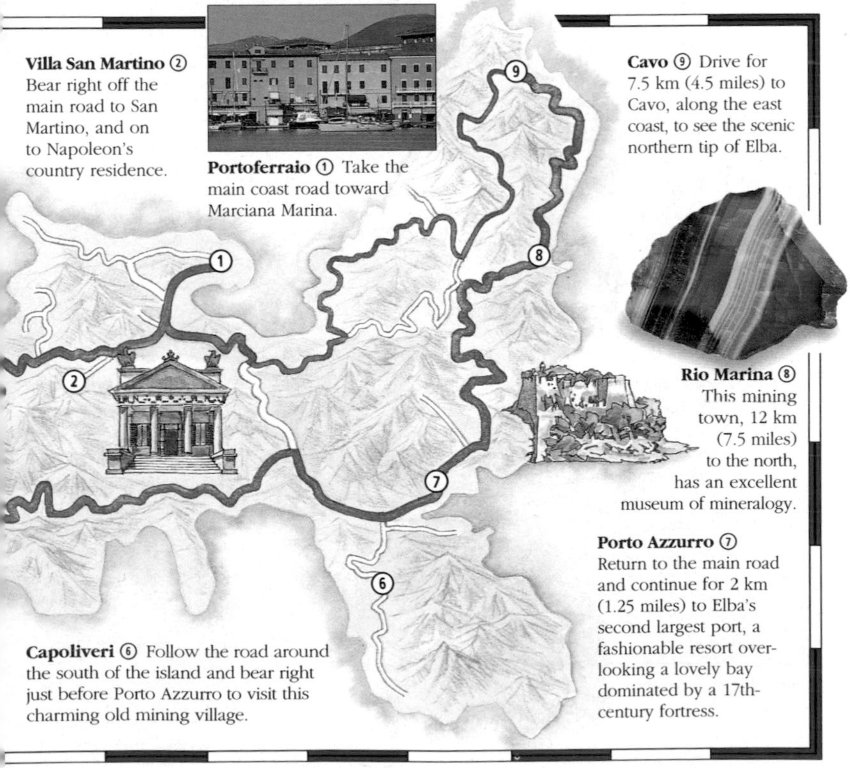


**Villa San Martino** ② Bear right off the main road to San Martino, and on to Napoleon's country residence.

**Portoferraio** ① Take the main coast road toward Marciana Marina.

**Cavo** ⑨ Drive for 7.5 km (4.5 miles) to Cavo, along the east coast, to see the scenic northern tip of Elba.

**Rio Marina** ⑧ This mining town, 12 km (7.5 miles) to the north, has an excellent museum of mineralogy.

**Porto Azzurro** ⑦ Return to the main road and continue for 2 km (1.25 miles) to Elba's second largest port, a fashionable resort overlooking a lovely bay dominated by a 17th-century fortress.

**Capoliveri** ⑥ Follow the road around the south of the island and bear right just before Porto Azzurro to visit this charming old mining village.

# The Maremma ❼

Maremma butterfly

THE ANCIENT ROMANS were the first to cultivate the marshes of the Maremma, but after the collapse of their empire, the area went virtually uninhabited until the 18th century. The land has since been reclaimed, the irrigation canals unblocked and farming developed on the fertile soil. The Parco Naturale dell'Uccellina was set up in 1975 to protect the abundant local flora and fauna and to prevent additional development.

**Wildlife**
*The undergrowth and marshes are home to wild boar and other wildlife.*

**Entry permits** are sold at Alberese.

**This salt marsh**, cut by irrigation canals, is home to herons, storks and other wading birds.

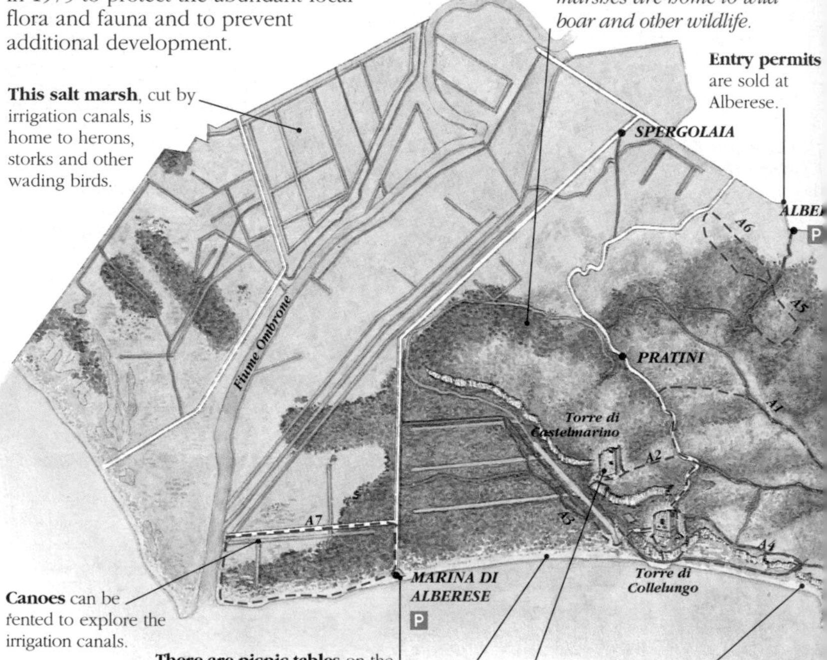


**Canoes** can be rented to explore the irrigation canals.

**There are picnic tables** on the beach in the shade of pine trees.

**Sea lilies and hollies** grow along the sandy shoreline, backed by groves of parasol pines, mastic trees and juniper.

**Beaches**
*The shoreline south of Marina di Alberese has wide, sandy beaches sheltered by steep cliffs.*

**Torre di Castelmarino**
*The cliffs are crowned by 16th-century watchtowers, part of a defense system built by the Medici to protect the coastal region from attack.*

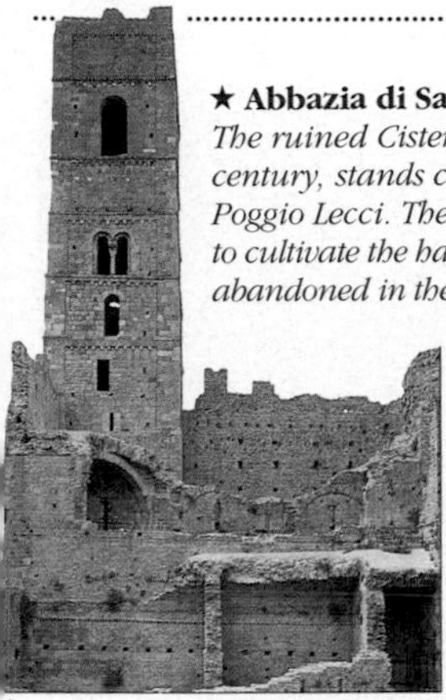

**★ Abbazia di San Rabano**
*The ruined Cistercian abbey, built in the 12th century, stands close to the park's highest peak, Poggio Lecci. The monks made a brave attempt to cultivate the harsh terrain, but the abbey was abandoned in the middle of the 17th century.*

**★ Marked Footpaths**
*Footpaths give access to areas where you can see butterflies, lizards and poisonous snakes, including vipers.*

**The hills** running parallel to the coast are cloaked in scrub called *macchia*, consisting of rosemary, broom, rock rose, sea lavender and rowan trees.

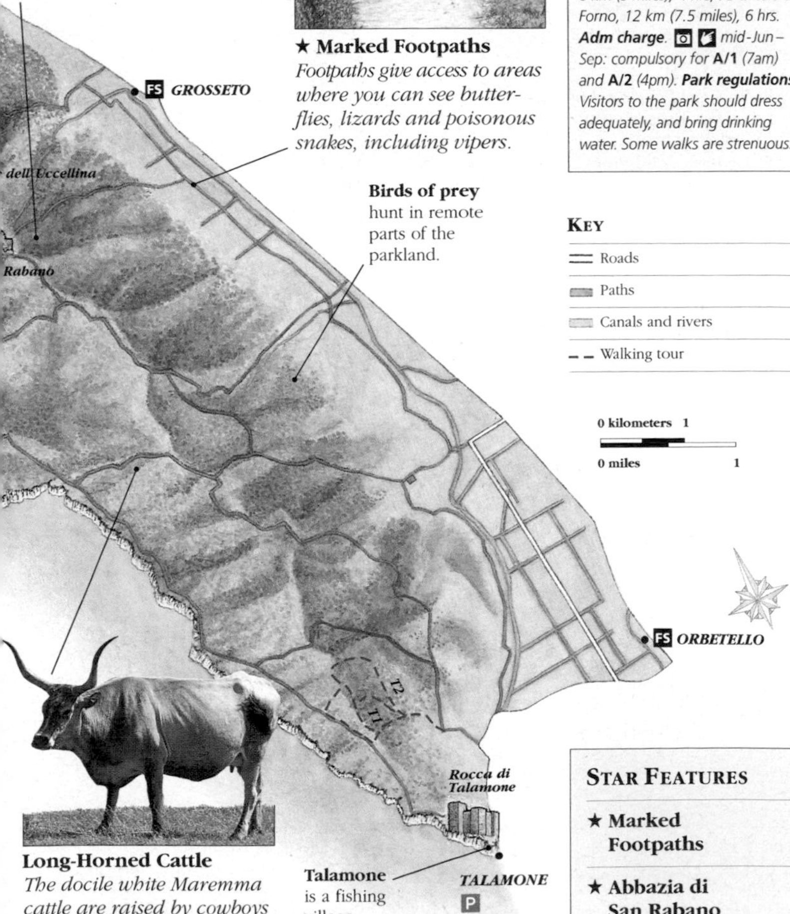


**Birds of prey** hunt in remote parts of the parkland.

**Long-Horned Cattle**
*The docile white Maremma cattle are raised by cowboys* (butteri) *who also stage rodeos.*

**Talamone** is a fishing village.

## Visitors' Checklist

Centro Visite di Alberese. **Road map** D5. (0564) 40 70 98. **Marginal areas open** *9am–1 hr before sunset daily (mid-Jun–Sep: 7:30–10am daily, also 4:30–6pm Wed, Sat, Sun & Aug).* **Entrances** *at Alberese, Marina di Alberese, Talamone.* **Walking tour: A/5, A/6**: *nature trails 5 km (3 miles), 3 hrs;* **A/7**: *Ombrone estuary, 4 km (2.5 miles), 3 hrs;* **T/1, T/2**: *short trails. adv booking.*
**Inner park areas open** *9am–1 hr before sunset Wed, Sat, Sun and public hols.* **Entrance** *Alberese. Transportation provided to tour departure point at Pratini, 9 km (5.5 miles).* **Walking tour: A/1**: *Abbazia di San Rabano, 6 km (3.75 miles), 5 hrs;* **A/2**: *Le Torri, 5 km (3 miles), 3 hrs;* **A/3**: *Le Grotte, 8 km (5 miles), 4 hrs;* **A/4**: *Cala di Forno, 12 km (7.5 miles), 6 hrs.*
***Adm charge***. *mid-Jun–Sep: compulsory for* **A/1** *(7am) and* **A/2** *(4pm).* **Park regulations:** *Visitors to the park should dress adequately, and bring drinking water. Some walks are strenuous.*

## Key

- Roads
- Paths
- Canals and rivers
- Walking tour

0 kilometers 1

0 miles 1

## Star Features

- ★ Marked Footpaths
- ★ Abbazia di San Rabano

## Rio Marina 5

**Road map** B4. *1800.*
*Piazza Salvo d'Acquisto. (0565) 96 20 09.* *Mon.*

AROUND RIO MARINA there are still open-pit mines which extract the ores that attracted the Etruscans to Elba. The **Museo dei Minerali Elbani** explains the geology of the island. Shops in the town center sell jewelry made of local semi-precious stones.

### Museo dei Minerali Elbani

Palazzo Comunale. *(0565) 96 27 47.* **Open** *Apr–Sep: daily.* **Adm charge**.

## Grosseto 6

**Road map** D4. *71,472.*
*Viale Monterosa 206. (0564) 45 45 27.* *Thu.*

GROSSETO IS the largest town in southern Tuscany. War damage destroyed many buildings, although the 16th-century city walls are still standing and several of the bastions are now parks.

### Museo Civico Archeologico e d'Arte della Maremma

Piazza Baccarini 3. **Open** *mid-1995.* **Adm charge**.
The museum has Etruscan and Roman artifacts from Vetulonia and Roselle, along with plans giving information about the sites. There is a collection of coins, intaglios (carved stones) and pottery.

**Grosseto, a busy town full of narrow streets and shops**

**Cascate del Gorello, free for all to enjoy in Saturnia**

## The Maremma 7

*See pp232–3.*

## Saturnia 8

**Road map** D5. *550.* *Via Aldobrandeschi. (0564) 60 12 08.*

VACATIONERS come to Saturnia to enjoy the good Maremma food or seek a health cure in the modern spa of Terme di Saturnia. Others prefer to bathe for free in the hot, sulfurous waters of the waterfall at Cascate del Gorello on the Montemerano road. This is a pretty spot, with its water pools and rocks stained coppery green.

## Sovana 9

**Road map** E5. *100.*

SOVANA SITS ON a ridge high above the Lente valley. Its main street is lined with cafés, restaurants and shops. The 13th-century Romanesque **Rocca Aldobrandesca**, named after the Teutonic family that ruled in the area until 1608, is now in ruins.

The medieval church of **Santa Maria** has frescoes of the late 15th-century Siena School, which were recently discovered under the white-washed walls. The main altar is sheltered by a 9th-century baldacchino that was originally in the Romanesque **Duomo**. This 12th-century building incorporates sculpture from earlier churches built on the same site.

The Etruscans dug tombs nearby in the soft limestone cliffs bordering the river Lente. Some are badly eroded but the most complete set of **Necropoli Etrusca** can be found in a valley just to the west of Sovana.

### Rocca Aldobrandesca

Via del Pretorio. ***Closed***.

### Santa Maria

Piazza del Pretorio. **Open** *daily.*

### Duomo

Piazza del Pretorio. **Open** *daily in summer; Sat & Sun only in winter.*

### Necropoli Etrusca

Poggio di Sopra Ripa. **Open** *daily.*

Cafés and shops in Sovana's medieval piazza

## Pitigliano ⑩

**Road map** E5. 4,361.
Via Roma 6. (0564) 61 44 33.
*Wed.*

PITIGLIANO IS spectacular, perched on a plateau high above cliffs carved out by the river Lente. The houses seem to grow out of the cliffs, which are riddled with caves cut out of a soft limestone called tufa. The caves have been used for many years to store locally made wines and olive oils.

A maze of tiny medieval streets, including Via Zuccarelli, passes through the Jewish ghetto, formed when Jews fleeing from Catholic persecution took refuge here in the 17th century. The Palazzo Orsini in the town center has its water supply brought in by an aqueduct built in 1545 that overhangs Via Cavour. The **Museo Zuccarelli** in the palazzo has a small exhibition of work by artist Francesco Zuccarelli (1702–88), who lived locally. He also painted two of the altarpieces in the medieval **Duomo**, whose massive bell tower supports a bell which weighs about 3 tons.

The new **Museo Etrusco**, opened in 1994, contains finds from ancient local settlements.

**Museo Zuccarelli**
Palazzo Orsini, Piazza della Fortezza Orsini.
(0564) 61 55 68.
***Open*** *Mar–Jul: Tue–Sun; Aug: daily; Sep–Dec: Sat & Sun.* ***Adm charge.***

**Duomo**
Piazza San Gregorio. ***Open*** *daily.*

**Museo Etrusco**
Piazza Fortezza.

## Orbetello ⑪

**Road map** D5. *15,455.* FS
*Piazza del Duomo. (0564) 86 80 10.* *Sat.*

ORBETELLO is a crowded resort bordered by two tidal lagoons. Part of the northernmost lagoon is managed by the World Wide Fund for Nature as a wildlife park.

The town was the capital of a tiny Spanish state, called the Presidio, from 1557 until 1808, when it was absorbed into the Grand Duchy of Tuscany. The Porta del Soccorso, a triple-arched gateway in the 16th-century city walls, bears the coat of arms of the king of Spain. Inside the gates is the **Polveriera Guzman**, which was originally used as an arsenal. It is now being restored and will contain an archaeological museum. The Duomo, **Santa Maria Assunta**, also has Spanish-style decoration, but the altar in the Cappella di San Biagio is typically Romanesque in design.

Coat of arms on the Porta del Soccorso

**Polveriera Guzman**
Viale Mura di Levante. ***Closed*** *indefinitely.*

**Santa Maria Assunta**
Piazza del Duomo. ***Open*** *daily.*

View over Pitigliano showing soft limestone cliffs and caves bordering the river Lente

Porto Ercole, near Monte Argentario

## Monte Argentario ⓬

**Road map** D5. *13,000.* *Corso Umberto 55, Porto Santo Stéfano. (0564) 81 42 08.* *Tue.*

MONTE ARGENTARIO was an island until the early 18th century, when the shallow waters separating it from the mainland began to silt up, creating two sandy spits of land, known as *tomboli*, that enclose the Orbetello lagoon. Orbetello itself was linked to the island in 1842, when a dike was constructed linking the mainland to Terrarossa.

The two harbor towns of Porto Ercole and Porto Santo Stéfano are both favored by wealthy yacht owners. There are good fish restaurants in both towns *(see p263)*, and from the Strada Panoramica there are views over rocky coves, cliffs and bays. Ferries from Porto Santo Stéfano go to the island of Giglio, popular with Italian tourists for its sandy beaches and rich wildlife.

During the summer months the Porto Santo Stéfano ferry also calls at Giannutri, which is a privately owned island where visitors are not allowed to stay overnight.

## Ansedonia ⓭

**Road map** D5. *300.*

ANSEDONIA is a prosperous village of luxurious villas and gardens, high on a hill above the coast. The ruins of the city of Cosa, founded by the Romans in 173 BC, are on the summit of the hill looking over Ansedonia. The **Museo di Cosa**, containing relics from the ancient settlement, is close by. East of Ansedonia is a long stretch of sandy beach and the remains of the Etruscan Canal. The date

## An Etruscan Tour

THE ETRUSCANS GAINED much of their wealth from Tuscany's vast mineral resources, and the Etruscan monied classes were cultured and worldly. Their elaborate burial sites and the artifacts found in the tombs give us an insight into their lives *(see pp40–41)*. Etruscan burial sites were carved into soft rock or built of huge stone slabs with rock-cut roads leading down to the tombs.

**Grosseto** ① The Museo Civico Archeologico has a collection of Etruscan artifacts found in local tombs.

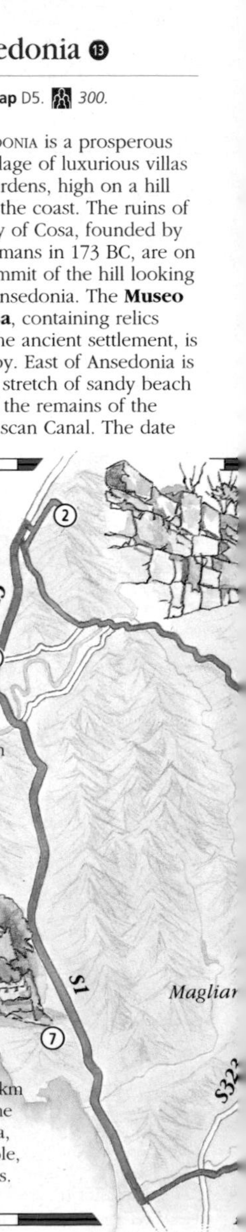


### ALSO WORTH SEEING

**Museo Archeologico**, Florence *(see p99)*.

**Museo Etrusco**, Volterra *(see p162)*.

**Vulci** and **Tarquinia** These excavated sites, just over the Tuscany border in Lazio, have impressive Etruscan ruins, painted tombs and art collections.

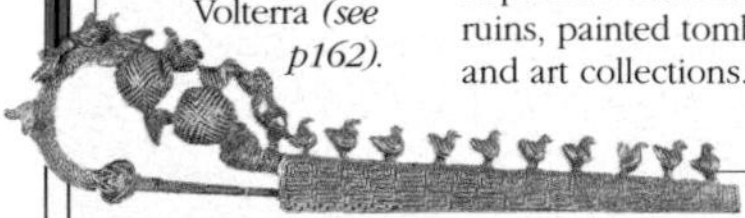

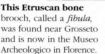

**This Etruscan bone** brooch, called a *fibula*, was found near Grosseto and is now in the Museo Archeologico in Florence.

0 kilometers 5

0 miles 5

**Talamone** ⑦ Follow the S74 up to the S1. Turn right and after 8 km (5 miles), fork off to the left, into the Maremma, for the Etruscan temple, Roman villa and baths.

The Etruscan Canal at Ansedonia

and purpose of the canal are debatable, but it may have been dug in Roman times to keep the harbor free of silt. Alternatively, it may have been part of a canal leading to the Lago di Burano, 5 km (3 miles) down the coast. This lagoon is 4 km (2.5 miles) long and has been turned into a wildlife refuge *(rifugio faunistico)* by the World Wide Fund for Nature. It is a very important habitat for wading birds.

### Museo di Cosa

Ansedonia. (0564) 88 14 21.
**Open** *daily.*

## Capalbio ⓮

**Road map** D5. *4,049.* *Wed.*

CAPALBIO is another village that is popular with wealthy Italians. The hilltop town has several restaurants and hotels and is busy all year round. Summer tourists come for the beaches, and winter visitors flock to hunt deer and wild boar in the surrounding woodland, which is now managed as a game reserve. A game festival is held in September each year.

### Giardino dei Tarocchi

Garavicchio, Pescia Fiorentina. *(0564) 238 72.* **Open** *Jun–Aug: Mon–Sat.*

At nearby Pescia Fiorentino, to the southeast of Capalbio, is a modern sculpture garden created by the French artist Niki de Saint-Phalle in 1982. It was inspired by the mystical figures of the Tarot and has been many years in the making. The bigger pieces each represent one card from the mystic Tarot pack. Among the sculptures already finished is *The Tower*, a glittering three-story edifice made almost entirely out of broken mirrors.

View across the rooftops of Capalbio

**Roselle** ② Head north on the S223 to the most important excavated Etruscan and Roman remains in Tuscany.

**Saturnia** ③ Continue east for 54 km (34 miles) for the rock-cut tombs below this tiny village of Etruscan origin.

**Sovana** ④ From Saturnia, drive toward Sovana to the famous Ildebranda Tomb in a valley to the west.

**Marsiliana** ⑥ Head west on the S74 through Manciano to the vast necropoli on the outskirts of Marsiliana.

**Pitigliano** ⑤ The town, on the junction with the S74, is built on tufa cliffs riddled with Etruscan tombs and tunnels, now used for storing produce.

**KEY**

Tour route

Other roads

# TRAVELERS' NEEDS

# Where to Stay

**Sign showing hotel rating**

Of all Italy's regions, Tuscany has some of the most charming places to stay. Inland these range from magnificent ancient villas to elegant town houses. A number of the smaller, family-run establishments excel in their cuisine and are filled with interesting antiques. Hotels on the coast tend to be less distinctive, but the popularity of coastal resorts in summer means that standards are high. Many visitors opt for low-cost, modest rooms. Often the accommodation is a small apartment or house on a farm, and the prices can be very reasonable. Other options include hostel or dormitory accommodation and, for walking enthusiasts, there are mountain huts throughout the region. For more information on hotels in Florence and Tuscany see the listings on pages 247–51.

**Terrace at Hotel Continental *(see p248)***

## Where to Look

Florence has a wide range of hotels, but prices can be high. The most attractive locations are along the north bank of the Arno, the historic center and in nearby Fiesole. Parking is a problem in the city center, so if you have a car it is best to choose a hotel that has parking facilities.

Accommodation in central Pisa is generally substandard but there are some lovely Tuscan villa hotels a short drive from the center.

Though large, Arezzo has relatively few hotels and those in the center are mostly geared to business people. If you can, stay outside the town and travel in to visit the center.

The hill towns of central Tuscany offer a number of quality villa hotels, manor houses and even former palaces. The Chianti region is rich in converted villa hotels, with excellent regional restaurants, particularly around Radda and Gaiole. Siena's more attractive options are outside the city, such as the tiny hamlet of Strove.

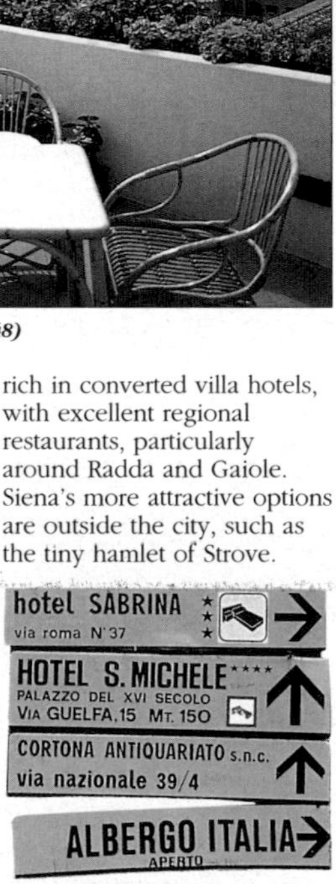

**Street sign showing the direction and location of hotels**

## Hotel Prices

During the low season (November to March) prices are cheaper and often negotiable. Florence is less busy than other parts of Tuscany in July and August, but this is the peak holiday season on the coast. Avoid the city during certain weeks of January and July when fashion shows fill the leading hotels, raising low-season prices.

Single-room rates are higher than individual rates for two people sharing a double room. Prices include tax and service. Bear in mind that accommodations in Florence and Siena are more expensive than elsewhere in the region.

## Hidden Extras

Before making a reservation, establish whether breakfast is included in the price. Garage parking, laundry and snacks in the hotel or from the minibar may be pricey, and telephone charges from your hotel room can be phenomenal. Check the rates first if you are concerned. Some hotels may expect you to take some or all meals during the high season.

## Hotel Gradings and Facilities

Hotels in Italy are classified by a star-rating system, from one to five stars. However, each province sets its own levels for grading; consequently, standards for each category may vary from one area to another. Some hotels may not have a restaurant but those that do will welcome nonresidents to stop by and eat.

Some of the converted castles and ancient villas are not air-conditioned, but the stone walls are thick, and the

The marvelous gallery entrance of Hotel Villa Villoresi *(see p248)*

midsummer heat barely penetrates the buildings.

Children are welcome but the smaller hotels generally have limited facilities. Often, the more upscale hotels will arrange a baby-sitting service. Sometimes the proprietor of a smaller hotel, or a member of the family, will mind your children, if they are not busy.

## What to Expect

In Florence, street numbers can be confusing *(see p274)*, so refer to the map references in the listings.

Hotel proprietors are obliged by law to register you with the police, so they will ask for your passport when you arrive. Make sure you take it back, as you will need some form of identification to change money or traveler's checks.

Even the most humble of *pensioni* should have a reasonably good bathroom, even if it's shared. Rooms without a bathroom will usually have washbasins and towels.

Hotel decoration may not always be first-class, and you may sometimes prefer to sacrifice fancy décor for the charm of an old establishment.

The Italian breakfast is light – a cup of coffee and French toast or cake *(brioche)*. Most hotels serve a continental breakfast of coffee, tea or hot chocolate, rolls and jam. However, it may be cheaper and just as good to go to a local bar or patisserie.

Florence can be very noisy. First-class hotels may have some form of soundproofing, but ask for a room facing away from the street if you are easily disturbed by noise.

Checkout time is usually noon in four- and five-star hotels and between 10am and noon in one- to three-star establishments. If you stay longer you will be asked to pay for an extra day.

## Booking and Paying

Book at least two months in advance if you want to stay in a particular hotel during the high season. The local tourist office will have listings of all the hotels in the area, and they will be able to advise you on the best hotels for each star category. Most hotels above the L100,000 price bracket take credit cards, but check which cards are accepted when booking. You can usually pay the deposit by credit card, or send a Eurocheque or international money order.

Under Italian law, a booking is valid as soon as the deposit is paid and confirmation is received. As in restaurants, you are required by law to keep your hotel receipt until you leave Italy.

## Disabled Travelers

Facilities for the disabled are usually limited. The hotel listings on pages 247–51 indicate which hotels have these facilities.

## Hotels in Historic Buildings

The Tuscany regional tourist board publishes a brochure that lists hotels in historic buildings or those of artistic interest. Some of the best are included in the listings here. The booklet is available from national Italian tourist offices worldwide. The **International Relais and Château** guide includes a number of high quality Tuscan hotels and hotel restaurants of historic interest.

Villa San Michele, a former monastery, in Fiesole *(see p248)*

Garden terrace at Villa La Massa *(see p248)*

## Residential Rentals

Farm and villa vacation accommodations abound in Tuscany. There is an **Agriturist** office in each region which will provide information on private rentals, often on a farm that is still working.

Two international agencies dealing with residential rentals around Florence are the **American Agency** and **Solemar**. Other agents include **Casa Club** in Siena, **Cuendet** in Monteriggioni and **Prima Italia** in Grosseto. Solemar and Cuendet have agents throughout the world, such as **Interhome** (Solemar) and **Cuendet USA.**

Prices for private rentals vary enormously depending on the season and location. Generally, a four-person villa within a complex in the low season will cost around L875,000 per week, while an individual villa in its own grounds can cost as much as L3,500,000 per week during the peak season.

## Staying in Private Homes

Rooms in private homes can usually be rented through one of the recreational associations such as **AGAP** (Associazione Gestori Alloggi Privati) in Florence. Meals are not provided but can sometimes be arranged on request.

## Residential Hotels

Throughout Tuscany there are former palaces or villas housing a complex of small apartments, with facilities such as a swimming

## Directory

### Historic Hotels

**Centre d'Information Relais & Chateaux**
11 E 44th St, Suite 707
NY, NY 10017.
*(212) 856-0115.*

### Residential Rentals

**Agriturist Ufficio Regionale**
Piazza di San Firenze 3
50122 Florence.
*(055) 28 78 38.*

**American Agency**
Via del Ponte Rosso 33r
50129 Florence.
*(055) 47 50 53.*

**Casaclub**
Via dei Termini 83
53100 Siena.
*(0577) 464 84.*

**Cuendet**
Località Il Cerreto, Strove
53035 Monteriggioni.
*(0577) 30 10 53.*

**Cuendet USA**
165 Chestnut St, Allendale
New Jersey 07401.
*(201) 327-2333.*

**Interhome**
124 Little Falls Road
New Jersey 07004.
*(201) 882-6864.*

**Prima Italia**
Viale Tirreno 19 Principina a Mare
58046 Grosseto.
*(0564) 300 09.*

**Solemar**
Via Cavour 80
50129 Florence.
*(055) 21 81 12.*

### Private Homes

**AGAP**
Via de' Neri 9
50122 Florence.
*(055) 28 41 00.*

### Residential Hotels

**La Bugia**
Via Santa Margherita a Montici 54
50125 Florence.
*(055) 68 81 89.*

**Mini Residence**
Via Giulio Caccini 20
50141 Florence.
*(055) 41 08 76.*

**Palazzo Mannaioni**
Via Maffia 9, 50125
Florence. **Map** 3 B2 (5 A5).
*(055) 28 00 59.*

**Palazzo Ricasoli**
Via delle Mantellate 2
50129 Florence.
**Map** 2 D3.
*(055) 35 21 51.*

**Residence Da-al**
Via dell'Ariento 3r, 50123
Florence. **Map** 1 C4 (5 C1).
*(055) 21 49 79.*

### Hotel Cooperatives

**Consorzio Sviluppo Turistico Mugello**
Via Palmiro Togliatti 6
Borgo San Lorenzo
50133 Florence.
**Map** 6 D2.
*(055) 845 80 45.*

**Coopal**
Il Prato 2r, 50123
Florence. **Map** 1 A4.
*(055) 21 95 25.*

**Family Hotel**
Via Faenza 77, 50123
Florence. **Map** 1 C4 (5 C1).
*(055) 21 79 75.*

**Florence Promhotels**
Viale Alessandro Volta 72
50131 Florence.
**Map** 2 F2.
*(055) 57 04 81.*

### Budget Accommodations

**Associazione Italiana Alberghi per la Gioventù**
Via Cavour 44
00184 Rome
*(06) 487 11 52.*

**Europa Villa Camerata**
Viale Augusto Righi 2–4
50137 Florence.
*(055) 60 14 51.*

### Mountain Refuges and Campsites

**Touring Club Italiano**
Corso Italia 10
20122 Milan.
*(02) 852 61.*

**Club Alpino Italiano**
Via Fonseca Pimental 7
20127 Milan.
*(02) 26 14 13 78.*

pool or a bar. The minimum period of stay is usually a week, but there is more flexibility in low season.

Residential hotels in the center of Florence include **Palazzo Mannaioni** and **Residence Da-al**. The local tourist office keeps a list of others in the region.

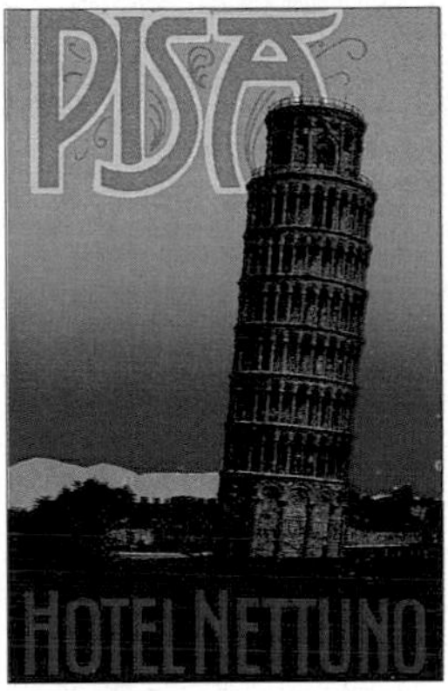


**Poster (about 1918) of a Pisan hotel**

### Hotel Cooperatives

These are not chains but consortiums of different hotel types. **Family Hotel** specializes in small, intimate family hotels or *pensioni*, while **Florence Promhotels** provide a wider range of accommodations. **Coopal** only accepts groups of a minimum of 10 people, and **Consorzio Sviluppo** deals with hotels south of Florence.

### Budget Accommodations

One- and two-star budget hotels charging from L35,000 to L60,000 per person per night are generally small, family-run establishments. These were originally known as *pensioni*, but the term is no longer much in use. However, many places retain the name and personal character that has made them so popular. Most offer breakfast, and some have rooms with private bathrooms, but you should not expect particularly high standards of service.

Hostel and dormitory accommodations can often be found in convents and religious institutions. Dormitory accommodations can be arranged through the local tourist office. The **Associazione Italiana Alberghi per la Gioventù** (Italian Youth Hostel Association) in Rome has lists of youth hostels in Italy. The main youth hostel in Florence is **Europa Villa Camerata**.

Full lists and booking facilities for youth hostels are available through the Italian tourist board (ENIT) worldwide or from the local tourist offices *(see p272)*.

### Mountain Refuges and Campsites

If you are likely to be trekking, backpacking or walking, there are mountain refuges or huts dotted throughout Tuscany. There are also campsites on the fringes of most towns. A list of campsites and mountain refuges is available from ENIT *(see p273)* or local tourist offices. **Club Alpino Italiano** in Milan owns most of the huts in the mountain districts of Italy, including Tuscany. The **Touring Club Italiano** publishes a list of campsites in *Campeggi e Villaggi Turistici in Italia*.

### Using the Listings

The hotels on pages 247–51 are listed according to area and price category. The symbols summarize the facilities at each hotel.

- all rooms have bath and/or shower unless otherwise indicated
- 1 single-rate rooms available
- rooms for more than two people available, or an extra bed can be put in a double room
- TV television in all rooms
- air-conditioning in all rooms
- swimming pool in hotel
- wheelchair access
- elevator
- P hotel parking available
- restaurant
- credit cards accepted

**Price categories** for a standard double room per night, including breakfast, tax and service:

- Ⓛ under L100,000
- ⓁⓁ L100,000–L160,000
- ⓁⓁⓁ L160,000–L240,000
- ⓁⓁⓁⓁ L240,000–L340,000
- ⓁⓁⓁⓁⓁ over L340,000

**Vaulted entrance hall of Hotel Porta Rossa *(see p247)***

# Florence's Best Hotels

In a city renowned for its splendid architecture, it is hardly surprising that many of Florence's hotels are favored by visitors for their charm and individual character. Former palazzi, monasteries such as Villa San Michele, and town villas offer accommodation in all price ranges. Original features are sometimes preserved at the expense of modern comforts: among the older establishments listed on pages 247–8, we try to include those which combine both. The hotels shown here are a selection of the best.

**Hotel Tornabuoni Beacci**
*This family-run former palace is particularly welcoming and furnished with fine antiques.* (See p247.)

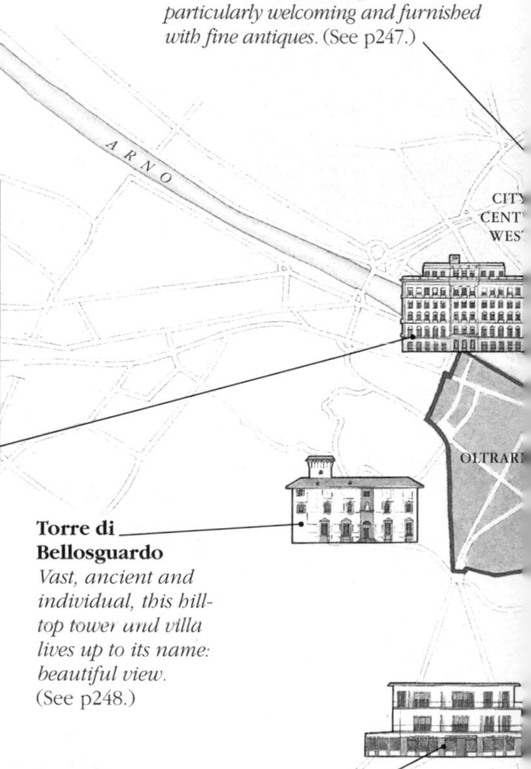


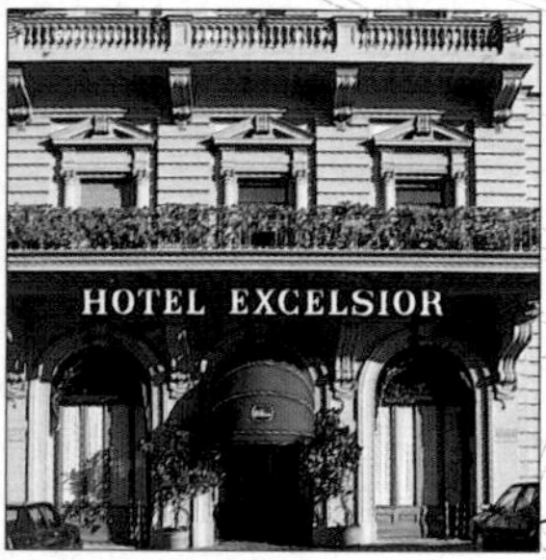


**Hotel Excelsior**
*On a 13th-century square near the river Arno, this beautiful hotel epitomizes luxury, with well-appointed rooms and 19th-century fittings.* (See p248.)

**Torre di Bellosguardo**
*Vast, ancient and individual, this hill-top tower and villa lives up to its name: beautiful view.* (See p248.)

**Hotel Villa Belvedere**
*This 1930s hillside hotel is set in 11 acres of landscaped gardens and has excellent views of the city. Inside, the décor is impeccable.* (See p247.)

0 meters 1,000

0 yards 1,000

**Villa San Michele**

*This peaceful monastery in Fiesole is said to have been designed by Michelangelo.* (See p248.)

**Pensione Bencistà**

*A haven in the hills behind the city, this lovingly kept* pensione *has luxurious period furniture.* (See p248.)

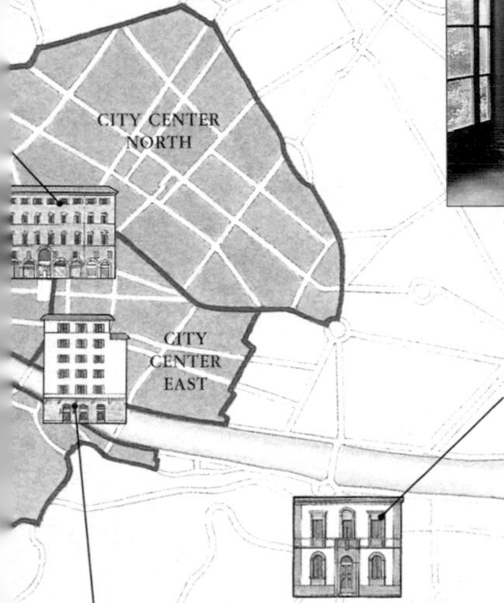


**Hotel Villa Liberty**

*A jewel-like bar and stylish bedrooms are special features of this turn-of-the-century villa on the southeastern side of town.* (See p247.)

**Villa La Massa**

*Surrounded by parkland, this former country home is one of Florence's most elegant hotels.* (See p248.)

**Hotel Hermitage**

*The drawing room overlooks the Ponte Vecchio in this comfortable and quiet hotel housed on the top floors of a tall medieval building.* (See p247.)

# Florence and Siena Hotels

THIS SELECTION CHART is a quick reference to hotels in Florence and Siena, many of which offer charming décor and surroundings even in the lower price categories. These hotels, and others in Tuscany, are listed in more detail on the following pages. For information on other types of accommodations, see pages 242–3.

| | | Number of Rooms | Family Rooms | Hotel Parking | Restaurant | Buildings of Historic or Artistic Interest | Attractive Views | Quiet Location |
|---|---|---|---|---|---|---|---|---|
| **Florence City Center** *(see pp247–8)* | | | | | | | | |
| **Hotel Locanda Orchidea** | Ⓛ | 7 | | | | ■ | | |
| **Pensione Maxim** | Ⓛ | 23 | ● | | | | | |
| **Hotel Porta Rossa** | ⓁⓁ | 85 | ● | | | ■ | ● | |
| **Hotel Silla** | ⓁⓁ | 35 | | | | ■ | ● | ■ |
| **Splendor** | ⓁⓁ | 31 | ● | | | | | |
| **Hotel Aprile** | ⓁⓁⓁ | 29 | ● | | | ■ | | |
| **Hotel Hermitage** | ⓁⓁⓁ | 29 | ● | | | ■ | ● | ■ |
| **Hotel Loggiato dei Serviti** | ⓁⓁⓁ | 29 | ● | | | ■ | | |
| **Hotel Tornabuoni Beacci** | ⓁⓁⓁ | 28 | ● | | ● | ■ | | |
| **Hotel Villa Liberty** | ⓁⓁⓁ | 16 | ● | ■ | | ■ | | |
| **Morandi alla Crocetta** | ⓁⓁⓁ | 9 | ● | | | ■ | | |
| **Pensione Annalena** | ⓁⓁⓁ | 20 | ● | | | ■ | | |
| **Hotel J and J** | ⓁⓁⓁⓁ | 19 | ● | | | ■ | | ■ |
| **Hotel Monna Lisa** | ⓁⓁⓁⓁ | 30 | ● | ■ | | ■ | | |
| **Hotel Villa Belvedere** | ⓁⓁⓁⓁ | 26 | ● | | | | ● | |
| **Rivoli** | ⓁⓁⓁⓁ | 65 | ● | | | ■ | | |
| **Grand Hotel Villa Cora** | ⓁⓁⓁⓁⓁ | 48 | ● | ■ | ● | ■ | | |
| **Hotel Brunelleschi** | ⓁⓁⓁⓁⓁ | 94 | ● | | ● | ■ | | ■ |
| **Hotel Continental** | ⓁⓁⓁⓁⓁ | 48 | ● | | | | ● | |
| **Hotel Excelsior** | ⓁⓁⓁⓁⓁ | 192 | ● | | ● | ■ | ● | |
| **Hotel Helvetia e Bristol** | ⓁⓁⓁⓁⓁ | 52 | ● | | ● | ■ | | |
| **Hotel Regency** | ⓁⓁⓁⓁⓁ | 34 | | | ● | ■ | | ■ |
| **Torre di Bellosguardo** | ⓁⓁⓁⓁⓁ | 16 | ● | ■ | | ■ | ● | ■ |
| **Florence Environs** *(see p248)* | | | | | | | | |
| **Pensione Bencistà** | Ⓛ | 50 | ● | ■ | ● | ■ | ● | ■ |
| **Ariele** | ⓁⓁ | 39 | ● | ■ | | | | |
| **Hotel Villa Bonelli** | ⓁⓁ | 20 | ● | ■ | | | ● | ■ |
| **Villa Le Rondini** | ⓁⓁⓁ | 31 | ● | ■ | ● | ■ | ● | |
| **Villa Carlotta** | ⓁⓁⓁⓁ | 27 | ● | ■ | ● | ■ | | ■ |
| **Hotel Villa Villoresi** | ⓁⓁⓁⓁⓁ | 28 | | ■ | ● | ■ | | |
| **Villa La Massa** | ⓁⓁⓁⓁⓁ | 42 | ● | ■ | ● | ■ | | |
| **Villa San Michele** | ⓁⓁⓁⓁⓁ | 28 | | ■ | ● | ■ | ● | ■ |
| **Siena** *(see p251)* | | | | | | | | |
| **Hotel Chiusarelli** | ⓁⓁ | 50 | ● | ■ | ● | | | |
| **Pensione Palazzo Ravizza** | ⓁⓁ | 30 | | | ● | ■ | ● | |
| **Santa Caterina** | ⓁⓁⓁ | 19 | ● | ■ | | | | |
| **Villa Patrizia** | ⓁⓁⓁⓁ | 33 | ● | ■ | ● | ■ | ● | |
| **Villa Scacciapensieri** | ⓁⓁⓁⓁ | 30 | | ■ | ● | ■ | ● | |
| **Hotel Certosa di Maggiano** | ⓁⓁⓁⓁⓁ | 17 | ● | ■ | ● | ■ | | |

**Price categories** for a double room per night, including breakfast, tax and service:
Ⓛ under L100,000
ⓁⓁ L100,000–L160,000
ⓁⓁⓁ L160,000–L240,000
ⓁⓁⓁⓁ L240,000–L340,000
ⓁⓁⓁⓁⓁ over L340,000.

**Restaurant**
The hotel has a restaurant on the premises serving breakfast, lunch and dinner. Nonresidents are usually welcome to use the hotel restaurant, but priority may be given to guests staying at the hotel. Breakfast is served in most of the hotels listed, but it is advisable to check before booking.

**Hotel Parking**
Hotels with parking facilities. Some hotels will only have limited spaces and there may also be a parking fee.

**Family Rooms**
Rooms for more than two people are available, or an extra bed may be put into a double room.

# FLORENCE

## CITY CENTER

### Hotel Locanda Orchidea

Borgo degli Albizi 11, 50122. **Map** 2 D5 (6 E3). *(055) 248 03 46.* ***Rooms**: 7.* 1 Ⓛ

This simple, family-run hotel is on the second floor of a 12th-century building. The rooms are cozy but show some signs of wear.

### Pensione Maxim

Via de' Medici 4, 50123. **Map** 6 D3. *(055) 21 74 74.* FAX *28 37 29.* ***Rooms**: 23.* *14.* 1 Ⓛ

Stairs lead from the side street up to the third-floor reception of the Pensione Maxim. Some of the bedrooms of this hotel overlook the pedestrianized Via dei Calzaiuoli.

### Hotel Porta Rossa

Via Porta Rossa 19, 50100. **Map** 3 C1 (5 C3). *(055) 28 75 51.* FAX *28 21 79.* ***Rooms**: 85.* *70.* 1 TV ⓁⓁ

Built as a hotel in 1386, this is Italy's second-oldest hotel. The vaulted entrance hall is furnished with leather suites. Some of the bedrooms are huge, and all are in different styles. The tower suite has good views over the town.

### Hotel Silla

Via dei Renai 5, 50125. **Map** 4 D2 (6 E5). *(055) 234 28 88.* FAX *234 14 37.* ***Rooms**: 35.* 1 ⓁⓁ

The 16th-century Hotel Silla is approached through an elegant courtyard with a grand staircase to the first floor. The reception areas are decorated in pretty shades of pink and blue.

### Splendor

Via San Gallo 30, 50129. **Map** 2 D4. *(055) 48 34 27.* FAX *46 12 76.* ***Rooms**: 31.* *25.* 1 TV ⓁⓁ

The dark-red décor and frescoed, stuccoed ceilings give the impression that this building is a grand mansion. Overall, this family hotel shows signs of wear.

### Hotel Aprile

Via della Scala 6, 50123. **Map** 1 A4 (5 A1). *(055) 21 62 37.* FAX *28 09 47.* ***Rooms**: 29.* *24.* 1 ⓁⓁⓁ

Traces of 16th-century paintings representing *The Triumph of David* cover the façade of this attractive hotel. Other parts of this scene are displayed in the reception area as well as antique *objets d'art*. There is a small bar and an old-fashioned tearoom leading off it. In the summer, breakfast is served in the courtyard garden.

### Hotel Hermitage

Vicolo Marzio 1, 50122. **Map** 3 C1 (6 D4). *(055) 28 72 16.* FAX *21 22 08.* ***Rooms**: 29.* 1 ⓁⓁⓁ

On the top floors of a six-story medieval building, this hotel is just yards from the Ponte Vecchio. Superb views can be enjoyed from the more expensive rooms on the top floor. The rooms on the lower floor are less expensive.

### Hotel Loggiato dei Serviti

Piazza della SS. Annunziata 3, 50122. **Map** 2 D4. *(055) 28 95 92.* FAX *28 95 95.* ***Rooms**: 29.* 1 TV ⓁⓁⓁ

Built in 1527, this hotel near the Spedale degli Innocenti has an old-style reception area with vaulted ceilings. The bar area is flanked by large stone columns.

### Hotel Tornabuoni Beacci

Via de' Tornabuoni 3, 50123. **Map** 1 C5 (5 C2). *(055) 26 83 77.* FAX *28 35 94.* ***Rooms**: 28.* 1 TV ⓁⓁⓁ

This former palace is situated on a busy central street. Wide, carpeted hallways lead to lounge areas with antique furniture and tapestries. The bedrooms are luxurious, with the beds piled high with pillows.

### Hotel Villa Liberty

Viale Michelangelo 40, 50125. **Map** 4 F3. *(055) 68 38 19.* FAX *681 25 95.* ***Rooms**: 16.* 1 P *for 6 cars.* ⓁⓁⓁ

Set back from an attractive but busy tree-lined road, this turn-of-the-century villa is on the south-eastern side of town. Curving stone steps lead into the homey old-style interior with archways, plants and a tiny jewel of a bar.

### Morandi alla Crocetta

Via Laura 50, 50121. **Map** 2 E4. *(055) 234 47 47.* FAX *248 09 54.* ***Rooms**: 9.* 1 TV ⓁⓁⓁ

Once a convent, this lovely old house is run by Mrs. Doyle, an Englishwoman who has lived here since the 1920s. The tasteful interior is decorated with antiques, rugs and an abundance of plants.

### Pensione Annalena

Via Romana 34, 50125. **Map** 3 A3. *(055) 22 24 02.* FAX *22 24 03.* ***Rooms**: 20.* 1 TV ⓁⓁⓁ

The entrance to this 15th-century hotel is through an attractive courtyard and up a flight of stone steps. The reception area, breakfast and sitting rooms are all contained within an enormous hall. The spacious bedrooms are simply, but attractively, furnished.

### Hotel J and J

Via di Mezzo 20, 50121. **Map** 2 E5. *(055) 24 09 51.* FAX *24 02 82.* ***Rooms**: 19.* TV ⓁⓁⓁⓁ

This pretty, peaceful hotel is set in a former 16th-century monastery. The attractive ground-floor exterior has full-length glass windows set between old stone arches with frescoed ceilings.

### Hotel Monna Lisa

Borgo Pinti 27, 50121. **Map** 2 E5 (6 F2). *(055) 247 97 51.* FAX *247 97 55.* ***Rooms**: 30.* 1 P ⓁⓁⓁⓁ

An impressive stone interior courtyard leads to the reception area of this Renaissance palazzo. Some of the bedrooms are huge, with old furniture and high ceilings. The modern extension lacks the charm of the main building.

### Hotel Villa Belvedere

Via Benedetto Castelli 3, 50124. **Map** 3 A5. *(055) 22 25 01.* FAX *22 31 63.* ***Rooms**: 26.* 1 TV ⓁⓁⓁⓁ

This spacious 1930s villa is set in landscaped grounds, close to the the Boboli Gardens. All the bedrooms have a safe and mini-bar, and the first-floor terraces have lovely views of the gardens.

### Rivoli

Via della Scala 33, 50123. **Map** 1 A4 (5 A1). *(055) 28 28 53.* FAX *29 40 41.* ***Rooms**: 65.* 1 TV ⓁⓁⓁⓁ

The weathered façade suggests the age of this 15th-century hotel. It is generally spacious, cool and decorated to a high standard, combining both modern and Classical styles with simple elegance.

For key to symbols *see p243*

## Grand Hotel Villa Cora

Viale Niccolò Machiavelli 18, 50125. **Map** 3 A3. *(055) 229 84 51.* FAX *22 90 86.* ***Rooms**: 48.* ⓁⓁⓁⓁⓁ

Shades of peach and gray windows highlight the Villa Cora's stunning Renaissance-style façades. There are many balustraded terraces segregated by Classical pillars and tall windows. Inside, reception rooms have frescoed ceilings and varnished wooden flooring.

## Hotel Brunelleschi

Piazza Santa Elisabetta 3, 50122. **Map** 6 D2. *(055) 56 20 68.* FAX *21 96 53.* ***Rooms**: 94.* ⓁⓁⓁⓁⓁ

Once a prison, this hotel houses a fascinating museum displaying Byzantine ceramics and old stone baths discovered during its reconstruction. The gray brick walls have been retained in the cool, airy reception area.

## Hotel Continental

Lungarno degli Acciaiuoli 2, 50123. **Map** 3 C1 (5 C4). *(055) 28 23 92.* FAX *28 31 39.* ***Rooms**: 48.* ⓁⓁⓁⓁⓁ

Decorated with pale gray marble-effect walls throughout, this hotel is in a prime location opposite the Ponte Vecchio. The bar lounge overlooks the river, as do the stunning top-floor suites.

## Hotel Excelsior

Piazza d'Ognissanti 3, 50123. **Map** 1 B5 (5 A2). *(055) 26 42 01.* FAX *21 02 78.* ***Rooms**: 192.* ⓁⓁⓁⓁⓁ

Occupying two houses rebuilt in 1815, this hotel has lovely views of the Arno. Inside it has a feeling of grandeur, with marble floors and columns, 19th-century staircases, statues, stained-glass windows and oil paintings.

## Hotel Helvetia e Bristol

Via de' Pescioni 2, 50123. **Map** 1 C5 (5 C2). *(055) 28 78 14.* FAX *28 83 53.* ***Rooms**: 52.* ⓁⓁⓁⓁⓁ

This luxurious 18th-century hotel is just a few steps from the Duomo. Beautiful antiques decorate the interior, and there is a domed, stained-glass ceiling as well as a splendid wood-and-marble bar.

## Hotel Regency

Piazza Massimo d'Azeglio 3, 50121. **Map** 2 F5. *(055) 24 52 47.* FAX *24 52 47.* ***Rooms**: 34.* ⓁⓁⓁⓁⓁ

Though well-maintained, the outside of this Florentine town house suggests little of the grandeur within. The Classical-style reception and bar area has wood-paneling and the front bedrooms overlook the pretty Piazza d'Azeglio.

## Torre di Bellosguardo

2.5 km (1.5 miles) SW Florence. Via Roti Michelozzi 2, 50124. *(055) 229 81 45.* FAX *22 90 08.* ***Rooms**: 16.* ⓁⓁⓁⓁⓁ

A long, sweeping road leads to this vast 14th-century tower and adjoining 16th-century villa. Inside, colossal wooden doors lead to huge rooms filled with antiques and Persian rugs. The bedrooms are decorated on an equally grand scale. The villa commands sweeping views over Florence.

# Florence Environs

## Pensione Bencistà

4 km (2.5 miles) NE Florence. Via Benedetto da Maiano 4, Fiesole, 50014. *(055) 591 63.* FAX *591 63.* ***Rooms**: 50.* *39.* Ⓛ

Inside this superior 14th-century villa are polished tiles, antique furniture and cool, airy bedrooms. There are small lounges off the reception. Watch the sun set across the Florentine countryside from the sunlit stone balcony.

## Ariele

2 km (1 mile) SE Florence. Via Magenta 11, 50123. *(055) 21 15 09.* FAX *26 85 21.* ***Rooms**: 39.* ⓁⓁ

This homey hotel is located on a residential side street. It has extensive lounge and bar areas with high ceilings, paintings and antiques. The bedrooms are a little austere, but generally spacious.

## Hotel Villa Bonelli

4 km (2.5 miles) NE Florence. Via F Poeti 1, Fiesole, 50014. *(055) 595 13.* FAX *59 89 42.* ***Rooms**: 20.* ⓁⓁ

This small, friendly hotel is simply but pleasantly furnished, with wonderful views of Florence from the top rooms. Half-board is obligatory during the high season.

## Villa Le Rondini

4 km (2.5 miles) N Florence. Via Bolognese Vecchia 224, Trespiano, 50139. *(055) 40 00 81.* FAX *26 82 12.* ***Rooms**: 31.* ⓁⓁⓁ

The Villa Le Rondini is set in secluded gardens and has stunning views of the Arno valley. The main house has very traditional furnishings, such as the beamed ceilings and antique fireplace in the split-level sitting room.

## Villa Carlotta

2 km (1 mile) S Florence. Via Michele di Lando 3, 50125. *(055) 233 61 51.* FAX *233 61 47.* ***Rooms**: 27.* ⓁⓁⓁⓁ

This gracious 19th-century building is hidden in a remote, secluded area. It is an attractive, friendly and airy villa with large windows and Neo-Classical decorations throughout.

## Hotel Villa Villoresi

10 km (6 miles) NW Florence. Via Ciampi 2, Colonnata di Sesto Fiorentino, 50019. *(055) 44 36 92.* FAX *44 20 63.* ***Rooms**: 28.* ⓁⓁⓁⓁⓁ

Built for military purposes in the 12th century, this villa was transformed into a country house during the Renaissance. The gallery entrance is covered with 19th-century murals of Tuscan landscapes interspersed with Egyptian symbols depicting Napoleon's campaign.

## Villa La Massa

6km (4 miles) SE Florence. Via la Massa 24, Candeli, 50012. *(055) 651 01 01.* FAX *651 01 09.* ***Rooms**: 42.* ⓁⓁⓁⓁⓁ

Three 17th-century villas make up this luxurious hotel with a river-side restaurant. The formal public rooms and wonderful bedrooms are decorated with antique furniture.

## Villa San Michele

4 km (2.5 miles) NE Florence. Via Doccia 4, Fiesole, 50014. *(055) 594 51.* FAX *59 87 34.* ***Rooms**: 28.* ⓁⓁⓁⓁⓁ

Said to have been designed by Michelangelo, the beautiful San Michele monastery stands in 15 ha (37 acres) of grounds. The panorama across the city is best seen from the loggia, where you can dine outside. Many of the bedrooms are simple, but retain an air of elegance.

# WESTERN TUSCANY

## ARTIMINO

### Paggeria Medicea

**Road map** C2. Viale Papa Giovanni XXIII 3, 50040. *(055) 871 80 81.* FAX *871 80 80.* ***Rooms****: 37.* 1 TV P ⓁⓁⓁⓁ

Ferdinand I de' Medici built this marvelous hilltop villa. The hotel, which is a mix of ancient and modern styles, is housed in what were once the servants' quarters.

## PISA

### Royal Victoria Hotel

**Road map** B2. Lungarno Pacinotti 12, 56126. *(050) 94 01 11.* FAX *94 01 80.* ***Rooms****: 48.* *40.* 1 P ⓁⓁ

This handsome, dignified hotel was built in the 19th century. Original features still remain, including the wood-paneled doors and some exquisite *trompe l'œil* drapery.

### Hotel d'Azeglio

**Road map** B2. Piazza Vittorio Emanuele II 18b, 56125. *(050) 50 03 10.* FAX *280 17.* ***Rooms****: 29.* 1 TV P ⓁⓁⓁ

The attraction of this tall, modern block is the view from the seventh-floor breakfast room and coffee bar. Windows on all sides look over Pisa to mountains beyond.

### Rest Hotel Primavère

**Road map** B2. Via Aurelia km 342 & 750, Migliarino Pisano, 56010. *(050) 80 33 10.* FAX *80 33 15.* ***Rooms****: 62.* 1 P ⓁⓁⓁ

This functional hotel is convenient for drivers. It is clean, well decorated and nicely laid out, with extensive lawns. Four rooms are specially equipped for the disabled.

## RIGOLI

### Hotel Villa di Corliano

**Road map** B2. Via Statale del Brennero 50, 56010. *(050) 81 81 93.* FAX *81 83 84.* ***Rooms****: 18.* 6. ⓁⓁ

Two sweeping driveways lead on either side of parkland to this magnificent late-Renaissance mansion. An architectural delight inside and out, it features restored Classical murals on the walls and ceilings. The enormous stately bedrooms are off the central hall.

## SAN MINIATO

### Hotel Miravalle

**Road map** C2. Via del Castello 3, 56027. ***Rooms****: 20.* *(0571) 41 80 75.* FAX *41 96 81.* 1 ⓁⓁ

The Miravalle is perched on a 10th-century castle wall adjoining what remains of the castle tower. The interior is somewhat worn, but the rooms have splendid views, especially from the restaurant.

## VOLTERRA

### Albergo Villa Nencini

**Road map** C3. Borgo Santo Stefano 55, 56048. *(0588) 863 86.* FAX *866 86.* ***Rooms****: 14.* *11.* 1 Ⓛ

This stone country hotel is situated in a small park, a few minutes' drive from the town. Bedrooms are cool and light, though not very large. There is a smart breakfast room and basement taverna, as well as a lounge bar and terrace.

# NORTHERN TUSCANY

## BALBANO

### Villa Casanova

**Road map** B2. Via di Casanova, 55050. *(0583) 54 84 29.* FAX *54 84 29.* ***Rooms****: 40.* *35.* 1 Ⓛ

Overlooking the valley, this huge 17th-century Tuscan farmhouse is perched on a small hill. The rooms are comfortable and simply furnished. This hotel is in an excellent location for walkers, cyclists and those wishing to get away from it all. There are also reduced prices for children.

## LUCCA

### Piccolo Hotel Puccini

**Road map** C2. Via di Poggio 9, 55100. *(0583) 554 21.* FAX *534 87.* ***Rooms****: 14.* 1 Ⓛ

This attractive, old stone building is a few steps from the fabulous Piazza San Michele. Inside it is small but fashionable, and there is a bar with tables beside a full-length window looking out on the pretty, narrow street.

### Hotel Universo

**Road map** C2. Piazza del Giglio 1, 55100. *(0583) 49 36 78.* FAX *95 48 54.* ***Rooms****: 60.* 1 ⓁⓁⓁ

Built in the 19th century, this big, slightly worn hotel has a cozy wood-paneled bar and a marbled reception area. The comfortable bedrooms have luxurious marble bathrooms; some rooms have pleasant views onto the square.

### Hotel Principessa Elisa

**Road map** C2. Via Nuova per Pisa, 55050. *(0583) 37 97 37.* FAX *37 90 19.* ***Rooms****: 10.* 1 TV ⓁⓁⓁⓁ

Recently refurbished, this stately home imitates 18th-century Parisian style. The beautifully decorated bedrooms have a mix of reproductions and genuine antique furniture, and each room is fitted with a safe. Free alcoholic drinks are kept out on a table in the smaller of the two drawing rooms, for guests to help themselves. This hotel is more suitable for individuals or couples wanting luxury and peaceful surroundings, than for families with children.

## PISTOIA

### Albergo Patria

**Road map** C2. Via F Crispi 8, 51100. *(0573) 251 87.* FAX *36 81 68.* ***Rooms****: 28.* *23.* 1 ⓁⓁ

On a pretty, narrow street in the center of Pistoia, this ancient hotel has a dark, modern interior. There are good-sized 1970s-style rooms, with fair-sized bathrooms, an older TV lounge and a pleasant bar and restaurant. The top bedrooms have good views of the Romanesque Duomo.

### Hotel Piccolo Ritz

**Road map** C2. Via A Vannucci 67, 51100. *(0573) 267 75.* FAX *277 98.* ***Rooms****: 21.* 1 ⓁⓁ

Close to the station on the Piazza Dante Alighieri, and in the historic center of Pistoia, the Piccolo Ritz lives up to its name. Inside it is attractive, but somewhat small. It has a pleasant café-style bar with an original frescoed ceiling.

For key to symbols *see p243*

## Pontenuovo

### Il Convento

**Road map** C2. Via San Quirico 33, 51030. *(0573) 45 26 51.* FAX *45 35 78.* ***Rooms****: 25.* ⓁⓁ

A pretty pathway leads to the reception and rather worn lounge area of this former convent. The tables in the intimate dining areas are set with crisp linen cloths. The main dining area still has the old wooden benches on which the nuns sat. The bedrooms are simple but comfortable.

## Viareggio

### Hotel President

**Road map** B2. Viale Carducci 5, 55049. *(0584) 96 27 12.* FAX *96 36 58.* ***Rooms****: 37.* ⓁⓁⓁ

The President is a smart villa-style hotel on the beachfront. Newly refurbished, the bedrooms of this hotel are particularly attractive. The rooftop restaurant has stunning sea views and can be reached via a panoramic glass elevator.

# Eastern Tuscany

## Arezzo

### Castello di Gargonza

**Road map** E3. Gargonza, Monte San Savino, 52048. *(0575) 84 70 21.* FAX *84 70 54.* ***Rooms****: 7.* ⓁⓁⓁ

More of a medieval "castle-cum-village," this guesthouse also provides 18 furnished apartments. A sweeping, tree-lined driveway curves around the castle walls to the entrance. There is a tiny garden and a pretty frescoed chapel where services are held once a week.

## Cortona

### Hotel San Luca

**Road map** E3. Piazzale Garibaldi 1, 52044. *(0575) 63 04 60.* FAX *63 01 05.* ***Rooms****: 56.* ⓁⓁ

Built into the hillside, the San Luca enjoys a panoramic view from the reception and dining rooms of the valleys below. The reception area is large, light and comfortably furnished, but the bedrooms are quite simple.

### Hotel San Michele

**Road map** E3. Via Guelfa 15, 52044. *(0575) 60 43 48.* FAX *63 01 47.* ***Rooms****: 32.* ⓁⓁ

The San Michele is a beautifully restored Renaissance palazzo, fronting onto a narrow town street. It retains the original tall, heavy wooden doors outside and paneled doors inside. A maze of corridors lead to the comfortable, homey bedrooms and there is a superb attic suite.

# Central Tuscany

## Castellina in Chianti

### Salivolpi

**Road map** D3. Via Fiorentia 89, 53011. *(0577) 74 04 84.* FAX *409 98.* ***Rooms****: 19.* ⓁⓁ

This restored country farmhouse has a smart rustic interior with whitewashed walls and warm terra-cotta floors. The bedrooms in the main farmhouse have low windows, beamed ceilings and gleaming bathrooms.

### Tenuta di Ricavo

**Road map** D3. Località Ricavo, 53011. *(0577) 74 02 21.* FAX *74 10 14.* ***Rooms****: 23.* *on request.* *closed Mon.* ⓁⓁⓁ

This charming hotel occupies the entire 1,000-year-old hamlet of Ricavo. Consequently, many of the rooms are in old country houses, half with their own terrace. The sitting rooms are styled in a harmonious blend of antiques and peasant furniture.

## Gaiole in Chianti

### Castello di Spaltenna

**Road map** D3. Spaltenna 53013. *(0577) 74 94 83.* FAX *74 92 69.* ***Rooms****: 21.* ⓁⓁⓁ

Sitting on a hill, the Castello di Spaltenna is in a beautiful, fortified former monastery. The owners take pride in their restaurant, where the food is cooked in a woodburning oven. Spacious rooms overlook the courtyard and some have the luxury of a jacuzzi.

## Panzano in Chianti

### Villa le Barone

**Road map** D3. Via San Leolino 19, 50020. *(055) 85 26 21.* FAX *85 22 77.* ***Rooms****: 25.* ⓁⓁ

This 16th-century family house once belonged to the della Robbia family, famous for their ceramics. Fresh flowers brighten the sitting rooms and antiques furnish the bedrooms.

## Radda in Chianti

### Villa Miranda

**Road map** D3. 53017. *(0577) 73 80 21.* FAX *73 86 68.* ***Rooms****: 42.* ⓁⓁ

Three buildings make up this hotel, which has been run by the same family since the original building, the post house, was built in 1842. Bedrooms have beamed ceilings and brass bedsteads.

### Relais Fattoria Vignale

**Road map** D3. Via Pianigiani 8, 53017. *(0577) 73 83 00.* FAX *73 85 92.* ***Rooms****: 27.* ⓁⓁⓁ

Inside this superb manor are attractive lounges with terra-cotta floors, murals, stone fireplaces, antiques and rugs. Bedrooms to the rear overlook the valley below.

## San Gimignano

### Hotel Belvedere

**Road map** C3. Via Dante 14, 53037. *(0577) 94 05 39.* FAX *90 03 27.* ***Rooms****: 12.* ⓁⓁ

This pretty terra-cotta villa has light, modern bedrooms, painted in soothing pastel shades. The garden is pretty, with a hammock slung between cypress trees.

### Hotel Leon Bianco

**Road map** C3. Piazza della Cisterna 13, 53037. *(0577) 94 12 94.* FAX *94 21 23.* ***Rooms****: 25.* ⓁⓁ

Parts of the original stone wall remain in this former palazzo. The rooms are airy with pleasant views and have terra-cotta floors.

## Villa San Paolo

**Road map** C3. Strada per Certaldo, 53037. *(0577) 95 51 00.* FAX *95 51 13.* ***Rooms**: 15.* ⓁⓁⓁ

This attractive hillside villa is set in spacious terraced gardens, which include a tennis court. Inside, there are intimate lounges and pretty bedrooms.

### San Gusmé

## Villa Arceno

**Road map** D3. Castelnuovo Berardenga, 53010. *(0577) 35 92 92.* FAX *35 92 76.* ***Rooms**: 16.* ⓁⓁⓁⓁⓁ

Large bedrooms are a feature in this 17th-century villa, set in beautiful woodland. The bedrooms are spacious and the vaulted public rooms are furnished with light, antique reproductions.

### Siena

## Hotel Chiusarelli

**Road map** D3. Viale Curtatone 15, 53100. *(0577) 28 05 62.* FAX *27 11 77.* ***Rooms**: 50.* *45.* ⓁⓁ

This pretty villa shows some signs of wear and tear, but the interior has recently undergone extensive restoration. Outside, the pleasant garden is filled with palm trees.

## Pensione Palazzo Ravizza

**Road map** D3. Pian dei Mantellini 34, 53100. *(0577) 28 04 62.* FAX *27 13 70.* ***Rooms**: 30.* *21.* ⓁⓁ

Within the city walls, this is a charming base. It has a lounge, library and bedrooms with excellent rural views over the Tuscan landscape. The restaurant is only open in the evening.

## Santa Caterina

**Road map** D3. Via Enea Silvio Piccolomini 7, 53100. *(0577) 22 11 05.* FAX *27 10 87.* ***Rooms**: 19.* ⓁⓁⓁ

This 18th-century house is one of Siena's inexpensive options. It is pleasantly furnished in rustic style and in keeping with its age. The bedrooms differ in style and size, and are decorated with antiques.

## Villa Patrizia

**Road map** D3. Via Fiorentina 58, 53100. *(0577) 504 31.* FAX *504 31.* ***Rooms**: 33.* ⓁⓁⓁⓁ

This rambling old villa is on the northern outskirts of the city. The bedrooms are simply furnished, but comfortable.

## Villa Scacciapensieri

**Road map** D3. Via di Scacciapensieri 10, 53100. *(0577) 414 41.* FAX *27 08 54.* ***Rooms**: 30.* ⓁⓁⓁⓁ

Set in attractive grounds, this villa features an old-style lounge with a huge stone fireplace. The spacious bedrooms have views of Siena and the Tuscan hills.

## Hotel Certosa di Maggiano

**Road map** D3. Via Certosa 82, 53100. *(0577) 28 81 80.* FAX *28 81 89.* ***Rooms**: 17.* ⓁⓁⓁⓁⓁ

Built in 1314, this former Carthusian monastery was the oldest in Tuscany. This amazing hotel – its rooms adorned with antique paintings – makes an exclusive, homey and peaceful retreat.

### Sinalunga

## Locanda dell'Amorosa

**Road map** E3. Località Amorosa, 53048. *(0577) 67 94 97.* FAX *67 82 16.* ***Rooms**: 15.* ⓁⓁⓁⓁ

This idyllic 14th-century villa is part of an estate with its own vineyard and farmland. Inside, the bedrooms are cool and airy.

### Strove

## Albergo Casalta

**Road map** D3. Comune di Monteriggioni, 53035. *(0577) 30 10 02.* ***Rooms**: 12.* *closed Wed.* Ⓛ

A tiny hamlet is home to this hotel in a 1,000-year-old stone building. The central hearth in the reception is warm and inviting, and there is an elegant restaurant.

## San Luigi Residence

**Road map** D3. Via della Cerreta, 53030. *(0577) 30 10 55.* FAX *30 11 67.* ***Rooms**: 46.* ⓁⓁⓁⓁ

The beautifully restored farm buildings belonging to the San Luigi Residence lie in an expansive park. Sporting facilities include tennis courts, a volley ball court and a children's play area.

# SOUTHERN TUSCANY

### Elba

## Capo Sud

**Road map** B4. Località Lacona, 57037. *(0565) 96 40 21.* FAX *96 42 63.* ***Rooms**: 39.* *on request.* ⓁⓁⓁ

This small villagelike resort has perfect views of the bay. The rooms are housed in a complex of villas, scattered around the hotel grounds. The restaurant serves produce from its own vineyard and orchard.

### Giglio Porto

## Castello Monticello

**Road map** C5. Via Provinciale, 58013. *(0564) 80 92 52.* ***Rooms**: 34.* ⓁⓁ

This castle hotel is on the lovely island of Giglio and was originally built as a private house. The hotel sits on a hill and enjoys superb views from the bedrooms.

### Punta Ala

## Piccolo Hotel Alleluja

**Road map** C4. Via del Porto, 58040. *(0564) 92 20 50.* FAX *92 07 34.* ***Rooms**: 42.* ⓁⓁⓁⓁ

This small seaside hotel has a stylish interior with simple, light furnishings. Some bedrooms have their own sitting rooms. There are tennis courts and a card room.

### Porto Ercole

## Il Pellicano

**Road map** D5. Località Cala dei Santi, 58018. *(0564) 83 38 01.* FAX *83 34 18.* ***Rooms**: 37.* ⓁⓁⓁⓁⓁ

Luxurious and exclusive with its own rocky beach area, this is an old-style Tuscan villa covered in vines. It is stylishly furnished with antiques and has quiet bedrooms.

For key to symbols *see p243*

# Restaurants, Cafés and Bars

Food is one of the great Italian passions, and eating out on a balmy summer's evening can be a memorable experience. Few restaurants in Tuscany serve anything but Italian food, and most concentrate on the robust fare that typifies the region's cuisine. Most Tuscans take their lunch *(pranzo)* around 1pm, and have dinner *(cena)* from 8pm. Restaurants may close for several weeks during the winter and also during the vacation season in summer. If in doubt, phone first to check that the restaurant is open. Finding the restaurants in Florence can be confusing due to the dual numbering of the streets *(see p274)*, so use the map references.

**Italian waiter at your service**

The restaurants listed on pages 258–263 have been selected from the best the city and region can offer across all price ranges.

## Types of Restaurants and Bars

Italian restaurants have a bewildering variety of names, but in practice there's little difference between a *trattoria*, *osteria* or *ristorante* in terms of price, cooking or ambience. Both a *birreria* and *spaghetteria* are more downmarket establishments, and sell beer, pasta dishes and snacks. A *pizzeria* is a cheap, informal restaurant with pasta, meat and fish on the menu as well as pizzas. It is usually open only in the evening, especially if it has wood-fired ovens.

At lunch time you could visit a *tavola calda*, one of the increasingly rare places selling a limited range of hot snacks. A *rosticceria* offers barbecued chicken to take out, often with other fast foods. Most bars sell filled rolls *(panini)* and sandwiches *(tramezzini)* and small pizza bars sell slices of pizza *(pizza taglia)* to eat on the street.

Old-fashioned wine bars *(vinaii* or *fiaschetterie)* are a dying breed, but they are atmospheric places to grab a snack or a glass of wine. Ice cream parlors *(gelaterie)*, by contrast, are thriving, and Florence has some of the best to be found in Italy.

## Vegetarian Food

Although most Italians find it hard to understand vegetarianism, and Florence boasts only a very few vegetarian restaurants, you should have no trouble assembling a meat-free meal, particularly if you eat fish and seafood. Starters *(antipasti)* will usually include some suitable dishes. There are also plenty of vegetable-based soups and pasta sauces commonly available, but check whether they are cooked with vegetable stock *(brodo vegetariano)*. Try the excellent salads, served with delicious dressings, and the vegetables.

**Outside Palle d'Oro *(see p258)***

## How Much to Pay

Prices are often higher in Florence than elsewhere. In the less expensive eating establishments and pizzerias you can have a two-course or a fixed-price *(menù turistico)* meal with half a liter of wine for around L15,000–L18,000. Average prices for a three-course meal are L25,000–L50,000, and in upscale restaurants you could easily pay L80,000–L100,000.

Nearly all restaurants have a cover charge *(pane e coperto)*, usually L2,000–L5,000. Many also add a 10 percent service charge *(servizio)* to the check *(il conto)*, so always establish whether or not this is the case. Where leaving a tip is a matter of your own discretion, 12–15 percent is acceptable.

Restaurants are obliged by law to give you a receipt *(una ricevuta)*. Scraps of paper with an illegible scrawl are illegal, and you are perfectly within your rights to ask for a readable check.

**Inside the established Le Fonticine in Florence *(see p259)***

Cash is the preferred form of payment in most cafés and bars, but many restaurants, particularly the more expensive, will accept major credit cards. Check which cards are accepted when booking.

### MAKING RESERVATIONS

FLORENCE'S BEST restaurants in all price ranges are well patronized. It is therefore advisable to try and reserve a table, even in the less expensive places. Where restaurants do not accept bookings, try to arrive early to avoid long waits.

### DRESS CODE

ITALIANS ARE RELAXED about eating out, but nevertheless like to dress up to dine. The restaurant listings indicate where formal dress is required.

**Trattoria Angiolino** ***(see p258)***

### READING THE MENU

A MEAL IN A RESTAURANT will usually start with *antipasti*, or hors d'œuvres (hams, olives, salamis, crostini), followed by *primi* (soups, pasta or rice). Main courses – *secondi* – will be meat or fish, either served alone or accompanied by vegetables *(contorni)* or a salad *(insalata)*.

To finish, there will probably be a choice of fruit *(frutta)*, cheese *(formaggio)*, desserts *(dolci)*, or a combination of all three. Coffee – always espresso, never cappuccino – is ordered right at the end of a meal, often with a *digestivo (see p257)*. In less expensive restaurants, the menu *(il menù* or *la lista)* may be written on a blackboard, and in many establishments the waiter *(cameriere)* will recite the chef's daily specials at your table.

**The 11th-century Badia a Coltibuono in Gaiole in Chianti** ***(see p262)***

### CHOICE OF WINE

HOUSE WINES will usually be Chiantis or some close cousin. The cheaper establishments usually have only house wine, or a small choice of other Tuscan wines. Those in the L75,000–L100,000 price range will have a fuller selection of regional wines, as well as wines from other parts of Italy. At the top of the scale, there should be a wide range of Italian and local wines, and, as at the Enoteca Pinchiorri *(see p259)*, a selection of French and other foreign vintages. *(See also pp256–7.)*

### CHILDREN

CHILDREN ARE GENERALLY welcome in restaurants, but less so in the evening and in more upscale places.

**Outdoor dining at the popular Rivoire café** ***(see p265)***

Special facilities such as high chairs are not commonly provided. Check the menu for the option of a small portion *(una porzione piccola)*: most restaurants will prepare a half portion *(mezza porzione)* if requested, and some charge less for these smaller portions.

### SMOKING

ITALIANS STILL SMOKE more than most. Few restaurants and virtually none of the bars or cafés set aside space for nonsmokers.

### WHEELCHAIR ACCESS

FEW RESTAURANTS make special provisions for wheelchairs, though a word when you are booking should ensure a conveniently situated table and assistance on arrival.

### USING THE LISTINGS

Key to the symbols in the listings on pp258–63.

- fixed-price menu
- jacket and tie required
- tables outside
- air-conditioning
- good wine list
- ★ highly recommended
- credit cards accepted. Check which cards are accepted when booking.

**Price categories** for a three-course meal for one including a half-bottle of house wine, cover charge, tax and service.

Ⓛ under L25,000
ⓁⓁ L25,000–L50,000
ⓁⓁⓁ L50,000–L75,000
ⓁⓁⓁⓁ L75,000–L100,000
ⓁⓁⓁⓁⓁ over L100,000

# What to Eat in Florence and Tuscany

Plum tomato

TUSCAN CUISINE still has its roots in peasant cooking, relying on basic staples such as olive oil, for which the region is renowned, tomatoes, beans, hams and salamis. Chewy, saltless bread or thick vegetable soups such as *ribollita* often take the place of pasta, followed by grilled or roast meats, the great standbys of rustic cuisine. Sheep's milk cheeses are common, especially *pecorino* and the creamy *ricotta.* Fruit or ice cream round off many meals, or try Siena's nougat-like *panforte* or the famous *cantucci* accompanied by *vin santo.*

**Brioche**
*These plain, jam or custard-filled buns are usually eaten for breakfast.*

**Panzanella**
*Basil, tomatoes, parsley, garlic and oil-soaked bread make up this summer salad.*

**Bruschetta**
*Pieces of toasted bread are rubbed with garlic and olive oil or spread with anchovy, olive, tomato or liver paste to make this delicious snack.*

**Ribollita**
*This thickened soup is a rich broth of cabbage, herbs, beans and vegetables.*

**Fagioli all'Uccelletto**
*A classic combination of beans in a tomato sauce, this is one of the most popular vegetable dishes in Tuscany.*

**Salame di Cinghiale**
*This is a strongly flavored salami made from wild boar.*

**Pappardelle alla Lepre**
*Typically Tuscan, these broad noodles are covered in a hare sauce. The hare is often cooked in its own blood, or in a rich beef stock.*

**Trippa alla Fiorentina**
*Tripe and a parmesan-topped tomato sauce are used to make this dish.*

**Bistecca alla Fiorentina**
*Grilled over an open fire, this large, tender steak can be seasoned with oil and herbs.*

**Baccalà**
*This is dried salt cod, most often prepared with garlic, parsley and tomatoes.*

**Scottiglia di Cinghiale**
*Prepared with wild boar chops, this dish is particularly popular in the Maremma.*

**Arosto Misto**
*This common rural dish is a mixture of roast meats, such as lamb, pork, chicken, liver and spicy sausages* (salsicce).

**Castagne Ubriache**
*Chestnuts are covered in red wine sauce and often served with baked custard.*

**Torta di Riso**
*Rice cakes can be served with a simple fruit sauce.*

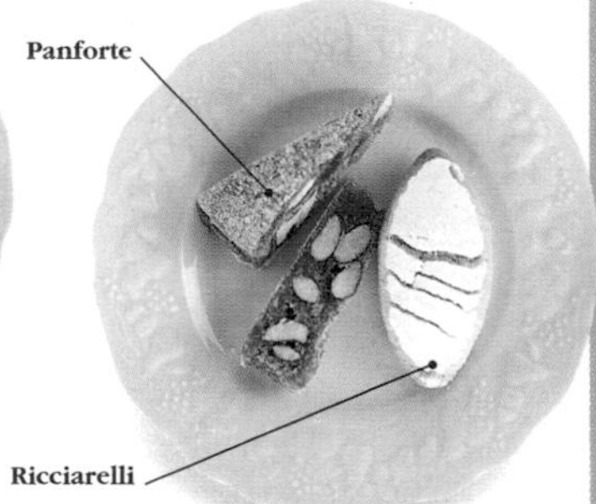


**Panforte and Ricciarelli**
*Panforte is a dense, dark cake spiced with cloves and cinnamon. Ricciarelli are made from ground almonds, candied orange peel and honey.*

**Pecorino**
*This sheep's milk cheese is either fresh and sweet, or well-matured and hard.*

**Ricotta**
*Made from sheep's milk whey,* ricotta *can be eaten with olive oil or honey.*

**Cantucci**
*These sweet cookies taste best dipped in* vin santo, *a delicious dessert wine.*

# What to Drink in Florence and Tuscany

Medieval engraving of a grape crusher

TUSCANY IS A MAJOR wine-producing region whose wines make ideal partners for the robust local food. Both reds and whites are made here, ranging from light house wine *(vino della casa)* to the very best Europe can produce. The most famous reds, notably Brunello di Montalcino, Vino Nobile di Montepulciano and Chianti, are made from the Sangiovese grape and are produced inland, on the hills of Tuscany. A number of estates, particularly in Chianti Classico, also experiment with non-Italian grape varieties with considerable success. Throughout Tuscany, bars and cafés are open all day, serving drinks from wine to beer and coffee. See also *A Day Out in Chianti* on page 225.

**Il Poggione** is an excellent producer of Brunello di Montalcino.

**Carmignano**, a good dry red, is made north of Florence.

## Red Wine

CHIANTI IS MADE in seven defined zones, but the best wines generally come from the hilly areas of Classico and Rufina. Brunello, from farther south, needs aging and can be expensive, but Rosso di Montalcino, made for younger drinking, often offers better value. Tuscan table wine can be cheap or expensive – the top-priced wines may not fit the traditional Chianti regulations, but are likely to be extremely good. Sassicaia, made from the French Cabernet Sauvignon grape, is an example. Other fine reds include Fontalloro, Cepparello and Solaia.

Tuscan table wine

Chianti produced by Ruffino

**Sassicaia** is made from Cabernet Sauvignon grapes.

## White Wine

Galestro

TUSCANY'S WHITE WINES are less interesting than the reds, although some producers are experimenting with a handful of quality whites from grapes such as Chardonnay and Sauvignon. Most Tuscan white wine is made from the Trebbiano grape, at its lightest in the spritzy style called Galestro, but usually sold as plain dry Bianco della Toscana. Vernaccia di San Gimignano, from the Vernaccia grape, is sometimes good and Montecarlo, from near Lucca, a blend of grapes, offers more interesting drinking. Most Tuscan whites need to be drunk young.

Vin Santo

## Vin Santo

VIN SANTO, or "Holy Wine," is a traditional wine once made on farms throughout the region and now seeing a revival of interest from modern producers. The best versions are sweet, though it can be found as a dry wine. It is often offered with *cantucci*, small almond biscuits, in Tuscan restaurants and homes. Vin Santo is made from Trebbiano and Malvasia grapes which are semi-dried, made into wine and then aged in small barrels for a number of years before bottling. The best are very concentrated in flavor. Quality varies, but superb versions are made by Avignonesi and Isole e Olena.

## How Chianti is Made

Chianti is made as soon as possible after the October harvest. The quality of the wine can be very high, as wineries have combined the best of traditional and modern techniques.

**Crushing and Stemming**

*The Sangiovese grapes are separated from the stalks. The tannin from the skins preserves the wine, but the stalk tannin is too harsh for fine wine.*

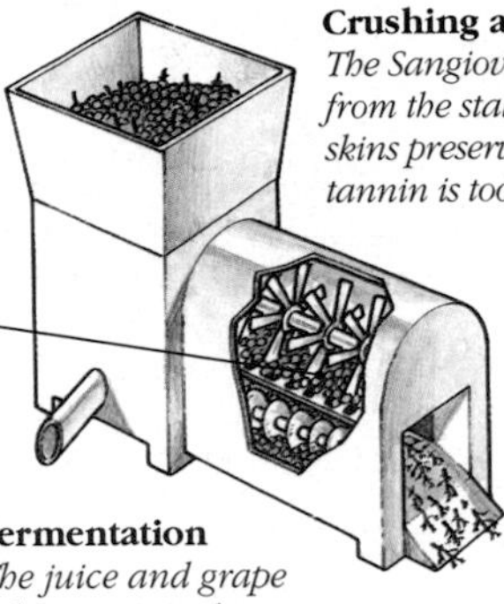


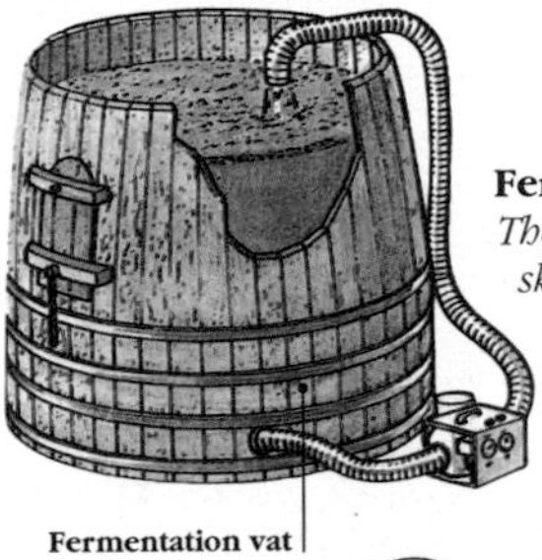


**Fermentation**

*The juice and grape skins go into the vat, where a pump circulates wine over the floating "cap" of skins to extract color, tannin and flavor. Fermentation may take up to 15 days or more.*

**Harvest at the Brolio estate in Gaiole in Chianti**

**Pressing the Residue**

*Once the new wine has been drained off, the remaining skins and seeds are pressed, producing dark, often harsh, press wine. Stored separately, this may be used in the final blend.*

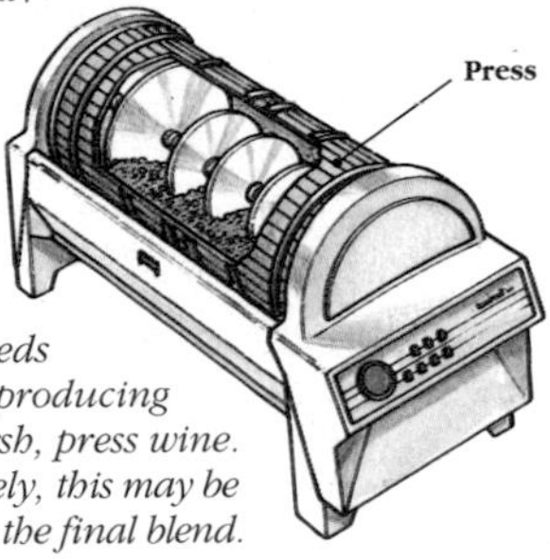


**The barrels** are topped off to prevent air from reaching the wine.

**Maturation**

*A second fermentation, the malolactic, occurs in the spring, softening the wine, which is then run into wooden barrels to mature.*

**Cinzano, a popular early evening *aperitivo***

### Aperitifs and Digestifs

Pre- and postmeal tipples include Campari, Cinzano and the artichoke-based Cynar, as well as Crodino, the best-known of several non-alcoholic early evening drinks. The herb-flavored *amaro* or an Italian brandy commonly round off a meal; otherwise try a *grappa* or the sweeter aniseed-scented Sambuca and almond-flavored Amaretto.

### Beer

Beer can be a great thirst-quencher, especially in the summer heat. Draft beer *(birra alla spina)* is less expensive than bottled beer and is sold by the measure. Good Italian lager-style beers include Peroni and Moretti.

### Other Drinks

Fruit juices are sold in small bottles *(succo di frutta)* or freshly squeezed *(una spremuta)*. A fruit milk shake *(un frullato)* can be delicious and, in summer, iced tea or coffee is very refreshing. Italian coffee is drunk with frothy milk for breakfast *(cappuccino)* or black after meals *(espresso)*.

**Espresso**

**Cappuccino**

# FLORENCE

## CITY CENTER

### Acquacotta

Via de' Pilastri 51r. **Map** 2 E5. (055) 24 29 07. ***Open*** *noon–2pm, 7:30–10pm Thu–Mon, noon–2pm Tue.* Ⓛ

This cheap, three-roomed restaurant takes its name from the house specialty, *acquacotta*, which literally means cooked water. It is in fact a Florentine vegetable soup served over toast and crowned with a poached egg. Grilled meats and other Tuscan foods also are featured, along with dishes that may require a stronger stomach, such as pigs' trotters, tongue, and *bollito misto e salsa verde* (boiled meat with a green sauce).

### La Maremmana

Via de' Macci 77r. **Map** 4 E1. *(055) 24 12 26.* ***Open*** *12:30–2:30pm, 7:30–10:30pm Mon–Sat.* Ⓛ

This restaurant's slightly outlying position on the edge of the Sant'Ambrogio market – but close to Santa Croce – means it sees far fewer tourists than some. It is a basic trattoria of the old school and is particularly popular for its reasonable fixed-price menu.

### Le Mossacce

Via del Proconsolo 55r. **Map** 2 D5 (6 E2). *(055) 29 43 61.* ***Open*** *noon–2:30pm, 7–9:30pm Mon–Fri.* Ⓛ

Multilingual menus and a chaotic lunchtime air shouldn't keep you from this 100-year-old restaurant, in an ideal location between the Bargello and the Duomo. Nor should the name, which means "discourteous." Tiny wooden tables and paper tablecloths are complemented by suitably robust Tuscan food, with barely a nod to dishes from outside the region. The fixed-price menu, even without a dessert, is a good buy. Tables cannot be reserved.

### Palle d'Oro

Via Sant'Antonino 43r. **Map** 1 C5 (5 C1). *(055) 28 83 83.* ***Open*** *noon–3pm, 7:30–10pm Mon–Sat.* Ⓛ

This sparse, spotlessly clean trattoria is as simple as they come. There are wooden booths and tables at the rear, and a takeout sandwich bar at the front. The food is basic but well-cooked.

### Trattoria Mario

Via Rosina 2r. **Map** 1 C4. *(055) 21 85 50.* ***Open*** *noon–3pm Mon–Sat.* Ⓛ

On the edge of the Mercato Centrale, this humble but popular spot resounds with the banter of students and market traders. Arrive early to be sure of a seat, and choose from a board of daily specials such as *ribollita* and *trippa*. Fish is offered on Fridays and *gnocchi* (dumplings) on Thursdays. There is no dessert or coffee on the menu, just fresh fruit and *cantucci* biscuits to dip into glasses of *vin santo*.

### Buca dell'Orafo

Volta de' Girolami 28r. **Map** 6 D4. *(055) 21 36 19.* ***Open*** *12:30–2:30pm, 7:30–10:30pm Tue–Sat.* ⓁⓁ

Packed with visitors during lunch and early evening and with locals later on, the friendly hole-in-the-wall Buca is a longtime favorite with Florentines looking for homestyle cooking. The pasta is homemade and daily specials feature fish on Friday, *pasta e fagioli* on Saturday and *ribollita* on Thursday, Friday and Saturday. The house *dolce*, a sponge cake oozing cream and topped with almonds and meringue, is renowned and should be tried.

### Buca Mario

Piazza degli Ottaviani 16r. **Map** 1 B5 (5 B2). *(055) 21 41 79.* ***Open*** *noon–2:30pm, 7:30–10:30pm Fri–Tue, 7:30–10pm Thu.* ⓁⓁ

Florentines and foreigners alike often form a little knot outside this restaurant. They wait patiently for one of the few tables down below in the cellar and a chance to enjoy homemade pastas and grilled meats at surprisingly good prices.

### Cafaggi

Via Guelfa 35r. **Map** 1 C4. *(055) 29 49 89.* ***Open*** *noon–2:30pm, 7–10pm Mon–Sat, noon–2pm Sun.* ⓁⓁ

This classic Tuscan trattoria – just two simple underfurnished rooms – has been in the Cafaggi family for 60 years. The oil and several of the wines used come from the family farm in Chianti, complementing fresh, well-prepared dishes. The *crostini*, *zuppa di farro*, *involtini* and crème caramel are particularly good. Stick to one of the three fixed-price menus for a reasonably priced meal – either the *turistico*, *leggero* (light) or *vegetariano* (vegetarian).

### Da Ganino

Piazza dei Cimatori 4r. **Map** 6 D3. *(055) 21 41 25.* ***Open*** *1–3pm, 7:30–10:30pm Mon–Sat.* ⓁⓁ

Pleasant and uncrowded restaurants are in short supply close to the Duomo and Via dei Calzaiuoli. This small restaurant, however, is friendly and popular with locals and tourists, and offers all the basics, such as *ravioli con burro e salvia* (ravioli with butter and sage), at a reasonable price. It has an old-fashioned interior and a few tables outside on a tiny and appealing piazza. If the tables are full, try the Birreria Centrale immediately next door *(see p265)*.

### Da Pennello

Via Dante Alighieri 4r. **Map** 4 D1 (6 E3). *(055) 29 48 48.* ***Open*** *noon–3pm, 7–10pm Tue–Sat, noon–3pm Sun.* ⓁⓁ

Book well ahead unless you're prepared to wait for some time to sit at the tables in the summer garden or bright dining room. This is a restaurant that has been well and truly discovered. It is best known for its wonderful variety of *antipasti* – a meal in themselves.

### Paoli

Via dei Tavolini 12r. **Map** 4 D1 (6 D3). *(055) 21 62 15.* ***Open*** *noon–2:30pm, 7–10:30pm Wed–Mon.* ⓁⓁ

The food here is not exceptional, but you are paying for an ambience scarcely bettered anywhere in the city. The dining area is a single, vaulted hall completely smothered in medieval frescoes. This, and its position just off Via dei Calzaiuoli, mean it is invariably full, so be sure to book or arrive early.

### San Zanobi

Via San Zanobi 33r. **Map** 1 C4. *(055) 47 52 86.* ***Open*** *noon–2:30pm, 8–10:30pm Tue–Sun.* ⓁⓁ

Dedicated cooking is evident at San Zanobi in everything from the delicacy and inventiveness of the cooking to the scrupulous attention to detail in the sedate and refined dining room. The dishes, based on a traditional Florentine theme, are light and superbly presented.

### Trattoria Angiolino

Via di Santo Spirito 36r. **Map** 3 B1 (5 A4). *(055) 239 89 76.* ***Open*** *noon–2:30pm, 7–10:30pm Tue–Sat, noon–2:30pm Sun.* ⓁⓁ

This atttractive restaurant in Oltrarno has a typically bustling Florentine atmosphere. However, the quality of the food – which can be excellent – and service is not always consistent. Particularly charming is the iron stove in the middle of the restaurant, which is lit during the winter months. Specialties on the menu include *penne ai funghi* (mushroom).

## Trattoria Zà Zà

Piazza del Mercato Centrale 26r. **Map** 1 C4. *(055) 21 54 11. **Open** noon–3pm, 7–10:30pm Mon–Sat.* ⓁⓁ

Both the upper and lower rooms of this canteen-like restaurant are packed with customers perched on stools, elbow-to-elbow at wooden trestle tables. Yellowing posters of 1950s film stars provide the decoration, shadowed by shelves of precariously stacked bottles of Chianti. The service is amiable and the food is robust and Tuscan. Soups such as *ribollita*, *pomodoro* (tomato) and *passato di fagioli* (bean purée) make good *primi*, while *arista* (roast pork) and *scaloppine* (veal) are dependable main courses. To finish off, try the house specialty, *torta di mele alla zà zà* (apple tart).

## Alle Murate

Via Ghibellina 52r. **Map** 4 D1 (6 E3). *(055) 24 06 18. **Open** 8–11:30pm Tue–Sun.* ⓁⓁⓁ

This increasingly popular restaurant is buoyed by the delicate cooking of a young female chef who, with dishes such as *ravioli di gamberi* (pasta stuffed with prawns), combines basic Italian staples with a dash of more far-flung Mediterranean cuisines. Desserts are light and innovative, and the wine cellar is among the best in the city.

## Cibrèo

Via de' Macci 118. **Map** 4 E1. *(055) 234 11 00. **Open** 12:50–2:30pm, 7:30–10:30pm Tue–Sat.* ★ ⓁⓁⓁ

Under the guiding hand of Fabio and Benedetta Picchi Cibrèo, this restaurant offers superbly prepared traditional Tuscan food in an unstuffy atmosphere. Cibrèo does not serve pasta but you can choose between thoroughly Florentine dishes such as tripe, pumpkin, sheeps' brains, cockscombs and kidneys, or more palatable items often lightly tinged with touches of *nouvelle cuisine* – such as duck stuffed with raisins and pine nuts, lamb with artichokes and some tasty soups. Also try the delicious desserts.

## Dino

Via Ghibellina 51r. **Map** 4 D1 (6 E3). *(055) 24 14 52. **Open** 12:30–2:30pm, 7:30–10:30pm Tue–Sat, 12:30–2:30pm Sun.* ⓁⓁⓁ

This well-regarded restaurant is situated on the edge of the Santa Croce district in a beautiful 14th-century palazzo. This restaurant has one of Florence's best wine cellars and its decorous and refined setting complement a long menu and excellent seasonal cooking. Dishes on the menu, which can be adventurous, include *talgliatelle all'erba limoncella* (pasta with herbs), several types of *baccalà* as well as the famous *filettino di maiale al cartoccio* (pork fillets baked in paper).

## I Quattro Amici

Via degli Orti Oricellari 29. **Map** 1 A5 (5 A1). *(055) 21 54 13. **Open** noon–2:30pm, 7:30–10:30pm Thu–Tue.* ⓁⓁⓁ

Four friends *(quattro amici)* with many years in the business came together to create this fish-only restaurant, located in the less-than-safe area around the railway station. The interior is cool, tending toward spartan, and though elegant, has little charm. However, the food has earned a Michelin star. Fish is brought directly from Porto Santo Stéfano on the Tuscan coast. The only weak point, as in many Italian restaurants, is that the desserts are made off the premises.

## Il Francescano

Largo Bargellini, Via di San Giuseppe 26. **Map** 4 E1. *(055) 24 16 05. **Open** noon–2:30pm, 7:30–10:30pm Thu–Tue.* ⓁⓁⓁ

After a superb start in the 1980s, standards have slipped and prices crept up in this smartly decorated restaurant of wood, marble and valuable *objects d'art*. The mainly young clientele has a choice of dishes such as *tartino di carciofi* (artichoke tart), soups and various meat dishes. The choice of wines at this restaurant is impressive.

## La Taverna del Bronzino

Via delle Ruote 27r. **Map** 2 D3. *(055) 49 52 20. **Open** noon–2:30pm, 7:30–10:15pm Mon–Sat.* ⓁⓁⓁ

The 15th-century palazzo that houses this restaurant has connections with the Florentine painter Bronzino, hence the name. Well-heeled business people on expense accounts make up the bulk of the restaurant's clientele. The atmosphere is reserved without being stuffy; the surroundings airy and beautifully finished. The *antipasti* and wide choice of pastas are safely Tuscan, while the main courses are more ambitiously Florentine. The cooking is of the highest quality.

## Le Fonticine

Via Nazionale 79r. **Map** 1 C4. *(055) 28 21 06. **Open** noon–2:30pm, 7–10:30pm Tue–Sat.* ⓁⓁⓁ

The owners of this long-established and well-known restaurant come from the neighboring Emilia Romagna region, famous for its cuisine, and give a more refined twist to solid Tuscan dishes such as *trippa*, *ossobuco* (veal) and *cinghiale*. The meats are generally of the highest quality and the pasta is homemade and delicious.

## Enoteca Pinchiorri

Via Ghibellina 87. **Map** 1 A5 (5 A1). *(055) 24 27 77. **Open** 12:30–2:30pm, 7:30–10:30pm Tue–Sat, 7:30–10:30pm Mon.* ★ ⓁⓁⓁⓁⓁ

The Pinchiorri is frequently described as Italy's finest restaurant, and also boasts what many have called the greatest wine cellar in Europe (over 80,000 bottles of French and Italian vintages). The setting on the ground floor of the 15th-century Palazzo Ciofi-Iacometti matches the excellence of the award-winning cooking, a mixture of Tuscan and French-inspired *cucina nuova*. The set-price *menù degustazione* includes glasses of wine appropriate to each course, thus allowing you to sample the cellar without having to buy whole bottles. Not everyone, however, will be comfortable with the ceremony and seriousness that is attached to eating and drinking at the Pinchiorri.

## Sabatini

Via Panzani 9a. **Map** 1 C5 (5 C1). *(055) 28 28 02. **Open** 12:30–2:30pm, 7:30–11pm Tue–Sun.* ⓁⓁⓁⓁⓁ

Once Florence's most eminent restaurant, Sabatini's glory days are now long gone. However, the critical backlash that flayed its reputation has done a disservice to the cooking – a mixture of Italian and international – that is always reliable and occasionally superlative. The ambience and service are as fine as ever, though neither the food nor the excellent selection of wines comes cheap.

For key to symbols *see p253*

## Florence Environs

### Caffè Concerto

2 km (1.25 miles) E Florence. Lungarno Cristoforo Colombo 7. *(055) 67 73 77. **Open** noon–2:30pm, 7:30–11pm Mon–Sat.* ⓁⓁⓁ

Gabriele Tarchiani's eclectic décor and *cucina nuova* aren't for all tastes. However, the view over the Arno from the veranda is almost reason enough to sample some of the innovative, if sometimes far-fetched, dishes.

# WESTERN TUSCANY

## Artimino

### Da Delfina

**Road map** C2. Via della Chiesa 1. *(055) 871 80 74. **Open** noon–2:30pm, 7:30–10pm Wed–Sun, noon–2:30pm Mon.* ★ ⓁⓁⓁ

Carlo Cioni has continued the authentic culinary traditions of his mother, Delfina, in this lovely restaurant, located in a walled medieval village just 22 km (14 miles) west of Florence. Game is a particular specialty of this restaurant. Pork with wild fennel and black Tuscan cabbage is just one of numerous outstanding local dishes.

## Livorno

### La Barcarola

**Road map** B3. Viale Carducci 63. *(0586) 40 23 67. **Open** noon–2:30pm, 7:30–10pm Mon–Sat.* ⓁⓁⓁ

Livorno may not be Tuscany's prettiest city, but it is undoubtedly the best place to eat fish. The one dish not to miss at this lively restaurant is *cacciucco*, the traditional Livornese fish soup. Other specialties include *zuppa di pesce* and *penne* with scampi.

### La Chiave

**Road map** B3. Scali delle Cantine 52. *(0586) 88 86 09. **Open** noon–2:30pm, 7:30–10pm Thu–Tue.* ⓁⓁⓁ

La Chiave offers extremely refined and elegant dining. The menu includes traditional local fare and Italian specialties from as far afield as Naples and Sicily.

## Pisa

### Al Ristoro dei Vecchi Macelli

**Road map** B2. Via Volturno 49. *(050) 204 24. **Open** noon–2:30pm, 7:30–10:30pm Thu–Sat & Mon–Tue, 7:30–10:30pm Sun.* ⓁⓁⓁ

Traditional bean soup with the addition of seafood is one of several innovative dishes in this pleasant, intimate restaurant that serves light Tuscan food with a twist. Fish, seafood and game specialties are all delicately prepared and the homemade desserts are sensational.

### Sergio

**Road map** B2. Lungarno Pacinotti 1. *(050) 58 05 80. **Open** noon–3pm, 7:30–10:30pm Tue–Sat, 7:30–10:30pm Mon.* ⓁⓁⓁⓁ

This restaurant appeals mainly to Pisan business people with expense accounts. The food is over-elaborate by Italian standards, but the execution is exquisite, and the setting, service and wines are correspondingly grand.

## Volterra

### Etruria

**Road map** C3. Piazza dei Priori 8. *(0588) 860 64. **Open** noon–2:30pm, 7–10:30pm Fri–Wed.* ⓁⓁ

In a town not blessed with good restaurants, the Etruria on Volterra's main square is your best bet. Try the game and roast boar specialties in season, usually in the autumn.

# NORTHERN TUSCANY

## Lucca

### Buca di Sant'Antonio

**Road map** C2. Via della Cervia 3. *(0583) 558 81. **Open** 12:30–3pm, 7:30–10:30pm Tue–Sat, 12:30–3pm Sun.* ⓁⓁ

This, Lucca's most famous restaurant, has been graced with compliments in the past. The heavy rustic cooking no longer excels, but the variety of dishes from the Garfagnana region makes it reliable and reasonably priced.

### Giulio in Pelleria

**Road map** C2. Via delle Conce 47. *(0583) 559 48. **Open** noon–2:30pm, 7–10pm Tue–Sat.* ⓁⓁ

You must book ahead to enter into the spirit of this bright, boisterous and extremely busy neighborhood restaurant. Here the hearty local dishes offer few surprises, but the prices are extremely reasonable.

### Solferino

**Road map** C2. Via delle Gavine 50, San Macario in Piano. *(0583) 591 18. **Open** noon–2:30pm, 7:30–10pm Fri–Tue, 7:30–10pm Thu.* ⓁⓁⓁ

Solferino has been in the same family for generations and is among the most famous and highly regarded restaurants in Tuscany. The menu is mainly Tuscan, but cooks Edema and Giampiero regularly come up with innovative interpretations. The wines are superb.

### Vipore

**Road map** C2. Pieve Santo Stefano. *(0583) 592 45. **Open** Apr–Oct: 12:30–3pm, 7:45–10:30pm Tue–Sat, 12:30–3pm Sun; Nov Mar: 12:30–3pm, 7:45–10:30pm Wed–Sat, 12:30–3pm Sun.* ⓁⓁⓁ

Situated on a hill top, this restaurant has magnificent views. Young chef-patron Cesare Casella produces food of unusual originality, using seasonal vegetables and game, dressed with herbs from his garden, and local olive oil.

## Montecatini Terme

### Pier Angelo

**Road map** C2. Viale IV Novembre 99. *(0572) 77 15 52. **Open** 12:30–2:30pm, 7:30–10pm Tue–Sat, 12:30–3pm Sun.* ⓁⓁⓁⓁ

A restored Art Nouveau villa provides the setting for this highly renowned restaurant. A previous tendency to indulge the worst aspects of *nouvelle cuisine* appears to have passed, though the food is still occasionally overly esoteric and bland.

## Pescia

### Cecco

**Road map** C2. Via Francesco Forti 94–96. *(0572) 47 79 55. **Open** 12:15–2:30pm, 8:15–10pm Tue–Sun.* ⓁⓁ

This quiet, easygoing restaurant is the best place to sample Pescia's famous *asparagi* (asparagus), though all the food prepared here can be outstanding. Try the dessert – *cioncia* – a delicious house specialty, on cold days.

## Pistoia

### Leon Rosso

**Road map** C2. Via Panciatichi 4. *(0573) 292 30.* ***Open*** *12:30–3pm, 7:30–10:30pm Mon–Sat.* ⓁⓁ

The Leon Rosso provides a modest culinary oasis in the center of Pistoia, a city that is otherwise something of a gastronomic desert. Dishes – which are reliable but rarely inspired – include *gnocchi al gorgonzola* (dumplings with cheese sauce) and *maccheroncini al cinghiale* (macaroni with boar).

## Prato

### Osvaldo Baroncelli

**Road map** D2. Via Fra' Bartolomeo 13. *(0574) 238 10.* ***Open*** *12:30–2:30pm, 7:30–10pm Mon–Sat.* ⓁⓁⓁ

Forty years of experience on the part of the eponymous Osvaldo ensure a high standard in dishes such as small tarts of potato and *porcini* mushrooms. Try the chicken stuffed with pistachios and the tasty sweet rolls, laced with honey and Calvados.

### Il Pirana

**Road map** D2. Via Valentini 110. *(0574) 257 46.* ***Open*** *12:30–2:30pm, 8–10:30pm Mon–Fri, 8–10:30pm Sat.* ⓁⓁⓁⓁ

Many rate this as one of the best fish restaurants in Italy, certainly in Tuscany. Do not be put off by the over-precious modern interior or by the factory-dotted location of this place, ten minutes' drive from the center of Prato.

## Viareggio

### Romano

**Road map** B2. Via Mazzini 120. *(0584) 313 82.* ***Open*** *12:30–2:30pm, 7:30–10pm Tue–Sun.* ★ ⓁⓁⓁⓁ

Romano is one of Tuscany's best fish restaurants. Although expensive, few other places are so well priced. Wines are fairly priced, and the set-price menu has ten full courses. Romano is on hand and unfailingly courteous, and his wife Franca prepares simple, often inventive and always immaculately presented food.

# EASTERN TUSCANY

## Arezzo

### Buca di San Francesco

**Road map** E3. Via San Francesco 1. *(0575) 232 71.* ***Open*** *noon–2:30pm, 7–10pm Wed–Sun, noon–2:30pm Mon.* ⓁⓁ

The food in the Buca di San Francesco is nothing to write home about. However, its medieval ambience and position alongside the church of San Francesco, with Piero della Francesca's fresco cycle, make it the first choice for most visitors to Arezzo.

## Camaldoli

### Il Cedro

**Road map** E2. Via di Camaldoli 20, Moggiona. *(0575) 55 60 80.* ***Open*** *12:30–2pm, 7:30–9pm Tue–Sun.* ⓁⓁ

Finely cooked specialties such as venison, boar and fried vegetables combine with the lovely position of this restaurant overlooking the forests and mountains of the Casentino. This small establishment is one of the most popular and appealing in the region.

## Castelnuovo Berardenga

### La Bottega del Trenta

**Road map** D3. Villa a Sesta, Via Santa Caterina 2. *(0577) 35 92 26.* ***Open*** *7:30–10:30pm Mon & Thu–Sun, noon–2:30pm Sun.* ⓁⓁⓁ

This is a serious and tasteful restaurant run by lively patron Franco Cameilia and his French wife, Hélène. Here, the occasionally adventurous cooking includes a renowned *petto di anatra con il finocchio selvatico* (breast of duck with wild fennel). Pastas may be too adventurous if you have become used to simple Tuscan cooking, but the desserts are excellent and the choice of wine is extensive.

## Cortona

### La Loggetta

**Road map** E3. Piazza Pescheria 3. *(0575) 63 05 75.* ***Open*** *12:30–2:30pm, 7–10pm Tue–Sun.* ⓁⓁ

La Loggetta sits plumb in the center of Cortona, looking down over a small square from its quaint medieval loggia. Inside, the atmosphere is cool and sedate, with scrubbed stone medieval walls. Be sure to try the home-made *cannelloni* stuffed with spinach and ricotta cheese.

## Sansepolcro

### Il Fiorentino

**Road map** E3. Via Luca Pacioli 60. *(0575) 74 03 70 or 74 03 50.* ***Open*** *12:30–2:30pm, 7–10pm, Sat–Thu.* ⓁⓁ

This central, amiable and unfussy hotel restaurant is dedicated to the regional cuisines of nearby Umbria and Marche. Pigeon with olives, a classic local dish, is an excellent choice, as are several of the herb-flavored pasta sauces. Try the assortment of local cheeses.

### Paolo e Marco Mercati

**Road map** E3. Via Palmiro Togliatti 68. *(0575) 73 50 51.* ***Open*** *7–10:30pm Mon–Sat.* ⓁⓁ

This is a new and dignified restaurant whose fixed-price menu is a very good buy. Dishes include Tuscan black cabbage cooked with white truffles, vegetable ravioli and truffles, roast pigeon, *gnocchi* (dumplings) in a sauce of tomatoes, and seafood.

# CENTRAL TUSCANY

## Colle di Val d'Elsa

### Antica Trattoria

**Road map** C3. Piazza Arnolfo 23. *(0577) 92 37 47.* ***Open*** *12:30–2:30pm, 8–10:30pm Wed–Sun, 12:30–2:30pm Mon.* ★ ⓁⓁⓁ

The more homey and relaxed of Colle's two excellent restaurants, the Antica Trattoria is a family-run concern dedicated – after some dabbling with *cucina nuova* – to traditional regional cuisine. The setting is medieval and the service, under the eye of patron Enrico Paradisi, is lively and attentive.

For key to symbols *see p253*

### Arnolfo

**Road map** C3. Piazza Santa Caterina 1. *(0577) 92 05 49.* ***Open*** *12:30–2:30pm, 7:30–10pm Wed–Mon.* ⓁⓁⓁⓁ

French-trained chefs have earned this intimate three-roomed restaurant one of Tuscany's few Michelin stars. The wines, food and service are all impeccable, but the dignified and reverential atmosphere is a little too solemn for an Italian restaurant. Typical dishes include pigeon cooked with wine, prunes and pine nuts, lamb with thyme and sesame seeds, a sublime *ribollita* and an asparagus and onion tart.

## Gaiole in Chianti

### Badia a Coltibuono

**Road map** D3. Badia a Coltibuono. *(0577) 74 94 24.* ***Open*** *Apr–Oct: 12:30–2:30pm, 7:30–10pm Tue–Sun (Nov–Mar: Wed–Sun).* ⓁⓁⓁ

The Badia, an 11th-century abbey, forms the heart of an eminent vineyard where wines and oils are used in the distinguished adjoining restaurant. The menu offers meats roasted on a spit and delicious desserts. Visitors can take a tour around the estate and there are also cookery courses available.

### Castello di Spaltenna

**Road map** D3. Via Spaltenna. *(0577) 74 94 83.* ***Open*** *12:30–2:30pm, 7:30–10pm Wed–Sun, 7:30–10pm Tue.* ★ ⓁⓁⓁⓁ. *See also* **Where to Stay**, *p250.*

This lovely stone-walled and flower-filled restaurant forms part of a peaceful hotel situated in a castle just outside Gaiole in Chianti. Popular with expatriates, it offers refined versions of Tuscan classics such as pigeon cooked in Chianti, fresh *porcini* mushrooms, chickpea soup and the occasional more offbeat innovation.

## Montalcino

### Taverna e Fattoria dei Barbi

**Road map** D4. Località Podernovi. *(0577) 84 93 57.* ***Open*** *12:30–2:30pm, 7–10pm Thu–Mon, noon–2:30pm Tue.* ★ ⓁⓁ

Magnificent Brunello wines from the surrounding vineyards complement the superb country cooking of this renowned restaurant south of Montalcino. Try to get a table outside, where you can admire the lovely views over the surrounding hills.

## Montepulciano

### Il Marzocco

**Road map** E4. Piazza Savonarola 18. *(0578) 75 72 62.* ***Open*** *noon–2:30pm, 7:30–10pm Thu–Tue.* ⓁⓁ

Part of a 19th-century hotel, Il Marzocco is just within the city walls. This pleasant family-run restaurant offers basic, well-executed food in unpretentious surroundings.

## Monteriggioni

### Il Pozzo

**Road map** D3. Piazza Roma 2. *(0577) 30 41 27.* ***Open*** *12:15–2:40pm, 7:45–10pm Tue–Sat, 12:15–2:40pm Sun.* ⓁⓁⓁ

The old stone-walled ambience of this restaurant is what you would expect from a village as thoroughly medieval as Monteriggioni. An ideal place for lunch, the food is rigorously Tuscan, simple and enthusiastically prepared. The homemade desserts of the owner Lucia are widely renowned.

## Pienza

### Da Falco

**Road map** D4. Piazza Dante Alighieri 7. *(0578) 74 85 51.* ***Open*** *12–2:30pm, 7–10pm Sat–Thu.* Ⓛ

This friendly restaurant is among the best of Pienza's handful of places to eat. The *antipasti* are excellent and there is a vast choice of *primi* and *secondi* on a long menu of regional specialties.

## San Gimignano

### Le Terrazze

**Road map** C3. Albergo La Cisterna, Piazza della Cisterna 24. *(0577) 94 03 28.* ***Open*** *12:30–2:30pm, 7–10pm Thu–Mon, 7–10pm Wed.* ⓁⓁ

The Terrazze's selling point, as its name suggests, is a terrace with views over the rolling hills of southern Tuscany. The dining room is medieval, with low ceilings and wooden beams, and forms part of a 13th-century palazzo, mostly occupied by the adjoining hotel. This is a good place for regional specialties, although the menu also boasts the occasional novelty.

## Siena

### Al Marsili

**Road map** D3. Via del Castoro 3. *(0577) 471 54.* ***Open*** *12:30–2:30pm, 7:30–10:30pm Tue–Sun.* ⓁⓁ

Standards in this long-term rival to Osteria Le Logge *(see below)* for the title of Siena's best restaurant, have been erratic. However, with Le Logge's prices now edging toward excessive, the Marsili's equally elegant and central setting once again looks tempting.

### La Torre

**Road map** D3. Via Salicotto 7–9. *(0577) 28 75 48.* ***Open*** *12:30–3pm, 7–10pm Fri–Wed.* ⓁⓁ

Despite its position immediately off the Campo, this tiny old-fashioned trattoria remained all but unknown for years. Now it has been discovered, so arrive early to grab one of the handful of tables in the narrow, noisy stone-arched dining room.

### Il Campo

**Road map** D3. Piazza del Campo 50. *(0577) 28 07 25.* ***Open*** *Sep–Jun: noon–2:30pm, 7–10pm Wed–Mon; Jul–Aug: noon–2:30pm, 7–10pm daily.* ⓁⓁⓁ

Most of the restaurants that ring the Campo are expensive and slipshod tourist traps. The most expensive, however, Il Campo, is the exception, and the place to come if you're going to treat yourself to a meal in arguably Italy's loveliest piazza. You can either eat *alla carta* or choose from the two fixed-price menus.

### Osteria Le Logge

**Road map** D3. Via del Porrione 33. *(0577) 480 13.* ***Open*** *noon–3pm, 7–10:30pm Mon–Sat.* ⓁⓁⓁ

Siena's prettiest, and often full, restaurant has a dark wood and marble interior. The tables are laid with crisp linen cloths and decorated with plants. Home-produced oils and Montalcino wines accompany dishes that wander slightly from mainstream Tuscan cooking. More exotic *primi* include stuffed guinea fowl *(faraona)*, chicken with lemon, duck and fennel, and meats stuffed with rabbit and capers. Book or arrive early to avoid waiting for a table.

### Ristorante Certosa di Maggiano

**Road map** D3. Via di Certosa 82. *(0577) 28 81 80.* ***Open*** *12:30–2:30pm, 7–10pm daily.* ⓁⓁⓁⓁ. *See also* **Where to Stay**, *p251.*

The Hotel Certosa di Maggiano, a restored 14th-century abbey, is the perfect place for a honeymoon. While the food in the restaurant doesn't quite live up to the idyllic surroundings, it's still a fine place to escape the city and enjoy – at quite a considerable price – rarefied and delicate Italian cooking. Meals are served in the dining room or in the quiet 14th-century cloisters.

## SOUTHERN TUSCANY

### Capalbio

### Da Maria

**Road map** D5. Via Comunale 3. *(0564) 89 60 14.* ***Open*** *12:30–2:30pm, 7:30–10pm Wed–Mon.* ⓁⓁ

Capalbio's vacation population of Roman politicians and media types sits down with locals and visitors to enjoy Maurizio Rossi's variety of soundly cooked authentic Maremman cuisine. Dishes include *cinghiale alla cacciatora* (wild boar in a rich "hunter's" sauce), *acquacotta, tortelli tartufati* (stuffed pasta with truffles), *fritto misto vegetale* (mixed deep-fried vegetables) and many more.

### Elba

### Publius

**Road map** B4. Piazza XX Settembre, Poggio Marciana. *(0565) 992 08.* ***Open*** *Apr–Oct: 12:30–2:30pm, 7–10:30pm daily; Nov–Mar: 12:30–2:30pm, 7–10:30pm Tue–Sun.* ★ ⓁⓁ

Not only does this pleasant and historic trattoria have perhaps the best wine cellar on the island, but it also provides a respite from the unfailing diet of fish and seafood that dominates most Elban restaurants. Here, in addition to fish, you can eat mountain mushrooms, game, wild boar, lamb roasted in herbs, and a wide choice of *pecorino* and other cheeses. There are fantastic views of the island from the restaurant.

### Rendez-Vous da Marcello

**Road map** B4. Piazza della Vittoria 1, Marciana Marina. *(0565) 992 51.* ***Open*** *Jul–Sep: noon–2:30pm, 7–10pm daily; Dec & Mar–Jun noon–2:30pm, 7–10pm Thu–Tue.* ⓁⓁⓁ

Outdoor tables on the harbor front at this noted fish restaurant make a pleasant retreat from the summer crowds of Marciana Marina. Most dishes are pleasantly simple and straightforward, but the menu may, at times, include the fashionable culinary fads of the moment.

### Massa Marittima

### Bracali

**Road map** C4. Via Pietro Sarcoli, Frazione Ghirlanda. *(0566) 90 20 63.* ***Open*** *12:30–2:30pm, 7:30–10:30pm Wed–Mon.* ⓁⓁ

For such a popular tourist town, Massa Marittima has few good central eating places. However, it is worth a few minutes' drive on the main road north out of town to sample Maremman cooking in a family restaurant that is not afraid to search farther afield for the best ingredients. Among the mouth-watering *secondi* are *brasato* of wild boar (thin-cut slices), pigeon with honey, cold duck with balsamic vinegar and blackcurrants, and guinea fowl with white grapes.

### Orbetello

### Osteria del Lupacante

**Road map** D5. Corso Italia 103. *(0564) 86 76 18.* ***Open*** *12:30–2:30pm, 7:30–10pm Thu–Tue.* ⓁⓁ

This pleasant *osteria* sticks to old ways in a place increasingly over-run by visitors and affluent out-of-towners. The cooking, which concentrates on fish and seafood, has a light touch but can nonetheless be adventurous. Dishes to look for include *cozze in salsa di Marsala* (mussels in a Marsala sauce), *risotto con gamberi e pinoli* (risotto with prawns and pine nuts) and fillet of sole with almonds and onions.

### Porto Ercole

### Bacco in Toscana

**Road map** D5. Via San Paolo 6. *(0564) 83 30 78.* ***Open*** *Apr–Sep: 1–2:30pm, 7:30–10:30pm daily; Oct–Mar: 1–2:30pm, 7:30–10:30pm Sat & Sun.* ⓁⓁ

This intimate restaurant serves excellent seafood dishes. Favorites are scampi with lemon, *spaghetti alle vongole* (clams) and *cozze* (mussels) with potato.

### Porto Santo Stefano

### La Bussola

**Road map** C5. Piazza Fucchinetti 11. *(0564) 81 42 25.* ***Open*** *noon–2:30pm, 7:30–10:30pm Thu–Tue.* ⓁⓁⓁ

This restaurant serves adventurous first-course dishes, often a seafood pasta. The traditional main course is less fancy and will usually include grilled fish. Dine on the terrace where there are lovely views across the peninsula.

### Saturnia

### I Due Cippi da Michele

**Road map** D5. Piazza Vittorio Veneto 26a. *(0564) 60 10 74.* ***Open*** *12:30–2:30pm, 7:30–10pm Wed–Mon.* ⓁⓁ

This is one of the region's most popular restaurants and a touch-stone for Maremman cuisine. Although its menu has been going through an uneven time, its more traditional offerings remain unbeatable at the price. Be sure to reserve a table.

### Sovana

### Taverna Etrusca

**Road map** E5. Piazza del Pretorio 16. *(0564) 61 61 83.* ***Open*** *12:30–2:30pm, 7:30–9:30pm Tue–Sun.* ⓁⓁ

The Etrusca's popularity is due, perhaps, to the exacting standards set by its two owners. This small restaurant has a medieval dining area that is beautifully appointed, and the food – Tuscan with sophisticated cosmopolitan touches – is excellent.

For key to symbols *see p253*

# Light Meals and Snacks in Florence

The traditional sidewalk café is not as much a part of local life in Florence as in other Italian cities. However, small, hole-in-the-wall bars can be found on most of the city's streets. Here, you can have alcoholic or soft drinks, as well as a range of tempting breakfast and lunchtime snacks. Old-fashioned wine bars provide alternative eating and drinking venues, and the city has plenty of takeout establishments, especially near Santa Maria Novella station, if you want to eat on the move.

Sitting down at a bar or café can be expensive, because there is a table charge. If you only want a quick snack, it may be cheaper to stand at the counter. It is also worth noting that some cafés and bars may close during the month of August.

## Bars

Locals generally patronize bars to pick up a coffee, quick snack, or an early morning apéritif, or to make a phone call or use the toilet *(il bagno)*. Some bars stay open late, particularly during the summer, but most are busiest during the day. Most have a counter for standing rather than tables.

Some bars also double as a pastry shop *(pasticceria)*; virtually all serve filled rolls *(panini)* or sandwiches *(tramezzini)* for lunch.

Breakfast is usually *un caffè* (a short espresso) or *un cappuccino* (milky coffee) with a plain jam or custard-filled croissant *(un brioche* or *un cornetto)*. Other drinks available are freshly squeezed fruit juice *(una spremuta)*, grappa and wine by the glass *(un bicchiere di vino)*.

The cheapest way to buy beer at a bar is from the keg *(una birra alla spina)*, either as a *piccola*, *media* or *grande* measure. Italian bottled beers such as Peroni are also reasonably priced, but foreign beers are expensive.

Once you have chosen what to eat or drink, you must first pay at the cash desk *(la cassa)*, and then take your receipt *(lo scontrino)* to the bar, where you will be served. A L100 tip on the counter will usually ensure quicker service.

There are numerous bars dotted around Florence, and many are convenient for the sights. **Caffè** is opposite the Palazzo Pitti, and **Gran Caffè San Marco** on the Piazza San Marco is also worth trying.

## Wine Cellars

Once a Florentine institution, wine cellars (*vinaii* or *fiaschetterie*) are now a dying breed. Locals meet in these wonderfully old-fashioned places to eat and drink. **Alessi**, like many other wine bars, offers *crostini* or a light meal, washed down with a glass of wine.

## Cafés

Four of Florence's handful of old-world cafés stand around the gloomy perimeter of Piazza della Repubblica. **Gilli**, renowned for its cocktails, dates back to 1733. It has two rear paneled rooms still evocative of an earlier age. **Giubbe Rosse**, once the haunt of the city's turn-of-the century literati, also evokes its former glory with dazzling chandeliers. However, like the neighboring cafés, it is over-priced and likely to be filled with wealthy foreigners rather than elegant Florentines. Instead, locals head for the **Rivoire**, also expensive but with more genuine class and a beautiful marble interior. **Manaresi** in Via de' Lamberti is a contender for the best coffee in the city.

The younger set go to **Giacosa**, the birthplace of the Negroni cocktail (vermouth, gin and Campari), or to **Procacci**, famous for its delicious truffle rolls *(tartufati)*.

## Takeout Food

Traditional street food includes tripe and *lampredotto* (pig's intestines) sandwiches, sold from the stalls at the Mercato Centrale *(see p88)*, around the Mercato Nuovo behind the Porcellino statue *(see p112)*, as well as in the Piazza dei Cimatori. The Mercato Centrale is a great place to buy picnic provisions if you are planning a day's excursion out of the city.

In the same areas you will also find vans selling *porchetta*, crispy slices of suckling pig in round rolls known as *rosette*. Small shops selling pizza by weight or slice *(pizza taglia)* are found all over the city, especially on the streets around Santa Maria Novella station.

Bars offer other takeout options including *panini*, *tramezzini* and ice cream. Some *vinaii* or *fiaschetterie*, notably in Via dei Cimatori and Piazza dell'Olio, also serve *crostini* and sandwiches that can be taken out.

Snack bars, such as **Gastronomia Vera**, selling burgers, fries and flavored milk shakes, are becoming increasingly popular.

## Ice Cream Parlors

Florentines often round off a meal or the evening *passeggiata* (walk) with an ice cream *(gelato)*. No day in the city is complete without at least one visit to an ice cream parlor *(gelateria)*. You can choose between a cone *(un cono)* and a cup *(una coppa)* and pay by size, usually starting at L1,500 and working up in L500 stages to enormous multiscoop offerings at L3,500.

Generally, it's best to avoid bars where the selection is limited, and the ice cream is made off the premises. Head instead for **Bar Vivoli Gelateria** *(see p71)*, thought by many to produce the best ice cream in Italy, or to the more outlying **Badiani** famed for its egg-rich *Buontalenti*. **Frilli** is also a popular spot.

## Directory

### City Center East

#### Bars and Cafés

**Bar 16**
Via del Proconsolo 51.
**Map** 2 D5 (6 E2).

**Break**
Via delle Terme 17.
**Map** 3 C1 (5 C3).

**Caffè Caruso**
Via Lambertesca 14–16r.
**Map** 6 D4.

**Caffè Meseta**
Via Pietrapiana 69.
**Map** 4 E1.

**Dolci Dolcezze**
Piazza Cesare Beccaria 8r.
**Map** 4 F1.

**Fantasy Snack Bar**
Via de' Cerchi 15.
**Map** 6 D3.

**Galleria degli Uffizi**
Piazzale degli Uffizi 6.
**Map** 6 D4.

**Il Rifrullo**
Via di San Niccolò 55r.
**Map** 4 D2.

**Manaresi**
Via de' Lamberti 16r.
**Map** 6 D3.

**Red Garter**
Via de' Benci 33.
**Map** 4 D2 (6 E4).

**Rivoire**
Piazza della Signoria 5.
**Map** 4 D1 (6 D3).

**Robiglio**
Via de' Tosinghi 11.
**Map** 6 D2.

**Santa Croce**
Borgo Santa Croce 31r.
**Map** 4 D1 (6 F4).

**Scudieri**
Piazza di San Giovanni 19.
**Map** 1 C5 (6 D2).

#### Wine Cellars

**Birreria Centrale**
Piazza dei Cimatori 38r.
**Map** 6 D3.

**Fiaschetteria al Panino**
Via de' Neri 2r.
**Map** 4 D1 (6 E4).

**Vini del Chianti**
Via dei Cimatori.
**Map** 4 D1 (6 D3).

**Vini e Panini**
Via dei Cimatori 38r.
**Map** 4 D1 (6 D3).

#### Takeout Food

**Cantinetta del Verrazzano**
Via dei Tavolini 18–20r.
**Map** 4 D1 (6 D3).

**Fiaschetteria al Panino**
Via de' Neri 2r.
**Map** 4 D1 (6 E4).

**Giovacchino**
Via de' Tosinghi 34r.
**Map** 6 D2.

**Italy & Italy**
Piazza della Stazione 25.
**Map** 1 B5 (5 B1).

#### Ice Cream Parlors

**Bar Vivoli Gelateria**
Via Isola delle Stinche 7r.
**Map** 6 F3.

**Festival del Gelato**
Via del Corso 75r.
**Map** 2 D5 (6 D3).

**Gelateria Veneta**
Piazza Cesare Beccaria.
**Map** 4 F1.

**Perchè No!**
Via dei Tavolini 19r.
**Map** 4 D1 (6 D3).

### City Center North

#### Bars and Cafés

**Da Nerbone**
Mercato Centrale.
**Map** 1 C4 (5C1).

**Gran Caffè San Marco**
Piazza San Marco.
**Map** 2 D4.

**Robiglio**
Via dei Servi 112.
**Map** 2 D5 (6 E2).

**Rex Café**
Via Fiesolana 23–25r.
**Map** 2 E5.

#### Wine Cellars

**Alessi**
Via di Mezzo 26.
**Map** 2 E5.

#### Ice Cream Parlors

**Badiani**
Via dei Mille 20.
**Map** 2 F2.

**Il Triangolo della Bermude**
Via Nazionale 61r.
**Map** 1 C4.

### City Center West

#### Bars and Cafés

**Alimentari**
Via Parione 12r.
**Map** 3 B1 (5 B3).

**Caffè Amerini**
Via della Vigna Nuova 61–63.
**Map** 3 B1 (5 B3).

**Caffè Strozzi**
Piazza degli Strozzi 16r.
**Map** 3 C1 (5 C3).

**Caffè Voltaire**
Via della Scala 9r.
**Map** 1 A4 (5 A1).

**Donini**
Piazza della Repubblica 15r.
**Map** 1 C5 (6 D3).

**Giacosa**
Via de' Tornabuoni 83r.
**Map** 1 C5 (5 C2).

**Gilli**
Piazza della Repubblica 39r.
**Map** 1 C5 (6 D3).

**Giubbe Rosse**
Piazza della Repubblica 13–14r.
**Map** 1 C5 (6 D3).

**Il Barretto Piano Bar**
Via Parione 50r.
**Map** 3 B1 (5 B3).

**La Vigna**
Via della Vigna Nuova 88.
**Map** 3 B1 (5 B3).

**Palle d'Oro**
Via Sant'Antonino 43.
**Map** 1 C5 (5 C1).

**Paszkowski**
Piazza della Repubblica 6r.
**Map** 1 C5 (6 D3).

**Procacci**
Via de' Tornabuoni 64r.
**Map** 1 C5 (5 C2).

**Rose's Bar**
Via Parione 3.
**Map** 3 B1 (5 B3).

#### Ice Cream Parlors

**Banchi**
Via dei Banchi 14r.
**Map** 1 C5 (5 C2).

### Oltrarno

#### Bars and Cafés

**Bar Ricchi**
Piazza di Santo Spirito 9r.
**Map** 3 B2 (5 A5).

**Bar Tabbucchin**
Piazza di Santo Spirito.
**Map** 3 B2 (5 A5).

**Caffè**
Piazza de' Pitti 11–12r.
**Map** 3 B2 (5 B5).

**Caffè Santa Trìnita**
Via Maggio 2r.
**Map** 3 B2 (5 B5).

**Caffeteria Henry**
Via dei Renai 27a.
**Map** 4 D2 (6 E5).

**Cennini**
Borgo San Jacopo 51r.
**Map** 3 C1 (5 C4).

**Dolce Vita**
Piazza del Carmine.
**Map** 3 A1 (5 A4).

**Gastronomia Vera**
Piazza de' Frescobaldi 3r.
**Map** 3 B1 (5 B4).

**La Loggia**
Piazzale Michelangelo 1.
**Map** 4 E3.

**Marino**
Piazza Nazario Sauro 19r.
**Map** 3 B1 (5 A3).

**Pasticceria Maioli**
Via de' Guicciardini 43r.
**Map** 3 C2 (5 C5).

**Tiratoio**
Piazza de' Nerli.
**Map** 3 A1.

#### Wine Cellars

**Cantinone del Gallo Nero**
Via di Santa Spirito 5–6r.
**Map** 3 B1 (5 A4).

#### Takeout Food

**Gastronomia Vera**
Piazza de' Frescobaldi 3r.
**Map** 3 B1 (5 B4).

#### Ice Cream Parlors

**Frilli**
Via di San Niccolò 57.
**Map** 4 D2.

**Il Giardino delle Delizie**
Piazza di Santa Felicita.
**Map** 3 C1 (5 C4).

# Shops and Markets

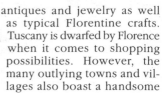

**Protective bag with designer label**

Shopping in Florence can be a unique experience as you wander through its ancient and medieval streets, exploring the city's renowned tradition of crafts and family-run businesses. Few cities of comparable size can boast such a profusion and variety of high-quality goods. Walking around the city you will find shops selling fashionable clothes, antiques and jewelry as well as typical Florentine crafts. Tuscany is dwarfed by Florence when it comes to shopping possibilities. However, the many outlying towns and villages also boast a handsome variety of local crafts and specialties, ranging from ceramics and handwoven materials to the region's many gastronomic delicacies. *(See also pp28–9.)*

**A colorful shop display of elegant handbags**

### When to Shop

Generally, shops open around 9am and close at 1pm. In the afternoon they are open from 3:30pm to 7:30pm in winter, and 4pm to 8pm in summer. In Florence, Siena and Arezzo, shops close on Monday morning in winter, and on Saturday afternoon in summer; in Pisa and Lucca they are shut on Monday morning throughout the year.

Bear in mind that shops and markets close by the score for two or three weeks around August 15, the national holiday *(ferragosto)*.

### How to Pay

Major credit cards and Eurocheques are usually accepted in larger stores, but smaller shops prefer cash. Traveler's checks are also widely accepted for payment of goods, though the rate is less favorable than at a bank.

Shopkeepers and market stallholders should by law give you a receipt *(ricevuta fiscale)*. If a purchased item is defective, most shops will exchange the article or give you a credit note, as long as you show the receipt. Cash refunds are uncommon.

### VAT Exemption

Visitors from non-EU countries can reclaim the 19 percent sales tax (IVA) on purchases from the same shop exceeding L300,000. Ask for an invoice when you buy the goods and inform the shop of your intention to reclaim the tax. The invoice must be stamped at customs as you leave the country. The shop will reimburse the tax in lire, once they have received the stamped invoice.

### Shopping in Florence

The center of Florence is packed with shops selling everything from designer clothes to secondhand books. The best time for bargains is during the January and July sales. Also explore the streets away from the center around Piazza di Santa Croce, Piazza dei Ciompi and Piazza di Santo Spirito, where craftspeople are busy at work.

**Window shopping in the Via de' Tornabuoni, Florence**

### Department Stores

The main chain store in Florence is **Coin**, which is also in Montecatini Terme and Livorno. Another possibility is **UPIM** in the Piazza della Repubblica and also found in towns throughout Tuscany.

### Fashion and Accessories

In Florence, the big names in Italian fashion are mostly found in Via de' Tornabuoni *(see p105)*, such as **Gucci** and **Enrico Coveri**, or Via della Vigna Nuova *(see p105)*, where you'll find **Giorgio Armani** and **Valentino**. Make an appointment to visit the showroom at **Emilio Pucci**'s family palace *(see p88)*, famous for his extravagant 1960s clothes. Alternatively, visit the shop in Via della Vigna Nuova. **Principe** sells classic menswear as well as women's and children's clothes. **Eredi Chiarini** has more casual styles or, for more flamboyant creations, go to **Ermanno Daelli**.

Florence abounds in shoe and leather shops. The classic styles and refined finishing of **Ferragamo**'s shoes are sought after by Hollywood stars. Alternatively, try the more affordable **Cresti** for a range of fashionable footwear, or stroll down Via de' Cerretani. Across the Arno is the tiny shop **Francesco**, selling simple, handmade shoes and sandals at modest prices. Piazza di Santa Croce and the adjoining streets are lined with leather shops. Elegant leather bags are sold at **Bojola** in Via de' Cerretani.

There are opulent fabrics at **Valli** and fine silks at **Lisio – Arte della Seta**. Embroidered linen can be found at **Taf**.

## TOILETRIES

TOILETRIES AND BEAUTY products can be bought at a *profumeria*. An *erboristeria* (herbalist) dispenses natural remedies and a range of natural products. Typical examples in Florence are **Erboristeria** (Palazzo Vecchio) *(see p75)* and **De Herbore**. Also well worth a visit is the **Farmacia di Santa Maria Novella**, a frescoed apothecary shop near Via dei Fossi *(see pp112–13)* selling products from the elixirs of the Camaldoli monks to herbal remedies and soaps.

**Interior design shop, Cesari**

## ART, ANTIQUES AND INTERIOR DESIGN

FLORENCE HAS ALWAYS been noted for its gold and silversmiths. Go to **Torrini**, whose family has produced jewelry in Florence for six centuries, and to **Buccellati**, renowned for its diamond-encrusted wedding rings.

For lovers of Art Nouveau and Art Deco furnishings there is **Fallani Best**, while **Cesari** sells decorating fabrics. For top-quality antiques go to **Neri**. **Romanelli** sells antique marble and bronze statuary.

**Alessi kitchenware at Rebus**

For modern art objects and gifts go to **Armando Poggi**. **Ugo Poggi** has a selection of household objects including elegant porcelain, while **Rebus** sells stylish Alessi kitchenware. **Il Tegame** stocks a more rustic range of kitchenware, such as copper kettles.

## BOOKS AND GIFTS

THE MAIN BOOKSTORES in Florence include **Seeber**, which sells publications in various languages, and **Feltrinelli**. **Salimbeni** sells art books and **Chiari** second-hand history, art and literature. For a selection of maps and guidebooks, try **Il Viaggio**.

Typically Florentine crafts include handmade marbled paper, used to decorate a variety of objects. These are available at **Giulio Giannini** or **Il Torchio**.

Go to **Ugolini** and **Mosaico di Pitti** for tables and framed pictures made with the old technique of marble inlay. For terra-cotta and decorative glazed ceramics visit **Sbigoli**, and **Arredamenti Castorina** for an astonishing selection of intricate intarsias. Via de' Guicciardini is packed with shops selling books, silver and other objects bound in colored leather.

## FOOD AND WINE

SHOPPING FOR FOOD should not pose too much of a problem. **Pegna**, a mini-supermarket in the heart of Florence, stocks fresh foods and a vast selection of delicacies. For typically British foods such as teas, gentleman's relish and whiskies go to **Old England Stores**.

For wines, one of the best-stocked shops is the **Enoteca Bonatti**, where you'll find a vast selection of Italian wines, and olive oil from Fiesole, bottled on the premises from a huge terra-cotta vase. Another place to buy wine is **Zanobini**, where you can join with the locals and have a *bicchiere*.

## FLORENCE MARKETS

FLORENCE'S CENTRAL street market is the **Mercato di San Lorenzo**, which caters mostly to tourists *(see p88)*. Nearby, in Via dell'Ariento, is **Mercato Centrale**, the city's main food market *(see p88)*.

In the city center, beneath the 16th-century Loggia del Porcellino, is the **Mercato Nuovo**, or Straw Market, which sells leather goods and souvenirs *(see p112)*.

The **Mercato delle Pulci** is a flea market, selling a range of antiques and bric-a-brac. On the last Sunday of each month (except July) the market swells to fill the adjoining streets for the Mercato del Piccolo Antiquariato.

Flower enthusiasts might want to check out the small **Mercato delle Piante**, selling herbs and ornamental plants.

**Fresh vegetables at a Florentine market stall**

## Shopping in Tuscany

Small towns throughout Tuscany have a multitude of shops selling a range of handicrafts, foods and some of the best wine in Italy. These are invariably displayed in small shops or at the frequent markets, seasonal fairs and local celebrations *(see pp32–7)* that are such an integral part of Tuscan rural life.

**Display of local pottery**

### Gifts and Souvenirs

Characteristic ceramics are found throughout the region, from the famed raw terra-cotta of Impruneta to the decorated glazed pottery of Montelupo and Siena. In San Gimignano, look for shops selling artistic ceramics *(see p28)* and handwoven fabrics.

The best in marble can be found in Pietrasanta and Carrara *(see p168).* The world-famous white marble of the Alpi Apuane continues to serve local craftsmen, who make busts and reproductions of sculpted works of art, as in Michelangelo's day.

The Etruscans mastered the art of working alabaster, and today the tradition lives on in Volterra, where many shops sell a range of souvenirs *(see p162).* The Etruscans also had knowledge of the minerals and precious stones characteristic of the volcanic Colline Metallifere, Maremma and the island of Elba, the latter famous for its quartz and opals *(see pp230–31).*

For textiles, Lucca lays claim to a rich tradition of silk manufacture, as well as embroidery and handwoven fabrics, reflecting the strong rural craft tradition of the nearby Garfagnana area. Rustic crafts are common in the Mugello and Casentino.

### Food and Wine

Excursions into Tuscany should include at least one visit to a local vineyard where wine is sold directly from the cellars. The Chianti region is studded with castles and farms producing their own wines *(see p225).* Greve has several good wine outlets, and during the third week of September there is the annual wine festival, the Rassegna del Chianti Classico *(see p36).*

The excellent Vernaccia, a white wine, is typical of the San Gimignano area. The vineyards around Montalcino produce some of the best wine in Italy *(see p220).*

Tuscany's rich gastronomic tradition is reflected in the profusion of local products. The main streets of towns such as Greve, Montalcino, San Gimignano and Pienza have a range of food shops.

Sheep's cheese *(pecorino),* produced around the area of Crete, can be bought directly from the farm or from shops in local towns. In Pienza, store shelves are laden with local

**A Tuscan delicatessen**

cheeses *(see p222),* cured meats, wines and grappas. In Grosseto you will find truffles.

Siena is renowned for its *panforte*, a dark cake spiced with cloves and cinnamon, that has been produced since the Middle Ages. Biscuits include *cavallucci* (ground walnuts and aniseed) and *ricciarelli* (ground almonds, candied orange peel and honey) *(see p255).*

### Markets in Tuscany

Markets are plentiful throughout the region. Particularly famous is the Mercato dell'Antiquariato, which sells goods from antique furniture to bric-a-brac. It is a sprawling affair that takes place in Arezzo on the Piazza Grande on the first weekend of each month, in Pisa on the Ponte di Mezzo on the second weekend, and in Lucca in Piazza San Martino on the third weekend.

**The Mercato dell'Antiquariato on the Piazza Grande in Arezzo**

## Florence Directory

### Department Stores

**Coin**
Via dei Calzaiuoli 56r.
**Map** 6 D3.
*(055) 28 05 31.*

**UPIM**
Piazza della Repubblica.
**Map** 1 C5 (6 D3).
*(055) 21 03 17.*

### Fashion and Accessories

**Bojola**
Via de' Rondinelli 25r.
**Map** 5 C2.
*(055) 21 11 55.*

**Cresti**
Via Roma 9r.
**Map** 1 C5 (6 D2).
*(055) 29 23 77.*

**Emilio Pucci**
Via della Vigna Nouva 97r.
**Map** 3 B1 (5 B3).
*(055) 29 40 28.*

**Enrico Coveri**
Via de' Tornabuoni 81r.
**Map** 1 C5 (5 C2).
*(055) 21 12 63.*

**Eredi Chiarini**
Via Roma 18–22r.
**Map** 1 C5 (6 D2).
*(055) 21 55 57.*

**Ermanno Daelli**
Via Roma 12r.
**Map** 1 C5 (6 D2).
*(055) 21 24 77.*

**Ferragamo**
Via de' Tornabuoni 14r.
**Map** 1 C5 (5 C2).
*(055) 29 21 23.*

**Francesco**
Via di Santo Spirito 62r.
**Map** 3 B1 (5 A4).
*(055) 21 24 28.*

**Giorgio Armani**
Via della Vigna Nuova 51r.
**Map** 3 B1 (5 B3).
*(055) 21 90 41.*

**Gucci**
Via de' Tornabuoni 73r.
**Map** 1 C5 (5 C2).
*(055) 26 40 11.*

**Lisio – Arte della Seta**
Via dei Fossi 45r.
**Map** 1 B5 (5 B3).
*(055) 21 24 30.*

**Principe**
Via degli Strozzi 21–29r.
**Map** 1 C5 (5 C3).
*(055) 29 27 64.*

**Taf**
Via Por Santa Maria 22r.
**Map** 6 D4.
*(055) 21 31 90.*

**Valentino**
Via della Vigna Nuova 47r.
**Map** 3 B1 (5 B3).
*(055) 29 31 42.*

**Valli**
Via degli Strozzi 4r.
**Map** 1 C5 (5 C3).
*(055) 28 24 85.*

### Art, Antiques and Interior Design

**Armando Poggi**
Via dei Calzaiuoli 114–118r.
**Map** 6 D3.
*(055) 21 65 28.*

**Buccellati**
Via de' Tornabuoni 71r.
**Map** 1 C5 (5 C2).
*(055) 239 65 79.*

**Cesari**
Via de' Tornabuoni 2.
**Map** 1 C5 (5 C2).
*(055) 28 98 46.*

**Fallani Best**
Borgo Ognissanti 15r.
**Map** 1 A5 (5 A2).
*(055) 21 49 86.*

**Il Tegame**
Piazza Gaetano Salvemini 7.
**Map** 2 E5 (4 E1).
*(055) 248 05 68.*

**Neri**
Via dei Fossi 57r.
**Map** 1 B5 (5 B3).
*(055) 29 21 36.*

**Rebus**
Borgo Ognissanti 114r.
**Map** 1 A5 (5 A2).
*(055) 28 39 11.*

**Romanelli**
Lungarno degli Acciaiuoli 74r.
**Map** 3 C1 (5 C4).
*(055) 239 60 47.*

**Torrini**
Piazza del Duomo 10r.
**Map** 2 D5 (6 D2).
*(055) 28 44 57.*

**Ugo Poggi**
Via degli Strozzi 26r.
**Map** 1 C5 (5 C3).
*(055) 21 67 41.*

### Books and Gifts

**Arredamenti Castorina**
Via di Santo Spirito 15r.
**Map** 3 B1 (5 A4).
*(055) 21 28 85.*

**Chiari**
Borgo Allegri 16r.
**Map** 4 E1.
*(055) 24 52 91.*

**Feltrinelli**
Via de' Cerretani 30–32r.
**Map** 5 C2.
*(055) 238 26 52.*

**Giulio Giannini**
Piazza de' Pitti 37r.
**Map** 3 B2 (5 B5).
*(055) 21 26 21.*

**Il Torchio**
Via de' Bardi 17.
**Map** 3 C2 (6 D4).
*(055) 234 28 62.*

**Il Viaggio**
Via Ghibellina 117r.
**Map** 4 D1 (6 E3).
*(055) 21 81 53.*

**Mosaico di Pitti**
Piazza de' Pitti 16r.
**Map** 3 B2 (5 B5).
*(055) 28 21 27.*

**Salimbeni**
Via Matteo Palmieri 14–16r. **Map** 4 E1 (6 F3).
*(055) 234 09 04.*

**Sbigoli**
Via Sant'Egidio 4r.
**Map** 6 F2.
*(055) 247 97 13.*

**Seeber**
Via de' Tornabuoni 70r.
**Map** 1 C5 (5 C2).
*(055) 21 56 97.*

**Ugolini**
Lungarno degli Acciaiuoli 66–70r. **Map** 3 C1 (5 C4).
*(055) 28 49 69.*

### Food and Wine

**Enoteca Bonatti**
Via Vincenzo Gioberti 66r (off Piazza Cesare Beccaria, **Map** 4 F1).
*(055) 66 00 50.*

**Old England Stores**
Via de' Vecchietti 28r.
**Map** 1 C5 (5 C2).
*(055) 21 19 83.*

**Pegna**
Via dello Studio 8.
**Map** 6 E2.
*(055) 28 27 01.*

**Zanobini**
Via Sant'Antonino 47r.
**Map** 1 C5 (5 C1).
*(055) 239 68 50.*

### Toiletries

**De Herbore**
Via del Proconsolo 6a.
**Map** 2 D5 (6 E2).
*(055) 234 09 96.*

**Erboristeria**
Via Vacchereccia 9r.
**Map** 3 C1 (6 D3).
*(055) 239 60 55.*

**Farmacia di Santa Maria Novella**
Via della Scala 16.
**Map** 1 A4 (5 A1).
*(055) 21 62 76.*

### Markets

**Mercato Centrale**
*See p88.*

**Mercato delle Piante**
Pellicceria. **Map** 6 D3.
***Open*** *Sep–Jun: 8am–5pm Thu.*

**Mercato delle Pulci**
Piazza dei Ciompi.
**Map** 4 E1.
***Open*** *8:30am–12:30pm, 3:30–7:30pm Tue–Sat.*

**Mercato di San Lorenzo**
Piazza di San Lorenzo.
**Map** 1 C5 (6 D1).
***Open*** *Apr–Oct: 8am–8pm daily; Nov–Mar: 8am–8pm Tue–Sat.*

**Mercato Nuovo**
Calimala. **Map** 3 C1 (6 D3). ***Open*** *Apr–Oct: 9am–7pm daily; Nov–Mar: 9am–7pm Tue–Sat.*

# SURVIVAL GUIDE

# PRACTICAL INFORMATION

VISITORS HAVE BEEN coming to Tuscany for centuries, drawn by its magnificent art and architecture, landscape and cuisine. These may all seem overwhelming at first, so try to plan your stay to make the most of this beautiful region. Start your day early and take time over lunch: most sights and shops close for several hours and open again in the afternoon.

Tourist board logo

Try to have a relaxed attitude to your sightseeing – opening hours can be erratic and may vary depending on the season. Bear in mind that most Italians take their vacation in August, so some places may be closed. If your stay in Florence is brief, you could take a city tour. You can also combine your stay with study courses, offered year round by various colleges.

Evening concert in Piazza del Campo in Siena

## MUSEUMS AND MONUMENTS

MUSEUMS IN ITALY often have irregular opening times, so plan ahead to avoid disappointment. Most museums open in the morning and close all day Monday. Privately owned museums have various opening hours and often open later in the afternoon. There is usually an admission charge, but some museums offer discounts. However, in Florence, on most evenings between June and September, a different museum is open free of charge between 9pm and 11pm. Ask at the tourist office for more details. The booklet *Florence and its Surroundings* lists the different museums and is available at most tourist offices.

Museum opening times may vary, due to lack of staff, restoration *(chiuso per restauro)*, or a strike *(sciopero)*.

In Florence, an entry ticket can be purchased that admits you to several museums, including the Palazzo Vecchio and Museo di Firenze com'era. It is valid for six months and can be bought from any one of their ticket booths.

A musician with an accordion entertaining outside the Uffizi

## TOURIST INFORMATION

FLORENCE, PISA and Siena have several **Ufficio Informazioni Turistiche** (tourist offices), and most small towns have at least one. However, most offices only have details on their particular town. Travel agents such as **CIT**, **American Express** and **World Vision Travel** have information on local tours and offer guidance on rail and bus travel in Italy. If you want to plan ahead, it may be worth contacting **ENIT** (the Italian Tourist Board) in your country before you leave for Italy.

Sign for tourist information

## ENTERTAINMENT INFORMATION

THE BEST GUIDE for entertainment is the daily *La Nazione*. It has a supplement for Florence, Siena, Pisa and Empoli. In Florence, the monthly magazines *Firenze Spettacolo* and *Florence Today* have restaurant and café guides, as well as details of concerts, exhibitions, museums and sporting events.

Another useful booklet is *Concierge Information*, written in Italian and English and available from most hotels. Tourist offices often have a selection of brochures on local entertainment and events.

During the summer evenings, concerts with local bands are often held throughout Tuscany. Most of the

**Listings magazines for Florence**

nightspots are found in the cities and beach resorts, although you are likely to find a bar just about anywhere.

## Guided Tours

Tours around Florence can be arranged through travel agents including **CIT** and **American Express**. Tour guides can often speak various languages. Guides for private groups can be rented from the **Società Cooperativa Giotto**, which also has multilingual guides.

In Siena, **Balzana Viaggi** organizes tours to the Chianti area and Volterra. Tourist offices and travel agents throughout Tuscany have lists of authorized guides for city and regional tours.

**A guided tour of Florence**

## Etiquette

Efforts to speak a few words of Italian will be appreciated, although most of the big hotels have multilingual staff.

Italians drink in moderation, but smoking is common everywhere, except in movie theaters and on public transportation.

## Visiting Churches

Italians are strict on dress codes in churches, and you may be refused entry if you are wearing shorts or if your upper arms are bare. Some churches charge an entrance fee. Most are dark, so make sure you carry plenty of small change (L200, L500) for the automatic lights.

## Tipping

Service in restaurants is included in the price, unless otherwise stated *(see p252)*. However, foreigners are expected to tip. Keep L1,000 and L2,000 notes handy for taxi drivers, porters, doormen and sacristans.

## Disabled Travelers

Facilities for the disabled traveler in Tuscany are limited. If you book a package tour, representatives can assist in arranging help at airports and finding the most convenient hotel room.

Some intercity trains have special facilities for wheelchair users. Some stations, such as Santa Maria Novella, have elevators to help those with wheelchairs on and off trains, but arrangements must be made 24 hours in advance.

## Public Toilets

There are few public toilets in Tuscany. Many galleries and museums have toilets, and most bars and cafés will also let you use theirs.

## Useful Addresses

**American Express**
Via Dante Alighieri 22r
Florence.
**Map** 4 D1 (6 E3).
☎ *(055) 509 81.*

**Balzana Viaggi**
Via Montanini 73–75, Siena.
☎ *(0577) 28 50 13.*

**CIT**
Via Cavour 56r, Florence.
**Map** 2 D4 (6 D1).
☎ *(055) 29 43 06.*

**ENIT**
Via Marghera 2, Rome 00185.
☎ *(06) 497 11.*

**ENIT US**
30 Fifth Avenue, Suite 1565, NY
NY 10111. ☎ *(212) 245-4822.*

**Società Cooperativa Giotto**
Viale Antonio Gramsci 9a
Florence. **Map** 2 F4.
☎ *(055) 247 81 88.*

**Ufficio Informazioni Turistiche**
Via Cavour 1r
Florence. **Map** 2 D4 (6 D1).
☎ *(055) 29 08 32.*
Piazza del Campo 56, Siena.
☎ *(0577) 28 05 51.*
Piazza del Duomo, Pisa.
☎ *(050) 56 04 64.*

**World Vision Travel**
Lungarno degli Acciaiuoli 4
Florence. **Map** 3 C1 (5 C4).
☎ *(055) 29 52 71.*
Piazza Repubblica 3, Pisa.
☎ *(050) 58 10 14.*

## Horse-Drawn Carriages

This is a very pleasant way to spend an hour seeing the historic part of Florence. Carriages carry up to five people and can be rented in Piazza della Signoria and Piazza del Duomo. They can be expensive, so first negotiate a price and the length of the ride. Be sure to establish whether the price is per person, or for the whole carriage.

**Carriage at the Piazza della Signoria**

## Immigration and Customs

European union (EU) residents and visitors from the US, Canada, Australia and New Zealand do not need visas for stays of up to three months. However, all non-EU visitors need to bring a full passport. British citizens may use a Visitor's Card. A visa is needed for stays longer than three months. Vaccination certificates are not necessary.

All visitors to Italy should by law register with the police within three days of arrival. Most hotels will register visitors when they check in. If in doubt, contact a local police department or phone the **Questura**.

Duty-free allowances are as follows: non-EU residents can bring in either 400 cigarettes, 100 cigars, 200 cigarillos or 500 grams of tobacco; 1 liter of spirits and 2 liters of wine; 50 grams of perfume. Goods such as watches and cameras may be imported as long as they are for personal or professional use. EU residents no longer have to declare goods, but random checks are often made to guard against any drug traffickers.

The refund system for Valued Added Tax (IVA in Italy) for non-EU residents is complicated and is only worth reclaiming if you have spent at least L300,000 in a single establishment *(see p266)*.

## Renting Private Residences

If you are traveling with a family, renting a private residence can be an economical alternative to staying in hotels *(see p242)*. However, be prepared for small inconveniences – a common problem is a shortage of water.

Italy has retained the small shops culture, so you may have to go to several different shops to get your necessities. Fortunately, even the smallest village usually has a grocery store *(alimentari)*. Some shops may close for one or two hours during lunch *(see p266)*. Laundromats *(lavanderie)* will do your laundry.

Student relaxing in the sun in Gaiole in Chianti

## Addresses

Red street number

Blue street number

Florence has a confusing dual address system. Each street has a double set of numbers: a red number indicates a shop, restaurant or business, while a blue or black number refers to a hotel or domestic residence. When writing to a business, insert an "r" after the number to distinguish it from a residential address. Each set of numbers has its own sequence, so business premises at, say, No. 10r, may well be next to a residential address at No. 23.

## Student Information

An international student Identity Card (ISIC) or a YIEE (Youth International Educational Exchange Card) will usually get reductions on museums and other charges. For discount travel, go to the **Centro Turistico Studentesco (CTS)**. **Villa Europa Camerata** youth hostel provides listings of hostels in Tuscany.

Discount air and rail tickets, such as the Transalpino/BIJ rail tickets for those under 26, can be bought from the **Wasteels** office at Santa Maria Novella station in Florence, the CTS or any travel agent displaying the green Transalpino sign.

## Educational Courses

There are numerous language and art schools in Tuscany. **The British Institute** in Florence is one of the better known, as is the **Centro di Cultura per Stranieri dell'Università di Firenze**. The **Istituto per l'Arte e Restauro** offers courses on art, restoration, upholstery, ceramics, drawing and painting. The **Centro Internazionale Dante Alighieri** or the **Università per Stranieri** in Siena has courses on Italian culture, history and cooking. A list of schools in Tuscany is available from the **Ufficio Promozione Turistica, Turismo Sociale e Sport**.

## Newspapers, TV, Radio

Tuscany's main newspaper is *La Nazione*, with regional supplements. European and American newspapers and magazines are also available, and *USA Today* and the *International Herald Tribune* are available on the day of issue.

Newspaper stall selling national and international publications

LA NAZIONE
Firenze
Somalia: ucci
Ferrovie, deraglia l'accordo
Brucia la Rondinella

*La Nazione* **with supplement**

The state TV channels are RAI Uno, RAI Due and RAI Tre. Satellite and cable TV transmit European channels in many languages, as well as CNN news in English. BBC World Service is broadcast on radio on 15.070 MHz (short wave) in the mornings and 648 KHz (medium wave) at night.

### Embassies and Consulates

If you lose your passport or need other help, contact your national embassy or consulate as listed below.

### Electrical Adaptors

Electrical current in Italy is 220V AC, with two-pin, round-pronged plugs. It is probably better to buy an adaptor before leaving for Italy. Most hotels above three star have electrical outlets for shavers and hair dryers in all bedrooms.

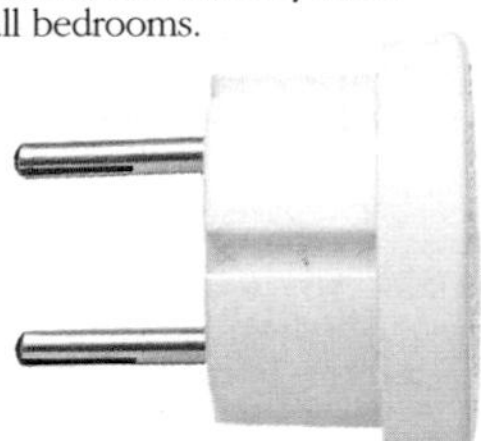

**Standard Italian plug**

### Tuscan Time

Tuscany is one hour ahead of Greenwich Mean Time (GMT). The time difference between Tuscany and other cities is as follows: London: -1 hour; New York: -6 hours; Perth: +7 hours; Auckland: +11 hours; Tokyo: +8 hours. These figures may vary for brief periods in the summer with local changes. For all official purposes the Italians use the 24-hour clock (eg 10pm = 22.00).

### Religious Services

The Florence Duomo has a mass in English at 5:30pm every Saturday *(see pp64–5)*. See below for other services.

### Conversion Table

**Imperial to Metric**
1 inch = 2.54 centimeters
1 foot = 30 centimeters
1 mile = 1.6 kilometers
1 ounce = 28 grams
1 pound = 454 grams
1 pint = 0.6 liters
1 US gallon = 3.8 liters

**Metric to Imperial**
1 centimeter = 0.4 inches
1 meter = 3 feet, 3 inches
1 kilometer = 0.6 miles
1 gram = 0.04 ounces
1 kilogram = 2.2 pounds
1 liter = 2.1 US pints

## Directory

### Immigration Information

**Questura**
Via Zara 2
Florence.
**Map** 2 D3.
*(055) 497 71.*

Via Castoro
Siena.
*(0577) 20 11 11.*

Via Lalli
Pisa.
*(050) 58 35 11.*

### Student Information

**Centro Turistico Studentesco**
Via de' Ginori 25r
Florence.
**Map** 2 D4 (6 D1).
*(055) 28 97 21.*

Via Angiolieri 49
Siena.
*(0577) 28 50 08.*

**Villa Europa Camerata**
Viale Augusto Righi 2–4
Florence.
*(055) 60 14 51.*

**Wasteels**
Santa Maria Novella Station, Florence. **Map** 1 B4 (5 B1). *(055) 28 06 83.*

### Educational Courses

**Centro di Cultura per Stranieri dell' Università di Firenze**
Via Vittorio Emanuele II 64
50134 Florence. **Map** 1 C1.
*(0577) 47 21 39.*

**Centro Internazionale Dante Alighieri**
La Lizza 10, 53100 Siena.
*(0577) 464 21.*

**Istituto per l'Arte e Restauro**
Palazzo Spinelli
Borgo Santa Croce 10
50134 Florence.
**Map** 4 D1 (6 F4).
*(055) 234 58 98.*

**The British Institute**
Lungarno Guicciardini 9
50125 Florence.
**Map** 3 B1 (5 B3).
*(055) 28 40 31.*

**Ufficio Promozione Turistica, Turismo Sociale e Sport**
Via Novoli 26
50127 Florence.
*(055) 438 21 11.*

**Università per Stranieri**
Piazzetta Grassi 2
53100 Siena.
*(0577) 492 60.*

### Embassies and Consulates

**Australia**
Via Alessandria 215, Rome.
*(06) 854 27 21.*

**New Zealand**
Via Zara 28, Rome.
*(06) 440 29 28.*

**UK**
Lungarno Corsini 2
Florence.
**Map** 3 B1 (5 B3).
*(055) 28 41 33.*

**US**
Lungarno Amerigo Vespucci 38, Florence.
**Map** 1 A5 (5 A2).
*(055) 239 82 76.*

### Religious Services

**American Episcopal**
Via Bernardo Rucellai 9
Florence. **Map** 1 A4.
*(055) 29 44 17.*

**Chiesa Evangelica Valdese**
Via Pier Antonio Micheli 26
Florence. **Map** 2 D3.
*(055) 247 78 00.*

**Church of England**
Via Maggio16, Florence.
**Map** 3 B2 (5 B5).
*(055) 29 47 64.*

**Jewish**
Tempio Israelitico
Via Luigi Farini 4, Florence.
**Map** 2 F5.
*(055) 24 52 52.*

**Methodist**
Via de' Benci 9, Florence.
**Map** 4 D2 (6 E4).
*(055) 29 26 73.*

# Personal Security and Health

TUSCANY AND ITS CITIES are generally safe as long as a few simple precautions are taken. As in many European cities, pickpockets are a common problem, especially around Florence and Pisa. Take extra care in crowded areas, particularly around popular tourist spots, and on buses. Leave valuables and any important documents in the hotel safe, and carry only the minimum amount of money necessary for the day. Make sure you take out adequate travel insurance before leaving for Italy, as it is very difficult to obtain once you are in the country.

**Florentine police officers helping a tourist with directions**

## Protecting Your Property

TRAVELER'S CHECKS OR Eurocheques are the safest way to carry large sums of money. Try to keep your receipts and traveler's checks separately, together with a photocopy of vital documents, in case of loss.

Be wary of pickpockets, especially around the Duomo and Santa Maria Novella in Florence, and around the Leaning Tower in Pisa. They are mainly children, operating in small groups, usually carrying newspapers or cardboard as a cover for their hands. "Fanny packs" or money belts are their favorite target, so try to keep them hidden. Thefts from cars are particularly common.

**Municipal police officer**

Buses are notorious for pickpockets. Be aware if someone bumps into you – they may be trying to distract you while somebody else takes your wallet. Bus No. 12/13 to Piazzale Michelangelo in Florence is a prime target, as are the buses to and from Pisa station.

To make an insurance claim you must report the theft to the police within 24 hours and obtain a statement *(denuncia)*.

## Personal Safety

ALTHOUGH THERE IS a fair amount of petty crime in the cities, such as pickpocketing and car theft, violent crime is rare. The streets are busy until late evening and women traveling alone are rarely harassed, and usually not very persistently. However, try to avoid badly lit areas late at night. Always use the official taxis, with the license number clearly displayed. When you call for a taxi, make sure you are given the code name of the driver, for example, Napoli 37.

## Police

THE VIGILI URBANI, or municipal police, wear blue uniforms in winter and white during the summer. They are most often seen in the streets regulating the traffic. The *carabinieri* are the military police. They dress in red-striped trousers and deal with a variety of offenses from theft to speeding. *La polizia* (the state police) wear blue uniforms, with white belts and berets. They specialize in serious crimes. Any of these should be able to help you.

### Emergency Numbers

**Ambulance**
Florence ☎ *(055) 21 22 22.*
Pisa ☎ *(050) 58 11 11.*
Siena ☎ *(0577) 28 00 28.*

**Automobile Club d'Italia** ☎ *116.*
*Car accidents and breakdowns.*

**Fire** ☎ *115.*

**General SOS** ☎ *113.*

**Medical Emergencies** ☎ *118.*

**Police** ☎ *112.*

**Traffic Police**
Florence ☎ *(055) 57 77 77.*
Pisa ☎ *(050) 58 05 88.*
Siena ☎ *(0577) 470 47.*

**A team of *carabinieri* in traffic police uniform**

## Personal Precautions

VISITORS FROM the European Union (EU) are officially entitled to reciprocal state medical care in Italy. Before you travel, pick up form E111 from the post office, which covers you for emergency medical treatment. You may want to take out additional medical insurance, as E111 does not cover repatriation costs or additional expenses, such as accommodation, food and flights for anyone traveling with you. Visitors from outside the EU should take out a comprehensive insurance policy that will cover them for emergency medical treatment.

Inoculations are not necessary for Tuscany, but take mosquito repellent, especially for the rural areas. One effective solution to repel mosquitos is a small electrical machine that burns a pill on a tiny hotplate. It repels insects for up to 12 hours and is available from most department stores, such as UPIM *(see p269)*. Also, do not underestimate the strength of the sun – drink plenty of water and use a high SPF sunscreen. You can drink the water from the taps but most Italians prefer bottled water.

## Medical Treatment

**Outside a Florentine pharmacy with red cross sign**

If you are in need of urgent medical attention, go to the *Pronto Soccorso* (outpatients) department of the nearest main hospital. Patients staying in hospitals are expected to supply their own silverware, plates, towels and toilet paper, but not bed linen. The nursing staff will also expect either friends or

**A volunteer for the Misericordia dressed in traditional black cassock**

relatives to help feed and wash hospital patients.

In Florence and Siena, the **Associazione Volontari Ospedalieri** has volunteer interpreters on call who can help with medical matters. The service is free and available in French, German and English. The **Tourist Medical Center** in Florence has English- and French-speaking doctors and specialists.

Dentists are expensive in Italy. You can find the nearest one in the yellow pages *(pagine gialle)*, or ask for a recommendation at your hotel.

Pharmacies in Tuscany rotate night and Sunday openings. Schedules are posted on their doors. The **Farmacia Comunale 13** at Florence's Santa Maria Novella station stays open 24 hours a day, as does the **Farmacia Molteni** in Via dei Calzaiuoli.

In Tuscany, the Misericordia *(see p193)* is one of the oldest charitable lay institutions in the world. It is responsible for a large part of the ambulance services. Most of the staff are trained volunteers, but there is also a team of fully qualified medical staff. Volunteers do not wear the traditional black cassock when out on a medical emergency.

**Ambulance run by the Misericordia, on the streets of Florence**

### Useful Information

**Associazione Volontari Ospedalieri**
Florence ☎ *(055) 40 31 26 or 234 45 67.*
Siena ☎ *(0577) 29 93 62.*

**Tourist Medical Center**
Via Lorenzo Il Magnifico 59 Florence.
**Map** 1 C3.
☎ *(055) 47 54 11.*

**Farmacia Comunale 13**
Santa Maria Novella station, Florence. **Map** 1 B4 (5 B1).
☎ *(055) 21 67 61.*

**Farmacia Molteni**
Via dei Calzaiuoli 7r, Florence.
**Map** 6 D3.
☎ *(055) 21 54 72.*

**Florence Hospital**
Arcispedale di Santa Maria Nuova.
Piazza di Santa Maria Nuova 1.
**Map** 6 F2.
☎ *(055) 275 81.*

**Siena Hospital**
Presidio Ospedaliero Santa Maria della Scala.
Piazza del Duomo.
☎ *(0577) 29 91 11.*

**Pisa Hospital**
Ospedale di Santa Chiara.
Via Roma 67.
☎ *(050) 59 21 11.*

**Lost Property Offices**
Via Circondaria 19, Florence.
**Map** 1 A1.
☎ *(055) 36 79 43.*
Via Castoro, Siena.
☎ *(0577) 20 11 11.*
Via Lalli, Pisa.
☎ *(050) 58 35 11.*

**Missing Credit Cards**
American Express.
☎ *(06) 722 82.*
Diners Club.
☎ *167 86 40 64 (toll-free).*
Eurocard, Access and Visa.
☎ *167 82 80 47 (toll-free).*

**Missing Traveler's Checks**
American Express.
☎ *167 87 20 00 (toll-free).*
Thomas Cook.
☎ *167 87 20 50 (toll-free).*
VISA.
☎ *167 87 41 55 (toll-free).*

# Banking and Local Currency

Visitors to Tuscany have a number of options available to them for changing money. Banks tend to give more favorable rates than bureaux de change, hotels and travel agents, but the paperwork is usually more time-consuming. Alternatively, credit cards or Eurocheques can be used for purchasing goods. When changing money you will need to show some form of identification, such as a passport. Try to keep a few coins in reserve for telephones, tips and for the coin-operated lights that illuminate works of art in churches.

**Exchange office at one of the Italian national banks**

## Changing Money

Banking hours can be erratic, especially the day before a bank holiday, so it is safest to acquire some local currency before you arrive. Exchange rates will vary from place to place, so you may want to shop around.

A more convenient way to change money is to use electronic exchange machines. These are found at Florence and Pisa airports, as well as in Florence and Siena. There are also some in smaller towns, such as San Gimignano. There are multilingual instructions and the exchange rate is displayed on the screen. You simply feed in up to ten notes of the same foreign currency, and you will get lire back.

## Cash Machines

Cash cards for US bank accounts may be used in cash machines displaying the appropriate system logo. Ask your bank for ATM locations before you travel.

Eurocheques, available to travelers with European bank accounts, can be used in cash machines with the Eurocheque logo or as direct payment for goods and services. The checks can also be cashed at most banks. A Eurocheque card will guarantee checks up to a maximum of L300,000.

**Eurocheque logo**

## Credit Cards

Credit cards are not as widely used in Italy as in the rest of Europe. However, most establishments in the cities will accept them. VISA and MasterCard (Access) are the most popular, followed by American Express and Diner's Club. Some banks and cash dispensers accept VISA or MasterCard for cash advances, but interest is payable as soon as the money is withdrawn. In Florence, banks with cash dispensers that accept credit cards are to be found around Piazza della Repubblica.

## Traveler's Checks

Traveler's checks are probably the safest way to carry large sums of money. Choose a well-known name such as Thomas Cook, American Express or checks issued through a major bank. There is a minimum commission charge, which may make changing small sums of money uneconomical. Some establishments will charge you for each check.

Check the exchange rates before you travel and decide whether, dollar or lire traveler's checks are more appropriate for your trip. Bear in mind that it may be more difficult to cash lire traveler's checks, especially in hotels, because it is not very profitable for the exchanger.

## Banking Hours

Banks are usually open between 8:30am–1:20pm, Mon–Fri. Most branches also open for an hour in the afternoon from about 2:45pm to 4pm. They close on weekends and for public holidays *(see p35)*, and they also close early the day before a major holiday. Exchange offices stay open longer but the rates are less favorable.

In Florence, the exchange office behind the station is open from 8am to late evening, depending on the season. In Pisa, the exchange offices in Piazza del Duomo and at the railway station stay open until the evening and on weekends.

## Using Banks

Changing money at a bank can at times be a frustrating process, as it inevitably involves endless forms and waiting in line. You must apply first at the window displaying the *cambio* sign, then go to the *cassa* to obtain your Italian money.

For security, most banks have electronic double doors. Press the button to open the outer door, then wait for it to close behind you. The inner door then opens automatically.

**Entering and leaving a bank through an electronic double door**

## CURRENCY

ITALY'S CURRENCY is the *lira* (plural *lire*) and is usually written as L or ₤. It became the national currency in the mid-19th century during Unification.

*Lira* means pound, so the English pound is referred to as the *lira sterlina.*

Telephone tokens *(gettoni)* have a value of L200 and can be used as ordinary coins. Initially, the thousands of units of currency seem very confusing, but the distinctive colors of the notes make distinguishing among them easy. Plans to alter the basic unit have not yet been put into practice, but you will generally find that the last three zeros are often ignored in spoken Italian: *cinquanta* will usually mean L50,000 and not, as you may think, L50.

Most shop and bar owners are not willing to accept large notes for small purchases, so you should try to get some small denomination notes when changing money.

**Bank Notes**

*Italian bank notes come in denominations of L100,000, L50,000, L10,000, L5,000, L2,000 and L1,000. Each one has a different color and a picture of a different historic person. Notes increase in size according to their value. The lira itself is never divided up into smaller units.*

1,000 lire

2,000 lire

5,000 lire

10,000 lire

50,000 lire

100,000 lire

**Coins**

*Coins, shown here at actual size, are in denominations of L500, L200, L100 and L50. Old L100 and L50 coins are still in use and there are L10 and L20 coins of minute value. Telephone* gettoni *are worth L200.*

50 lire (new) 100 lire (new) 500 lire

50 lire (old) 100 lire (old) 200 lire *Gettone* (200 lire)

# Using Tuscany's Telephones

THERE ARE PLENTY of public phones throughout Tuscany but telephoning, especially abroad, can at times be frustrating. Do not be surprised if you get a crossed line or if you get cut off in midconversation. There are phone kiosks on the streets of all main towns, and public phones can also be found in bars, tobacco stores and post offices.

## Telephone Offices

TELEPHONE OFFICES *(Telefoni)* are run by the Italian telecom companies SIP and ASST. When making international or long-distance calls you may find it easier to get a connection using one of these offices. Each *Telefoni* has several soundproof booths with a metered phone. You will be assigned a booth by an assistant, and your call will be metered once you are connected to the number you want. No premium is charged for this service, but the opening hours of *Telefoni* rarely coincide with Italy's low rate calling hours. The calls are measured in *scatti* (units) costing L200 per unit.

**Telephone sign**

Most major post offices and SIP offices throughout Tuscany have *Telefoni*, including Florence's main post office. The one at Florence station stays open until 8pm, and has telephone directories for all of Italy. There is a *Telefono* at Pisa train station, which is open until 9:45pm, and one at Pisa airport. The SIP office in Siena is at Via dei Termini 40.

To send an international telegram go to a post office or call **Italcable**.

**Italcable**
*1790.*

**Telephone company logo**

## Call Charges

CALLS WITHIN ITALY are cheapest between 10pm and 8am from Monday to Saturday and all day Sunday. It is also relatively inexpensive to call between 6:30pm and 10pm weekdays and after 1pm on Saturdays.

International calls within Europe are cheapest between 10pm and 8am and all day Sunday. Calls to Canada and the United States are cheapest from 11pm to 8am weekdays, and 11pm to 2pm on weekends. For Australia, call between 11pm and 8am Monday to Saturday and all day Sunday. There are no cheap rates for Japan.

Hotels will charge a higher rate to call from your room. Also, calls from Italy cost more than the equivalent call from the US or the UK.

## Using a SIP Coin and Card Telephone

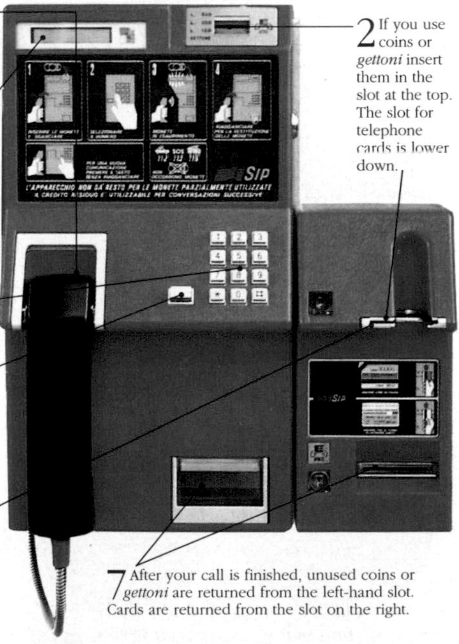

1 Lift the receiver and wait for the dial tone.

2 If you use coins or *gettoni* insert them in the slot at the top. The slot for telephone cards is lower down.

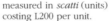

3 The display shows how much credit is left.

4 Dial the number and wait to be connected.

5 If you still have credit and want to make a second call, press the "follow-on call" button.

6 If your telephone card is about to expire, place a new one in the telephone card slot. When the old card expires, it will feed through automatically.

7 After your call is finished, unused coins or *gettoni* are returned from the left-hand slot. Cards are returned from the slot on the right.

**Telephone cards** have values of L5,000 or L10,000.

**To use a card,** break off the marked corner and insert, arrow first.

**L200** **L500**

**L100** ***Gettone***

### Reaching The Right Number

- Dialing codes are: Florence 055; Siena 0577; Pisa 050; Viareggio 0584; Arezzo 0575; Lucca 0583; and Pistoia 0573.
- European information is on 176.
- European operator assistance is on 15. You can make reverse charge and credit card calls on this number.
- Intercontinental operator assistance is on 170.
- General telephone information is on 1800.
- With the Italcable service you can dial directly to an operator in your own country to make a collect or credit card call. Dial 172 followed by: 0044 for UK; 1061 for Australia; 1011 for AT&T, US; 1022 for MCI, US; 1877 for US Sprint; 1001 for Canada.
- *See also* Emergency Numbers, *p276*.

**Telephone kiosk**

### Using Public Telephones

You can dial long-distance and international calls from SIP public telephones. When making long-distance calls, have at least L2,000 in change ready. If you don't put enough coins in to start with, the telephone disconnects you and retains your money. The most up-to-date payphones also take SIP telephone cards *(carta* or *scheda telefonica)*. You can buy these from bars, newspaper kiosks and tobacco shops displaying the black-and-white "T" sign.

The older-style phones, found in more remote villages, only accept tokens *(gettoni)*. *Gettoni* cost L200 each and can be bought from bars, newsagents and post offices. However, for long distance calls on older telephones it is best to find a metered phone. Ask a bar owner if you can use the phone and the meter will be set. You pay when you have finished your call.

**Telephone cards, *gettoni* and stamps are available from here**

## Sending Letters

The Italian postal service is notoriously inefficient. Expect anything sent abroad to take some time, especially during the August holiday season. Postcards to the UK can take up to a month if sent during the summer, and letters sent within Italy can take up to a week to reach their destination. For urgent or important communications, it is better to use the more expensive express system, which is quicker.

You can buy stamps *(francobolli)* from any tobacconist with the black-and-white "T" sign as well as from post offices. Branch post office hours are usually from 8:30am – 2pm, Mon–Fri and from 8:30am–noon on Saturday and the last day of the month. Main offices stay open until early evening.

**City letters** **Other destinations**

**Italian post box**

**Post Office sign**

### Sending Parcels

Sending parcels from Italy can be extremely difficult. Certain rules must be adhered to, otherwise your package will not be accepted for mailing. The package must be placed in a rigid box, wrapped in brown paper and bound with string and a lead seal. You will also need to fill in a simple customs declaration form. Often a stationery or gift shop in the major towns will, for a fee, wrap your package. Very few post offices offer this service.

### Poste Restante

Letters and parcels should be sent care of (c/o) Fermo Posta, Ufficio Postale Principale, then the name of the town in which you wish to pick them up. Print the surname clearly in block capitals and underline it to make sure the letters are sorted correctly. To collect your mail you need to show some form of identity and pay a small fee.

### Main Post Offices

Pellicceria 3, Florence. **Map** 6 D3.
*(055) 21 41 29.*

Piazza Matteotti 37, Siena.
*(0577) 28 30 17.*

Piazza Vittorio Emanuele II, Pisa.
*(050) 450 80.*

# TRAVEL INFORMATION

Alitalia aircraft

TUSCANY is most easily reached by air, but although planes arrive from European airports, there are no direct intercontinental flights, and visitors from outside Europe have to transfer. The nearest intercontinental airports are Milan and Rome. Tuscany's main airport is in Pisa; it receives both domestic and European flights as well as most charter traffic. Florence's airport is smaller and is located slightly north of the city, a short bus ride away from the center. Almost exclusively, it deals with scheduled flights. Florence is also the main arrival point for the far-reaching European train and bus network, and Pisa has good international rail connections. However, overland travel to Tuscany is much slower than flying, and the savings on cost are negligible. It is only worthwhile if you have particular reasons for doing so.

The main entrance hall at Pisa airport

## ARRIVING BY AIR

DIRECT FLIGHTS connect Pisa and Florence to London, Paris and Frankfurt all year round. There are also flights to Florence from Barcelona and Brussels. During the summer months, Pisa can be reached directly from Madrid, Manchester and Glasgow.

There are no direct intercontinental flights to Pisa or Florence, but you can transfer at Rome or Milan. Alitalia also run a fast (though expensive) train link between Rome Fiumicino airport and Florence. You may find it cheaper to get a budget flight to London, Paris or Frankfurt and transfer to another carrier.

Daily scheduled flights to Pisa are operated by **British Airways**, **Alitalia**, Air France and Lufthansa from London, Paris, Munich and Frankfurt. During the summer, Viva Air flies from Madrid, while companies such as Britannia operate charter flights all the year round from London.

**Air UK** operates a daily scheduled flight to Florence from London Stansted, and Meridiana flies direct from Gatwick and Barcelona. Sabena flies from Brussels.

APEX, PEX or SuperPEX fares generally offer the best deal in scheduled flights, but they must be purchased well in advance; at least 14 days in the UK and 21 days in the US.

The train station at Pisa's Galileo Galilei airport

They are subject to penalty clauses, so it is advisable to take out insurance against unforeseen cancellation. There are offices worldwide of the national travel agency, **CIT**, which should be able to help with budget travel. If you wish to book flights during your stay in Tuscany, travel agents such as CIT or the **American Express** office in Florence can help.

### USEFUL NUMBERS

**Air UK**
*(055) 28 40 43.*

**Alitalia**
Florence
*(055) 278 88.*
Pisa
*(050) 50 15 70.*

**British Airways**
*(055) 21 86 55.*

**TWA**
*(055) 239 68 56 or 28 46 91.*

**CIT**
Florence
*(055) 239 69 63.*
London
*081-686 0677.*
Sydney
*(2) 299 4754.*

**American Express**
Via Dante Alighieri 22r, Florence.
*(055) 509 81*

**Airport Information**
Florence
*(055) 37 34 98.*
Pisa
*(050) 50 07 07*

## Package Vacations

Package vacations are almost always cheaper than traveling independently, unless you are traveling on a very tight budget and prefer camping and youth hostels. Florence is often offered as part of a two- or three-center vacation with Rome and Venice, or with a stay in the Tuscan countryside. Different tour operators may use the same hotels in Florence, so it is worth looking around for the best deal. Transfer from the airport on arrival is usually included in the package price and saves both money and effort.

## Pisa Airport

**Sign to the trains at Pisa airport**

Trains run directly from Pisa's Galileo Galilei airport to Florence's Santa Maria Novella station. To reach the trains, turn left as you leave the airport arrivals hall. Train tickets can be bought from the information kiosk at the airport. The journey to Florence takes an hour, and the service runs at 40 minutes past the hour, but is less regular or frequent in the early morning and late evening. There is also an infrequent train serving Lucca and Montecatini.

The through train to Florence stops at Pisa Centrale, and Empoli, where you can change on to the local line that serves Siena.

**Cart attendant at Pisa airport**

The No. 7 bus runs from Pisa airport to the town center. Buy tickets before you get on the bus from the airport information kiosk. There is also a taxi rank at the front of the airport.

There are baggage carts at the airport, but you must have L2,000 ready to pay the attendant. You will need to buy some lire before landing, because there are no facilities available for changing money in the baggage claim hall.

## Florence Airport

Florence's Amerigo Vespucci airport, often known as Peretola, is very small. The local SITA bus *(see p287)* to the city center leaves from the front of the airport building. The service is timed to coincide with flight arrivals. There is usually one bus an hour between 9:40am and 10:30pm, and the journey takes 20 minutes. Buy tickets in advance from the bar at the airport.

Take only a taxi from the official rank. They will charge for the ride coming from the airport plus a charge for luggage. There is also an extra charge on Sundays and holidays.

Most drivers are honest, but check that the meter is switched on and showing the minimum fare before you begin your journey.

## Car Rental

All the major rental car firms have rental offices at both airports. However, it is wise to make rental arrangements before your departure *(see p290)*, because it will cost you far less than renting after you arrive in Italy.

Leaving Pisa airport by car, it is quickest to get on the two-lane highway linking Pisa and Florence. At Florence airport, it might be easier to take public transportation into the center and arrange to pick up your rental car there *(see p291)*.

## Airport Car Rental

**Avis**
Florence Airport ☎ *(055) 31 55 88.*
Pisa Airport ☎ *(050) 420 28.*

**Hertz**
Florence Airport ☎ *(055) 30 73 70.*
Pisa Airport ☎ *(050) 432 20.*

**Maggiore**
Florence Airport ☎ *(055) 31 12 56.*
Pisa Airport ☎ *(050) 425 74.*

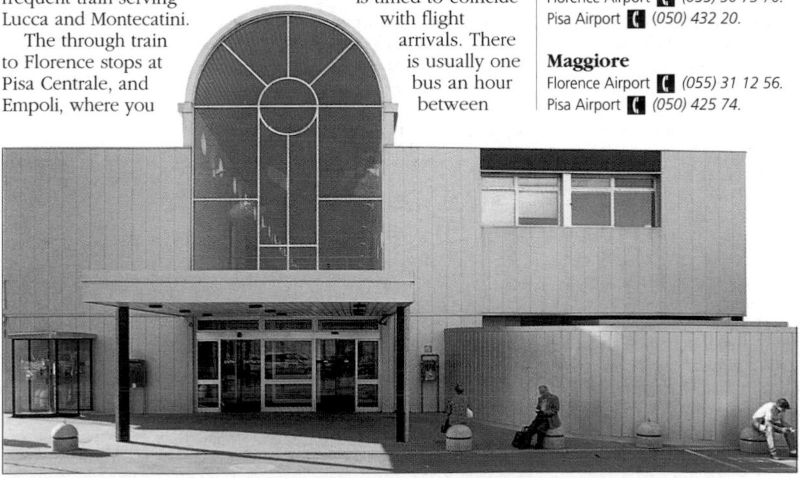

**Florence's Amerigo Vespucci airport, which has only recently started accepting international flights**

# Traveling by Train

TRAVELING OVERLAND can be a very pleasurable way of getting to and traveling around Tuscany. Italy's state railway (Ferrovie dello Stato, or FS) has a train for every type of journey, from the quaintly, maddeningly slow *locali* (stopping trains) through various levels of rapid intercity service to the luxurious, superfast *pendolino*, which rushes between Italian cities at a speed to match its ticket price. The network between large cities is very good, but journeys to towns on branch lines may be quicker by bus *(see p287)*.

An Alitalia train at Florence station

## Arriving by Train

FLORENCE AND PISA are the main arrival points for trains from Europe. The Galilei from Paris and the Italia Express from Frankfurt travel direct to Florence. Passengers from London have to change in Paris or Ostend.

From Florence, there is also a direct Alitalia train link with Rome's Fiumicino airport, but this is very expensive.

Europe-wide train passes, such as EurRail (US), or Inter-Rail for those under 26 (Europe), are accepted on the FS network. You may have to pay a supplement, however, to travel on fast trains. Always check first before using any private rail lines.

A *pendolino* – Italy's fastest train

## Train Travel in Italy

TRAINS FROM all over Italy arrive at and depart from Pisa Centrale and Florence's Santa Maria Novella station *(see p286)*, while the *pendolino* uses Florence's Rifredi station. If you are planning to travel around, there are passes that allow unlimited travel on the FS network. These include a travel-at-will ticket *(biglietto turistico libera circolazione)* for non-residents, available from the station; and the *biglietto chilometrico*, which allows 20 trips totaling no more than 3,000 km (1,865 miles) for up to four people, so a family of four could make five trips. These are available from international and Italian **CIT** offices *(see p282)*, and from any travel agent selling train tickets. There are facilities for disabled travelers on some intercity services *(see p273)*.

## Making Reservations

BOOKING AHEAD IS obligatory on the *pendolino* and on some other intercity services, indicated on the schedule by a black R on a white background. The booking office is at the front of Florence station. Be prepared for long lines: telephone reservations are not accepted. Travel agents can book your railway tickets free of charge.

Reservations are advisable if you wish to travel at busy times: during the high season or on weekends. Buying your intercity ticket at least five hours before traveling entitles you to a free seat reservation, well worth it when trains get very crowded. For a small fee, you can reserve a seat on any train, except local trains.

## Booking Agents

**CIT Viaggi**
Piazza della Stazione 51, Florence.
**Map** 1 B5 (5 B1). ☎ *(055) 239 69 63.*

**Seti Viaggi**
Piazza del Campo 56, Siena.
☎ *(0577) 28 30 04.*

**World Vision Travel**
Lungarno Acciaiuoli 4, Florence.
**Map** 3 C1 (5 C4). ☎ *(055) 29 52 71.*
Piazza della Repubblica 3, Pisa.
☎ *(050) 58 10 14.*

## Tickets

ALWAYS BUY a ticket before you travel. You can pay on the train, but you will be surcharged by at least L6,000 and a percentage of the ticket price. You can upgrade to first class or sleeper by paying the conductor.

If the ticket office is busy, try one of the self-service ticket machines found at most stations. They accept L100, L200 and L500 coins, and

Ticket windows at Florence's Santa Maria Novella station

notes up to L50,000. There are instructions in six European languages.

If you are traveling no more than 200 km (124 miles), you can buy a short-range ticket *(biglietto a fasce chilometriche)* from a station newsstand. Your station of departure will usually be stamped on the ticket, but if it is not, write it on the back. You must then validate the ticket by stamping it in one of the gold-colored machines situated at the entrance to most platforms. These machines must also be used to time-stamp the return portion of a ticket. Both the outward and return portions of a round-trip ticket must be used within three days of purchase. One-way tickets are issued in 200-km (124-mile) "bands" and are valid according to band: for example, a ticket for 200 km lasts for a day, a ticket for 400 km (250 miles) lasts for two days, and so on.

On all intercity trains you must pay a supplement *(supplemento)* even if you have an InterRail card. This includes the *pendolino* and Eurocity services. The cost depends on the distance.

### Tickets for Local Journeys

*Ask at newsstands at the station for a* biglietto a fasce chilometriche *to the destination you require.*

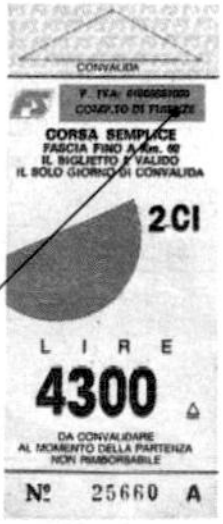


**Station of departure**

**Stamp ticket here**

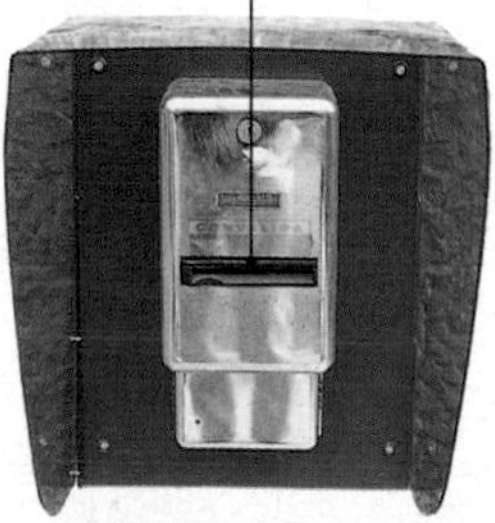

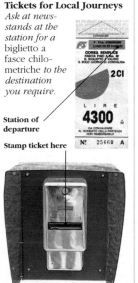

**Machine for validating tickets**

## Machines for FS Rail Tickets

These machines are easy to use, and most have instructions in six languages on a printed panel.

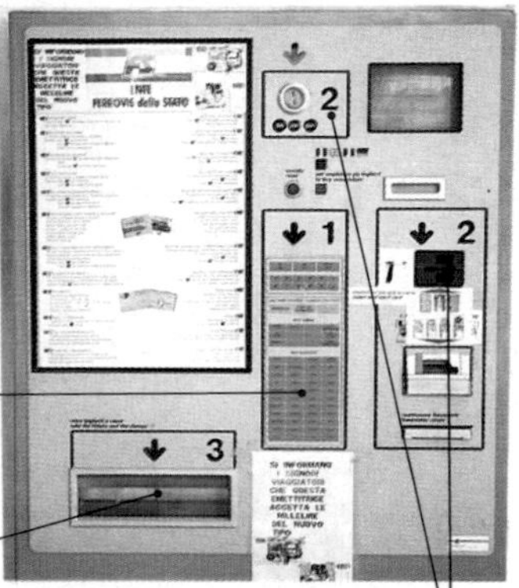

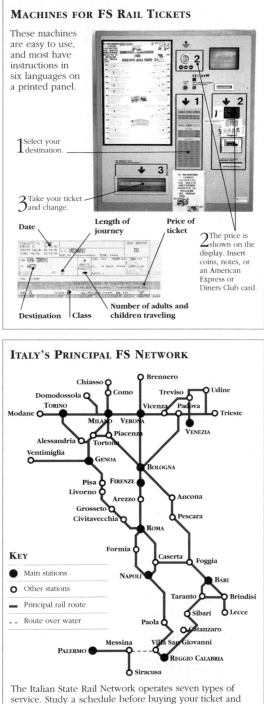

1 Select your destination.

2 The price is shown on the display. Insert coins, notes, or an American Express or Diners Club card.

3 Take your ticket and change.

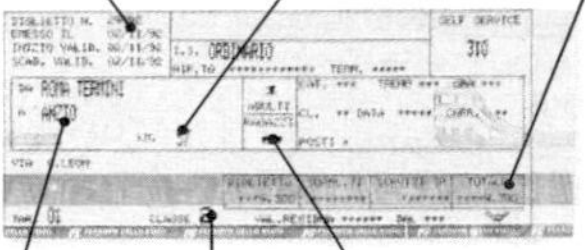

**Date**

**Length of journey**

**Price of ticket**

**Destination**

**Class**

**Number of adults and children traveling**

## Italy's Principal FS Network

**Key**

- Main stations
- Other stations
- Principal rail route
- Route over water

The Italian State Rail Network operates seven types of service. Study a schedule before buying your ticket and choose a service to suit both your pocket and agenda.

## Santa Maria Novella Station, Florence

Santa Maria Novella station is Florence's central railway station, although the *pendolino (see p284)* uses Firenze Rifredi. Santa Maria Novella is always busy, and like most major termini attracts some unsavory characters; it is not a place to linger. There is a taxi rank at the front, and local buses *(see p288)* depart from the side of the station.

In summer, long lines form at the main ticket office, so it is worth tackling the self-service machines *(see p285)*. There is another ticket office, usually less crowded, on platform *(binario)* 16.

The baggage check office *(deposito bagagli)* is also on platform 16, as is a Wasteels student travel office *(see p274)*, and the *Polfer*, the railway police.

The large train information office has do-it-yourself international information machines: you key in your destination, and it prints out a relevant schedule. There are display screens for national train information in the station foyer, with multi-lingual instructions. Line up for the staffed information booths, take a ticket and wait for your number to come up. There are some staff who speak French and English.

Other facilities in the foyer include a 24-hour pharmacy, an office with a hotel booking service and stalls selling international magazines, papers and city bus tickets. The international telephone office is near platform 5, where there is an air terminal for Pisa airport *(see p283)*. There is a bank and a bureau de change inside the station, and in the ticket office foyer there is also an automatic exchange machine.

**Do-it-yourself help points with train information on screens**

**Tourist information office outside Santa Maria Novella station, Florence**

The tourist information office is outside the station: you should leave by the exit nearest the pharmacy, cross to the walkway and walk to your right to the gray marble building at the end.

**Entrance to Santa Maria Novella station, with departure board**

## Siena Station

Situated outside the city walls on Piazzale Carlo Roselli, Siena station is quite small and is about a 20-minute walk from the center. Buses Nos. 2, 3, 4, 6, 9 and 10 leave from opposite the station for the city center.

Train information is available at the ticket office, and there are also automatic help points with information available in English, French and German. Other facilities include a baggage check office, a snack bar and a newspaper stand. In addition to the services leaving from the city center, the TRA-IN bus company runs some buses to Montepulciano, Montalcino and Buonconvento. These depart from the front of the station. Tickets must be bought from the bus ticket window or self-service machines in the station foyer before you board.

## Pisa Centrale

Pisa's central station is fairly large, with most of the usual facilities situated either in the foyer or on platform 1: a restaurant and bar, newspaper kiosks that sell bus tickets and telephone cards, and several do-it-yourself information and self-service ticket machines.

An exchange booth, open until 7pm, is on the left of the foyer, along with the train information and booking office. The international telephone office, which is open until 9:45pm, is on the right. The baggage check office and the *Polfer* (railway police) are on platform 1.

The tourist information office is out at the front of the station, near the Banca Nazionale di Lavoro. Most local buses, including the No. 1 for the Campo dei Miracoli *(see pp154–5)* and No. 7 for the airport, stop in front of the station. You will find a bus information and ticket office close to the bus stops, on your right as you leave the station. There is also a machine selling tickets. There is another station at Pisa airport *(see p283)*.

# Traveling by Bus

Lazzi bus, for travel all over Italy

FLORENCE IS LINKED by bus to most major European cities and local companies operate an extensive network of services within Tuscany. Buses are quicker where there is no direct train link, particularly in the countryside. Although the train is faster for long journeys, the bus may be cheaper. To plan trips around Tuscany by bus, maps and schedules are available from all the bus companies' offices, which you will usually find situated near city railway stations.

## ARRIVING BY BUS

SANTA MARIA NOVELLA railway station in Florence is Tuscany's main arrival and departure point for all long-distance bus journeys, and the hub of the extensive local bus network. The **Lazzi** company runs bus links with many major European cities from Florence and sells tickets for Euroline buses. Reserve tickets at their office by Santa Maria Novella station. Express services to Rome are run by Lazzi from Florence and **TRA-IN** from Siena.

## FLORENCE

FLORENCE HAS FOUR main bus companies. Lazzi serves the region north and west of Florence and **SITA** serves the southern and eastern region. The **COPIT** bus company connects the city with the Abetone/Pistoia region and **CAP** links Florence to the Mugello area north of the city. All these companies have ticket and information offices a stone's throw from Santa Maria Novella railway station.

## SIENA

SIENA'S MAIN BUS company is TRA-IN, which runs urban and local as well as long-distance regional services. Local services leave from Piazza Antonio Gramsci and regional buses from Piazza San Domenico. There is an information/ticket office in both squares. TRA-IN operates buses to most parts of Tuscany, as well as a direct bus to Rome twice daily.

Lazzi office in Florence

## PISA

THE CITY BUS COMPANY **APT** also serves the areas around Volterra, Pontedera, Livorno and San Miniato. These buses leave from Piazza Sant'Antonio, where there is an APT office. **Lazzi** runs a service to Viareggio, Lucca and Florence from Pisa, departing from Piazza Vittorio Emanuele II, which has a Lazzi ticket office.

## DIRECTORY

### FLORENCE

**CAP**
Largo Fratelli Alinari 9. **Map** 1 C4 (5 B1). *(055) 21 46 37.*

**COPIT**
Piazza di Santa Maria Novella 22r. **Map** 1 B5 (5 B2). *(055) 21 54 51.*

**Lazzi**
Piazza della Stazione. **Map** 1 B5 (5 B2). *(055) 21 51 54 (Tuscany); (055) 21 51 55 (national).*

**SITA**
Via di Santa Caterina da Siena 15r. **Map** 1 B5 (5 A1). *(055) 48 36 51 (Tuscany); (055) 21 47 21 (national).*

### SIENA

**TRA-IN**
Piazza Antonio Gramsci *(local);* Piazza San Domenico *(regional).* *(0577) 20 41 11 (all services).*

### PISA

**APT**
Via Cesare Battisti 55. *(050) 233 84.*

**Lazzi**
Piazza Vittorio Emanuele II. *(050) 462 88.*

One of Florence's bus lines

SITA bus arriving at the station in Florence

# Getting Around on Foot and by Bus

Pedestrian zone sign

TUSCAN CITIES are compact enough to get around reasonably comfortably on foot. City buses cover the city well, and service is cheap and regular. A single ticket will take you up to 15 km (10 miles) out of town, making the bus ideal for trips from the city center to outlying areas of Florence, Pisa or Siena. The buses get very hot in the summer and are popular with pickpockets, so take care when they're crowded.

## WALKING

SIGHTSEEING ON FOOT in Tuscan cities is made all the more pleasurable by the fact that there are plenty of squares in which to rest and watch the world go by, or cool churches to pop into when the heat gets too much. Moreover, there are limited-traffic zones in the center of most towns, which makes life slightly easier for pedestrians.

Signs for sights and landmarks are usually quite clear, especially those in Siena. In Florence it is easy to pick out the Duomo and the river and orient yourself in relation to them. A gentle stroll around the main sights of Florence can take just a couple of hours. The Duomo, Santa Maria Novella, Ponte Vecchio and the Accademia are all within ten minutes' walk of one another. The main sights in Pisa are all in the same square. Siena is also compact but hilly, so be sure to wear comfortable shoes.

The cities can, however, be unbearably hot in summer. Plan your day so that you are inside for the hottest part. Recuperate Italian-style, with a leisurely lunch followed by a siesta. Shopping is more pleasant in the early evening when it is cooler, and the streets start to come alive.

**Signposting for pedestrian routes to sights in Florence**

## CROSSING ROADS

USE THE *sottopassaggio* (underpass) wherever possible. The busiest roads also have signals to help you cross: the green *avanti* sign gives you right of way, in theory, but *never* expect drivers to recognize this as a matter of course. Seize your opportunity and walk out slowly and confidently, glaring at the traffic and maintaining a determined pace: the traffic should stop or at least swerve. Take extra care at night: traffic lights are switched to flashing amber and crossings become free-for-alls.

**Stay on the pavement at all costs**

**It is marginally less dangerous to cross**

## CITY BUSES

FLORENCE'S CITY BUS company is called **ATAF**, Pisa's is **APT**, and Siena's **TRA-IN**. All the buses are bright orange. Most lines run until at least 9:30pm, with the most popular running until midnight or 1am in Florence.

In Siena, the narrow streets keep buses from going close to the center, but in Pisa and Florence, buses run near all the main sights. Among the most useful Florentine routes for visitors are the No. 12 and No. 13, which make hour-long clockwise/counterclockwise circuits of the city, and the No. 7 to Fiesole.

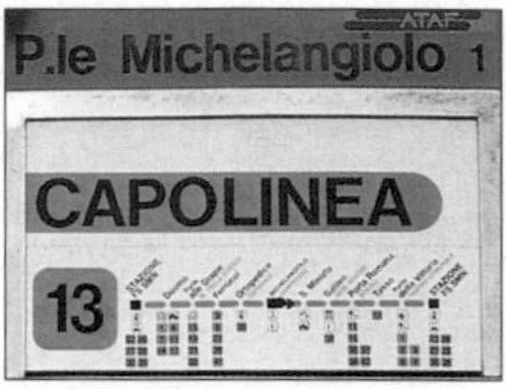


**Bus stop displaying the route**

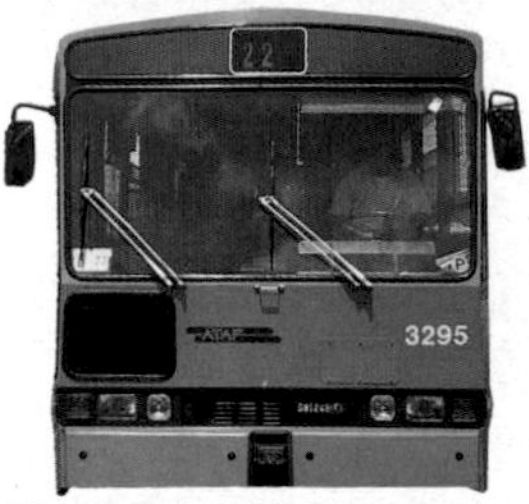


**Florence's No. 22 bus from the station to Piazza della Repubblica**

## USING LOCAL SERVICES

FLORENCE DOES NOT HAVE a main terminus, but most buses can be picked up alongside Santa Maria Novella station. In Pisa, most buses stop at the railway station and Piazza Vittorio Emanuele II; in Siena, at Piazza Antonio Gramsci and Piazza San Domenico. There are bus information kiosks at all these points, but they are not always open. Tourist information offices can usually help.

Using Italian buses is an art. The theory is to enter the bus at the front or back and get off through the middle doors. In practice, you have to struggle on and off wherever you can when the bus is full. Fare dodging is common, but so are inspectors. The fine is 50 times the cost of a ticket.

## BUS TICKETS

TICKETS FOR CITY BUSES must be bought before you travel, from newsstands, bars displaying the bus company sign (ATAF, APT, TRA-IN) or tobacco shops, or at the bus termini. If you are likely to make a few trips, buy several tickets at once; they become valid when you time-stamp them in the machine at the front or rear of the bus.

There are also ticket vending machines in the streets, usually near stops, which take any coins and L1,000 and L5,000 notes.

Ticket prices and validity vary from town to town. You can usually buy a ticket valid for one, two or sometimes four hours' unlimited travel. The time limit starts when you stamp your ticket on the first bus. You can also buy daily passes, or a *tesserino* consisting of one or two tickets, each valid for a number of rides. A *tesserino* is slightly cheaper than the same number of single tickets. You just stamp it as and when needed until you have made the permitted number of trips.

### Long-Term Passes

If you are staying for a long time in one town, a monthly pass for unlimited travel is a good idea. In Florence and Siena, you need an identity card with your photograph. These are available for a small charge from the **Ufficio Abbonamenti** on the walkway by Santa Maria Novella station. Make sure you take along two photos and your passport. In Siena, photocards are available from the TRA-IN office in Piazza San Domenico. Once you have the photocard you can buy monthly passes wherever bus tickets are on sale.

If you are not resident in Tuscany, you can buy a *carta arancio*, valid for seven days on trains and all bus lines within the province of Florence, covering trips to, say, Vallombrosa, Empoli, Vinci and Certaldo. You can buy it from any train, coach or bus company ticket office.

**Main bus stop at Florence's Santa Maria Novella station**

**Ticket valid for 2 hours**

**Price varies with journey time**

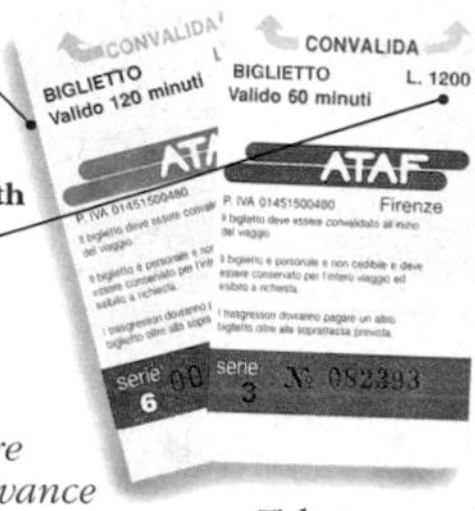


**Validating Tickets**

*Bus tickets are bought in advance and only become valid when stamped in special machines on the bus.*

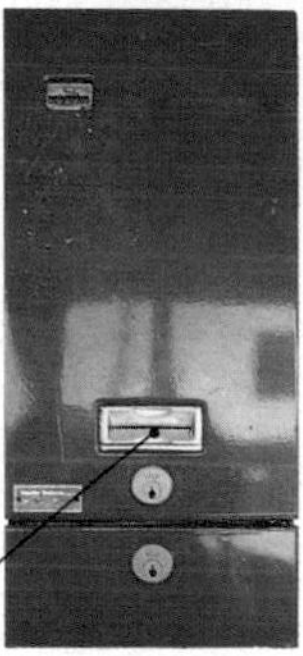

**Ticket inserted here**

**Stamping machine**

### Useful Addresses

**ATAF**
Ufficio Informazioni, Piazza della Stazione, Florence. **Map** 1 B5 (5 B1).
*(055) 58 05 28.*

**APT**
Ufficio Informazioni, Via Cesare Battisti 56, Pisa. *(050) 233 84.*

**TRA-IN**
Piazza Antonio Gramsci, Siena.
*(0577) 20 41 11.*

**Ufficio Abbonamenti ATAF**
Piazza Adua, Florence. **Map** 1 B4.

### Taxis in Tuscany

Official taxis are white in Tuscan cities, with a "Taxi" sign on the roof. Only take taxis at official ranks, not offers from strangers at the stations. There are added charges for baggage, for rides between 10pm and 7am, on Sundays and on public holidays, and for journeys to and from the airport. If you phone for a taxi, the meter starts to run from the moment you book the taxi; by the time it arrives, there could already be several thousand lire clocked up. Generally, traveling by taxi is costly. Taxi drivers are usually honest, but make sure you know what any extra costs are for. Italians give very small tips or nothing at all, but 10 percent is expected from visitors.

In Florence, there are ranks at Via Pellicceria, Piazza di Santa Maria Novella and Piazza di San Marco. In Siena, taxis can be found in Piazza Matteotti and Piazza della Stazione, and in Pisa at the Piazza del Duomo, Piazza Garibaldi and Piazza della Stazione.

**Taxi waiting for a fare at an official rank in Florence**

#### Booking Numbers

**Florence Radiotaxi**
*(055) 47 98 or 42 42 or 43 90.*

**Siena Radiotaxi**
*(0577) 492 22.*

**Pisa Radiotaxi**
*(050) 54 16 00.*

# Driving in Florence and Tuscany

The classic Fiat 500

A DRIVING TOUR through Tuscany makes a memorable trip, if you are prepared for high fuel costs and erratic Italian driving. But if you are staying in Siena or Florence, with no plans to travel around, there is little point in having a car: both are small enough to walk around and parking can be difficult and expensive. If you are staying in the countryside and visiting towns by car, it is best to park on the outskirts and walk or take a bus into the center.

## Arriving by Car

DRIVERS FROM THE United States should ideally have an international driver's license. Fill out an application form (available from your travel agent) and submit it with the required photos. Allow 30–60 days for delivery.

The **ACI (Automobile Club d'Italia)** provides excellent maps and invaluable help. It will tow anyone free, and offers free repairs to members of affiliated associations, such as the Automobile Association of America (AAA), the AA or RAC in Britain, the ADAC in Germany, the AIT in France, the RACE in Spain and ANWB in Holland. SOS columns on highways allow instant, round-the-clock access to the emergency services.

## Car Rental

CAR RENTAL in Italy is expensive and should be organized through a travel agent before leaving for Tuscany. Cars can be reserved through any rental company with branches in Italy. If you rent a car when you are in Tuscany, a local firm such as **Maggiore** may be cheaper.

To rent a car you must be over 21 and have held a license for at least a year. Visitors from outside the EU need an international license, though in practice rental companies may not insist.

Make sure the rental price includes collision damage waiver, breakdown service and both car and contents theft insurance.

Getting around Florence by scooter

## Bike and Moped Rental

A DAY SPENT cycling around a town such as Lucca (where cycles can be rented from the tourist office) or out in the countryside can be delightful, and a moped or scooter makes lighter work of the Tuscan hills. Bicycles can be rented for around L3,000 per hour or L15,000 for the day; moped prices start at about L35,000 per day. You may have to leave a credit card as a deposit.

## Driving in Town

CITY CENTERS are usually fraught with one-way systems, limited traffic zones and erratic drivers, and are only recommended for the confident driver. In Lucca, Siena and San Gimignano, only residents and taxis may drive inside the city walls. Visitors may go in to unload at their hotel but must then park outside the walls.

Pisa has limited traffic zones around the Arno, and the rule for tourists unloading also applies in Florence, with its *zona traffico limitato* or *zona blu*, which covers most of the center. There is a pedestrian zone around the Duomo, although pedestrians here should be prepared, nevertheless, to step aside for taxis, mopeds and bicycles. The latter two often do not comply with traffic light instructions.

**Rules of the Road**

*Drive on the right and, generally, yield to the right. Seat belts are compulsory in the front and back, and children should be properly restrained. You must also carry a warning triangle in case of breakdown. In town centers, the speed limit is 50 km/h (30 mph); on ordinary roads 90 km/h (55 mph); and on highways 110 km/h (70 mph) for cars up to 1099cc, and 130 km/h (80 mph) for more powerful cars. Penalties for speeding include spot fines and license points, and there are drunk-driving laws as elsewhere in the EU.*

One-way street

Speed limit (on minor road)

End of speed restriction

Pedestrianized street – no traffic

Yield to oncoming traffic

Yield 320 m (350 yd) ahead

Danger (often with description)

**Automatic tollbooths on the highway outside Florence**

## Parking

Official parking areas are marked by blue lines, usually with meters or an attendant nearby. There are two large underground parking garages in Florence: at Santa Maria Novella station, open daily 6:30am until 1am; and on the northeast side of Piazza della Libertà.

The *disco orario* system allows free parking for a fixed period, mainly outside city centers. Set the disk to your time of arrival and you then usually have one or two hours *(un'ora* or *due ore)*. Rental cars have disks; gas stations also sell them.

**Parking disk**

If you park illegally, your car could be towed away. In Tuscany, one day a week is set aside for street cleaning, and parking is forbidden. This is indicated by signs saying *zona rimozione* with the day and time. Beware of residents-only parking areas, marked *riservato ai residenti.* If your car is towed away, phone the **Vigili**, the municipal police, to find out where it has been taken.

**Official parking area patrolled by attendant**

## Driving in the Countryside

Driving on the quiet Tuscan country roads can be a pleasure. However, distances can be deceptive. What looks like a short trip on the map may take much longer because of winding roads. Some back roads may not be surfaced, so beware of blowouts. You may also find driving at night disorienting as roads and signs are poorly lit.

## Tolls and Gasoline

Tolls operate on all highways north of Rome, although there are a couple of free two-lane highways in Tuscany. Tollbooths take cash or prepaid magnetic "swipe" cards called Viacards, available from tobacconists and ACI.

Highway service stations occur at irregular intervals, and there are fewer gas stations in the countryside than the cities. Few outside the cities take credit cards. Many close at noon and reopen about 3:30pm until about 7:30pm; few open on Sundays and many in the countryside close in August.

At gas stations with self-service pumps, put L10,000 notes in the machine. Lead-free gas is *senza piombo.*

## Directory

### City Car Rental

**Avis**
Borgo Ognissanti 128r, Florence.
**Map** 1 A5 (5 A2).
☎ *(055) 21 36 29.*
c/o de Martino Autonoleggi
Via Simone Martini 36, Siena.
☎ *(0577) 27 03 05.*

**Hertz**
Via Maso Finiguerra 33, Florence.
**Map** 1 B5 (5 A2).
☎ *(055) 239 82 05.*

**Maggiore**
Via Maso Finiguerra 11r, Florence.
**Map** 1 B5 (5 A2).
☎ *(055) 21 02 38.*

### Cycle and Moped Rental

**Motorent**
Via Zanobi 9r, Florence.
☎ *(055) 49 01 13.*

**Ufficio Turismo**
Piazzale Giuseppe Verdi, Lucca.
☎ *(0583) 41 96 89.*

**Bici-Bike**
Via della Spina 25, Pisa.
☎ *(050) 202 00.*

**DF Moto**
Via dei Gazzoni 14, Siena.
☎ *(0577) 415 59.*

### Breakdowns

**Automobile Club d'Italia**
Viale G. Amendola 36, Florence.
**Map** 4 F1. ☎ *(055) 248 61.*
Via San Martino 1, Pisa.
☎ *(050) 59 86 00.*
Viale Vittorio Veneto 47, Siena.
☎ *(0577) 490 01.*

Emergencies ☎ *116.*

### Towing

**Vigili (Municipal Police)**
Florence ☎ *(055) 328 31.*
Pisa ☎ *(050) 50 14 44.*
Siena ☎ *(0577) 29 25 50.*

### 24-Hour Gas Stations, Florence

**AGIP**
Via di Rocca Tedalda.

**MOBIL**
Via Pratese.

# General Index

# D

# G

# L



# M

## S

# T

# U



# V

## W



## Y



## Z

# Acknowledgments

DORLING KINDERSLEY would like to thank the following people whose contributions and assistance have made the preparation of this book possible.

### MAIN CONTRIBUTOR

Christopher Catling has been visiting Florence and Tuscany for 20 years since his first archeological dig there while he was a student at Cambridge University. He is the author of several guide books on the city and region.

### ADDITIONAL PHOTOGRAPHY

Jane Burton, Philip Dowell, Neil Fletcher, Steve Gorton, Frank Greenaway, Neil Mersh, Poppy, Clive Streeter.

### ADDITIONAL ILLUSTRATIONS

Gillie Newman, Chris D. Orr, Sue Sharples, Ann Winterbotham, John Woodcock, Martin Woodward.

### CARTOGRAPHY

Colourmap Scannning Limited; Contour Publishing; Cosmographics; European Map Graphics. Street Finder maps: ERA Maptech Ltd. (Dublin), adapted with permission from original survey and mapping by Shobunsha (Japan).

### CARTOGRAPHIC RESEARCH

Caroline Bowie, Peter Winfield, Claudine Zante.

### DESIGN AND EDITORIAL ASSISTANCE

Louise Abbott, Rosemary Bailey, Julee Binder, Hilary Bird, Lucia Bronzin, Cooling Brown Partnership, Vanessa Courtier, Camela Decaire, Joy FitzSimmons, Natalie Godwin, Steve Knowlden, Neil Lockley, Georgina Matthews, Alice Peebles, Andrew Szudek, Dawn Terrey, Tracy Timson, Daphne Trotter, Glenda Tyrrell, Nick Turpin, Janis Utton, Alastair Wardle, Fiona Wild.

### SPECIAL ASSISTANCE

Antonio Carluccio; Sam Cole; Julian Fox, University of East London; Simon Groom; Signor Tucci at the Ministero dei Beni Culturali e Ambientali; Museo dell'Opificio delle Pietre Dure; Signora Pelliconi at the Soprintendenza per i Beni Artistici e Storici delle Province di Firenze e Pistoia; Prof. Francesco Villari, Direttore, Istituto Italiano di Cultura, London.

For special assistance in supplying the computer-generated image of the Gozzoli frescoes in the Palazzo Medici Riccardi: Dr. Cristina Acidini, Head of Restoration, and the restorers at Consorzio Pegasus, Firenze; Ancilla Antonini of Index, Firenze; and Galileo Siscam SpA, Firenze, producers of the CAD Orthomap graphic program.

### PHOTOGRAPHIC REFERENCE

Camisa I & Son, Carluccio's, Gucci Ltd.

### PHOTOGRAPHY PERMISSIONS

DORLING KINDERSLEY would like to thank the following for their permission to photograph: **FLORENCE**: Badia Fiorentina; Biblioteca Mediceo-Laurenziana; Biblioteca Riccardiana; Centro Mostra di Firenze; Comune di Firenze; Duomo; Hotel Continental; Hotel Hermitage; Hotel Villa Belvedere; Le Fonticine; Museo Bardini; Museo di Firenze com'era; Museo Horne; Museo Marino Marini; Museo dell'Opera del Duomo di Firenze; Ognissanti; Palazzo Vecchio; Pensione Bencistà; Rebus; Santi Apostoli; Santa Croce; San Lorenzo; Santa Maria Novella; Santa Trìnita; Soprintendenza per i Beni Ambientali e Architettonici delle Province di Firenze e Pistoia; Tempio Israelitico; Trattoria Angiolino; Ufficio Occupazioni Suolo Pubblico di Firenze; Villa La Massa; Villa Villoresi. **TUSCANY**: Campo dei Miracoli, Pisa; Collegiata, San Gimignano; Comune di Empoli; Comune di San Gimignano; Comune di Vinci; Duomo, Siena; Duomo, Volterra; Museo della Collegiata di Sant'Andrea, Empoli; Museo Diocesano di Cortona; Museo Etrusco Guarnacci, Volterra; Museo Leonardiano, Vinci; Museo dell'Opera del Duomo, Pisa; Museo dell'Opera del Duomo, Siena; Museo delle Sinopie, Pisa; Opera della Metropolitana di Siena; Opera Primaziale Pisana, Pisa; Soprintendenza per i Beni Ambientali e Architettonici di Siena; Soprintendenza per i Beni Artistici e Storici di Siena; Soprintendenza per i Beni Ambientali, Architettonici, Artistici e Storici di Pisa.

### PICTURE CREDITS

t = top; tl = top left; tc = top center; tr = top right; cla = center left above; ca = center above; cra = center right above; cl = center left; c = center; cr = center right; clb = center left below; cb = center below; crb = center right below; bl = bottom left; b = bottom; bc = bottom center; br = bottom right; (d) = detail.

Every effort has been made to trace the copyright holders and we apologize in advance for any unintentional omissions. We would be pleased to insert the appropriate acknowledgments in any subsequent edition of this publication.

The publisher would like to thank the following individuals, companies and picture libraries for permission to reproduce their photographs:

ARCHIVI ALINARI, FIRENZE: 104b; THE ANCIENT ART AND ARCHITECTURE COLLECTION: 77tl; ARCHIVIO FOTOGRAFICO ENCICLOPEDICO, ROMA: Giuseppe Carfagna 36t, 37b, 199t, 199c; Luciano Casadei 36b; Cellai/Focus Team 36c; Claudio Cerquetti 31bl; B. Kortenhorst/K & B News Foto 19t; B. Mariotti 37c; S. Paderno 21t, 37t; G. Veggi 32c.

THE BRIDGEMAN ART LIBRARY, LONDON: Archivo dello Stato, Siena 45clb; Bargello, Firenze 68t, 69t; Biblioteca di San Marco, Firenze/K & B News Foto 97t; Biblioteca Marciana, Venezia 42br; Galleria dell'Accademia, Firenze 94b; Galleria degli Uffizi, Firenze 25br, 43b, 45cla, 80b, 81tl, 81tr, 83t, 83b; Musée du Louvre, Paris/Lauros-Giraudon, 105t; Museo di San Marco, Firenze 50tl, 51t, 97cb; Museo Civico, Prato 184t; Sant'Apollonia, Firenze 89t (d), 92c (d); Santa Croce, Firenze 72b; Santa Maria del Carmine, Firenze 127bl(d); Santa Maria Novella, Firenze 111cr; © THE BRITISH MUSEUM: 40b.

BRUCE COLEMAN: N. G. Blake 31br, Hans Reinhard 31cla, 31cra; JOE CORNISH: 30–31, 34t, 35, 129t, 201t, 223t; GIANCARLO COSTA, MILANO: 32t, 43t, 53clb, 54ca, 54bl, 145 (inset), 256tl.

MARY EVANS PICTURE LIBRARY: 44t, 46b, 48bl (Explorer), 53b, 54br, 74c, 175c, 192c.

GALLERIA DEL COSTUME, FIRENZE/ SOPRINTENDENZA DEI BENI ARTISTICI: 121tr.

ROBERT HARDING PICTURE LIBRARY: 56–7; ALISON HARRIS: Museo dell'Opera del Duomo, Firenze 25bl, 67t, 67c; Palazzo Vecchio, Firenze/Comune di Roma/Direzione dei Musei 4t, 50cb (Sala di Gigli), 51clb, 79t; San Lorenzo, Firenze/ Soprintendenza per i Beni Artistici 91c; Santa Felicità, Firenze 119t (d); Santo Spirito, Firenze 118b; 116; HOTEL PORTA ROSSA, FIRENZE: 179b; PIPPA HURST: 179cr.

THE IMAGE BANK: 58t, 100; Guido Alberto Rossi 11t, 11b; IMPACT PHOTOS: Piers Cavendish 5b; Brian Harris 17b; INDEX, FIRENZE: 182t (d), 182b, 182c (d), 183t; Biblioteca Nazionale, Firenze 9 (inset); Biblioteca Riccardiana, Firenze 57 (inset), 239 (inset) 271 (inset); Galileo Siscam, S.p.A, Firenze 54–5; P. Tosi, 66cr; ISTITUTO E MUSEO DI STORIA DELLA SCIENZA DI FIRENZE: 74b, 75t.

FRANK LANE PICTURE AGENCY: R. Wilmshurst 31crb.

THE MANSELL COLLECTION: 45b; MUSEO DELL'OPIFICIO DELLE PIETRE DURE, FIRENZE: 95c.

GRAZIA NERI, MILANO: R. Bettini 34b; Carlo Lannutti 55b; PETER NOBLE: 5t, 16, 168b, 218tr, 218cra, 276c.

OXFORD SCIENTIFIC FILMS: Stan Osolinski 232tr.

ROGER PHILLIPS: 198cra, 198crb; ANDREA PISTOLESI, FIRENZE: 220b, 277t; EMILIO PUCCI S.R.L, FIRENZE: 55cla.

RETROGRAPH ARCHIVE, LONDON: © Martin Breese 169c, 180b, 243t, 257bl; ROYAL COLLECTION: © HER MAJESTY QUEEN ELIZABETH II: 53t (d).

SCALA, FIRENZE: Abbazia, Monte Oliveto Maggiore 207t; Galleria dell'Accademia, Firenze 92b, 94t, 95t; Badia, Fiesole 47clb; Badia, Firenze 70b; Bargello, Firenze 39t, 42bl, 44b, 47cla, 47b, 49cr, 52br, 66tr, 68b, 69cla, 69cra, 69clb, 108c; Battistero, Pisa 154b; Biblioteca Laurenziana, Firenze 90c; Camposanto, Pisa 152b; Cappella dei Principi, Firenze 48tl, 90t; Cappelle Medicee, Firenze 51crb, 91t; Casa del Vasari, Arezzo 195t (d); Chiesa del Carmine, Firenze 126–7, (126t, 126b, 127br all details); Cimitero, Monterchi 26c; Collegiata, San Gimignano 208cb; Corridoio Vasariano, Firenze 106t; Duomo, Lucca 176b; Duomo, Pisa 155t; Duomo, Prato 26t (d), 27t (d) 27c (d), 27b (d), 26–7; Galleria Comunale, Prato 184b; Galleria d'Arte Moderna, Firenze 52cb, 121tl; Galleria Palatina, Firenze 53crb, 122–3; Galleria degli Uffizi, Firenze 17t, 41cla, 41br, 46c, 48c, 48br, 49t, 49cl, 49b, 50cl, 50b (Collezione Giovanna), 80t, 81ca, 81cb, 81b, 82t, 82b, 83c (d); Loggia dei Lanzi, Firenze 77tr; Musée Bonnat, Bayonne 69b; Musei Civici, San Gimignano 38, 209b, 211b; Museo Archeologico, Arezzo 195c; Museo Archeologico, Firenze 40ca, 41clb, 41bl, 93cb, 99t, 99b, 236b; Museo Archeologico, Grosseto 236c; Museo Civico, Bologna 46tr; Museo degli Argenti, Firenze 51b, 52t, 52ca, 120b; Museo dell'Accademia Etrusca, Cortona 41t, 42ca; Museo dell'Opera del Duomo, Firenze 45t, 63t (d); Museo dell'Opera Metropolitana, Siena 24t; Museo di Firenze com'era, Firenze 71t, 125t, 161b; Museo Diocesano, Cortona 200b; Museo Etrusco Guarnacci, Volterra 40t; Museo di San Marco, Firenze 59t, 84, 96t (d), 96c, 96b, 97ca, 97b; Museo Mediceo, Firenze 48tr; Museo Nazionale di San Matteo, Pisa 153t; Necropoli, Sovana 237crb; Palazzo Davanzati, Firenze 103c (Sala dei Pappagalli), 108t; Palazzo Medici Riccardi, Firenze 2–3; Palazzo Pitti, Firenze 120c, 121bl; Palazzo Pubblico, Siena 44–5, 215t; Palazzo Vecchio, Firenze 50–51 (Sala di Clemente VII), 78t (Sala dei Gigli); Pinacoteca Comunale, Sansepolcro 193b; Pinacoteca Comunale, Volterra 162cr; San Francesco, Arezzo 196–7, (196t, 196b, 197t, 197b, 197cl all details); San Lorenzo, Firenze 25t; Santa Maria Novella, Firenze 24b, 44c (d), 47t (d), 110b; Santa Trìnita, Firenze 102t; Santissima Annunziata, Firenze 98b; Tomba del Colle, Chiusi 40cb, 224t; Tribuna di Galileo, Firenze 52–3; Vaticano 39b (Galleria Carte Geographica); SYGMA: G. Giansanti 218cla, 218 crb, 218bl; Keystone 55t.

THE TRAVEL LIBRARY: Philip Enticknap 94cr, 214t, 272c.

Front Endpaper: THE IMAGE BANK: tl; SCALA, FIRENZE: tr.

# Phrase Book

## Emergency Phrases

| | | |
|---|---|---|
| Help! | **Aiuto!** | *eye-**yoo**-toh* |
| Stop! | **Fermate!** | *fair-**mah**-teh* |
| Call a doctor. | **Chiama un medico** | *kee-**ah**-mah oon **meh**-dee-koh* |
| Call an ambulance. | **Chiama un' ambulanza** | *kee-**ah**-mah oon am-boo-**lan**-tsa* |
| Call the police. | **Chiama la polizia** | *kee-**ah**-mah lah pol-ee-**tsee**-ah* |
| Call the fire department. | **Chiama i pompieri** | *kee-**ah**-mah ee pom-pee-**air**-ee* |
| Where is the telephone? | **Dov'è il telefono?** | *dov-**eh** eel teh-**leh**-foh-noh?* |
| The nearest hospital? | **L'ospedale più vicino?** | *loss-peh-**dah**-leh pee-**oo** vee-**chee**-noh?* |

## Communication Essentials

| | | |
|---|---|---|
| Yes/No | **Si/No** | ***see/noh*** |
| Please | **Per favore** | *pair fah-**vor**-eh* |
| Thank you | **Grazie** | ***grah**-tsee-eh* |
| Excuse me | **Mi scusi** | *mee **skoo**-zee* |
| Hello | **Buon giorno** | *bwon **jor**-noh* |
| Good-bye | **Arrivederci** | *ah-ree-veh-**dair**-chee* |
| Good evening | **Buona sera** | ***bwon**-ah **sair**-ah* |
| morning | **la mattina** | *lah mah-**tee**-nah* |
| afternoon | **il pomeriggio** | *eel poh-meh-**ree**-joh* |
| evening | **la sera** | *lah **sair**-ah* |
| yesterday | **ieri** | *ee-**air**-ee* |
| today | **oggi** | ***oh**-jee* |
| tomorrow | **domani** | *doh-**mah**-nee* |
| here | **qui** | ***kwee*** |
| there | **la** | ***lah*** |
| What? | **Quale?** | ***kwah**-leh?* |
| When? | **Quando?** | ***kwan**-doh?* |
| Why? | **Perchè?** | *pair-**keh**?* |
| Where? | **Dove?** | ***doh**-veh* |

## Useful Phrases

| | | |
|---|---|---|
| How are you? | **Come sta?** | ***koh**-meh stah?* |
| Very well, thank you. | **Molto bene, grazie.** | ***moll**-toh **beh**-neh **grah**-tsee-eh* |
| Pleased to meet you. | **Piacere di conoscerla.** | *pee-ah-**chair**-eh dee coh-**noh**-shair-lah* |
| See you soon. | **A più tardi.** | *ah pee-**oo** **tar**-dee* |
| That's fine. | **Va bene.** | *va **beh**-neh* |
| Where is/are ...? | **Dov'è/Dove sono ...?** | *dov-**eh**/doveh **soh**-noh?* |
| How long does it take to get to ...? | **Quanto tempo ci vuole per andare a ...?** | ***kwan**-toh **tem**-poh chee voo-**oh**-leh pair an-**dar**-eh ah...?* |
| How do I get to ...? | **Come faccio per arrivare a ...?** | *koh-meh **fah**-choh pair arri-**var**-eh ah..?* |
| Do you speak English? | **Parla inglese?** | ***par**-lah een-**gleh**-zeh?* |
| I don't understand. | **Non capisco.** | *non ka-**pee**-skoh* |
| Could you speak more slowly, please? | **Può parlare più lentamente, per favore?** | *pwoh par-**lah**-reh pee-**oo** len-ta-**men**-teh pair fah-**vor**-eh* |
| I'm sorry. | **Mi dispiace.** | *mee dee-spee-**ah**-cheh* |

## Useful Words

| | | |
|---|---|---|
| big | **grande** | ***gran**-deh* |
| small | **piccolo** | ***pee**-koh-loh* |
| hot | **caldo** | ***kal**-doh* |
| cold | **freddo** | ***fred**-doh* |
| good | **buono** | ***bwoh**-noh* |
| bad | **cattivo** | *kat-**tee**-voh* |
| enough | **basta** | ***bas**-tah* |
| well | **bene** | ***beh**-neh* |
| open | **aperto** | *ah-**pair**-toh* |
| closed | **chiuso** | *kee-**oo**-zoh* |
| left | **a sinistra** | *ah see-**nee**-strah* |
| right | **a destra** | *ah **dess**-trah* |
| straight ahead | **sempre dritto** | ***sem**-preh **dree**-toh* |
| near | **vicino** | *vee-**chee**-noh* |
| far | **lontano** | *lon-**tah**-noh* |
| up | **su** | ***soo*** |
| down | **giù** | ***joo*** |
| early | **presto** | ***press**-toh* |
| late | **tardi** | ***tar**-dee* |
| entrance | **entrata** | *en-**trah**-tah* |
| exit | **uscita** | *oo-**shee**-ta* |
| toilet | **il gabinetto** | *eel gah-bee-**net**-toh* |
| free, unoccupied | **libero** | ***lee**-bair-oh* |
| free, no charge | **gratuito** | *grah-**too**-ee-toh* |

## Making a Telephone Call

| | | |
|---|---|---|
| I'd like to place a long-distance call. | **Vorrei fare una interurbana.** | *vor-**ray far**-eh oona in-tair-oor-**bah**-nah* |
| I'd like to make a collect call. | **Vorrei fare una telefonata a carico del destinatario.** | *vor-**ray far**-eh oona teh-leh-fon-**ah**-tah ah **kar**-ee-koh dell dess-tee-nah-**tar**-ree-oh* |
| I'll try again later. | **Ritelefono più tardi.** | *ree-teh-**leh**-foh-noh pee-oo **tar**-dee* |
| Can I leave a message? | **Posso lasciare un messaggio?** | ***poss**-oh lash-**ah**-reh oon mess-**sah**-joh?* |
| Hold on. | **Un attimo, per favore** | *oon **ah**-tee-moh, pair fah-**vor**-eh* |
| Could you speak up a little please? | **Può parlare più forte, per favore?** | *pwoh par-**lah**-reh pee-**oo for**-teh, pair fah-**vor**-eh?* |
| local call | **la telefonata locale** | *lah teh-leh-fon-**ah**-ta loh-**kah**-leh* |

## Shopping

| | | |
|---|---|---|
| How much does this cost? | **Quant'è, per favore?** | *kwan-**teh** pair fah-**vor**-eh?* |
| I would like ... | **Vorrei ...** | *vor-**ray*** |
| Do you have ...? | **Avete ...?** | *ah-**veh**-teh.. ?* |
| I'm just looking. | **Sto soltanto guardando.** | *stoh sol-**tan**-toh gwar-**dan**-doh* |
| Do you take credit cards? | **Accettate carte di credito?** | *ah-chet-**tah**-teh **kar**-teh dee **creh**-dee-toh?* |
| What time do you open/close? | **A che ora apre/chiude?** | *ah keh **or**-ah **ah**-preh/kee-**oo**-deh?* |
| this one | **questo** | ***kweh**-stoh* |
| that one | **quello** | ***kwell**-oh* |
| expensive | **caro** | ***kar**-oh* |
| cheap | **a buon prezzo** | *ah bwon **pret**-soh* |
| size, clothes | **la taglia** | *lah **tah**-lee-ah* |
| size, shoes | **il numero** | *eel **noo**-mair-oh* |
| white | **bianco** | *bee-**ang**-koh* |
| black | **nero** | ***neh**-roh* |
| red | **rosso** | ***ross**-oh* |
| yellow | **giallo** | ***jal**-loh* |
| green | **verde** | ***vair**-deh* |
| blue | **blu** | *bloo* |
| brown | **marrone** | *mar-**roh**-neh* |

## Types of Shops

| | | |
|---|---|---|
| antiques dealer | **l'antiquario** | *lan-tee-**kwah**-ree-oh* |
| bakery | **la panetteria** | *lah pah-net-tair-**ree**-ah* |
| bank | **la banca** | *lah **bang**-kah* |
| bookstore | **la libreria** | *lah lee-breh-**ree**-ah* |
| butcher's | **la macelleria** | *lah mah-chell-eh-**ree**-ah* |
| delicatessen | **la salumeria** | *lah sah-loo-meh-**ree**-ah* |
| department store | **il grande magazzino** | *eel **gran**-deh mag-gad-**zee**-noh* |
| drugstore | **la farmacia** | *lah far-mah-**chee**-ah* |
| fish market | **la pescheria** | *lah pess-keh-**ree**-ah* |
| florist | **il fioraio** | *eel fee-or-**eye**-oh* |
| greengrocer | **il fruttivendolo** | *eel froo-tee-**ven**-doh-loh* |
| grocery store | **alimentari** | *ah-lee-men-**tah**-ree* |
| hairdresser | **il parrucchiere** | *eel par-oo-kee-**air**-eh* |
| ice cream parlor | **la gelateria** | *lah jel-lah-tair-**ree**-ah* |
| market | **il mercato** | *eel mair-**kah**-toh* |
| newsstand | **l'edicola** | *leh-**dee**-koh-lah* |
| pastry shop | **la pasticceria** | *lah pas-tee-chair-**ee**-ah* |
| post office | **l'ufficio postale** | *loo-**fee**-choh pos-**tah**-leh* |
| shoe store | **il negozio di scarpe** | *eel neh-**goh**-tsioh dee **skar**-peh* |
| supermarket | **il supermercato** | *su-pair-mair-**kah**-toh* |
| tobacco shop | **il tabaccaio** | *eel tah-bak-**eye**-oh* |
| travel agency | **l'agenzia di viaggi** | *lah-jen-**tsee**-ah dee vee-**ad**-jee* |

## Sightseeing

| | | |
|---|---|---|
| art gallery | **la pinacoteca** | *lah peena-koh-**teh**-kah* |
| bus stop | **la fermata dell'autobus** | *lah fair-**mah**-tah dell **ow**-toh-booss* |
| church | **la chiesa** | *lah kee-**eh**-zah* |
| | **la basilica** | *lah bah-**seel**-i-kah* |
| closed for the public holiday | **chiuso per la festa** | *kee-**oo**-zoh pair lah **fess**-tah* |
| garden | **il giardino** | *eel jar-**dee**-no* |
| library | **la biblioteca** | *lah beeb-lee-oh-**teh**-kah* |
| museum | **il museo** | *eel moo-**zeh**-oh* |
| tourist information | **l'ufficio turistico** | *loo-**fee**-choh too-**ree**-stee-koh* |
| train station | **la stazione** | *lah stah-tsee-**oh**-neh* |

## Staying in a Hotel

| | | |
|---|---|---|
| Do you have any vacant rooms? | **Avete camere libere?** | ah-**veh**-teh **kah**-mair-eh **lee**-bair-eh? |
| double room | **una camera doppia** | oona **kah**-mair-ah **doh**-pee-ah |
| with double bed | **con letto matrimoniale** | kon **let**-toh mah-tree-moh-nee-**ah**-leh |
| twin room | **una camera con due letti** | oona **kah**-mair-ah kon **doo**-eh **let**-tee |
| single room | **una camera singola** | oona **kah**-mair-ah **sing**-goh-lah |
| room with a bath, shower | **una camera con bagno, con doccia** | oona **kah**-mair-ah kon **ban**-yoh, kon **dot**-chah |
| porter | **il facchino** | eel fah-**kee**-noh |
| key | **la chiave** | lah kee-**ah**-veh |
| I have a reservation. | **Ho fatto una prenotazione.** | oh **fat**-toh oona preh-noh-tah-tsee-**oh**-neh |

## Eating Out

| | | |
|---|---|---|
| Have you got a table for ...? | **Avete una tavola per ... ?** | ah-**veh**-teh oona **tah**-voh-lah pair ...? |
| I'd like to reserve a table. | **Vorrei riservare una tavola.** | vor-**ray** ree-sair-**vah**-reh oona **tah**-voh-lah |
| breakfast | **colazione** | koh-lah-tsee-**oh**-neh |
| lunch | **pranzo** | **pran**-tsoh |
| dinner | **cena** | **cheh**-nah |
| The check, please. | **Il conto, per favore.** | eel **kon**-toh pair fah-**vor**-eh |
| I am a vegetarian. | **Sono vegetariano/a.** | **soh**-noh **veh**-jeh-tar-ee-**ah**-noh/nah |
| waitress | **cameriera** | kah-mair-ee-**air**-ah |
| waiter | **cameriere** | kah-mair-ee-**air**-eh |
| fixed price menu | **il menù a prezzo fisso** | eel meh-**noo** ah **pret**-soh **fee**-soh |
| dish of the day | **piatto del giorno** | pee-**ah**-toh dell **jor**-no |
| starter | **antipasto** | an-tee-**pass**-toh |
| first course | **il primo** | eel **pree**-moh |
| main course | **il secondo** | eel seh-**kon**-doh |
| vegetables | **il contorno** | eel kon-**tor**-noh |
| dessert | **il dolce** | eel **doll**-cheh |
| cover charge | **il coperto** | eel koh-**pair**-toh |
| wine list | **la lista dei vini** | lah **lee**-stah day **vee**-nee |
| rare | **al sangue** | al **sang**-gweh |
| medium | **al puntino** | al poon-**tee**-noh |
| well-done | **ben cotto** | ben **kot**-toh |
| glass | **il bicchiere** | eel bee-kee-**air**-eh |
| bottle | **la bottiglia** | lah bot-**teel**-yah |
| knife | **il coltello** | eel kol-**tell**-oh |
| fork | **la forchetta** | lah for-**ket**-tah |
| spoon | **il cucchiaio** | eel koo-kee-**eye**-oh |

## Menu Decoder

| | | |
|---|---|---|
| **l'abbacchio** | lah-**back**-kee-oh | lamb |
| **l'aceto** | lah-**cheh**-toh | vinegar |
| **l'acqua** | **lah**-kwah | water |
| **l'acqua minerale gasata/naturale** | **lah**-kwah mee-nair-**ah**-leh gah-**zah**-tah/ nah-too-**rah**-leh | mineral water carbonated/still |
| **l'aglio** | **lahl**-yoh | garlic |
| **al forno** | al **for**-noh | baked |
| **alla griglia** | ah-lah **greel**-yah | grilled |
| **l'anatra** | **lah**-nah-trah | duck |
| **l'aragosta** | lah-rah-**goss**-tah | lobster |
| **l'arancia** | lah-**ran**-chah | orange |
| **arrosto** | ar-**ross**-toh | roast |
| **la birra** | lah **beer**-rah | beer |
| **la bistecca** | lah bee-**stek**-kah | steak |
| **il brodo** | eel **broh**-doh | broth |
| **il burro** | eel **boor**-oh | butter |
| **il caffè** | eel kah-**feh** | coffee |
| **il carciofo** | eel kar-**choff**-oh | artichoke |
| **la carne** | la **kar**-neh | meat |
| **carne di maiale** | **kar**-neh dee mah-**yah**-leh | pork |
| **la cipolla** | lah chee-**poll**-ah | onion |
| **i fagioli** | ee fah-**joh**-lee | beans |
| **il formaggio** | eel for-**mad**-joh | cheese |
| **le fragole** | leh **frah**-goh-leh | strawberries |
| **frutta fresca** | **froo**-tah **fress**-kah | fresh fruit |
| **frutti di mare** | **froo**-tee dee **mah**-reh | seafood |
| **i funghi** | ee **foon**-gee | mushrooms |
| **i gamberi** | ee **gam**-bair-ee | shrimp |
| **il gelato** | eel jel-**lah**-toh | ice cream |
| **l'insalata** | leen-sah-**lah**-tah | salad |
| **il latte** | eel **laht**-teh | milk |
| **i legumi** | ee leh-**goo**-mee | vegetables |
| **lesso** | **less**-oh | boiled |
| **il manzo** | eel **man**-tsoh | beef |
| **la mela** | lah **meh**-lah | apple |
| **la melanzana** | lah meh-lan-**tsah**-nah | eggplant |
| **la minestra** | lah mee-**ness**-trah | soup |
| **l'olio** | **loll**-yoh | oil |
| **l'oliva** | loh-**lee**-vah | olive |
| **il pane** | eel **pah**-neh | bread |
| **il panino** | eel pah-**nee**-noh | roll |
| **le patate** | leh pah-**tah**-teh | potatoes |
| **patatine fritte** | pah-tah-**teen**-eh **free**-teh | french fries |
| **il pepe** | eel **peh**-peh | pepper |
| **la pesca** | lah **pess**-kah | peach |
| **il pesce** | eel **pesh**-eh | fish |
| **il pollo** | eel **poll**-oh | chicken |
| **il pomodoro** | eel poh-moh-**dor**-oh | tomato |
| **il prosciutto cotto/crudo** | eel pro-**shoo**-toh **kot**-toh/**kroo**-doh | ham cooked/cured |
| **il riso** | eel **ree**-zoh | rice |
| **il sale** | eel **sah**-leh | salt |
| **la salsiccia** | lah sal-**see**-chah | sausage |
| **secco** | **sek**-koh | dry |
| **succo d'arancia/ di limone** | **soo**-koh dah-**ran**-chah/ dee lee-**moh**-neh | orange/lemon juice |
| **il tè** | eel **teh** | tea |
| **la tisana** | lah tee-**zah**-nah | herb tea |
| **il tonno** | **ton**-noh | tuna |
| **la torta** | lah **tor**-tah | cake |
| **l'uovo** | loo-**oh**-voh | egg |
| **l'uva** | **loo**-vah | grapes |
| **vino bianco** | **vee**-noh bee-**ang**-koh | white wine |
| **vino rosso** | **vee**-noh **ross**-oh | red wine |
| **il vitello** | eel vee-**tell**-oh | veal |
| **le vongole** | leh **von**-goh-leh | baby clams |
| **lo zucchero** | loh **zoo**-kair-oh | sugar |
| **gli zucchini** | lyee dzo-**kee**-nee | zucchini |
| **la zuppa** | lah **tsoo**-pah | soup |

## Numbers

| | | |
|---|---|---|
| 1 | **uno** | **oo**-noh |
| 2 | **due** | **doo**-eh |
| 3 | **tre** | treh |
| 4 | **quattro** | **kwat**-roh |
| 5 | **cinque** | **ching**-kweh |
| 6 | **sei** | **say**-ee |
| 7 | **sette** | **set**-teh |
| 8 | **otto** | **ot**-toh |
| 9 | **nove** | **noh**-veh |
| 10 | **dieci** | dee-**eh**-chee |
| 11 | **undici** | **oon**-dee-chee |
| 12 | **dodici** | **doh**-dee-chee |
| 13 | **tredici** | **tray**-dee-chee |
| 14 | **quattordici** | kwat-**tor**-dee-chee |
| 15 | **quindici** | **kwin**-dee-chee |
| 16 | **sedici** | **say**-dee-chee |
| 17 | **diciassette** | dee-chah-**set**-teh |
| 18 | **diciotto** | dee-**chot**-toh |
| 19 | **diciannove** | dee-chah-**noh**-veh |
| 20 | **venti** | **ven**-tee |
| 30 | **trenta** | **tren**-tah |
| 40 | **quaranta** | kwah-**ran**-tah |
| 50 | **cinquanta** | ching-**kwan**-tah |
| 60 | **sessanta** | sess-**an**-tah |
| 70 | **settanta** | set-**tan**-tah |
| 80 | **ottanta** | ot-**tan**-tah |
| 90 | **novanta** | noh-**van**-tah |
| 100 | **cento** | **chen**-toh |
| 1,000 | **mille** | **mee**-leh |
| 2,000 | **duemila** | **doo**-eh **mee**-lah |
| 5,000 | **cinquemila** | **ching**-kweh **mee**-lah |
| 1,000,000 | **un milione** | oon meel-**yoh**-neh |

## Time

| | | |
|---|---|---|
| one minute | **un minuto** | oon mee-**noo**-toh |
| one hour | **un'ora** | oon **or**-ah |
| half an hour | **mezz'ora** | medz-**or**-ah |
| a day | **un giorno** | oon **jor**-noh |
| a week | **una settimana** | oona set-tee-**mah**-nah |
| Monday | **lunedì** | loo-neh-**dee** |
| Tuesday | **martedì** | mar-teh-**dee** |
| Wednesday | **mercoledì** | mair-koh-leh-**dee** |
| Thursday | **giovedì** | joh-veh-**dee** |
| Friday | **venerdì** | ven-air-**dee** |
| Saturday | **sabato** | **sah**-bah-toh |
| Sunday | **domenica** | doh-**meh**-nee-kah |

Road Map of Tuscany
A
B
C
1
2
3
4
5
EMILIA-ROMAGN
PIEMONTE
Lunigiana
Appenino Tosco-Emiliano
Garfagnana
Alpi Apuane
Versilia
Mare Ligure
TOSCAN
Colline Metallifere
Arcipelageo Toscano
Canale di Piombino
Golfo di Follónica
Mar Tirreno
CORSICA
Aulla
S. Stefano di Magra
Sarzano
La Spezia
Carrara
Massa
Castelnuovo di Garfagnana
Barga
Bagni di Lucca
Pistoia
Collodi
Pescia
Montecatini
Montecatini Terme
Viareggio
Balbano
Lucca
Torre del Lago Puccini
Rigoli
Ponte Buggianese
Vinci
Pisa
Certosa di Pisa
Empoli
Tenuta di San Rossore
Marina di Pisa
San Piero a Grado
San Miniato
Tenuta di Tombolo
Collesalvetti
Livorno
Ísola di Gorgona
San Gimign
Volterra
Vada
Saline di Volterra
Cecina
Ísola di Capraia
Capraia
St. di Campiglia Marittima
Massa Maritt
Piombino
Follónica
Montepesc
Portoferraio
Rio Marina
Marciana
Porto Azzurro
Punta Ala
Ísola d'Elba
Pianosa
Ísola di Pianosa
Porto S Sté
Scoglio d'Affrica
Ísola di Montecristo
Í. del Giglio
Í. di Gia
Serchio
Arno
Cecina
Lima
Reno
Elsa
Panaro
A12
A15
A11
A11-E74
S235
S1
S62
S63
S12
S324
S435
S439
S436
S67
S429
S206
S68
S322
KEY
Airport
Ferry service
Railway station
Private railway station
Railway line
Highway
Major road
Minor road
0 kilometers 20
0 miles 20